Praise for Stephen E. Ambrose

Citizen Soldiers
'An unforgettable testament to the World War II generation'
The New York Times

'The most gripping account of the Second World War
that I have ever read' Joseph Heller

'History boldly told and elegantly written . . . Gripping'
Wall Street Journal

'Ambrose proves once again he is a masterful historian . . .
spellbinding' *People*

D-Day
'*D-Day* is mostly about people, but goes even further in evok-
ing the horror, the endurance, the daring and indeed, the
human failings at Omaha Beach . . . Outstanding'
The New York Times Book Review

'Packed with drama and information, never losing sight of the
horrors of combat, Ambrose's *D-Day* is the best book yet on
what many historians consider to be the most important day
of the 20th century' *San Francisco Chronicle*

Pegasus Bridge
'All the vividness of a movie and all the intelligence – in every
sense – of fine military history. One of the best single battle
accounts to come out of World War II' *Los Angeles Herald*

'An illuminating account of an operation as strategically
important as any fought on D-Day' *New York Times*

Wild Blue
'Mr Ambrose's storytelling ability is unparalleled'
Wall Street Journal

'Brilliant' *USA Today*

'Ambrose is a superb historian'
New York times Book Review

Other books by Stephen E. Ambrose

CRAZY HORSE AND CUSTER

The Epic Clash of Two Great Warriors at the Little Bighorn

Stephen E. Ambrose

POCKET
BOOKS

LONDON • SYDNEY • NEW YORK • TOKYO • SINGAPORE • TORONTO

This edition published by Pocket Books, 2003
An imprint of Simon & Schuster UK Ltd
A CBS COMPANY

7 9 10 8

Simon & Schuster UK Ltd
1st Floor
222 Gray's Inn Road
London WC1X 8HB

www.simonandschuster.co.uk

Simon & Schuster Australia
Sydney

A CIP catalogue record for this book is available
from the British Library

ISBN: 978-0-7434-6864-0

Printed and bound in Great Britain by
CPI Cox & Wyman, Reading, RG1 8EX

For Moira, who took me to Wounded Knee,
and for Stephenie, Barry, Andrew, Grace,
Hugh, Bib, and Blackness, who came along.

A WORD OF SPECIAL THANKS

To the Oglala Sioux at Pine Ridge and Wounded Knee, South Dakota; to the Brulé Sioux at Rosebud, South Dakota; to the Shoshonis and Arapahoes at Wind River, Wyoming; to the Crows at Crow Agency, Montana; and to the northern Cheyennes at Lame Deer, Montana, for allowing me and my family to camp with them on their land;

and to the National Park Service officials at Gettysburg, Pennsylvania; Fort Laramie and Fort Phil Kearny, Wyoming; and Custer Battlefield, Montana, for their many kindnesses;

and to the state officials at Custer State Park in the Black Hills of South Dakota and at Camp Robinson, Nebraska, for their excellent campgrounds and generous assistance;

and to all the people of the Great Plains, red and white, for their hospitality.

CONTENTS

LIST OF PHOTOGRAPHS

1. One of Crazy Horse's "dress" shirts.
2. He Dog, a life-long friend of Crazy Horse.
3. Custer in his 1861 West Point graduation photograph.
4. A Sioux encampment along the Platte River.
5. Custer, the boy general of the Civil War, dressed in atypical fashion.
6. Pawnee Killer, the Sioux warrior who led Custer on a wild chase.
7. Custer, the leader of the Washita campaign.
8. Elizabeth Bacon Custer in the late 1860s.
9. Custer in 1874, after the Black Hills expedition.
10. Touch-the-Clouds, the seven-foot-tall war chief of the Miniconjous.
11. Tom Custer, devoted brother and gallant soldier.
12. Young-Man-Afraid-of-His-Horses, probably the most intelligent Sioux leader of the period.
13. Custer and his Indian scouts during the Yellowstone River expedition of 1873.
14. Spotted Tail, Crazy Horse's uncle, fearless Brulé warrior.
15. Custer's camp in the Black Hills, 1874, near the spot where gold was first discovered in South Dakota.
16. Custer and Libbie at Fort Abraham Lincoln, 1875.
17. Little Big Man, one of Crazy Horse's wildest warriors.
18. Elizabeth Bacon Custer in 1874.
19. Red Cloud, an Oglala leader, a champion of peace, an able and unscrupulous politician.
20. The famous Hunkpapa leader Sitting Bull.
21. Libbie Custer at the turn of the century.
22. He Dog in old age.

LIST OF MAPS

INTRODUCTION

This is the story of two men who died as they lived—violently. They were both war lovers, men of aggression with a deeply rooted instinct to charge the enemy, rout him, kill him. Men of supreme courage, they were natural-born leaders in a combat crisis, the type to whom others instinctively looked for guidance and inspiration. They were always the first to charge the enemy, and the last to retreat.

Just as they shared broadly similar instincts, so did they have roughly parallel careers. Born at about the same time, they died within a year of each other. Both had happy childhoods, both had become recognized and honored leaders in their societies at an astonishingly young age (Custer at twenty-three, Crazy Horse at twenty-four), both were humiliated and punished at the height of their careers for violating the fundamental laws of their societies in an attempt to be with the women they loved, both recovered from the blows and re-established their claims to leadership roles, both had younger brothers who were even more daredevil risk takers than they were, and both were in a position when they died that, with a little luck, could have given them the supreme political direction of their people.

There were other parallels. Neither man drank. Both were avid hunters, for whom only the excitement of combat exceeded the joy of the chase. Each man loved horses, and riding at full gallop across the unfenced Great Plains of North America, day after day, was a source of never-ending delight for both of them.

Yet Crazy Horse and Custer, like their societies, were as different as life and death.

Crazy Horse and Custer spent their adult lives on the Great Plains, riding, hunting, fighting. They met only twice, on the battlefield, the first time on the banks of the Yellowstone in 1873, the second time on the banks of the Little Bighorn in 1876. The trail each man followed to the Little Bighorn is the subject of the following story.

Stephen E. Ambrose
Started in June 1971 at
Wounded Knee, South Dakota;
finished in July 1974 at
Camp Robinson, Nebraska.

"I said, 'Does this mean that you will be my enemy if I move across the creek?' Crazy Horse laughed in my face. He said, 'I am no white man! They are the only people that make rules for other people, that say, "If you stay on one side of this line it is peace, but if you go on the other side I will kill you all." I don't hold with deadlines. There is plenty of room; camp where you please.'"

> He Dog, close friend and associate of Crazy Horse, in an interview in 1930

"In years long-numbered with the past, when I was verging upon manhood, my every thought was ambitious—not to be wealthy, not to be learned, but to be great. I desired to link my name with acts & men, and in such a manner as to to be a mark of honor—not only to the present, but to future generations."

> George Armstrong Custer

"So much to win and only life to lose."

> John Neihardt, *The Song of the Indian Wars**

* From *The Song of the Indian Wars* by John Neihardt. Copyright 1925 by Macmillan Publishing Co., Inc., renewed 1953 by John G. Neihardt. Reprinted by permission of Macmillan Publishing Company, Inc.

Part One

CHAPTER ONE

The Setting and the People: The Great Plains

"As far as the eye could reach the country seemed blackened by innumerable herds [of buffalo]."

Captain Benjamin Bonneville, 1832

"Indians are so excessively indolent and lazy, they would rather starve a week than work a day."   James Mackay, 1835

The Great Plains of North America, on a cloudless day, stretch out forever under an infinity of bright blue sky. During the violence of a tornado or a snowstorm, however, the vision is limited to the length of an arm. The Plains can be hot, dusty, brown, flat, and unfit for life; they can be delightfully cool, abundantly watered, a dozen shades of green, marvelously varied in appearance, ranging from near mountains to level valleys, and hospitable to all forms of life.

The Plains can be a source of endless delight, or of misery, as well they might be, considering their extent. They stretch from the Mexican border north to and beyond the Canadian frontier, from the 100° meridian west to the Rocky Mountains. The Plains are relatively flat, semiarid, and essentially treeless.[1] In the midnineteenth century they were unfenced, covered by an endless sea of prairie grass, grass that sent its roots down twenty-four inches or more to withstand the droughts and which offered some of the most nutritious plant food in the world. Innumerable small streams cut through the Plains; many of them were dry beds in summer and only a few would be dignified by names or used as reference points in a humid area, but every one carried a name and a legend on the Plains. Trees, mostly cottonwoods, grew along the stream beds, and there men and animals tended to congregate. Among the cottonwoods they found shade, a little water, and perhaps an escape from the sense of limitless space, with its constant reminder of the insignificance of mankind.

Men and animals also congregated in the tree groves to escape the weather. The weather. On the Plains it cannot be ignored. There is, first of all, the nearly constant need for rain. The average yearly rainfall is less than twenty inches, so every storm is welcome. Or rather nearly every storm, because at times the sky can open, dump five inches of rain in a matter of hours, fill the stream beds to over-flowing, and flood the surrounding countryside. Spring and summer storms often touch off tornadoes, too, which level everything in their path, or they become hail storms, beating plants to the ground and destroying them. No one can do anything about the storms—those who live on the Plains must accept them.

They must also accept the wind, which blows harder, and more consistently, on the Plains than anywhere else on the continent, save at the seashore. And the average wind velocity on the Plains is equal to that on the seashore.

"Does the wind blow this way here all the time?" asked the eastern visitor.

"No, mister," answered the cowboy. "It'll maybe blow this way for a week or ten days, and then it'll take a change and blow like hell for a while."[2]

There are all kinds of winds on the Plains, winds from every di-rection, sometimes it seems from every direction at once. A chinook can roar over the mountains in the early spring and change the weather in minutes. There is a recorded case in South Dakota that only a Plainsman could believe: within three minutes of the ar-rival of the chinook the temperature rose from ten degrees below zero to forty-two degrees above zero. In the winter, blizzards reverse the process—the Plains are replete with stories of men working in their barns on a bright, fairly warm midwinter day who did not see the blizzard coming and who then got lost and froze to death trying to find their way from the barn to the farmhouse. In the summer the wind is hot, dry, and mostly from the south. Sometimes it kicks up a dust storm, with winds reaching eighty miles per hour. It al-ways blows.[3]

Despite the excesses of the Plains weather, however, it is an invigo-rating climate for man and beast. Spring and fall are temperate and even in the summer the nights are usually delightfully cool. Most winter days are bracing, the sun bright on the snow and warm on the body, the cold clean air filling lungs and heart with the joy of life.

Across the immense oceanlike prairie, in the middle of the nine-teenth century, animals abounded, healthy animals, possessing great vitality, nurtured as they were on the luxuriant Plains grass. The

Plains squirrels, called prairie dogs, for example, were there in such numbers that, like much else on the Plains, they had to be seen to be believed. One observer estimated that in 1901 Texas alone had eight hundred million prairie dogs.[4] Jack rabbits were nearly as numerous. Antelope and deer numbered in the millions, as did the wolves and coyotes, and there were thousands of elk, bear, and other game.

But most of all, there were buffalo. Enormous beasts—a full-grown bull weighed nearly a ton and a half—they looked a little like oversized cattle, except for the humps on their backs and their shaggy hair. They moved back and forth, up and down the Great Plains like nothing ever seen on this earth. Stupid, shortsighted, hard of hearing, slow of gait, clumsy in movement, the buffalo had only his sense of smell to warn him of danger—and that sense was of no use when a hunter approached from down wind.

The buffalo provided an apparently inexhaustible meat supply, unrivaled by anything else known to man before or since. The beasts bunched together in huge numbers, migrating over the Plains in search of fresh grass and water. In 1832, on a high bluff near the North Fork of the Platte River, Captain Benjamin Bonneville reported that "as far as the eye could reach the country seemed blackened by innumerable herds." In the spring of the next year an observer in the Platte Valley in Nebraska* stopped on the rise of a hill, caught his breath, and saw "one enormous mass of buffaloes. Our vision, at the least computation, would certainly extend ten miles; and in the whole of this vast space, including about eight miles in width from the bluffs to the river bank, there apparently was no vista in the incalculable multitude." In northwestern Texas a pioneer saw a herd which he said covered fifty square miles. The Republican River herd in Kansas alone was estimated to contain more than twelve million buffalo. The total Great Plains herd may have contained more than seventy-five million head.[5]

Here was meat for the taking, and not just meat either, for when proper use was made of the buffalo it provided nearly all the necessities of human life. Shelter and clothing could be made from the skin, while weapons, utensils, toys, and much else could be fashioned from the bones. Add the wild vegetables and fruits of the Plains, a few trees to provide lodge poles, and material for the bow and arrow, and the basic problems of sustaining human life were solved.

---

* I will hereafter refer to places according to the modern state boundaries, on the grounds that it might help the reader's orientation.

The buffalo even provided fuel for the treeless prairie—dried buffalo droppings, called chips, fed the campfires of all those living on the Plains.

The buffalo was a magnet drawing men onto the Plains even before they had solved the problem of transportation across the vast spaces. Indeed, the first men in what is now the United States may have lived on the Plains; some ten thousand years ago men using Folsom points killed prehistoric buffalo in Colorado and Texas.[6] Most Indians, however, passed over or around the Plains, for without the horse, men could not survive in great numbers on the prairie.

Over the centuries Indians did build civilizations on the Plains, but the small tribes stayed in the river bottoms, where they established permanent villages, raised vegetables, and only occasionally took advantage of the plentiful wild game on the upland. Tribes like the Mandan, Arikara, Omaha, and Osage sallied forth once or twice a year in pursuit of the buffalo, the entire village participating in an arduous collective hunt. They would try to surround a herd or drive it over a cliff or into a prepared impoundment. The stampeding buffalo created much danger for people, of course, but the chief difficulty seems to have been getting the heavy carcasses back to the village. For this job the Indians developed an ingenious device, the travois, pulled by a dog, their only domesticated animal. It was a simple affair, two sticks tied together behind the dog and to his shoulders at the front, providing a platform on which to load the meat and skins. But the dog's carrying capacity was limited, and for the most part these sedentary Indians relied on beans, squash, and corn for their food.[7]

Then came the horse, introduced by the Spanish to the Americas and soon spread among the Indians. By 1690 the horse was in use among the tribes of the southern Plains; within less than a century it was in wide use as far north as the Canadian Plains.[8]

These horses, or more properly ponies, were mainly pintos—called "piebalds" in England—the basic coloration being white on brown or bay, or brown or bay on white. How this color characteristic came to predominate among the ponies of the Plains is a mystery; there is a fascinating literature on the subject, a literature long on impassioned arguments and short on proven conclusions.[9] There was at least one pinto among the first sixteen horses to set foot on the continent, brought by Hernando Cortes to Mexico in 1519. However it happened, the pinto gave the Indians great pleasure, so much so that when they acquired a gray or brown horse the first thing they did was to paint the skin. For all their admirable features, the

Plains are drab, especially in late summer; the pintos added a splash of color that was highly welcome.

Pintos had more practical advantages over their larger cousins. Descended from wild herds, they could care for themselves, which was absolutely necessary, since the Plains Indians were notoriously neglectful of their herds. Small of stature—they stood about fourteen hands in height and the average weight was not much more than seven hundred pounds—large of head, with thin legs, the pintos had impressive endurance. Early white visitors on the Plains swore that Indians could gallop their ponies all day, turn them out at night, and then gallop them through the following day. The source of their endurance is as much a mystery as is the source of their color; the Canadian historian Frank Roe suggests that it came from the nutritive content of the prairie grass, which was higher in protein than tame grasses, possibly as a result of centuries of buffalo manuring of the prairie. Whatever the cause, it is certain that the Indian pony could run farther (although not faster), turn quicker, and take better care of himself than the white man's larger horse.[10]

Indians had no great problems in learning how to train and ride ponies or in acquiring them. By the eighteenth century the wild herds were enormous, running into the millions, for the horse took to the Plains as readily as did the game animals. Left unchecked by fences or horse catchers, the wild horses might have equaled the buffalo in number, competing with the buffalo for grass.[11] Aside from capturing feral stock, Indians got ponies via trade with other tribes or through theft.

As the horse came onto the Plains another white man's innovation, the gun, was forcing the hunting and gathering tribes of the Mississippi Valley westward. French and English fur traders, starting with the East Coast Indians, exchanged weapons for furs. The gun gave the eastern tribes great advantages over their western neighbors—its noise had a psychological effect; the bullet had more hitting power than the arrow; the range was greater. With the gun the eastern tribes drove their enemies westward. As the white fur traders penetrated farther into the interior of the continent the process was repeated. Most of the famous Plains tribes were pushed out onto the prairie by military defeats, the Crow, Arapaho, Blackfoot, and Cheyenne among them. The last major tribe to arrive on the Plains was the Sioux; trekking out of the woods of Minnesota, their ancient enemy the Chippewa at their heels, the Sioux did not cross the Missouri River or acquire the horse in any great numbers until 1776, the year of American Independence.[12]

With the horse and the gun, the Plains Indians set up the most effective barrier the Europeans met in their drive to settle the continent. As Walter Webb reminds us, "for two and a half centuries [the Plains Indians] maintained themselves with great fortitude against the Spanish, English, French, Mexican, Texas, and American invaders, withstanding missionaries, whiskey, disease, gunpowder, and lead."[13] None resisted more fiercely than the Sioux, the only Indian nation to defeat the United States in war and force it to sign a peace treaty favorable to the red man.

The Sioux, a large tribe with many divisions, came onto the Plains at an ideal time. First of all, the horse was there in abundant numbers. Second, the vast region of the high Plains, teeming with buffalo, was up for grabs. The Mandans and the Arikaras, who with their fortified villages along the river valleys had held back the flow of eastern Indians onto the Plains, had been decimated by three or more great epidemics of smallpox.[14] Third, the Teton Dakota branch of the Sioux, consisting of the Blackfeet, Brulé, Hunkpapa, Miniconjou, Sans Arcs (also called No Bows), Two-Kettle, and Oglala tribes, came in far greater numbers than the possessors of the prime buffalo range. Finally, the Sioux tribes acted more or less in concert, while the Crow, Cheyenne, Pawnee, and other tribes could not or would not combine their forces for defensive purposes. By 1800 the Sioux had acquired more than enough horses to take control of a vast region stretching from the Missouri River on the east and north to the Black Hills on the west, to the Platte River on the south.

The horse gave the Sioux a previously undreamed of mobility. With their pintos they were vastly superior hunters and warriors than they had been on foot. They could now strike quickly and get away fast. They stole ponies constantly from their neighbors, as their neighbors did from them. Indeed, most war parties went out for the sole purpose of stealing horses.

The horse gave the Sioux personal property and became the medium of exchange and the measure of wealth. In the nature of things, nomads have few material possessions. Property was for use, not for accumulation. Without the horse, there were almost no distinctions between individuals within a village; with the horse there was an easily recognizable distinction. Still, the Sioux did not succumb to the development of hereditary classes, nor did they divide themselves into the rich and powerful on one side, the poor and weak on the other. Rather, they brought an egalitarian philosophy onto the Plains with them. Societal pressure and economic necessity forced the temporarily rich man to give away his possessions—i.e., his extra ponies—in order to block the growth of a privileged class *and* to make certain that every able-bodied man had a horse for the communal hunt or for war. The sanctity of private property could go only so far in a society that required every man to have a horse for the buffalo hunt or to defend the village. Successful horse thieves, then, did not become rich in horses, though they did grow rich in prestige.

The Sioux had no individuals who were wealthy, but as a tribe they were, in effect, rolling in money. With one successful buffalo hunt in the spring and another in the fall they could supply nearly all their needs. Their diet was superb. Buffalo muscle was an excellent source of protein (and it tasted better than beef, according to whites on the frontier who ate both), while the beast's vital parts supplied vitamins and minerals in abundance. Cut into thin strips and dried in the hot Plains sun, its meat was relatively easy to store. Indian women would gather cherries and other wild fruit to pound into the dried meat, thus making pemmican which was almost a complete diet in itself. There were no cases of scurvy among Plains Indians at a time when it was a common complaint among European sailors, even though the Indians lived in an area that was devoid of fresh fruits and vegetables from October until May.

The fur traders and trappers, French and English, followed the Indians out onto the prairie. Working for such giant outfits as the American Fur Company, they lived among the tribes, often married Indian women, learned the language, and did all they could to get the Indians to trap or shoot fur-bearing animals, especially the beaver that filled the streams. To these men the main problem with the Plains Indians was that they were too rich. Because of their affluence, they would not work. The Indians exhibited an independence— like "the air they breathed or the wind that blew," according to one trader—that was the despair of the white man, who tried to create in them wants that could be satisfied only through the fur trade.[15] Without much luck, however, because the Indians were terribly lazy, or so it appeared to the white men on the make. One trader, James Adair, referred to the red men as "great enemies to profuse sweating" and insisted that an Indian hurried "only when the devil is at his arse." James Mackay, a Scottish explorer, thought the Plains Indians "so excessively indolent and lazy" that they "would rather starve a week than work a day."[16]

The fur traders, in their letters back to headquarters explaining their difficulties, provide a fascinating view of Sioux life on the

Plains before extensive contact with the whites had unalterably changed that life-style. The traders judged the Indians from a European perspective, of course, but the white men were in such a minority—hardly ever more than one to a village, if that many—that they made no attempt to force their value system or culture on the Indians, save for their futile and frustrating efforts to induce the Indians to work.

The traders found much to comment upon—the Indians' bravery, endurance, horsemanship, and so on—but nothing impressed them so deeply as Indian gluttony. As the fur-trade historian Lewis Saum puts it, "They stood in awe of the red man's ability to eat." Pierre-Antoine Tabeau decided that in gluttony the Indian experienced his foremost happiness. Food monopolized most conversations. Edwin Denig tried to describe the Indians' "incredible" gastronomical achievements but gave it up as hopeless—no one who did not know the Indians could even approach the truth, for "it can not be realized."[17] One Indian could consume five, even ten pounds of buffalo meat at a single sitting.

The other side of the coin was Indian improvidence. Most traders complained that the Indians did not have the slightest idea of a future, refused to lay up stores against a rainy day, and trusted to nature to supply needs as they arose. But the Indians did store food; what the traders really meant was that the Indians could not be made acquisitive, cared little if at all for manufactured products, and refused to run a trap line in order to earn knives, cloth, beads, or even firearms. The only item that the Indian wanted badly enough to work for was whiskey, which soon dominated the fur trade.

Even whiskey, however, was an insufficient spur. When they were not on a war party or a buffalo hunt, Sioux men liked nothing better than lazing around camp, smoking a pipe, telling stories, playing with the children, enjoying themselves. In 1822 Jedediah Smith described in his journal the serenely pastoral setting of a Sioux camp on the Plains and remarked that it would "almost persuade a man to renounce the world, take the lodge and live the careless, Lazy life of an Indian."[18] Francis Parkman, who lived among the Oglala Sioux in the summer of 1846, described a typical afternoon. He lay in a buffalo-skin lodge, "overcome by the listless torpor that pervaded the encampment. The day's work was finished, or if it were not, the inhabitants had resolved not to finish it at all, and were dozing quietly within the shelter of the lodges. A profound lethargy, the very spirit of indolence, seemed to have sunk upon the village . . . The spirit of the place infected me; I could not think consecutively;

I was fit only for musing and revery, when at last, like the rest, I fell asleep."[19]

Everything about the Indian was, for the white man, extreme. His laziness and improvidence had a counterpoint: once aroused, the Indian was capable of prodigious bursts of energy. Parkman was always impatient for action, for example, but when the time came he could not begin to keep up with the Oglalas on a buffalo hunt. A Sioux warrior could run all day, and the next, and on through the week if necessary to escape pursuers. The Sioux could pack up a village and be on the move in fifteen minutes. A war party, returning from a raid on the Crow camps near the Bighorn Mountains, would dance all night in celebration when the men arrived home with their loot, even though the men had been on the move for two weeks or more, chased by the Crows, with little sleep or food.

Indians were an enigma to the whites. As fur trader Henry Boller put it, "I could 'paint' you . . . two pictures: The One would represent the bright side of Indian Life, with its feathers, lances, gayly dressed & mounted 'banneries,' fights, buffalo hunting &c.

"The other, the dark side, showing the filth, vermin, poverty, nakedness, suffering, starvation, superstition, &c. *Both would be equally true—neither exaggerated, or distorted; both totally disimillar!*"[20]

Of all the puzzlements, none exceeded the Sioux method of making war. As in European armies, there were grades of honors which entitled the brave man to wear distinguishing marks, medals among the Europeans, feathers among the Indians. Unlike the whites, however, the Indians did not fight to kill, but to win prestige. With the red men the highest honors went to the man who touched a live enemy with a bow, spear, or hand, which was called "counting coup." Killing an enemy from a distance with an arrow or bullet carried almost no prestige with it, for in the red man's view it took no great bravery to fire a weapon at a distant enemy. Although the Indians would never have admitted it, their system of honors—common to all Plains tribes—had the salutary effect of holding down losses. And since the Plains were underpopulated and every able-bodied man was required for the hunt, holding down losses was crucial.

Intertribal "battles" hardly ever became full-scale fights, with one side or both committing all its strength. Rather, they tended to be individual duels. The Crows would gather on one side of a valley, the Sioux on the other. They would shout taunts back and forth. Occasionally, a young brave, eager to win honors, would dash forward on his pinto, gallop into the Crow line, arrows flying everywhere, count coup, and ride like hell to get out of there. The main idea was to make sure that everyone was watching. After a few casualties had been sustained, the two sides would ride off in opposite directions. That night they would mourn the dead, then celebrate the new honors won.

A missionary who lived with the Sioux from 1835 to 1845, Reverend S. W. Pond, recorded the results of the constant warfare between that tribe and the Sac, Pottawatomie, Chippewa, and Ojibway. In that decade the Sioux killed or wounded one hundred twenty-nine of their enemies and lost in killed or wounded eighty-eight people. Since more than half the total in both cases were children and women, the Sioux lost less than four warriors per year. Hunting accidents were probably a more serious cause of manpower losses.

Pond cited Little Crow, a Santee Sioux, who in 1819 told an Army officer (who had urged him to give up the war with the Chippewas), that "it is better for us to carry on the war in the way we do than to make peace, because we lose a man or two every year, but we kill as many of the enemy during the same time." Little Crow said if the Santees made peace, the Chippewas would overrun Sioux territory. "Why, then, should we give up such an extensive country to save the life of a man or two annually?"

Pond reported that "the Indians spent a good deal of time at war, but their attempts to kill their enemies were not often very successful." Small parties of warriors were more successful than large ones, although both types usually returned to the village without any scalps. Pond gave examples of opportunities to strike a foe which the Sioux passed up and concluded, "Indeed, Indians consider it foolhardiness to make an attack where it is certain some of them will be killed."[21]

Although boundaries between tribes were always changing, the Sioux did not drive the Ojibways or the Crees or the Crows out of an area; it would be more nearly correct to say that the Sioux forced their enemies back simply because of their superior numbers, which gave them a presence in the region that by itself was sufficient to deter opponents from attack and even to force them to withdraw. If the Sioux came upon a Pawnee hunting party, they would drive off the Pawnees. Or rather, they would if they outnumbered the Pawnees; and if they outnumbered them badly enough, they might slaughter the entire tribe—such cases, although rare, did happen. Otherwise the Sioux would count a few coup and wait for the Pawnees to ride off. When faced with superior numbers, Indians nearly always retreated, which was how it happened that the Sioux took over the prime buffalo range without having to fight any pitched battles, much less campaigns. Certainly there were few tribal victories or defeats. To the disgust of the fur traders, Indian warfare was little more than individual combat.[22]

The fur traders could hardly understand the Indians' attitudes toward war. William Laidlaw was delighted when the Sioux went on the warpath against the Arikaras, because the Sioux were trading with him and the Arikaras were not. But after killing only a few Arikaras the Sioux had grown tired of the war and were arranging peace. Laidlaw's disgusted comment was, "so much for Indian Warfare——." To illustrate the red man's "great aversion to going to the 'Spirit Land' before his allotted time," Henry Boller described an unexpected encounter between three Assiniboine and three Sioux. Although the two tribes were traditional enemies, both groups simply stood and looked at each other, so confounded were they by the equality of numbers. "What was to be done?" Boller wrote rhetorically. "Fight it out? Far from it——!" The Indians decided to hell with it, sat down, smoked a pipe, stripped, exchanged clothes, smoked again, and rode off in opposite directions. Boller said the story was "as true as it is ridiculous."[23]

Fur traders generally found little to admire in the Indians, but then they were trying to make money off the red men and exploiters seldom find many admirable characteristics among the group they are exploiting. Francis Parkman saw them differently. Not yet twenty-three years old and fresh out of Harvard when he lived among the Oglala Sioux in 1846, Parkman was so steeped in James Fenimore Cooper's romantic view of the red man that he once said he sometimes felt he could not say for sure where Cooper left off and his own observations began.[24] Where the trader saw a lazy, filthy Indian, Parkman tended to see a noble savage. His views were tempered, however, by living among the Indians. As a proper Bostonian he was shocked by the Oglalas' laziness and obscenity, horrified by their manners, dress, and smell, and entirely disapproving of their habits.

"For the most part," Parkman wrote in a final judgment, "a civilized white man can discover very few points of sympathy between his own nature and that of an Indian. With every disposition to do justice to their good qualities, he must be conscious that an impassable gulf lies between him and his red brethren. Nay, so alien to himself do they appear, that, after breathing the air of the prairie for a few months or weeks, he begins to look upon them as a troublesome and dangerous species of wild beast."[25] The generalization was obviously too wide. Many civilized white men formed fast friendships with individual Sioux, while a goodly number married into the tribe and lived the wild life, refusing to return to civilization. The view was too extreme even for Parkman himself, who elsewhere indicated that he found much to admire in the Oglalas. Sioux historian George E. Hyde points out that Parkman "had an instinctive understanding of the Indians; they were neither Noble Red Men nor scurvy savages to him, but human beings each with his own characteristic faults and virtues." Hyde also flatly and correctly states, "There is no other picture of these people in their wild, free state that is to be compared with" Parkman's.[26]

Parkman hired a guide, Henry Chatillon, an illiterate hunter who was married to an Oglala woman; Chatillon took him to Old Smoke's band south of the Platte River. It is probable that Crazy Horse, who was about five years old that summer of 1846, was living with the band at the time. When Parkman first saw the village, it was camped near the Platte River across from the recently opened Oregon Trail. The village covered several acres. "Warriors, women, and children swarmed like bees," Parkman wrote. "Hundreds of dogs, of all sizes and colors, ran restlessly about; and, close at hand, the wide shallow stream was alive with boys, girls, and young squaws, splashing, screaming, and laughing in the water. At the same time a long train of emigrants with their heavy wagons was crossing the creek, and dragging on in slow procession by the encampment."[27]

Despite the juxtaposition of moods that Parkman pointed out, the two races got on well. The emigrants were allowed to pass through Sioux territory without being molested, while the Sioux got coffee and sugar (to which they were addicted and wanted as much as they did whiskey) and some crackers. Indeed, Old Smoke's band of Oglalas had traveled for three days just to reach the Oregon Trail and enjoy some sweet coffee and baked food. It was established custom that the emigrants had to feed all Indians who came to visit. The whites didn't much like it, but it was better than fighting their way through the Plains.[28]

The red man-white man relationship, in short, was of mutual benefit. This had usually been the case when the Indians' contact with whites was limited to traders, and it continued to be so before the Oregon Trail began to fill with emigrants, whom Parkman found uncouth and unpleasant, but with whom the Sioux had good rapport —until the trickle of white men passing over the Plains became a great flood.

Parkman was a keen observer of Indian life. Speaking of the Oglala children, he complained that the parents "indulged to excess" their youngsters, showering them with love and never punishing them for any transgressions. Nearly all whites commented on this phenomenon and attributed various Indian shortcomings to it; the Sioux, for their part, were horrified at the emigrants' practice of beating their children, which the Indians decided was done in order to teach youngsters that the earth belongs to the powerful, who can do as they wish. In writing about Indian upbringing, Parkman let his prejudices show: "Their offspring became sufficiently undutiful and disobedient under this system of education, which tends not a little to foster that wild idea of liberty and utter intolerance of restraint which lie at the foundation of the Indian character."[29] Shocked as he was at the Oglalas' lack of discipline and unable to recognize how necessary the wild bravery of the Sioux male was to a warrior-nomad society, Parkman was nonetheless wise enough to recognize that it was a *system* of education and that it worked.

As was typical of Plains Indians, the Old Smoke band moved frequently while Parkman was living in the village. The Indians moved at least once a week, usually twice, during the summer months (in winter they hunkered down in a cottonwood valley and stayed put). Parkman was amazed at how quickly Old Smoke's people could be on the road. He awoke one morning to find that the encampment was disappearing: "Some of the lodges were reduced to nothing but bare skeletons of poles; the leather covering of others was flapping in the wind as the squaws pulled it off." Looking around, he noted that "where the great circle of the village had been only a few moments before, nothing now remained but a ring of horses and Indians, crowded in confusion together." The camp grounds looked like a garbage dump, with kettles, stone mallets, ladles of horn, buffalo robes, dried meat, and other items scattered everywhere. But before the sun had dried the dew, everything was securely packed and the village was on the move.

Parkman rode to the top of a bluff to observe: "Here were the heavy-laden pack-horses, some wretched old women leading them, and two or three children clinging to their backs. Here were mules or ponies covered from head to tail with gaudy trappings, and mounted by some gay young squaw, grinning bashfulness and pleasure. . . . Boys with miniature bows and arrows wandered over the plains, little naked children ran along on foot, and numberless dogs scampered among the feet of the horses. The young braves, gaudy with paint and feathers, rode in groups among the crowd, often galloping, two or three at once along the line, to try the speed of their horses." With the rough prairie and broken hills for background, Parkman found the restless scene "striking and picturesque beyond description."

The elders walked at the head of the column. "These were the dignitaries of the village, the old men . . . to whose age and experience that wandering democracy yielded a silent deference."[30]

When the moving village crossed a stream, utter confusion reigned, in marked contrast to the emigrant trains. The horses and dogs plunged right in, their travois floating along behind. Little children, clinging to a horse or an adult, screamed constantly, while the dogs barked and howled in chorus and the old women shrieked. Stray horses and colts dashed back and forth. "Buxom young squaws, blooming in all the charms of vermilion, stood here and there on the bank, holding aloft their master's lance, as a signal to collect the scattered portions of his household. In a few moments the crowd melted away; each family, with its horses and equipage, filing off to the plain; here, in the space of half an hour, arose sixty or seventy of their tapering lodges," and the camp quickly settled into lethargy, the old men sitting and talking in front of their lodges, the children playing.[31]

After many more moves and a successful buffalo hunt, the village started for the Black Hills to obtain poles for the winter lodges. Again Parkman was struck by the practices of that wandering democracy. "Amid the general abundance which . . . prevailed, there were no instances of individual privation; for although the hide and the tongue of the buffalo belong by exclusive right to the hunter who has killed it, yet any one else is equally entitled to help himself from the rest of the carcass. Thus the weak, the aged, and even the indolent come in for a share of the spoils, and many a helpless old woman, who would otherwise perish from starvation, is sustained in abundance."[32]

Parkman's over-all impression of the Oglalas was that they were a happy people, an impression shared by most whites who saw the Indians before the final struggle between the red man and the white man for control of the Plains began. They were well-fed, beautifully clothed, and nicely sheltered in a home that could be taken down and put up again in less than an hour. They had excellent personal relations. Their life was simple, their implements few, their plans for the future non-existent (beyond assuring an adequate meat supply for the winter). They had not the faintest idea of progress, which left them free to please themselves, which they did.

Nothing pleased them more than riding horseback across the prairie. As Frank Roe puts it, "The Indian set himself to *discover* the combined potentialities of horse and rider. The *act* of riding was a joy to him, as it is to most people whose fortune it has been to ride in conditions of untrammeled freedom such as the Indian's Plains environment bestowed. In this field of achievement (and for very practical ends) the Indians may be said to have begun where the circus trainer (for money) left off."[33]

But despite their conservatism, order, stability, and self-sufficiency, the Sioux at the time of Crazy Horse's birth were in a state of flux. Although they would not exert themselves enough to satisfy fur traders, they were tempted by the white man's goods, as signified by Old Smoke's journey to the Oregon Trail for coffee. They were caught in a dilemma. Having no desire to change their way of life, they nevertheless wanted the whiskey, coffee, metal, and guns of the whites, none of which they could have without changing their habits. Contact with the whites, although beneficial to the Indians, created a tension among them. Some bands located more or less permanently along the Oregon Trail, where they made pests of themselves as they begged the emigrants for this or that item of white culture, or they settled down beside the forts of the American Fur Company, especially Laramie, sold their women to the traders, and worked on a trap line during the day in order to have a little whiskey at night. Other villages stayed far away from the Oregon Trail and scornfully referred to their brothers as "Hang-Around-the-Forts" or "Laramie Loafers."

The Indian response to white intrusion, in short, was divided. Some became friends of the whites, while others turned hostile, a division that grew ever more pronounced and was crucial to the white man's eventual victory.

When Crazy Horse was still a small boy, the not-yet-famous Sitting Bull, a Hunkpapa Sioux, urged his people to leave the Oregon Trail and withdraw to the ways of their ancestors. "I don't want to have anything to do with people who make one carry water on the shoulders and haul manure," Sitting Bull declared. "The whites may get me at last, but I will have good times till then. You are fools to make yourselves slaves to a piece of fat bacon, some hardtack, and a little sugar and coffee."[34]

But half or more of the Sioux did not see things the way Sitting Bull did. They thought they could obtain what the white man offered without having to give up anything of their own. Thus the Sioux nation was split.

Crazy Horse was born into this tension and lived his whole life with it; in the end the divided Indian response to the challenge of the white man was directly responsible for his early death.

CHAPTER TWO

The Setting and the People: Ohio

"I know of no country, indeed, where the love of money has taken stronger hold on the affections of men, and where a profounder contempt is expressed for the theory of the permanent equality of property."   Alexis de Tocqueville

In 1839, the year of George Armstrong Custer's birth, the United States was a country of striking diversity in its physical features, its economy, and its people. There were immigrants from all over Europe and Africa, speaking a variety of languages and carrying on equally varied cultural traditions. There were scores of religions, and although nearly all were within the Christian framework, wide differences marked the various rituals. Within the two basic types of economy, slave labor south of the Ohio River and wage labor to the north, there were hundreds of ways a man could make a living. Frontiersmen, filling up the empty land east of the Mississippi River, worked from dawn to dusk to become self-sufficient. Their tools and work habits were hardly more sophisticated than those of the Indians whom they had only recently replaced. On the East Coast, meanwhile, a complex culture had arisen; American merchants, lawyers, doctors, politicians, and sometimes even manufacturers could match the best Europe had to offer. In the South, despite its political domination by the planters and the slave economy, great opportunities existed for the artisan, the merchant, the small farmer, and even the ironmaker.

The land itself encouraged diversity. With the single exception of Russia, no other country had such a wide pattern of different land forms, soil types, and climate.

Yet there was a unity to the United States, a unity born of many factors, of which possibly the most important was the political genius of the Founding Fathers, who in writing the Constitution had managed to achieve a unique balance between national and local interests and governmental power. If there were few national institutions, there were national feelings and traditions. Americans had unbounded respect for republican government, a deep loathing of monarchy, and a common conviction that their country was without peer. They embraced the idea of political equality, as demonstrated by the position of the Northwest Territories, which—unlike any previous colonies—enjoyed full participation in the central government.

Nearly every white American believed in the future, in the doctrine that things were getting better all the time, for individuals and for the country as a whole. Faith and ambition helped draw Americans together; so did their mobility. Although they were by no means nomads, Americans moved longer distances, and more often, than Europeans had ever dreamed possible. In the process, Americans came to know men of widely separate backgrounds and heritages, giving to most Americans a breadth of experience unknown elsewhere.

No region of the country was typical, just as no man could be said to be a typical American, but there was one state in the United States that pulled together most of the traits usually associated with Americans and produced a blend that could at least be called representative. That state was Ohio. Its population came from both sides of the Ohio River and included people from every part of Europe and most of Africa. In 1850, out of a state-wide population of almost 2 million, 62 per cent had been born in Ohio, 27 per cent elsewhere in America, and 11 per cent in Europe. Ohio's location, fertility, and opportunities made it equally attractive to Yankees and Southerners; New York State contributed 86,000 emigrants to Ohio's total, while Virginia also had sent 86,000 settlers to the state. There were 36,000 residents of Ohio who had been born in Great Britain, 51,-000 born in Ireland, and 112,000 in Germany.[1] Africa contributed 25,000 free blacks to the population, half born in Ohio, half in the slave states.[2] Taken together, Ohio had a wonderful mixture of peoples.

In the first decade of Custer's life, Ohio enjoyed an economic boom. Population increased from 1.5 million to 2 million. Most of the growth was non-agricultural, which meant that Ohio was becoming more complex, specialized, and richer. While there were still settlers trying to scratch out a living on newly cleared land, there were thousands of solid, well-established commercial farmers, artisans of all kinds, lawyers, ministers, doctors and other professional men, and industrialists. In 1840, 272,000 Ohio men were involved in farming; by 1850 that number had dropped to 270,000.

The number of men engaged in commerce, trade, manufacturing, or the mechanical arts had grown from 76,000 in 1840 to more than 140,000 in 1850. The number of professional men had grown from 5,600 to 9,000.[3] Almost everyone worked. The "whole number of Paupers supported in whole or part," as the census taker put it in 1850, was 1,250.[4]

It was a young population. In 1850 only 16 per cent of Ohio's people were over forty years of age; another 11 per cent was between thirty and forty years old; 73 per cent were under thirty.[5] Ohio's people were even more diverse in their religion than they were in origin or employment; fifty-one distinct religious denominations sponsored nearly four thousand churches in Ohio.[6]

Ohio was wealthy. The sources of that wealth were the labor of the people—just plain hard work, with lots of sweat, from dawn to dusk—the influx of speculative capital from Europe and the eastern states, and a furious assault on the state's natural resources, designed to change the environment to one more suitable—i.e., one more immediately productive. All three elements were crucial. Without the back-breaking labor nothing could have been done. But the workers needed tools, and the settlers needed money to purchase their land and equipment, and the towns needed money to build and grow. The risk capital could only come from the East. All the work and money in the world, however, by themselves could not have turned Ohio into the "Garden of the World," as her residents liked to call the state. Fertile land, virgin to the plow, and minerals within easy reach beneath the earth were also necessary to success.

There has been much speculation about the origin of the American's penchant for hard work, most of it starting with some reference to Calvinist doctrine. Undoubtedly Calvinism played a role, but few Virginians in Ohio were Calvinists, and yet they evidently worked as long and as hard as did their Yankee neighbors. No dry religious doctrine, not even a burning faith, could account for the way Americans labored. They worked so much that work became a psychic need with them; Americans were fidgety and nervous when they were not "doing something," anything, as long as it was important enough to be called "work."

Americans worked because they believed it was godly to do so, because of the vastness of the task facing them, and because the work would be rewarded. They were filled with a feeling that there was much to do—as a western traveler in the 1850s put it, "the forest to be felled, the city to be built, the railroad surveyed, the swamp cleared, political, social, and religious systems to be organized . . ."[7]

Americans saw the land different from what it was; looking to the future, they imagined bridges over the rivers, roads over the mountains, the forest replaced by the garden, towns springing up at every bend of every river, great cities growing wherever two rivers came together. They lived in a fantasy world, except that the fantasies were for the most part realistic and came true. With all that work around waiting to be done, Americans were always itchy to get at the job and transform dream into reality.

Ohioans knew that the work would pay off. Nowhere else on the globe, as Henry Steele Commager puts it, "had nature been at once so rich and so generous, and her riches were available to all who had the enterprise to take them and the good fortune to be white." Ohioans realized, as did every American, the truth of Commager's statement: "Nothing in all history had ever succeeded like America."[8]

The riches were there to be had, and everything in the society and the environment encouraged the citizen to think big and work hard. There was a sense of spaciousness, an invitation to mobility—physical, economic, and social—and an encouragement to enterprise that made Americans forever optimists. Progress was no mere philosophical notion or ideal; it was all around, visible everywhere, a commonplace. The American, Commager points out, "planned ambitiously and was used to seeing even his most visionary plans surpassed; he came at last to believe that nothing was beyond his power and to be impatient with any success that was less than triumph" or, one might add, with any success that took longer than immediately.[9]

The political system protected a man's right to possess exclusively whatever he had earned or built. Squatters were sometimes forced off the land by speculators and lawyers, to be sure, and often enough a frontiersman had to fight for what was his, but within the organized states a man's property was secure both in law and custom. That security encouraged him to earn or build more, a process that could go on for a lifetime, for there was no limit on how much property or money a man could possess.

Just as the system encouraged each man to work, so did it encourage him to look out for himself and to hell with others. Nearly every European visitor to the United States before the Civil War commented on the extreme individualism of Americans with regard to matters of money or property and wondered how such a dog-eat-dog society could function. To the American mind, the answer was simple: every individual's economic advance redounded to the benefit of the whole. Every tree felled, every bridge built, every industry established strengthened the nation and made it richer, and the richer the nation was, the greater the opportunity for individuals to get rich. Both federal and state governments, meanwhile, would see to it—at least in theory—that the race for riches was fairly run and that to the victor belonged the spoils.

The stability of the political system, the willingness of the men of the West to work, and the persistent image that in the West lay the Garden of Eden, or the marketplace and manufactory of the world, or a combination of both, all led to making the West a prime investment opportunity for European and eastern capital. Very few men in the West itself ever got rich, at least by eastern standards; the largest share of the profits usually wound up in New York, Philadelphia, Boston, or London. Speculators of all kinds poured investment capital into the West, as they had from the beginning of the white man's conquest of the New World. Like the squatters, the speculators saw in the West "a prospect into unlimited empires,"[10] or, more succinctly, a pot of gold. Speculators, or rather their agents, were always stirring up emotions in the West, encouraging men to push on even farther west to extend the frontier, to build new towns, new farms, new factories, anything, everything. The settlers hardly had to be convinced, for they shared with the speculators a sense of bigness and of power and an assumption of destiny.

From the time of the founding of Jamestown, Americans had been optimists, but the size and shape of their optimism were intensified in the 1840s. A world was beginning to open for them, justifying the high hopes of the past and enriching the fantasies about the future. Before the 1840s those who crossed the mountains and descended into the valley of the Ohio cut themselves off from regular contact with the outside world. But the coming of the railroad made travel back and forth, and within the valley, much easier. New printing techniques, meanwhile, cut printing costs and made penny newspapers available to the Ohio people, and the telegraph provided the mass circulation papers with all the news from Europe and the East Coast. In 1828 there were sixty-six newspapers and periodicals published in Ohio; in 1840 there were one hundred twenty-three; by 1850 there were two hundred thirty-seven.[11]

The forties were a time of increasing specialization of labor. The sewing machine, patented in the decade, relieved women of the task of making men's clothing by hand; factories took over that job. Saddles and shoes were also factory made. The frontiersman, who could do a tolerable piece of work on any job that needed to be done, gave way to various specialists, who by sticking to one task did it better and simultaneously released time for his customers so that they could concentrate on their specialties. Custer's father was part of the process, and of the westward movement; in the 1830s he left Maryland to become a blacksmith in the village of New Rumley, Ohio.

New uses for steam power, and new iron boilers to hold the steam inside, extended the American's power over his environment and provided something of a symbol for the most dynamic people the world had ever seen. Max Lerner sees dynamism as the key to the American character, for it permeated everything. There was the dynamism of the pioneer and the mechanic, the farmer and the inventor, the financier and the managers, the salesmen and the speculators, the lawyer and the politician, the intellectual and the soldier.[12]

It was a dynamism dedicated to transformation, and nowhere was it seen more clearly than in the assault on nature. The magnificent forests of the Ohio Valley, unsurpassed anywhere, were in the eyes of Ohioans nothing more than obstacles to progress. Standing trees were an affront to Americans because they were worse than useless—they took up sunlight and soil nutrients that could better be used by corn. Although everyone used wood as a source of heat or as building material, few thought of the forest in productive terms since there was more wood than could ever possibly be used, or so the settlers believed. Ohioans were united in their desire, nay passion, to destroy the forest, and much of their working time went into the task.

Clearing the land challenged even the Americans' capacity for work. One began by girdling the big timber, which would kill the tree in a year. Meanwhile the settler grubbed out all bushes less than six inches in diameter and cut down and burned all saplings. It took a good farmhand sixteen days to clear an acre for the plow. The heavy deadened timber remained. These half-cleared fields were a familiar sight to anyone living in Ohio before the Civil War. One Ohio resident, David S. Stanley, who later attended West Point and then became a major general and served with Custer in the Indian-fighting Army, described the scene: "Huge trees dotted over the field, their bare bodies and naked limbs in the dusk of the evening or the pale light of the moon, having a most dismal and ghost-like appearance."[13] Beautiful black walnut, oak, maple, and other prime lumber stood dead and pathetic—and hated—wherever one traveled in the Ohio Valley.

Removing the huge crop of dead trees was an arduous task. Workers cut the tree down, then chopped the top limbs into ten-foot lengths. These they piled on the main trunk and set afire. Once the great log had burned in half, a team of horses or oxen swung the sections around so that they were parallel to each other. Then came the hardest job of all, rolling the largest logs together. The aid of half a dozen or more neighbors was necessary because one or two men could not handle the big logs. When that task was accomplished, the men piled smaller logs crosswise on the trunks, with all the smaller timber and limbs thrown on top, and started the fire.

"To see ten or fifteen acres on the day or more particularly on the night of firing," Stanley wrote of his Ohio boyhood, "was to see a grand sight. . . . The adjoining woods are lighted up, fences stand out in bright relief, the sky is red with reflected forms and firelight, and saddest part of all, hundreds of cords of the finest firewood and thousands of feet of the most beautiful timber—all consumed and for no purpose but to get rid of it."[14]

"Getting rid of it"—with "it" meaning anything or anyone who stood in the way of progress—was a universal American passion and a commonplace experience for all those living in the Old Northwest. It took time; by as late as 1850 nearly half the land in Harrison County, Ohio, where Custer lived, was still uncleared.[15] But the determination was there, and the job was finished. Arthur Moore describes the results: "Whole forests of oak, beech, poplar, maple, and walnut, standing since Columbus, collapsed . . . from girdling and deadening with fire. There was in the heart of the new race no more consideration for the trees than for the game until the best of both were gone; steel conquered the West but chilled the soul of the conqueror. This assault on nature, than which few more frightful spectacles could be imagined, owed much to sheer need, but something also to a compelling desire to destroy conspicuous specimens of the fauna and flora of the wilderness. The origin of this mad destructiveness may be in doubt, but there is no question about its effect. The Ohio Valley today has neither trees nor animals to recall adequately the splendor of the garden of the Indian which the white man found and used so profligately."[16]

From the beginning, then, the American tendency was to attack and destroy, then build. The Americans eliminated the forest and the game; even earlier they had eliminated the native human inhabitants of the valley. Twelve years before Custer's father Emmanuel was born, "Mad Anthony" Wayne had opened Ohio to settlement by defeating the Indians at the battle of Fallen Timbers (1794). Emmanuel Custer was himself a member of the local militia, which was something of a joke as a military institution by the 1840s but nevertheless a vivid reminder of the day when the settlers had engaged in combat with the Indians. Western boys took as their heroes the Indian fighters; killing Indians was the noblest activity a resident of the valley could engage in. Hunting Indians was, besides, incomparably more exciting than hunting game, as frontiersman Adam Poe candidly admitted. "I've tried all kinds of game, boys!" he exclaimed. "I've fit bar and painter [panther] and catamount, but," he added regretfully, with a vague, unsatisfied longing in his voice, "thar ain't no game like Ingins—no, sir! no game like Injins."

Arthur Moore, after an intensive study of the thought of the residents of the Ohio Valley, has concluded that although Indian-initiated atrocities doubtless produced many an Indian hater, "the white man's desire for fame possibly took as many Indian lives as his passion for revenge." The Indian, Moore writes in a penetrating passage, "was the finest instrument of the hero's ambition, for notable deeds wrought against him earned the adulation of the public."[17] As the frontier advanced, newspaper reporters kept up with it, to send back East impassioned, heroic stories about the mighty conquerors of the red man. The stock adventure stories of the 1840s, sold in cheap paperback editions by the thousands to eager young readers, including Custer, recounted the deeds of the Indian fighters.

The Indian fighter was the advance agent of civilization, doing good and necessary work for the future benefit and · rosperity of the United States. For the American public, as Andrew Jackson's and William Henry Harrison's careers illustrated, no reward was too great for those who drove the Indian out of the path of progress.

But if the frontiersman saw the Indian as only a more exciting and challenging obstacle than a tree, in the eastern states there was a growing sentiment that the Indian was a noble savage. The number of Indian lovers grew in direct relationship to the distance from the frontier. Here, as in so many things, Ohio stood in the middle: if there was no Indian threat, there were old Indian fighters around to remind people of what it had been like. So too, however, were copies of the *Leatherstocking Tales*, James Fenimore Cooper's romantic confession of his own ambivalence toward the Indian.

Like so many of his fellow Americans, Cooper was drawn to the ideas of a primitive, free access to the bounty of nature, the rough equality of all men in a society, and of a natural, intuitive theology. These themes enjoyed something of a vogue in the America of Custer's youth, especially among intellectuals and reformers, who were disappointed at (or resentful of) America's failure to become a "new society" in a New World. In their eyes, the United States had repeated all the mistakes of Europe, with individual appropriation and inviolable property rights locking the many out from access to the wealth of the few, leading to a social stratification based on unequal distribution of property.[18]

Indian lovers tended to be reformers, or vice versa, and they saw so much to be done in the nation—starting with the elimination of slavery (Indian lovers and reformers were hard to find in the South) —that they had little time for the Indians themselves. Living on land only recently conquered from the Indians, they were content to defend verbally the rights of the Indians out West. Certainly they never developed the methods necessary to study the Indians. Rather, the Indian lovers, like the Indian haters, were satisfied with their own image of the red man.

Thus two myths existed together, irreconcilable but alive, available as a set of ideas, however contradictory, to any American who wanted to absorb them as part of his thought. To the American, the Indian was simultaneously always honest—and forever a liar; always courageous—and forever a coward; always happy—and forever downcast; always colorful and attractive in appearance—and forever dirty and disgusting. The Indian was faithful and kind—and disloyal and cruel.

Ambivalence always characterized American thought about Indians, but everyone used the Indian to prove some theory. To Southerners, Indians provided evidence of the inferiority of nonwhite peoples. To frontiersmen, Indian atrocities proved that the primitives were beasts, to be treated as such. Settlers used the Indians to prove their own economic ideas—removal of the red men was just, because they had not improved the land; putting it the other way around, settlers had a right to exclusive title to the land because they had worked on it and improved it, while the Indians who had neglected the land had no just claim to it.[19] To reformers, Indians were living proof that a rough form of social equality, with equal distribution and ownership, and a closeness to nature, made for a happy life, in contrast to the "miserable conditions" under which the bulk of the American people lived.

Another element in the attraction of the Indians, or at least the idea of Indians, was that of wildness. The Indians were wild; whites were civilized—and tame. Indians knew the mysterious ways of the forest; whites did not. Indians wore rough, loose fitting, comfortable clothes; whites wore smooth, tight, constraining outfits. Indians were tough and manly; civilized whites were soft and feminine. Indians were at one with nature, while whites had somehow lost touch with the elemental forces.

"It is perhaps the consummate irony," Arthur Moore writes, "that at each step up from savagery the human race has regarded the fruits of progress with a degree of misgiving and often longed against reason for a return to a simpler condition."[20] This desire for the not-here and the not-now has always existed, of course, nor without reason, but the point is that it added to the American's ambivalent attitude toward Indians. Officers in the Indian-fighting Army after the Civil War were often heard to say that they much preferred the wild Indians to the tame ones, or that if they were Indians, they would most certainly be out with the hostiles, not drunk on the reservation. Custer expressed such sentiments frequently. These same officers took the lead in making certain that there were no more wild Indians.

So if Americans could not agree on what to think about the Indian, they did agree on what to do about him. If he stood in the way, he had to be moved. This fixed idea sprang, in part, from the nearly universally held notion that the United States had a "manifest destiny" to overspread the continent. Nothing could stand in the way of that achievement, not treaties, not truth, not courage, not suffering, nothing. No boundary lines were fixed and final, not until they became American boundaries. Each time any section or group within the United States cast jealous eyes on neighboring territory, be it Indian, or Spanish, or French, or Mexican, or British, the Americans readily agreed that the true, natural God-given boundaries of the country in actuality lay thither.[21]

Nineteenth-century Americans went on a campaign of military conquest unrivaled in world history, a campaign that was crucial to keeping alive the fundamental ideas of American life. The conquered land was "unsettled," and long before 1893, when Frederick Jackson Turner delivered his famous address on the meaning of the frontier, Americans knew the central importance of free land to the American way of life. For not only did the conquest of the continent add to the strength of the nation, it also nurtured in the breast of millions of young men the hope that they too could get rich. Expansion by conquest, in short, kept the economic boom, and the boom psychology, alive.

Even an Indian lover like Thomas Farnham, a Vermont lawyer who traveled in the Old Northwest in 1839, accepted the prevailing philosophy. "The Indians' bones must enrich the soil, before the plough of civilized man can open it," Farnham declared in a grisly passage. "The noble heart . . . must fatten the corn hills of a more civilized race! The sturdy plant of the wilderness droops under the enervating culture of the garden. The Indian is buried with his arrows and bow." Those Indians who did not serve as fertilizer, meanwhile, could be educated and civilized—i.e., made over into white men.

Here again the Indian lover and the Indian hater came together; once the Indian was removed from the path of progress, he should be civilized and Christianized. The problem was, how to do it? How could one change the virtually anarchic Indian, who was in the habit of doing as he pleased, into a stable and productive citizen? The answer was simple and direct, as it had been throughout the period of white contact with the red men.

First, make them dependent. Meriwether Lewis and William Clark saw this in a flash after their initial encounter with the Sioux, of whom they said, "These are the vilest miscreants of the savage race, and must ever remain the pirates of the Missouri, until such measures are pursued, by our government, as will make them feel a dependence on its will for their supply of merchandise."[22] All that would then be needed to put the Indian on the road to civilization was, in the words of Henry Knox, the Secretary of War in 1789, to give the Indian "a love for exclusive property."[23]

That statement cut through all the verbiage and philosophical dispute about what an Indian was or was not and neatly defined what he must be, if he were to "be" at all. It was the guiding light for the missionaries and other friends of the Indians; they taught their wards that a love for private property and a love for the missionaries' Bible went hand in hand. Moreover, the statement recognized *the* fundamental difference between white and red society, the difference from which all others sprang. The Indians had a communal ideal and practice, while the whites had an individual ideal and practice.* The Indians had no real notion of the meaning of private property; the whites not only understood it, they embraced it and all of the consequences that went with it. Even those consequences that led to excesses, such as extreme competitiveness, were exalted into virtues when they furthered the acquisition of wealth or fame.

* Obviously, as will be seen later, things were not quite that simple. Within the context of a communal society in which material goods were shared more or less equally, the Indians followed their own conscience and did whatever it was they wanted to do; within an individualistic society in which everyone was free to keep whatever he could get his hands on, most white individuals were tightly constrained in their actions by social and legal mores.

The way to make the red men into acceptable neighbors or even someday into members of the community was to nurture in them "a love for exclusive property," for this was the glue binding white society together. Alexis de Tocqueville, looking at America with the eyes of a French aristocrat, was most struck by the "general equality of condition among the people."[24] What he meant was not equality of possession, but rather that Americans were equally free to get rich or famous. "I know of no country, indeed," he wrote, "where the love of money has taken stronger hold on the affections of men, and where a profounder contempt is expressed for the theory of the permanent equality of property."[25]

The absence of a feudal tradition, the presence of natural wealth in uncountable amounts, and a political system that put its stress on equality of opportunity, all combined to make America the most open society in the civilized world. Anyone could become rich, anyone could become famous. Social and economic mobility, down as well as up the ladder, was the rule rather than the exception. So was the assumption that every man should stand on his own feet, which meant in practice that he should regard all his fellow men as competitors. The co-operation between people that was so central to primitive life and feudal tradition was, if not entirely absent from American life, only incidental to it. Farmers got together to share the work that no individual could do by himself, and cornhusking or logrolling or haymaking became social festivals, but essentially a man farmed by himself and kept what he grew.

In the end, the American was lonesome. De Tocqueville captured this feeling when he wrote, "Thus, not only does democracy make every man forget his ancestors, but it hides his descendants and separates his contemporaries from him; it throws him back forever upon himself alone, and threatens in the end to confine him entirely within the solitude of his own heart."[26]

And the American was ambitious, always, to improve himself and his station in his society. "The first thing which strikes a traveller in the United States," De Tocqueville noted, "is the innumerable multitude of those who seek to emerge from their original condition."[27] Opportunities to improve himself lay all around the American, but precisely because they did and because a man could fall even easier than he could rise, the American carried a heavy burden. There was no real security, no real sense of place, not even for the rich and famous, who necessarily wanted to become richer or more famous.

In pre-Civil War America a son was expected to do better in life

—i.e., make more money or own more land or become more famous or powerful—than the father had done. This expectation hung over the head of every boy in the United States. It was a revolutionary expectation. Never before, anywhere, had the mass of the citizenry expected an improvement in their condition, or acted on the assumption that things were getting better all the time, or—most of all—that where the father had eighty acres or a thousand dollars, the son would have one hundred sixty acres or ten thousand dollars. It put an immense strain on the boys, for if they just held onto what the old man had, they would be failures. The American definition of success was something new in world history; the pressure of that definition, that need to improve, to do better, was felt by every lad in the land.

The thought that a man could and should improve his station in life was, I think, what De Crèvecoeur had in mind when he wrote, "The American is a new man who acts on new principles." Certainly he did not mean that Americans had left European influences behind, not when he saw Christian churches in every village he visited, European technology on every farm, European-style merchants in every town, selling European goods; not when every lawyer he met had read Edward Coke and every politician had read John Locke, not when he saw Americans enslaving black men and calling Indians savage inferiors. What was new in America was individual expectation of personal betterment. It made Americans into the hardest working people in the world, and the most ambitious.

Ambition was the key to the American character. It was the motive power that got the work done, and the one sentiment shared by all white Americans, who were otherwise so diverse. George Armstrong Custer knew it well; late in his life he wrote: "In years long-numbered with the past, when I was verging upon manhood, my every thought was ambitious—not to be wealthy, not to be learned, but to be great. I desired to link my name with acts & men, and in such a manner as to be a mark of honor—not only to the present, but to future generations."[28] In the end his ambition was directly responsible for his early death.

CHAPTER THREE

"Curly"

"When we were young all we thought about was going to war with some other nation; all tried to get their names up the highest, and whoever did so was the principal man in the nation; and Crazy Horse wanted to get to the highest station and rank."

Chips, an Oglala Sioux

The Black Hills, one of the oldest mountain ranges in the world, rise up in the middle of the northern Great Plains. The highest point, Harney Peak, is slightly over 7,200 feet above sea level. About one hundred miles long, north and south, and some sixty miles wide, the Hills were not extensive enough to provide permanent homes for the Sioux, who in any case were people of the Plains unsuited for long habitation in mountains. The Sioux used the Hills as a refuge in periods of bad weather, for occasional hunting, and as a source of their lodge and travois poles. Generally, however, they must have felt somewhat uncomfortable in the mountain forest; in a vague sort of way the Hills became, for the Sioux, a place where spirits dwelled, a holy place, called *Pa Sapa*. In 1874 George Armstrong Custer led an expedition that opened the Hills to white gold miners, but until that time *Pa Sapa* belonged to the Sioux.

Just northeast of the Hills a volcanic bubble erupts out of the earth. Called Bear Butte, it gives an unsurpassed view of the Plains stretching out to the north, east and west, and of the Hills to the south. The Belle Fourche River runs along the northern base of Bear Butte, which has a special place in Indian mythology. The great Cheyenne lawgiver, Sweet Medicine, received the Four Sacred Arrows and the laws of his tribe from spirits who lived in a cave on Bear Butte.[1] The Sioux often gathered at the foot of the butte for what amounted to an annual convention, most of the scattered bands coming together at the beginning or end of the summer to exchange news and gossip, to trade for goods, and to carry out various religious rituals.

At one of these gatherings, in the fall of the year 1841,[2] a Brulé woman, her name unknown to history, wife of Oglala holy man Crazy Horse, went down to the stream, where, on a piece of soft deerskin placed over a bed of sand, assisted by a midwife, she quietly delivered her second child and first son. If the baby cried, she pinched his nose with her thumb and first finger, holding her palm over his mouth, until he stopped. No one, not even an infant, could be allowed to give away the tribe's position, not when an enemy might be lurking nearby.

The boy's first meal was a community project. The Sioux believed that the colostrum (the first secretion from the milk glands) was poison for the baby, so mothers did not offer the breast until there was a good stream of perfect milk. Relatives and friends prepared the baby's first meal; they gathered the best berries and herbs the prairie afforded and put the juice from these into a buffalo bladder, which served as a nursing bottle. The mother, meanwhile, had the colostrum sucked from her breast by an older woman who had been commanded in her dreams to perform this office.[3]

This boy was different from other Oglala babies. He had light, curly hair and a light complexion. As he would not receive his real name until he had accomplished a notable deed or had a memorable dream, the Indians called him by various nicknames, all connected to his distinguishing physical characteristics. Sometimes he was "Curly Hair," sometimes the "Light-Haired Boy"; as he grew older he usually was called "Curly."[4]

Curly's family was a solid, respected one among the Indians, rather than prominent. His father, Crazy Horse, was not a warrior but a healer, a dreamer and an interpreter of dreams. He had two wives, although the older one had died; both women were Brulés and both were sisters of Spotted Tail, already a famous young warrior although only about twenty years old when Curly was born. Eventually Curly's uncle would be head of all the Brulés, their leader for nearly three decades.[5] It was customary for Sioux men to have more than one wife; ordinarily they would marry sisters, as did Crazy Horse, on the sensible basis that if two women were going to live with one man under the same roof, the chances of their getting along together were better if they were sisters.

Curly spent most of his infanthood on a cradleboard. He was fed on demand, not on schedule. By the time he was one year old he was receiving supplementary feedings, such as a piece of buffalo meat chewed first by his sister and dipped in soup, on which he sucked. When he was two he ate soup from a spoon. These extra feedings, however, had little to do with weaning, for he was free to take the breast as long as he wanted to do so—most Sioux children were off the breast by the age of three or four, but sometimes a child would nurse until he was six. In any event, the decision to stop nursing was the child's. White observers often saw Sioux children of two or three years of age stop their play, casually nurse for a few moments from the nearest woman, then return to play. The system gave the mothers more freedom than they could have enjoyed had they been solely responsible for the nurture of their children, while it implanted in the children the fundamental Sioux doctrine that everything the tribe had was to be shared equally.[6]

As soon as he learned to talk, Curly called all his maternal female relatives "mother" and all his paternal male relatives "father"; the aged, whether related or not, were "grandmother" and "grandfather." He had a strong sense of being welcome and of belonging, for he had a wide variety of personalities to deal with and a knowledge that his well-being was a tribal, not just a family, responsibility. He was free to stop in any tipi anytime he chose, to be feasted and petted.[7]

The Sioux treated their children with great love and tenderness. Fathers and other men would play with children for hours on end. That they would do anything for their children was exemplified by the fact that as long as a child was nursing, his parents slept apart because intercourse might lead to pregnancy which would stop the flow of milk. Once Curly was permanently off the cradleboard and free to roam the village, he knew practically no restraint. He was never struck by an adult.[8]

Some dangers the children learned about from their older friends; others they discovered on their own. When infants went creeping around the tipi floor, for example, no one stopped them from reaching into the fire. The children thus learned a quick and probably permanent lesson without being yelled at or yanked away from the source of danger. The adults did not frustrate the child's natural curiosity or take onto themselves the blame for hurt and pain that rightly belonged to the fire. Nor did the Sioux directly threaten the child who irritated them. Instead, they warned that if he did not cease the "owl" or the "sioko" (frightener of children) would "take him away." Later, the threat was that "the white man is going to take you away."[9]

Curly ran naked much of the time before his seventh or eighth birthday, especially in summer and even in winter within the tipi. Toilet training was in the hands of older children in the village, and it was done by example, not force. Indian children quickly learned

to follow slightly older siblings to designated spots outside the village to relieve themselves. This was, incidentally, a sanitary method
of disposal, partly because of frequent moves and partly because
the sun, wind, and rain soon broke down the feces on the open
prairie. The white man's outhouse kept the elements out but let the
flies in.[10]

Toilet training was but one aspect of a general socializing pattern;
Sioux children learned by imitating older children, not from
adults.[11] Games were an important part of the process. Curly's first
games revolved around home life; older children would make little
tipis, travois, and implements for the youngsters so that they could
play house. During these play sessions and by observing what was
going on in the village, Curly absorbed the basic social customs of
his people. A married man, for example, never spoke directly to his
mother-in-law, something Curly learned when he played the role of
husband in a game or when his father asked him to say something
to his grandmother. The children gossiped incessantly, again imitating their elders, gossip being a basic form of social control among
the Sioux.

As Curly grew toward adolescence his games became rougher and
more diverse. The main, unspoken and unacknowledged, object of
the games was to prepare him for adult tasks. Skill, endurance, brute
force, and the ability to withstand pain were the major elements
within the myriad of games the boys played. There was a wide diversity to the games, involving every physical activity, most skills needed
for survival on the Plains, and much excitement, for the Sioux were
gamblers and even the children gambled on their games, using their
toys for bets. The children played on the snow or grass or ice or
whatever suited their fancy.

A favorite boys' game was "Throw at Each Other with Mud."
Teams of boys would attack each other with mud balls which they
threw from the tips of short springy sticks. In the "Buffalo-Hunt"
game a boy attached a large cactus to a five-foot stick; the center
had been cut from the cactus to represent the buffalo's heart. As
the boy walked about holding the cactus above him, playmates tried
to pierce the heart with their arrows. If they missed, the "buffalo"
chased them a little with the cactus, but if an arrow went through
the heart, he chased the hunter until he could poke him on the
buttocks with the cactus.

In the "Fire-Throwing" game teams of boys would set fire to piles
of brush. After each player had picked up a few flaming sticks, the
teams attacked each other, the players hurling the sparkling brands

at the "enemy." The object was to drive the other team away from its brush pile, but if neither team retreated the players would meet in the center and strike at one another amid sparks and smoke. One player recalled, "In close fighting after you have hit an enemy two or three times, your torch goes out. Then you get your share until his stick dies out."[12]

Perhaps the most popular boys' game was stealing meat from the drying racks. Sioux women cut buffalo meat into long, thin strips, which they hung on a rack in the sun to dry before storing for the winter. The racks were high enough to keep the dogs from the meat, but not the boys. The women kept guard over the racks and would shoo away Curly or any boy they caught near them; worse, they would tease the boy for getting caught, making him an object of ridicule with his age mates. But the boys got their share of meat, too, and in the process learned stealth, daring, and the other essential attributes of the successful thief—all of which they would use when they grew up and began stealing horses from neighboring tribes.[13]

By the time Curly was stealing meat and playing the "Fire-Throwing" game, there was a sharp division between his activities and those of girls his age. Girls never stole meat or participated in the rough-and-tumble games. Instead, they played with infants or dolls and were beginning to learn beadwork, food preparation, and other household tasks.

Shooting arrows from a bow was a major pastime of Sioux boys, nicely suited to stirring up Curly's competitive instincts. His father or an uncle probably made Curly's first bow, but by the time he was ten years old he was making his own, and testing himself with them against his peers. Who could shoot the farthest, the quickest, the straightest? Day after day, year after year, Curly and his friends found out. Most Indians became amazingly proficient; Colonel Richard Dodge stated that a Plains Indian could "grasp five to ten arrows in his left hand, and discharge them so rapidly that the last will be on its flight before the first has touched the ground, and with such force that each would mortally wound a man . . ." A full-grown Sioux warrior could drive an arrow clear through a buffalo.[14]

As soon as Curly could saddle a pony, his father Crazy Horse gave him a colt of his own. This became Curly's pony to do with as he wished and was his responsibility. He also assumed responsibility for the village herd when it was his turn to keep watch at night for wandering horse thieves. During the day he rode to his heart's content, while at night he observed the herd and came to understand horses' habits and their needs. And he was always learning—how to sleep while riding, how to get the most out of a horse, how to gallop past a fallen comrade and jerk him up onto the back of the horse, and a thousand other tricks.[15]

During the long winter nights, when the village was snugly settled in a valley, Curly learned the tribal traditions. Grandmothers and grandfathers were the storytellers, satisfying the children's curiosity about where the Sioux came from, why a tipi always opened to the east, where and how a particular animal species acquired its distinctive character traits, the origin of Sioux law and political organization, and much else. The myths usually had a moral—tricksters would get tricked, the evil were punished, generosity brought rewards—and, along with gossip, were fundamental to the socialization process.

The myths emphasized the relatedness of life, for in them plants and animals talked and exhibited other human characteristics. The myths taught young Curly that everything had its place and function and that all things and animals were important. The stories also gave him a feeling of balance; one, for example, told how the animals got together one day and decided to get back at mankind for killing and eating them. Each animal decided on a different disease he would give to man in retribution. Upon hearing of this, the plants got together and each one decided to provide a remedy for a specific disease. The telling of this myth might lead to the handing down of ancient wisdom about the medicinal properties of various leaves, bark, roots, and herbs.[16]

Sioux boys often paired off in special friendships, called "kolas"; they agreed to be partners in all undertakings, to share material belongings, and to hunt and make war together. Kolas were above all loyal, and it was considered good to be a kola. Curly's kola was High Back Bone, called "Hump" for short, a Miniconjou-Oglala slightly older than Curly.[17] Curly and Hump did everything together. They organized hunting parties, which mimicked those of their elders, except that the game was not buffalo but rabbit, small birds, and the like. They acted as leaders, persuading others to go along and directing them once on the hunt.[18]

By the time he was ten, Curly was well on his way to knowing the significance of everything that happened around him. The prairie was his schoolhouse. Each morning when he left the tipi, his father, Crazy Horse, would tell him to study his environment. When Curly returned in the evening, Crazy Horse would sit with him for an hour or so and question him about the day. Curly had to know which side of the trees had lighter-colored bark and which side had the more regular branches. He had to be able to describe the birds he had seen that day and their activities. Crazy Horse would then explain to him the meaning of the jay's call or that when swallows flew with their mouths empty they were going to water but if their mouths had mud in them, they were coming from water. From these and scores of other signs, Curly learned the most fundamental lesson of survival on the Plains; as Thomas Mails puts it, "wherever he was, a first requirement was that by merely looking at the country, a warrior should be able to judge accurately in what direction water could be found and the approximate distance to it."

Curly learned that there were signs everywhere on the Plains. If the wild horse herd was strung out and walking steadily along, it was headed for water; if the horses were scattered and grazing they were coming from water. Crazy Horse and other adults encouraged Curly to study all the animals, unobserved, for they had much to teach. Eagles and hawks gave lessons in patience and how to strike; coyotes showed how to elude capture. Tracks told their own story, to those who could read them, as did droppings.

The idea of the animals as teachers was deeply ingrained in Indian life and was one aspect of what the French anthropologist Claude Lévi-Strauss calls the "science of the concrete." To illustrate his point, Lévi-Strauss quotes a North American Indian: "We know what the animals do, what are the needs of the beaver, the bear, the salmon, and other creatures, because long ago men married them and acquired this knowledge from their animal wives. Today the priests say we lie, but we know better. The white man has been only a short time in this country and knows very little about the animals; we have lived here thousands of years and were taught long ago by the animals themselves. The white man writes everything down in a book so that it will not be forgotten; but our ancestors married the animals, learned all their ways, and passed on the knowledge from one generation to another."[19] Plains Indians knew the medicinal properties of more than two thousand plants, they understood weather patterns, and so on. All this information was passed on from one generation to the next. Thus, though Curly's society had no written language to pass on information, he was nevertheless the recipient of a vast amount of knowledge.

By keeping his eyes open, both when he was moving with the tribe or wandering alone or with Hump, Curly could draw a basic map of the High Plains in his mind. He came to know every ridge and valley, every stream, every landmark between the Platte River and the Black Hills and beyond. He developed an acute sense of direction, common to all Plains Indians. The country looked distressingly similar to whites, but an Indian seldom got lost.

Curly often went off camping, either alone, with Hump, or with a group of age-mates. The boys learned to cook their meals using a buffalo paunch as a kettle to boil the water holding the meat. They would suspend the paunch from four green poles, half fill it with water, place the meat in the water, and then drop in heated stones, which made the water boil and cooked the meat, providing a nice soup as a bonus. Curly also learned to move his sleeping robe a few hundred yards away from the fire so that he could not be surprised at night by an enemy.[20]

Curly was a full-fledged hunter before he became a teen-ager. Most boys participated in their first tribal hunt at ten or eleven years of age, or as soon as they were strong enough to kill a buffalo with an arrow. Parkman saw an Oglala boy, called Hail-Storm, drop a buffalo, and described the scene in detail: "A shaggy buffalo-bull bounded out from a neighboring hollow, and close behind him came a slender Indian boy, riding without stirrups or saddle, and lashing his eager little horse to full speed. Yard after yard he drew closer to his gigantic victim, though the bull, with his short tail erect and his tongue lolling out a foot from his foaming jaws, was straining his unwieldy strength to the utmost. Hail-Storm . . . dropped the rein on his horse's neck, and jerked an arrow like lightning from the quiver at his shoulder.

"'I tell you,' said Reynal [Parkman's white companion] 'that in a year's time that boy will match the best hunter in the village. There, he has given it to him!—and there goes another! You feel well, now, old bull, don't you, with two arrows stuck in your lights! There, he has given him another! Hear how the Hail-Storm yells when he shoots! Yes, jump at him; try it again, old fellow! You may jump all day before you get your horns into that pony!'

"The bull sprang again and again at his assailant, but the horse kept dodging with wonderful celerity. At length the bull followed up his attack with a furious rush, and the Hail-Storm was put to flight, the shaggy monster following close behind. The boy clung in his seat like a leech, and secure in the speed of his little pony, looked round towards us and laughed." Soon after, the bull fell dead.[21]

Hail-Storm's accomplishment, impressive as it was in the telling, was commonplace among the Oglala boys. So were other hazardous feats. When Curly was eleven he joined Hump and others on a horse-catching expedition. The boys went south to the Sand Hills of present-day northwestern Nebraska, where the wild herds roamed. They pushed a bunch of horses until the animals tired, then moved in on them and secured the horses with rawhide ropes. Curly was the first boy to mount and break one of the wild horses. When the party returned to the village, Crazy Horse gave his son a new name, His Horse Looking, but it did not stick and most Oglalas continued to call him Curly.[22]

Throughout his childhood, Curly was encouraged to emulate the young warriors of the village. They were the center of attention, the ones that the children and the women and the aged discussed, the heroes who brought in meat or went off on war parties. The warriors were extraordinary braggarts, entitled (and expected) to sing their own praises at all opportunities, but especially at tribal dances, with the women, children, and old men sitting around in a great circle while the young braves danced and showered themselves with boasts about their accomplishments.

They were an impressive sight, those young braves, sticking together for the most part and highly picturesque when bedecked for war. They wore crests of feathers, robes of individual and colorful design, with scalp locks of their enemies hanging from the fringes. Many carried shields, painted and fluttering with eagles' feathers. Some wore war bonnets with feathered streamers that trailed to the earth. All had bows and arrows at their backs; some carried long lances and one or two might have had a gun. Their ponies, too, were individually decorated.

Francis Parkman described the return of a group of braves to his Oglala village in the summer of 1846: "The warriors rode three times round the village; and as each noted champion passed, the old women would scream out his name, to honor his bravery, and excite the emulation of the younger warriors. Little urchins, not two years old, followed the warlike pageant with glittering eyes, and gazed with eager admiration at the heroes of their tribe."[23] Curly may have been present on that occasion; if not, he would have witnessed similar scenes frequently throughout his childhood.

As one of the most daring boys in his group, Curly knew that someday he too would ride around the village to the adulation of the multitude. It could not happen soon enough, however; like most Sioux youth, Curly probably snuck off on his first war party when he was eleven or twelve years old. Mothers nearly always tried to stop their fledglings from going off to war, and fathers and other adults made pro-forma objections, but with most boys nothing could hold them back. They would listen as the braves planned an expedition, watch as the party left the village, and then that night crawl out of their tipis, catch their ponies, and ride off to join the warriors. When a boy arrived at the first night's camping place the braves would try to talk him into returning to the village, but they did not try very hard, since each of them had likely gone on his first war party under similar circumstances. Instead, the warriors made the neophyte's trip rather miserable, appointing him water boy, horse watcher, and general servant. He had to stay behind and hold the horses when the men crept into the enemy camp to steal horses; thus he would be far from the scene of action and consequently out of serious danger. But though he had no opportunity to win honor for himself, he did get the feel of an expedition and he had broken the bonds of childhood through his own initiative. Now he could smoke the pipe with the other men, speak in the presence of his elders, and strut in front of his peers.[24]

Not all boys chose to be hunters and warriors. Pretty One, for example, son of Bad Face and grandson of Old Smoke, chose a different path. Pretty One was Curly's childhood friend and later played a crucial role in his career, but by the time he was ten Pretty One wore paint and quilled buckskin and beads every day. He did not enjoy the rough boys' games that Curly reveled in. Pretty One was well on his way to becoming a *winkte*, or homosexual, a man who dressed in fancy clothes, sometimes even wearing a dress, did bead and quill work as well as a woman and often became a shaman. The *winkte* was recognized as *wakan*, or holy; a Sioux woman told Royal Hassrick that "there is a belief that if a *winkte* is asked to name a child, the child will grow up without sickness."[25]

Even the bravest warriors sometimes slept with a *winkte*, although the general attitude toward homosexuality was negative. There was obvious ambivalence; the *winkte* was held in awesome respect on the one hand and in disdainful fear on the other. Curly and his friends sometimes teased Pretty One, but usually ignored him. The important thing was that no one questioned his choice, for his life role had been revealed to him in a dream, and no Sioux would ever consider arguing with someone's dream. As Erikson points out, there was no conscious deceit involved in the process, but a true psychological wisdom, for "the dreamer was not conscious of and was not held individually responsible for the psychological reality which alone could have made his experience visionary and convincing, namely, the strength of this own abnormal wishes."[26]

Others of Curly's childhood friends chose different occupations, selecting hunting or becoming wild-horse catchers, medicine men, or holy men like Curly's father. Most, however, became warriors, or at least thought of themselves as such, for in truth they would spend most of their active hours during their adult lives hunting. But if successful hunting brought respect and some prestige, it did not give a young man the right to sing of his exploits before the camp circle.

A Sioux boy was constantly reminded of his duty as a warrior. He heard the old men recite their exploits, saw his mother and sister celebrate victories in the Scalp Dance. He saw teen-aged braves proudly displaying their feather badges of honor. In the tipi he studied the war record painted on the warrior's shield or on the tipi cover; he rode on a pony stolen from the Crows or Pawnees. And he heard, time and again, from women, old men, and braves that it was best to die young in battle and in glory.[27]

Everything in his society encouraged Curly to be brave. The Sioux were not born brave, and certainly they had their share of cowards as well as reasonably prudent men who saw no point to taking unnecessary risks. But the tribe had techniques of self-encouragement to help these warriors live up to society's expectations, such as growling like a grizzly in times of danger or uttering the war whoop; these sounds frightened the enemy and, more important, encouraged those who made them. Bragging about one's exploits in front of the assembled village served the same purpose, as did the feats of physical endurance Sioux boys underwent.[28]

The emphasis on bravery and self-assertion, however, led to problems. On communal hunts, for example, when it was crucial to strike the buffalo herd as a unit, young braves had to be closely watched to prevent them from dashing forward into the herd in the hopes of killing the first, or the largest, or the most buffalo. The same problem plagued Sioux war parties; just when an ambush was about to succeed, a young hot-shot might dash forward into the enemy's ranks and spoil everything.

Some system was necessary to channel the impulsive bravery of the youth into acceptable and useful activity; the Sioux found it with the *akicita* societies. The primary purpose of the societies was to serve as a men's club, and at its lodge a member would lounge, sleep, eat, dance, sing, and gossip with his fellows. The societies were private and membership was open by invitation only. Cowards, men guilty of murder or adultery, or those who amassed wealth by not giving away their extra ponies were excluded. So were the poor hunters or inept warriors; as one Sioux put it, "Such men just live."[29]

There were a number of such societies in each village, such as the
Brave Hearts, the Crow Owners, the Kit Foxes, and the Lance Owners. Each had its own traditions, songs, regalia, and ceremonies.

The original function of the *akicita* societies seems to have been
military; leaders were always men of proven valor and their songs
were designed to encourage members to brave deeds done for the
benefit of the whole tribe. The Kit Fox song ran:

> I am a Fox
> I am supposed to die
> If there is anything difficult,
> If there is anything dangerous,
> That is mine to do.[30]

By the nineteenth century, however, *akicita* societies had taken
on new functions, serving as legislative and executive bodies and
thereby becoming more powerful than the nominal tribal chiefs.
The *akicita* societies decided on new law when events required it,
then acted as police to enforce the law and to punish the guilty. As
Parkman noted, "While very few [Oglala] chiefs could venture without risk of their lives to strike or lay hands upon the meanest of
their people, the 'soldiers' in the discharge of their appropriate functions, have full license to make use of these and similar acts of
coercion."[31] The *akicita* kept order in camp, when the tribe was on
the move and most of all during tribal hunts or on war parties. They
beat offenders who broke ranks, exiled murderers from the village,
destroyed the tipi of a man who had stolen property, stopped fights,
and generally upheld law and order. Anthropologist Robert Lowie
sees in the *akicita* the germ of civil government, the origin of the
state.[32]

The Sioux had a number of devices to keep any one *akicita* society
from becoming dictatorial. First and foremost, they rotated the authority; the Kit Foxes would be the police one month, the Brave
Hearts the next, and so on. Second, no man could simultaneously
be a head of an *akicita* society and a tribal chief or member of the
governing council. Third, the Sioux did not delegate real power to
an individual, be he a head of an *akicita* society, tribal chief, or
simply a brave individual. As Lowie puts it, "in normal times the
chief was not a supreme executive, but a peacemaker and an orator."
Chiefs—all chiefs—were titular, "and any power exercised within the
tribe was exercised by the total body of responsible men who had
qualified for social eminence by their war record and their generos-

ity."[33] Whites could never understand this point, incidentally; because they could not conceive of a society without a solid hierarchy, the whites insisted that the Indians had to have chiefs who would be a final authority and able to speak for the entire tribe. Later, much difficulty grew out of this basic white misunderstanding of Indian government.

The freedom of life on the Plains helped prevent the rise of dictatorship. The Sioux would not subject themselves to ineffectual or dominating leadership, primarily because they did not have to do so. If a war-party commander blundered and lost two or three men—or even one—the Sioux demoted him to the ranks by the simple process of not following him on any further expeditions. If a chief picked poor camping grounds or was unsuccessful in locating the buffalo herds, the people moved to another village. Families and groups were always separating from the village, drifting off to join another band, or establishing a new one themselves. Political, economic, and social secession, in short, caused no trauma. The Sioux felt no loyalty to an individual chief, or a village, or even a tribe—Brulés frequently came to live with Oglalas, for example, and there were usually a few Sioux families living with the Cheyennes or Arapahoes, and vice versa. The Sioux were loyal to themselves, their families, their close friends, and a set of ideas, not to an office or an institution.[34]

The Sioux lived without compulsion. While the society most assuredly and most vigorously tried to steer children in certain directions, it would probably be most correct to say that the Sioux had hopes, rather than expectations, for their children. No stigma was attached to those who chose other than the normal roles, nor did they suffer from punishment or in any material way. They did not become leaders or people of prestige, of course, but their choice was respected. Indeed, the Sioux could not imagine *not* following one's inner voice, one's feelings, usually expressed in a dream or vision but always authentic.

The Sioux had plenty of room for those who thought differently from the majority, as Curly found out. By the time he was well into his teen-age years many of his age-mates had gone through the Sun Dance, a religious ceremony involving excruciating self-torture, done for the well-being of the tribe and consequently an act of great prestige and an act that thoroughly tested a boy's ability to withstand pain. Curly had always been among the most daring and courageous members of his age group, one of the first to kill a buffalo and to go on a war party. He now had a younger brother, Little

Hawk, whom he had taught the lessons of the Plains, and he had joined an *akicita*, the Crow Owners Society. But Curly chose not to undergo the ordeal of the Sun Dance. His status was not affected by his decision, nor was any pressure put on him to do otherwise than as he felt.

Curly had always been physically different from other Oglala children; as a teen-ager, additional differences developed. Curly was quiet and modest, not boastful like most Oglala boys. He had a sense of reserve that was unusual—Curly was somewhat offended by the Sioux custom of wild displays of emotion at moments of tragedy or victory. He did not object; he just didn't much like it and removed himself from such scenes. Nor did he like to hear the warriors brag about themselves, and he refused to do it himself. He did not enjoy the rough jokes and loud singing at the *akicita* societies, either, so he joined the Crow Owners on expeditions but seldom in the society lodge. Nor did he feel he had to prove anything at the Sun Dance. He was earning enough respect to satisfy him as it was, as a promising hunter and warrior.[35]

As a mature war leader, Curly would discover the full cost the Sioux had to pay for their individualism. The absence of compulsion, the freedom to do what one felt like doing, so long as no one got hurt, made the Sioux a woefully inefficient people. They could not build or produce material goods in any quantity, their transportation system remained primitive, and their ability to withstand attack from a stronger outside force was severely limited. By granting priority to the individual's need to be himself, the Sioux precluded unified military, economic, and political action. They had national heroes and sometimes effective tribal leaders, but they never developed a true national leader. Or a national policy. From the time they emerged onto the Plains until they went onto the reservations (and, in truth, down to the present day), the Sioux were divided against themselves, incapable of rallying around a cause or a leader, and thus in the end unable to defend their way of life.

Curly knew that his people were divided as soon as he became aware of events outside the tipi. Indeed, in the year of Curly's birth his band, the Oglala, split into two feuding factions, a split that continued until well into the twentieth century. Details on the origin of the feud are few, and those that do exist are disputed, but the general outline is clear enough.

In a way the whites were responsible. Fur traders first entered the Laramie region of the North Platte River in 1834, and the Oglalas soon fell into the habit of spending much of their time in that vicinity, where they became victims of a bitter rivalry between the American Fur Company and its competitors. The traders knew that their most potent weapon in the struggle for the Indian trade was whiskey, and they used it indiscriminately. Many Oglala men soon became nothing more than common drunks, nearly all became irritable and quarrelsome, and petty differences between individuals were escalated into serious trouble. Incidents previously unheard of among the Oglalas, such as stealing in order to have something to trade for whiskey or fights within the village between members of the same band became routine.

Adding to the difficulty was the rivalry between Bull Bear, a loud, aggressive, powerful chief who came closer than anyone else to dominating the Oglalas, and Old Smoke, a fat and jovial chief. Bull Bear was a chief of the Koya band of the Oglalas, while Old Smoke led the Bad Faces. The white traders evidently tried to push Old Smoke to the forefront, as he was easier to deal with than the tyrannical Bull Bear. Furious at this turn of events, Bull Bear paraded through the Bad Face camp, loudly challenging Old Smoke to come out and fight. When Old Smoke refused to leave his tipi, Bull Bear killed Smoke's favorite horse and triumphantly marched back to the Koya camp.

A few years later, in the fall of 1841, the Bad Faces got their revenge. Bull Bear and a few followers rode into Old Smoke's camp on the Chugwater, an eastern branch of the Laramie River, and started a quarrel. The American Fur Company men were in Old Smoke's camp, trading liquor for robes, and Old Smoke's people were drunk. Soon enough arrows were flying, and old Bull Bear fell dead, some say at the hands of a young Bad Face warrior named Red Cloud.

Following this incident the Koyas, now known as the Cut-Offs, drifted southeastward, occupying the lands between the Platte and Smoky Hill rivers in Kansas. The Bad Faces moved northward, toward the Black Hills and even further westward toward the headwaters of the Powder River, where they were soon associating with the northern Cheyennes and the Miniconjous. These associations were more geographical than political; the various tribes formed no firm alliance. Each little group acted independently.[36]

When Parkman joined the Old Smoke band five years later, he found the Oglalas divided and leaderless. To his disgust, they could not even get together to strike their enemies. Much of Parkman's journal consists of his complaints at the Sioux inability to organize a grand revenge expedition against the Shoshonis, who had whipped an Oglala war party the previous summer. All the Oglalas were sup-

posed to participate, along with some Miniconjous and others, but
nothing came of it.

Nor could the Indians agree on when and where to move. One
morning Parkman asked Eagle Feather, a warrior, if the village would
move the next day. "He shook his head, and said that nobody could
tell, for since old Mahto-Tatonka [Bull Bear] had died, the people
had been like children that did not know their own minds. They
were no better than a body without a head."[37]

The Oglalas divided just as they faced their most serious challenge.
Shortly after Bull Bear's death increasing numbers of white emigrants began to file through their country, following the Platte River
on their way west. Over the years the Sioux gradually became aware
that these whites were spoiling the Platte Valley, destroying the
timber, trampling down or overgrazing the grass, driving off e
game animals, and altogether turning the valley into a white ma 's
country "where the Indian was only tolerated as an unwelcome in-
truder and was expected to conform to the white man's laws and
regulations, which he did not understand."[38]

Because Old Smoke liked his coffee, Curly spent much of his
childhood on or near the Platte, where he saw the friction between
the whites and the Indians grow and flourish. Given the cultural
differences between the two groups, the clash was inevitable. Indians
took stray cattle and horses from the emigrants. To the red man
this was no more than simple duty, but to the white man it was
a crime demanding punishment. Young warriors sporadically raided
the wagon trains, then visited the same emigrants the next day to
beg coffee and sugar. Whites complained that whatever was not tied
down was stolen; Indians complained that the whites were stingy.

In the summer of 1845 the first white soldiers came into Sioux
country to protect the emigrants. Colonel Stephen W. Kearny
marched up the Platte at the head of a force of dragoons to quiet
the tribes through a display of strength. Kearny met with the Bad
Faces and other Oglalas on Laramie River, warning them sternly
that if they molested the emigrants they would be severely punished.
Despite the troubles, the Oglalas continued to hang around the
whites, drawn to the Oregon Trail by the good things white society
had to offer.[39]

In 1849 disaster struck. White man's diseases, including cholera,
smallpox, and measles, hit the Sioux. Cholera especially raged all
across the Plains; Cheyennes fleeing southward came across other
Cheyennes fleeing northward, both groups trying to get out of cholera country. The Brulés and Oglalas fled northward, back toward

their old homes on the White River in South Dakota, where they discovered a ghost camp, the tipis all standing, and all full of dead people. The cholera hung on for a year, killing nearly half the Cheyenne tribe and causing dreadful losses among the Sioux. It was followed in 1850 by a smallpox epidemic, which carried off hundreds of additional Indians. The Sioux and Cheyennes began to talk of vengeance against the whites, whom they blamed. Many were convinced that the cholera was a wicked magic that the whites had deliberately introduced among them.[40]

By 1851 the epidemics had dissipated, but not the white men. They wanted all the tribes that lived on or near the Platte River to come to a council at Fort Laramie—since 1849 a government post with a small detachment of troops garrisoned there—to sign a general peace and friendship treaty. The soldiers were supposed to protect the emigrants on the Oregon Trail from the Indians, but given the extent of the territory involved, the minuscule force (one company of infantry) could do little more than maintain Fort Laramie as a way station. The whites decided to pay for the privilege of walking through Indian lands, a realistic policy since the U. S. Army could not possibly bring enough strength to the Platte Valley to shoot a path through.

So government agents went out to all the tribes of the Platte region, including Old Smoke's. The agent promised him handsome gifts of beads, blankets, guns, and utensils if he and his people would come down to Fort Laramie for the peacemaking. Old Smoke consulted with his tribesmen; everyone wanted to go; and they were off.

They arrived in August 1851, along with 10,000 other Indians. They made a great splash of color on the brown, burned-out prairie dirt. There were Shoshonis there, from beyond the Bighorn Mountains, and Crows from the Yellowstone River; Sioux from the Missouri River and both sides of the Platte River, Cheyennes from the Powder River. Curly had never seen anything like it—the Laramie Council was the largest assembly of Indians on the Plains that had yet taken place.

Curly was about ten years old at the time of the Laramie Council, and one can suppose that he had a marvelous time, riding from camp to camp, getting to know his sworn enemies, meeting Cheyennes, racing on horseback, counting playful coups, asking questions, observing. The boys had no difficulty communicating with each other, because all were proficient in the sign language, that unique skill of the Plains Indians that cut across all language barriers. The atmosphere of the council was probably somewhat like that of the county fair eleven-year-old George Custer attended that summer in Ohio, although the Indian council lasted longer.

Certainly Curly feasted. The tribes vied with each other as hosts, and the eating was continuous. Father De Smet, the famous Catholic missionary, who was there, declared that "no epoch in Indian annals probably shows a greater massacre of the canine race."[41] The Indians were camped at Fort Laramie for nearly a month before the treaty was finally signed and the presents distributed, so Curly had plenty of time to get to know, and eat with, many new people.

The completed treaty gave the whites the right to use the Oregon Trail (the "Holy Road," the Indians dubbed it), which was the point of it all. The Indians promised not to make war on each other or on the whites—clauses impossible of fulfillment—and to respect the boundaries drawn on a map to mark their respective territory. Within the year, of course, the Sioux were ignoring the treaty and pushing the Crows out of the Powder River country. In return for the right of passage, the whites promised to pay annuity goods to the value of $50,000 yearly to the Indians. They insisted that each of the tribes have a single chief, so that he could take charge of the distribution and speak for the tribe. For an unexplained reason they passed over Old Smoke and chose Conquering Bear as chief of all the Sioux, a previously unheard of position.*

But Conquering Bear became, instantly, a man of power—more power than any Indian had ever dreamed of; he became a man to inspire awe. Father De Smet described how the process began: the Indians had all gathered in a gigantic circle, with the white officials in the middle. Conquering Bear and the selected chiefs of the Shoshonis, Cheyennes, and Crows walked to center stage, where with much pomp they were presented with gaudy uniforms. "You may easily imagine their singular movements upon appearing in public and the admiration they excited in their comrades. . . . The great chiefs for the first time in their lives pantalooned: each was arrayed in a general's uniform, a gilt sword hanging at his side. Their long coarse hair floated above the military costume and the whole was crowned with the burlesque solemnity of their painted faces."[42]

---

* Conquering Bear was a Brulé. The whites thought they were making him chief of all the Sioux, but he seems to have assumed that he was now chief of the Oglalas and Brulés. There is great confusion on this point because the Indians could not conceive of anyone being chief of even the Oglalas or Brulés, much less *all* the Sioux.

But if they looked funny to De Smet, they looked impressive as hell to the Indians.

Conquering Bear and the other chiefs now had everyone's attention. When they began to distribute the white man's presents, they got everyone's gratitude. And a hold over their fellow tribesmen in the future, because the goods would come every year and the white man would deal only through the chiefs.

So now the Oglalas had a chief, and lots of the white man's good things. Everyone had had a fine time. Curly and the Bad Faces left Laramie in a happy mood. They went north for a buffalo hunt and then to settle down for the winter. After the hunt the following spring they returned to the Laramie region, where they harassed passing wagon trains and waited for their annuity goods. Curly may have participated in some of the raids on the emigrants, for they were well-nigh continuous and exclusively the work of the hot-blooded young warriors. Amos Robinson, who passed over the Oregon Trail en route to California in 1852, the year after the Laramie treaty, recalled that his train was met by a party of Sioux one day's march east of Laramie. The Indians plundered the train, taking what they wanted and killing a herder. The next day Robinson saw the same Indians hanging around Fort Laramie. The emigrants rested one day at the fort, then pushed on, only to be followed by the same Indians who again plundered the train a few miles away from the fort.[43] During this period scarcely a train got through the Plains without being hit at least once by the Sioux.[44]

Friction was continuous. The emigrants hated the Indians and resented having to pay tribute to them; the Indians were furious at the ever-increasing flow of emigrants, whom they blamed for the disappearance of the buffalo herds from the Platte Valley and for the diseases that were wracking the tribes. Conquering Bear did all he could to keep the warriors quiet, but it was impossible, for the young braves were sure they were strong enough to destroy all the whites on the Plains. The soldiers at Fort Laramie, meanwhile, were just as sure they could teach a lesson to the disorderly, undisciplined, ill-armed Sioux and were itching for a chance.

In June of 1853, when the Indians had again begun to gather around Laramie to receive their summer hand-outs, there was more trouble. A young Miniconjou, visiting the Oglalas, asked a soldier for a ride across the river in a skiff. The soldier told the Miniconjou to go to hell; the Indian fired an arrow at him. The next day the soldiers, twenty in all, marched into the Oglala camp to arrest the offender. Some troublemaker, whether white or red is not known, fired a shot; the men in uniform unloosed a volley, and five Oglalas lay dead. The Miniconjou got away. A few days later the Oglalas got revenge, attacking a small emigrant camp near the fort and killing a family of four. The soldiers marched out of the fort again and fired on the first Indians they met, killing one and wounding another. The pattern was typical—neither side, in the struggle for the possession of the Plains that was now underway, ever distinguished the guilty from the innocent. If Indian blood was spilled, white blood must run, even if the white victims had been miles away from the original incident; so too with the whites, who attacked the first red men they came across whenever an Indian outrage was committed.[45]

In 1853 Conquering Bear, who seems to have realized that his power was dependent on his favored status with the whites, was able to smooth things over and there was no general war. After the Indians got their annuity goods they drifted off again, with promises to return the next summer.

Throughout this period Curly continued to grow and learn. He and Hump, his kola, had added Little Hawk (Curly's younger brother) and Lone Bear to their group. The four were always together, on raiding parties, watching the pony herd at night, making their bows, arrows, and other implements, hunting, or just loafing and talking. Curly had grown to nearly six feet in height, although he was on the thin side. His hair remained sandy brown, or even medium blond, and his complexion was light. Short Bull, who grew up with Curly, said "his features were not like those of the rest of us. His face was not broad, and he had a sharp, high nose. He had black eyes that hardly ever looked straight at a man, but they didn't miss much that was going on, all the same."[46] He was shy, quieter and more reserved than his fellows; he was already showing that characteristic that his childhood acquaintance, He Dog, would later emphasize. He Dog said of Curly, "He never spoke in council and attended very few. There was no special reason for this, it was just his nature. He was a very quiet man except when there was fighting."[47]

Chips, a medicine man slightly older than Curly, said that "when we were young all we thought about was going to war with some other nation; all tried to get their names up the highest, and whoever did so was the principal man in the nation; and Crazy Horse [Curly] wanted to get to the highest station and rank."[48]

As a teen-ager, then, Curly was set on his life's path. He would be a warrior and a hunter, protecting and providing for the helpless ones of his tribe. He wanted prestige and fame and was willing, nay, anxious, to take great personal risks to achieve his goal. He thought of the Crows, Shoshonis, and Pawnees as his main enemies. He had seen much of the white man, but had at best a limited understanding of white culture or practices. He was a free young man, living his life the way he wanted to live it.

CHAPTER FOUR

Curly's Vision

"I give him a new name, the name of his father, and of many
fathers before him—I give him a great name. I call him Crazy
Horse."
                                                    Crazy Horse's father

In the summer of 1854, following the annual Sun Dance and the
buffalo hunt, the northern Oglalas and the Brulés returned to the
Fort Laramie region, there to await their presents from the government. The troubles of the previous summer were, they felt, of no
more significance than the passing of a dark cloud over the face of
the moon. They traded buffalo robes for whiskey, coffee, and other
items at Jim Bordeaux's trading house and at the American Fur
Company post a few miles east of Fort Laramie, held feasts for each
other, and pestered the emigrants on the Holy Road. Conquering
Bear was there, camped with the Brulés, and so were Curly, Hump,
Little Hawk, and Lone Bear, all living in the Oglala camp headed
by Old-Man-Afraid-of-His-Horses* (Old Smoke was a very old man
by this time and lived permanently at Fort Laramie, in retirement).[1]
The boys probably joined other youngsters on raiding parties
against the emigrant wagon trains. Almost every day young braves
would nip off a horse here, a cow there, or sneak into a camp at night
and take an iron cooking pot or even a rifle. It was great fun, of
course, and profitable; best of all, the emigrants did not pursue the
thieves as the Crows or Pawnees would have done, and the tiny
infantry garrison at Fort Laramie was much too small to do anything
about it.

Or so the Sioux believed. Inside the fort, however, a young officer
fresh out of West Point, twenty-four-year-old Lieutenant John L.
Grattan, was itching to get at the Indians. Grattan had never seen
the Sioux in battle, but he was certain that such an ill-organized,

* Usually called simply Man Afraid. His son had the same name (which meant
his enemies were afraid even of his horses). In this work, the father will be
called Old Man Afraid, the son—about Curly's age—Young Man Afraid.

undisciplined bunch of savages could never stand up to a force of U. S. Infantry. Like so many other whites on the frontier, Grattan was a heavy drinker—there not being much else to do on such an isolated post—and when drunk he often said that with twenty soldiers and a field piece he could whip the whole Sioux nation.[2]

For Grattan and the other troops inside Fort Laramie the situation was fast becoming intolerable. They were supposed to be protecting the lives and property of American citizens on the Holy Road, but it was almost as if they themselves were being besieged. They could do little more than offer the emigrants a place to rest, while every day the Sioux grew bolder. Bored, hot, and resentful at being sent to such a Godforsaken place, the officers (Lieutenant Hugh B. Fleming, twenty-eight years old and two years out of West Point, in command) decided that the Sioux had to be taught a lesson before they started carrying off the wagons themselves, instead of just a stray stock animal and a few utensils.

Their chance came on August 17, 1854. A Mormon wagon train passed the Brulé camp. At the rear of the wagons a Mormon was leading a lame old cow. Some young Miniconjous were staying with the Brulés, the same troublemakers from the previous summer; one of their number, High Forehead, shot the old cow with an arrow, perhaps as the result of a dare or just for the hell of it. The Mormon, terrified, fled the scene, hurried to Fort Laramie, where he told his story, with embellishments, and demanded that the Army do something.[3]

Fleming sent a runner to fetch Conquering Bear. When the old chief appeared, Fleming demanded that he bring in High Forehead and turn him over to the white authorities for proper punishment. Conquering Bear was astonished; here was a mere boy with less than one hundred men under his command telling a venerable chief of the Sioux, who had a thousand and more warriors in the vicinity, what to do. (One is struck by the extreme youth of the frontier Army leadership; Fleming was a very young man to be in such a responsible position—at twenty-eight, he was the chief representative of the United States Government on the whole upper Platte River.)

Conquering Bear told Fleming that the cow was lame and nearly dead, and that High Forehead's action was no more than what other Indians had done a hundred times over. Why all the fuss? But Fleming said enough was enough and insisted on the surrender of High Forehead. Not wanting any trouble, Conquering Bear offered to take the Mormon to his personal herd of ponies and allow him to pick one for himself, in payment for the cow.

According to Frank Salaway, a fur trader who was there, Fleming brushed the offer aside and insisted, "I want you to bring that man in here." Conquering Bear replied, "That man does not belong to my band. He is a Sioux, but he belongs to the Miniconjou band." Fleming said that was immaterial; he wanted High Forehead brought in. Well, said Conquering Bear, "if you want him why don't you go up there and arrest him? That is what your soldiers are here for." Fleming was furious. The whites had made Conquering Bear chief of all the Sioux so that they could deal with the tribe through him, and here was Conquering Bear saying he had no power at all, no way to force a hot-blooded young warrior to toe a line. Conquering Bear's gratuitous advice to be careful because High Forehead was hot-tempered did not help Fleming's mood. He told Conquering Bear his soldiers would be in the Brulé camp the following morning. "All right," replied Conquering Bear. "I'll show you his lodge; I'll show you the man."[4]

Conquering Bear passed through the Oglala camp on his way back to his own village and told the Oglalas what Fleming had said he was going to do. It struck the Oglalas as a foolish thing, making such a fuss about one old cow, especially in view of all the far superior stock the Indians had run off over the past months and about which nothing had been done. But foolish or not, the threat was real; armed men were preparing to march into a Sioux camp with the announced intention of taking a Sioux warrior prisoner. Nothing remotely like that had ever happened to the Sioux and their immediate reaction was to begin preparing themselves for war. Curly must have watched fascinated as the men began to paint themselves, prepare their medicine, and sing their brave-heart songs. The older men, led by Old Man Afraid in the Oglala camp and Conquering Bear in the Brulé camp, tried to keep everyone calm. The last thing they wanted was an open clash with the whites, who were, after all, in possession of the yearly annuity goods, which had not yet been distributed. On the white side, meanwhile, older men like trader Bordeaux were trying to get the young Army officers to cool off, also without success.

The next morning Lieutenant Grattan, who had begged Fleming for the honor of commanding the expedition, led a volunteer force of thirty-one men, a 12-pounder field piece, and a small mountain howitzer past the Oglala camp. He either did not notice or did not care that the Oglalas had driven in their pony herd in preparation for a fight. There were six hundred or more Sioux lodges in the Laramie region; at an average of two warriors per lodge, there were 1,200 warriors in the area.[5] Most of them had already gathered around the

Brulé village. Grattan stopped at the Bordeaux trading post and tried to induce Bordeaux, who had the trust of the Sioux, to go along and act as interpreter. But Bordeaux told Grattan that he was a damned fool and refused to do so. Outside the post, meanwhile, hundreds of mounted Indians, painted for war, were milling around.

Grattan had an interpreter with him, a half-French, half-Iowa Indian named Wyuse, but Wyuse did not speak Dakota well. Furthermore, he was drunk (Salaway says Grattan was drunk too). The Sioux hated Wyuse and had often asked Fleming to hire a new interpreter, but nothing had been done, and now Wyuse, backed up by the infantry and artillery, was whipping his horse back and forth, just as the Sioux did before a battle in order to give their ponies a second wind. Wyuse shouted insults and taunts at the watching warriors. He said the soldiers would give the Sioux a new set of ears, so that they could better understand the white man's orders.[6]

Grattan marched on to the Brulé village, posted his men on its outskirts, and moved to the front of the line with Wyuse at his side, Wyuse shouting that he would cut out the Sioux hearts and have them for breakfast. Conquering Bear came out of his lodge and warned Grattan that there would be trouble. Grattan insisted on the surrender of High Forehead. Conquering Bear said he would see what he could do, consulted with the Miniconjou warrior, and returned to inform Grattan that High Forehead would not give himself up. The parley went on for half an hour or more, Conquering Bear moving back and forth between Grattan and High Forehead. Curly, along with hundreds of other Indians, watched the whole scene from the surrounding bluffs.

Grattan lost what little patience he had. He snapped out an order, then jumped aside. His men fired two volleys into the encampment. The howitzer had been laid too high and the grapeshot tore through the tops of the tipis without doing any real harm, but Conquering Bear—standing right in the middle, directly in front of the line of infantry—had nine bullet wounds and lay in a pool of blood in the dust.

The Brulés poured out of their lodges; the Oglalas rode down on the Grattan party from the bluffs. One quick volley of arrows and it was over. Grattan and all his men were dead.[7]

Wyuse escaped into a nearby tipi, but the Indians dragged him out, killed him, and mutilated the body. Then the warriors rode off for Bordeaux's place, with the intention of shooting it up and taking his stock of goods.

Curly watched the whole thing. When the warriors left, he and Lone Bear rode down to the village, where they examined the bodies. Standing over Wyuse, they offered him the ultimate insult of the Sioux—each boy jerked up his breechcloth and stood bare before the staring eyes of the dead man. Then they rode back to the Oglala village.[8]

The main body of warriors, meanwhile, were whooping and hollering around Bordeaux's place. The wily old trader had fortunately hidden his whiskey. He had many close friends among the Sioux and with the help of these men, plus a liberal distribution of his stocks, he managed to survive the night. The Indians argued with each other. Young braves were all for riding on to Fort Laramie, killing the handful of soldiers left there, and taking the annuity goods stored in the warehouse. The older men counseled against this and advised moving north instead. They could return later for their presents, but if they took them now, by force, there would be none the next year and the whites would be even more inclined to retaliate for the killing of Grattan and his men.

The young men were most interested in winning honors and loot, of course, but they may also have realized that war with the whites, so long brewing, was now upon them and that they were unlikely to ever again have as good an opportunity. Old Man Afraid and the other headmen wanted to deny the plain facts. They hoped that the whites would pass over the Grattan massacre as merely an incident, brought on by Grattan's foolishness and a few unmanageable young Indians. For the elders, heavy with honors won against the Crows and Pawnees and accustomed to all the good things the whites had brought them, war made no sense at all.

The younger men either refused to see that their style of life was now dependent on the white man's favors, or they were willing to reject that life-style and return to the ways of their ancestors. They had had enough of the whites and wanted to drive them, soldiers, emigrants, and even the traders, out of Sioux territory. The older men said that was impossible; they had heard from Bordeaux and from the Pawnees and other eastern tribes of the overwhelming power of the whites, but the young braves refused to believe such stories. Besides, the evidence to the contrary was right before their eyes—thirty-one dead white soldiers lay in and around the Brulé village. The Indians had suffered no losses, save for the badly wounded Conquering Bear. The braves indignantly demanded to know if the elders were going to allow the whites to march into a Sioux village and shoot down a chief. The headmen shouted back that the braves were fools if they thought they could overrun Fort Laramie and escape unpunished.

All through the night the argument raged, Bordeaux right in the middle of it, pleading and cajoling the braves, emptying his shelves. In the end the Brulé and Oglala women decided the matter. Their impulse was to get away from trouble, and they had packed up their lodges and started north. Pointing out that the Sioux warrior's first obligation was to protect the helpless ones who were now moving undefended over the prairie, the elders convinced the braves to ride away from Fort Laramie.[9]

Thus the first battle between the Sioux and the whites revealed the fatal weakness of the Indians. Without leadership, the Sioux were unable to turn a battle into a campaign. There is no doubt that they could have overrun Fort Laramie and then blocked the Holy Road, preventing the retaliatory force that the headmen so feared from even getting into Sioux country. The Holy Road was an extraordinarily vulnerable supply line or invasion route. There were dozens of ideal places for ambush, hundreds of spots from which the Indians could harass a moving column. The whites had no knowledge of the terrain, no maps, and no inclination to leave their supply wagons and cut overland in pursuit of enemies they could never catch anyway. The soldiers were roadbound, like most American soldiers before and since, but the Indians made no effort to exploit that weakness. Instead, having inflicted what they thought was a heavy blow, the red men split their forces and retired—just as they would have done had the thirty-one dead men been Crows.

The Sioux failure to follow up their advantage, however, was inevitable. They could not have done otherwise. To have mounted a sustained campaign they would have had to delegate real authority to one man, or at most a small group of men, who would have had to have the power to give orders and see to it that they were enforced. It would have required putting small groups of men along the Holy Road, there to wait in endless boredom for the white columns to come along. It would have meant attacking in concert, Brulés and Oglalas and others acting together with the object of destroying the enemy, not winning personal honors. It would have required specialization, with some men hunting all the time in order to support those who were full-time soldiers.

A sustained campaign, in short, would have meant an end to the Sioux way of life just as surely as defeat at the hands of the whites meant an end to the old life-style. The Sioux could not simultaneously be free and be effective soldiers. They chose to remain free.

Even the hot-blooded braves around Bordeaux's place that terrible night, so eager to strike another blow, would never have submitted to the discipline that alone could have made the follow-up campaign work. Knowing this, the headmen thankfully turned their ponies' heads north and rode away from the battlefield.

Curly rode with the Brulés, probably because his mother was a Brulé. The mortally wounded Conquering Bear was carried along with the tribe, which had headed east. Curly, who had just turned thirteen, must have been confused by the dramatic events he had witnessed. Conquering Bear was dying of his wounds; evidently Curly and Hump caught a glimpse of the old man wasting away on his robe on the lodge floor. Deeply moved, Curly rode out on the prairie alone.[10] He was now in western Nebraska, country that Custer—at the time a fifteen-year-old Ohio farm boy—would later cross and recross on horseback.

Curly had decided to seek a vision. For the Sioux male, the vision quest was central to life. It was usually preceded by a fast, complicated purification rites, and a series of lectures from a holy man. The teen-agers then stayed alone in some sacred place, forcing themselves to remain awake until the vision came. A holy man interpreted the dream and it became the guiding star for the remainder of the dreamer's life. From the vision the Sioux drew their inspiration. Their dreams might lead them to become medicine men, or warriors, or horse catchers, but whatever the vision proscribed for the dreamer, it was *wakan* and never to be disregarded.

The vision gave a man his power. Without it, he was nothing; with a vision he was in touch with the sacred forces. The power obtained in dreams became as much a part of the individual as his arms and legs or his character. It was usually bestowed through animals, who spoke to the dreamer, and like the power of animals was specific and limited to particular areas. Further, as a trust it carried grave responsibilities.

The vision forced a boy to make a choice, to decide what he would be. The successful vision seeker knew who he was, and what he was, and what he must do. It gave the Sioux an amazing degree of self-confidence. The dreams obviously reinforced choices that had already been made. Boys like Curly and Hump usually had a vision that compelled them to be warriors, while youngsters like Pretty One ordinarily had dreams that forced them to be *winktes*. The more or less established pattern of dreams (and their standard interpretations) were well within the structural needs of the society.[11] The overwhelming majority of Sioux males had broadly similar dreams, propelling them down similar warrior paths, but each individual Sioux felt that his dream was his own, and it gave him an unshakable sense of self.

The Sioux were not secretive about their dreams; indeed, they were anxious to tell them to others. Thus we know what Curly dreamed out on the prairie of the lake country in the Nebraska Sand Hills, for he later described it on a number of occasions to Indians and at least once to a white man. He also made a drawing of his vision in sand rocks after the Little Bighorn battle, twenty-two years later.[12]

After two days of fasting and keeping himself awake by placing sharp stones under his body when he had to lie down, Curly began to fear that he had made a terrible mistake. No dream came, perhaps because he had not made the proper preparations, perhaps because he was not worthy. He had given up and started down the hill to his pony, which he had hobbled beside a lake, when the dream came (most likely, he had fainted).

A man on horseback rode out of the lake. The horse kept changing colors, and it floated above the ground, so light was it, the man too, who sat well forward on the horse. He wore plain leggings and a simple shirt. His face was unpainted and he had only a single feather in his long brown hair. He had a small brown stone tied behind his ear. He did not seem to speak, but Curly heard him clearly nonetheless.

The man told Curly never to wear a war bonnet, nor to tie up his horse's tail (it was the Sioux custom to tie up their ponies' tails in a knot), because the horse needed his tail when he jumped a stream and in summer time to brush flies. He said that before going into battle Curly should pass some dust over his horse in lines and streaks, but should not paint the pony. And he should rub some of the dirt over his own hair and body. Then he would never be killed by a bullet or by an enemy. But he should never take anything for himself.

All the while the man and horse were floating, brushing aside constant attacks from a shadowy enemy. But he rode straight through them, straight through the flying arrows and lead balls, which always disappeared before striking their target. Several times the man and horse were held back, it seemed by his own people coming up from behind and catching his arms, but he shook them off and rode on. A storm came up and on the man's cheek a little zigzag of lightning appeared and a few hail spots on his body. Then the storm passed, and the man's people closed in around him, grabbing and pulling, while overhead a hawk screamed. Then the dream faded and Curly was awake.[13]

It did not seem to Curly to be much of a dream—it was not like any others he had heard about, especially such parts as not painting himself or not wearing a war bonnet—so he stayed on the prairie and continued to fast, hoping for a more suitable dream. But he finally fell asleep, and when he woke his father and Hump were standing over him. They were angry. He had left the village without telling anyone, at a time when all were concerned with the dying Conquering Bear, and gone into a country where Crow or Pawnee raiding parties might stumble over him. When Curly said he was seeking a vision, Crazy Horse was furious. His son had made no preparations, had not been purified, had received no advice from the wise ones for guidance. Chastened, Curly followed the others back to camp. He did not tell of his dream.

A few days later Conquering Bear died. After wrapping his body in a buffalo robe and placing it on a scaffold, the Brulés went off on a fall hunt. Curly was the first to locate a herd—he did so by placing his ear to the ground and listening for the thundering hoofs—and in the communal hunt he killed the first buffalo. Hump, the previous incident forgotten, sang Curly's praises that night in the camp circle.[14] In November four Brulés, led by Curly's uncle Spotted Tail, went on the warpath seeking revenge for Conquering Bear's death. They attacked the mail wagon on the Holy Road, killed two drivers and a passenger, and picked up $20,000 in paper money, which was never found (George Hyde suggests that the trader Jim Bordeaux got it, which seems likely).[15]

The following spring, 1855, the young Brulés, joined by some Miniconjous and Oglalas, made a series of unco-ordinated raids against the Holy Road. They concentrated on driving off livestock but engaged in no pitched battles or even any individual combat. They killed no whites, but they were a nuisance, enough to make the whites even more determined to revenge Grattan and teach the Sioux a lesson.[16] The Brulés, in other words, fought as if they were engaged in a campaign against another Indian tribe. They appear to have felt that successful horse and cattle raids would be sufficient to convince the whites to abandon the Holy Road.

During this period the Old Man Afraid Oglalas stayed well north of Fort Laramie, out of trouble, but many of the young warriors—including Curly—lived with the Brulés, where the action was. This was typical of the Sioux and led to much difficulty. Chiefs like Old Man Afraid could claim that their tribes were peaceful, which was true, but the whites could counter that the young braves were on the warpath, which was also true. The situation made it extremely difficult, indeed impossible, for the whites to figure out which Indians to punish.

In the summer of 1855 the Brulés, fat with buffalo and the white man's cattle and rich in horses, gave up their war with the whites (at a time when the whites were most vulnerable, the Holy Road being filled with more-or-less defenseless wagon trains). Little Thunder, Spotted Tail, and other leaders led the warriors in a great expedition to the lower Platte country against the Pawnees and the Omahas. One group swung down to the Loup River to steal Pawnee horses, but the Pawnees were out hunting and could not be found. A second group of Brulés, with Curly along, ran into the Omahas, who had left their cornfields to hunt buffalo. The Sioux managed to steal a few horses; the Omahas came charging after them; a big fight followed, with three Omahas being killed.

Curly made his first human kill that day. He noticed an Omaha sneaking through the brush, fired an arrow, and saw the enemy straighten up, then fall forward, dead. Curly jumped from his horse and raced to the brush, scalping knife in hand. But when he lifted the hair, he saw with astonishment that he had killed a woman.

This was hardly a shameful act. According to ancient Sioux custom there was great honor in counting coup upon or killing an enemy woman within sight of her own warriors, the theory being that the warriors would fight even harder to protect or avenge one of their women than one of their men. Curly tried to lift her scalp, but when he saw that she was as young and pretty as his own sister, he got a little sick and left the scalp to another. Curly's uncle Spotted Tail held the Omahas off while the Brulés collected their spoils and rode away. When they were safe, the men teased Curly for abandoning the scalp, even making up a little song about the experience:

> A brave young man comes here
> But a foolish one,
> Without a good knife.

Curly said nothing, although years later he told a white Army officer that he disapproved of the ethics of the Sioux custom with regard to enemy women.[17]

While the Sioux were out stealing a few horses, committing the best of their warriors, and acting as if the war with the whites were over for the season, the whites were mounting a major expedition against the Sioux. A new agent had been appointed for the Indians of the Platte, Thomas S. Twiss, another West Point graduate. The War Department, meanwhile, had ordered Brigadier General W. S. Harney, a hero of the Mexican War, to assemble a force at Fort Leavenworth in eastern Kansas and then march against the Sioux. The size of the force Harney gathered—six hundred men—indicated that the whites still held the Sioux in contempt, even after the Grattan massacre, although it was also true that by the United States Army standards of the time six hundred men was a large force. Harney's orders were to follow the Oregon Trail to Laramie, then turn back and march northeastward, through the heart of the Oglala and Brulé country, to Fort Pierre on the Missouri River. He was to strike terror into the heart of any Sioux he met along the way. The orders were an open invitation to disaster—if the Sioux acted in concert they could crush six hundred men like so many flies.[18]

But the Sioux had no intention of acting together. The headmen had stifled the talk of the wild young warriors about war with the whites, and when Agent Twiss sent out runners to all the Sioux tribes, ordering them to move south of the Platte River or be considered hostile, more than half the bands, including the Oglalas, obeyed. By September, Twiss had assembled four hundred lodges of Sioux near Fort Laramie. Practically all the Brulés and Miniconjous "stayed out," as the expression of the time had it, and were therefore considered hostile.

Among the hostiles was Little Thunder's band of Brulés, which was camped on the Bluewater River, a few miles north of the North Platte River and a little more than one hundred miles east of Fort Laramie. Little Thunder was thought of as a friendly, but his band did contain young men who had been on raids against the Holy Road in the spring, and Little Thunder was well aware that by camping where he was he had placed his people in a dangerous position. Bordeaux sent out three special runners to urge Little Thunder to "come in" before Harney arrived, but the Brulés would not move. They had had a successful hunt and wanted time to prepare the buffalo meat and robes for the winter.[19]

The Brulés made no move to avoid a battle. While the women worked on the buffalo carcasses, the young braves went back to raiding the Oregon Trail. When Harney arrived in the vicinity on September 2, 1855, he found a train of emigrants which had been compelled to corral and defend itself three times that day. The Brulés had not attacked, but they had demanded arms and ammunition. The Indians said they needed the weapons to fight the soldiers. Obviously, Little Thunder expected trouble; just as obviously, he knew nothing of white warfare and had no idea of the striking power of a mixed force of six hundred cavalry, infantry, and artillery. He believed either that Harney would pass by his camp or that Harney's six hundred men would fall as easily as Grattan's thirty-one had done.[20] He obviously forgot, or ignored, the simple fact that nearly all (about two thousand) the Brulés and Oglalas had fought against Grattan, while he had only a handful of Brulés with him (about one hundred).

Little Thunder was not much of a leader. At this critical moment in the life of his band, his fighting strength was scattered all across the country. Curly, for example, who was living with the Little Thunder people that summer, was out hunting, along with three other teen-agers. But there was already plenty of meat in the camp and these youngsters could have been acting as scouts. Little Thunder had no scouts out to watch for the approach of the enemy. Other young warriors were pestering the whites on the Holy Road, rather than preparing themselves for the fight of their lives. The camp was in a valley surrounded by heavily wooded hills—about the worst possible position for a defensive action.

Given what the Brulés knew about Harney's intentions and Twiss's orders, one can only conclude that the Indians simply could not believe that anyone would dare attack a Sioux camp in Sioux territory. It had never been tried before Grattan marched into Conquering Bear's camp the previous summer, and Grattan's fate indicated to the Brulés that it would be a long time before anyone tried again. The Brulés were cocky, overconfident, unorganized, badly located, and wasteful of their fighting power. They were a long way from being "the finest light cavalry in the world," as the Sioux have often been described.

At dawn, on September 3, 1855, Harney moved. In what would become the classic method of attacking a Plains Indian encampment, he sent the cavalry through the hills to get to the far end of the village, while he prepared to attack from the front with the infantry and artillery. With Harney was Lieutenant Alfred Pleasonton, who later, as a Civil War brigadier general, gave Custer one of his early breaks.

Without scouts, the Brulés did not know of Harney's presence until the soldiers were nearly in position. Little Thunder then rode out beyond the village to meet Harney, Spotted Tail at his side carrying a white flag. A council followed, each side trying to fool the other. Harney wanted to buy time for his cavalry to get into position; Little Thunder also hoped for delay so that the women and children could pack up and get away.

Little Thunder professed great friendship for the whites and explained his reasons for not obeying Twiss's orders. Harney humored him until he received word that the cavalry was in place, then he said he had come to fight and Little Thunder had better get ready. Little Thunder and Spotted Tail fled back to the Brulé camp, Harney and the infantry hot on their heels. When Little Thunder got within hailing distance of the camp he called out to the Indians to run. They did so—and ran right into the cavalry.

What followed was more a massacre than a battle, although individual warriors—especially Spotted Tail—covered themselves with glory. But the Indians could not stand up to the fire power of the troops. There were about two hundred fifty Indians in Little Thunder's camp. Within half an hour Harney's men had killed eighty-six of them and captured seventy women and children. Harney also had possession of the camp. The survivors, less than one hundred, scattered in every direction, without food or shelter.[21]

This was unmitigated disaster, on a scale undreamed of by the Sioux. Curly returned from his hunting trip, drawn by the smoke and noise, to the carnage. What he witnessed no Sioux had ever seen before—a Sioux camp completely destroyed. Curly had been brought up to believe that the loss of one or two warriors on a raiding party was a shocking business, the loss of three or four a tribal disaster. Now he saw dozens of dead warriors stretched out before him, Sioux women dead too, their dresses thrown over their heads, their pubic hair taken as scalps by the soldiers, right in the middle of a Sioux camp. For Curly, as for the entire Sioux nation, this was a new kind of warfare, totally beyond their imagination.

Late in the afternoon Curly found a survivor hiding in the bushes, a dead infant at her side. Her name was Yellow Woman; she was a Cheyenne who had been visiting with the Brulés. Her husband and son had been killed by the soldiers. Curly put together a travois and carried her away to safety. It turned out that she was a niece of Ice, a famous Cheyenne medicine man; thus began Curly's long and close association with the Cheyennes.[22]

Harney, meanwhile, pressed his advantage. He marched his captives up the Oregon Trail to Fort Laramie, where he called all the chiefs from the friendly camps to a council. Twiss had been preparing to hand out the annuity goods to the friendlies, but Harney ordered him not to do so. He then spoke very roughly to the headmen, telling them there would be no more presents until the four

Brulés who had attacked the mail wagon in November 1854 and stolen the $20,000 were turned over to the military. Until that was done, Harney said, the war would continue. He then dismissed the chiefs, telling them he would march the next morning to Fort Pierre, attacking any Indians he encountered along the way.[23]

Three events in quick succession showed that Harney had accomplished his objective and that the Sioux were absolutely terrorized. First, he marched from Fort Laramie to Fort Pierre through the heart of Sioux territory without seeing a single Indian; they all fled from his path. Second, Spotted Tail and the other culprits from the mail-wagon affair gave themselves up, surrendering at Fort Laramie within two weeks of Harney's demand; before Harney's attack on Little Thunder, no one would have believed it possible to induce a Sioux warrior to surrender voluntarily.[24] Third, Harney held a council at Fort Pierre in March 1856. Most of the Sioux headmen were there and they readily agreed to stop molesting emigrants on the Oregon Trail and to permit travel on a road from Fort Laramie to Fort Pierre. In return, Harney promised to start issuing annuity goods again.[25]

At the council Harney tried to impress the Indians with the power of the whites. Chloroform was just then coming into use as an anesthetic and Harney told the chiefs, "Why, we can kill a man and then restore him to life. There, surgeon, kill that dog and then restore it." The surgeon administered a dose of chloroform to an Indian dog and Harney then passed it around among the Indians, who pronounced it "plenty dead." "Now," said Harney, "bring it to life." The surgeon tried hard, applying all known restoratives, but the dog was plenty dead, sure enough. The Indians laughed boisterously. "White man's medicine too strong," they said.[26]

Unknown to Harney, the Sioux decided at the end of the council to meet again the next summer at Bear Butte, just north of the Black Hills. They sent runners out with the sacred pipes to call all the Sioux people together. The headmen hoped to work out some unity among the Sioux, enough to make resistance to white encroachment possible.

Despite the call for a meeting at Bear Butte, with its promise of future resistance, Harney had won the campaign for control of the Platte River Valley. The Brulé, Oglala, and other Sioux tribes stayed away from the Holy Road, except to go to Fort Laramie for their yearly hand-outs. Curly wandered from band to band; everywhere he found the Sioux confused and frightened. He spent the winter of 1856–57 with the Cheyennes, Yellow Woman's people; Young Man

Afraid, son of the Oglala headman Old Man Afraid, was with him. Medicine-man Ice had a special fondness for Curly and taught him the ways of the Cheyennes that winter, on the Smoky Hill River in Kansas, well south of the Platte, and ten years later the site of Custer's first Indian campaign.

In the spring of 1857 the Cheyennes had a number of small skirmishes in central Kansas with the white soldiers. The visiting Sioux told them that the whites would soon come in force, so the Cheyennes made ready. Ice and another medicine man took the warriors down to a small lake, where they dipped their hands into the water while they sang medicine songs and made ritual gestures. Satisfied, they asked a warrior to shoot at them with his gun. The warrior took a shot at each man from close range, but neither was injured—the bullets bounced off their hands. Here was strong medicine indeed. The Cheyennes rushed to the water to dip their hands into it, Curly among them. Now let the soldiers come.†[27]

On July 29, 1857, the troops came, six companies of cavalry under the command of Colonel E. V. Sumner. The Cheyennes were on the Solomon River in north-central Kansas. They rode out to meet the soldiers, Curly with them, the stream on their left and high bluffs on their right. After giving their ponies their second wind, the Indians formed themselves into a line of battle—one of the few recorded instances of this happening in Plains warfare—and began a slow advance. The cavalry at the other end of the valley also formed a battle line, three deep, and came forward at a gallop. The whites were struck by the extreme confidence the Indians displayed. Most of the Cheyennes had their weapons at their sides or over their backs and held their open hands toward the whites, in order to catch the bullets so that they would fall harmlessly to the ground.

But no gun sounded. At the last minute, Sumner ordered his men to draw their sabers and charge. They did so with a whoop. The Cheyennes scattered in total confusion. They put up no fight at all, but simply fled, so confounded were they by the saber charge and the soldiers' failure to use their guns. Four Cheyennes lay dead; the rest, panic-stricken, ran away as fast as they could. The women and children joined them, and the Cheyennes abandoned their camp, lodges and all, retreating far south. Curly stayed with them a day or so, then started north to rejoin the Sioux.[28]

Curly had much to think about as he rode north. Just fifteen years old, he had seen three Indian camps destroyed or abandoned in the

† The probable explanation is that the shells were underloaded. Perhaps Ice was in collusion with the warrior, who may have cheated on the powder load.

past three years, and except at the Grattan battle in 1854 few soldiers had been harmed. He knew that the whites had taken the Platte River Valley away from the Sioux and made it their own. He had learned that Indian medicine did not work against the whites, and that no single Indian village could stand up to an assault by white soldiers. Perhaps, however, if the Sioux could act together, they could preserve what was left of their territory.

Curly set out for the great council at Bear Butte. Most of the Teton Dakotas were there, the Oglalas, Miniconjous, Sans Arcs, Blackfeet, Two Kettles, and Hunkpapas. The wild Sioux from the north country, led by the Hunkpapas, had seen few whites and suffered no defeats at their hands—they, at least, were not intimidated. It was the largest gathering of the Sioux people in years. Its objective was to set a national policy for dealing with the whites; surely something good would come of it. Only the Brulés had not come to Bear Butte—Spotted Tail and Little Thunder had had enough of fighting the whites and were now interested only in their perpetual war against the Pawnees.[29]

There were over 5,000 and perhaps as many as 7,500 Sioux camped at the base of the butte, their tipis making one gigantic circle. Curly was reunited with his parents, sister, and his brother Little Hawk, already a daredevil warrior, veteran of at least two war parties at the age of twelve. Hump was there, along with Young Man Afraid, Lone Bear, and Pretty One. Scores of pretty girls tormented the teen-age boys with their shy smiles and subdued giggles. There was much feasting and exchange of gossip, and, of course, courting. Curly's favorite seems to have been Red Cloud's niece, Black Buffalo Woman.

As Curly renewed friendships and struck up new ones, he observed the great men of the Sioux, men he heard about around the winter campfires. Old Four Horns, the Hunkpapa, and his nephew Sitting Bull; Long Mandan of the Two Kettles; Crow Feather of the Sans Arcs—heroes all. And the headmen of the northern Oglalas were there too, Old Man Afraid, Red Cloud, perhaps the most famous of the warriors, and others. The Miniconjous were led by Lone Horn and his seven-foot warrior son, Touch the Clouds.[30]

The Dakotas were pleased with themselves, delighted to see how many they were, and how strong. The chiefs decided that they had made a mistake in giving in to Harney so easily, and they agreed to act together to stop any further white encroachments on their land. The Sioux of the north country set the tone of the council, a tone of defiance toward the whites. Solemn vows were taken, promises made.

According to some accounts, Curly was moved to pledge to his father that he would fight the whites the rest of his life. Whether true or not, that was the spirit and atmosphere of the Bear Butte Council.

But there was no follow-up. Having made their vows and completed the Sun Dance, the Sioux went off their separate ways. They had not elected a head chief or indeed done anything to provide for an institutional basis for resistance. No generals were appointed, no scouts organized, no system for exchanging information set up, no provision made for arming the warriors with guns instead of bow and arrow (a general guess would be that one in one hundred warriors had a gun at this time, and probably less than half of the guns worked). Nor was there any discussion on *how* to fight the whites. Nothing but promises.

At the conclusion of the council, Curly and Crazy Horse went off alone. Curly was fifteen now, nearly a full-grown warrior, and he had traveled far and seen many things. Crazy Horse wanted to instruct him in his duties and responsibilities, so they built a sweat lodge, fasted, then purified themselves. Crazy Horse said Curly must always look after the helpless ones, provide food for the hungry, and be brave. Curly then told his father of his dream, the dream he had had while Conquering Bear was dying.

Crazy Horse interpreted the dream for his son. He said Curly must be the man in the dream, must do as he said, dress as he dressed, wear a single hawk feather in his hair, a small stone behind his ear. He must lead the people and never take anything for himself.[31]

Father and son then moved south, to the western edge of the Black Hills, where they joined some Oglalas and Miniconjous on a buffalo hunt. They had located a herd, along the line separating South Dakota and Wyoming, but the buffalo did not have their full growth of hair as yet, so the Sioux were herding the animals, holding them in place until the hair was satisfactory for winter robes. The *akicita* kept the young braves from disturbing the main herd—hunters picked off only a few stragglers from time to time for food—and posted scouts to the south to keep the buffalo in place. Curly enjoyed the fine fall weather and lazy days in camp.

But there was no escaping the whites. One bright afternoon Lieutenant Gouverneur K. Warren, a U. S. Army topographical engineer at the head of a small surveying party, stumbled onto the Sioux camp. The younger warriors were for attacking the soldiers at once —the whites had no business being in the Black Hills and the Sioux had just agreed at Bear Butte to resist further white encroachments on their land—but the older men stopped the braves. The elders were afraid that if they killed Warren and his party, General Harney would march again. In the conference that followed, Warren emphasized that retribution would be swift and terrible if he were attacked.

Still, the encounter could have led to disaster had not both sides displayed common sense. Warren was only twenty-six years old, but he had graduated second in the West Point class of 1850 and was an outstanding officer. He listened sympathetically as the Indians explained the situation and begged him not to proceed, because he would drive the buffalo away. "For us to have continued on," Warren wrote in his report, "would have been an act for which certain death would have been inflicted upon a like number of their own tribe had they done it." Further, Warren did not want a war, as he explained in his report. "I felt that besides being an unnecessary risk to subject my party and the interests of the expedition to, it was almost cruelty to the Indians to drive them to commit a desperate act which would call for chastisement from the government." If the Army had had more officers like Warren on the frontier, there would have been much less bloodshed to mark Indian-white relations.

The Sioux told Warren there were other reasons why they wanted him out of the Black Hills. The agreement with Harney gave the whites the right to use the Oregon Trail and a road from Fort Laramie to Fort Pierre, but otherwise they were to stay out of Indian territory. One old man told Warren that "having already given up all of the country they could spare to the whites, these Black Hills must be left wholly to themselves." Besides, if Warren made his survey it would be a great advantage to the whites in the event of another red man-white man war. "I was necessarily compelled to admit to myself the truth and force of these objections," Warren wrote. He agreed to stay where he was until Bear's Rib, a prominent Miniconjou, returned from a war party he had led against the Crows.

Warren waited a few days but Bear's Rib did not show up, so the survey party started east, across the base of the Black Hills and away from the buffalo herd. Bear's Rib caught up with the whites two days later. After a long conference, Bear's Rib agreed that Warren could head north for Bear Butte, but then he must march east, away from *Pa Sapa*, the holy place. Warren agreed to do so. "In return for this," Warren reported, Bear's Rib "wished me to say to the President and to the white people that they could not be allowed to come into that country; that if the treaty presents were to purchase such a right that they did not want them. All they asked of the white people was to be left to themselves and let alone; that if the presents were to induce them not to go to war with the Crows and their other enemies, they did not want them. War with them was not only a necessity, but a pastime."

Clearly Bear's Rib was no Conquering Bear, a peace-at-any-price headman. He said that "the annuities scarcely paid for going after them," and that the Sioux wanted no part of the whites any longer. Bear's Rib had just heard about the Yankton Sioux of the Missouri selling their lands along that river to the whites, and he told Warren he wanted the Yanktons "informed that they could not come to his people's lands. They must stay with the whites." If the Yanktons came west, the Miniconjous and Oglalas would drive them back.

Both men were as good as their word. Warren proceeded to Bear Butte, then marched east and away from the Black Hills. The Indians let him alone, as Bear's Rib had promised.[32]

Bear's Rib had spoken for all the Sioux of the Black Hills country. By this time the whites had destroyed the good hunting along the Platte River. The grass was trampled down or overgrazed by emigrant stock, and the great buffalo herds were gone. For the first time since they left Minnesota eighty years earlier, the Sioux of the Plains were feeling a pinch. The main buffalo herds were now north and west of the Black Hills, in the Powder River country, and the Sioux had to follow the herds. Economic necessity dictated their attitude toward their cousins the Yanktons, and toward their enemies the Crows and the whites. They could not stay in the Fort Laramie region, or, rather, they could stay there only by becoming agency Indians, "Hang-Around-the-Forts" (or "Laramie Loafers," as the wild Indians and frontiersmen contemptuously called them), accepting handouts from the whites to stay alive. And they could not make peace with the Crows, because they had to have Crow land (the same factors were the basic cause of the endemic Brulé-Pawnee war).

For the next decade and more the Oglalas, Miniconjous, and other northern Sioux were to be engaged in a struggle with the Crows, Shoshonis, and Arapahoes for possession of the Powder River country. It had been a sort of no man's land, a place where war parties stumbled across each other and where hunting parties constantly looked back over their shoulders for signs of the enemy. By 1857, however, the Sioux had determined to drive the Crows and Shoshonis and Arapahoes back to the Bighorn River and beyond, right into the mountains. Just as the whites had conquered their land, so they would take the land of the Crows. Until the very end, this Sioux war with the western Plains Indians would be the central fact of

Curly's life; conflict with the whites was only incidental, a bothersome nuisance.

In his sixteenth summer, 1858, Curly joined Hump, Lone Bear, Little Hawk, and other young warriors on a war party headed west. They went farther than any Oglalas had previously traveled, all the way to the Wind River, in central Wyoming, the land of the Shoshonis (or Snakes, as the Sioux called them) and the Arapahoes, just south of Crow country. A scout located an Arapaho village with many fine horses. The Sioux had never seen the Arapahoes, did not understand their language, but were confident that they were more than a match for these strange people, so they decided to attack immediately.

Curly prepared himself in the proper way, as he had been told in the dream and as he would do before every battle of his life. He already wore a small stone behind his ear; now he put a single hawk's feather in his hair, painted a zigzag line with red earth from the top of his forehead downward and to one side of his nose on to the base of his chin. He then put a few spots to represent hail on his body, passed some dust over his horse, and finally sprinkled a little dust on his hair and body. He was ready.[38]

The Arapahoes had discovered the Sioux presence and before the war party reached the village, Arapaho warriors started firing. The Arapaho held the high ground. Hump led an attack, but the Arapahoes held firm. The Sioux had a man wounded, managed to kill one enemy, but for two hours the fight was a standstill.

Suddenly, Curly gave a whoop and charged straight toward the Arapaho position. Arrows and bullets flew around him, but he rode on, right into the enemy. Curly counted one, two, three coup, then turned his horse and retreated, whooping and hollering, while the Sioux at the foot of the hill called out his name in honor of his bravery. Curly charged again and then again. His medicine, it seemed, was powerful; like the man in the dream, he rode through volley after volley of arrows and bullets without getting hit.

The last time Curly charged, two Arapahoes came forward to meet him. Curly killed one with an arrow, leaped his horse over the dead man, whirled, and shot the second man with another arrow. Then, with arrows from above and below him flying over his head, the air filled with the whoops of Arapaho and Sioux warriors, Curly jumped from his horse and took the scalps of the two dead men. Just as he lifted the second scalp, an arrow hit him in the leg. His horse jerked loose, and he had to flee downhill on foot.

Hump pulled the arrow from Curly's leg, then dressed the wound with a fresh piece of skin from a dead horse. Curly threw away the scalps—he had forgotten that he should never take anything for himself: because he had forgotten, the power of his dream had failed him and he was wounded. With one exception, he would never again take a scalp.

As soon as Curly's wound was dressed the Oglalas decided that enough was enough and rode away, heading back to camp. When they arrived there was a victory dance. Twice, Curly was pushed forward into the circle and told to make a song in praise of his brave deeds, but each time he backed out, saying nothing.

The next day Curly's father put on his ceremonial blanket and picked up his sacred pipe. Then he walked through the village, singing a song he had composed, a song that would give Curly a new name, a name he could hold to with pride for the rest of his life:

> My son has been against the people of unknown tongue.
> He has done a brave thing;
> For this I give him a new name, the name of his father,
> and of many fathers before him—
> I give him a great name
> I call him Crazy Horse.

After that the father was no longer called by the name he had given away, but by a nickname, Worm. And Crazy Horse joined Worm, and all the others, at a great feast in honor of his new name.[34]

CHAPTER FIVE

Autie

"My voice is for war!"   George Armstrong Custer, aged seven

"What a pretty girl he would have made."
              Sara McFarland, on the sixteen-year-old Custer

George Armstrong Custer was born on December 5, 1839, in the
tiny village of New Rumley, in Harrison County, Ohio. His father
was Pennsylvania Dutch, descended from solid German citizens of
the Rhineland who had immigrated to America in the eighteenth
century in search of a better life. A sturdy people, these Custers had
their full share of progeny, including Emmanuel Henry Custer, born
in 1806 in Cresaptown, western Maryland. When he was eighteen
years old Emmanuel followed the advancing frontier—and members
of the large Custer clan who had already made the trek—to New
Rumley, a town that had been laid out by his uncle Jacob in 1812.[1]

Emmanuel, who wore a long flowing beard and had the stern
countenance of the German burger, was a part-time farmer, part-
time blacksmith. He married Matilda Viers, who gave him three
children before dying untimely in 1835. Seven months later Emmanuel married Maria Ward Kirkpatrick, a widow from Burgetts-
town, Pennsylvania, who had three children of her own. Maria had
an imposing chin, a narrow, hard-set mouth, slightly shrunken
cheeks, and a thin but prominent nose that looked a little like a
hawk's beak. George, one of her sons by Emmanuel, inherited these
physical characteristics.

Emmanuel and Maria had children of their own at closely spaced
intervals; the first two died as infants, and George—nicknamed
"Autie" by his family—was in effect the oldest child of the union.
But in terms of his family experience, he was almost smack in the
middle, with six older children from the previous marriages to look
after him and four younger ones for him to lord it over. Remarriage
on the frontier was common enough, and the Custers merged into a

solid family with evidently no difficulty at all. Although the family was by no means isolated, it was clannish—Autie spent his infancy almost entirely within the family nest. He was probably a pet of both Ma's kids and Pa's kids, who to him were simply brothers and sisters —as an adult, Custer could not recall who was whose child. As far as he was concerned, they were all Custers, no more, no less. That simple fact speaks eloquently for a healthy, warm, and happy family.[2]

The Custers were fairly typical Americans, a part of the vast melting pot like so many other residents of Ohio. Maria was Scotch-Irish, Emmanuel was German, but the Custer family was American. The fact that the Custers were Methodists was one example of their rejection of the Old World ways; the Methodist Church played a leading role in bringing together Americans of different European backgrounds.

Autie's experiences as an infant are unrecorded. He was probably nursed at Maria's breast, although by 1840 bottle feeding was growing in popularity. Weaning, that first basic lesson in discipline, almost certainly came early, perhaps as early as eight months and clearly before he was much over a year old, for his brother Nevin was only eighteen months younger than he was. Toilet training was probably complete by that time, too; the child-raising literature of the period expressed disgust at wetness and lack of control and urged mothers to complete the job as quickly as possible. Training was accomplished through frequent changes of the child's clothing, by placing the child on the "chair" for hours on end, and, in Autie's case, through the example of older brothers and sisters. The training instilled in him the habits of cleanliness, regularity, obedience, and discipline, and probably something like a sense of shame at his own body's functions. If he engaged in infantile masturbation he was probably warned off and punished if he persisted, for nineteenth-century Americans believed that masturbation would ruin a child, leading to disease, insanity, and even death.[3]

As Autie grew older he was physically punished for transgressions, but although the Pennsylvania Dutch were noted for beating their children to force submission, Autie probably did not have it as bad as most boys his age, for Emmanuel Custer was a fun-loving sort who much preferred playing with his kids—or yelling at them—to whipping them. The atmosphere around the Custer home seems to have been joyous, especially in comparison to the mood at neighboring homes. Emmanuel was a practical joker and so were his children—Autie, worst of all. Chairs were always being pulled from under someone just sitting down; the object of the joke laughed as loud as the others, for he or she knew that the shoe would probably be on the other foot next time around.

Maria was a strong woman who devoted herself to her children. They were at the center of her life, her only real care and concern. She fed and clothed them, hugged them when they needed it, listened carefully and sympathetically to their stories of their adventures, and generally fulfilled the idealized role of motherhood in American society. Not well educated herself, she did all she could to see to it that her children got the best possible educations. After the Civil War she wrote a revealing letter to Autie that began, "My loveing son," and continued: "When you speak about your boyhood home in your dear letter I had to weep for joy that the recollection was sweet in your memory. Many a time I have thought there was things my children needed it caused me tears. Yet I consoled myself that I had done my best in making home comfortable." Not for herself, Maria added, and she regretted that "I was not fortunate enough to have wealth to make home beautiful, always my desire. So I tried to fill the empty spaces with little acts of kindness. Even when there was a meal admired by my children it was my greatest pleasure to get it for them."

A cynic might have seen her as not much more than a maid, or even a slave, ministering to every little want and desire of her children, denying herself always. Maria would not have agreed. She found her satisfaction, her reason for being, in raising happy, healthy children, a task she carried out with great success. As she wrote her son, "It is sweet to toil for those we love." Autie returned her love in abundance. Throughout his life, even when he was a world-famous general, he hated partings from his mother; the partings were always emotional, with great hugs and flowing tears.[4]

Emmanuel was a strong-willed, self-confident man who liked to roar out his opinions to make certain that everyone knew where he stood and understood him perfectly. He was also a free thinker: in a county of Whigs, he was the leading Democrat. He enjoyed debating the public issues of the day and did so at all opportunities. He took his politics seriously and regarded party loyalty as important as church denominational loyalty. "My first vote was cast for Andrew Jackson," he wrote at the close of his life, "my last for Grover Cleveland. Good votes, both!"

Emmanuel was quietly but deeply religious. He helped found the Methodist Church in New Rumley and would go there to pray for guidance on the burning political questions of the times. He regarded card playing, drinking liquor, dancing, and a host of other pleasures as sinful, did not indulge himself, and was rather successful in keeping his children away from forbidden fruit. During the Civil War he wrote his daughter-in-law, "I have every confidence in my dear son Autie, surrounded as he is by temptations . . . but, Libbie, I want you to counsel Thomas [Autie's younger brother, also in the Army]. I want my boys to be, foremost, soldiers of the Lord."[5]

Emmanuel was no soldier himself, although as a respectable member of the community he did belong to the local militia, grandly called the New Rumley Invincibles. Emmanuel took Autie to drill meetings with him, dressing the boy in a tiny suit of velvet with brave big buttons. By the time he was four years old Autie could go through the manual of arms perfectly; the militiamen called him "a born soldier."[6]

Autie was impulsive and somewhat precocious. Emmanuel later described a childhood incident: "When Autie was about 4 years old he had to have a tooth drawn, and he was very much afraid of blood. When I took him to the Doctor to have the tooth pulled it was in the night & I told him if it bled well it would get well right away, and he must be a good soldier. When we got to the Doctor he took his seat, and the pulling began. The forceps slipped off, and Doc had to make a second trial. He pulled it out, and Autie never even scrunched. Going home, I led him by the arm. He jumped & skipped, and said, 'Pop, you & me can whip all the Whigs in Ohio!' I thought that was saying a good deal, but I didn't contradict him!" In fact, Emmanuel quoted him to everyone he met for weeks afterward.

When Autie was seven years old, war with Mexico loomed. The Democrats were hawks, the Whigs doves. At militia drill one day Autie waved a penny flag and called out loudly, "My voice is for war!" Emmanuel quoted the battle cry so often, and others like it, that Autie learned a life-long lesson—the outrageous statement or action was a sure way to draw attention to himself.[7]

Starting at the age of six or seven, Autie spent a few months each year in school. Prior to that time his education had been in family hands; now society took over a part of the task. By the 1840s most Ohioans supported the idea of public education and saw to it that a majority of the children got some book learning. By 1850 Harrison County had only 1,507 illiterates out of a total population of 20,157.[8]

Autie's first teacher was probably a woman, but whether male or female, the teacher inculcated in him the values of the society. In so doing, of course, the teacher was seconding, reinforcing, and extending the lessons he had already learned at home. The whole idea was to make Autie inner-directed, in David Riesman's phrase, or as Erich Fromm expresses it: "In order that any society may function well, its members must acquire the kind of character which makes them *want* to act in the way they *have* to act as members of the society or of a special class within it. They had to *desire* what objectively is *necessary* for them to do. *Outer force* is to be replaced by *inner compulsion* and by the particular kind of human energy which is channeled into character traits."[9] Fromm's insight, of course, applied also to Crazy Horse and the Oglalas.

Autie's teachers taught him, first of all, discipline and respect for authority. A large and growing body of literature on education instructed the teachers on their duties, of which the most important was training good citizens for the Republic. The common theme in the pedagogical literature was that the maintenance of rigid discipline and authority in the schoolroom was by far the best means of inculcating respect for law and order.[10] Corporal punishment was common. The schools also were used to pull the diverse population together; in the words of the superintendent of public instruction in Indiana, the policy was "to make of all the varieties of population among us, differing as they do in origin, language, habits of thought, modes of action, and social custom, one people, with one common interest."[11] The accepted method for accomplishing that goal was a heavy emphasis on American history, especially on the Revolution and the Constitution. Autie learned that his country was uniquely blessed, had the finest form of government ever conceived by man, was the freest the world had ever known, and had a Manifest Destiny to overspread the continent. He heard no criticism of past American actions, only praise for what his predecessors had accomplished.[12]

The schools laid great emphasis on the principle of the equality of white Americans, but in practice openly recognized the existence of a class society. Indeed, teachers sold the idea of public schooling on the grounds that they would teach the poor to respect other men's property. One professional educator minced no words in putting the question, "What surer guaranty can the capitalist find for the security of his investments, than is to be found in the sense of a community morally and intellectually enlightened?" while another spokesman observed that "to the owner of property, no economy is more important than that which shall reform those who have it in their power to plunder and destroy."[13] David Page, the leading writer on education for nearly half a century, emphasized the duty of teachers to instruct children with regard to "the sacredness of all property"; similar lessons were taught by Noah Webster's *Elementary Speller*.[14]

So young Autie learned what was expected of him and how to prosper in his society. He had a happy disposition and seems to have been everyone's favorite. Strong, handsome, and athletic, he had a daredevil spirit and an infectious grin. Having had so much experience wrestling, fighting, racing, and playing other sports with his older brothers and sisters, he outstripped all his classmates at school in athletics. Emmanuel had moved from New Rumley to a farm a couple of miles outside the village, so Autie worked hard, ate well, and grew stronger every day. He knew a great deal about the care and use of domestic animals and about growing a crop. He was especially good with horses; Emmanuel had kept up his blacksmith business and Autie frequently helped him with that work too. Most of all, Autie was responsible—by the time he was ten he could be trusted to feed the stock or clean the stables, or do other tasks.

A classmate of young Autie, Judge R. M. Voorhees, later described him during this period: "Without advantages, despite the hard work of the farm, he was a leader in sports, by nature manly, exuberant, enthusiastic, with a noble, knightly countenance." It must be said that when the judge delivered his opinion, Custer was dead and famous; one can doubt that as a child anyone thought of Autie as "knightly" or "noble."[15]

By the time Autie was ten years old his parents had three more boys of their own—Nevin, Thomas, and Boston—and the house must have been crowded. At least one of the older children had moved out, however; in 1845 Autie's half sister, Lydia Kirkpatrick, married David Reed of Monroe, Michigan, and went there to live. The young bride became lonesome in a home of her own without a gang of kids running around all day long. And she especially missed Autie, who had always been her favorite, almost a son—she had helped make his baby clothes and his velvet military suit. (The only physical scar Autie had—or would ever have—came because of Lydia. When Autie was a tot she had put him on a skittish heifer for a joke. The heifer bucked and Autie was thrown to the ground, receiving a bad cut on his forehead.)

Lydia wanted Autie to come to Monroe to live with her, help David in his draying business and on the farm, and attend school. Maria agreed—she had more than enough children to look after and Monroe's schools were thought to be superior to those of New Rumley.[16]

So Autie left home. Monroe had a population of 3,500 in 1849, equal parts French, English, and German. The second oldest town in southern Michigan, it had pretensions of sophistication. There was an established class, a group of leading citizens who owned or controlled the community's economic life and liked to think of itself as composing an elect society. In Monroe, in short, Autie encountered snobbery for the first time. He saw it from the underside, too, for the Reeds were not members of the better classes.

A retired Army officer with aristocratic pretensions, Major Joseph R. Smith, dismissed the Reeds with a verbal back of the hand: "Of course we did not associate with them." Another resident of Monroe commented: "We did not associate with the [Reeds and] Custers. They were quite ordinary people, no intellectual interests, very little schooling."[17]

We can only conjecture as to how Autie reacted to the new situation. A bright, inquisitive, sensitive youngster, he probably noticed the difference between his family's standing in New Rumley and in Monroe. He does seem to have worked harder at his studies. He could never stand to be second at anything and he had the American faith that education was the best ladder for social and economic climbing.

He got a job working for the town's leading resident, Judge Daniel S. Bacon, a man of imposing position, power, and wealth. Everyone in town knew and respected the judge, a widower with one daughter; she was much the prettiest girl in town. Elizabeth "Libbie" Bacon was about two years younger than Autie,* but she caught his eye nonetheless. One day Autie was walking down Monroe Street when he ran into Libbie swinging on her front gate. "Hi, you Custer boy!" she called out, grinning, before fleeing to the house.[18]

Libbie fascinated Autie—she was so pert, sprightly, and out of reach. He asked the judge if he could do odd jobs in the yard and the judge agreed. But whatever happiness Autie felt was soon dashed, as he quickly learned his place. A neighbor related: "Young Custer got a little job working for the Bacons. He used to hang around the back yard and wait for Libbie. He was not received in her home. He was of good character but the family just couldn't see him."[19] One can imagine Autie standing at the back door of the judge's home, digging a toe in the dirt, receiving a few coins from the judge for the day's work, trying to peek around his rather corpulent figure to catch a glimpse of the interior of the finest house in Monroe—it even had a piano![20]

After two years in Monroe, Autie went back to New Rumley. The reason is unknown. He stayed in Ohio for two years, working on

---

* Libbie's birthdate seems to be unrecorded, and Libbie refused to ever set it straight. A good guess is that she was born in 1841.

Emmanuel's farm and continuing his studies, then returned to Monroe, probably because of its better schools. At the age of fourteen Autie entered Alfred Stebins' Young Men's Academy, which he attended for the next two years. He was the top scholar in his class, so good that he could hold his position without studying. His deskmate, John Bulkley, recalled how Autie often smuggled novels into class and read them behind the textbook during geography hour. His favorite reading was military fiction.

Autie had a fierce temper and was astonishingly impetuous. He was a good speller and led his class in spelling bees. On one occasion a truant rival stood outside the schoolhouse window as Autie was struggling with a difficult word. The rival made faces and ornery gestures at Autie. Angry beyond endurance, Autie sprang to the window, smashed his fist through the glass, and bloodied his tormentor's nose.[21]

Autie graduated from the Academy at the age of sixteen and immediately got a position as principal of a school back in Harrison County, Ohio—"principal" meaning that he was the only teacher in the one-room schoolhouse. He was paid $25 per month, with board. When he received his first month's pay he rushed home to New Rumley, where he found his mother sitting in a rocker. Breathlessly, he threw the money into her lap. "My first earnings," he managed to gasp. "For you." He later said it was one of the happiest moments of his life.[22]

Autie was a popular teacher. His students reca' ed that he tusseled with the boys on the playground, washed the girls' faces in the snow, and played an accordion for opening exercises. He enjoyed arguing politics, just as Emmanuel did, and used to roar out denunciations of "Black Republicans" (abolitionists). A staunch Democrat, he once assigned a student, Sara McFarland, the theme topic "James Buchanan, Our Honored President." Sara changed the title to "Ten-Cent Jimmie," but Autie did not punish her for the impudence. Sara also remembered Autie's dancing blue eyes and his curly redgold hair which he brushed back over his ears. She thought, as she watched him, "what a pretty girl he would have made."[23]

Autie boarded in the home of a substantial farmer, and there he fell in love with the farmer's daughter, Mary Holland. After school he would write of his emotions to her. Custer biographer Jay Monaghan writes, "Boy and man, Custer preferred to express himself on paper rather than orally." "You occupy the first place in my affections, and the only place as far as love is concerned," he wrote Mary. "If any power which I possess or control can aid in or in any way hasten our marriage, it shall be exerted for that object. But I will talk with you about it when I see you next at the trundle-bed." He ended one note, "Farewell, my only Love, until we meet again—From your true & faithful Lover, Bachelor Boy."

Whichever of the joys of intimacy Autie and Mary were discovering on the trundle bed on the Holland farm, they were enough to lead the love-struck Autie to poetry:

To Mary

I've seen and kiss'd that crimson lip
  With honied smiles o'erflowing,
Enchanted watch'd the opening rose,
  Upon thy soft cheek glowing.

Dear Mary, thy eyes may prove less blue,
  Thy beauty fade to-morrow;
But Oh, my heart can ne'er forget
  Thy parting look of sorrow.[24]

By this time the sixteen-year-old Autie was interested in going to the United States Military Academy at West Point. It was the only place, besides the Naval Academy, in the country where he could get a free higher education; it would give him immediate social standing (and he had learned from both the Bacons and the Hollands that his social standing needed improvement) and a secure future. He wanted Mary to marry him before he left but she did not like the idea of being a soldier's wife. At this point her father seems to have intervened. He knew that West Point cadets could not marry, evidently felt besides that his daughter was much too young to be contemplating marriage, and may have wanted her to do better for herself in the husband line. In any event, Holland evidently played a major, though discreet, role in getting Autie his West Point appointment.

Custer's biographers have been mystified by Autie's desire to go to West Point, but the reasons seem clear enough. He had gone as high as he was likely to go in Harrison County, Ohio; he had no real future in Michigan; he was ambitious; his parents couldn't possibly afford a higher education and West Point was free; he wanted adventure; and the idea of soldiering appealed to him. His major difficulty was securing an appointment, for the local congressman, John A. Bingham, was a Whig turned Republican, and appointments to West Point were in the hands of the district representative. The Custers were notorious Democrats and Americans of the period took their politics seriously.

At this point Holland may have helped. He was a prominent member of the community, a Republican, a friend of Bingham's, and he wanted the impetuous, love-struck Autie out of his daughter's life. Possibly Holland talked to both Autie and Bingham about West Point. In any event, Autie wrote Bingham, described himself as a "Democrat boy" so that there would be no confusion on that score, and asked for an appointment on the grounds that he wanted to be a soldier. Struck by Autie's boldness and originality, Bingham wrote a favorable response, saying he had already made an appointment for 1856 but would keep Autie in mind for the next year if Autie would send the required particulars.

Autie replied immediately, thanking Bingham for the opportunity and describing himself as seventeen years of age (which added six months to his real age), "above the medium height, and of remarkably strong constitution & vigorous frame." Later that summer, when Bingham was in Ohio, Autie paid him a visit and impressed the congressman with his frankness and determination. Bingham said Autie could have the next appointment. Maria Custer was opposed, Autie wrote his sister Lydia in Monroe, for the mother did not want her son to be a soldier. But Autie added, "Pop favors it very much." Indeed, Emmanuel was so pleased at the idea of his son's getting a college education that he sold his small farm and gave Autie the buyer's $200 down payment for expenses.[25]

And so the young man prepared in the summer of 1857 to go forth and make his mark on the world. With the help of his elders he had survived an intense teen-aged love affair more or less unscathed. By the standards of the time he was well educated already, and about to join America's elite, for West Point was the outstanding engineering school in the country. If he completed the course, an officer's commission would automatically make him a gentleman, a welcome guest at the best social functions. He was more experienced and independent than his age-mates, had lived in different places, and contributed to his family's income while being responsible for himself.

The prospective cadet was a strikingly handsome lad, beautifully built, with everything in proportion—broad shoulders, strong arms, muscular legs, and a powerful chest. His health was excellent. He enjoyed life and was forever laughing, joking, playing. A free soul who hated restraint, he had nevertheless accepted the need for discipline and realized that his advancement depended upon his superiors, who had to be respected and obeyed.

He was ambitious. Whatever he felt personally about such men as Judge Bacon or Mr. Holland, he was envious of their position in society and looked up to them as men to be emulated. He knew that getting ahead required him to curb his fun-loving, impulsive spirit. He was determined to channel his vast physical energy in the right directions.

He was not an original or an independent thinker, nor even intellectually curious. He accepted what he was taught. Autie echoed his father's politics, denouncing abolitionists and Black Republicans at every opportunity, praising Democrats, and urging his fellow Ohioans to allow the South to work out its own problems. He had no sympathy for the underdog but great interest in and admiration for the rich and powerful.

He was a young man of action, direct action, speeding toward his goals. If a boy teased him during a spelling bee, he punched the boy in the nose, even if he had to go through a window pane to do it. If he fell in love, he tried to get married right away. If he wanted to go to West Point, he wrote directly to the man who could get him there, regardless of the unfavorable circumstances. He had, in short, all the qualities of a good junior officer.

He had a strong sense of self and of family. He consulted with his mother and father, and with Lydia and David Reed, before accepting the West Point appointment. He got on famously with his brothers and sisters; young Tom, in turn, worshiped Autie and imitated him whenever possible. Autie did not question his parents' values and did his best to curb his spirits and make those values his own. Late in his life, he tried to express some of his feelings (and his gratitude) toward his parents. Typically, he wrote them out in a letter to Emmanuel: "You and Mother instilled into me principles of industry, self-reliance, honesty. You taught me the value of temperate habits, the difference between right and wrong. I look back on the days spent under the home-roof as a period of pure happiness, and I feel thankful for such noble parents."[26]

CHAPTER SIX

Custer at West Point

"The Academy stands *in loco parentis* not only over the mental but the moral, physical and, so to speak, the official man. It dominates every phase of his development."   A West Point official

In July 1857 seventeen-and-a-half-year-old George Armstrong Custer entered the United States Military Academy at West Point. Save for one short summer vacation at the end of his second year, he would not leave again until July 1861. Custer himself set the theme for his biographers in their treatment of those four years: "My career as a cadet," he wrote, "had but little to recommend it to the study of those who came after me, unless as an example to be carefully avoided."[1]

One of Custer's biographers describes him as "a slovenly soldier and a deplorable student . . . a tardy and a clumsy recruit who persistently was punished for slackness in drill, dirty equipment, or disorderly uniform."[2] Another biographer asserts that "it is safe to say that in all the long history of the Military Academy it was never afflicted with a less promising or more cantankerous pupil."[3] Custer's biographers delight in recording anecdotes about his life as a cadet, detailing his pranks, his free spirit and fun-loving nature, his refusal to live by the regulations, and his woefully bad record in his studies. The over-all picture is one of an irresponsible and irrepressible adolescent who came perilously close to being thrown out of the Academy on numerous occasions because of his violations of the rules and regulations, and of a lazy, indifferent student who graduated last in his class.

There is some truth in the assessment. Throughout his cadet career Custer found an outlet for his vast energy in forbidden activities. With his curly locks he looked more like a boy than a man, and he did the bare minimum to survive in his studies. His fellow cadets regarded him as a fun-loving prankster.

But the portrait of Custer as a cadet who thumbed his nose at the authorities and who successfully maintained his individualism in the face of West Point's pressure toward dull conformity, misses the point. Custer survived four years at the Academy intact, but hardly unchanged. At West Point, Custer learned the meaning of institutional discipline and the importance of selective obedience. He learned to regard all his fellow cadets (and future fellow officers) as competitors in the race for position and honors. He came to expect to be judged, and ranked, every day. He developed a cool contempt for civilians, especially civilian soldiers, and an exalted view of the United States Army and its officers. He absorbed enough of the social graces to be able to mingle freely with America's elite. He learned a little military and much civil engineering, some mathematics, a smattering of Spanish, the Army's technical jargon, a few ideas about tactics, and almost nothing about strategy.

Most of all, Custer developed his sense of timing, a characteristic too often ignored in accounts of the great and near-great. All comedians have it, and Custer had it as a child—timing is the essence of the practical joke, and as a boy (and a man) Custer was above all else a practical joker. Nor was young Autie's sense of timing limited to knowing the precise moment when pulling a chair from under someone would be funny rather than hurtful—he could also pick the exact place in a conversation to interrupt and call out, "My voice is for war!"

As a cadet, Custer learned to use his sense of timing for practical and immediate results. Any cadet who received more than one hundred demerits in a six-month period was automatically dismissed from the Academy, and Custer (and his biographers) made much of the fact that he had ninety-four demerits in one six-month period, ninety-eight in the next, and so on. What stands out, however, is not that he could not curb his impulsiveness and thus was always on the brink of dismissal, but rather that he *could* curb himself when it was necessary. Once, when he gathered over ninety demerits in the first three months of a reporting period, he went the following three months without collecting a single one.[4] At West Point, that was an accomplishment even the most serious-minded, mature cadet found it difficult to match.

In his studies, Custer did what had to be done. He may have been last in his class, but he *did* graduate, and in any case emphasizing the fact that he was thirty-fourth in a class of thirty-four is entirely misleading. There were one hundred eight candidates for admission to his class, but only sixty-eight passed the entrance examination— Custer among them. Of the sixty-eight admitted, only half graduated

—Custer among them (twenty-two Southerners resigned to join the Confederacy, while a dozen other cadets were dismissed for academic or disciplinary reasons). Further, western and southern boys always brought up the tail end of the West Point class, because their preparation was not equal to that enjoyed by cadets from the East Coast. Most importantly, Custer always knew exactly where he stood in his class and exactly what he had to do to graduate—and he did it. "At least 20% will probably 'flunk out,' " he wrote his sister in May, 1861, "but I have no intention of being among the number."[5] And he was not.

Throughout his West Point career, Custer knew what he could get away with without being thrown out of the Academy and he delighted in going right to the line but never beyond it. He knew when he had to study, or behave, and he did what was necessary. Thousands of Americans before and since have gone through college in just that style, of course, but what makes Custer's record impressive is the place that he made it. Nowhere else in the country, and perhaps in the world, did a stricter discipline or more rigid enforcement of rules exist than at West Point, nor did any other institution require as much memorization of scholastic detail. Every cadet was graded, every day, in every subject, and all those marks went into a cadet's final class ranking. Cadet Custer took advantage of most opportunities to taste of forbidden fruit, but in comparison to his fellows at civilian colleges he was a scholastic monk.

When Custer entered West Point he delivered himself into the hands of an administration and faculty obsessed with the development of character. They pushed, pulled, shaped, and hammered the boys into the accepted mold of a Christian soldier, emphasizing the virtues of duty, loyalty, honor, and courage. The methods used in building moral fiber were simple: required attendance at church, minute regulation of daily life, cold rooms in winter and hot ones in summer, inferior food and uncomfortable clothing, and no recreation. The Academy, in the words of one official, "stands *in loco parentis* not only over the mental but the moral, physical and, so to speak, the official man. It dominates every phase of his development. . . . There is very little of his time over which it does not exercise a close scrutiny, and for which it does not demand a rigid accountability."[6]

When the cadets did have some time off, as on Sunday afternoons, the authorities did their best to see to it that there was nothing to do. There were no organized activities and the only voluntary associations permitted were debating clubs—which by regulation could not debate political questions. No outside lectures were allowed and the cadets could subscribe to no more than one periodical per month. The cadets never got leaves and had no cash to spend. The over-all effect of all this was one of stifling boredom—West Point was oppressively dull. At West Point, one cadet said, "all is monotony," while one of Custer's classmates told his father, "I don't like this mode of life at all; it is too much like slavery to suit me."[7]

At West Point the cadets were not "boys" but "men," and their superiors said they expected them to act as such. The rules and regulations, however, expressed a different view; the authorities assumed the cadets were wild youngsters who had to be watched and from whom temptation had to be removed. One official claimed that "the moral discipline of the institution is perfect; the avenues to vice are closed, and the temptations to dissipation . . . have been vigilantly guarded against." Custer and his fellows were forbidden to drink liquor, play cards or chess, gamble, use or possess tobacco, keep any cooking utensils in their rooms, participate in any games, go off the post, bathe in the Hudson River, or play a musical instrument. They could possess only certain items and each of these had to be in its assigned place in their rooms.[8]

Supervision was minute. Officers in the Tactical Department were no more nor less than spies, forever looking for offenses to mark in their books. Custer was cited on page after page: late for parade, talking on parade, face unshaven, hair unkempt, equipment dirty, uniform disordered (he lay down on the floor to study in order to keep the press in his uniform, but it did little good—then and later, Custer's clothes were sloppy), shoes unpolished, slackness in drill, failure to salute a superior, sitting down on sentry duty, room out of order, gambling in quarters, tobacco smoke in quarters, late for class, and so on.[9]

Demerits meant punishment tours—marching back and forth, in full uniform and carrying a rifle, on weekends. Custer later said he spent sixty-six Saturdays marching post to pay for his transgressions, four hours at a time, without speaking to anyone.[10] But here, as usual, he was in control of the situation, for he had made the choice. Pulling a prank in class meant four hours on the parade ground marching, but it also meant getting a laugh from his fellow cadets, so he willingly paid the price. In one letter home, after describing the hardships he was undergoing because of all the extra marching, Custer commented: "Everything is fine. It's just the way I like it."[11]

Custer, like every cadet, was required to march to and from chapel, where he was supposed to sit in an erect posture on a hard wooden bench and listen to a two-hour sermon from the Episcopalian chaplain—the Army having decided that the Episcopalian faith was the ideal one for an officer and a gentleman. Custer may have wondered why attendance was required, for as one cadet put it, "all excesses are without our reach and in fact we are everywhere so hemmed in that it is almost as difficult to sin here as it is to do well in the world at large."[12]

Custer had no privacy and precious few comforts, even in his room, which, like those of all other cadets, was always open and could be inspected at any time by one of the Tactical Department officers. He learned to do without luxuries; his furniture consisted of an iron bedstead, a table, a straight-backed chair, a lamp, a mirror, a mattress and blanket, and a washstand. That was all that was allowed—any additional items would be confiscated and earn him demerits. His uniform was ill-fitting and always constraining. The shoes were heavy and clumsy, the pantaloons too tight, while the coat, with its three rows of eight yellow brass bullet buttons in front, inspired a cadet verse:

Your coat is made, you button it, give one spasmodic cough,
And do not draw another breath until you take it off!

The crowning adornment was a bell-crowned black leather cap, seven inches high, with a polished leather visor and an eight-inch black plume. It weighed five pounds and, as Cadet John Pope put it, "hurt my head extremely." Superintendent Robert E. Lee confessed in 1852 that the hat caused "headaches and dizziness."[13]

All the hardships of West Point life paled beside the food. The authorities did their best to keep it as cheap, unappetizing, and unnourishing as possible. The menu was short and to the point: boiled potatoes, boiled meat or fish, boiled pudding, bread, and coffee. One cadet reported that although he became accustomed to the sight, and even the smell, of the boiled fish, in four years he had never been able to eat it.[14] Cadets supplemented the diet with impromptu meals cooked over the small fireplaces in their rooms; Custer once stole a rooster from an officer's chicken coop and presided over such a feast.[15] He also received demerits when cooking utensils were discovered hidden in his fireplace.

That Custer survived four years of such a prisonlike existence was testimony to his determination and ambition and to the Academy's ability to persuade its cadets that what it had to offer was worth the cost. Day after day, in small ways and large, the faculty and staff told the cadets that they were the best, the cream of the crop, members of the elite "long gray line." There were constant references to graduates who had reached high positions in both civil and military life, daily reminders that the cadets would soon be the first line of defense of the nation.[16] Civilians were objects of contempt, enlisted men beneath any notice at all. When Cadet Oliver O. Howard paid a visit to an old friend who was serving as a sergeant in a company of troops stationed at West Point, he was roundly criticized by his fellow cadets and by the officers, one of whom called him in and said, "You must remember that it will be for your own advantage to separate yourself from your friend while he is in the unfortunate position of an enlisted man."[17]

In some ways the Corps of Cadets was as elite as the authorities were always telling Custer and his comrades that it was. Because of the method of congressional selection, the cadets tended to come from families of importance in the congressional district, for it did a politician little good to select a boy whose parents could not help him in the next election. Custer was an exception to this general rule, but sons of some of America's leading families regularly appeared to take the oath as a cadet. In 1858 the Corps contained a Washington from Virginia, a Buchanan from Pennsylvania, a Breckinridge from Kentucky, a Huger and a Mordecai from South Carolina, a Du Pont from Delaware, and a Hasbrouck and a Vanderbilt from New York.[18]

For a boy like Custer, without a distinguished family background, wealth, or political position to push him ahead, West Point was an ideal place for social climbing and general advancement. Custer found himself on a plane of total equality with the Vanderbilts or the Du Ponts. Cadets, rich or poor, had no money to spend. They never saw their pay of $30 per month, which went to the commissary for mirrors, razors, clothes, and other essentials. They were forbidden to receive money from home; for two years Cadet Henry A. Du Pont could not leave the post because he was in debt at the commissary.[19] Since there were no fraternities nor indeed any social organizations of any type, cadets divided themselves along the lines of their barracks, squads, and class assignments, not according to background or wealth. And because all the cadets shared the same hardships and all were told that together they constituted an elite, they tended to set themselves off as a group against the civilian world, rather than dividing internally. Western boys quickly learned formal table manners under the watchful eyes of the authorities, so that at dress balls or at dinners Custer could mix easily with the sons and daughters of the American elite.

The intensity of the experience of living four years at West Point was so overwhelming that most cadets formed lifelong friendships there. They drew much closer to each other than most college students of the period, even those who were in the same fraternity. As will be noted below, West Point encouraged the cadets to compete with each other, and they did, but overriding the competition was the strong sense of all the cadets being in the same fix together. Each cadet had the same enemy—the Tactical Department officers and the authorities generally—and the boys came together to protect each other from the spies and the absurd regulations. In the Army, then and now, non-West Point officers referred sneeringly (and jealously) to the "West Point Protective Association," an unofficial and informal—and entirely effective—organization that saw to it that West Pointers got the rewarding assignments, that covered up West Pointers' mistakes, and generally insured favored treatment within the Army for an Academy graduate. The WPPA worked because it was based on the common experience of nearly all graduates—as cadets, they had seen themselves as a small embattled group that could survive only by helping each other against the malevolent forces of the authorities.

Custer made excellent contacts while at West Point, contacts with the rich and powerful, with people who could see to it that he got good positions in the military, political, or business worlds—the kind of positions in which a young man couldn't miss. Being a member of the WPPA almost insured success.

At West Point, Custer and his fellows learned absolute rules. Right was right and wrong was wrong. The cadet honor code emphasized the point. A cadet did not lie, steal, or cheat; he answered all questions fully and truthfully. He was honor bound to report any violation of the regulations that came to his attention. These requirements looked good on paper, and the honor code has long been the most cherished possession of the Corps of Cadets, setting the Corps off from all other college students. But the trouble with the honor code was that no one really lived by it. Obviously Custer did not turn himself in when he violated the regulations, although he was supposed to do so, and neither he nor any other cadet ever reported that someone had sneaked off to a local tavern for a drink or two. West Point pretended that it lived up to an impossibly high moral standard, which in practice meant that the cadets quickly absorbed the most important rule of all: don't get caught, have a story prepared if you are caught, and be ready to cover for other cadets when necessary. Cadets may not have lied, stolen, or cheated, but they did quibble—all the time.

At West Point the course of studies was so rigorous that only those with outstanding ability or excellent preparation could stay in the school at all. The Academy thought of itself as the best educational institution in the country, and while it was not that good, it certainly was the toughest. Cadets who had been to other colleges before coming to West Point were amazed at how much they were expected to know and how well they were required to know it. Students back home, one of Custer's contemporaries wrote, "have not the faintest idea of what hard study is." "You can not and you dare not slight anything" at West Point, he added, for you may be called on at any time, on any aspect of the course. West Point, he claimed, covered more ground in one month than the ordinary college did in three, and the level of work was higher. Cadet Henry Du Pont found West Point at least twice as difficult as the University of Pennsylvania, which he had attended for a year before coming to the Academy.[20]

So the cadets learned a great deal and thought of themselves— and endlessly told themselves and were endlessly told by their superiors—that they were the top college students in the country. In fact, however, it was nearly all rote learning, memorization pure and simple. West Point turned out competent civil engineers; because it was almost the only civil engineering school in a country that had an insatiable appetite for building, it served a real function and gave its graduates lifetime job security. If all else failed, they could always make a handsome living as civil engineers.

But there was no intellectual questioning, no real curiosity, no attempt to experiment or discuss difficult issues. Custer had daily assignments, but no time to reflect on them; he had to recite in every class, but was never encouraged (or permitted) to discuss the implications of the subject matter. He was told what he must know and never urged to exercise his imagination or curiosity to seek out new fields of knowledge. West Point assumed that it knew what he had to know to be an effective officer and that his only job was to commit that body of knowledge to memory.

Mathematics was by far the most important subject, both because it was the basis for later study in engineering and because it counted most in making up the academic merit roll. To those who had difficulty with the subject, mathematics became an obsession. One cadet told his father, "I can't write as good a letter as I used to—as I am always thinking of Math. —I have a nightmare every night almost of it.—Gigantic X's and Y's, +'s and —'s squat on me—and amuse themselves in sticking me with equations, and pounding me on the head."[21] Another cadet put his feelings more succinctly when he inscribed on the flyleaf of his calculus book, "God damn all the mathematics to the lowest depths of hell!!"[22]

West Point was not unique. The idea that regurgitation of trivial facts constituted an education was common to the pre–Civil War American college, although nowhere did it go as far as it did at West Point. Thus the more they regurgitated the more superior the cadets felt themselves to be.

The daily recitations also helped reinforce the spirit of competition that was so marked a feature of cadet life. If to the outside world the cadets presented a solid front of superiority, within their own class cadets were expected to fight each other for higher rank, based solely on their classroom performance and demerits. The principle of pure competition, the fighting for higher standing and rank, permeated every aspect of Academy life. That it generally made the cadets work harder and produced good results is obvious, but there were other results. "I cannot find as good open hearts among the cadets as among my friends at home," one cadet said. "There is a species of lurking selfishness hanging around cadets, for in class every man is in a degree jealous of his neighbor, in some greater or less according as the feeling is called forth by circumstances of position."[23] Inasmuch as there was a weekly posting of grades and inasmuch as a man's career hung on the result, it could hardly have been otherwise. For Custer, however, the competition was not as intense as it was for those at the top of his class, who were fighting each other for final standing as number one or two. He was just trying to get by, so he threatened no one and no one threatened him.

Custer was popular with his fellow cadets, possibly the most popular cadet of the late 1850s. Aside from the negative fact that he threatened no cadet's class standing, his popularity was based on solid appeal. He was a natural athlete and much admired for it. As Jay Monaghan notes, "He enjoyed athletic stunts, like twisting his legs behind his head or bounding to his feet from a prone position." Although only average in height and slightly below average in weight, he was the second strongest boy in his class, yet he was easygoing, slow to take offense, and neither violent nor vicious. There is no record of his engaging in any fist fights as a cadet.[24]

Custer was a "character," bringing some amusement into the drab lives of the cadets. He was always and forever laughing, so it was pleasant just to be around him. His pranks became legends. In French class he was asked to translate at sight, "*Léopold, duc d'Autriche, se mettait sur les plaines,*" and he set out boldly enough, "Leopold, duck and ostrich . . ." In Spanish class, Custer interrupted the instructor and asked him to translate into Spanish, "Class is dismissed." When the teacher did so, Custer marched the class out of the room.[25]

He loved attention and was an expert at getting it. At West Point his lifelong ambivalence about his hair style began. He always attracted nicknames—among the cadets, a sure sign of acceptance into the group—and his nicknames usually referred to his current hair style. When he showed up at the Academy for the first time, his curly blond locks immediately won him the nickname "Fanny." After a week or so of being called by a girl's name, Custer shaved off most of his hair. But a crew cut stood out as much in the 1850s as did flowing, shoulder-length hair, so he bought a toupee and wore it for nearly a year. When his own hair had grown out again, Custer splattered it with hair oil—and picked up the nickname "Cinnamon" from the scent. By the time he graduated, he had acquired Crazy Horse's childhood name, "Curly."

Custer was very much "one of the boys," a member of the in-group who could be counted on to participate in any extralegal caper. Aside from stealing a chicken, duck, or goose and roasting it over the fireplace, this usually consisted of sneaking away from the Academy grounds and having a forbidden glass of whiskey or rum at a local tavern, Benny Haven's. Custer later said he went to Haven's more often than he should have, which in translation meant that he may have had a few drinks on three or four occasions each year.

By the time Custer entered West Point, the sectional controversy that would tear the country apart was threatening to divide the Corps of Cadets into two political groups, but as a pro-South Democrat from Ohio, Custer had no difficulties. He got on easily with the southern cadets and there was only a handful of abolitionists among the northern boys. With his happy-go-lucky nature, his strong support of the Union, and his equally strong denunciation of Republicans as threats to the Union, he was a favorite with cadets from both sides of the Mason-Dixon line.[26]

In the summer of 1859 Custer had his only leave. He went to see his parents in Ohio, then to Michigan to spend some time with the Reeds. He may have seen Mary Holland—he had sent her a formal invitation to the 1858 West Point ball. When he returned to West Point, Cadet James B. Washington, a relative of George Washington, remembered hearing "Here comes Custer!" Historian Jay Monaghan notes that "the name meant nothing to [Washington], but he turned, and saw a slim, immature lad with unmilitary figure, slightly rounded shoulders, and a gangling walk."[27]

"West Point has had many a character to deal with," Cadet Morris Schaff later wrote, "but it may be a question whether it ever had a cadet so exuberant, one who cared so little for its serious attempts to elevate and burnish, or one on whom its tactical officers kept their eyes so constantly and unsympathetically searching as upon Custer. And yet how we all loved him."[28]

Schaff, who was also from Ohio, a year behind Custer and one of his closest friends, wrote the classic volume on the pre–Civil War Academy, *The Spirit of Old West Point*. Speaking of Custer's nature, Schaff said it was "full of those streams that rise, so to speak, among the high hills of our being. I have in mind his joyousness, his attachment to the friends of his youth, and his never-ending delight in talking about his old home . . ."[29] Schaff records numerous examples of Custer's ability to bring some laughter into the dull routine of West Point. One summer Jasper Myers of Indiana arrived to take the oath as a cadet. Myers had a long beard. Custer walked up to Myers and gravely informed him that a mistake had been made. Myers should go home at once and send his son, because it was the boy that the government meant should have the appointment, not the full-bearded old man.[30]

Custer's popularity also rested on his willing, even joyful, acceptance of group standards. He challenged no one's intellect. He was far from being an original thinker and he did not question the clichés of his day. Like his father he loved to argue politics, but again like Emmanuel Custer he did so in a friendly spirit and had nothing new to say—he merely repeated whatever the current wisdom of the Democratic party might be. He filled his letters and his conversations with political slogans, which enlightened no one, not even Custer, who never thought very hard or long about what he was saying. But his clichés did not offend or make him many enemies.[31]

West Point had a small library, from which cadets were allowed to check out books from time to time. Custer was not much of a reader—during his last two years he took out nothing—and what he did read tended to be romantic adventure stories. He tried John Pendleton Kennedy's *Swallow Barn*, which gave him a picture of a friendly, hospitable South with happy black folks bossing their masters around, and William Gilmore Simms's *Eutaw*, a romance about the Revolution. Both books were filled with admirable heroes, men of unbelievable courage who always won against overwhelming odds.[32]

Custer also read Cooper's *Leatherstocking Tales*, which led him to write an essay for English class entitled "The Red Man." In painstaking handwriting, he traced in two pages the history of the Indians on the North American Continent. Before the white man came, "they were the favored sons of nature, and she like a doting mother, had bestowed all her gifts on them." But now "the familiar forests, under whose grateful shade, he and his ancestors stretched their weary limbs after the excitement of the chase, are swept away by the axe of the woodman." The Indian's hunting grounds were gone. "We behold him now on the verge of extinction, standing on his last foothold, clutching his bloodstained rifle, resolved to die amidst the horrors of slaughter, and soon he will be talked of as a noble race who once existed but have now passed away."[33]

In both English and ethics class (Custer said later these were the two least helpful subjects he studied) Custer continued to mix his metaphors and confuse the singular and plural as he gushed out his schoolboy views. The "Elements of Ideal Moral Perfection," he wrote in an essay for ethics, were "Benevolence, Justice, Truth, Purity, and Order." In an analysis of "Christian precepts concerning obedience and command," Custer quoted the Bible to support such lofty moral ideals as "Duty of obedience of children to parents," "Disobedience mentioned among the signs of perilous times," "Duties between servants and masters," "Servants, be obedient to them that are your masters," "Slaves bound to their masters," and so forth. It was rote work, nothing more nor less, but it was as close to a liberal education as a cadet could get at West Point.[34]

Although he got low grades in his English and ethics classes, Custer enjoyed writing. He became addicted to setting thoughts, feelings, emotions, and anecdotes down on paper. He wrote countless letters to his family (and possibly to Mary Holland) during his cadet days. The cadet schedule was so tight that the boys were allowed only seven hours' sleep per night, but Custer got by on even less, because he needed the time to write. He would prop up a blanket in bed, then light a candle and crawl into the hideaway with pen and paper. Later, during his Indian campaigns, he would sit up through half or more of the night, jotting down the experiences of an exhausting day.

On May 5, 1860, Custer wrote an eight-page letter to a boyhood companion in Ohio. After describing life at West Point in some detail, he concluded: "I will change the subject by saying a few words on politics." The "few words" occupied two and a half closely written sheets of the usual clichés denouncing the "Black-Brown-Republicans" who "will either deprive a portion of our fellow citizens of their just rights or produce a dissolution of the Union."[35] In his letters to his family he described his life in detail, asked after all his brothers and sisters and his parents, regretted that he was not sending money home to support the family, handed out advice about the children not smoking tobacco or getting into fights, and generally used written communications to help him feel as if he were still an intimate member of the family. He also wrote the kind of thing he knew the home folks wanted to hear: "I would not leave this place," he told his sister Ann, "for any amount of money, for I would rather have a good education and no money than a fortune and be ignorant."[36]

Throughout his life, Custer's obsession with writing continued. He jotted down everything; nothing was too insignificant to escape his notice or his written description. If the total outpouring could ever be collected and counted, it would surely rank him with some of the most productive professional writers of the century, at least in terms of the number of written words. His style was convoluted and polite, like much of nineteenth-century American literature, and most of it dealt with what Custer had seen, heard, thought, or felt. He considered himself to be the most fascinating character he knew and therefore loved to write about himself, confident that others would find his experiences equally fascinating. But most of all, he wanted to leave a record, an ultimate proof that he had existed and that he was important. That burning need to write, to set down for posterity his own experiences, was as integral a part of Custer's character as his courage, his ambition, or his joyful nature.

The United States Military Academy, like every other institution in America, was torn apart by the Civil War. The Academy was one of the last to divide. After the Democratic convention of 1860, the Academy and the Catholic Church remained as the only truly national institutions left in the United States. It was not surprising that this was so, for as the "national academy" it had consistently tried to eliminate sectional prejudice and foster national sentiments. But no matter what the authorities did, they could not totally isolate the cadets from events in a rapidly polarizing nation. In the late fifties at the Academy, fist fights, especially during election periods, became more frequent. In the aftermath of John Brown's raid on Harpers

Ferry in 1859, there were many heated arguments and at least one duel, which involved Custer's friend Pierce M. B. Young of Georgia.[37]

For Custer it was an exciting and distressing period. Exciting because of the prospect of war, now on everyone's lips. War would mean immediate service, promotions, an opportunity to win fame. Distressing, because Custer did not want to fight against his southern friends, did not want to see the Union broken, and did not want to fight for a Republican Administration against the institution of slavery, which he continued to defend. Rumors flew among the cadets about who was going to do what, and there were countless quiet discussions in barracks far into the night, with cadets asking one another what they should do.

From the time of Abraham Lincoln's nomination for President by the Republicans, and the division of the Democratic party into northern and southern wings, talk of secession was rampant. It was generally understood that secession would mean war. Cadets had a number of choices. Southerners could resign from the Academy, return to their home states, and expect a commission—at a much higher rank than second lieutenant—in either the prospective Confederate Army or their home state militia. Resignation came hard, however, especially to those who had endured four years of hell at the Academy and who, by resigning, would have nothing to show for it. Pierce Young told his parents, "You and others down there don't realize the sacrifice resigning means." He reminded them that "it is a hard thing to throw up a diploma from the *greatest* Institution in the world when that diploma is in my very grasp and you know that diploma would give me pre-eminence over other men in any profession."[38]

Northern cadets could also resign, return to their states, and expect to become captains, majors, or even lieutenant colonels in their state forces. Or cadets could stay at the Academy, graduate, receive their regular Army commissions as second lieutenants, and then hope for a combat assignment. The problem with that last course of action was that promotion in the regular Army was governed by seniority and was exceedingly slow, while promotion in a state force for a trained professional soldier promised to be rapid indeed.

Many cadets agonized over their choice, but not Custer. Throughout the 1860 election campaign, when excitement was building every day, he damned Lincoln and the Republicans, expressed great sympathy for the southern position, and hoped that the Democrats would somehow win the election and avert a civil war. But no matter how deeply he felt about the justice of the southern cause, Custer was no traitor. He never considered the possibility of joining the South or of doing anything less than his duty to the United States, a duty he had assumed when he took his oath of loyalty. He was a Democrat, but a Jacksonian Democrat. He believed in America and its mission. He could not abide the thought of breaking up the Union.

Many of Custer's closest friends were Southerners, but concerned though he always was about politics, he never took them so seriously as to allow political differences to interfere with friendships. During and after the war he maintained a close rapport with his southern friends, even though he had fought many a bloody battle against them. All this had been prophesied; during the secession winter Pierce Young told Custer, "We're going to have war. It's no use talking; I see it coming. . . . Now let me prophesy what will happen to you and me." Young said they would both become colonels of a cavalry regiment, Custer from Ohio and Young from Georgia. "And who knows but we may move against each other during the war." Young added that "we'll get the best of the fight in the end, because we will fight for a principle, a cause, while you will fight only to perpetuate the abuse of power."[39]

On election night Custer, with many friends, stayed up long after "lights out" waiting for the final returns. By midnight the cadets knew that Lincoln had won. Some southern cadets hanged his body in effigy from a tree in front of the barracks; Custer and other northern cadets cut it down before dawn.[40]

In November 1860 two South Carolina cadets resigned from the Academy and returned home; in December the remainder of the South Carolina contingent, along with three Mississippians and two Alabamians also left. One of the Alabama cadets was Charles P. Ball, first sergeant of Company A, heir to the first captaincy of the Corps and one of the most popular cadets. When he was about to leave he called the cadets to attention in the mess hall and declared, "Good-bye, boys! God bless you all!" Thereupon the members of his class hoisted Ball onto their shoulders and carried him to the wharf. Custer was paying the usual penalty for demerits by extra marching. As Ball passed, Custer's sense of loyalty to the Corps and his friendship for a classmate led him to halt, click his heels together and present arms.[41]

On Washington's Birthday, February 22, 1861, the band marched at dusk into the barracks area, playing "The Star-Spangled Banner." It was a warm late-winter evening. "Every room fronting the area was aglow," Morris Schaff recorded, "every window up and filled with

men. With the appearance of the band at the Sally Port a thundering cheer broke, and, upon my soul! I believe it was begun at our
window by Custer, for it took a man of his courage and heedlessness
openly to violate the regulations." The band then struck up "Dixie,"
and Tom Rosser of Texas, another of Custer's close friends, led a
southern cheer. "Ah, it was a great night!" Schaff remembered. "Rosser at one window, Custer at another," cheering madly.[42]

A week or so later Custer learned that a tall, muscular Southerner
had threatened Schaff. Like Custer, Schaff was a Democrat, but he
had come to the defense of Ohio Republican Senator Benjamin
Wade when the southern cadet had damned Wade to eternity. Schaff
was short and slim, but Custer told him not to worry: "If he lays
a hand on you, Morris, we'll maul the earth with him."[43]

Throughout the secession period, Custer continued to spend much
of his free time with southern classmates, even though they became
louder and more boastful every day. Custer didn't mind their swagger
—he was that way himself. Nor did he object to their defense of
slavery. But he did tell them, flatly, that to resign and go South to
fight for the Confederacy was treason, pure and simple, and a direct
violation of the oath of allegiance they had solemnly taken. But he
said it as a statement of fact, without rancor, and lost no friends
thereby.[44]

On April 10, 1861, Custer wrote his sister Lydia, "In case of war,
I shall serve my country according to the oath I took . . ." He predicted war within a week—it came three days later. Custer noted the
contrast of feelings among the cadets: "Those leaving for the South
were impatient, enthusiastic, and hopeful. Their comrades from the
North, whom they were leaving behind, were reserved almost to sul-
lenness—were grave almost to stoicism."[45]

It was a trying time for the northern cadets. Day after day their
southern comrades resigned and returned home, there to pick up
prized commissions in the Confederate or state volunteer forces.
Meanwhile the northern boys fumed and fussed—they were stuck
with their daily classes and recitations. They felt an acute sense of
isolation. The war news from all over the country was intensely exciting, but at West Point, now that the Southerners had left, everything
was quiet and normal—maddeningly so. All over the North, volunteer
companies and regiments were being formed, men were marching off
to war to the tune of "The Battle Hymn of the Republic," with
pretty girls' kisses on their cheeks, and the great crusade was under
way. But at West Point, nothing. The young heroes, eager to save

their nation, were ignored. To make a bad situation worse, high rank in the volunteer outfits was going to untrained civilians.

Like many Americans, the cadets assumed the war would consist of one gigantic battle, with the winner marching on and capturing the loser's capital. The relative inactivity and isolation at West Point, the continuation of regular classes, and the seeming blindness of the authorities who refused to call them immediately into active service, all made the cadets frantic. They were certain the great battle would be fought without them. The nation needed all the help it could get, but the authorities were ignoring the dozens of potential Napoleons at West Point. The First Class (seniors) sent a petition to the Secretary of War begging for an early graduation; he granted it and on May 6 the senior cadets received their commissions and set out for active duty in Washington. Custer's class was next in line—it was not due to graduate until June 1862, but it also sent a petition for graduation a full year early and had it granted.[46]*

With his final examinations coming up, Custer worked harder than he ever had in his life. He was determined not to miss his opportunity. "We study incessantly," he wrote Lydia on May 31. "I and others only average about four hours' sleep in the twenty-four. I work until one at night, and get up at five. All my classmates are becoming pale and thin. I lost five lbs. already! We do not complain. On the contrary, everyone is anxious and willing." He knew there were risks involved, but he wanted to meet the challenge. "It is my great expectation to fight for my country," he wrote, "and to die for it if need be. The thought has often occurred to me that I might be killed in this war; and if so, so be it."[47]

Custer's family asked him to apply for a furlough and come home for a farewell visit. He would have none of it. "I would not ask for a leave when all are needed," he explained. "It is my duty to take whatever position they assign me." By this time, early June 1861, he had developed a realistic view of what lay ahead: "It is useless to hope the coming struggle will be bloodless or of short duration. Much blood will be spilled and thousands of lives, at the least, lost." But he was neither dismayed nor afraid. "If it is to be my lot to fall in the service of my country and my country's rights, I will have no regrets."[48]

On June 24, 1861, Custer graduated. As the last member in his class, he bowed solemnly as he received his diploma. His classmates cheered. He was now an officer in the United States Army.

* In the 1850s West Point had a five-year course.

For the next week, Custer and his classmates killed time as well as they could while waiting for orders. It must have been almost intolerable—the armies of the South and North were gathering between Richmond, Virginia, and Washington, D.C., in preparation for the first great battle of the war, while the new second lieutenants of the West Point Class of 1861 cooled their heels on the banks of the Hudson River. Custer had endured four years at the Academy. He had done what he could to relieve the boredom and oppression of cadet life, but withal he had taken the worst the Academy could throw at him and never stumbled. Despite his hundreds of demerits, Custer had met the Academy's minimum standard. But enough was enough —he wanted to be off to war, not serving as an Officer of the Guard at the summer encampment, watching the antics of entering cadets.

As historian Jay Monaghan tells it: "On the evening of June 29, 1861, two newly arrived candidates got in a fight over their respective places before a water faucet. Instead of stopping the fisticuffs, Custer had stopped intervention, saying, 'Let there be a fair fight.' He himself became so engrossed in the contest that he did not notice the circle of onlookers melting away; they had spied Lieutenant William B. Hazen, Officer of the day, coming from the guard tent. Custer was placed under arrest and charges were preferred."

Under arrest! Four years as a cadet and nothing remotely as serious had ever happened to him; now, an officer for less than a week, expecting to be sent to the battle front at any time, he was under arrest. His luck had run out. Not even Custer could make a joke out of this situation, especially not on the next day, when he watched from the guardhouse as the remainder of his class received orders and started out for active duty in Washington, leaving Custer behind.

The Commandant of Cadets, Lieutenant Colonel John F. Reynolds, interviewed Custer the next day. After getting all the facts, Reynolds asked Custer if he knew what his duty had been as Officer of the Guard.

"My duty," Custer replied forthrightly, "was plain and simple. I should have arrested the two combatants and sent them to the guard tent for violating the peace and regulations of the Academy." And why, Reynolds asked, had Custer not done his duty? "The instincts of a boy," Custer responded, "prevailed over the obligations of an Officer of the Guard."[49] Custer went back to the guardhouse while Reynolds prepared court-martial proceedings.

The incident was revealing. Throughout his career, Custer allowed the instincts of the boy to prevail over his obligations as an officer. West Point had taught him how to behave, but it had not broken his youthful spirit. Time and again he would neglect his "plain and simple duty" when an irresistible impulse led him off on another lark. But he had learned at the Academy how to play the system, how to violate the regulations and get away with it, how to appear contrite when contriteness was demanded.

For two weeks Custer remained in the guardhouse, while the West Point Protective Association came to his rescue. In Custer's words, "My classmates who had preceded me to Washington interested themselves earnestly in my behalf to secure my release . . . and an order for me to join them at the national capital. Fortunately some of them had influential friends there, and it was but a few days after my trial that the superintendent of the Academy received a telegraphic order from Washington, directing him to release me at once, and order me to report to the Adjutant-General of the Army for duty. This order practically rendered the action and proceedings of the court-martial is my case nugatory."[50]

When his trial came, on July 15, it was, in Custer's words, "brief, scarcely occupying more time than did the primary difficulty." Lieutenant Hazen, who had arrested Custer, spoke up for him. The court, acting under instructions from the War Department, let Custer off with a reprimand. He was immediately handed his orders directing him to report to Washington at once.[51]

Custer had made it through West Point and into the Army. That he had only just made it mattered not at all—he had his commission in his pocket and his future ahead of him. He was sure of himself, without any doubts as to his proper course of action. He wanted to fight and lead others into combat. He was as determined to stand out in battle as Crazy Horse was to count coup. Custer realized that he had a rare opportunity—under ordinary circumstances, a West Point graduate could expect to be a second lieutenant for five or more years, a first lieutenant for ten years, and a captain only when he reached middle age. But there was a war on, the biggest in the nation's history, and for the young would-be hero there were opportunities at every hand. He would have to prove his courage to others, and to himself. He desperately wanted to rise rapidly in the Army, where he expected his West Point diploma would help him with the high command. In perfect health, bursting with strength and energy, twenty-one years old, Custer was ready.

CHAPTER SEVEN

Custer and Crazy Horse on the Eve of Manhood

Crazy Horse and Custer had happy childhoods. Each infant boy was loved and cherished by his parents and by a wider group—in Custer's case by his large family, in Crazy Horse's case by the whole of Old Smoke's Oglala village. They were both well fed, adequately clothed, and nicely sheltered. Each boy was carefully taught by his society the skills necessary to survival, and each learned what was expected of him with regard to behavior and belief. Neither boy came from a prominent family, but by the time they were in their late teens both Custer and Crazy Horse stood out in their societies as individuals of unusual daring, drive, and initiative. Both red and white societies were sufficiently practical and realistic to recognize these valuable traits despite the boys' modest backgrounds.

Both boys traveled extensively and learned to deal with different cultures and personalities. Although Custer had lived in only two states before he went to West Point, he had dealt with a wide variety of strong-willed personalities, beginning with his multitude of brothers and sisters and including most residents of New Rumley, Ohio, and Monroe, Michigan. At West Point, he met and lived with other youngsters from all across the United States. Crazy Horse had roamed across the northern Great Plains, living with different Sioux bands and with the Cheyennes.

Crazy Horse had lived near the whites and knew something of their ways. Custer knew next to nothing about Indians. Crazy Horse had seen combat at first hand, both against the whites and against other Indians. He had killed enemies. Custer had never seen combat and of course had never killed.

Both boys lived in a society that exalted individualism, but in Custer's culture only the elite males could really practice it, while in Crazy Horse's village everyone expressed themselves in his or her own way. Custer's society was so complex that there was a wide scope available for self-expression in work, at least for the men, who had a variety of occupations to choose from. Within that scope, however, there were rather narrow restrictions on how a man could act, be he a lawyer, doctor, warrior, common laborer, or whatever, and there was societal pressure pushing men toward certain jobs. Crazy Horse's society offered only a limited number of occupational options, but within those narrow confines a man was free to make his own choices and act as he pleased. Custer's society was strictly ordered in terms of functions—nearly every man had someone telling him what to do. Although there was some freedom of movement within the hierarchy—enough to allow a blacksmith's son like Custer to become a cadet at the elite Military Academy—the fact that there were bosses and those who were bossed never changed. Crazy Horse's society was, essentially, bossless—no man could tell another what to do.

Custer was disciplined. Crazy Horse was not. On innumerable occasions Custer forced himself to do something he did not want to do, but which his society required him to perform. He accepted orders. When he was told he had to study, he studied; when he was told to march, he marched; when he was required to keep his uniform and his room neat and tidy, he kept them neat and tidy. He never liked it, but he knew that if he did not do as he was told he would be a failure. Crazy Horse did as he wished. When he felt like seeking a vision, he sought one, ignoring tribal tradition. When he wanted to live with the Cheyennes, he did, even if his services were required by the Oglalas. He ate when it pleased him to do so, not according to a clock, and he slept when he was tired. He neither took nor gave orders.

Because it was disciplined, Custer's culture was infinitely more productive than Crazy Horse's, better able to get things done. Custer's people could act in concert for a common objective, while Crazy Horse's could not.

Custer's society was specialized. Thus, despite his range of choices, once Custer settled into an occupation, he knew relatively little about what other men in his society did for their daily bread. After becoming a soldier, Custer knew almost nothing about medicine or law or manufacturing. He never really understood how his society worked. Crazy Horse knew how to do everything required to make his society function. He could put up a tipi, kill buffalo, skin animals, cook, make war, treat injuries or illness, and so on. Put Crazy Horse down naked and alone on the Great Plains and within a month he would have a full set of weapons, shelter, stocks of food, and be in good shape to face the future.

Custer's culture was inventive and progressive. Never satisfied with the present, it lived for the future, embracing whatever was new. It had an almost manic desire to reach out and overwhelm nature, to force it to submit, to exploit it. When Custer looked on a virgin forest, he generalized or abstracted. He envisioned sawmills, planks rolling out of them, houses being built all across the country, and on the land itself small farms, cleared of trees, carefully cultivated by a happy yeoman. Crazy Horse saw the trees as they were at that moment, perhaps noting an immediate use for the saplings as lodge or travois poles, but otherwise casting a practiced eye over the scene to calculate what animals lived where in that particular forest.

Living for the future almost had the effect of making Custer's society live *in* the future, while Crazy Horse, caring only for the present, lived in it. Custer believed in progress, in the doctrine that things were always getting better, most notably gadgets, such as new rifles, or trains, or the telegraph. Crazy Horse's world view was circular, while Custer's was linear. Custer saw history sequentially —that is, events marched forward in a recognizable order, with cause and effect being known and understood, the whole leading ever onward and upward.

Crazy Horse, on the other hand, saw history as an integral part of the present, unknown as cause and effect or in any sequential way, but nevertheless incorporated into his daily life. Much of what Crazy Horse did he did because that was the way "it has always been done." Crazy Horse's myths had no time sequence to them, except obviously for the genesis stories; rather, the myths explained to him *why* things were done a certain way, rather than *when* a certain event happened. For all Crazy Horse knew, it could have happened ten or a thousand years before his birth. That did not matter; what mattered was that the myth lived in the present.

Custer was taught countless details about the past. He had dead heroes, while Crazy Horse had only live ones. Custer knew of innumerable battles and of the individuals involved in them, from the time of the Mexican War back to the Peloponnesian Wars. Crazy Horse knew nothing about any individuals from the Sioux past, not even their names, and he was hardly aware of what life had been like when his people lived without horses on the Minnesota meadows —which was less than seventy years before his birth. For Custer, what had happened was known and past. For Crazy Horse, what had happened was unknown in detail but present in spirit.

Custer's fantasy life was terribly constricted, while Crazy Horse's was boundless. Custer could imagine only what he felt, saw, touched, understood. Crazy Horse could imagine almost anything. Custer's culture taught him to be practical; Crazy Horse's culture encouraged him to dream. Custer spent his teen-age years trying to do something, to be somebody; Crazy Horse spent his teen-age years seeking a vision. Custer thought of animals only in terms of their usefulness, as objects; Crazy Horse thought of animals as a different, not distinct, form of life, to whom he was closely connected and with whom he could get in touch via the vision. Custer could not imagine talking to animals or plants; Crazy Horse could not imagine *not* communicating with all forms of life. Custer dismissed the non-Christian supernatural, while Crazy Horse embraced it.

Crazy Horse believed that he was connected to all that there was, the earth, the sky, the sun and moon, the plants and animals, even the insects—everything was part of *Wakan Tanka*, the Great Spirit. Custer saw himself as distinct from, and superior to, everything—most of all, the animals and even some of his fellow human beings, such as blacks or Indians (Crazy Horse also saw himself as distinct from, and even superior to, human beings who were not Sioux; his society was as willing as Custer's to kill or exploit outsiders).

Burial practices illustrated the two men's different outlooks. Custer believed a body should be buried in a long-lasting metal casket, thus removing the body from the ecological system by preventing bacteria from breaking it down and feeding it back into the soil. Crazy Horse believed in wrapping a body inside a buffalo robe and placing it on a scaffold on an open hillside, where the elements could break it down in a year or two. It would then come up again as buffalo grass, to be eaten by the buffalo, which would then be eaten by the Sioux, completing the circle.

Custer's religion was constricting. Everything was sharply defined, from God to the smallest sin, and all action, belief, and thoughts were described as good or evil. Like other Christians, Custer was expected to adhere to a strict code of behavior and belief, with the emphasis on work, faith, discipline, and morality. At West Point, he wrote extensive lists of what was good and what was bad, what was required and what was forbidden. As a bearer of the truth, it was his duty to carry that truth to others. Custer was always being measured, and was measuring himself, against a fixed and impersonal standard. He believed he had to do what was required of him or he would be punished. He embraced the concept of a stern male God and of God's authority. He believed that his soul was immortal and that it belonged to God. If he lived up to the standard, God would reward him in an afterlife. His religion required him to be other than, and better than, his instincts.

Crazy Horse's religion was all-embracing. *Wakan Tanka* was the All, the One, the Great Mystery, but not in any recognizable form, for *Wakan Tanka* was *in* everything, *of* everything. The Sioux believed in gods and goddesses, but they were vague, shadowy figures, never sharply defined as to appearance or authority. The gods laid no requirement as to action or belief on the Sioux beyond such ritual observances as the Sun Dance. All that existed was precious in Crazy Horse's religion—whatever a man did or thought was good, was *wakan*, so long as he obeyed his own inner voice, for that too was *wakan*. The concept of an afterlife was absent; instead, the Sioux emphasized the cycle of life on this earth.

Custer had to account for his actions and beliefs to his mortal superiors and to God. Crazy Horse did not have to answer to anyone for his actions or beliefs, not to other Sioux nor to *Wakan Tanka*. He did have to answer to himself.

The ultimate difference between the two men was their mood. Custer was never satisfied with where he was. He always aimed to go on to the next higher station in his society. He was always in a state of *becoming*. Crazy Horse accepted the situations he found himself in and aimed only to be a brave and respected Sioux warrior, which by the time he was a young adult he had been, was then, and would be. He was in a state of *being*. Custer believed that things could be better than they were. Crazy Horse did not.

Part Two

CHAPTER EIGHT

War and Love Among the Oglalas

"He wanted to be sure he hit what he aimed at."

He Dog, on Crazy Horse

The years following 1858 were good to the Oglalas. They were relatively free of the white soldiers, who from 1861 to 1865 were busy fighting their own war east of the Mississippi River. The Oglalas, meanwhile, along with other Sioux bands, drove the Shoshonis and Crows from the Powder River country, making that prime buffalo range their own. Those were fat times for the Oglalas, the smell of roasting buffalo ribs rising up from their campfires, plenty of good skins for the lodges, the horse herds growing every year at the expense of the Crows and Shoshonis. War parties went out each summer, giving ambitious young braves opportunities to count coup, steal horses, and win honors. It was glorious warfare, for the most part, exactly suited to the Oglala style. Nearly all the fighting was done in the summer; the Oglalas would set the war aside for the spring and fall buffalo hunts and during the winter, taking it up again only after the Sun Dance in early summer. Losses in battle against the Crows and Shoshonis were minimal, nothing like the number of lives taken when the Oglalas found themselves at war with the white soldiers.

The Oglalas were no longer begging handouts from whites on the Holy Road, no longer drinking themselves into a stupor on the white man's whiskey, no longer catching the white man's diseases. They had returned to the old ways, the ways of the people before the Holy Road was opened and Fort Laramie established. Best of all, the Oglalas and their allies were living in what must have been, at that time, the finest hunting country in North America.

These were the years of Crazy Horse's maturity. During them he experienced a wide range of human emotions—deep satisfaction at providing a fresh-killed elk for a temporarily hungry village; the joy and excitement that came from riding pell-mell into a herd of stampeding buffalo and shooting down one, two, three, a dozen fat cows for the women to butcher; exaltation at counting coup upon or stealing a few horses from his Indian enemies; anger and helplessness at the violent death of his closest comrades; pleasure and ego enrichment at being selected a leader of the people; and the despair and blackness of heart that engulfs a rejected lover.

Crazy Horse was a free man. He traveled all across the northern Great Plains, visiting other Sioux bands, living with the Cheyennes, staying alone for weeks at a time on the prairie. He never underwent the ordeal of the Sun Dance, but he was one of the best hunters among the Oglalas and the most daredevil of their warriors, so he rose in prestige. He remained quiet and introspective, dressed modestly, gave away the ponies he had stolen from the Crows or the meat he had brought into camp from his solitary hunting trips, but still his exploits became legends, told and retold around the winter campfires.

The mature Crazy Horse spent much of his time in camp, making his bows and arrows, listening to gossip, perhaps contributing a bit of information himself from time to time, smoking his pipe, training his ponies, just sitting in the sun on a warm June day, watching the pretty young maidens and the old squaws at their work. Occasionally he would go to his *akicita* lodge to sing songs or listen to others boast of their brave deeds.

His major activity—what he "did for a living," as the whites put it —was hunting. He usually brought down the most cows at the tribal buffalo hunts, but he was even more notable for his success as a lone hunter, quietly slipping away from the village in the morning and returning at dusk with an elk, a deer, a couple of antelope, or, during the spring and fall migrations, with scores of fat, juicy ducks or geese.

Crazy Horse went on innumerable war parties and fought countless battles. The expeditions were usually successful, in part because the other Oglalas thought that Crazy Horse's medicine was most powerful and when it was known that he was going on a war party, other braves were eager to go along. For the Oglala warriors, it was axiomatic that no wounded brave nor the body of a dead one would be left on the battlefield if Crazy Horse could help it. Some of these battles were recorded, but establishing a chronology for them is impossible. The Indians gave them names, often after the nearest geographical feature (they would speak of the "Arrow Creek Fight" or the "Captive Butte Battle") or some notable event of the fight ("where Red Feather did his brave deed"). But it is not clear in what year a specific battle occurred or in what order the fights came. The most that can be said is that there were skirmishes nearly every summer between the Sioux and their allies against the Crows and Shoshonis, with the Sioux consistently winning and gradually forcing their enemies back up against and beyond the Bighorn Mountains.[1]

One big fight that can be dated with some precision came in June 1861. Crazy Horse was living with the Cheyennes at the time. A runner came flying into camp to report that the Oglalas were organizing a war party against the Shoshonis, who were hunting along the Sweetwater River, just south of where the Wind River joins the Bighorn River. Washakie himself, for decades the famous headman of the Shoshonis, was with the camp. A few of the younger Cheyennes, along with the twenty-year-old Crazy Horse, decided to go along.

After a long march of several days, the Oglalas and Cheyennes came to the Shoshoni village. While the *akicita* kept the warriors under control, scouts checked on conditions in the village. They reported a large pony herd, ripe for the picking. Following a sleepless, fireless night, Crazy Horse and his comrades rode to a bluff from which, at first light, they could make out the sleeping Shoshoni camp. With a whoop, they rode at full gallop down the bluff and into the village.

The old Shoshoni women, first risers in the camp, began screaming, "The Sioux are upon us! The Sioux are here!" Dogs barked, ponies neighed, children shrieked, while the Shoshoni warriors yelled at their women to get them their weapons. The attackers never paused. Galloping through the camp, they went straight to the pony herd and cut out four hundred head, more than half the total herd and started the captured ponies back toward the bluff and the faraway Oglala territory.

The Shoshonis kept their war horses tethered outside their lodges for just such a situation, but the Sioux had stampeded most of them as well, so it took Washakie's people some time to organize a pursuit. The Sioux were slow in getting away, however, because they had taken so many ponies that it was difficult to keep the captured herd together as they headed toward the east. Crazy Horse, along with seven or eight others, dropped behind to fight a delaying action against the pursuing Shoshonis.

It was just the sort of fight Crazy Horse loved best. He never liked to stay with the mass of warriors, preferring to do battle on his own or with only a few others. He leaped from his pony, got behind a rock or tree, and fired a dozen or so well-aimed arrows at the enemy, checking the pursuit and giving the main body of Sioux with the herd a chance to get away. When the Shoshonis pressed too close or attacked his position in overwhelming numbers, Crazy Horse jumped back on his pony and rode away. After he and the others in the rear guard had put some distance between themselves and the enemy, Crazy Horse found another protected spot and repeated the process. If a small body of Shoshonis got out ahead of the rest, Crazy Horse charged them, forcing them to fall back to their slower companions. Little Hawk, Crazy Horse's younger brother, was along, and the two brothers fought side by side.

At one stand-off, with Crazy Horse and Little Hawk firing arrows as fast as they could and the Shoshonis returning the fire (thus providing Crazy Horse with more ammunition, as he could pick up their arrows from the ground), Crazy Horse's pony was hit in the leg. Then Little Hawk's pony was wounded. The brothers found themselves alone, Shoshonis pressing toward them, the brothers' comrades riding as fast as they could to the east. So furiously did Crazy Horse and Little Hawk keep fighting, however, that the Shoshonis feared to press home the attack. Instead, they encircled the trapped Sioux, firing arrows and shouting taunts. Then two brave Shoshonis rode forward for individual combat, intending to ride down Crazy Horse and Little Hawk.

As the two Shoshonis charged, Crazy Horse shouted to Little Hawk, "Take care of yourself—I'll do the fancy stunt."* Stepping forward from his protected position, Crazy Horse stood directly in the path of a charging Shoshoni. When the man and pony were almost upon him, Crazy Horse, with his head and shoulders, feinted to his right. The Shoshoni took the fake and turned his horse in the direction he expected Crazy Horse to move. But at the last second Crazy Horse twisted to his left, grabbed the leg of the passing Shoshoni, and jerked him from the pony. The man hit the ground with a thud, knocked unconscious. Crazy Horse jumped on the Shoshoni pony, looked around, and discovered that Little Hawk had hit the other enemy with an arrow, unseating him from his pony. Little Hawk mounted up and the brothers dug in their heels and took off for the east, laughing gaily.[2]

Still the Shoshonis came on, anxious now for revenge and desperate to get their ponies back. They were furious, too furious for their own good, because no longer did they stay together. Instead, each Shoshoni rode as fast as he could to get at the retreating Sioux,

---

* The quotation is from Short Bull, who in 1930 recalled hearing that these were Crazy Horse's words.

which left them stretched out and incapable of delivering a telling, collective blow.

One Shoshoni got way ahead of the others. Soon he came up on Crazy Horse and the rest of the Sioux rear guard. Instead of checking his pony and waiting for help, he came right on, riding smack into the middle of the eight Sioux. He shot one Oglala with each of his pistols before someone brought him down with a lance. The Sioux immediately recognized him as the son of Washakie and proudly took his scalp before resuming the retreat. Later, they returned the scalp to Washakie, telling him how brave his son had been.

The running fight continued for three hours. Once Washakie led his warriors around the Sioux flank, cut into the tiring herd of ponies from the side, and recaptured half the animals. Finally the Sioux found a good stand of trees along a stream and hustled the remaining captured stock into the grove, then set up a defensive perimeter around the edge of the woods. The Shoshonis charged several times but were unable to dislodge the defenders, much less get at the ponies. When darkness came the Sioux got away, carrying three dead Oglalas and one dead Cheyenne with them, along with the captured ponies. In a few days they were safely back in their own village, where they mourned the dead, then held a victory dance. Then the camp settled back into its accustomed lethargy. That was enough war for one summer.[3]

Nearly every summer for the rest of his life, Crazy Horse went out on war parties against the Crows or Shoshonis. In 1862 or 1863 a medicine man named Chips, a friend of his youth, made him a special charm to ward off danger, a little white stone with a hole through it, suspended from a buckskin string that Crazy Horse wore slung over his shoulder and under his left arm. Six decades later Red Feather, who fought in many a battle with Crazy Horse, was still awed by the power of that stone. Crazy Horse, he said, had been slightly wounded twice before he began to wear it, but afterward, although he had eight horses killed under him, he was never wounded by an enemy of the Oglalas.[4]

Crazy Horse was no fool, however, nor was he suicidal. Warriors who had a blackness in their hearts, from whatever cause, would sometimes throw away their bows and arrows and charge the enemy with a war club, singing their death songs at the top of their lungs. In 1930 Eleanor Hinman of the Nebraska State Historical Society, who was interviewing Crazy Horse's associates, asked his childhood friends if the rumor were true that Crazy Horse often fought in that manner. He Dog denied it with a chuckle. Crazy Horse, he said, "always stuck close to his bow or rifle. He always tried to kill as many as possible of the enemy without losing his own men." By the mid-1860s, Crazy Horse was a recognized war-party leader among the Oglalas. He Dog characterized his activities in that role: "Crazy Horse always led his men himself when they went into battle, and he kept well in front of them. He headed many charges."

He Dog was struck by another typical Crazy Horse action in combat against other Indians: "All the times I was in fights with Crazy Horse, in critical moments of the fight Crazy Horse would always jump off his horse to fire. He is the only Indian I ever knew who did that often. He wanted to be sure that he hit what he aimed at. That is the kind of a fighter he was. He didn't like to start a battle unless he had it all planned out in his head and knew he was going to win. He always used judgment and played safe. His brother and Hump were reckless."[5]

A word about Eleanor Hinman's interviews with Crazy Horse's friends is perhaps in order here. Obviously anything they said is suspect, sixty or more years having passed between the event and the telling. Direct quotations are especially open to question. But it should also be mentioned that though these old men were illiterate, illiterate people everywhere are noted for their excellent memories. The early Greeks passed on the long Homeric tales from one generation to the next with hardly a phrase out of place, a phenomenon that occurs again and again among primitive cultures. Further, Hinman often interviewed the old Indians in groups, so that they could check on this or that fact with each other. They seldom disagreed, and when they did it was over some minute detail. In any event, those old men's memories are all we have to go on for many of the details of Crazy Horse's life.[6]

One such disagreement, for example, involved the Second Arrow Creek Fight, which took place around 1870. In a sketch of the battle Bad Heart Bull had numbered the warriors who counted first, second, third, and fourth coup on a fallen Crow. He Dog disagreed with the order in which Bad Heart Bull had placed the fortunate Oglala coup-counters, saying that the man listed as third was really second.

It was at the Second Arrow Creek Fight, with the Crows, that Crazy Horse came closest to death at the hands of his enemies. The Crows had great admiration for Crazy Horse and said he was the bravest Sioux they had ever known. They tried by special means and select warriors to put an end to his life and had made a special trip to the country of the Nez Percés, west of the Rockies, to buy medicine that would make it possible for them to shoot Crazy Horse's pony from under him.[7] Red Feather told the story of one such attempt: "Crazy Horse charged the Crows, his horse was shot under him, and he was surrounded by the enemy. The Oglalas tried to help him but could not get near him. A man named Spotted Deer made a last effort to reach him. He broke through the enemy and Crazy Horse got onto his pony behind him and they made a charge for the open."[8]

In the summer of 1865 the Oglalas decided to revive a governmental system that had fallen into disuse after they started hanging around the Holy Road. The system had been given to them early in the century by a great medicine man who had learned it from the Blackfeet. It called for seven older leaders, men over forty, called the "Big Bellies," to act together as a chiefs' society. The Big Bellies would advise and govern the people when they camped or moved, hunted or made war. To execute their orders, the Big Bellies selected four strong young men, called "shirt-wearers." All this was done on a rather haphazard basis. The people chose the Big Bellies by common consent, without anything like a formal election, and for both the chiefs and the shirt-wearers their duties and responsibilities were exacting and precise, although their powers were somewhat vague.

The installation ceremony was impressive. The Oglalas were camped on a creek about seventy miles northwest of Fort Laramie. The camp was a circle with an opening to the east. A large lodge, comparable to a circus tent, stood in the middle of the circle. Billy Garnett, a white trader and interpreter, was there, and he later described the scene.

Warriors on horses, bedecked in all their finery, rode around the inside of the circle, as the people stood in front of their tipis. Four times the warriors made the circuit, each time selecting a young man from the people and leading him to the center lodge. As the shirt-wearers were selected, the women made the trilling and called out the names of the heroes—Young Man Afraid, Sword, and American Horse. All were sons of Big Bellies, and it was expected that the fourth man selected would also come from a prominent family. But the horsemen passed by the obvious choices, went behind the mass of warriors, and from the rear of the crowd selected Crazy Horse.

He was led to the center lodge, where he joined the others, the rest of the people following and filling up the huge tipi. The selected shirt-wearers sat in the middle; across from them were the Big Bellies, the greatest of them all, Old Man Afraid, in the center of the chiefs. Garnett went in, too, and was treated to a feast of buffalo and boiled dog.

When the food had been cleared away an old man noted for his wisdom and knowledge of the way things had been done in the past rose to address the young men in the middle of the group. They would head the warriors in camp and on the march, he said, and see to it that order was preserved and no violence committed. They were required to make certain that every Oglala man, woman, or child had their rights respected. They must be wise and kind and firm in all things, counseling, advising, and then commanding. If their words were not heard, they could use blows to enforce their orders; in extreme cases, they even had the right to kill. But they must never take up arms against their own people without thought and counsel and must always act with caution and justice.

Then the actual shirts, made of two bighorn sheepskins, were given to the four men. Each shirt was beautifully quilled, fringed with hair, each lock of hair representing a brave deed accomplished. Crazy Horse had over two hundred forty locks on his shirt.

Another, even older man, now rose and addressed the four shirt-wearers. He told them that from now on they must always help the others, never thinking of themselves. They were obliged to look out for the poor, the widows, the orphans, and all those of little power. As shirt-wearers they could think no ill of others, nor notice any harm done to themselves. Using a favorite Sioux expression, the old man said that if someone damaged the shirt-wearers, they should pay no more attention to it than if a dog lifted his leg at their tipi. The old man acknowledged that it would indeed be difficult to follow such strong injunctions, but the Big Bellies had chosen the four because they were greathearted, generous, strong, and brave, and he knew they would do their duty gladly and with a good heart.[9]

So Crazy Horse became a leader of his people. It brought him no riches; to the contrary, he was expected to live modestly (as he did anyway), keep only those ponies he actually needed for the hunt or war and give away the others, distribute his meat to the helpless ones, especially the choicest cuts such as the tongue or hump of the buffalo, saving only the stringy leg muscle for himself. He did have much honor and prestige, of course, and the right to enforce his orders, even up to the point of killing a hot-blooded young warrior who persisted in ruining a buffalo hunt or an ambush. But his power was strictly personal. He was not given an *akicita* to see to it that his orders were enforced, nor any special policemen, nor indeed any outside force at all.

A year or so later, in 1867, Crazy Horse and He Dog were given the lances of the Crow Owners Society, an *akicita*. The lances were reputed to be three or four hundred years old; it is certain that the Sioux had brought them across the Missouri River in the eighteenth century. He Dog recalled the occasion: "Crazy Horse and I went together on a war trip to the other side of the mountains [the Bighorns, called the White Mountains by the Sioux]. When we came back the people came out of the camp to meet us and escorted us back and at a big ceremony presented us with two spears, the gift of the whole tribe, which was met together. These spears were given by the older generation to those in the younger generation who had best lived the life of a warrior." Again, there was great honor involved, and many duties and responsibilities, but no material benefits.[10]

At about the time of his twenty-first birthday in 1862, Crazy Horse had fallen in love. Her name was Black Buffalo Woman, a Bad Face Oglala, niece of Red Cloud. Crazy Horse had known her most of his life, watched her grow into her womanhood, stood beside the path to catch a glimpse of her swinging braids and laughing face as she carried water back to camp. By now a full-grown man, Crazy Horse was under some pressure from his parents and friends to take a wife. He began to formally court Black Buffalo Woman.[11] To do so, he had to act within a rigid framework.

Relations between the sexes among the Sioux were as complicated as they are in most societies. Although Sioux women had some basic constitutional rights that were secure in both custom and practice, in general men disposed of women as if they were so much property. The only acceptable role for women was that of wife, housekeeper, and mother, and although there were exceptions, the woman living outside her assigned role in Sioux society was as rare as a businesswoman in nineteenth-century white society. Indeed, at no other point were red and white cultures so close as in the relationships between the sexes.

Indian men expected their daughters to be chaste, their wives faithful. Teen-age girls were forced to wear a chastity belt, or submit to having their legs tied together each night. In part this was a realistic protection against the young braves, who were constantly encouraged to be bold and daring in all their activities and who liked nothing better than robbing a girl of her virginity. The boys considered it the equivalent of counting coup upon an enemy. But the father was also concerned with protecting his property. A virgin

bride would bring many horses when she was given to a proper
suitor, while the deflowered girl would be lucky to find a husband
at all, and even if she did, her father would receive no presents. The
gifts themselves were relatively unimportant, for the parents of the
bride had to return presents of equal value, but the prestige involved
in giving away a virgin daughter was, to the Sioux, crucial.

In legal theory the girls had no say in the choice of a husband, but
in practice most Sioux fathers would bend with the wishes of their
daughters. In the usual case, the father of the prospective bride
would put the matter to her. If she was willing to marry the suitor,
she put the matter back into his hands, meekly submitting to her
father's will. If she disapproved she let her feelings be known; when
that happened, the father would refuse the ponies and other gifts
offered by the suitor. But the father might insist, in which case the
duty of the girl to submit to his wishes was clear.[12]

The girls had little basis for making a choice, because courtship
among the Sioux was terribly restricted. Teen-age boys were warriors
and hunters, while teen-age girls were housewives and mothers in
training. The two sexes seldom if ever did things together. The girls
were always chaperoned by older women. Intimacy between unmarried teen-agers was well-nigh impossible. The Sioux placed such a
high value on chastity for the unmarried and loyalty for the married
women that the woman who could live up to the standard attained
a goddesslike quality. Standing on a pedestal, however, sometimes
made them more vulnerable, because it made it even more difficult
for young men to get to know young women as human beings. Instead they became objects, a challenge to the young man's masculine
qualities of boldness and self-assertion.

The prescribed courtship procedure which Crazy Horse was now
following with Black Buffalo Woman had the young man meet the
girl of his choice at dusk in front of her tipi. There Crazy Horse
would enfold Black Buffalo Woman in his robe; together, their heads
covered from view, they could converse privately. But Black Buffalo
Woman was popular; she had a long line of suitors waiting, blanket
in hand, outside her tipi each evening. After only a few minutes with
Crazy Horse, she would move gaily on to the next in line. When
Black Buffalo Woman finally went into her lodge for the night, her
mother tied her legs; the following day her mother saw to it that
she had no opportunity to be alone with any of her amorous young
men, not even one so widely respected as Crazy Horse. Young people, in short, had almost no chance of getting to know one another

intimately. Most of what they knew about each other came from public gossip and observation.[13]

Despite these handicaps, the Sioux did get married, usually successfully—i.e., the ordinary Sioux marriage seems to have lasted throughout the lives of the partners and was marked by mutual consideration, respect, and love. Worm and Crazy Horse's mother, for example, remained together for fifty years. The Sioux had no marriage ceremony, either religious or civil, although there usually was a dance following the exchange of presents between the bride's and groom's families. By custom and practice, however, all that was required to seal a marriage was for the young man and woman to spend a night together. This arrangement neatly solved the problem of elopement, which usually came when a girl was being pressured by her father to marry someone she did not want to live with. In such cases the girl would sometimes run off with a boy she loved. When the elopers returned they presented the girl's family with a *fait accompli*. Then the couple would settle down to the routine of married life, the woman doing all the household work, such as preparing the meat for storage, gathering the vegetables and berries, hauling water, putting up and taking down the tipi, packing for a move, making clothes, and so on, while the men hunted and made war.[14]

Both husband and wife expected their partner to be faithful. Divorce, which was easily accomplished, resulted more often than not from adultery (the laziness of a husband or the sharp tongue of a wife were also frequent causes of divorce). A wife could divorce a husband simply by throwing all his belongings out of the tipi, which was her private property. Sometimes, if angry enough, she would destroy his bow and arrows, his medicine bag, his robes and clothes, and so on. But the balance of legal prerogatives weighed heavily in favor of the men. While the woman could throw the husband out of her life, she had no regularized legal right to punish him. The husband, on the other hand, enjoyed that privilege with embellishments. If a husband caught his wife in adultery, he had the right not only to an immediate divorce, but also to cut off her braids and even her nose. Such a disfigurement not only marked his wrath upon her for life and reduced her attractiveness to other men, but it also made permanently public the male's position of dominance and authority. Statistics on this gruesome practice are not available for the Sioux; among the Cheyenne, a tribe with similar custom, there was only one known case of cutting off a nose, in the second half of the nineteenth century. Still, the threat was always there.[15]

Under the circumstances, women were much better off if they

broke cleanly with their husbands and went to live openly with another man. This happened often enough—Crazy Horse himself got involved in one such case—but how it came out depended on the aggrieved husband. He was expected to accept the situation and usually did, taking the attitude that a runaway wife was not worth bothering about. The more important the man, the more likely he was to ignore the affair. Chiefs and shirt-wearers were formally required to pay no attention whatever to a wife's defection. "His fellow chiefs would think less of him if he weakened," was the way the Cheyennes put it.[16] Among the Sioux, chiefs and other leaders were enjoined to pay no more attention to a defecting wife than they would to a dog pissing on the tipi. It did not fit a Sioux warrior's ideal conception of dignity to chase after a woman who did not want him. Instead, most Sioux men would simply accept the pony or two that the new bridegroom offered as a token for the runaway wife, a practice that itself emphasized the concept of women as property.

The injunction to ignore the fleeing wife proved to be too much for some Sioux men, however, as Crazy Horse was to learn. Angry and humiliated, the aggrieved husband might shoot the favorite pony of the man who had taken his wife or, in extreme cases, shoot the man himself. Murder within the tribe was by far the worst crime known to the Sioux, and most murders occurred as a result of a wife leaving her husband for another man.

In day-to-day life women always took second place to the men, and the two were usually separated. When food was served, even in the privacy of the tipi, the woman waited upon the man and ate only after he had finished. At public gatherings, such as a dance or religious ceremony, men and women sat on opposite sides of the circle. Men danced or women danced; the two sexes did not dance together.[17]

Woman's work was constant, but not terribly arduous. There was a gay, lighthearted spirit to their work, as they usually toiled together at their tasks. Unlike their white sisters who had settled on the prairie and who found themselves isolated from any companionship outside the immediate family, Sioux women had scores of female friends with whom they could exchange gossip, ideas, information, and experiences. What they chatted about among themselves we do not know—historians who interviewed old-time Sioux in the early twentieth century never thought to ask, and if the Sioux males knew, which is unlikely, they did not say—but the fact that Sioux women were a close-knit group is obvious.

One of the many factors holding them together was the attitude of Sioux men in general toward women. The Sioux warrior loved, cherished, and cared for his woman, but he also feared her. Nowhere does that fear show so clearly as in menstrual segregation. The menstruating women moved to separate, communal lodges, where they were brought food and water and otherwise cared for by female friends. There they remained until menstruation ceased. This practice meant, incidentally, that every woman had four days a month of freedom from labor, a chance to catch her breath and restore her energy. The menstruating woman was segregated because Sioux men believed that their sacred objects and war paraphernalia were subject to contamination from such a woman. Women, even when not menstruating, were considered a sufficiently corrupting influence that for them to touch a man's medicine or equipment was to defile it.[18]

Sioux men also believed that having intercourse with a woman before performing a religious ceremony or going on the warpath would be destructive, so they abstained from acts of love for four or more days before undertaking any important activity. Indeed, Sioux men believed that intercourse at any time weakened the body and mind, which may have had something to do with Crazy Horse's late marriage. It is possible that he may have feared being contaminated or weakened if he lived with a woman. Sioux men used to speak proudly of mastering their sexual urges and directing that energy toward war.[19] Roman Nose, a famous Cheyenne warrior whom Crazy Horse knew well and admired, was one of many Plains Indians who relied upon his "no-woman medicine" to help him in combat. These Indians had a vague idea that as the father of none they were the protector of all, defending the tribe as a husband and a father defended his helpless ones.[20]

Crazy Horse, in other words, had just as hard a time in figuring out where he stood with regard to the opposite sex as Custer did. How he handled his ambivalence we do not know, but we do know that at about the age of twenty-one years he began courting Black Buffalo Woman with the thought of making her his wife. But she was popular, and he had to wait his turn. Besides, although he was a highly respected hunter and warrior, his family was of no great standing among the Oglala, and Black Buffalo Woman, as a niece of Red Cloud, could expect to make a better match. Among her suitors, for one, there was No Water, brother of Black Twin, a leading man in the council. Still, Crazy Horse hoped, and continued to court.

In the early summer of 1862 matters came to a head. Red Cloud sent word that he would lead a big war party against the Crows.

Black Twin and No Water were going along, as well as Crazy Horse's oldest friend, Hump. Little Hawk and Crazy Horse joined up. The morning the expedition started out, however, No Water sat on the ground, moaning and holding his face with his hand. He had a great pain in his tooth. Since No Water's medicine was the two fierce teeth of the grizzly bear, none questioned his decision to stay home on the grounds that his medicine was of no use when he had a toothache.

The war party was gone two weeks. It captured some Crow horses, killed one enemy, and in general had a fine time. When it was still a day or so away from the village, Woman's Dress rode out to meet the returning warriors. Woman's Dress was a *winkte*; a grandson of Old Smoke and known as a boy as Pretty One, he had grown up with Crazy Horse, as we learned earlier. Bursting with news, Woman's Dress grabbed Crazy Horse by the arm and led him off, away from the others, to whisper in his ear that Black Buffalo Woman had married No Water while the war party was away.

Crazy Horse went immediately to his mother's lodge, where he stayed for two or three days, no one daring to disturb him. Then he packed his horse and started once again for Crow country, this time alone. No one ever heard him say what he did there, but when he came home toward the end of the summer he threw two Crow scalps to the dogs—the only scalps he had taken in five years.[21]

Over the next half decade Crazy Horse continued his travels, but he frequently returned to the Bad Face camp of the Oglalas, where he could see and on occasion chat with Black Buffalo Woman. Soon he was paying so much attention to her that they became objects of gossip. According to He Dog, "No Water did not want to let the woman go," which might indicate that Crazy Horse or Black Buffalo Woman had approached No Water on the subject. In any event, it was common knowledge that Crazy Horse loved Black Buffalo Woman, that she was at least willing to flirt with him, that No Water was furious about the situation, and that consequently trouble was coming.[22] When he became a shirt-wearer in 1865, however, Crazy Horse was under a strong injunction to do nothing that would bring discord to the tribe, so he stuck to his no-woman medicine, did not marry, and put his energies into fighting. That he did so was fortunate for the Oglalas, because in 1866 the white soldiers had returned and were marching into the Powder River country.

CHAPTER NINE

Guerrilla Warfare, Indian Style

"Crazy Horse and Little Big Man carried on a lively business in
horse-stealing and the killing of white men."

Billy Garnett

By the early 1860s the Sioux were in a position not only to stop the
flow of emigrants through their territory or to defend what was still
theirs, but even to drive the whites away from the Platte River country that the Indians had lost in the 1850s. The whites were busy from
1861 to 1865 fighting a ferocious civil war which required nearly the
full military strength of the United States, and the frontier of the
American empire was left almost defenseless. The Sioux opportunity
to strike was even more glittering because never before had there
been so many emigrating whites along the Holy Road or so few
soldiers to protect them. Draft dodgers, fortune seekers, deserters,
bounty jumpers, every white man who wanted to avoid the Civil
War, it seemed, was headed west. They came in small, ill-organized
groups, which made them an ideal target for the Sioux hit-and-run
tactics.

But the Sioux did not strike an effective blow. At first they failed
to do anything to take advantage of the situation, and they never
attacked as a whole tribe. Crazy Horse's northern Oglalas were fat,
happy, and secure in the Powder River country, wanting nothing
more than to be left alone. They were content to hunt buffalo and
send out war parties against the Crows. While the other Indians
were fighting the whites to the north, west, south, and east of the
Powder River, the Oglala Sioux continued until 1865 to act as if they
had solved the problem of white encroachment for all time by the
simple expedient of moving out of the way of the whites.

The "might have beens" in the situation are too numerous to enu-
merate in detail, but it is possible that had the Plains Indians produced a leader with the vision, organizing ability, and charisma of the
great Shawnee chief Tecumseh, they might have rolled back the

white frontier. Certainly they could have forced the whites to pay a far higher price for the conquest of the Plains and, perhaps, in the process made the whites accept a compromise that would have left the Indians with more freedom and larger reservations than they got. One cannot go too far with this kind of speculation, however, because white society had an enormous latent power, even in the midst of a civil war; when the whites made that power real and directed it against the Sioux, there was no doubt as to the final outcome. Still, whatever the long-term results, the Sioux and their allies certainly missed a grand opportunity during the Civil War.

Crazy Horse was as blind to the possibilities as his comrades. For the first three years of the Civil War he stayed in the Powder River country. To the southwest, the Shoshonis were raiding the whites on the Holy Road and cutting their telegraph wires; to the east, the Santee Sioux had staged a bloody uprising in Minnesota, which soon led to trouble all along the Missouri River north of Oglala territory; to the south, the Cheyennes and Arapahoes were engaged in constant struggle with white soldiers. From Fort Laramie to the Bighorn Mountains and north to the Yellowstone River, however, all was peace.

Eventually Crazy Horse joined the war against the whites; he left the northern Oglalas and moved south to participate with the Cheyennes and his southern relatives in raids on white outposts. It is impossible to tell what his motives were, but the circumstantial evidence indicates that he was drawn into the conflict by the mere promise of excitement and the chance to win additional honors. The Indians south of the Platte River were having a fine time, shooting up whites, stealing their stock, raiding their wagon trains and supply depots. While Old Man Afraid and the other big men among the northern Oglalas continued to argue for peace and kept their bands out of the way of the whites, young braves like Crazy Horse rode south on their own and joined in the fray. They had a great fondness for such a war—they were getting big American horses for themselves, and cattle, and all kinds of fine goods, such as new rifles, ammunition, canned food, blankets, and so forth. By attacking isolated outposts and ranches and by killing all the inhabitants, the Indians made retaliation impossible. The raids on the whites, in short, were much more profitable than attacking the Crows or Shoshonis, and less dangerous. For the Cheyennes there was a vengeance motive involved, at least after the Sand Creek massacre of 1864 (see below), but for most of the Sioux braves, including Crazy Horse, it was all just fun.

Indeed, far from hating the whites, Crazy Horse had formed a fast friendship with a white Army officer, Lieutenant Caspar Collins. Young Collins was stationed at Fort Laramie, where his father, Colonel William O. Collins, was in command. Lieutenant Collins enjoyed traveling alone through the Indian country, stopping off at various camps for a few days, getting to know the Sioux as people rather than as savages or enemies. He spent much of the winter of 1863–64 with the Oglalas, where Crazy Horse taught him the ways of the Sioux, taking him on hunts, showing him how to make a bow and arrows, helping him learn the Dakota language. It is one of the great misfortunes of American Indian history that Lieutenant Collins did not record his experiences.[1]

Colonel Collins was a man of common sense and decency, playing a significant role in the maintenance of peace north of Fort Laramie. His men were itching for a fight. The 11th Ohio Volunteer Cavalry had been raised for the Civil War and the men who volunteered expected to do their bit to save the nation, but the War Department had sent it west following the Santee uprising in Minnesota. Finding themselves in what Lieutenant Collins called "one of the most desolate regions on the American continent,"[2] bored, frustrated, and resentful at the injustice of it all, they wanted a go at the sea of Indians surrounding them. Rather like Lieutenant Grattan a decade earlier, the Ohio soldiers were sure they could send the Indians packing with a show of force.

Discarding their uniforms, the Ohio boys decked themselves out in buckskins and moccasins and acquired Indian ponies. ("The laziest things on earth," Caspar Collins called the ponies, "unless it is their Indian masters." He added that the pintos "have two good traits: one is being able to live on sage brush . . . and the other is that they can travel on a slow lope for almost incredible distances."[3]) Thus dressed, the Ohio soldiers assured each other that they were as tough as the toughest frontiersmen, and they eagerly awaited their chance to show their prowess as Indian fighters.

That they did not bring on a war was due to Colonel Collins, who realized that his major responsibility was to keep the peace. The men wanted to go out on search-and-destroy missions, but he kept them close to Fort Laramie. Collins was one of those rare Army officers who was able to see both sides to a question. He did not want war and he knew that the Sioux leaders were also men of peace. In May 1865, following a year of almost continuous fighting south and east of Fort Laramie, Collins reported that the Indians in his region were still friendly and wanted to remain so. Collins also had a nice feel for the difficulties the chiefs were having in keeping their dare-devil warriors in check, problems so similar to his own. Probably basing his observations on verbal reports from his son, Collins informed the War Department about the number of Indians in the vicinity, who the headmen were, and so on. Colonel Collins said there were 350 lodges of Oglalas north of the Platte, 150 south of the river; the Brulés had 350 lodges, while there were 80 lodges of hostile Cheyennes and 100 or so of friendly Cheyennes; the various bands of Sioux near the Yellowstone and Little Missouri rivers numbered 350 lodges. This is probably the most accurate census available on Sioux numbers at this time. The usual estimate is that there were two to three warriors living in each lodge; that number would include boys of twelve and men over forty years of age.

"It is proper to remark," Colonel Collins concluded, "that almost all the Indians are just now liable to become hostile. The rush of emigrants through their country is immense, and their game is being rapidly destroyed or frightened away; the whites who come in contact with them generally know nothing of Indian habits or character and often do them injustice; and then they [the Indians] complain that the treaty promises of the Government are not kept. War with somebody is also the natural state of an Indian people. Every tribe has some hereditary enemies with whom it is always at war and against whom it makes regular expeditions to get scalps and steal ponies . . . To heal these difficulties perfectly is impossible, as there is always some wrong unavenged. It is by war that they obtain wealth, position, and influence with the tribe. The young men especially look up to and follow the successful warrior rather than the wise and prudent chiefs."[4]

Throughout Colonel Collins' report one can hear the voice of his son, telling him of the things he had learned from his Indian friends. Colonel Collins was a stranger to the frontier, having been there less than a year, but thanks to his son and his own wisdom he had come to understand the Sioux better than any Army officer west of the Mississippi. Of Old Man Afraid, for example, Collins wrote: "This chief is prudent and sensible, and has always been, and I think still is, friendly to the whites. He does all in his power to restrain his people, but complains that some of his young men are bad."[5] (Crazy Horse was almost certainly one of those Old Man Afraid regarded as "bad.") If other white officers had possessed Collins' ability to understand and even sympathize with their opposite numbers among the Indian tribes, much tragedy on the Plains would have been avoided.

But Collins was not typical. President Lincoln needed every officer of ability he could get his hands on to direct his armies in the Civil War; the Army on the Plains got what was left. With the notable exception of Colonel Collins, that wasn't much. Most of the generals and colonels on the frontier were nothing more nor less than buffoons. As George Hyde puts it, "the ignorance of some of these superior officers was really amazing."[6] One general reported in August 1864 that "the Snakes, Winnibigoshish, and Minnesota Sioux" were raiding west of Fort Laramie. The Minnesota Sioux (Santees) were in fact on the Missouri River, hundreds of miles north and east of Fort Laramie, while Winnibigoshish is a lake.[7] These officers had their poorly disciplined and badly organized troops marching back and forth across the Plains in futile search-and-destroy missions, while the Indians went merrily about their way, attacking settlements and stagecoach stations. The Indians then disappeared onto the prairie, and the soldiers trudged their way to the scene of the outrage, getting there days after the attack. The Indians, meanwhile, would hit the area the soldiers had vacated.

Soldiers chasing the Santees shot at every Indian they saw, provoking such widespread hostility that all the whites along the frontier, from Fort Laramie clear down to Texas, feared for their lives. They demanded protection so loudly that the Lincoln government had to respond. The fresh troops shot more Indians and a general Indian uprising followed.

Throughout the summer of 1864 the southern Oglalas, Cheyennes, and other tribes raided or otherwise harassed the whites. It was a classic guerrilla campaign, albeit that the Indians acted haphazardly and without any hint of central direction. Most often, the Indians attacked in very small groups, a half dozen men or less. The Plains and its people were the ocean in which these fish swam, and the white soldiers could not keep up with them. The United States was discovering that for all its industrial might, it was exceedingly difficult to bring its power to bear on its frontier or, once having gotten the power there, to use it effectively. The Indians knew the terrain; the whites did not. Indians could live off the country; the whites could not. The Indians were mobile; the whites were not. The Indians had the initiative; the whites did not. So there was a terrible anger among the whites, and a humiliating frustration. When these elements were combined with inept leadership, the resulting brew was dangerous.

Crazy Horse was a part of the campaign. According to fur-trader Billy Garnett, Crazy Horse and a childhood friend, Little Big Man, operated as a team that summer, living in one of the hostile villages for a few days, then striking out again. Together, Garnett said, they "carried on a lively business in horse stealing and the killing of white people."[8] Along with hundreds of similar small teams they managed to stop the western flow of white emigration. Crazy Horse and the other Indians burned wagon trains and ranches, robbed and destroyed stagecoach stations and telegraph offices, laid waste to private dwellings for hundreds of miles on all the various lines of travel from the Missouri River to the Rocky Mountains, most especially the Holy Road. It was not a thought-out campaign, nor a concerted one—Old Man Afraid never brought the main body of northern Oglalas into it—but it was marvelously effective.[9]

Under the circumstances, it was hardly surprising that panic seized the frontier. Governor John Evans of Colorado Territory issued a proclamation in August 1864, urging citizens to form themselves into parties to hunt down the Indians, killing every hostile they might meet. The proclamation was about as harmful as anything could have been. It put every friendly Indian in jeopardy, at the mercy of the whites; it created what amounted to free-fire zones; it invited revengeful emigrants who had been harassed by hostiles and any white man who coveted an Indian's pony or wife to shoot to kill. Of course, the only Indians they could find were friendly, and for every one they shot, five friendlies or more turned hostile. Evans had armed bands of whites roaming the countryside, murdering innocent Indians, while the Indians had their armed war parties out murdering whites. In this struggle, the Cheyennes and their Sioux and Arapaho allies got much the best of it.[10]

The military commander in Colorado was Colonel John M. Chivington, a boastful, arrogant, stupid man. He was urging every white man he met to kill all Indians seen, "little and big."[11] In November 1864, in collusion with other Army officers, Chivington induced Black Kettle and his Cheyenne band to camp at Sand Creek, southeast of Denver between the Smoky Hill and Arkansas rivers. Black Kettle was a leading friendly who wished to avoid war with the whites at all costs. His young braves were certainly guilty of many outrages, but neither he nor his band could properly be blamed. With fighting going on all around him, Black Kettle wanted to find a safe place to camp for the winter. The Army officers promised him protection if he would move to Sand Creek, about forty miles from Fort Lyon, Colorado. Black Kettle did as he was told, running up an American flag on a pole in the center of the village.

Chivington had raised an infantry regiment of hundred-day volunteers in Denver, the 3rd Colorado, composed of all the riffraff on the frontier. Fortune seekers of every type, drunks, cardsharps, gun fighters, and all the Indian haters of Denver signed up for a grand campaign. Their sole aim, and Chivington's, was to kill as many Indians as possible, as quickly and safely as it could be done, and then get back to the warm comforts of the whorehouses and gambling dens of Denver. It never occurred to them that killing friendlies only made more hostiles or that the whites did not have enough power on the frontier to cope with the general Indian uprising that would surely result from a massacre.

At dawn on November 29, 1864, Chivington and his six hundred men attacked Black Kettle's camp at Sand Creek, which held about two hundred warriors and five hundred women and children. Chivington struck hard, but the Indians recovered and put up a stiff fight for three or four hours, inflicting forty-seven casualties. Indian losses in dead alone were three times that high. (Chivington later boasted that he had killed five hundred Cheyennes but, as was typical of officers' reports during the Plains fighting, that was a grossly exaggerated body count.) Two thirds or more of the dead Indians were women and children. The white soldiers scalped the dead and cut up and mutilated the bodies. A few days later, between the acts of a theatrical performance in Denver, they displayed the scalps, including the pubic hair of the Cheyenne women. Yellow Woman, the Cheyenne whom Crazy Horse had rescued nine years earlier after Harney's attack on Little Thunder's village, was among the dead.[12]

The Cheyennes who escaped now sent around a war pipe (although Black Kettle himself still held out for peace). Around eight hundred lodges of Indians, including southern Oglalas, Brulés, Arapahoes, and some southern Cheyennes soon gathered at the headwaters of the Smoky Hill River. If Old Man Afraid and the northern Oglalas received the war pipe they paid no attention to it, but individual warriors did set out to join the big camp, Crazy Horse among them. Most of these Indians had never before been on a winter war party, but they were so furious that they could not wait for spring. On January 7, 1865, they hit the stagecoach station at Julesburg, Colorado, on the South Platte River, southeast of Fort Laramie. After running the small cavalry detachment at Camp Rankin into its stockade a mile away, the Indians plundered the station, the store, and the stage company's warehouse. The women brought up pack ponies, loaded them with plunder, and late in the day started back toward camp, the ponies so heavily burdened that they could barely move.[13] Over the next few days the Indians continued to raid up and down the South Platte River, causing pandemonium. They took control of an area that would, three years later, be the scene of Custer's first Indian campaign.

Fighting the United States could have its rewards. Crazy Horse had never seen so much loot in his life—this was ten, twenty, one hundred times better than raiding the Crows. George Bent, the half-Cheyenne son of an old trader, who went over to the Indian side after Sand Creek, later told George Grinnell, "I never saw so much plunder in an Indian camp as there was in this one. Besides all the ranches and stage stations which had been plundered—and most of these places had stores at which the emigrants and travelers traded—two large wagon trains had been captured west of Julesburg. The camp was well supplied with fresh beef, and there was a large herd of cattle on hoof." Bent said the Indians had sacks of flour, corn meal, rice, sugar, and coffee, crates of hams and bacon, boxes of dried fruit, and big tins of molasses. There were all kinds of clothing and other manufactured articles. The Indians kept Bent busy explaining to them what this or that was used for. Canned oysters were a particular favorite. When Bent told one group of Indians that catsup, candied fruits, and imported cheese were indeed excellent fare, they mixed it all together for a huge meal—and were violently sick.[14]

Crazy Horse and Little Big Man, who went along on other small war parties, continued to go out at night to raid the settlers. So completely had the Indians taken control of the South Platte Valley that their big allied village kept huge fires burning all night, to guide the returning war parties. When the braves were not out on raids, they danced through the night. Captain Eugene F. Ware, who was stuck inside Camp Rankin, could look at the blaze of the campfires. "We could hear them shrieking and yelling, we could hear the tum-tum of a native drum, and we could hear a chorus shouting. Then we could see them circling around the fire, then separately stamping the ground and making gestures. . . . We knew that the bottled liquors destined for Denver were beginning to get in their work and a perfect orgy was ensuing. It kept up constantly. It seemed as if exhausted Indians fell back and let fresh ones take hold . . ."[15]

On February 2, 1865, the big village packed up and started north, the chiefs having agreed to strike out for the Powder River country, where they could join forces with Old Man Afraid's Oglalas. As the women began to pack, some one thousand warriors set off for another attack on Julesburg. Crazy Horse served as a decoy, riding out with a small group to the gates of Camp Rankin, hoping to draw out the cavalry and lead the soldiers into an ambush. But the whites would

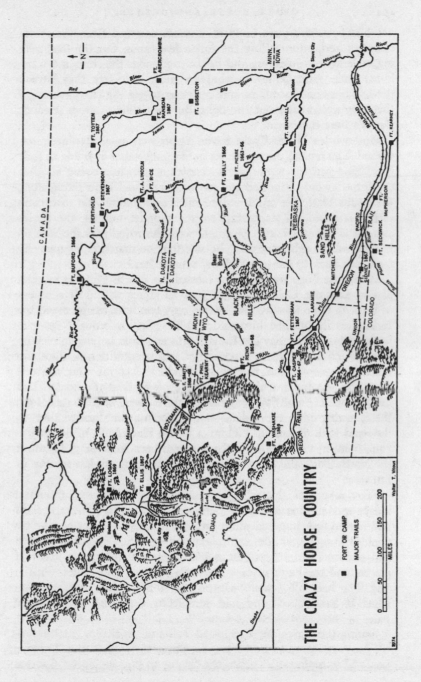

THE CRAZY HORSE COUNTRY

■ FORT OR CAMP

— MAJOR TRAILS

MILES

0 50 100 150 200

Walter T. Vitous

1974

not budge, so the main body of warriors emerged from their concealment and, after circling the fort a few times, shooting and yelling, rode over to Julesburg and began to plunder the store and warehouse again. After removing whatever goods were left, they burned the buildings one by one in another effort to get the troops so angry that they would come out and fight. But the soldiers, rather sensibly, stayed where they were.[16]

Most whites in the Platte River region were now absolutely terrorized. The ranking Army officers outdid each other in trying to shift the blame for this unmitigated disaster, meanwhile doing all they could to stay out of the Indians' path. One colonel, after riding along the South Platte for one hundred miles and finding the road completely wrecked, all stage stations and ranches burned, the horses and cattle driven off, the telegraph poles destroyed and the wire removed, was so aghast at what he saw that he marched his men immediately back to the safety of the nearest fort.[17]

When the huge Indian camp crossed the North Platte, southeast of Fort Laramie, Colonel Collins tried to attack with a detachment of his 11th Ohio Cavalry, but he had only two hundred men and the Indians easily brushed him aside. When Collins brought up reinforcements the next day the Indians attacked him, hoping to pick up some American horses and more arms and ammunition. Collins corralled his wagons, put the horses inside the corral, and made it clear that the Indians would have to work to take any horses from his command. An all-day, long-range fight ensued, with no casualties; the following dawn the Indians started north again, headed through the Sand Hills of western Nebraska to the Black Hills of South Dakota, then on to the Powder River in northern Wyoming. North of the North Platte there were virtually no whites, much less soldiers or forts.[18]

"The march of this village of seven hundred to one thousand lodges was an amazing feat," George Hyde writes. "These Indians had moved four hundred miles during the worst weather of a severe winter through open, desolate plains taking with them their women and children, lodges, and household property, their vast herds of ponies, and the herds of captured cattle, horses, and mules. On the way they had killed more whites than the number of Cheyennes killed at Sand Creek and had completely destroyed one hundred miles of the Overland Stage Line."[19]

During the march north, Spotted Tail and his Brulés left the hostile camp to return to Fort Laramie, where they joined the "Laramie Loafers," sometimes also called the "Hang-Around-the-Forts." Spotted

Tail wanted to put the war with the whites aside for the coming season, so that he could concentrate on buffalo and Pawnees. The Arapahoes also left, traveling southwest. The Cheyennes and Sioux continued on, reaching the Oglala camps on the Powder River early in March 1865. The stories the hostiles told the Oglalas of the outrage at Sand Creek and of the retribution they had exacted from the whites greatly excited Old Man Afraid's warriors. They were even more excited by the sight of all those captured horses, cattle, and general plunder. It must have been at just this time that Old Man Afraid lost his hold over his people—even his own son now began to talk of going on the warpath against the whites.[20]

Throughout the month of April 1865, the Cheyennes and Oglalas went about their business, hunting some buffalo, killing a few Crows, but mainly giving their ponies a chance to put on some weight. In May, George Bent told Hyde, the headmen of the *akicita* (called "war chiefs" by the whites) held a meeting. Young Man Afraid and Red Cloud took the lead in the council, which decided to attack the whites on the North Platte in midsummer; meanwhile, small war parties would conduct raids along the Holy Road.

The *akicita* chiefs told the members of the raiding parties, Crazy Horse among them, to bring back as much information as possible, so that they would know where to strike the most effective blow in July, when the Indians would be at full strength. By making small raids the Indians would keep the whites stirred up, with troops marching hither and yon in vain attempts to catch them, wearing out their horses and themselves in the process.

In late May 1865 some Cheyennes attacked near Deer Creek, on the Oregon Trail, while Young Man Afraid led a few Sioux warriors in an attack farther to the east on the Holy Road. These pinpricks accomplished exactly what the Indians wanted; the commander at Fort Laramie, Colonel Thomas Moonlight (the War Department, with its usual wisdom, had removed Colonel Collins) set off with most of his cavalry. Finding no Indians, he continued to march west, all the way to the Wind River. The Indians had a glorious time behind him, raiding along the Holy Road.[21]

While Moonlight was off on his wild goose chase, the tiny garrison remaining at Fort Laramie managed the remarkable feat of turning the Laramie Loafers into hostiles. These Loafer Indians had hardly hunted for years or joined war parties; they were completely dependent on the whites at Laramie for their livelihood. The hostile Sioux despised the Hang-Around-the-Forts, but as Hyde so nicely puts it, "There are at least two sides to every issue, and the people in the

Loafer camp returned the scorn of the wild Sioux of the north, treating them like country bumpkins who came to visit the sophisticated Sioux at the fort. These wild bulls from the Powder River were full of airs and big talk about fighting the whites, but what did they know about the whites and their strength? They imagined that a fight among fifty warriors, in which two men were killed, was a big fight. The Loafers at the fort had heard details of the mighty three-day struggle at Gettysburg, and they knew what the white men meant when they spoke of a battle."22

Even the Loafers, however, had a limit to what they could take from the whites. Two minor Oglala chiefs, Two Face and Blackfoot, came into Laramie with a captured white woman, Mrs. Eubanks, who had been taken by the Cheyennes the previous winter. Blackfoot and Two Face had bought her from the Cheyennes and brought her to Fort Laramie as a kind of peace offering; they had been hostiles but now, for whatever reason, they wanted to join the Loafers and were returning Mrs. Eubanks as evidence of their good faith.

The temporary commander at Fort Laramie was drunk when they came in, and he listened eagerly while Mrs. Eubanks told an amazing tale. She said the Cheyennes had raped her continuously, then sold her to Two Face for three horses; Blackfoot had bought her from Two Face. They had all raped her, she said, and on the morning they brought her to the fort they had taken her swimming in the Platte, where a whole horde of Sioux raped her. The drunken officer never asked the obvious question: why, if Two Face and Blackfoot had so shockingly mistreated her, did they voluntarily accompany her into the fort and thereby place themselves in the custody of the soldiers? Instead, he ordered the two Indians hanged, which was immediately done, the soldiers attaching big iron balls to their legs. The Loafers were not even allowed to cut the dead men down—a soldier kept guard over the bodies—and they hung there, twisting in the wind, until the balls pulled the legs off the bodies.23

The stupidity of the white officers was limitless. The Civil War had ended by now and a new set of officers was taking over on the Plains, backed up by plenty of reinforcements. Major General G. M. Dodge took command of the military Department of the Missouri. He was astonished to learn that a large group of Sioux were camped next to Fort Laramie and by telegraph demanded to know why they had not been attacked. Local officers carefully explained to him that they were friendlies, living under the protection of the military. An able commander might have seen these Loafers as potentially valuable allies. They would have made excellent scouts and many of them would have jumped at the chance to get a uniform, an American horse, regular pay, and a repeating rifle. But Dodge decided that they were an intolerable burden. He ordered them all moved to Fort Kearney, Nebraska, on the lower Platte River. When Spotted Tail, who was at Fort Laramie, learned of the order, he protested. It would be a march to death, he said, because the soldiers had disarmed most of the Loafers, who were also without ponies. It would be murder to send such a helpless people into Pawnee territory, for the Pawnees would surely kill them all.

But Dodge insisted, and on June 11, 1865, between fifteen hundred and two thousand Loafers and Brulés started southeastward under the guard of one hundred thirty-five soldiers of the 7th Iowa Cavalry. Along the march, the Sioux passed the site of the Brulé village of 1854, where Lieutenant Grattan and his men had been killed; farther down they came to Horse Creek, where in 1851 at the big council the whites had signed a treaty promising eternal friendship and recognizing the Sioux right to all land from Laramie northward.

The march was a nightmare for the Sioux. Small boys caught racing or otherwise cutting up were tied to wagon wheels and whipped. The soldiers kept throwing children into the springtime floods of the Platte River, laughing at their frantic efforts to get out. At night, the troops took young maidens from the village.

When the Oglalas learned what was taking place they sent a group of warriors to the scene to help plan and execute an escape. Crazy Horse went along, and on the night of June 13, he slipped into the Loafer camp, where he conferred with the headmen. There were warriors across the river, on the north bank, Crazy Horse reported, and they were anxious to help. Spotted Tail and the Loafers decided to make a break for it the next day, leaving the tipis and equipment behind. Crazy Horse recrossed the river to prepare the warriors on the north side.

At dawn on June 14, 1865, when the captives failed to pack and start moving, an Army captain with a few men rode into the Indian camp to see what was holding things up (the soldiers had camped on the opposite side of Horse Creek). As the captain was cursing and ordering the Indians to get moving, a warrior shot him dead. The remaining soldiers fled. The Indians raced for the North Platte, crossing it on foot and picking up horses on the other side, where the Oglalas were waiting for them. Everyone got away, except for one poor Loafer man who had displeased the whites and had a ball and chain on his leg. The soldiers killed him and took his scalp. The

Loafers and Brulés scattered northward, greatly swelling the ranks of the hostiles. When the soldiers tried to pursue, Crazy Horse joined other warriors, Spotted Tail among them, to drive the whites back across the North Platte.[24]

Colonel Moonlight provided a fitting climax to this bitter comedy. He returned to Fort Laramie from his foray to the Wind River just in time to hear the news and immediately gathered every available cavalryman to set off in pursuit. Up by White River, near the Nebraska-South Dakota boundary, he went into camp, turning his horses out to graze. His scouts warned him not to let the horses run loose in Indian country, but Moonlight told them to shut up. A minute later Crazy Horse and a band of warriors came swooping down, yelling, firing, and waving buffalo robes. They stampeded the cavalry horses and made off with them, leaving Moonlight and his men horseless on the prairie. Moonlight's troops had to walk all the way back to Laramie, their saddles and equipment on their backs.[25]

Early in June 1865 Young Man Afraid, Little Big Man, Crazy Horse, and the other warriors who had been out on raids returned to the main camp near the Powder River. The Cheyenne and Oglala headmen then sent around orders that no more war parties would be allowed to go on expeditions. They appointed one of the *akicita* societies to police the camp and make certain that no warriors slipped away to make little raids, which would alarm the whites and put them on their guard. Then the Cheyennes made their medicine-lodge ceremonial, while the Sioux held a Sun Dance. Black Wolf, an Oglala who had taken the responsibility for guiding the women and children of the Loafers across the North Platte during the great escape from Horse Creek, had vowed to undergo torture in the Sun Dance if he succeeded in getting the people across safely. He now lived up to his vow, and it is said that all the Indians present marveled at his endurance of the torture.[26]

Following the Sun Dance the Indians began to prepare themselves for a full-scale expedition against the whites, the whole of both tribes to participate. Throughout the vast encampment young warriors consulted with the old men to learn the sacred ways, what to wear, the words to the old-time war songs, and what paraphernalia to take along. The medicine men did a thriving business. Crazy Horse got a new medicine from Chips, a little stone pebble to tie into the tail of a fast bay horse that he had taken from the Crows and did not want to lose.

Crazy Horse was about twenty-four years old at this time. He was slightly below medium height and remained rather thin, weighing only around one hundred forty pounds. His color was deepening, but he was still of a lighter complexion than his comrades. His hair was light and long, hanging below his waist when combed out; he almost always wore it in braids. His idiosyncrasies had hardened into habits. Before going into battle he always threw a handful of dust over himself and his pony and never wore anything more than a breechcloth and leggings, a single hawk feather in his hair, his ever-present small stone behind his ear, and another stone from Chips under his left arm. He did not boast about his accomplishments and refused to participate in the wild, emotional mourning scenes the Sioux indulged themselves in when a loved one died. Nor would he smoke the pipe if the tobacco had been packed down in the bowl with a stick, as was the almost universal custom; unless the tobacco was pressed down with the thumb by all the smokers quaffing the pipe, Crazy Horse would not touch it. But no one objected to his quirks of character because he was already one of the most famous Oglala warriors, the youngest of the newly appointed shirt-wearers.[27]

As the grand expedition against the Holy Road prepared to move out, the warriors dressed themselves, taking hours and even days at their toilet. Shields, bonnets, war shirts, and every article and weapon the warriors might need received careful attention. There were over one thousand lodges in the village, mainly Oglala and Cheyenne but including some Miniconjous, Brulés, Sans Arcs, Loafers, and Arapahoes. The lodges were laid out in a circle; within the circle the warriors held a final parade, riding around the inside, dressed in all their war finery, their ponies painted and decorated with eagle feathers. The men sang the old war songs, then rode out of the camp circle and started up the Powder River. *Akicita* policemen were on each side of the column, to keep everyone in his place.

The headmen marched in front, carrying the war pipes. George Bent, who was a member of the expedition, told Hyde that the men who led the march were Roman Nose of the northern Cheyennes and Young Man Afraid and Red Cloud of the Oglalas. This would seem to indicate that Old Man Afraid, Spotted Tail, and the other older leaders did not approve of the offensive.[28]

The war chiefs had made an ambitious plan. Runners had established regular contact between the Powder River camp and Sitting Bull's Hunkpapas of the far-north country in Montana and North Dakota. Sitting Bull, always an enemy of the whites, agreed to attack Fort Rice on the Missouri in North Dakota at the same time that the Oglalas and their allies hit the Holy Road, at Platte Bridge. Both offensives were designed to cut the white man's communications and make it impossible for him to proceed any farther into Indian country. The leaders had the right idea, but their strategy was deficient. The Oglalas should have gone farther east, at least to Fort Laramie and even better to Fort Kearney in central Nebraska, while Sitting Bull should have attacked farther south, at Fort Sully or Fort Randall in South Dakota. A successful assault on Forts Sully and Kearney, followed by a determined effort to hold both places, would have isolated the forts upstream on the Missouri and the Platte. Forts Laramie and Rice would have quickly fallen of their own weight without a steady flow of supplies. Still, not having a line of communications themselves, the Indians can hardly be blamed for failing to understand fully the vulnerability of the whites.

Despite the strategic shortcomings, this was an impressive campaign. It was as close as the Sioux and Cheyennes ever came to making a concerted, unified *offensive* movement. The two-pronged attack was the right idea—it kept the soldiers from one area from reinforcing those under attack in another region. Indian morale was high. After the easy victories over the whites in 1864, the warriors were full of confidence. They were also impressed by their own numbers; never having seen such a large war party before (there were perhaps as many as three thousand warriors in the Oglala-Cheyenne camp alone), they were certain that nothing could stand in their path.

On the evening of July 24, 1865, after a three-day march, the expedition camped just below the Platte Bridge near Fort Casper (the site of present day Casper, Wyoming). The Oregon Trail crossed the North Platte River where the bridge stood and there was a small garrison stationed on the south bank to protect the bridge. The Indians could have attacked the garrison itself, with overwhelming numbers, or they could have burned the bridge and then, through sniping, prevented the soldiers from repairing it. Either way, they would have cut the white man's line of communications. But the Indians' idea of fighting was getting the enemy out into the open, where the red men's numbers and skill as horsemen would be most telling and where their casualties would be lightest. So Roman Nose, Red Cloud, Young Man Afraid and the others decided to use the old decoy trick.

Twenty men would make up the decoy party. George Bent was one of them, Crazy Horse another, joined by the other shirt-wearers. The idea was that the decoys would draw a pursuit from the soldiers. Crazy Horse would lead the cavalry into the hills beyond the north bank of the river, where the main body of warriors would be waiting over the rise, held in check by an *akicita* from each tribe.

At dawn, July 25, Crazy Horse was ready. Tossing a little dust over his hair and on the bay he had gotten from the Crows, he mounted up and trotted off with the decoys. They rode down toward the bridge, Crazy Horse motioning toward the herds of American horses and mules on the opposite bank. As they approached the bridge, Crazy Horse and the others shook out their buffalo blankets, as if in preparation for a stampeding of the herd. A company of troops with a howitzer came dashing out of the fort protecting the bridge, raced across the bridge, and stopped on the north bank. Holding the bay in check with one hand, Crazy Horse pretended to be beating his horse with the other, hoping to convince the soldiers that he was in a panicky retreat and thereby inducing them to follow. But the troops stayed put, so Crazy Horse and a young Cheyenne jumped from their horses and fired a few well-aimed shots at the soldiers. The whites responded by lobbing some howitzer shells in the direction of the decoy party.

When the warriors hidden behind the hills heard the heavy firing, they could not be restrained. First one or two broke ranks, an *akicita* policeman chasing them; then the multitude galloped to the top of the hills, to see what was happening. The soldiers below took one look, saw perhaps three thousand warriors staring down on them, and retreated to the safety of the fort. With Red Cloud and Young Man Afraid roaring at them, the members of the *akicita* finally caught up with the warriors and started herding them away from the hilltops, striking the stubborn ones with their quirts. The furious headmen then sent a Cheyenne, High Back Wolf, to tell the decoy party to return.[29]

When High Back Wolf passed on the message, one of the decoys spoke angrily: "Now, when I see anything and go to get it, I want to succeed in getting it." Crazy Horse shouted his approval—he too wanted some action. "All right," High Back Wolf said. "I feel just as you do about that, but I am trying to do what the headmen have asked me to do." Then, after thinking about it for a minute, High Back Wolf decided to hell with his orders. "Come on now," he called out. "Let us swim the river and get close to the soldiers." With a whoop, Crazy Horse and the others did so.

A half dozen soldiers, returning from a hunting expedition, were riding up the river on the south bank and had nearly reached the post. Crazy Horse and the decoy party charged through these soldiers, giving them the fright of their lives. At such close quarters, moving at top speed, the Indians could not use their weapons, but they had an orgy of coup counting as they rode through the terrified troops. Turning to charge again, the decoys ran into another small party of soldiers, who had come out from the fort to help their comrades. These troops shot High Back Wolf, who fell dead. (High Back Wolf had a powerful bullet-proof medicine, but it worked only on the condition that he put no metal, especially a bullet, into his mouth on the day of a fight. In the excitement just before he was killed, High Back Wolf had put a bullet into his mouth while reloading his six-shooter.) Crazy Horse tried to retrieve the body but could not, and the decoys retreated across the river, their heads hanging. The next dawn Crazy Horse, High Back Wolf's father, and some Cheyennes sneaked down to the fort and retrieved the body.[30]

Later that day, July 26, Crazy Horse and the decoy party went out again, to try to accomplish their mission once more. The decoys went through their whole bag of tricks, pretending that their ponies were crippled or that they had fallen off—anything to get the troops to come out. But the soldiers just watched. Then, when the decoys had about given up, a party of troops on gray horses came riding out and crossed the bridge. The decoys thought they were finally being pursued, but in fact the troops (under the command of Lieutenant Caspar Collins) were headed upriver, going to escort a wagon train that was coming down the trail and about which the Indians knew nothing.

This time Red Cloud, Roman Nose, and Young Man Afraid had made a more complex plan. The Oglalas were stationed downriver from the bridge, the Cheyennes upstream. As Lieutenant Collins swung to his left on the north bank, the Oglalas below the bridge rode out to cut the soldiers off from the bridge. Then the Cheyennes swung down on Collins' flank. Collins fled back toward the bridge, shouting that he was a friend and wanted no fight. Some Oglalas recognized him and gave way, yelling at each other over the noise of the battle not to shoot, this was a friend. But just as Collins reached the bridge, most of his men safely across, his horse bolted and took him back into the hills, where the Cheyennes killed him. They kept his horse for a long time, but it was always uncontrollable and no one could ride it.[31]

The Cheyennes were angry with the Oglalas for letting the soldiers get away. The Indians outnumbered the troops by one hundred to one or more, but only eight soldiers had been killed. The Sioux had counted lots of coup on the retreating soldiers, but what good was that? A body of nearly three thousand warriors had spent weeks in preparation, then made a three-day march, and all they had to show for it was eight scalps and some coup counted. True, the Sioux were less experienced in fighting whites than the Cheyennes, and had fewer guns,* but still the Cheyennes muttered that their allies should have killed more. Later in the day the Cheyenne mood softened when they discovered the wagon train, pillaged, and burned it, killing all the drivers except for two men who swam the river and got away.[32] That night the Indians held a victory dance; the next day most of them began riding back to the Powder River.

That was the end of the great allied Indian expedition of 1865. The Indians had put the war "in the bag," as the Indians phrased it, never mind that the troops still held the upper Platte Bridge, their stockade intact. The leaders could not hold the warriors together and the Indian army melted away. Up at Fort Rice, the Hunkpapa warriors had also broken through the *akicita,* spoiling Sitting Bull's ambush. The white man's line of communications remained secure.

Unknown to the Indians, while they were taking the war to the Holy Road, the United States Army was trying to bring the war to them. In late summer of 1865 three strong columns of troops, more than two thousand soldiers in all, set out from Fort Laramie for the Powder River country. They wanted to teach the wild Sioux and Cheyennes a lesson, then force them back into an agency on the Missouri or, even better if everything went well, down to Oklahoma. Gold had been discovered in Montana and the whites wanted a road through the country, along the shortest route between the Holy Road and the mines. It was called the Bozeman Trail.

But the troops the Army sent were Civil War regiments of draftees or volunteers, and the men were full of resentment. They wanted to be mustered out, not sent off to the farthest reaches of the Wild West to get killed by savage Indians. Those who did not desert to go to the mines spent their time sulking and cursing the Army; one regiment even pulled off a mutiny. To understate the case, their hearts were not in their work, and they blundered their way around the countryside, never managing to find any Indians who did not want to be found. Occasionally, the Oglalas or Cheyennes would run off some of the soldiers' horses and otherwise pester them, but mainly the Indians left them alone. In September the soldiers, by then badly confused and often lost, were slaughtering their own horses for food. When they finally reached Fort Laramie, the soldiers

---

* Hyde estimates that the Oglalas had one gun per hundred warriors at this time.

were in a frightful condition, mere crowds of ragged, hungry, and footsore men. One captain said they looked like tramps.[33]

While the Army was out making futile marches, the United States Government inaugurated a new Indian policy. The Radical Republicans were just coming into full control in Congress, anxious to remake the image and reality of America. They wanted to force the United States to live up to its obligations to blacks and other minority groups, including Indians. In their view, the trouble on the Plains came because the Army was always starting Indian wars; the solution was to buy a peace with the hostiles. These Indian lovers were just as determined to open the Bozeman Trail (and thus further the national purpose) as the bitterest Indian hater. The only real difference between the two groups was that the Indian lovers thought it would be cheaper to get control of the Powder River country through bribery than through fighting.

So a peace commission went out, loaded with presents, and all the friendlies signed whatever the commissioners told them to sign, took their gifts, and were happy. The Indians who made their marks on the treaty gave the whites the right to build posts and open roads in the Powder River country, a region none of the friendlies had been in for decades, if ever. The commissioners then proclaimed that peace had arrived. Meanwhile, there were three thousand or more Sioux and Cheyenne warriors on the Little Missouri and Powder rivers who had no intention of allowing any whites to enter their land.

Not until December 1865 did some bureaucrat realize that when the soldiers started out for the Powder River the next spring they would meet with opposition, a treaty with the Sioux being not much good when it did not include any of the hostile Sioux. So government agents sent a copy of the treaty up to Fort Laramie, with instructions to get the hostiles to sign. Runners went out to bring the chiefs into the fort, but only one or two minor chiefs came in. The others, including Young Man Afraid, Red Cloud, and Roman Nose, stayed out.

Thus did the year 1865 come to an end. Both sides had made a big effort, but nothing of consequence had been accomplished by either one. Still, something had been learned. The Indians had reorganized, Crazy Horse becoming a leader of the Oglalas, and Young Man Afraid and Red Cloud were now big men. The whites, too, were choosing new leaders. Both sides were preparing for an all-out struggle in 1866.

CHAPTER TEN

War and Love Among the Americans

"We went out a skouting yesterday. We got to one house where
there was Five Secessionests and they broke and run and Arch
haloed out to shoot the ornery Suns of bitches and they all let
go there fire. They may say what they please, but goddamit pa,
it is fun." From a letter from an Ohio recruit, writing home
after his first brush with the enemy

George Armstrong Custer was a war lover. The Civil War was the
great event in his life. He won national prominence and thoroughly
enjoyed himself during those four bloody years. He responded enthusiastically to every aspect of war—being with "the boys," drinking,
swearing, loving the pretty young maids, fighting, marching. Custer
had as much endurance as any Plains Indian and far more than his
fellow whites; he actually enjoyed spending two or three days in the
saddle, without rest or food. A 2 A.M. breakfast of hardtack and black,
unsweetened coffee has little appeal to most men, but Custer reveled
in such moments. He could imagine few things finer than the hearty
comradeship, the rough good humor of the campfire. Always curious,
always anxious to see new places or to have new experiences, Custer
made the most of his wartime travels, which took him up and down
the eastern seaboard of the United States and threw him into daily
contact with the great and near great. So often was he in the right
place at the right time that "Custer's luck" became a byword in the
Army.

Most of all, Custer discovered that he loved the smells, sights, and
sounds of the battlefield. For him, no thrill compared to the saber
charge. He was most thoroughly himself when he stood in his stirrups, bullets whizzing all around him, drew his saber, turned his
head, and called out to the thousands of men behind him,
"Charge!" Like George S. Patton, Jr., and hundreds of other generals
through the ages, Custer was disappointed when "his" war ended,
and he hardly knew what to do with himself. Only twenty-five years

old at Appomattox, he had done it all, seen it all. Everything that
followed, until the last week of his life, was anticlimactic.

Custer fought in innumerable battles in the Civil War. They have
all been recorded. Incredibly small details are known about what he
did, what his unit did, how a battle as a whole was fought. We know
where Custer was on each day of the four-year war and what he was
doing there. There is no need to go into such details here, fortunately, because Custer's biography has been written, accurately and
wisely, by Jay Monaghan. Indeed, Monaghan's *Custer* is a model
biography—scholarly, detailed, and lively. It cannot be surpassed and
hardly needs to be summarized. General remarks about Custer's
Civil War, however, coupled with an attempt to understand why he
did what he did, may help illuminate the man and his culture.

The first thing that stands out about Custer's Civil War is that he
was not engaged in a crusade. Custer shared his opponents' assumptions and prejudices about the nature of the world, just as Crazy
Horse did not object to the way the Crows lived but simply enjoyed
fighting them. In politics, Custer was a War Democrat, loyal to the
Union but opposed to the destruction of slavery or indeed any assault on the southern way of life. His proclivities in that direction,
already pronounced when the war began, were immeasurably
strengthened by service on the staff of General George B. McClellan,
commander of the Army of the Potomac. McClellan gave Custer his
first big break and Custer idolized him: "I have more confidence in
General McClellan than in any man living," he wrote in March 1862.
"I would forsake everything and follow him to the ends of the earth.
I would lay down my life for him."[1]

The source of McClellan's magnetism for Custer was obviously not
"Little Mac's" fighting style—McClellan avoided pitched battle
whenever possible, while Custer embraced it. Custer did admire the
way McClellan carried himself—he looked and acted like a soldier—
but even more Custer responded to the atmosphere McClellan created around his headquarters. There were any number of French
dukes and even princes there, and for Custer just being around royalty was a heady experience. In addition, prominent Democrats were
always hanging around McClellan's headquarters. They drank their
whiskey straight and told rough, barrack room jokes about "niggers,"
Lincoln, and the "Black Republicans." Custer joined in the fun.

They also plotted against the government. In the summer of 1862
Fernando Wood, the recent mayor of New York City, visited Mc-
Clellan's headquarters. Wood was a leader of those northern Demo-
crats who allowed their sympathy for the South, their hatred of

blacks, and their opposition to the Republican party to carry them to the brink of treason. Wood and his friends were grooming McClellan for the 1864 Democratic nomination for the Presidency—or possibly for a *coup d'état*. It was an improbable proposition at best and seems impossible today to take seriously, but Wood was serious, and McClellan may have been. The "Young Napoleon" felt that he had been stabbed in the back by the Republicans, who in his view had deliberately withheld reinforcements from him during his Peninsula campaign of 1862 in order to bring on a humiliating defeat and thus get rid of him.

In addition, McClellan had basic policy differences with the Lincoln Administration. The general wanted a "soft" war, while Lincoln was inclining to the view that it would have to be a "hard" war, much of the difference between the hards and the softs centering around the problem of slavery. Lincoln was moving closer to abolishing it, and just before Wood arrived at McClellan's headquarters, the latter had written to Lincoln, telling the President to change policy "or our cause will be lost. . . . Neither confiscation of property, political executions of persons, territorial organization of states or forcible abolition of slavery should be contemplated for a moment." McClellan showed Wood a similar, although apparently more inflammatory note. When Brigadier General William F. Smith, one of McClellan's closest friends, saw the second document, his hair stood on end and he mumbled, "It looks like treason." On Smith's advice, McClellan destroyed the document, but he certainly discussed the gist of it with Wood.[2]

McClellan's staff, of course, knew what was going on and gossiped about it constantly. Since to Custer, McClellan's views were so close to those of his father Emmanuel, his West Point friends, and his own, he felt himself to be a patriot when he joined in campfire talk about marching on Washington and putting Little Mac at the head of the government. On November 7, 1862, when Lincoln finally removed McClellan from his command of the Army of the Potomac, replacing him with Major General Ambrose E. Burnside, Custer and his fellow aides—all West Pointers, save for the foreigners—began drinking and swaggering around the headquarters tents. They were "talking both loudly and disloyally," according to young Lieutenant James H. Wilson, and there was whiskey talk about "changing front on Washington" and setting McClellan up as a dictator. McClellan put such talk to rest when he took his leave of the Army, ordering it to "stand by General Burnside as you have stood by me," but the attitude lingered, poisoning the Army of the Potomac throughout its existence.[3]

On leaving the Army, McClellan went to New York to write his final report. Custer went with him. Little Mac was as much drawn to Custer as Custer was to him, and had requested his services in preparing his report. For Custer, then almost twenty-three years old, the experience of working with McClellan on the report reinforced all his prejudices. There was, first of all, McClellan's disdain for civilians generally and politicians especially. In the report, McClellan declared, "A statesman may, perhaps, be more competent than a soldier to determine the political objects and direction of a campaign; but those once decided upon, everything should be left to the responsible military head, without interference from civilians." That "may, perhaps," is priceless, but neither McClellan nor Custer thought it in any way remarkable.[4]

While he was in New York, Custer met more Democratic politicians, who seemed always to gather around McClellan, and indulged in more silly talk about the "treason" of the Republicans. Custer would later cultivate his contacts with the leading East Coast Democrats. He could not help but be impressed, young as he was, by the rich and powerful men he saw and talked with, and he was awed by the social life of New York's upper crust. McClellan's Democratic admirers in New York had presented the general with a house; Custer told his sister he had never seen such a palatial residence. Monaghan points out that the experience of helping McClellan prepare his report also taught Custer that no commander ever admits defeat, especially in his reports. In a number of instances, Custer knew that McClellan was indulging in plain and simple lies, most of all in his statements on enemy numbers.[5]

But Custer never wavered in his loyalty to McClellan, not even when it became obvious that being known as a "McClellan man" was a positive detriment to his career. Custer fought his way to the top; he earned his general officer rank despite, rather than as a result of, his politics. He stuck with his principles and never signed on for a crusade against slavery, but he also stuck with the Army and the Union.

One reason, perhaps, was that war was so much fun. An aspect of Custer's joyful response to combat may have been that he did not hate his enemy. Few men were as effective in making war on the Confederacy as Custer, but no Union officer exceeded him in admiration for the southern way of life or in friendship for individual Confederate officers. The war had some of the aspects of a game about it, at least to Custer; it was as if he were a modern college football player, congratulating his opponents at the end of a hard-fought game. "I rejoice, dear Pelham, in your success," he wrote West Point classmate John Pelham, who was making a name for himself in the Confederate artillery. After one of the early battles, Custer went to see "Gimlet" Lea, a West Point friend who had been captured. Tears welled in Lea's eyes as he embraced "Fanny." Custer brought him a meal and they chatted into the night, exchanging news of classmates on both sides. When Custer left he gave Lea some clothes and money. Bystanders wondered if they were brothers.[6] And at the end of the war, while Grant and Lee were signing the surrender terms at Appomattox, Custer was fraternizing with his rebel friends, as he had done at every opportunity throughout the past four years.[7]

Custer was really a very young man, and nothing reminds us more forcibly of his youth than an incident of the Peninsula campaign. While McClellan was disembarking his massive Army from the Peninsula (a time when there were tasks aplenty for his staff), Custer prevailed on his commander for a two-week furlough. He spent it visiting with Gimlet Lea, who was on parole and about to be married. At the Tidewater house where Lea was staying, Custer made himself at home. Lea's bride-to-be was there, along with her cousin. "What do you think of the girls?" Lea whispered in Custer's ear the first evening.

"Beautiful, both of them. Beautiful."

Lea had pushed forward the date of his wedding so that Custer could be there. It was an Episcopalian service, highly dignified. After the ceremony, Lea noticed that his Cousin Maggie was crying.

"What are you crying for?" he asked. "Oh, I know. You are crying because you are not married; well, here is the minister and here is Captain Custer, who I know would be glad to carry off such a pretty bride from the Southern Confederacy."

"Captain Lea," the girl said between sobs, "you are just as mean as you can be." Going in to dinner that evening, Custer took Maggie's arm and whispered, "I don't see how such a strong Secessionist can take the arm of a Union officer."

"You *ought* to be in *our* army," she snapped back.

It was a gay two weeks for the four young people. They sang songs in the evening around the piano ("For Southern Rights, Hurrah!" "Dixie," and other southern favorites), played cards, or just chatted merrily, teasing each other. Custer stayed in the delightful surroundings so long that he was the last Union officer to leave the Peninsula. The Army of the Potomac was gone before Custer had even said his good-byes to his rebel friends, and he had to book passage on a private steamer to get back to Washington.[8]

McClellan never asked Custer where he had been—Little Mac had enough problems at the time, since Lincoln at the end of August 1862 had taken much of his Army from him and given it to General John Pope for the second Bull Run campaign—so Custer's luck held. Indeed, as mentioned above, it was always good. His Civil War record is replete with incidents in which he was in the right place at the right time. When Custer left West Point to take up his duties in Washington, for example, his classmates had a two-week jump on him. They had been where the action was while he had sat in the guardhouse at West Point. On the train to Washington, Custer probably fretted that his friends had taken all the choice assignments and that he would get off to a poor start on his Army career.

He arrived in Washington on the eve of the first battle of Bull Run. Reporting to the Adjutant-General's office, he had to wait a few hours before finding an officer with time enough to accept his papers. The officer glanced at them, looked at some records, and informed Custer that he had been assigned to the 2nd Cavalry. Then, almost as an afterthought, the officer casually inquired, "Perhaps you would like to be presented to General Scott, Mr. Custer?" Then, according to Monaghan, "Young Armstrong stood dumfounded [sic]. He had glimpsed the grand figure of Winfield Scott when that dignitary visited the Academy for reviews, but the general had been as untouchable as the upper social set back in Monroe. He stammered assent . . ." (Winfield Scott, an old man by this time and soon to be retired, made something of pets of the West Point cadets and was always willing to do something special for them.)

After an exchange of greetings, Scott told Custer that his classmates were drilling recruits. "Now, what can I do for you? Would you prefer to be ordered to report to General Mansfield to aid in this work, or is your desire for something more active?"

What a choice! Custer indicated that he wanted to go into the line.

"A very commendable resolution, young man," Scott replied. "Go and provide yourself with a horse, if possible, and call here at seven o'clock this evening. I desire to send some dispatches to General Mc-Dowell at Centerville, and you can be the bearer of them. You are not afraid of a night ride, are you?" (Brigadier General Irvin McDowell was in command of the Union troops in northeastern Virginia.)

"No, sir," Custer replied, snapping into a salute. His luck continued to hold. He found a horse by great good fortune, made the ride to McDowell's headquarters, handed over Scott's dispatches, got to meet McDowell's chief staff officers, joined his regiment, participated in the battle of Bull Run, got himself mentioned in the reports on the engagement, and had a quiet laugh at his classmates who had missed the battle. And it all happened because he had been court-martialed at West Point and was thus late in reporting for duty.[9]

A second example of Custer's penchant for being where it counted came the following year during the Peninsula campaign, the occasion of his first meeting with McClellan. One day McClellan rode to the south bank of the Chickahominy River, attended by his usual retinue of princes, counts, rich Democrats, and distinguished regular Army officers. Custer, a fresh second lieutenant attached to a division staff, was at the rear of the column. When McClellan got to the riverbank he stopped, looked up- and downstream, and then said reflectively: "I wish I knew how deep it is." No one stirred, but his question was passed down the line. Custer rode out from his place in the ranks, trotted up to the bank, put his spurs to his horse, and plunged into the river with the remark, "I'll damn soon show how deep it is." He quickly reached the other shore, turned around and forded the river again, came ashore, and called out, "That's how deep it is, General." Then he quietly rode back to his place in line.

McClellan called him forward. "Do you know," the general said, "you're just the young man I've been looking for, Mr. Custer. How would you like to come on my staff?" And so Custer got a promotion to captain and a place near the center of power.[10]

The next day McClellan began to cross the Chickahominy and he gave Custer the honor of leading a company in the van of a charge. "Why, that's Armstrong Custer!" the men of Company A, 4th Michigan shouted when Custer took his place at the head of the column. The company had been recruited in Monroe, Michigan, Custer's second home. Custer greeted the men cheerfully, shook hands all around, then straightened up in his saddle and shouted, "Come on, Monroe!" After leading the company across the river, Custer got involved in a fire fight with the rebel outposts. He had been scouting the area for more than a week and persuaded his immediate superior that by recrossing the river, riding downstream a mile, then crossing once again, he could bring Company A onto the enemy's rear. Permission granted, Custer led the flanking expedition. When he had Company A in place he called out, "Go in, Wolverines! Give 'em hell!" and led a charge that sent the rebels running. He was the first into the fight and the last man to leave the field. "Custer was simply a reckless, gallant boy, undeterred by fatigue, unconscious of fear," McClellan wrote in his memoirs. "His head was always clear in danger and he always brought me clear and intelligible reports. . . . I became much attached to him."[11]

Custer's luck was a major factor in his success, but as both incidents (and dozens of others) illustrate, luck was not the only thing on his side. There was, to start with, the West Point Protective Association. West Pointers took care of their own, and West Pointers ran the Union Army. But in addition to his luck and the assistance of the WPPA, Custer had unique qualities that pushed him to the fore. He was always eager for action, ready to take any risk, willing to seize the initiative. When McClellan had trouble finding someone willing to go up in a balloon to observe Confederate positions, Custer volunteered for the dangerous duty and carried it out with success. Staff officers in the Civil War, unlike their successors in the twentieth century, did precious little paperwork, much less planning for future campaigns. Instead, they did errands for their generals, odd jobs that no one else could or would do. Custer, ever the man of action, served with credit on the staffs of some half dozen generals during the first two years of the war.

All the generals under whom Custer served liked having him around. It was not only that he could be relied upon to get a job done; Custer also appealed to his superiors because of his fun-loving nature and droll ways. Perpetually cheerful, always full of practical jokes, he made those around him happy, and all generals appreciate a good-humored staff and cheerful headquarters environment. Custer was something of a character, with his slouch hat, his practice of cutting his hair, then letting it grow out and smearing it with cinnamon hair oil, his hodgepodge uniform, forever in need of washing, and his oversize boots. Custer was a dandy in reverse, almost what the Sioux called a "contrary." Amid all the glitter and polish of his fellow staff officers, especially around McClellan's headquarters, Custer stood out because of his deliberately sloppy exterior. He took to wearing captured Confederate boots, the bigger the better, and his outlandish footwear provided a standing joke. So did his tight hussar jacket and black trousers trimmed with gold lace. He looked, another staff member remarked, "like a circus rider gone mad."[12]

Another factor in Custer's success was his amazingly good health and endurance. He was little bothered by disease—he took sick leave only twice in the four-year war—in an Army that was wracked by fatal illness. More men died in the Civil War of looseness of the bowels than fell on the field of combat; in the Army of the Potomac there were 57,000 deaths from diarrhea and dysentery as against 44,-000 killed in battle. Thousands more died from other diseases and it was not uncommon for new regiments to have two thirds of their strength on the sick list. But Custer came out of the war in perfect health, just as he had entered it.[13]

Over and above all his other qualities, Custer was firm in his principles and physically courageous. For his entire adult life Custer was on the unpopular side of the political fence, both in terms of national and Army politics. He was also willing to face death. It is easier to describe his courage than to account for it. He was at the head of every charge, never faltered, and always kept his head no matter how deadly the hail of bullets.

Like Crazy Horse, Custer lived his life to the full; again like Crazy Horse, he was so involved with living that he did not have time to fear death. He was not suicidal. His life was precious to him, but only if he lived up to his own image of himself. He would rather die than ignore his duty or shirk danger. Many Civil War soldiers shared that attitude; Bell Wiley's magnificent account of the common soldier of the Union Army, *The Life of Billy Yank*, is full of accounts of men whose dying words were, "Have I not always done my duty?" or similar statements.[14]

In a way, Custer's courage sprang from the fear of looking bad in front of comrades. His account of his first combat experience illustrates the point. Six days after leaving West Point, he was involved at Bull Run in his first cavalry charge. "I realized that I was in front of a company of old and experienced soldiers," he later recalled, "all of whom would have an eye upon their new lieutenant to see how he comported himself when under fire." Custer tried, more or less successfully, to appear calm. Riding beside him was another young lieutenant, Leicester Walker, fresh from civilian life and holding a political commission. As the column rode toward the enemy on the other side of a hill, Walker anxiously inquired, "Custer, what weapon are you going to use in the charge?"

"From my earliest notions of the true cavalryman," Custer wrote later, "I had always pictured him in the charge bearing aloft his curved saber, and cleaving the skulls of all with whom he came in contact." So he promptly replied, "The saber," flashed his bright new blade from its scabbard, and rode forward, totally unconcerned. Walker, figuring that was the way it was done at West Point, also drew his saber. But then Custer began to have doubts. "I began arguing in my own mind as to the comparative merits of the saber and revolver as a weapon of attack. If I remember correctly, I reasoned *pro* and *con* about as follows: 'Now the saber is a beautiful weapon; it produces an ugly wound; the term "saber charge" sounds well; and above all the saber is sure; it never misses fire. It has this drawback, however; in order to be made effective, it is indispensable that you approach very close to your adversary . . . So much for the saber. Now as to the revolver, it has this advantage . . . one is not compelled to range himself alongside his adversary before beginning the attack . . . As this is my first battle, had I not better defer the use of the saber until after I have acquired a little more experience?' "

He returned his saber to its scabbard and drew his revolver. Walker, seeing Custer's action, did the same. But Custer argued some more with himself, finally replacing the revolver and again drawing his saber. Walker did the same. So it went until they reached the top of the hill, to discover the enemy had already withdrawn.[15]

Custer knew how to overwhelm or at least overcome his fears, but there was more to his courage than that. He positively enjoyed combat. He would have understood perfectly the cavalryman who wrote after the battle of Brandy Station, "I never felt so gay in my life as I did when we charged with the Saber" or the artilleryman who remarked after Gettysburg, "I felt a joyous exaltation, a perfect indifference to circumstances through the whole of that three days fight, and have seldom enjoyed three days more in my life."[16] As much as any man who fought in the Civil War, Custer felt that exaltation that comes to some after a fight gets under way. "There is something grand about it—it is magnificent," one rebel wrote. "I feel elated as borne along with the tide of battle."[17] In addition, as an officer at the head of a column of cavalry, Custer felt an awesome sense of power as he cried out, "Charge!"

Combat, for Custer, held some of the fascination of the hunt. In writing home about his battle experiences he used words like "the chase" or "the sport" and referred to his enemies as "the game." In one of his early actions he was leading ten men in pursuit of a small body of Confederate cavalry. It was, Custer wrote home, "the most exciting sport I ever engaged in." He saw a rebel officer mounted on a magnificent blooded bay horse. "I selected him as my game, and gave my black the spur and rein. . . . Seeing a stout rail fence in front of him, I concluded to try him at it. I reasoned that he might attempt to leap it and be thrown, or if he could clear it so could I. The chase was now exciting in the extreme."

The Confederate cleared the fence. So did Custer. By avoiding a swamp, Custer gained on his quarry and called on him to surrender. When the rebel rode on, Custer fired his pistol. He missed. Again Custer called on him to surrender, but the man rode on. Taking care-

1. Crazy Horse's photograph was never taken. He refused to pose because he held the Indian belief that to steal his shadow would shorten his life. This is one of Crazy Horse's "dress" shirts, fringed with hair from ponies' tails. It is not the shirt he was awarded to go with his position of shirt-wearer.

2. He Dog in 1879. He Dog was a lifelong friend of Crazy Horse and his chief lieutenant in battle. They were also related by marriage. He Dog was one of the few Oglalas who remained loyal to Crazy Horse until the very end. The cross around his neck was typical of the Indians after they came into the reservation and posed for formal portaits. It did not indicate conversion.

3. George Armstrong Custer, in his West Point graduation photograph, 1861. He led a monk's life at the Academy, where he learned a little mathematics, some civil engineering, a smattering of natural science, and a great deal about discipline.

4. A Sioux encampment along the Platte River in western Nebraska, with Chimney Rock in the background, in a painting by William de la Montaigne Cary (1840–1922). As a boy, Crazy Horse frequently lived in small camps like this one along the Platte.

5. Custer, the boy general of the Civil War, in a typical formal attire. Throughout his life, Custer was constantly changing his hair style. When he wore it short, he liked to slick it down with cinnamon oil, which led his friends to nickname him "Cinnamon." When he wore it long, they called him "Curly."

6. Pawnee Killer, the southern Oglala warrior who was beside Crazy Horse at Fort Phil Kearny, then went south to Kansas, where throughout the summer of 1867 he led Custer on a merry chase.

7. Custer in the outfit he wore during the Washita campaign in Texas and what is now Oklahoma 1868. He drove his men, and himself, very hard to get in shape for the campaign, and it paid off as they made prodigious marches through deep snow without complaint.

8. Elizabeth Bacon Custer—Libbie—in the late 1860s, when her husband was fighting Indians on the Plains and telling her to join him at the frontier forts. "Come as soon as you can," he commanded. "I did not marry you for you to live in one house, me in another. One bed shall accommodate us both."

9. Custer in 1874, after the Black Hills expedition. He is wearing his only civilian suit; he could afford no more. When he and Libbie made a trip to New York the following year, they stayed in a boarding house to save money and went on forty different occasions to see their actor friend Lawrence Barrett in *Julius Caesar*, because they could get in free.

10. Touch-the-Clouds, the seven-foot-tall war chief of the Miniconjous. A tower of strength and dignity, Touch-the-Clouds fought beside Crazy Horse until the very end. He was respected by both red and white men and much feared by his enemies.

11. Captain Tom Custer, the bravest of the brave, winner of the Congressional Medal of Honor during the Civil War. Custer often said that Tom, not he, should have been the general. Tom idolized his older brother and followed him everywhere, even to the very end at the Little Bighorn.

12. Young-Man-Afraid-of-His-Horses, usually called simply Young Man Afraid (his full name, in Lakota, meant that the enemies of the Sioux were afraid even of his horses). His father, Old-Man-Afraid-of-His-Horses, was a big chief among the Oglalas. Young Man Afraid was probably the most intelligent Sioux leader of the period. Never a lackey for the whites, he was nevertheless an advocate of peace after 1868, when he realized that the red men could not win a war with the whites. He worked thereafter for the good of his people, with some success.

ful aim, or as careful as he could from the back of a galloping horse, Custer fired again. A hit, right in the head. Custer kept the Confederate's horse for himself, as well as his handsome saddle, fancy sword, and double-barreled shotgun. In reporting on his experience to his family, Custer concluded: "It was his own fault; I told him twice to surrender, but was compelled to shoot him."[18]

For all of his sportsman's attitude toward combat, however, Custer could get as sentimental about death as the most romantic Civil War soldier. In early 1862, when he was all of twenty-two years old, Custer told of burying a few dead Union soldiers. "Some were quite young and boyish," he wrote, "and looking at their faces, I could not but think of my own younger brother. One, shot through the heart, had been married the day before he left Vermont. Just as his comrades were about to consign his body to the earth, I thought of his wife, and, not wishing to put my hands in his pockets, cut them open with my knife, and found knife, porte-monnaie and ring. I then cut off a lock of his hair and gave them to a friend of his from the same town who promised to send them to his wife. As he lay there I thought of that poem: 'Let me kiss him for his mother . . .' and wished his mother were there to smooth his hair."[19]

In early spring 1863 Custer became an aide to Brigadier General Alfred Pleasonton, who commanded one of the three cavalry divisions in the Army of the Potomac, now commanded by General Joseph Hooker. Pleasonton was a tough old regular, a West Point graduate with twenty years' service. He had fought with General Harney in the attack on Little Thunder's camp of Brulés on the Bluewater River in 1855. It is easy enough to imagine the general and his young West Point aides sitting around the campfire eight years later, Pleasonton regaling his staff with stories of fighting against the Sioux. It was Custer's first close contact with a real Indian fighter and he probably was fascinated by Pleasonton's anecdotes.

Custer reveled in his new position, especially the daily rides through the command with his chief. He idolized Pleasonton, who in turn had a high opinion of the eager young staff officer. They lived well. Pleasonton sent to Baltimore daily for vegetables and other delicacies. "We have onions, radishes, and *ripe tomatoes*," Custer told the home folks, plus "asparagus, fresh fish, mackeral, beef, mutton, veal, *Bacon*, pound cake, oranges, ginger snaps, candies, *peas*, warm biscuits (instead of hard bread), fresh milk, butter, cheese, & everything."[20] He was always a man of extremes. In the field, Custer often went three or four days with virtually no food or sleep, but in camp he lived the good life to the full.

The enlisted men hated all staff officers, especially young squirts like Custer fresh out of West Point and full of airs, and they bitterly resented the privileges the staffers enjoyed. The men could be disarmingly frank in making their feelings known. "You are God damned trash," a Michigan private told his captain. "You think you can do just as you God damn please. . . . I'll be God damned if I will [obey your orders]. I'll see you in hell before I will." An Irish soldier, when ordered by a headquarters aide to keep quiet while serving a term in a guardhouse, replied, "I will not keep quiet for you, you God damned low-lived son of a bitch, you shit-house adjutant." "You order me!" an Ohio recruit snapped at another aide. "You ain't worth a pinch of shit!" Staff officers were dubbed "buggers," "dogs," "green-horns," "whore-house pimps," and more frequently the time-honored "son of a bitch."[21]

Clearly there was something of a gap between the leaders and the led in the Union Army—a situation totally foreign to Crazy Horse and the Oglalas—but Custer did not mind. Army discipline ensured that the men would do what they were told, and West Point had taught him that as an officer he was entitled to special privileges. Like other Union officers, he indulged himself in every comfort he could. By early 1863 Custer had a black woman cook, a teen-aged white boy who followed him everywhere and did all his cleaning and took care of his personal needs, two dogs, and a great pile of souvenirs. He was hardly alone; as a Massachusetts soldier pointed out, "Every private wants & Every officer has his colored servant whom he feeds scantily, clothes shabbily, works cruelly & curses soundly & in his curses includes the whole race."[22]

Officers in the Army of the Potomac lived better than did their counterparts in other theaters, and the cavalry officers did best of all. Civil War cavalry officers have often been compared to the hotshot Air Force pilots of the twentieth century—each service attracted the boastful, swaggering, devil-may-care, courageous young heroes. More than any other group, the young cavalry officers gave the Army of the Potomac its well-earned reputation for being the hardest drinking, hardest swearing outfit in the land. "I will be a perfect Barbarian if I should Stay hear 3 years," wrote one soldier, while another confessed that "I have seen but little of the wickedness and depravity of man until I Joined the Army." Another soldier commented, "The swearing especially is terrific, and even to a man accustomed to hear bad language, and with sensibilities not very easily shocked, it is really disgusting."[23]

Freed from the restraints of his Methodist parents and family, and from the petty regulations of West Point, Custer joined in the fun, swearing and drinking the way a cavalryman should and enjoying the fleshpots of Washington when on leave. But he did not neglect his duty, nor did the others, for they were all filled with ambition. The standard toast among the aides, at the beginning, middle, and end of a drinking bout, was "To promotion—or death!"

That was the only check on Custer's happiness—he was still a captain while some of his classmates were moving ahead rapidly, especially in the Confederate Army. Custer did his best to please all the generals he served—he brought captured booty to Pleasonton, including a magnificent horse and, by rumor at least, a female companion—but the only way to get ahead, it seemed, was via politics. In May 1863 Custer went to Pleasonton to ask two favors. First, he wanted Pleasonton to appoint Lieutenant George Yates, a friend from Monroe, to the staff (throughout his life Custer liked to surround himself with friends and relatives). Pleasonton agreed. Then Custer made the request closest to his heart. Would Pleasonton recommend him to Republican Governor Austin Blair for command of a Michigan cavalry regiment, newly organized? Again Pleasonton agreed, for like most West Pointers he wanted other Academy graduates to serve as the colonels of the volunteer regiments, not the politician who had raised the outfit.

With Pleasonton's recommendation, Custer was ready to make his application. He had already lined up four other generals to make recommendations for him, and he wrote to Judge Isaac Christiancy of the Michigan Supreme Court, a founder of the Republican party and a Monroe resident, asking for his help. Then he wrote his sister, confessing his fears: the politicians would never forgive him for being a "McClellan man," he said, and his politics would prevent his rise in the Army.[24]

He was right. Politics did count for more than ability. Governor Blair turned him down, and not because of his age. There were West Pointers no older than Custer serving as colonels at the head of Union volunteer regiments, but they were Republicans.

If coming of age for young men in America meant hard drinking, hard cussing, and hard riding, Custer was finding the maturing process an easy one. But there is more involved in becoming a man than just being tough, and in one crucial area Custer experienced great

difficulty. Relations between young men and women were as complicated among the whites as they were among the Oglalas. White society emphasized the sanctity of marriage every bit as much as the
Sioux did and forbade premarital and extramarital intercourse just
as firmly as did the Indians. White girls were trained to be wives
and taught to serve their husbands. There was not, of course, equality
among white women. Those fortunate enough to be married to a
member of the elite were able to hire someone else to do the household tasks, but that did not free them to pursue their own careers;
rather, they were expected to give their husbands moral support and
serve them as ornaments.

There were other divisions among white women not found among
their Indian counterparts. White males tended to regard white
women as objects, and those at the lower ends of the social and e o-
nomic scale were fair game for any man who had the money a.d
inclination to try to buy their time and bodies. Under these circumstances, Custer tended, not surprisingly, to divide women into two
groups; those who were fast and loose and those who were pure. He
used the first group and treated such women with contempt, while
he idealized the second group and treated those women with venera-
tion. Getting to know women as human beings was almost impossible
for him, for like Crazy Horse he had been indoctrinated by his culture to view *all* women as weak and inferior, to be taken seriously
only around the home or in bed.

Custer had had limited experience with women. Before going to
West Point he had developed a close relationship with Mary Holland, but nothing had come of the affair. At the Academy, he lived
a monk's life, not even seeing any women his own age. Crazy Horse
had more of an opportunity to get to know females than did Cadet
Custer. After joining the Army of the Potomac, Custer knew only
prostitutes on an intimate basis. Women of his own age and social
status were a mystery to him, and a challenge.

In the late fall of 1861, Custer returned to Michigan on sick leave.
His illness was brief, as would always be the case with him, and he
had more than a month to make his reputation in Monroe's social
circles. The handsome and dashing young bachelor strutted up and
down the streets of Monroe or held forth at parties or church functions, explaining to the civilians how the war was fought. Custer enjoyed every minute of it, but he was most delighted when he could
be with the eligible young ladies of Monroe, laughing, talking, teasing. He proposed marriage to at least one and possibly more.

Custer reveled in the role of the young hero returned from the

wars. After escorting Fanny Fifield or another beauty home from singing class, he went on drinking sprees with his boyhood companions,
filling their ears with combat stories—in Custer's stories, he always
led the charge, always killed his enemy, always swept the field. It
was a glorious vacation.

In February 1862 Custer returned to active duty, but he was back
in Monroe on a furlough in November of that year. This time he
had more war stories to tell, and as McClellan's aide he was near
enough to the seat of power to command attention from the town's
dignitaries. He spoke at banquet halls and on platforms at public
meetings. As a speaker he was awkward and embarrassed, but he
struck the older men as being properly modest and began receiving
invitations to the elite social affairs.[25]

On Thanksgiving evening, at a party held at the local girls' finishing school, Custer was presented to Miss Elizabeth Bacon, daughter
of Judge Daniel Bacon, the town's most prominent resident. Usually
full of talk, Custer for once was speechless; in addition to her social
position, Libbie Bacon was easily the prettiest girl at the party, indeed
one of the most beautiful Custer had ever seen. Libbie had been
well-trained and knew how to keep a conversation with a bashful
swain from floundering. She had one infallible question, flattering
to male vanity: "And what do you *really* think of Higher Education
for Women?" But on this occasion she too was tongue-tied and only
managed to say, "I believe your promotion has been very rapid?" Custer, then a captain, replied modestly, "I have been very fortunate."[26]
And that was about all, at least for that night. But it was as close
to love at first sight* as ever happens in real life, and Custer set
his cap to catch her if he could.

Libbie felt the same way toward him. She saw Custer on the streets
of Monroe the next day and he glanced at her. "Oh, how pleased
I was," she wrote of the experience. In church that Sunday, Custer
couldn't keep his eyes off Miss Bacon; as she put it, he "looked
such things at me." Like other love-struck young girls, she could not
believe that anyone so attractive as Custer could be interested in
plain old Libbie Bacon, and she took to comparing herself, unfavor-
ably, to her friends. Those young ladies, she was convinced, were far
better looking than she was, wore finer clothes, and were in constant
competition with her for men in general and Custer in particular.
"Yet without the least intention," she later wrote, "I captured the
greatest prize of all."[27]

---

* Custer had seen Libbie often as a child but had never been properly introduced because of the social gap between them.

Libbie hardly needed to worry about her competition. Her seminary graduation photograph, taken in the summer of 1862, shows her practicing her sweet, demure look, and she brought it off well. Her dark, long, curly hair fell over her shoulder in ringlets. She had just the hint of a smile, barely enough to reveal her dimples. Her ivory-colored skin set off her dark hair and eyebrows. Later full-length photographs show an ample bosom and a dangerously thin waist—the perfect figure, in other words, for wearing the sweeping dresses of the day. She was twenty-one years old that fall of 1862, so she tried terribly hard to look mature and almost made it. But her eyes did her in. They sparkled with life, vitality, youth. They seemed to promise adventure, enthusiasm, energy, and indicated that here was a woman ready for fun and excitement, always anxious to try something new, no matter how dangerous.[28]

Libbie Bacon was one of the most remarkable American women of the nineteenth century. As will be seen, she had unbounded energy, but she never worked a day in her life. She was as courageous as Custer himself, although she hid her bravery behind shrieks, screams, and her supposed need for a male protector from all dangers, big and little. She was a superb horsewoman, again as good as Custer himself, although her society forced her to ride sidesaddle. She was highly intelligent, even though she hid her intelligence just as carefully as she did her bravery. And she was a marvelously effective writer. She has left us some of the best descriptive material available on the Great Plains in the nineteenth century. But she devoted the twelve years of her married life and the fifty-seven years of her widowhood to her husband. He was the only human subject she ever wrote about and, as far as one can tell, almost the only human being she ever thought about. She lived to serve him and his memory. What a waste! Had Libbie been a boy, given the good start in life a child of Judge Bacon would have enjoyed and the talents and energy Libbie had, she would probably have gone right to the top of the American scene in any one of a number of fields. As it was, she was fated to be known only as a wife and then as a widow.

Libbie understood herself and her role. She was contented, even happy. She knew how to get what she wanted, which in truth was not much, as she never sought power or prominence or a career for herself. Her mother had died when she was quite young, and although her father remarried when she was in her late teens, she grew up without any close female companions. She did have schoolmates, of course, but they knew even less of the world than she did. So her views on what a woman was and how she should behave came primarily from her father, and Judge Bacon was a stern man who was firm in his views and set in his ways. He protected his little Libbie from the evils of the world. In fact, Libbie needed to be protected about as much as Custer did, but she learned to use her father's attitude to win her own small triumphs.

"Libbie Bacon has no mother! Poor motherless Libbie Bacon! How shamelessly I traded on this," she confessed late in her life. "What an excuse I made of it for not doing anything I didn't want to do! And what excuses were made for me on that score!" Judge Bacon had sent her to a seminary for young ladies in Grand Rapids, where she learned to sew, play the piano, and engage in other ornamental arts pleasing to the nineteenth-century American male. She spent her summers with the judge and his new wife in Monroe; Mrs. Bacon would not suffer her "young responsibility" to assume the slightest household task, so Libbie read edifying Christian literature. One year the Bacons kept Libbie in Monroe and out of school for the entire term, lest a summer cold cause her to "catch a consumption."[29]

When Custer met Libbie in 1862 she had just graduated from the seminary. As her lifetime friend, Marguerite Merington, put it, she was now a thoroughly educated young lady. "Her main preoccupation from that time onward would be to find a husband—or, more modestly, to be found by a husband acceptable to herself and family. Home, thanks to the second Mrs. Bacon, was all that a young lady could desire. She took up painting in the interval between one security and another—she looked forward in marriage to the sheltered life."[30]

Then occurred what Libbie ever afterward referred to as "that terrible day." Custer went on an afternoon drinking spree in Monroe, got roaring drunk, and staggered his way home along the sidewalk, weaving from side to side, falling, vomiting, and generally making a spectacle of himself. His path took him along Monroe Street, right past Judge Bacon's house. Libbie happened to be at the window upstairs, while the judge was downstairs, also looking toward the street. Both Bacons were disgusted by the sight of Custer.

"Home" for Custer in Monroe was, of course, the Reed house, where his older sister Lydia ran the household. She took one look and hustled the drunken soldier boy up to his room, locked the door behind her, and began her lecture. Frederick Whittaker, Custer's close friend and first biographer, tells the story of what happened as only a nineteenth-century author could: "What passed at that interview between the anxious loving sister and the impulsive erring boy, already repenting of his degradation and error, will never be fully known until the last day. Far be it from us to strive to lift the veil. It was a season of tears, prayers, and earnest pleading on one side, overcoming all resistance on the other. The result was that George Armstrong Custer then and there, in the presence of God, gave his sister a solemn pledge that never henceforth to the day of his death should a drop of intoxicating liquor pass his lips. That pledge he kept in letter and spirit to the last. His excess in Monroe was his last anywhere, and henceforth he was a free man."[31]

Custer did indeed keep his pledge. He would not even touch wine at formal dinner parties. He also took a pledge to refrain from cursing; on this point the evidence is not as clear as it was with regard to drinking, but most of Custer's Army associates testify that after 1862 he seldom swore. It obviously took a man of strong character to keep either pledge, much less both, but Custer's self-discipline was so strong that somehow he managed to do it.

The temptations not to do so were great throughout his life. The U. S. Army was hardly a teetotaling institution and Custer spent his adult years in close association with hard-drinking, hard-swearing officers. At no time was he more severely tested than during the first months of his pledge. According to Captain Charles Francis Adams of the 1st Massachusetts Cavalry, "During the winter [of 1862–63] . . . I can say from personal knowledge and experience, that the Headquarters of the Army of the Potomac was a place to which no self-respecting man liked to go, and no decent woman could go. It was a combination of barroom and brothel." Custer nevertheless remained steadfast; his character was as solid as a rock.[32]

Libbie was soon enough ready to forget, or at least to forgive, Custer's spree, but the judge was not. He had invited Custer to his home on one occasion, but it was a stiff, formal affair and he had told Libbie to stay upstairs, out of sight. The judge himself never introduced his daughter to Custer, nor did he allow her to meet other soldiers. "Oh, Wifey, Wifey!" he would cry out to the second Mrs. Bacon, "one of those mustached, gilt-striped and button critters will get our Libbie yet!" Custer had other disadvantages aside from his occupation—he came from a lower-class family and the judge could never forgive his drunken spectacle.

By this time Custer and Libbie were seeing each other regularly at social events, exchanging long looks in church, and otherwise flirting. The judge ordered his daughter never to see Custer again. To seal the matter, he told Libbie to go to Toledo, Ohio, until young Custer left town. A friend from Toledo, Annie Cotton, had been visiting Libbie in Monroe, so a return visit was easily arranged. Custer came to the train station to see Libbie off. Judge Bacon watched, aghast, as Custer gallantly touched Libbie's elbow to help her onto the train. The judge had not dreamed that their intimacy had gone so far. When he got home, he wrote his daughter a stern letter, deeply critical of her loose ways.

Libbie replied with some heat. "You have never been a girl, Father,"† she began, "and you cannot tell how hard a trial this was for me. At the depot he assisted Annie Cotton just as much as he did me." She informed her father that she had told Custer "never to meet me, and he has the sense to understand. But," she added, refusing to give in to her father's dictatorial orders, "I did not promise never to see him again." Monroe people, she said, "will please mind their own business, and let me alone. If the whole world Oh'd and Ah'd it would not move me . . . Do not blame Captain Custer. He has many fine traits and Monroe will yet be proud of him."[33]

Custer, meanwhile, did his best to please the judge. He made sure that Bacon knew of his temperance pledge, and in any case the judge, as a leading politician in town, could hardly ignore Monroe's young war hero (though they were of different political parties). The two were thrown together often at Union rallies. After he returned to the war, Custer corresponded with the judge, keeping him abreast of the war news and doing all he could to impress the older man with his sincerity and maturity. At the same time, Custer was corresponding secretly with Libbie—he addressed his letters to Nettie Humphrey, one of Libbie's Monroe friends, who read them to Libbie. He was desperate by this time to have Libbie for his own and he knew that could happen only if he married her. He also knew he could marry her only with the judge's consent, and that consent would come only if he proved himself. In effect, the judge and the captain were dickering over Libbie as if she were a piece of property, but Libbie accepted the rules. Strong-willed as she was, she would never dream of marrying without her father's blessing. So Custer went back to active duty more determined than ever to make a name for himself.

Throughout the spring of 1863, Custer shone. When General Robert E. Lee started his invasion of the North in early June, Pleasonton's cavalry had the task of breaking through Confederate General J. E. B. ("Jeb") Stuart's cavalry, crossing the Blue Ridge

† This classic line, so typical of Libbie, would fit well on the mantelpiece of every man who has a daughter.

Mountains, and obtaining information on the size and direction of the Army of Northern Virginia. Custer fought in the various skirmishes and battles that resulted, frequently getting his name mentioned in dispatches. As McClellan's aide, Custer had been a captain, but now that he was an aide to a corps commander (Pleasonton headed the Cavalry Corps) he reverted to his permanent rank of first lieutenant.

Custer was used to giving orders by this time, especially in a combat situation. Joseph Fought, a drummer boy who attached himself to Custer for most of the war (and wore oversize boots and long hair in emulation of his hero), described the situation that prevailed: "Genl. Pleasonton, a very active officer, was always anxious to be posted about what was doing in front of him. He himself could not be in front all the time, and in that respect his Trusties [aides] were more valuable to him than his brigade commanders. If Lt. Custer observed that it was important to make a movement or charge he would tell the commander to do it, and the commander would have to do it, would not dare question, because he knew Lt. Custer was working under Genl. Pleasonton who would confirm every one of his instructions and movements."[34]

On the night before Pleasonton moved out to attack Stuart, June 8, 1863, Custer wrote a long letter to his sister Lydia. He described every detail of his duties, said he would wake Pleasonton at 2 A.M. for a 4 A.M. march, remarked that his health was excellent and that he never felt better in his life. But there was a good chance he would be killed in the campaign. "In case anything happens to me," he wrote, "my trunk is to go to you. Burn all my letters."[35]

The following day, just at daylight, Custer helped lead a charge into the midst of some rebel cavalry cooking breakfast, thus beginning the battle of Brandy Station. For the first time in the war, Union cavalry fought Stuart on even terms. Custer took command of the 8th New York Cavalry when its colonel was killed. He led a series of charges, got himself and his men surrounded and outnumbered, cut his way out, and was lucky enough to have Pleasonton observe some of the action. The general was pleased with the way his aide took over in a crisis.

On June 17, 1863, Brigadier General Judson Kilpatrick, who had been a year ahead of Custer at West Point and who now commanded a brigade of three regiments (which fact made Lieutenant Custer burn with envy), attacked Stuart's horsemen. Custer got into the fight but his horse, a favorite named Harry, bolted and carried him through the Confederate lines and into their rear. He described what followed in a letter home: "I was surrounded by rebels, and cut off from my own men, but I made my way out safely, and all owing to my *hat*, which is a large broad brim [straw hat], exactly like that worn by the rebels. Every one tells me that I look like a rebel more than our own men. The rebels at first thought I was one of their own men, and did not attack me, except one, who rushed at me with his saber, but I struck him across the face with my saber, knocking him off his horse. I then put spurs to 'Harry' and made my escape."[36] Michigan newspapers played up the incident, making it appear that Custer saved the day by charging through the rebel lines.

On June 26 Pleasonton's cavalry crossed the Potomac, close on Lee's heels. The next day, when they were in Frederick, Maryland, the cavalrymen heard astonishing news. Lincoln had replaced Hooker with Major General George Gordon Meade as commander of the Army of the Potomac. The Cavalry Corps was being reorganized on the march: three new division commanders had been named, and new brigade commanders were expected to take over. (A Union cavalry division ordinarily had three brigades in it; each brigade contained three or four regiments. A regiment at full strength contained one thousand soldiers, but by 1863 the average size of a regiment was below five hundred. A cavalry brigade, then, contained between one thousand five hundred and two thousand troopers, while a division was five thousand to six thousand strong.) Kilpatrick, only a year older than Custer, became one of the division commanders, with a brigadier's star on each shoulder to go with it. Custer hid his jealousy, blurted out congratulations to Little Kil, then went off on the disagreeable task of inspecting the pickets in a pouring rain. His mood was hardly a good one when he returned to the aides' tent, dripping wet, and threw back the flap.

Some wag called out, "Gentlemen, General Custer!" Custer cringed. He had told his fellow aides countless times that he was "determined to be a general before the war was over," and he took a lot of ribbing because of the boast. "How are you, General Custer?" another voice taunted. "You're looking well, General," called out a third.

"You may laugh, boys," Custer retorted. "Laugh as long as you please, but I *will* be a general yet, for all your chaff. You see if I don't, that's all."

The aides slapped their sides and roared with laughter. Custer looked ready to fight. His Monroe friend, Lieutenant Yates, came to his rescue.

"*Look on the table*," Yates told Custer.

There was a large official envelope addressed to "Brigadier General George A. Custer, U.S. Vols." Custer took one look and sank into a chair. He was afraid he might cry.[37]

It was a volunteer rank, of course—in the regular Army Custer remained a first lieutenant—but still, at twenty-three years of age, Custer was a brigadier general, responsible for the lives and successes of a brigade of cavalry. How had it been done? How could it be done?

First and foremost, there was Custer's record. Pleasonton, who had made the recommendation, had seen Custer in action and come to trust him. The man and the youth had a close relationship. Custer wrote later, "I do not believe a father could love his son more than Genl. Pleasonton loves me. He is as solicitous about me and my safety as a mother about her only child."[38] Pleasonton desperately needed to shake up the Cavalry Corps, which had not been doing well in its battles with Stuart, and he wanted fresh young men at the top. Politics played no role in Custer's remarkable promotion. Pleasonton was a Republican and Custer's intimate contacts with the McClellan Democrats hurt rather than helped him. Pleasonton simply wanted the hardest driving, most ambitious young officers to give his cavalry some spirit, and Custer was an obvious choice.

It should be recalled that the Civil War was fought by very young men, at all levels. Three out of every four soldie : in the Union Army were under thirty years of age, and half had not celebrated their twenty-fifth birthday.[39] At the start of the war the officers tended to be somewhat older, but as the battles became fiercer and the political appointees began to drop out, their places were taken by young West Pointers. In 1860 and 1861 the Academy graduated a total of one hundred twenty cadets; of this number, fourteen became general officers in the Union Army, three in the Confederate service. Custer was by no means the only "boy general" of the war, although at age twenty-three he was the youngest man in the history of United States Armed Forces to ever wear stars on his shoulders.

Custer took charge of the 2nd Brigade in Kilpatrick's 3rd Division of the Cavalry Corps. The 2nd Brigade included the 1st, 5th, 6th, and 7th Michigan Cavalry Regiments, along with a battery of artillery. The 5th Michigan was the regiment Custer had asked to command as a colonel, only to be turned down by Governor Blair —oh, sweet is revenge! Custer led his brigade recklessly and with great success in the Gettysburg campaign, gaining wide publicity and becoming something of a national pet. "The Boy General with his flowing yellow curls," a New York *Herald* correspondent called him.[40]

In September 1863 Custer led his brigade on a brilliant saber charge against some Confederate cannon at Brandy Station. He captured some of Jeb Stuart's artillery, in itself a glorious feat, and added to the glory by taking Stuart's headquarters, including the rebel general's dinner. In so doing, Custer had his horse shot from under him (one of a dozen horses killed under him in combat in the war). Pleasonton had seen it all, accompanied by Colonel Theodore Lyman, a Harvard graduate serving as an observer for General Meade. After the battle, Custer came galloping up to Pleasonton and Lyman. "His aspect though highly amusing," Lyman wrote, referring to Custer's outlandish costume, "is also pleasing, as he has a very merry blue eye, and a devil-may-care style. His first greeting to General Pleasonton, as he rode up, was: 'How are you, fifteen-days'-leave-of-absence? They have spoiled my boots but they didn't gain much there, for I stole 'em from a Reb.'" Custer stuck out his foot to show the boot leg torn by the shell that killed his horse. Pleasonton gave Custer his requested fifteen days' leave and added ten more.[41]

So Custer returned to Monroe in late September 1863, now a national hero with his picture in *Harper's Weekly*. Custer met Libbie at once, and after he explained that he had been carrying on with Fanny Fifield and other Monroe girls only to stop gossip about himself and Libbie, she accepted his proposal of marriage. Custer promised to ask Judge Bacon's consent, but could not muster the courage —he would rather charge a division of Stuart's cavalry. He returned to active duty without becoming formally engaged.

The correspondence that ensued between Custer, Judge Bacon, Libbie, and Nettie Humphrey (who still acted as go-between for Custer and Libbie) is a priceless collection, providing a day-by-day account of the difficulties involved in getting married for respectable people of that era. Custer took forever to screw up his courage and write the judge; the judge sent an evasive reply; Custer pressed the point; the judge eventually gave in. Then began a long correspondence between the betrothed, page after page of it. Much of the material appears in Marguerite Merington's loving memoir, *The Custer Story: The Life and Intimate Letters of General George A. Custer and His Wife Elizabeth*, so only a few examples need be quoted here.

Custer selling himself to the judge: "It is true that I have often committed errors of judgment, but as I grew older I learned the necessity of propriety. I am aware of your fear of intemperance, but surely my conduct for the past two years—during which I have not violated the solemn promise I made my sister, with God to witness, should dispel that fear. [As usual, Custer exaggerated; he had stopped drinking less than a year earlier.] . . . I left home when but sixteen, and have been surrounded with temptation, but I have always had a purpose in life."[42]

Custer selling himself to Libbie (via Nettie): "Often I think of the vast responsibility resting on me, of the many lives entrusted to my keeping . . . and to think that I am just leaving my boyhood makes the responsibility appear greater. This is not due to egotism, self-conceit. I try to make no unjust pretensions . . . I ask myself, 'Is it right?' Satisfied that it is so, I let nothing swerve me from my purpose."[43]

Custer claiming that he would do anything for Libbie, which in practice meant anything that would not interfere with his career (again to Nettie): "However much I might wish to add a star to the one I wear, yet would one word of disapproval from Libbie check my aspiration. Yet I do not anticipate that she would wish me to lose that laudable ambition to which I already owe so much."[44]

Libbie urging Custer to put off their wedding date (he kept pressing her to push it forward): "Ah, dear man, if I am worth having am I not worth waiting for? The very thought of marriage makes me tremble. Girls have so much fun. Marriage means trouble, and, never having had any . . . If you tease me I will go into a convent for a year. The very thought of leaving my home, my family, is painful to me. I implore you not even to mention it for at least a year."[45] . . . "Father accuses me of trifling, says 'You must not keep Armstrong waiting.' But neither you nor he can know what preparations are needed for such an Event, an Event it takes at least a year to prepare for."[46]

Libbie told her stepmother that she was afraid that if she gave in and agreed to an early marriage, she would always have to give in to Custer's whims. "No, No," Mrs. Bacon replied. "For I consented to hasten my own wedding because my former husband Mr. Pitts insisted on it. . . . And I always had my own way afterwards, in Everything!"[47] What she meant by "Everything," of course, was control of household arrangements, probably what Mr. Pitts wore, and possibly their social life. But then Libbie's ambition was limited, too—she wanted only security, an opportunity to run her loved one's private life, and a famous husband.

In Monroe, class and social lines were so closely kept that Libbie had not yet met Custer's family, even though now they lived only one block from the Bacon home. (Custer's mother and father had moved to Monroe to be with the Reeds; Custer helped support them on his general's salary.)

Libbie to Custer: "Now I am going to surprise you. I know your family by sight. I stood near them at the Lilliputian Bazaar. I think they knew me. I could have kissed your little sister, she was so considerate of her mother."[48] Libbie did meet Custer's parents before the marriage.

Libbie to Custer, describing herself: "My own faults are legion. I am susceptible to admiration. In church I saw a handsome young man looking at me, and I blushed furiously. Mother says I am the most sarcastic girl, and say the most *withering* things."[49]

Libbie thinking about what she was getting herself into—and what it meant—in a letter to Custer: "Blessings brighten as they take their flight. How I love my name Libbie BACON. Libbie B-A-C-O-N. Bacon. Libbie Bacon."[50] (Libbie had no luck in holding onto her own name. In the index to the innumerable Custer books, she always appears under the name, "Custer, Mrs. George Armstrong.")

And finally, Libbie telling Custer that in return for giving up her name, she expected to share his life with him: "I had rather live in a tent, outdoors with you than in a palace with another. There is no place I would not go to, gladly, live in, gladly, because . . . Because I love you."[51]

The wedding took place on February 9, 1864, at the First Presbyterian Church in Monroe. Custer wore his full-dress uniform and was surrounded by his aides, all resplendent. Libbie wore a hoop-skirted, mist-green wedding dress, trimmed with yellow cavalry braid. She had her dark hair parted, rolled over each ear, and coiled in a knot on her neck under a green-silk wedding veil.[52] There were hundreds of guests; some had to be turned away because the church was overflowing. It was said to be the most splendid wedding ever seen in Michigan.[53]

The couple spent their honeymoon visiting cities between Michigan and New York. They stopped off at West Point for a day. There Libbie learned that her husband could be just as jealous, protective, and possessive of her as her father. Custer was furious at the way she flirted with the cadets and because she had kissed one of the professors. Years later, Libbie described the aftermath: "In the train [going down to New York] I was amazed to see my blithe bridegroom turned into an incarnated thundercloud. 'But,' I tearfully protested, 'the professor who claimed the privilege of kissing the bride was a veritable Methuselah. And the cadets who showed me Lover's Walk were like school-boys with their shy ways and nice, clean, friendly faces . . .' Oh, I quite expected to be sent home to my parents, till I took courage to say, 'Well, you left me with them, Autie!' "⁵⁴

From West Point the couple went to New York, then on to Washington. Custer received orders to report to his brigade. He told Libbie to stay in a boardinghouse in the capital. Not on your life! Libbie was going with him to the front, no matter what he said. Autie caved in. Libbie went to be with him at his winter headquarters five miles south of Brandy Station, Virginia. For better or for worse, she was in the Army now. Custer made her as comfortable as he could in a tent, introduced her to his black cook, his other servants, his dogs and horses, and his fellow officers. Then he turned his attention back to making war.

CHAPTER ELEVEN

The Boy General and the Glorious War

"Fighting for fun is rare. Only such men as . . . Custer and some others, attacked whenever they got a chance, and of their own accord." Colonel Theodore Lyman, member of General Meade's staff

"In the excitement of a charge, or in the enthusiasm of approaching victory, there is a sense of pleasure which no one should attempt to underrate." General Horace Porter, aide-de-camp to General Grant

Custer rode to the top of his profession over the backs of his fallen soldiers. As a general, Custer had one basic instinct, to charge the enemy wherever he might be, no matter how strong his position or numbers. Throughout his military career he indulged that instinct whenever he faced opposition. Neither a thinker nor a planner, Custer scorned maneuvering, reconnaissance, and all other subtleties of warfare. He was a good, if often reckless, small-unit combat commander, no more and no less. But his charges, although by no means always successful, made him a favorite of the national press and one of the superstars of the day. He and Libbie came to rank high on the Washington social list of sought-after couples.

Gleefully accepting every risk himself, Custer personally earned his reputation as the most daring, gallant, courageous, and successful Union cavalry general of the war, but the real price for his reputation was the lives of the hundreds of men who fell following his flag. Most Civil War generals were remarkably spendthrift about their men's lives, of course, and Custer can hardly be censured for emulating older and presumably wiser generals. Of the tens of thousands of men who died in combat in the war, possibly as many as half lost their lives in vain. Lee's charges at Malvern Hill and Gettysburg, Burnside's at Fredericksburg, Grant's at Vicksburg, and many others left the dead strewn everywhere for no discernible military gain. The

Sioux would never have followed men who led such bloody, futile assaults, but the Americans made heroes out of these generals—and the higher a general's losses, it seemed, the greater the hero he became. Of all the division commanders in the war (Custer became a major general in September 1864, and at that time took command of the 3rd Cavalry Division, Army of the Potomac), Custer was the most famous.

He almost certainly suffered the highest losses. At Gettysburg in July 1863, where he had a brigade of approximately 1,700 men under his command, he lost 481 in killed, wounded, and missing. He personally led the 1st Michigan Cavalry regiment, about 400 strong, in a saber charge against an entire enemy division. The charge did halt a Confederate advance, although that probably could have been done with less bloodshed by placing his men in a defensive position and throwing up breastworks. As Custer did the job, however, he lost 86 men in a few brief moments. But he also drew attention to himself and received high praise from his superiors for his boldness and willingness to seize the initiative.[1] The previous Army of the Potomac commander, General Hooker, had supposedly once complained that his cavalry would not fight and that he had never seen a dead cavalryman. Custer gave him plenty to look at.

In the Wilderness campaign of May 1864, Custer lost more than a third of his brigade (98 killed, 330 wounded, 348 missing, a total of 776 casualties in a force of 1,700).[2] Again, however, it must be pointed out that he was only doing what all the other generals were also doing, only he was doing it better. After General Ulysses S. Grant took command of the Union Armies in early March 1864, the sole idea the Union Army had was to kill as many Confederates as possible, no matter what the cost to the North. It was a strategy of annihilation, if annihilation can be called a strategy.[3]

Custer was only a small cog in Grant's killing machine. But Union generalship was at a low point during most of the Civil War, which provided an ideal opportunity for Custer, whose limited skills and talents were well suited to Grant's purpose. As the Army of the Potomac heavily outnumbered Lee's force, Grant wanted action, all the time, all across the front. Custer was one of those who gave it to him.

Custer was lucky to become a general officer when he did. By the time he took over his brigade and even more after he became a division commander, the Confederate cavalry was worn out, run-down, badly outnumbered, and absolutely incapable of meeting the Union cavalry on even terms. Custer's opponents in his most successful battles were poorly equipped in weapons and horses, exhausted, half starved, suffering the agonies of dysentery and other enervating diseases, while Custer's men, newly conscripted and in good health, had fresh, strong mounts, repeating rifles, and plenty of artillery and infantry to support them. Still, the rebel units he defeated were veteran outfits, fighting desperately under proven leaders, so Custer did not have every advantage. Even in the last campaign, around Appomattox, the Confederate cavalry put 377 men out of commission in Custer's division of 4,800. That loss cannot be regarded as excessive, however, for in return Custer captured thousands of prisoners and stopped Lee's flight to the West, forcing Lee to call off his retreat and surrender the Army of Northern Virginia.[4]

Only at Appomattox, however, did Custer get a decent return on the investment of his men's lives. One reads his battle reports today (and those of other generals) with a sense of wonderment. Heavy casualties were almost a point of pride with the Union generals, something to brag about, as they proved that the general had not shirked his duty, that he was willing, nay anxious, to get out there and fight. One hundred killed, three hundred wounded, two hundred missing, for no conceivable military advantage, but what did it matter, as long as a superior officer saw the charge or the newspapers reported on it? The reality behind the figures escapes us today, but it was there—farm boys without an arm or a leg, dragging out their existence, unable to work or support themselves or their families, men whose minds as well as their bodies were permanently scarred, young wives who never saw their husbands again, teen-age boys whose lives were cut short. The Union cause was about as just as men are ever likely to find in any war, certainly more noble and inspiring than most, but the price the North paid for victory was far higher than it should have been. And clearly, Custer was one of the leading spendthrifts.

Of course, he never saw it that way. To lead men in combat in the manner Custer did, he had to be able to ignore the horrors of war, and he did. Custer's eyes were blind to the field hospitals after a battle, with their stacks of amputated arms and legs. All he saw were the backs of his retreating enemies, never the dead cavalrymen lying around him.

Custer wallowed in romanticism. As with so many nineteenth-century romantics, he was unmoved by the deaths of thousands but tremendously affected by the suffering of one. During the Wilderness campaign he wrote Libbie: "One of my men of the 5th Mich. was shot in the heart by a sharp-shooter, and fell in a position as still exposed to enemy fire. He was even then in the death-struggle, but I could not bear the thought of his being struck again, so rushed forward, and picking him up, bore him to a place of safety. As I turned a sharp-shooter fired at me—the ball glanced, stunning me for a few moments."[5]

In the fall of 1863, after a cavalry skirmish on the Rappahannock River (which Custer with his usual enthusiasm pronounced "the greatest cavalry battle ever witnessed on this continent"), Custer wrote home: "Oh, could you but have seen some of the charges that were made! While thinking of them I cannot but exclaim 'Glorious War!' "[6]

It *was* a "glorious war" for Custer, but what of his men? How did he get them to follow him into the teeth of Confederate artillery or on a charge against rebel infantry lined up behind a stone wall? It is a crucial question, for nowhere is the contrast between white man and red more marked than in this area. White soldiers followed their leaders into near-certain death, something Indian warriors would never do. Indeed, it might almost be said that a major distinction between civilization and savagery is that the civilized give far more power (and fame) to their leaders than the savage would even dream possible. Civilized men obey their leaders, while savages do not. Discipline is what makes an army—and civilization.

Custer's men were disciplined, of course. Still, it seems incredible that he could get thousands of Michigan boys to follow him in a charge against an obviously impregnable position. But they did. One reason was that Custer identified with his men. He praised them at every opportunity, always in the grandiloquent style of the age and with the added ingredient of Custer's own enthusiasm. He and his staff worked hard at getting top-quality horses and arms for the men and saw to it that they were well fed and quartered whenever possible. Further, both with his brigade and his division, Custer created an atmosphere of closeness, even uniqueness, in a conscious attempt to make his outfits into one big happy family. In October 1863, after returning to his brigade following a leave, Custer wrote home, "I feel that here, surrounded by my little band of heroes, I am loved and respected."[7]

If Custer was the head of the family, his staff was the wife, taking care of the details of housekeeping. He picked his staff carefully, for he wanted a happy, close-knit group around his headquarters. He had begun by persuading General Pleasonton to give him Lieutenant Yates, his Monroe friend, as an aide, and for the next dozen years, Yates would serve on his staff. For adjutant, Custer got Nettie

Humphrey's suitor, Lieutenant Jacob Greene. For inspector general, quartermaster, commissary officer, ordnance officer, ambulance officer, and the other posts on his staff, Custer picked men of proven competence who also happened to be friends. They all admired Custer enormously, although none quite so extravagantly as Chaplain Theodore Holmes, who told Custer in March 1865, "I cannot express my gratefulness to the Almighty that He should have made you such a General and such a man."[8]

Custer's favorite aide was his younger brother Tom, who had enlisted as a private in 1864 and quickly received a commission, thanks to his older brother's influence. Tom joined his brother's staff in November 1864. Nepotism was common in the Union Army; General Philip Sheridan's brother served on his staff, Lincoln's son was on Grant's staff, and so on. Tom did not have a cushy job. Although when they were alone the two Custer officers tussled like the youths they were, in public they maintained a stiff formality. And, as Tom put it, "If anyone thinks it is a soft thing to be a commanding officer's brother he misses his guess."[9]

Tom idolized his older brother and emulated him in all things, most especially in risk taking. Custer described Tom's heroism at one of the battles in the Appomattox campaign: "Tom led the assault upon the enemy's breastworks, mounted, was first to leap his horse over the works on top of the enemy while they were pouring a volley of musketry into our ranks. Tom seized the rebel colors and demanded their surrender. The colorbearer shot him through face and neck, intending to shoot him through the head. So close the muzzle Tom's face was spotted with burnt powder. He retained the colors with one hand, while with the other he drew his revolver and shot the rebel dead. . . . With blood pouring from his wound he asked that someone might take the flag while he continued with the assaulting column." Custer had to put Tom under arrest in order to get him to go to the rear and see a surgeon. For his actions that day, Tom Custer received the Congressional Medal of Honor. Custer remarked that it was Tom, not he, who should be the commanding general.[10]

Custer's household staff also consisted of Custer worshipers. To do the cooking, he hired a runaway slave named Eliza, who said that she "jined up with the Ginnel" to try "this freedom business." A cadaverous waif named Johnnie Cisco, who had adopted Custer with the prescience of a stray dog, helped care for his horses and did errands. The drummer boy Joseph Fought deserted his outfit at every opportunity to be with Custer. In addition, Custer surrounded himself with dogs, goats, a pet squirrel, and a raccoon that slept with him at night, the animal's head on the pillow next to Custer. To complete his happiness, Libbie lived with him whenever he was in permanent camp, and she added to the atmosphere around headquarters. When Tom Custer joined the staff, Libbie wrote a friend that "he adds much to our family circle—for as such I consider the staff."[11]

Tom gave Libbie a second nickname. After a raid in the Shenandoah Valley, Custer and Tom returned to camp brimming with funny stories, of which the best was about a Dutchman who refused to allow the Union soldiers to use his house for a field headquarters, because "the Old Lady was agin it." From then on, Tom and Custer started calling Libbie their "Old Lady," especially whenever she disapproved of something they wanted to do. The name stuck for the rest of her married life, and Libbie always claimed to enjoy it.[12]

Custer's hand-picked and molded staff was an important factor in his successful leadership, but there was more involved in his rise to fame. His own flamboyance helped his men identify with him. He dressed and acted in such a way as to make certain that he stood out from the crowd, that he would always be the center of attention. Most enlisted men respond positively to the eccentric commander (if he is professionally competent and fair with them) and Custer's were no exception. Joseph Fought described Custer's uniform: "He wore a velveteen jacket with five gold loops on each sleeve, and a sailor shirt with a very large collar. . . . The shirt was dark blue, and with it he wore a conspicuous red tie—top boots, a soft hat, Confederate, that he had picked up on the field, and his hair was long and in curls almost to his shoulders."[13] The bright red tie turned out to be the best touch of all. First the staff, then the field officers, and finally the enlisted men all took to wearing red neckerchiefs around their necks, and the red tie became the proud distinguishing mark of the 3rd Cavalry Division.

A Michigan captain who met Custer for the first time at Gettysburg was surprised by the general's extreme youth, his blue eyes, girlish complexion, and the curls on his shoulders. Noticing Custer's brilliant red tie, dashing black hat with a gold star pinning up the right side, and gold spurs on high-topped boots, the captain thought Custer must be a courier or an aide, surely not a commanding general.[14]

In combat Custer was an inspiring sight. Usually out front deliberately exposing himself to enemy fire, and always at the head of the column when engaegd in a saber charge, waving his hat, pointing with his sword toward the enemy, shouting encouragement to the men, he was as close to being the perfect cavalryman as the Civil War produced. Monaghan describes Custer on the march: "Surrounded by his red-necktied staff, Armstrong trotted along the road, restless as a game animal, popping his whip on his boot, whistling a tune to the accompanying band, his sharp nose turning watchfully from side to side with quick jerks that flipped his long hair."[15] In that romantic age, who could help but love him?

Confederate Major General Joseph B. Kershaw, who fought against Custer at Appomattox, told of meeting Custer on the last day of the war: "The sun had gone down, peaceful evening settled on the scene of recently contending armies, when a cavalcade rode up briskly. A spare, lithe, sinewy figure; bright, dark, quick-moving blue eyes; florid complexion, light, wavy curls, high cheek-bones, firm-set teeth—a jaunty close-fitting cavalry jacket, large top-boots, Spanish spurs, golden aiguillettes, a serviceable sabre . . . a quick nervous movement, an air telling of the habit of command—announced the redoubtable Custer."[16]

Custer backed his appearance with performance. He embraced the time-honored advice to all combat leaders: never send your men to do something you wouldn't do yourself. To begin with, Custer always rode with his men. In camp he lived like a king, but on a raid or campaign he ate what the enlisted men ate, slept less than they did, and pushed himself harder. In March 1865 he told Libbie about one experience: "Last night I slept on the ground by the roadside, the rain coming down in torrents, our wagons several miles in the rear. Nothing to eat since daylight. My only protection was the fine rubber poncho given me by Captain Lyon. For pillow I had a stick laid across two parallel rails. Before I got the rails I slept a little, then woke to find myself in a puddle about two inches deep. Later I slept soundly. When the wagons came and I told Eliza about it she said, 'Oh, I 'spect you wanted Miss Libbie with you . . . and she just as willing, and she'd have said, "Oh, isn't this nice!" ' "[17]

In the Union Army, Custer's endurance was legendary. One observer wrote, "On the eve of the surrender . . . in one of those last strenuous days I came upon General Custer, sitting on a log, upright, a cup of coffee in his hand, sound asleep."[18]

Custer's bravery was equally legendary and a source of pride and inspiration for his men. At Gettysburg he attacked a division with a squadron, without reconnaissance. "I'll lead you, boys," Custer called out as soon as he spied the huge enemy force blocking his path. "Come on!" The charge utterly failed, but he was cited for gallantry.[19] On the third day at Gettysburg, Custer rode to the head of his brigade. "Come on, you Wolverines!" he shouted, his voice clear and defiant as a bugle. Those who fought behind Custer testify to the magic of that call. He rode four lengths ahead of his men and headed straight for the enemy, under Major General Wade Hampton, who was simultaneously charging the Union lines with his division. An officer far off to one side heard the two lines meet. The sound reminded him of the roaring crash when a woodsman felled a great tree. In leading the charge, Custer was disobeying a direct order (a practice that would soon become a habit), and he left dead Michigan boys everywhere, but he was pleased. "I challenge the annals of warfare to produce a more brilliant or successful charge of a cavalry," he wrote in his report on the engagement.[20]

At Brandy Station in the fall of 1863, Custer was surrounded (he was also surprised on three occasions and surrounded on two others). Riding ahead of the 5th Michigan, deployed in columns of squadrons, Custer stood up in his stirrups and shouted, "Boys of Michigan. There are some people between *us* and home: I'm going home, who else goes?" He ordered the band to strike up "Yankee Doodle" (Custer had the band with him always; it played stirring marches for his charges). Tossing his hat aside with a dramatic gesture, he drew his sword and rode back and forth at the head of the regiment, mad with battle ecstasy. "You should have heard the cheers they sent up," Custer wrote. "I gave the command 'Forward!' And I never expect to see a prettier sight. I frequently turned in my saddle to see the glittering sabers advance in the sunlight . . . After advancing a short distance I gave the word 'Charge!'—and away we went, whooping and yelling like so many demons."[21]

Sad to relate, the charge was not a model of cavalry in action. An unseen ditch caused horses and men to pile up in an impossible mêlée. Custer lost his horse, then another; finally he got the men re-formed and managed to cut his way through to safety.[22]

On May 11, 1864, at Yellow Tavern, Custer's men were getting pounded by Jeb Stuart's artillery. Custer dashed over to Major General Wesley Merritt, a fellow West Pointer who commanded the division Custer then served in. "Merritt," Custer said, "I'm going to charge that battery."

"Go in, General," Merritt responded. "I will give you all the support in my power."

Just then the two young generals saw Phil Sheridan riding up (Sheridan had replaced Pleasonton as head of the Cavalry Corps after Grant took command in March 1864). Custer hurried off to start the action while Sheridan was watching but before Sheridan could countermand the order to charge. At the head of eighteen hundred cavalrymen, their red neckties bright in the sun, with the band playing "Yankee Doodle," Custer galloped into the Confederate lines, then through their defensive works, onto their artillery. His brigade captured two guns and a hundred prisoners; best of all, Jeb Stuart had been mortally wounded and Sheridan had seen the whole thing. He sent his congratulations to Custer and soon thereafter made Custer a major general, with a division to command.[23]

In his first battle experience as a division commander, in October 1864, in the Shenandoah Valley, Custer was pitted against Tom Rosser, a close friend at the Academy and now a major general of Confederate cavalry. Spreading his regiments to his right and left in line of battle, Custer rode toward the enemy, his staff and billowing flags beside him. He halted his aides in a prominent position and rode forward alone. Tom Rosser had to know who he was up against. Custer reined in his horse, lifted his broad-brimmed hat, and bowed. Then he charged, with overwhelming numbers. The Union troops sent Rosser's men running; Custer chased them for ten miles in what was called "the Woodstock Races." He took six cannon, Rosser's supply train, ambulances, and headquarters wagons. Next day Custer appeared before his men dressed in Rosser's uniform, which was far too large for Custer. He wrote a note to Tom asking him to have his tailor make the tails shorter next time.[24]

Custer was a newspaperman's delight. Sketches of him in action appeared in the popular magazines of the day, while reporters outdid each other in singing his praises. "Custer, young as he is, displayed judgment worthy of a Napoleon," the New York *Times* wrote of his actions at Cedar Creek, Virginia, later in October 1864. At the outset of the spring campaign of 1865, E. A. Paul, the *Times*'s war correspondent, attached himself to Custer's division, telling his editors that was the best place to be to get news.[25] Paul was a Custer worshiper, enthusiastically so. In March 1865 he reported in the *Times* on a Custer raid: "General Custer deserves the credit for planning and executing one of the most brilliant and successful fights in this or any other war."[26] Such attention greatly pleased Custer's men and added to the luster of being a member of Custer's outfit.

Custer knew how to get publicity for himself and his men. He did his best to appear modest (with some success) and made it a rule to always praise his outfit, never himself, although he knew full well that honors for his division were honors for him and vice versa. His men felt the same way. On the eve of the presidential election of 1864, when the Lincoln Administration needed all the encouraging publicity about the progress of the war that it could get, Custer rode into Washington with rebel flags taken in the Shenandoah Valley, to present to the War Department. He also brought along the soldiers who had actually captured the flags. His timing was perfect. Together, Custer and his men rode a street omnibus up Pennsylvania Avenue, a rebel flag flying from each window. The press reported, "Washington has not had many such sensations. The soldiers in the city were jubilant . . . and some of the old soldiers would kiss Custer's hand." At the presentation, in Secretary of War Edwin Stanton's office, Lincoln's cabinet officers and other high officials "all flocked round" Custer "and were as proud of him as if he were their own flesh and blood."[27]

Custer made a little speech explaining how each flag was captured and pointing out the soldier who had taken it. At the conclusion of the ceremony, Stanton turned to the crowd and, taking Custer's hand, declared, "General, a gallant officer always makes gallant soldiers." One of Custer's privates piped up, "The 3rd Division wouldn't be worth a cent if it wasn't for him!" A friendly press reported, "The embarrassed looks of General Custer, as he bowed his thanks, showed that his modesty was equal to his courage."[28]

As the incident illustrates, Custer was learning to soft-pedal his politics, indeed, to simply keep his mouth shut. Libbie did not know which of the presidential candidates he supported, Democrat McClellan or Republican Lincoln. Most probably he did not vote at all. His only expression of political views was in a letter to Libbie during the 1864 political campaign: "I believe that if the two parties, North and South, could come together the result would be a union closer than the old union ever was. But my doctrine has ever been that a soldier should not meddle in politics."[29] Personally loyal to McClellan, he would hardly turn on the Lincoln Administration, which had promoted him to two-star rank.

The flag-presentation incident also illustrates Custer's popularity with his men. In general, they seem to have responded enthusiastically to his leadership. There were exceptions, of course, and most of what we know about how Custer's men felt about him comes from his own writings, which makes it suspect, since Custer always saw what he wanted to see. Nevertheless, he was popular. After a fight near Front Royal, Virginia, Custer wrote Libbie: "Imagine my surprise . . . to see every man, every officer, take off cap and give

'Three Cheers for General Custer!' It is the first time I ever knew of such a demonstration except in the case of General McClellan."[30] More telling was an earlier petition signed by 370 soldiers in the 1st Michigan, asking to be transferred to Custer's division. Later, 102 boys in the 7th Michigan also petitioned to join his outfit.[31]

But for all of Custer's popularity, his dash, his willingness to take risks, his identification of himself with his men, and his other qualities, the question of how he got his men to do what they did remains unanswered. He once marched them one hundred miles in thirty hours,[32] and in battle they fell in droves behind him. How did he do it? The question becomes even more intriguing in light of information developed in World War II by military historian S. L. A. Marshall. The remarkable facts Marshall discovered cannot be disputed, so careful and thorough was he in developing them, but they have never been applied to the Civil War.

Marshall's key finding is nicely summed up in his own words: "The thing is simply this, that out of an average one hundred men along the line of fire during the period of an encounter, only fifteen men on the average would take any part with their weapons. This was true whether the action was spread over a day, or two days, or three." Marshall found that this was the case in both the Pacific and European theaters, in small unit actions as well as big battles. The majority of American soldiers in World War II would not fire their weapons at the enemy, under any circumstances; of those few who would fire, less than half would take careful aim—the remainder just shot in the general direction of the enemy.[33] Why wouldn't they fire? Marshall puts the heaviest stress on the Christian injunction against killing. Most American soldiers simply refuse to kill other human beings.

It could be argued that Civil War soldiers were different, although certainly the Christian tradition was at least as strong in the 1860s as it was eighty years later. It is true that Civil War enlisted men were more likely to be farm boys than the GIs of World War II and that probably more of them were hunters and thus accustomed to taking life. But World War II soldiers were far better trained and thus much more familiar with their weapons than their Civil War ancestors. The GI in World War II had spent hours on the firing line, becoming familiar with his weapon. The Civil War soldier was handed a muzzle-loading rifle and shoved into the front line. Since we cannot subject Civil War troops to the post-combat-group-critique (Marshall's method for determining what happened in a battle), we cannot tell if they did better or worse in terms of firing at the enemy than did the World War II GIs. Even if the Civil War soldiers did three times better, however, that would still mean that less than half of Custer's men were willing to fire at the enemy.

The point is that while Custer attracted hot-blooded young adventurers into his command and certainly brought out the fighting qualities in his men, the vast majority of the 3rd Division were ordinary American boys. They had no intention of playing the hero, they did not share Custer's battle lust, and their desire to close with the enemy was nil. In one way, however, Custer was better off than infantry officers in World War II—his troopers did not have to fire their weapons to be effective. It is even possible that he recognized that most enlisted men would not shoot; that may be one reason he preferred the saber to the revolver or even to the repeating rifle. A mounted trooper, galloping into enemy lines, his saber glistening in the sun, was a fearsome sight, even if he never struck at the enemy. Cavalrymen in a charge don't have to kill to get the job done.

But they did have to ride into danger, something few men do willingly, and even making allowance for the emotional fervor of a cavalry charge, which sweeps men up into a high tide of passion despite themselves and even infects the horses, Custer's ability to get his men to charge continues to defy explanation. Certainly Crazy Horse would have liked to have known how Custer did it. No one has ever questioned the bravery of the Sioux, which makes the contrast between the way they fought and the way Custer's men fought even more marked.

The crucial difference was discipline. Custer got his men to charge because he could threaten them with something worse than the risks of the battlefield if they did not.

In the Union Army, soldiers who failed to do their duty in combat were court-martialed and given such sentences as a year at hard labor with forfeiture of all pay or dishonorable discharges, with such tokens of disgrace as head shaving and drumming out in the presence of comrades. On occasion, branding the letter C for coward with a red-hot iron on the culprit's hip or cheek was part of the penalty.[84] Punishment for cowardice in the face of the enemy was only part of the disciplining process. Custer's soldiers were well disciplined when they entered the Army, at least in comparison to Crazy Horse's warriors, but the Army made the discipline stick in ways that went far beyond anything encountered in civilian life. Custer had a reputation for tough discipline, and although among Europeans the Union Army was regarded as not much more than an armed mob, in fact to have a reputation as a disciplinarian in that Army meant that Custer was very tough indeed.

In the Army of the Potomac cavalry, petty offenders were required to carry saddles about the camp or were confined to the guardhouse on bread and water or were made to do exhausting labor. In some instances, commanders had offenders tied to the wheels of artillery pieces. One soldier described the brutality of that penalty: "Feet and hands were firmly bound to the felloes [rims] of the wheel. If the soldier was to be punished moderately he was left bound in an upright position on the wheel for five or six hours. If the punishment was to be severe, the ponderous wheel was given a quarter turn . . . which changed the position of the man being punished from an upright to a horizontal one . . . I have frequently seen men faint while undergoing this punishment . . . To cry out, to beg for mercy, to protest ensured additional discomfort in the shape of a gag being tied into the suffering man's mouth . . . No man wanted to be tied up but once."[35]

No wonder Custer's men obeyed his orders. The only alternative was to desert, but desertion was an act of total desperation; if caught the punishment was death. Bell Wiley reports that between July 1 and November 30, 1863, in the Army of the Potomac, 592 men were tried for desertion (the Army's total strength averaged slightly over 100,000 for that period). Of these, 291 were found guilty, 80 were sentenced to death, and 21 were eventually shot. In all, the Union Army executed 267 Union soldiers during the war, one third of them for murder or rape, the others for desertion.[36]

Custer himself, incidentally, although he had abundant self-discipline, was far from being a model soldier. Like so many officers before and since, he regarded the Army's rules and regulations as something for enlisted men. He frequently disobeyed direct orders from superior officers in combat situations, but he got away with it by pleading that he possessed information not available to his commanding officer. On a number of occasions he was technically guilty of deserting his command in the face of the enemy. Libbie spent part of the winter of 1864–65 in Custer's Winchester camp, and, as she reported to her parents after he had gone on a raid, "Autie always gets back ahead of his command. When within five miles, he lets his black horse fly, and 'tis all the staff can do to keep up with him."[37] Had an enlisted man tried that stunt, he would have been drummed out of the Army.

As an officer, Custer had the entire power of the state behind him when he gave an order. The Army and the government would go to great lengths to protect an officer's position. When Private John Williams of the 1st New Jersey Cavalry told his lieutenant, "If I ever get liberated I will shoot you and all such sons of bitches," his bid for personal freedom earned him forfeiture of all pay, confinement in the penitentiary for the rest of his enlistment, and dishonorable discharge. An Ohio artilleryman who cursed and slapped his lieutenant was sentenced to be shot; President Lincoln commuted his sentence to forfeiture of all pay and imprisonment during the remainder of his enlistment.[38]

Examples could go on endlessly, but the point is clear enough. Drawing upon the experiences and traditions of European armies, the Union Army practically guaranteed Custer that his men would do what he told them to do, no questions asked. One result was that Custer never had to face the problems of leadership that Crazy Horse did. Another was that Custer got an exalted and unrealistic view of his own leadership abilities.

It was probably inevitable, however, that Custer would come to see himself as bigger and more important than he really was. Seldom, if ever, has so young a man been so overwhelmingly subjected to praise and even adulation. The wonder is not that the boy general became as conceited as he did, but rather that he retained any sense of balance and perspective at all. To be compared by the New York Times to Napoleon at twenty-four years of age is, after all, a heady experience, but that was only part of the silly praise heaped on Custer.

"I can't tell you what a place Autie has here in public opinion," Libbie wrote her parents from Washington in March 1864. "I thought that a Brigadier [General] would not be anything, but I find that mine is someone to be envied. It astonishes me to see the attention with which he is treated everywhere. One day at the House [of Representatives] he was invited to go on the floor, and the members came flocking round to be presented. . . . The President [Lincoln] knew all about him when Autie was presented to him, and talked to him about his graduation [from West Point].

"None of the other generals receive half the attention, and their arrivals are scarcely noticed in the papers. I am so amazed at his reputation that I cannot but write you about it. I wonder his head is not turned. Tho not disposed to put on airs I find it very agreeable to be the wife of a man so generally known and respected."[39]

At a reception the following month, Libbie shook hands with President Lincoln "and I felt quite satisfied and was passing on, but it seems I was to be honored by his Highness. At mention of my name he took my hand again very cordially and said, 'So this is the young woman whose husband goes into a charge with a whoop and a shout. Well, I'm told he won't do so any more.'" Libbie said yes, he would. "Oh," Lincoln responded, "then you want to be a widow, I see." They both laughed. "Was I not honored?" Libbie wrote. "I am quite a Lincoln girl now."[40]

On a visit to the capitol, Libbie found that "People in the hall stared and pointed me out to each other: 'Custer's wife . . . That's the wife of Custer!'" And Secretary Stanton solemnly informed her, "General Custer is writing lasting letters on the pages of his country's history."[41]

Libbie was even younger than her husband and no more prepared to handle the flattery than he was. She passed every hint of praise that she heard on to him, and there was a great deal of it, partly inspired by the fact that she was the prettiest girl in Washington and a great flirt. Senators, congressmen, Cabinet officers, and other high officials fell all over each other trying to get to her side at a ball or other social gathering. She loved hearing her Autie praised, so the men laid it on thick. She would then tell Autie of what had been said, always ending with a solemn warning to avoid vanity.

The adulation Custer received gave him a far different life experience from anything known to Crazy Horse. As a shirt-wearer, Crazy Horse had approximately the same status among Indian warriors as Custer did with white soldiers, but nothing remotely like the praise, honors, and privileges Custer enjoyed. White society fed the egos of its leaders, constantly telling them how great they were. White leaders stood out, above and beyond ordinary folk. In the most notable cases, such as Custer's, they became heroes. Lesser leaders and the public fawned upon them, politicians flocked around them in the hope of catching some of their glory, and the newspapers reported on their every move.

One result was that the heroes came to objectify themselves, to confuse their public image with reality. Their "careers" came to be something beyond themselves, something "out there" to be encouraged, bolstered, or extended. In the summer of 1864, for the first time, Custer began writing about "my career" and enlisting the aid of others to help him advance it. Libbie, who lived in a fashionable boardinghouse in Washington when Custer was on campaign, was a great help. She told her parents of meeting Speaker of the House Schuyler Colfax at a White House reception. Colfax said, "I have been wishing to be presented to this lady, but am disappointed she is a Mrs.!" Libbie smiled, took his arm, and chatted away. At the capitol a month later, she reported to her husband, she "met Speaker Colfax and Oh he said lovely things about you." Two weeks later Colfax began to push Custer for a promotion, prompting Custer to write, "Mr. Colfax's note was certainly complimentary and it affords me great pleasure that so able and deservedly honored a man should be at all interested in my career."[42]

Obviously Libbie was moving that career along; in so doing, she was following the stern injunction of Judge Bacon, who wrote his daughter in June 1864, "Be calm, submissive and composed is the wish and prayer of your Father."[43] Libbie accepted her role; as she wrote Custer, "I cannot love as I do without my life blending with yours. I would not lose my individuality, but would be, as a wife should be, part of her husband, a life within a life. I never was an admirer of a submissive wife, but I wish to look to my husband as superior in judgment and experience and to be guided by him in all things."[44]

She meant what she said. During the Wilderness campaign, Custer wrote Libbie to say that he was surprised and pained to learn that she had not called upon Mrs. Francis William Kellogg, wife of an influential congressman from Michigan. Representative Kellogg, Custer told Libbie, "feels the omission deeply. . . . I should rather you had failed to call on any other person in Washington. I really feel quite badly about it. For my sake please be good and do so, won't you?" Libbie did not want to go. "Scarcely anybody here likes Mr K," she told Custer. "Some say he is dishonest and licentious."[45] But she hid her feelings and did as she was told. Through the remainder of the war, Libbie spent much of her social time with the Kelloggs.

Libbie knew how to use influence, too, as a letter to her father in October 1864 illustrates: "Mr. Kellogg has just returned from the front. He wants to go to Monroe and deliver a speech telling them what a man General Custer is. Now, Father, do have some of your friends invite Mr. K. to do this. But don't let anybody know you did so. For when he praises Autie they might think us proud. We have a right to be, but not to be 'set up.'"[46]

Another result of being a hero was that Custer found himself in intense competition with others who aspired to that degree of celebrity, especially his classmates who had also become boy generals. West Pointers did all they could to protect each other from outsiders, older graduates helped junior Academy-trained officers get ahead, but at the top the West Point Protective Association was ineffective and it was every man for himself. Throughout his life Custer retained warm feelings for his fellow West Pointers who had gone over to the Confederacy, partly because he was never in direct competition with them, but came to despise those few West Pointers of his age who vied with him for position and status. The two major culprits for Custer were Judson Kilpatrick and James Harrison Wilson, who graduated one and two classes, respectively, ahead of Custer.

Custer's problem with Kilpatrick began early. For one thing, Little Kil became a division commander when Custer took over his brigade, and Custer had to fight under Kil's orders. For another, the two youths seem to have shared a girlfriend in the summer before Custer got married, and they evidently quarreled over her.[47] But the major factor was professional jealousy. They fought each other over honors after successful battles and blamed each other when something went wrong. Custer claimed that a thrashing he had taken from the Confederates in the fall of 1863 was all Kilpatrick's fault.[48]

Shortly thereafter Custer toyed with the idea of going to the Western theater, where he would be free of Kilpatrick and more likely to be able to operate on his own. He hesitated, however, because "in leaving I should leave those with whom I have what reputation I now have," while "were I to go West . . . I should have to have success unmarred for a considerable time, to establish myself." But there was an advantage not to be overlooked: in the West, he would serve under Major General George Thomas, who "is Colonel of my regiment in the regular army, and would give me every opportunity to acquire distinction." On the other hand (Custer was forever making a list of plusses and minuses before coming to a decision), Thomas "could scarcely do more for me than Genl. Pleasonton."[49]

Custer wavered for a month. He possibly recognized that going West would cost him in publicity, for he could never draw as much attention to himself in Georgia as he could in Virginia. In any event, what mattered most to him was his relationship to Kilpatrick, and that settled the issue. "I heard that Kilpatrick is to be made Major-General and ordered West," he wrote home. "I am pleased because he is my senior. Had I been promoted and he not, his friends in Washington and in Congress would have attempted to defeat the confirmation. If he does not go West, I will." Kilpatrick went, and Custer stayed.[50]

Custer rode over to Kilpatrick's headquarters for a farewell dinner Little Kil was throwing. "Fellow officers," Monaghan writes, "jealous of his [Kilpatrick's] bravery, yet hating the brisk brutality with which he could order others to their deaths, drank to his health and sang his praises. This was the army Custer knew so well."[51]

Custer was even more jealous of Wilson than he was of Kilpatrick, possibly because Wilson was the best officer of the three, certainly because Wilson was General Grant's pet and Grant had made him a division commander when Custer wore only one star. Grant had picked Wilson to help him prepare a report on the Vicksburg campaign. A lucky Army pet, Custer called Wilson. The jealousy burned bright in large measure because Custer was identified with McClellan, whose star had disappeared, while Wilson had hitched himself to Grant, whose star was ascending.

Custer blamed one of his defeats on Wilson. After a battle in which he lost 480 men, Custer wrote Libbie: "Wilson proved him 'lf an imbecile and nearly ruined the corps by his blunders. Genl. S! .i-dan sent for me to rescue him." Afterward, Custer reported, "one of Genl. Sheridan's highest staff officers said, 'Custer saved the Cavalry Corps,' and Genl. Sheridan told Col. Alger 'Custer is the ablest man in the Cavalry Corps.'" Typically, Custer added, "This is for you only, my little one. I would not write this to anyone but you. You may repeat it to our own people in Monroe . . ."[52] In later correspondence, Custer referred to Wilson as "that upstart and imbecile," and even had the gall to call Wilson "an inexperienced and untrained officer."[53]

Wilson had no use for Custer, either. After Yellow Tavern, where Custer's men mortally wounded Jeb Stuart, Wilson was incensed. He felt that the press was giving credit to Custer that belonged to him.[54] Still, when Wilson went to the western theater for the last year of the war, he stifled his feelings and requested Custer's services; as ambitious as Little Kil or Custer himself, Wilson wanted the best cavalryman as his chief subordinate. Custer refused, but Wilson could be forgiving; at the end of a distinguished career, he wrote in his memoirs of those glorious Civil War days, "The modest man is not always the best soldier. . . . Some of the best, while shamelessly sounding their own praises, were brave, dashing, and enterprising to an unusual degree."[55]

When Wilson went to the western theater, Sheridan gave his division to Custer; this was the beginning of a Custer-Sheridan relationship which became mutually dependent and lasted to the end of Custer's life. Sheridan was a bullheaded little man, given to intense rages, mad with battle lust during an engagement, quick to censure and slow to forgive, bursting with energy, forever demanding the impossible of his men. He was a perfect superior for Custer and the two generals got on famously.

Custer usually had good relations with his superiors—it was his equals who gave him fits. After the Shenandoah Valley campaign of late 1864, General Merritt officially objected to the praise Custer received in the press. Merritt said Custer was claiming honors that rightfully belonged to his division, specifically, that Custer had told newspaper correspondents that his men had captured guns actually taken by Merritt's division. Custer demanded a board of inquiry to determine who actually took the guns.[56] And so it went, throughout the Civil War. The ambitious boy generals squabbled with each other like the immature men they were.

That they did so can hardly be wondered at, considering the stakes. They all knew that when the war ended they would lose their handsome general officer's pay and revert to their regular Army rank, lieutenant in most cases. Only one or two could become regular Army colonels, and they would be the ones with the most distinguished records. Custer was as careless with money as he was with the claimed number of enemy he had met and overcome; he had not saved a penny—could not, really, with Libbie buying $100 dresses to attend her social functions and his tastes were as expensive as Libbie's. Beyond the money, the rewards that white society gave its famous leaders were much desired, and no one enjoyed them more than Custer and Libbie.

Libbie especially cashed in on Custer's fame and on her own beauty. She became the leading light of the Washington social scene in the last year of the war. She knew all the right people, went to all the right balls, wore the right clothes, and charmed every man she met. "Such style as we go in!" she told her parents in the spring of 1864 when she was living in camp with Custer. "Most army officers' wives have to ride in ambulances, but my General has a carriage with silver harness that he captured last summer, and two magnificent matched horses. We have an escort of four or six soldiers riding behind."

When Custer left the Shenandoah Valley for the start of the Wilderness campaign in May 1864, he and Libbie rode the train to Washington in a special car assigned to General Grant, who was just then coming to the capital to take command of the Union Armies. The twenty-three-year-old Libbie had a gay time chatting about Army life with General Grant. "I was the only lady, and he was so considerate he went out on the platform to smoke his cigar, fearing it might be disagreeable to me, till Autie begged him to return. He smoked 5 on the journey."[57]

From Washington Libbie wrote Custer daily letters recounting her social triumphs. She went to a "hop" with Senator Zachariah Chandler of Michigan and found him to be "an old goosey idiot." His wife was away and he was drunk "and O, so silly."[58]

In August 1864 Congressman Kellogg arranged a trip for high-ranking officers' wives to City Point, Virginia, the great supply depot for the Union Army besieging Petersburg. Libbie wanted to go. "Mr K was here to-night," Libbie wrote Custer. "Very cordial. Too much so, for I avoided his attempt to kiss me by moving aside and offering him a chair. Any lady can get that man to do anything. But all I want is that he shall take me on that trip, to you." (Custer's jealousy and possessiveness faded when Libbie was flirting with someone who could advance his career.) Kellogg asked Libbie to come along. The ladies rode down on the presidential yacht, the *River Queen.* At City Point, General Sheridan brought his band on board, and the party danced and laughed far into the night, while the guns boomed like thunder at the Confederate defensive works around Petersburg.

Slim and beautiful, Libbie was much in demand as a dancing partner. "You should have seen Genl. Sheridan dance; it was too funny," Libbie wrote a friend. "He had never danced until this summer and he enters into it with his whole soul. He is short and so bright— He is like Genl. Pleasonton except that Genl. P is quieter and has exquisite taste."[59]

The following March, Libbie went to Lincoln's Inaugural Ball, escorted by Senator Chandler. "I promenaded with him and he introduced me to some of the distinguished people—Admiral Farragut the most so; he is right jolly and unaffected. The ladies' costumes were superb;—velvets, silks, diamonds dazzled my eyes."[60]

The climax to the Civil War for the two glamorous Custers was almost unbelievably romantic and glorious. Custer was in the van of Grant's entire force in the chase to cut Lee off from his supplies. His division brought the retreat to a halt and thereby forced Lee to surrender. Custer personally received Lee's white flag (which he kept and later gave to Libbie). While Grant and Lee discussed the terms, Custer tussled with Gimlet Lea and Fitzhugh Lee, Confederate generals. They rolled around on the ground, laughing like schoolboys. Sheridan took the small table on which the terms were written, then gave it to Custer to give to Libbie. Custer rode away laughing and balancing the table on his head. With the gift, Sheridan sent Libbie a note: "My dear Madam—I respectfully present to you the small writing-table on which the conditions of the surrender of the Confederate Army of Northern Virginia were written by Lt. General Grant—and permit me to say, Madam, that there is scarcely an individual in our service who has contributed more to bring this about than your very gallant husband."[61]

Libbie, meanwhile, had accompanied Senator Chandler and other members of Congress on a journey to Richmond. Somehow she managed to get the Confederate Executive Mansion assigned to her for her quarters, and that night she slept in Jefferson Davis' bed. Custer, without bothering to wait for permission for a furlough, rode all night to get to her side. As he bounded into Davis' room, he quipped, "So, after all these years of fighting, you beat me into Richmond."[62]

On May 23, 1865, the Army of the Potomac held its Grand Review in Washington. It was a spectacular parade down Pennsylvania Avenue—and Custer led the whole thing. At Fifteenth Street the van of the 3rd Cavalry Division turned around the Treasury Building and started toward the White House and the presidential reviewing stand. Some three hundred girls, all dressed in white, began to shower Custer with flowers and sing patriotic songs. He leaned over to catch a bouquet. At that moment, his horse bolted.

Custer's horse carried him at a full gallop down the parade route, lined with thousands of spectators. At the presidential reviewing stand, Custer tried to give a saber salute but lost the sword and his hat too. Then, displaying marvelous horsemanship, he brought his frantic beast under control, right in front of the President. Cheers went up. A newspaper reporter wrote, "In the sunshine his locks unskeined, stream a foot behind him . . . It was like the charge of a Sioux chieftain."[63]

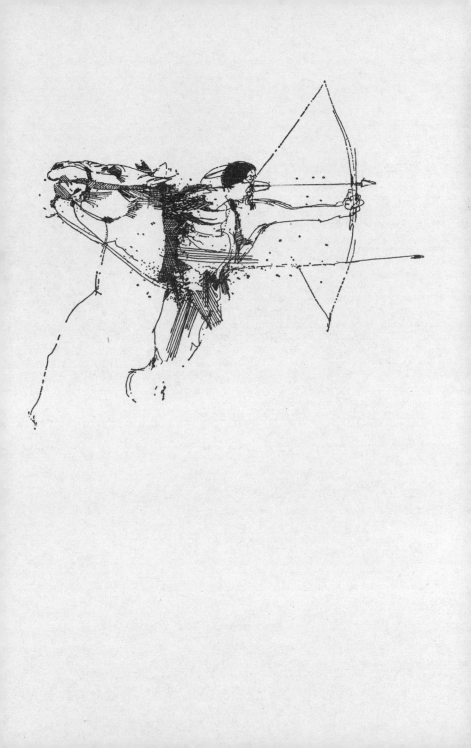

Crazy Horse and Custer as Young Warriors

Custer did not look like a Sioux chieftain, no matter what the newspapers said, nor did he think or act like one. To describe him as such, even though he rather liked the description and saved the clipping, only revealed how little the Americans understood Indians. The phrase also indicated the gap between reality and romance in Custer's Civil War. It was pure romance to describe him as anything other than what he was, a young soldier who had led a series of charges, most of them successful and all of them bloody, against an outgunned and outnumbered opponent. By one Sioux test— bravery—Custer had covered himself with honors, but by another Sioux test—bringing home the loot with minimal losses—he was a miserable failure. For the Sioux, reality was life, not fame and power. For Custer, the reverse was true—fame and power were real, while life was cheap. "To promotion—or death!" always continued to be his watchword.

Crazy Horse, judged by white standards, was also a failure. His bravery was there for all to see and earned him his promotion to shirt-wearer. But he could not hold his fighting men together, could not make them act as a unit, could not inspire them to carry out a sustained campaign, could not obey orders himself.

It was bravery, above and beyond all other qualities, that Custer and Crazy Horse had in common. Each man was an outstanding warrior in war-mad societies. Thousands upon thousands of Custer's fellow whites had as much opportunity as he did to demonstrate their courage, just as all of Crazy Horse's associates had countless opportunities to show that they equaled him in bravery. But no white warrior, save his younger brother, Tom, could outdo Custer, just as no Indian warrior, save his younger brother, Little Hawk, could outdo Crazy Horse. And for both white and red societies, no masculine virtue was more admired than bravery. To survive, both societies felt they had to have men willing to put their lives on the line. For men who were willing to do so, no reward was too great, even though there were vast differences in the way each society honored its heroes.

Beyond their bravery, Custer and Crazy Horse were individualists, each standing out from the crowd in his separate way. Custer wore outlandish uniforms, let his hair fall in long, flowing golden locks across his shoulders, surrounded himself with pet animals and admirers, and in general did all he could to draw attention to himself. Crazy Horse's individualism pushed him in an opposite direction—he wore a single feather in his hair when going into battle, rather than a war bonnet. Custer's vast energy set him apart from most of his fellows; the Sioux distinguished Crazy Horse from other warriors because of Crazy Horse's quietness and introspection. Both men lived in societies in which drugs, especially alcohol, were widely used, but neither Custer nor Crazy Horse drank. Most of all, of course, each man stood out in battle as a great risk taker.

Custer's men went into battle in uniform, perhaps partly so that they could not be told apart. Any single soldier, it was hoped, would act just as would any other soldier in the same situation. Crazy Horse's men went into battle in the most extreme, individualistic manner possible, painting weird figures all over their bodies and their horses, so that they would stand out as individuals; an observer, they hoped, would be able to pick them out from among a hundred other warriors. Both Custer and Crazy Horse led by example, but Custer knew that his men would follow because they were disciplined, while Crazy Horse could only hope that his example would suffice to get the warriors to follow him.

But if Custer's society gave him invaluable aid in his leadership role by making certain that his men would do what he told them to do, it also thrust upon him an enormous responsibility. At age twenty-four, he was in command of a body of troops that outnumbered the warrior population of the entire Sioux tribe. He was responsible for their well-being, their organization, their battle tactics, their behavior, and much else. Crazy Horse had no comparable experience; as a young warrior promoted to shirt-wearer he assumed certain duties and made stringent vows, but he was not responsible for his warriors to any degree as Custer was for his soldiers.

Which was one reason Custer got more rewards than Crazy Horse. Both men fought for prestige, although in Crazy Horse's case it was prestige for its own sake, while in Custer's case the prestige led to additional power. Until the very end Crazy Horse never had real power over other men. Nor did his great prestige lead to additional material comforts; indeed, in accord with his sworn oath, Crazy

Horse had less of those than did the majority of his tribesmen. Custer's camp life was much more comfortable than that of his soldiers, but his real goals were power and fame. He wanted power for its own sake, not to use to bring about some reform or revolution, as Custer was in perfect agreement with the prevailing structure and ideology of his society and had no intention of changing it in any way.

Least of all did Custer want any change in the status of women. Like Crazy Horse, he regarded women as inferior, mentally as well as physically, and treated them almost as a species of property. Custer expected Libbie to devote her life, her time, her talents, and her energy to him, just as Crazy Horse would have expected the same from Black Buffalo Woman had things worked out between them. This attitude, of course, was precisely that held by both red and white societies and by the women themselves. Both societies were sufficiently flexible and realistic to allow such young men as Custer and Crazy Horse, each from a modest background, to assume leadership roles, but made absolutely no provision for any woman of any age or ability to assume any institutionalized leadership position. A patriarchy is a patriarchy, whether civilized or primitive, and patriarchs think alike about women.

But not about other things. Custer embraced ambition; Crazy Horse hardly knew ambition at all. Custer worked hard, driving himself to get ahead. He never really relaxed—even his entertainment had to have a purpose beyond the immediate moment. Thus, in his social life, he chose his friends on the basis of what they could do for him, not how well he got along with them, much less liked them. Crazy Horse hardly worked at all—as Claude Lévi-Strauss points out, the notion that savages have to struggle for their existence is not altogether correct. Certainly Crazy Horse and his friends did not have to struggle—two or three successful buffalo hunts a year, plus some occasional sporadic hunting for other game, was sufficient to feed and shelter the tribe. Three or four war parties per year might set out from Crazy Horse's village, although by no means would he go on every expedition. The rest of the time Crazy Horse, like other Sioux men, enjoyed himself, courting girls, talking, sleeping, telling stories.

There were obvious vast differences between the two men, but at bottom they shared a fundamental trait. Both were aggressive. As a hunter Crazy Horse killed for a living; as a soldier, so did Custer. Both found the rush of hot, fresh blood exciting. Both would take great personal risks to make the blood flow. Crazy Horse was most completely himself when he rode pell-mell into a herd of buffalo, shooting his arrows clear through the beasts, or when he charged the enemy alone and unaided, or when during a winter hunt he drove a herd of elk out of a valley and into the deep drifts, then, on snowshoes, caught them and moved quickly from one elk to the next, cutting their throats as he proceeded, the bright red blood spurting out to cover him and the snow. Custer was most completely himself when on a hunt, or when he led his troops with a whoop and a shout on a charge into the heart of the enemy lines, cutting and thrusting with his saber, his horse falling beneath him, the band playing, and the newspaper correspondents watching. Neither man hated his enemy, nor did either man fight for a cause. They fought for honors and because their societies expected them to fight, and in Custer's case for personal power and fame. But the overriding reason they fought was that they enjoyed it. As a result, they both became heroes.

Part Three

CHAPTER THIRTEEN

Crazy Horse and the Fort Phil Kearny Battle

"With eighty men, I can ride through the entire Sioux nation."
                                        Captain William Fetterman

In the spring of 1866 the red-white crisis on the northern Great Plains began to move toward a climax. Crazy Horse, newly appointed as a shirt-wearer, faced the most significant challenge of his career as a military leader. He and his comrades were determined to keep the white man out of the Powder River country, which meant they had a defensive mission—to protect the boundaries of their hunting grounds. But because Crazy Horse and the Oglalas failed, in the summer of 1866, to prevent the whites from establishing a fort in the heart of their territory, they were on the defensive only for strategic purposes; in their tactics they necessarily assumed the offensive. Red Cloud provided the over-all leadership for the ensuing campaign, one of the most impressive in the annals of Indian warfare, while Crazy Horse served as one of his field commanders, directing the day-to-day tactics in dozens of skirmishes and fights. Crazy Horse was as successful in his role as Custer had been as a combat leader in the Civil War.

Also, as had been true in Custer's case, Crazy Horse was lucky in his opposition. The whites were divided on the question of how to carry out a campaign against the Sioux, indeed, on whether or not to even undertake a military campaign to clear the northern Plains of the troublesome red men. The United States was war-weary. People had had enough—enough of slaughter, of conscription, of war-encouraged corruption, of the cost of war, of war news generally. The Civil War Armies had been demobilized, the fighting strength of the nation dissipated. Of those few troops left, most were needed for occupation duty in the southern states.

The whites had turned their attention away from war and back to the real business of the nation: expansion. The South was defeated and demoralized, but the triumphant North was bursting its britches, full of swagger, ambitious plans, grandiose hopes. The two questions that had plagued the nation since its founding, slavery and the nature of the Union, had been settled on the field of battle. Now that the South had been reunited with the North, it was time to spread the American eagle over the whole continent, bringing the Far West into contact with the remainder of the nation by conquering the Great Plains and then crisscrossing them with railroads that would tie the Union together and complete the task begun in the Civil War.

Nowhere was the dynamic quality of post-Civil War America seen more clearly than in the various projects to span the Plains with continental railroads, nor did any other project so completely reflect the national purpose or so thoroughly capture the imagination of the American people. In the spring of 1866 the progress of the Kansas Pacific (which by then had reached Manhattan, Kansas, 115 miles from the Missouri), the Union Pacific (194 miles west of Omaha, at Fort Kearney, Nebraska), and the Central Pacific coming from California to meet the Union Pacific (tearing at the summit of the Sierra Nevada) were topics of daily discussion and achievements in which Americans took deep pride. The Army protected the railroad builders from marauding Indians, and the railroads had no better friends than the Army officers, especially Major General William Tecumseh Sherman, in St. Louis, in command of the Department of the Mississippi, a vast domain stretching from the Mississippi River to the crest of the Rocky Mountains.[1] "I hope the President and Secretary of War will continue, as hitherto, to befriend these roads as far as the law allows," Sherman wrote his superior, General Grant, in the spring of 1866. As for the Army, "it is our duty . . . to make the progress of construction of the great Pacific railways . . . as safe as possible."[2]

With good reason, Sherman feared that the Army would not be allowed to show that it could do to the Indians what it had done to the rebels. The Radical Republicans had inaugurated a peace policy for the Plains tribes, their idea being, as noted above, that it was cheaper to buy a way through the Plains than to fight a way through, and easier on the national consciousness. Putting the Sioux and other tribes on welfare certainly would have been cheaper, had it worked, but the government was miserly in its offers. Crazy Horse, Red Cloud, and the other Indians had no head for figures, but they could recognize a bad deal when they saw one. The government was offering $15,000 annually in annuities for a tribe of 5,000 or 6,000 people, hardly a sum sufficient to provide for their real necessities.

Each individual Sioux would get from his annuities less than he could secure from a trader for a single buffalo robe.[3]

Here was the real tragedy of the Plains wars. The peace-policy advocates, so much scorned by nearly every white Westerner at the time and by almost all historians who have written on red-white relations, were in fact victims of a governmental determination to cut taxes, lower expenditures, and balance the budget. A genuine offer to the Indians of nicely located, adequately supplied reservations, with sufficient annuities, would have attracted the bulk of Red Cloud's and Crazy Horse's warriors away from the Powder River country and out of the path of the advancing railroads. Expenditures of a quarter of a million dollars annually might have done the trick. Instead, the government tried to get by with $15,000 annually. And when that did not work, the Army had to spend millions subduing the hostiles. Red Cloud, Crazy Horse, and the other Indian leaders who were determined to resist white encroachment no matter how high the bribes went were the principal beneficiaries of the government's balanced budget, for it kept the Sioux moderates on their side.

Governmental blunders were constant. The route of the Union Pacific, which generally followed the Oregon Trail, had already been cleared of hostiles, while the Army was blasting a path through the central Plains for the Kansas Pacific. That left only the Powder River Sioux as obstacles to westward expansion, but in the spring of 1866 those Indians were bothering only the Crows. There were no white settlers in their area and the Northern Pacific was years away from entering their territory. It was true that they controlled the shortest route to the Montana mines, the Bozeman Trail, but they had been allowing whites to proceed along the trail just as they allowed emigrants to use the Holy Road years earlier. Miners on their way to Montana would give the Sioux some coffee and sugar, then go their way in peace. The Montana Historical Society has preserved a number of diaries of men who traveled the Bozeman Trail at this time, and they all indicate that there were relatively few difficulties with the Indians.[4] The United States Government had an obligation to protect its citizens, to be sure, but not when they did not require protection. It certainly had no obligation to provoke a crisis, but it did when it allowed the Army to carry through with plans to establish forts in the heart of Oglala Sioux territory.

The Army could be as stupid as the government. Badly understrength following the demobilization, the Army already had more tasks than it could handle. It was in no way prepared to send a sizable force into the Sioux country to cow or conquer the hostiles, nor was there any need to do so. Nevertheless, the Army did build the forts. Under the circumstances, it is difficult to avoid the conclusion that Grant, Sherman, and their associates wanted to deliberately provoke the Sioux into an all-out war, which the Army believed would lead to the extermination of the Sioux and thus a "final solution" to the Indian problem. Having conquered the Confederacy, the United States Army officers were full of optimism. They had, in short, made the classic military blunder of underestimating their enemy.

Sherman's policy in 1866 was based on his *idée fixe* that the initiative belonged to the Army. In the early summer of 1866, after starting minuscule forces on their way into the vast area of the Powder River country with orders to establish forts along the Bozeman Trail, Sherman wrote Grant's chief of staff, "All I ask is comparative quiet this year, for by next year we can have the new cavalry enlisted, equipped, and mounted, ready to go and visit these Indians where they live."[5] To make matters worse, Sherman assigned the command of the newly created "Mountain District" to a garrison officer with no experience in Indian warfare, Colonel Henry B. Carrington, and gave him a tiny force that consisted almost entirely of raw recruits.[6] Sherman evidently believed that the Indians would sit and watch while he established forts, reorganized the Army, raised new cavalry regiments for Indian warfare, and then attacked the Sioux in their villages at a time of his own choosing.

The campaign began in the spring of 1866, when Sherman started Carrington's column marching up the Holy Road toward the Powder River, while E. B. Taylor of the Indian Office called the Sioux to a council at Fort Laramie. Taylor was a leading advocate of the peace policy. By promising plenty of presents, including some arms and ammunition, he had induced the friendly chiefs to sign a treaty giving the whites the right to use the Bozeman Trail. Now he wanted to sign up the hostiles, so he sent runners to their camps to tell them that there was a rich store of presents awaiting them at Fort Laramie. Crazy Horse and most of the younger warriors did not want to go. They argued that the Oglalas and other tribes were living fat and had no need of the white man or his presents. But Red Cloud, the older chiefs, and Young Man Afraid decided it would do no harm to see what Taylor had to offer, the chief inducement being the possibility of getting arms and ammunition, always in desperately short supply among the Indians.

So Red Cloud and Young Man Afraid made the journey to Fort Laramie, leaving Crazy Horse and the warriors who were unwilling to consider compromise behind. When the delegation arrived at Fort Laramie, Red Cloud immediately demanded that Taylor explain to them, in detail, what the white men wanted. Taylor deliberately attempted to deceive them; he said nothing about the Army's building forts and declared that the whites wanted nothing new, only a legal right to use the old road, meaning the Bozeman Trail. He was upping the ante, too, offering $75,000 in yearly annuities, or about $10 per Indian, plus guns for hunting. The white travelers would not disturb the Indians' hunting grounds, Taylor promised, nor in any other way disrupt their way of life. All they wanted was free passage on the old road.

This was strong inducement indeed—guns and ammunition in return for simply touching the pen—and Red Cloud might have signed. But just at the critical moment, when he was wavering, a Brulé chief named Standing Elk came to Fort Laramie with the news that Colonel Carrington and his column of troops were a few miles away to the east. Standing Elk said that he had talked with Carrington, who casually informed him that the soldiers were marching to the Powder River, where they were going to build forts and guard the new road. The Brulé chief informed Carrington that "the fighting men in that country have not come to Laramie, and you will have to fight them." Standing Elk then rode on to Fort Laramie, where he told Red Cloud what had happened.

Wrapping his robe around him in a dramatic gesture, holding his head high, his eyes blazing, Red Cloud declared, "The Great Father sends us presents and wants us to sell him the road, but White Chief goes with soldiers to steal the road before Indians say Yes or No." He stormed out of the council tent, followed by Young Man Afraid and the other hostiles.[7]

That left Taylor and the friendlies. He got them all to sign up again, an unnoteworthy accomplishment if there ever was one, then telegraphed Washington, "Satisfactory treaty concluded with the Sioux. . . . Most cordial feeling prevails." He mentioned Red Cloud only in passing, saying he was an unimportant leader of a small group of malcontents. The government really believed it had peace on the Plains. Early that winter, on the eve of one of the worst defeats in the history of the U. S. Army, President Johnson assured the nation that the Sioux had "unconditionally submitted to our authority and manifested an earnest desire for a renewal of friendly

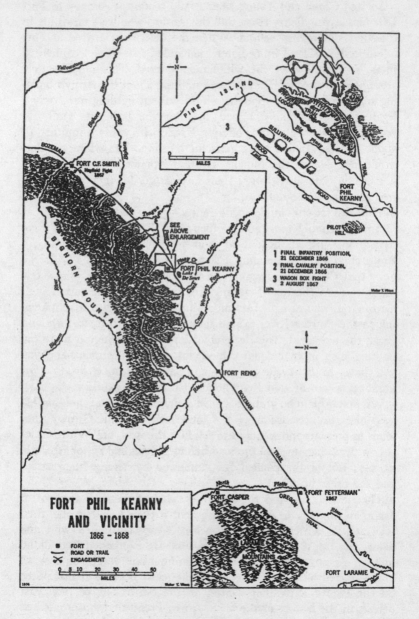

PINE ISLAND

BOZEMAN TRAIL

FORT C.F. SMITH
Mayfield Fight
1867

SEE ABOVE
ENLARGEMENT

FORT PHIL KEARNY
Lake De Smet

BIGHORN MOUNTAINS

Yellowstone River
Bighorn River
Little Bighorn River
Tongue River
Clear Creek

Crazy Woman's Fork
Powder River

FORT RENO

BOZEMAN TRAIL

1 FINAL INFANTRY POSITION,
  21 DECEMBER 1866
2 FINAL CAVALRY POSITION,
  21 DECEMBER 1866
3 WAGON BOX FIGHT
  2 AUGUST 1867

LODGE TRAIL
SULLIVANT HILLS
PINEY
BOZEMAN ROAD
WOOD ROAD
FORT PHIL KEARNY
PILOT HILL

North Platte River

FORT CASPER
OREGON TRAIL
FORT FETTERMAN
1867

LARAMIE MOUNTAINS

FORT LARAMIE
Lt. Laramie River

FORT PHIL KEARNY
AND VICINITY
1866 - 1868

■ FORT
✕ ROAD OR TRAIL
⚔ ENGAGEMENT

0 5 10   20   30   40   50
MILES

Walter T. Wisse

relations."⁸ The Army was more realistic but Sherman allowed Carrington to proceed under the impression that there would be no conflict on the Plains until the Army initiated it.

Carrington proceeded to Piney Creek, just northwest of Lake De Smet and about half-way between the Powder and Bighorn rivers, on the eastern foothills of the Bighorn Mountains. There he built Fort Phil Kearny. On August 3, 1866, he detached two of his seven infantry companies, sending them on north along the Bozeman Trail to establish Fort C. F. Smith on the Bighorn River near the point where the river cut its way out of the mountains. That left Carrington with 350 soldiers to guard a hundred miles of the Bozeman Trail.

Thus was the stage set for an epic tale. The leading actors were Red Cloud and Crazy Horse on the Indian side, Carrington and Captain William Fetterman on the white side. Crazy Horse was in his late twenties at this time, at the height of his powers. He was an intrepid but skillful and prudent combat leader; unlike Custer he had tasted defeat from his enemies, both red and white, and had a realistic idea of what could and could not be accomplished with the warriors who followed him. Red Cloud took no active part in the fighting that ensued (and he has been much criticized for this alleged shortcoming, but it should be obvious that middle-aged men—Red Cloud was forty-five years old—do not make combat leaders). Instead, he directed the strategy and, more important, was the organizing genius that made the whole campaign possible. Red Cloud had an extremely forceful personality. He was an adept politician in both inter- and intratribe dealings and with the possible exception of Spotted Tail he understood the whites better than any other important Indian on the Plains.

Like Red Cloud, Carrington was middle-aged and no fighter, but he was an able administrator, an excellent engineer, and a man of unusual talents (he read some portion of the Bible every morning in either Greek or Hebrew, and was the author of several histories of the American Revolution).⁹ He was the perfect choice for Sherman's fantasy—to establish forts along the Bozeman Trail and prepare them for an active offensive campaign the next year, to be directed by a more experienced combat soldier—but he was about the worst possible choice for the situation that actually existed. Captain Fetterman, in his midtwenties, was Carrington's principal tactical officer. He had established an outstanding combat record in the Civil War but had not enjoyed the breaks that had come to Custer and had consequently not risen in rank, a fact that preyed on his mind. He was determined to advance his reputation and could imagine no better tool for that purpose than the Sioux, whom he held in contempt. "With eighty men," he was often heard to say, he could "ride through the entire Sioux nation."[10] Like his opposite number, Crazy Horse, Fetterman was itching for a fight; unlike Crazy Horse, Fetterman knew next to nothing of his enemy. That simple fact gave Crazy Horse an enormous advantage.

Red Cloud also enjoyed an advantage over Carrington. The Indian leader was not only an executor of policy, but a maker of it as well. Carrington was an agent, doing what he was told, carrying out a policy set by men hundreds of miles from the scene. He did that part of his job superbly—Fort Phil Kearny was perhaps the most secure military establishment ever built during the Plains wars—but he could not begin to compete with Red Cloud as a strategic leader, nor could he convince his government to give him proper manpower or material support.

Red Cloud, Crazy Horse, and the other hostiles believed that a final struggle for control of the Powder River country was underway, that their existence as a nation was at stake, and they acted with great vigor and enthusiasm. Red Cloud assembled a large force of warriors and held it together for three full years of fighting. Even more impressive, it was an allied command, containing Oglalas, Miniconjous, some Hunkpapas, Sans Arcs and Brulés, along with northern Cheyennes and Arapahoes. After storming out of Fort Laramie, Red Cloud traveled throughout the northern Great Plains, carrying a war pipe and trying to convince all the Indians of the area that the time had come to put aside their endemic wars with each other and co-operate in an all-out offensive against the whites. He even went to his hereditary enemies the Crows, where the young warriors were willing to sign up but the old chiefs refused. (Red Cloud's attitude toward the Crows contrasts sharply with Carrington's. After the Crows refused Red Cloud's offer of an alliance, they went to Carrington and asked to be included in his force, but he scornfully turned them down.)[11]

Within a week of Carrington's establishment of Fort Phil Kearny, Red Cloud had established his own camp along the Powder River, from which place warriors went out each day to harass the travelers on the Bozeman Trail. Crazy Horse was one of Red Cloud's chief lieutenants. Together, they carried out what was virtually a three-year siege. In the first five months of fighting alone—from early August to mid-December 1866—the Indians killed 154 soldiers and travelers, wounded 20 more, and captured nearly 700 horses, cattle, and mules. They made 51 attacks on the fort itself during that time and did not allow a single wagon train to make it through without the loss of at least some of the emigrants. By the spring of 1867 they had brought all travel along the Bozeman Trail to a halt.[12]

It was warfare ideally suited to Crazy Horse's talents. He was active almost daily, usually working together with Hump, Little Hawk, their friend Lone Bear, and Young Man Afraid. Crazy Horse led war parties as far south and east as Fort Laramie, attacking wagon trains. Sometimes he would join Red Cloud on the ridges overlooking Fort Phil Kearny. Using smoke signals or mirror flashes, Crazy Horse and the other warriors co-ordinated their efforts, attacking any party of soldiers that dared to venture out of the fort. Carrington had located the fort on a grassy plateau, so the Indians could not approach it unseen, but he had to have wood for fuel and construction, and the nearest stand of pines was some five miles to the west, along the slopes of the Bighorn Mountains. Although Carrington provided a strong escort for the woodcutters, the Indians attacked at every opportunity, killing a soldier here, wounding another there, and generally adding to the depression within the fort.

So confident had Sherman been that the Indians would not resist the building of the fort that he had urged officers to bring their wives along, and most of them did. One of these women, Frances Grummond (who became a widow that winter and in 1871 married Carrington) described a typical attack. In September 1866 a group of miners set up camp outside the walls of the fort. They had lost two men getting as far as Fort Phil Kearny and decided to stay where they were; they would do their prospecting for gold in the Bighorn Mountains where they enjoyed the protection of the garrison. On the morning of September 19, Mrs. Grummond reported, "Quite a large body of Indians suddenly appeared at the summit of the hill in full warpaint, brandishing their spears, giving loud yells and lifting their blankets high in the air as they moved down in an attempted charge upon the miners' camp. Between one and two hundred Indians were scattered along the crest of that hill."[13] The Indians, perhaps led by Crazy Horse, attacked with spears and bow and arrow; the miners repulsed the attack with their carbines. After both sides suffered slight losses, the Indians broke off the engagement. Crazy Horse was much too wise to try to press home a charge against such well-armed opponents.

Carrington sent a small detachment in pursuit of the Indians, but as always it was no use. The Indians dropped out of sight as if by magic, a process that was repeated over and over. Carrington himself once made an attempt to lead a pursuit, chasing Crazy Horse all the way to the Tongue River in the hope of recovering some beef cattle the Indians had run off. Crazy Horse gleefully led him in the direction of Red Cloud's main camp, hoping to achieve a spontaneous ambush, but at the last minute Carrington realized what he was getting into and beat a hasty retreat.[14]

Throughout the fall of 1866 Carrington begged Sherman for more men, more arms, more ammunition, more supplies. He got virtually nothing, the authorities in Washington being certain that peace had come to the Plains and that Carrington was an alarmist who had only a small group of malcontents to deal with. While the garrison at Fort Phil Kearny suffered from the lack of nearly everything, Red Cloud's camps were bursting with provisions. Red Cloud even had sufficient ammunition for the few rifles his men possessed. He had a line of communication between Fort Laramie and his Powder River camp that surpassed Carrington's. Friendly Indians, mainly young Brulés, made a regular run between Fort Laramie and the hostile camp, bringing ammunition and other supplies with them; on the return trip they carried buffalo robes for which they found a ready market among the traders. Occasional hunting parties provided more meat than the hostiles could use. In every respect, in short, Red Cloud supported and equipped his army better than the government supported Carrington.[15] When winter came on, Red Cloud moved the allied camp to the base of the Bighorns, near the headwaters of the Tongue River, where he found shelter in the cold weather and from which he could send war parties out against Fort Phil Kearny on clear days.

Following one last big buffalo hunt, Red Cloud prepared to rub out the garrison. He now had over five hundred lodges of Indians gathered together, including a few Gros Ventres; the camp covered a forty-mile stretch of the Tongue Valley. There were smaller camps along the Powder River. In all, Red Cloud had a thousand or more warriors on active duty. For the final offensive, he called up his reserves—the young Brulés and Hang-Around-the-Forts who ordinarily spent the winter at or near the agencies, coming to the Powder River country only during the summer. But in December of 1866, Red Cloud had most of these youngsters with him, swelling the ranks of the hostiles by perhaps as many as a thousand additional warriors.

Crazy Horse and his fellow shirt-wearers knew that they could not hope to destroy the whites, despite a nearly six-to-one superiority, unless they could draw a portion of Carrington's command into the open. All the soldiers had single-shot rifles, while only a handful of warriors possessed firearms. But if a large number of soldiers could be lured into the open, where the Indians could fire volleys of arrows at them or overwhelm them by sheer numbers, using clubs and spears as the principal weapons, something significant could be accomplished. Accordingly, the shirt-wearers did not even bother to discuss attacking the fort; instead, they laid plans for a decoy party for the whites.[16]

On the morning of December 6 Crazy Horse joined Red Cloud and the shirt-wearers on Lodge Trail Ridge to watch the action. Behind them were about three hundred mounted warriors, while another large group of braves was over the ridge on the other side of the valley. Blanket wavings and mirror signals made it possible for the two groups to communicate. When all was ready, Red Cloud signaled for a force of about one hundred to attack the wood train (Carrington's Achilles' heel was his need for wood). Using captured binoculars, Red Cloud then turned to watch the fort to see what Carrington's reaction would be.

Carrington sent Captain Fetterman and forty cavalrymen to deal with the Indians attacking the wood train. Expecting the enemy to retreat to the north, along the western slope of Lodge Trail Ridge, Carrington then took forty mounted infantrymen around the Sullivant Hills in an attempt to ambush the hostiles. Neither side got what it wanted. Fetterman pursued the decoys just as Red Cloud wanted him to do, but before they had even arrived at Carrington's position the decoys turned to fight. They evidently believed that they could take care of Fetterman's command by themselves. The Indians across the valley from Crazy Horse, meanwhile, prematurely broke ranks and attacked Carrington's forty-man detachment. Both ambushes failed. After some lively hand-to-hand fighting, Fetterman and Carrington joined forces and retreated safely to the fort. They had lost two men killed and seven wounded; Indian losses were about the same.[17]

Fetterman returned to the fort fuming. He practically accused Carrington of cowardice (for sounding the retreat) and grumbled even more than usual about inept leadership. For weeks Fetterman had been turning the officers and men of the command against Carrington, second-guessing his decisions, wondering aloud when the Army would send a real soldier to take charge, demanding that Carrington take offensive action against the Indians. After December 6 such talk increased and became more vicious, but Carrington did nothing to stop it. His single foray against the enemy had risked almost a quarter of his troop strength (not to mention his own annihilation), and he became more determined than ever to avoid any further risks until reinforced in the spring.

Crazy Horse also fumed. He spoke to Hump and some of the shirt-wearers about it, hoping that they would speak up in front of the warriors, Crazy Horse not being an orator himself. Crazy Horse said the Indians would never get anywhere unless they could learn to hold their place in line and then act as a unit. Nothing would come of counting coup, he said, and most of all the decoys must learn to play their role properly. There had been too many of them on December 6 and there should be less next time. Then they would not be tempted to turn and fight on their own, but would bring the soldiers to a spot where all the warriors could get at them.[18] Red Cloud, meanwhile, had come to a more hopeful conclusion based on the lesson of the December 6 fight. He believed, from what he had seen, that his forces could overpower and destroy any force of soldiers Carrington might send out from the fort. He decided that on the first auspicious day after the full moon he would lay a great trap with two thousand warriors, make another feint at the wood train, draw out the soldiers, work the decoy trick, and kill all the pursuers.[19]

Red Cloud made his first attempt on December 19, but when Carrington sent a party out to relieve the wood train he put it under the command of his most cautious officer, with explicit orders not to pursue the Indians beyond Lodge Trail Ridge. Despite everything the decoys did, the soldiers would not follow, so there was no ambush that day. Red Cloud and his warriors made a temporary camp for the night, disappointed but still determined. The next day it snowed, so the Indians stayed in camp.

That night Fetterman and Captain Fred Brown called on Carrington, proposing that they lead an offensive expedition of fifty men to Red Cloud's main camp on the Tongue River, where they could destroy the village and thus raise the siege. Carrington told the two captains, with some heat, that he could not possibly spare fifty men for a hazardous expedition and in any event he had only forty-two serviceable horses. Brown muttered as he left that "he knew it was impossible, but that he just felt he could kill a dozen [Indians] himself." Within half a day, he would get his chance.[20]

While Carrington was dealing with his daredevil young officers, Red Cloud revised his plans. After some discussion, the shirt-wearers themselves decided to lead a small decoy party the next morning. There would be a separate attack on the wood train; when the soldiers rode out of the fort to chase away the attackers, the decoys would appear from behind Sullivant Hill and lure the pursuers into Peno Valley, beyond Lodge Trail Ridge. If Crazy Horse and the decoys could get the soldiers to follow that far, they would be out of view and beyond supporting distance from the fort.

Later that same night, December 20, the Miniconjous sent out a *winkte*, who was thought to have special powers, to see what their luck would be. Pulling a black cloth over his head, the *winkte* rode over a hill, zigzagging one way and another as he went, tooting on his whistle. Presently he rode back, came to where Red Cloud and the shirt-wearers had gathered, and said, "I have ten men, five in each hand; do you want them?" The leaders shook their heads; "No, we do not wish them. Look at all these people here. Do you think ten men are enough to go around?" The *winkte* rode away again. He soon returned, riding faster, swaying on his horse. "I have ten men in each hand," he gasped. "Twenty in all. Do you wish them?" Red Cloud said no, it was not enough. Again the *winkte* rode off; when he returned he said, "I have twenty in one hand and thirty in the other. The thirty are in the hand on the side toward which I am leaning." The shirt-wearers said it still wasn't enough. Without a word, the *winkte* rode off. On the fourth return he rode up fast and as his horse stopped, he fell off and struck the ground with both hands. "Answer me quickly," he said. "I have a hundred or more." All the warriors yelled their approval. That was what they wanted. Let the sun come up quickly—it was going to be a glorious day.[21]

December 21 dawned bright and cold. The mass of warriors deployed on each side of Peno Valley, but not until they had been harangued by Hump and others about holding their positions until the decoys, ten in all, gave the signal to attack. The Sioux graciously gave their allies, the Cheyennes, Arapahoes, and others, the sunny side of the valley ridge, while they took their places on the shaded, colder side. Red Cloud watched from a distance.

Two Arapahoes, two Cheyennes named Little Wolf and Wolf Left Hand, and Hump and Lone Bear joined the Sioux shirt-wearers American Horse, Young Man Afraid, He Dog, and Crazy Horse to form the decoy party. It was so cold that Crazy Horse did not strip for battle as he usually did, but instead kept his blanket belted around him. He led the decoy party into a little gulley, where it could not be seen from the fort and where the men could escape the biting wind, to wait for the attack on the wood train.

Almost as soon as the woodcutters reached the pine woods, a small group of Indians rode to the attack. Carrington had prepared a relief party of seventy-nine men, mixed infantry and cavalry, giv-

ing the command to the same cautious officer who had led the
pursuit on December 19. It was a wise choice, but just as the troops
were about to leave the fort Captain Fetterman caught Carrington's
arm and demanded that he be given command, as he was the senior
officer next to Carrington himself at the fort. Carrington acquiesced,
with obvious misgivings, as he gave Fetterman a cautious written
order: "Support the wood train. Relieve it and report to me. Do
not engage or pursue Indians at its expense. Under no circumstances
pursue over the ridge, that is, Lodge Trail Ridge." So worried was
Carrington about Fetterman, in fact, that he twice verbally repeated
the order not to pursue beyond Lodge Trail Ridge. As Fetterman
mounted up, Captain Brown appeared. He was scheduled to be
transferred in a few days, but he begged Carrington for "one more
chance to bring in the scalp of Red Cloud myself." When Carrington gave his permission, Fetterman had exactly the number of men
he said he needed to ride down the whole Sioux nation.[22]

When Fetterman emerged from the fort, Crazy Horse led the
decoy party out of hiding. From this point on it was Crazy Horse
versus Fetterman. Red Cloud and Carrington had done all they
could; victory would now belong to the side that had produced the
best combat leader.

As Fetterman swung his command to the left and started out to
relieve the wood train, Crazy Horse and the decoys popped up on
his right. Carrington fired a field artillery piece in their direction,
knocking one of the decoys from his horse. The others began whooping and yelling, running in all directions, zigzagging, looking as if
they were terrified. Red Cloud, meanwhile, signaled to the party attacking the wood train, and those Indians broke off their action
and began retreating in the general direction of Lodge Trail Ridge.
With all this happening in front of him in a matter of seconds,
Fetterman must have been confused. It was the critical moment
of the battle, Fetterman turning his head every which way wondering what to do. Crazy Horse seized the moment. He caught and
held Fetterman's attention, charging toward the eighty soldiers
alone, whooping and waving his blanket, giving the impression that
he was covering a retreat for the remainder of the decoy party. Fetterman decided to give chase. Instead of proceeding to his left toward the wood train, he struck out to the north, directly away from
the fort, following a path that would take him past the east slope of
the Sullivant Hills and onto Lodge Trail Ridge.

The ambush was working. Crazy Horse took one look at the advancing soldiers, checked his own pony, and turned back toward

Lodge Trail Ridge, using the old trick of pretending to beat the horse with one hand while actually holding it back with the other. Fetterman and his officers knew all about the decoy game, or thought they did, but Crazy Horse's performance was so realistic that they were convinced that finally, for once, they had caught a small group of Indians in the open and could give them the thrashing they deserved. If Fetterman thought at all about the wood train and the Indians who had attacked it, he evidently reasoned that they had already gotten away and he had better concentrate on the ten-man decoy party. After months of frustration, he would show Carrington what could be done by offensive tactics.

The decoys, with Crazy Horse in the rear, stayed just out of effective range of the soldiers' guns, a tantalizing target. Fetterman's command was about half infantry, half cavalry, so he moved forward slowly in order to keep his men together. The decoys, consequently, could not just ride off and hope for the soldiers to follow them into the ambush. They needed to maintain their distance, not getting so far ahead that Fetterman would give up and return to the fort, yet not falling back close enough to get shot. Several times Crazy Horse leaped off his horse, once pretending to tie his war rope closer, once to lift up a foot of the animal and shake his head disgustedly as if the horse had gone lame. He led the animal by the jaw bridle, running awkwardly. The other decoys, meanwhile, circled around him, as if to protect his retreat. When the distance between the decoys and the soldiers became too large, Crazy Horse sat down behind a bush and built a small fire. The other decoys yelled at him to get out of there, but he gestured that his horse was finished and indicated that he was giving up. Bullets began to zing over his head, kicking up puffs of dust and snow around him, the decoys reluctantly riding off and leaving him to his fate. At the last minute, when he was about to be overwhelmed, Crazy Horse jumped on his pony and rode off, whipping after the other decoys. He plunged down over the end of Lodge Trail Ridge toward Peno Valley, the soldiers following fast, Fetterman shouting at them to come on.

When Crazy Horse caught up with his fellow decoys he glanced over his shoulder, saw that all the soldiers had entered the valley behind Lodge Trail Ridge (about five miles from the fort), and felt his heart lift. It had worked! The warriors had remained hidden, the decoys had done their job, Fetterman had fallen for the oldest trick in Plains warfare, and the *winkte's* vision was about to come true. Crazy Horse divided the decoys and had them ride back and forth across each other's trail, the signal to the waiting warriors to attack. Some two thousand Cheyennes, Sioux, and Arapahoes came charging down on both sides of Peno Creek, hitting Fetterman's command on its front, rear, and both flanks. The sound of so many hoofs on the frozen ground made a noise like thunder.

Fetterman glanced in the direction he had come, but the bulk of the warriors were on his rear and he had no chance to retreat to the safety of the fort. He ordered his command to move to the right, up the slopes of a nearby hill—a difficult task at best because snow and ice made the going slippery. Arrows were flying everywhere— in the forty-minute battle the Indians fired forty thousand arrows— and the soldiers were looking for any shelter they could find. There were some boulders scattered about on the ground, and the infantry- men began to duck behind them. At this point Fetterman made his second major error—he allowed the cavalrymen to break loose from the infantry and lead their horses up the hill, where abundant rocks provided more protection. As a result, the cavalry watched while the infantrymen fought for their lives.

No one directed the Indian assault—it was every man for himself. First one, then two or three warriors rode through the infantry, counting coup and yelling at the top of their lungs. Eats Meat, a Miniconjou, tried it and fell. Then a Cheyenne rode into the in- fantry, only to be cut down. A young Oglala warrior charged through the smoke on foot toward a soldier who had just fallen with an arrow in his head. Grabbing the soldier's rifle, the warrior came dashing back, waving the weapon and shouting like a crazy man, "I have a gun! I have a gun!" All the while arrows flew through the air, so thick that the Oglalas were hitting Miniconjous, Chey- ennes were wounding Arapahoes. The Indians' heaviest losses that day came from their own fire.

But in less than twenty minutes the white infantry was wiped out. The Indians began to crawl up the hill in pursuit of the cavalry. The horse soldiers let their mounts loose, hoping that the Indians would chase the loose stock and leave them alone. Some of the war- riors took the bait, but most stuck to the business at hand. A few warriors remained mounted, but the majority were on foot, sneaking forward, using rocks for protection, talking to each other, shouting warnings to keep down. Occasionally an Indian would pop up and take careful aim; soldiers' heads appeared from behind the rocks as the white men tried to bring down the brave individual; the Indians would then fill the air with arrows. There was no need to save ammunition that day, as there were arrows lying all around, so the warriors only had to pick them up and keep firing. In a short time, less than fifteen minutes, the mass of warriors was close enough to the cavalry position to rush it.

"Be ready," the warriors called to each other. "Are you ready?" And others would call back, "We are ready." With a whoop they charged, clubbing to death any whites who were still alive. Captains Brown and Fetterman, at the last minute, placed their pistols against each other's temples, counted quickly to three, and fired. The battle was over.[23]

There was a temporary quiet on the battlefield. The Indians stared in wonderment at what they had done. Eighty-one soldiers lay dead before them, at a cost of ten Sioux, two Cheyennes, and one Arapaho, many of them victims of arrows. Most of the soldiers had been killed by arrows, too; only four of the eighty-one had been hit by bullets, an eloquent commentary on how many firearms the Indians possessed.

A dog belonging to one of the dead soldiers came running and barking out of the rocks. A Cheyenne warrior cried, "All are dead but the dog. Let him carry the news to the fort." But another warrior said, "No. Do not let even a dog get away," and he shot the animal through with an arrow.[24] The incident relieved the tension, and the warriors began screaming, dancing, lifting scalps, congratulating each other, working themselves into a frenzy. They stripped the soldiers, then mutilated the dead in every imaginable way. In his official report, Carrington described what they did: "Eyes torn out and laid on rocks; noses cut off; ears cut off; chins hewn off; teeth chopped out; joints of fingers, brains taken out and placed on rocks; entrails taken out and exposed; hands cut off; feet cut off; arms taken out from sockets; private parts severed and indecently placed on the person; eyes, ears, mouth, and arms penetrated with spearheads, sticks, and arrows; ribs slashed to separation with knives; skulls severed in every form, from chin to crown, muscles of calves, thighs, stomach, breast, back, arms and cheek taken out. Punctures upon every sensitive part of the body, even to the soles of the feet and palms of the hand."[25]

Whether Crazy Horse participated in this savage butchery or not is unknown. This was the first big victory the Indians had won against the soldiers, and certainly he was as worked up, as excited, as beside himself as his fellow warriors. Years of frustration and rage poured forth as the mutilations took place, coupled with the exultant feeling of triumph. An old white scout, Frank Grouard, however, claimed that Crazy Horse and Hump disappeared immediately after the battle, that they went off to search for their hard-luck friend Lone Bear, the warrior who was always getting wounded or having his galloping horse step into a prairie-dog hole. They eventually found him lying among the rocks, so badly wounded that he could not crawl out from the place where he had been hit. The blood from his wounds had already frozen. According to Grouard, Lone Bear "died in the arms of Crazy Horse while Hump stood by, weeping."[26]

That sounds terribly romantic, but it may be true, as it is known that Lone Bear died that day and that Hump and Crazy Horse stayed together throughout the fight. In any event, the bloody orgy was real enough. Cutting up the soldiers' bodies helped the Indians relieve their tension and made the victory more satisfying and complete. It was not a typical Indian action. In tribal warfare, the Sioux seldom got possession of their dead enemies' bodies, and certainly never in any numbers. Most Indian battles were running fights and, as previously mentioned, casualties hardly ever exceeded two or three on a side. Individual mutilation was common enough, but there was simply no opportunity to chop up bodies on a mass scale until the Fetterman fight. The orgy of December 21, 1866, revealed the Indians' savagery and their extreme hatred of white soldiers, who, after all, mutilated Indian bodies when they got hold of them.

About an hour after the battle, Captain R. Ten Eyck with sixty-seven men came out from Fort Phil Kearny to reinforce Fetterman. Ten Eyck stayed far away from the mass of Indians, contenting himself with watching them from a nearby hill. The warriors taunted the relief column, challenging it to come down into Peno Valley to fight, but Ten Eyck refused to accept the challenge. After an hour or so, the Indians rode off. A big storm was coming up; it was bitter cold; enough had been done. Ten Eyck's men later recovered the bodies of Fetterman's command.

Carrington feared an attack on the fort itself. He laid fuses into the powder supplies in the magazine, which he packed with ammunition, then surrounded the magazine with three rings of wagons. "We had ten women and several children with us," an officer inside the fort reported. "The colonel [Carrington] gave orders that as soon as the Indians made the expected attack, the women and children should enter the magazine, and the men should hold the fort as long as possible. When they could hold it no longer, they were to get behind the wagons that surrounded the magazine, and when the colonel saw that all was lost, he would himself blow up the magazine and take the lives of all, rather than allow the Indians to capture any of the inmates alive."[27]

No one inside the fort slept that night, but there was no attack. Whites had a notion that Indians would not fight at night because they feared dying in darkness would prevent them from getting to the Happy Hunting Grounds, but that was nonsense. Indians did not fight at night because the dew got their bowstrings wet and they could not fire. And, being expert weather predictors, they had felt the storm coming on and wanted to get to shelter. Perhaps most important, all the warriors, including Crazy Horse, were satisfied with what they had accomplished. They withdrew, leaving some scouts to make sure Carrington did not try to get out but making no effort themselves to get into the fort. It is remarkable but nonetheless true that these Indians, who could so horribly mutilate dead bodies, lacked a killer instinct. Custer never let a defeated opponent get away that easily.

CHAPTER FOURTEEN

Custer Comes to the Plains

> "Talk about regulars hunting Indians! They go out, and when night comes, they blow the bugle to let the Indians know that they are going to sleep. In the morning they blow the bugle to let the Indians know that they are going to get up. Between their bugle and their great trains, they manage to keep the redskins out of sight." *A Kansas settler*

> "I did not marry you for you to live in one house, me in another. One bed shall accommodate us both." *Custer to Libbie*

The Red Cloud-Crazy Horse victory at Fort Phil Kearny had a direct impact on Custer's life. It was the first time that anything Crazy Horse had done affected Custer, but from that point onward the two men were slowly, almost imperceptibly, drawn ever closer to each other and their final face-to-face encounter. From December 1866 to June 1876 Crazy Horse's activities influenced Custer's responses, while Custer's campaigns came to dominate Crazy Horse's plans and actions. Their careers became intertwined. Each man did what he had to do, sparing no one, least of all himself.

The influence of one upon the other began with the aftermath of the Fetterman disaster. The Army was shocked and outraged. "We must act with vindictive earnestness against the Sioux," said General Sherman, who was as responsible for the defeat as Fetterman, "even to their extermination, men, women, and children."[1] Western newspapers echoed the call, even accusing the Army of cowardice for not searching out and destroying the hostiles. Railroad and stagecoach companies sent lobbyists to Washington to urge Congress to allow the Army to go out and shoot all the red devils. It was in 1867, in response to these cries, that Custer got his first command on the Great Plains, where he would spend the bulk of the remainder of his life.

On the Plains, Custer and Libbie found happiness. They responded to the region as few couples before or since have done. Everything delighted them, from the majestic views to the smallest wild flower putting forth its first bloom on a warm spring day. Horses and riding became, if possible, even more central to their lives than they had been during the Civil War. They rode almost daily, for miles at a time, enjoying the freedom of the unfenced prairie. Custer became an avid, almost fanatic hunter, taking full advantage of the bountiful wild game. For the most part he enjoyed independent commands, which added to his and Libbie's sense of freedom. It was exactly the kind of life Custer wanted to lead, and he silently might have thanked Crazy Horse and the hostiles for making it possible. Certainly the Fetterman defeat and the Army's response to that disaster rescued Custer from a bad situation. The year and a half since the end of the war had not been a good time for him.

Custer's first postwar assignment was to accompany General Sheridan to Texas on an expedition that had three objectives: first, to force Confederate General Edmund Kirby-Smith and the last rebel force to surrender (which was accomplished on May 26, 1865, before Custer got to the scene); second, to provide an occupation force for Texas; third, as a show of force against French adventurers in Mexico. Indeed, Sheridan informed Custer that he might march into Mexico at the head of a volunteer division to drive Emperor Maximilian and his cohorts out of the country. Nothing came of this, so in the end Custer stayed in Texas solely as a conqueror imposing order on a defeated people.

Libbie went along, as did everyone else close to Custer whom he could persuade the Army to add to his party. Most of his Civil War staff accompanied him—George Yates, Tom Custer, and the others—as did his cook Eliza, his father (Custer got him on the payroll as a forager), his horses, and his pets (including a flock of turkeys he had acquired and a dozen or so dogs, some picked up along the way). Custer and Tom never lost their boyish impulsiveness and they played countless practical jokes on their father, on Libbie, on a steamboat captain, indeed on anyone unfortunate enough to come to their attention. The trip down the Ohio and Mississippi rivers went by quickly, marked by much laughter and rough good humor. In New Orleans the boy general and his dashing young wife enjoyed that delightful city to the full, indulging themselves at the famous restaurants, having their portraits painted, shopping, squandering money on dresses for Libbie (by the time she got back to civilization, a year later, the dresses were out of style and she never got to wear them), enjoying themselves.[2]

The party rode another steamboat up the Red River to Alexandria, Louisiana, where Custer took command of his volunteer division and prepared for the march into Texas. He cut his flowing locks—July in Louisiana is about as hot as any place on earth—but Libbie continued to wear her full outfit, with its floor-length, sweeping skirt.

While in Alexandria, Custer spoke out against slavery for the first time in his life. In the mansion where he was living, he wrote his father-in-law, "there is a young negro woman whose back bears the scars of five hundred lashes given at one time, for going beyond the limits of her master's plantation. If the War has attained nothing else it has placed America under a debt of gratitude for all time, for removal of this evil."[3] Nor did he find the Deep South as attractive as he had found Virginia. Neither did Libbie. "Everything here is so behind-hand," she wrote her parents. "'Ancestral Halls' and 'Parental Mansions' are nothing but old-style roomy houses, not so good as that of a Michigan farmer. . . . They need the advent of the thrifty ingenious Yankee."[4]

The march into Texas, in the middle of a Gulf Coast summer, must have been a trial for all concerned, but Custer was delighted to be on an active campaign again, and if her man was happy, Libbie was happy. Custer fixed up an ambulance for her to ride in, but the heat inside—and her own eagerness to see everything, do everything—gave her an excuse to travel horseback. She rode sidesaddle, despite a dress that was so heavily weighted at the hem that she could not lift it over her head unaided. Reveille came well before sunrise. Libbie, terrified that she might hold up the column, learned to make her morning toilet, dress, and be ready to mount up in seven minutes flat. During the midday break she and Custer found relief from the blazing sun under the southern pines, but even there they could not relax because of the ever-present poisonous snakes. More irritating, if less dangerous, were the chiggers. Libbie later described the ordeal: "They bury their heads under the skin, and when they are swollen with blood, it is almost impossible to extract them without leaving the head imbedded. This festers, and irritation is almost unbearable. If they see fit to locate on neck, face or arms, it is possible to outwit them in their progress; but they generally choose that unattainable spot between the shoulders, and the surgical operation of taking them out with a needle or knife-point, must devolve upon some one else."

Libbie wouldn't dream of halting the column so that she could remove a chigger; instead she endured the torment throughout the rides and had Custer remove the insects at night.[5]

As the column swung out of the Louisiana swamps and onto the Texas prairie, rabbits increased in size and number. Custer's hounds would take off after a startled rabbit, Custer would give a whoop and follow, and Libbie would give her horse a tap with her little switch and set off to join the adventure. One of the hounds would catch the rabbit, break its back with one bite, and bring it back toward the galloping couple. The dog would wag its tail, Custer would beam at the dog, and Libbie would beam at her man.[6]

"Horseback riding is one of our chief pleasures," Custer wrote home. "Libbie—I never saw her in better health—is now an expert horse-woman, so fearless she thinks nothing of mounting a girthless saddle on a strange horse. You should see her ride across these Texas prairies at such a gait that even some of the staff officers are left behind."[7] Libbie had only one complaint—she did not have enough room in her ambulance bed to kneel at night to say her prayers, but had to wait until she had crawled under the rough Army blanket. But even that difficulty was easily brushed aside, "since I had nothing to ask for, as I believed the best of everything on earth had already been given to me."[8]

At Hempstead, Texas, Custer went into semipermanent camp. Here Lieutenant Jacob Greene and his new bride, Nettie Humphrey, joined up. Nettie was Libbie's old friend from Monroe; Greene had served with Custer during the war and was glad to be back in the Army after failing in civilian life as an insurance salesman. Together with Tom, George Yates, and the other Custer hangers-on, they went on late-afternoon hunting parties, held dances, played jokes on each other, and generally did their best to enjoy the situation.

Custer needed all the relaxation he could get, for his problems were serious and never-ending. A mere twenty-five years of age, he had been given an assignment that would have taxed the statesmanship of a Lincoln. As senior military officer in Texas, he was expected to see to it that the freed men and women received fair treatment, that unsubdued rebels behaved themselves, that the rowdy frontiersmen obeyed the government, that the conquered rebels were punished, and that his own troops refrain from individual acts of lawlessness directed against the people they had so recently conquered. In addition, Custer was offered great temptation. Cotton had shot up in price during the war and was stored in great quantities throughout

Texas. Speculators offered him vast sums—$25,000 in one case—to allow them to sneak it out of the state and sell it in New Orleans. Custer was guilty of nepotism, of seeking political favors, and of enhancing his own exploits, but he was not a crook and he refused the bribes. Still, as Libbie pointed out, it was highly irresponsible for the government to place such a young man in such a demanding and tempting position.[9]

Custer's worst problems were with his own troops. The men in the cavalry division were Westerners, unused to the heavy discipline of the Army of the Potomac. In addition, they wanted to go home, not serve on occupation duty in Texas. One regiment, the 2nd Wisconsin Cavalry, staged a mutiny. A mob of enlisted men, with the help of several of their junior officers, attacked the regimental commander, demanding his resignation or his life. Custer put an end to the mutiny by arresting sixteen of the officers and reducing seventy-six noncommissioned officers to the ranks. Another problem was with troops who assailed civilians, pillaged their houses, insulted their women, and in general stole everything not nailed down. Custer adopted drastic measures to bring these marauders into line, including this order: "Every enlisted man committing depradations on the persons or property of citizens will have his head shaved, and, in addition, will receive twenty-five lashes on his back, well laid on." He was denounced by the Radical Republican press for "flogging men who had fought for their country, while favoring those who had turned traitor to it," but he stuck to his hard line.[10]

Desertion was another major concern. Civil War volunteers were no more anxious to sweat in Texas than they were to fight Crazy Horse in Wyoming, and they deserted in droves. Custer had at least one deserter shot, and although it evidently lowered the desertion rate, the action got him into further trouble. As reported in the northern press, here was Custer hobnobbing with former rebels, engaging in horse races and trades with former Confederate generals, enjoying the supposed luxuries of southern plantation living, and meanwhile flogging or shooting the brave boys who had saved the Union.

Custer's politics were not helping him any, either. His new-found opposition to slavery did not cause him to change his views about blacks in any significant way. "I am in favor of elevating the negro to the extent of his capacity and intelligence," he wrote, using the code words so common to nineteenth-century American racists, "and of our doing everything in our power to advance the race, . . . but I am opposed to making this advance by correspondingly debasing any portion of the white race. As to trusting the negro with the most sacred and responsible privilege—the right of suffrage—I should as soon think of elevating an Indian Chief to the Popedom of Rome."[11] As usual, Custer's political sentiments were derivative, a reflection of the commonplace judgments he heard daily from his southern friends. He hardly thought about what he was saying, and his impulsiveness, so necessary to his battlefield success, was beginning to damage his career. By taking the stand that he did he was placing himself in direct opposition to the most powerful political party in the country on the key political issue of the day, the freedman's right to vote.

Sheridan had recommended Custer for a permanent two-star rank in the regular Army, and throughout the second half of 1865 argued his case hard. But the Republicans controlling Congress were suspicious of pro-South officers, with good reason, as they were sabotaging national policy and undermining basic programs of elementary justice for freedmen and southern unionists. On January 31, 1866, Custer received the bad news—his volunteer commission had expired and he was reduced to his regular Army rank of captain in the 5th U. S. Cavalry and transferred to the east. He sold most of his horses, more than half of his dogs, disbanded his beloved staff, and started on the long road back to Monroe. He arrived in April, moved into Judge Bacon's house, received a thirty-day leave of absence, and began to think about the future.

The possibilities were glittering. Michigan Democrats, eager to have a war hero bear their party's standard, sought him out—would he be interested in political office? That was a path many of his fellow officers, including Judson Kilpatrick, had already trod. Custer put the politicians off, telling them he could not decide. There were also business possibilities—several firms figured Custer's name as vice president would be an asset and offered him a job, but he put them off too. Sitting in an office had no appeal to Custer. Much perplexed, he finally decided to go to Washington to see what Secretary of War Stanton, General Grant, or others of his war-time friends might have to offer. In order to save money he left Libbie in Monroe. He had been earning $8,000 a year as a major general, but now his salary was down to $2,000 a year and he and Libbie had no savings. Libbie, much put off by that fact, lamented the injustice of seeing her Autie go away as poor as when he left Monroe to go off to the Civil War.[12] She was learning that a man could fall as fast in America as he rose, but still she could hope. Custer may have been poor in money but he was rich in reputation, and that might prove to be worth something in postwar Washington.

Custer arrived in Washington in time to be caught up in the political tornado that left in its wake the Gilded Age of American politics. Everyone was on the make, it seemed, from President Andrew Johnson down to the lowest clerk or Army officer begging to retain his commission. And they all wanted Custer's support. He had by no means lost his position with the Radical Republicans, who wanted the war heroes on their side in the struggle for control of Reconstruction policy. Representative John A. Bingham of Ohio, who had appointed Custer to West Point and supported him throughout the war, and Senator Zachariah Chandler of Michigan, another leading Radical Republican, showered young Custer with attention. So did Secretary of War Stanton, another Radical soon to be at the center of a presidential impeachment struggle. When Custer first went to Stanton's office to inquire about possible future assignments, Stanton looked at him and declared, "Custer, stand up. I want to see you all over once more. It does me good to look at you again!" Custer asked for, and got, regular Army commissions for his brother Tom and for George Yates. "I tell you, Custer," Stanton said, "there is nothing in my power to grant I would not do, if you would ask me." Custer remarked that this was offering a great deal. Stanton replied, "Well, I mean it."[13]

But Custer's real friends were the McClellan Democrats, who also descended upon him, urging him to support President Andrew Johnson in the fight between the President and Congress over Reconstruction. Johnson's friends offered Custer a diplomatic post, possibly an ambassadorship, and he considered accepting. Eventually, Custer turned it down because it would mean resigning his commission. That commission he regarded as his most valuable possession, an attitude reinforced by the number of ex-volunteer officers he met hanging around Washington hoping for regular Army appointments. And, as had happened in Michigan, Democratic politicians beguiled him with political possibilities—he could be a representative from Michigan, they said, or a senator or governor. "Political combinations," he wrote Libbie. "I dare not write all that goes on underhand . . . I never knew political excitement to run so high. Even the ladies are excited and engaged in these matters."[14]

Custer put off the political offers, just as he toyed with and then turned down an opportunity to take a position in the Mexican Army at $10,000 per year. But he could not help discussing politics daily as he made the social rounds in Washington, where he still was much sought after. He had not taken open sides in the controversies agitating Washington, but he naturally drifted closer to the Democrats, as the major issue separating them and the President from the Radicals in Congress was civil rights. He did not believe that blacks were the equal of whites and he did not want them to have legal equality. Further, like Johnson, he wanted the South brought back into the Union immediately, with no strings attached. "My confidence in the strength of the Constitution is increasing daily," he wrote Libbie, "while Andy [Johnson] is as firm and upright as a tombstone."[15]

Late in March 1866 Custer went to New York, where he met with more McClellan Democrats and dined at the Manhattan Club. "Oh, these New York people are so kind to me," he told Libbie. They offered him attractive business positions and continued to whisper in his ear about his bright political future. Custer was again tempted by a business career, naturally enough, as he had expensive tastes and was broke. "I would like to become wealthy in order to make my permanent home here," he wrote Libbie from New York. McClellan's friends took him driving through Central Park behind the finest horses he had ever seen. He visited Wall Street, and the Brokers' Board adjourned to give him three cheers. At a breakfast arranged for him, Custer met the historian George Bancroft, the poet William Cullen Bryant, and other celebrities, experiences all very heady for a twenty-six-year-old Army captain making $2,000 a year.[16]

Back in Washington, Custer dined with Chief Justice Salmon P. Chase at his home, while Senator Chandler took Custer to meet his family. Custer testified before a Congressional Reconstruction committee about conditions in Texas—his dim view of the prospects for the freed blacks did not endear him to the Radicals. Nor did a public statement he made about the necessity of returning to former Confederates their rights, including the right to vote and hold office.[17]

In May 1866 Libbie's father, Judge Bacon, died. After settling his estate, which left her with a modest income, Libbie joined Custer in Washington. In July Custer received an appointment as lieutenant colonel in the 7th U. S. Cavalry, one of the new regiments being formed to fight the Indian wars. He had hoped for something better and continued to hope, but meanwhile accepted the position as second-in-command of the 7th Cavalry (in the event, the commander was always on detached duty, so Custer became the *de facto* commander of the regiment).

But for the moment Custer's time was taken up with politics, in which he was becoming more deeply involved with each passing day.

On August 9 he went to Detroit for a mass meeting to endorse the National Union party (the label under which Lincoln and Johnson had run in 1864 against McClellan and the Democrats) and was elected one of the four delegates to the national convention in Philadelphia. He possibly thought that supporting Johnson would garner him something better than a lieutenant colonelcy. At the convention, which began on August 14, delegates from South Carolina and Massachusetts walked into the opening session arm in arm. Custer heartily approved of this show of national unity and he mingled freely with his old southern friends, some of whom had already been elected to Congress from the former Confederate states. Custer also signed a call for all former soldiers and sailors, northern and southern, to attend a grand National Union rally in Cleveland on September 17, 1866, the anniversary of McClellan's battle at Antietam.[18]

After firmly establishing his credentials as a National Union man and, not incidentally, lending his prestige to the party, Custer wrote to the President, applying for a full colonelcy, even a colonelcy of infantry, he said, so long as it was not with a black regiment.[19] But Johnson needed Custer for more important work and in reply invited the boy general and his wife to join the presidential party on "a swing around the circle." Custer accepted.

The ostensible purpose of the swing was to place the cornerstone for a monument being erected to Stephen A. Douglas in Chicago and to visit Lincoln's grave in Springfield, but Johnson's real motive was to campaign for the fall congressional elections. The President was breaking openly with the Radical Republicans and wanted National Union men or Democrats (the two parties were becoming indistinguishable) elected to Congress. He intended to use Custer, in other words, for partisan political purposes. General Grant and Admiral Farragut were also along on the swing to provide luster.

From start to finish, Johnson's "swing around the circle" was a disaster. One problem was the President's intemperate speech making; he engaged in the lowest kind of name-calling and fell into the trap of trying to outshout Republican hecklers in his audiences. Grant was so disgusted that he took to drinking whiskey at every stop, thus providing an excuse for not appearing on the platform with Johnson. But the bigger problem was the President's politics. The North was by no means ready to forgive and forget, to welcome former Confederates back into Congress, to hand control of the southern states back to the men who had run affairs there before 1861 and had then made war on the government. Nor was the North willing to abandon the newly freed blacks to the tender mercies of their former masters.

Johnson wanted to build a strong National Union party, which would take the place of the Democratic party. Economic differences between Johnson and the Republicans were minimal, and economics did not become an issue in that critical congressional election of 1866.[20] The real issues, which were interconnected, were civil rights, the status of former Confederates, and the question of white supremacy. Most northern voters held prejudices against blacks, obviously, but few were willing to go so far in abandoning them as Johnson and his supporters wanted to do.[21]

Johnson and the National Union party stood for white supremacy. "No man can advocate an amalgamation of the white & black races and so create a mongrel nation," as Frank Blair, one of Johnson's more important allies, put it. Blair thought it important that the states have the right to send black convicts to penal colonies outside the country, for example, and that the South be allowed to induce manufacturing companies to come into Dixie by educating poor whites while restricting the blacks "to the ruder trades and to the producing of the raw material." Above all, Blair and the National Union party stood for racial segregation: "The policy of the country must therefore be a gradual segregation of the Races."[22] Having just paid an awful price to free the slaves, the northern public was not ready to accept such a policy.

Republican leaders feared the appeal of white supremacy, but voters were more concerned about the elevation of former Confederates. While Democrats and Johnson's supporters tried to portray the issue as simply involving white supremacy, the majority of northern voters were not prepared to forget wartime animosities toward Confederates or paternalistic idealism toward blacks. In trying to sell his lenient Reconstruction program through appeals to racial antipathy, Johnson merely widened the gap between himself and northern public opinion. And northern voters alone voted for congressmen in 1866. Unable to seat the southern delegations in 1865–66, Johnson's political gambit had backfired.

Custer gradually came to recognize that fundamental truth. The "swing around the circle" was exciting enough in a way—Custer and Libbie enjoyed hobnobbing with all the notables Johnson had collected, including Secretary of State William H. Seward, Secretary of the Navy Gideon Welles, General George H. Thomas, and others—

but Custer could hardly be blind to the increasingly hostile reaction Johnson received from the crowds whenever he spoke. On the few occasions Custer tried to speak, he was shouted down. Accustomed to adulation, he was not prepared for criticism. When the presidential party was in Michigan, local politicians again offered Custer a nomination, this time for congressman. After giving it some consideration, he said no—he wanted nothing more to do with politics.[23]

Custer's worst moment came at Scio, Ohio, nearest railroad point to his birthplace. When the presidential train pulled into the station, Custer swung to the ground. He noticed anti-Johnson placards among the crowd but ignored them to shake hands with old friends of the family. The crowd began badgering the President, calling out ugly remarks about his parentage and his patriotism. Custer, disgusted, faced the mob and shouted, "I was born two miles from here, and I am ashamed of you." He climbed back into the train and told Libbie he would never visit Scio again, a resolution he kept. As always, he had to write his feelings down immediately, and he dashed off a letter to the Scio citizens telling them he considered the reception a personal insult. Shortly thereafter Custer and Libbie left the presidential party. That was the end of his political activities, an attitude that was immeasurably strengthened in November 1866, when the Republicans won smashing victories in the congressional elections.[24]

Being back in Washington had initially done wonders for Custer's spirits. He had discovered that he was still loved, admired, honored. But he had been in a difficult position; as a war hero he had strong ties with such Radical Republicans as Chandler, Stanton, and Bingham, but he could not agree with their politics. These men did not want to desert him—he and his reputation could do as much for them as they could do for him—but the Republicans were put off by his doleful description of the freedmen in Texas, his gloomy predictions about the future of blacks, and his general adherence to a southern-Andrew Johnson line. Custer had gone too far, finally, when he joined Johnson on "the swing around the circle." The trip was also a climax for Custer. Never seeing that there were real issues involving real people at stake in the presidential-congressional struggle, he denounced the whole thing as "typical politics" and withdrew from the field, somewhat horrified at what he had seen. It was time for him to get out of Washington.

In early 1867 Custer joined his regiment, the 7th Cavalry, stationed at Fort Riley, Kansas. He took along his usual retinue, including Libbie, Eliza, a black jockey he had acquired in Texas and who rode his horses in races, four favorite horses, Byron (a greyhound), Turk (a white bulldog), and several hounds. He looked forward to the hunting at Fort Riley.

On their way to Kansas, Custer and Libbie had stopped off for an exposition in St. Louis. There they saw an American classical actor, Lawrence Barrett, in a play. Custer was much impressed and went backstage after the performance to meet the actor. Barrett noticed that Custer had direct and penetrating eyes, yet seemed bashful and reticent. The actor said Custer's voice was "earnest, soft, tender and appealing," and that his personality was one of rare charm. Custer took Barrett to his hotel to meet Libbie and the three became lifelong friends.[25] Custer usually impressed eastern or European sophisticates; that winter, which he spent at Fort Riley, Custer entertained a prominent New York newspaperman, Charles Godfrey Leland, who wrote in his memoirs: "There was a bright and joyous chivalry in that man [Custer], and a noble refinement mingled with constant gaiety in the wife, such as I fear is passing from the earth."[26] As Leland's remarks indicate, Custer had a fine time that winter. There was plenty of good hunting an easy ride from the fort, Libbie and the whole gang were with him, and he loved riding on the Plains. Once, galloping side by side with Libbie, he reached out with one hand and lifted her from the horse's back, held her at arm's length, then gently put her, breathless, back again.

Shortly after he arrived at Fort Riley in 1867 Custer heard the shocking details of the Fort Phil Kearny battle. He may have heard the name Crazy Horse via the Army's rumor mill, although he did not read it in newspaper accounts because Crazy Horse was not yet famous among the whites generally. In any event, Custer realized—everyone at Fort Riley realized—that there would be a grand campaign against the Indians in the spring, the peace policy advocates to the contrary notwithstanding. Perhaps nothing could be done immediately about Crazy Horse and the Powder River Indians, but sure as hell the Indians were going to be cleared out of Kansas and Nebraska. The Kansas Pacific Railroad had reached out from Kansas City, Missouri, to Abilene and beyond, while the Union Pacific was in central Nebraska. Both lines were anxious to push westward when good weather returned. No bunch of redskins could be allowed to stand in the path of these carriers of the nation's destiny. Knowing that the government and the Army had determined to punish the Indians—any Indians—for the Fetterman disaster, with an active campaign to look forward to, and with Libbie to share his life, Custer thoroughly enjoyed his first winter on the Plains.

That same winter, 1866–67, on the Powder River, Red Cloud and Crazy Horse were having trouble holding their force together. It was a terribly hard winter, bitterly cold, the snowdrifts so deep that most of the elk and buffalo left the country in their search for food. In one gulch, it was said, a herd of three hundred buffalo were trapped and froze to death and were now covered with snow. Even the wolves would have to wait for the spring thaw to get at the carcasses. Snow-blindness was common, but the Indian remedy—sprinkling a little snow in the eyes—made that problem manageable. Hunger was not so easily handled. Crazy Horse and Little Hawk spent much of their time hunting on snowshoes. Once they bagged eight elk in a protected canyon, catching the beasts in the deep snow and cutting their throats with knives.[27] Other hunters were not so lucky and by mid-January Red Cloud's army was gradually disappearing. Young braves from the Laramie Loafers or Spotted Tail's Brulés returned to the white man's agencies, promising to come back the next summer; until then they would live on government hand-outs (Army officers, naturally enough, grew livid at the mere thought of the government feeding the hostiles in the winter so that they could fight in the summer). Red Cloud kept some scouts posted around Fort Phil Kearny to make certain the soldiers there did not try to get away, but with the snow so deep and the weather so cold there was not much danger of that happening. Besides, the Indians had had enough war for one season. The defeat of Fetterman satisfied them and they had no inclination to attack the fort itself.

By February 1867 there were massive desertions from the Red Cloud camp. The southern Cheyennes, who had come in force to fight beside their relatives, the northern Cheyennes, on the Powder River, returned to Kansas. They did not think much of the cold northern winters and wanted to be back on the relatively mild central Plains. Some southern Oglalas went south too. Crazy Horse accompanied them part of the way, but he and Little Hawk dropped out of the moving village when it reached the vicinity of Fort Reno, at the southern end of the Bighorn Mountains along the Bozeman Trail. For the remainder of the winter, Crazy Horse and Little Hawk harassed the whites in and around Fort Reno.[28]

The southern Cheyennes and the southern Oglalas thought they were returning to a land of peace. Kansas had been quiet all through

1866, with only some minor Indian troubles being reported from the southwestern corner of the state and that consisted of a few small Kiowa raids. The red men in Kansas thought they had a treaty with the United States Government and felt secure. Custer and the Army were about to show them that they were wrong.

Sherman was determined to teach the redskins a lasting lesson. He wanted most of all to get at Red Cloud's Indians on the Powder River in Wyoming. On December 30, 1866, he wrote his brother, a senator from Ohio, John Sherman, "I expect to have two Indian wars on my hands . . . The Sioux and Cheyennes are now so circumscribed that I suppose they must be exterminated, for they cannot and will not settle down, and our people will force us to it."[29] Sherman had sent for Custer to join him on the frontier with the idea that Custer would provide the cutting edge of his extermination campaign. Writing to his brother in February 1867, Sherman said, "G. W. [sic] Custer, Lieutenant-Colonel Seventh Cavalry, is young, very brave, even to rashness, a good trait for a cavalry officer." Sherman had not known Custer during the Civil War, but Custer came recommended by both Grant and Sheridan and he made a strong impression on Sherman when they talked in St. Louis. Custer "came to duty immediately upon being appointed," Sherman wrote, "and is ready and willing now to fight the Indians." Custer's outstanding characteristics, Sherman believed, were "youth, health, energy, and extreme willingness to act and fight."[30]

Sherman did not have the backing of the government in Washington for action against the Indians, however, since the government was still controlled by the peace party. President Johnson appointed a new set of commissioners to go to Fort Laramie in June 1867 to try to induce Red Cloud to sign a treaty. The United States could hardly send a peace commission and a military expedition into the same area at the same time, so Sherman was forced to call off a planned Powder River offensive. In the central Plains no such obstacle blocked the Army, and if Sherman's first priority was to kill some Indians somewhere in retaliation for the Fetterman massacre, he was equally concerned with protecting the transcontinental railroads. He decided to send Major General Winfield Scott Hancock, commanding the Department of the Missouri and stationed at Fort Leavenworth, on a grand campaign to clear the Indians out of Kansas and Nebraska. Custer would lead the way.[31]

General Hancock looked every inch the soldier. His appearance was so impressive, General Grant wrote, that he "would attract the attention of any army as he passed." He had earned the label "Hancock the Superb" for repulsing Pickett's charge at Gettysburg and had indeed fought superbly in almost every major battle of the Army of the Potomac. He seemed the perfect choice for over-all command in Sherman's offensive, with Custer as the ideal tactical officer.[32] The trouble was that neither Hancock nor Custer knew anything about Indians or about the Plains, while they both had an exaggerated idea of their own abilities.

The United States Army has been unjustly maligned for its record in the wars with the Plains Indians. It is accused of starting most, if not all the wars, and of then blundering once hostilities broke out. But the Army was badly served by its political masters, given conflicting orders, hardly ever knowing from one month to the next what the policy of the government might be; it was poorly equipped and inadequately supplied. It was the clear duty of the Army to protect the advancing frontier and the transcontinental railroads, and the Indians *were* in the way. They had to be removed if the nation's destiny were to be realized. And in view of the expanding white population (and the growing world demand for foodstuffs), the red men could not be allowed to retain hundreds of square miles of prime grazing or wheat country in order to support a few thousand Indians.

There were two ways to remove the Indians: drive them onto reservations or bribe them there. The government never made the bribe attractive enough, as we have seen (and it may be doubted if any amount of presents could have induced Crazy Horse to sell his birthright), so the dirty job of removing them fell to the Army. In the process, though the Army made its share of blunders, showed its share of stupidity and cruelty, and initiated its share of hostilities, it also fought with great skill and bravery, tried on any number of occasions to avoid war, and blamed the government and its Indian agents, rather than the red men themselves, for its troubles.

It was really more a police force, less an Army, and it would be altogether wrong to think that its officers had no sympathy for the Indians. They did, but they also had a higher calling. Having spent four years fighting a bloody civil war to keep the nation unified, they intended to finish the job by seeing the transcontinental railroad completed and the Plains thoroughly integrated into national life. They hoped to realize their objectives without excessive bloodshed, for in truth there was little glory in Indian fighting by that time. Custer is almost the only Plains Indian fighter whose name is remembered today, and his is remembered primarily because of the circumstances surrounding his death.

The Army was damned if it did, damned if it didn't. If an Army

column found and destroyed an Indian village, Easterners generally
and the peace-policy advocates especially denounced the officers as
bloodthirsty butchers. If the Army tried to negotiate with the Indians, Westerners generally and frontiersmen especially denounced
it for neglect of duty at best, or even cowardice. But for the Army,
as General John Pope put it, "Whatever may be the right or wrong
of the question . . . the Indian must be dispossessed. The practical
question to be considered is how the inevitable can be accomplished
with the least inhumanity to the Indian."[33]

The Army's over-all record in the Indian wars, in short, was a
mixed one. Having said that, it must then be added that no campaign
the Army ever undertook matched the Hancock campaign of 1867
for sheer stupidity. In the first place, there was no reason at all to
send a force of 1,400 infantry, artillery, and cavalry chasing around
the central Plains looking for Indians. There had been no trouble
in Kansas or Nebraska nor any reason to expect any. Nevertheless
Hancock marched forth from Fort Riley looking for war, at a time
when he had a total force of only slightly more than 4,000 soldiers
to hold the vast spaces of the central Plains.[34] To make the comic
turn ridiculous, he set out with infantry, artillery, and heavy pontoon
trains (temporary movable bridges) to catch Indians somewhere, *anywhere*, in Kansas, Nebraska, or eastern Colorado. He never explained
how he proposed to catch wild Indians with infantry and pontoon
trains.

Hancock's main idea was to show the flag, or so he said. The immediate problem was, whose flag—the Army's, or the Indian Bureau's, or the government's? The Army's policy was to drive the
Indians onto reservations north of the Platte or south of the Arkansas
rivers; the Indian Bureau's policy was to bribe them there; the government's policy shifted from month to month. Legally, the Indians
were under the control of the Indian Bureau (which was under the
Department of the Interior) and more especially the Bureau's agents
in the field. The agents insisted that the Indians were peaceful, while
the Army charged that the agents lied and then compounded the
lie by selling arms and ammunition to the hostiles. Cheyenne agent
Edward W. Wynkoop took the brunt of this criticism—Custer accused him of being a direct accomplice to outright murder.[35] The
Army was supposed to support the Indian Bureau's policies, but no
one in the Bureau, least of all Wynkoop, wanted a huge force of
soldiers wandering around the Indian country, frightening the red
men and possibly spurring them to go on the warpath. The
Cheyennes would be especially fearful after the Chivington massacre

at Sand Creek three years earlier. Nevertheless, Hancock determined to march toward the Cheyennes living in western Kansas with all the pomp and display he could muster, then bully the Indians out of the path of the advancing railroads.

The expedition set out on March 22, 1867, from Fort Riley. The 1,400 soldiers comprised the largest force yet sent out on the Plains. Custer commanded the 7th Cavalry, about 400 men. Hancock had arranged for publicity; for the first time in America's Indian wars, newspaper correspondents accompanied a military expedition in the field. Theodore R. Davis, an artist-reporter for *Harper's Weekly*, was there, along with the not-yet famous Henry M. Stanley, a correspondent for the New York *Tribune*.[36]

Hancock told agent Wynkoop, who also accompanied the expedition, that there would be no war unless the Indians started it. He said he was prepared to aid the agents in controlling, arresting, or punishing any warrior who might be guilty of outrages, but otherwise he intended to leave the tribes alone. To his troops, however, Hancock expressed more hawkish sentiments. "We go prepared for war," Hancock proclaimed in his general orders, "and will make it if a proper occasion presents . . . No insolence [from the Indians] will be tolerated."[37]

Early in April 1867, Hancock arrived at Fort Larned on the Arkansas River in central Kansas. Here he had Wynkoop call in the Cheyenne chiefs for a conference. Hancock had promised Wynkoop that so long as the Indians left the travel routes alone the agent would remain in charge of all negotiations, but when the council began, Hancock broke his promise and would not allow Wynkoop to speak. Instead, the general lectured the Cheyennes on their responsibilities, held them guilty of depradations they had had no connection with, and told them that he intended to march his force to the Cheyenne village on Pawnee Fork, about thirty-five miles west of Fort Larned. Wynkoop protested the decision, saying it would terrify the Cheyennes to have such a huge force suddenly appear in their vicinity, but Hancock insisted.[38] Finally Wynkoop persuaded the general to remain at Fort Larned a few days and allow the Indians to come to him to talk.

The Cheyennes agreed to bring in the whole village on April 10, but on the ninth Kansas caught the tag end of the hard winter Crazy Horse and his comrades had been suffering through up north. There was an eight-inch snowfall followed by bitterly cold weather, so cold in fact that the American horses survived only by having their oats ration doubled and by having troopers whip them through the night to keep them moving. After the storm had blown over, the Cheyennes set out for Fort Larned, but they ran into a buffalo herd on the way and decided to stop and make a hunt. On April 14 Hancock, furious at what he regarded as betrayal, set off for Pawnee Fork. By noon of the next day the soldiers were within a few miles of the Indian camp.

Coming over a rise, Custer saw a sight he would never forget. It was, he later wrote, "one of the finest and most imposing military displays . . . which it has ever been my lot to behold. It was nothing more nor less than an Indian line of battle drawn directly across our line of march; as if to say: thus far and no farther. Most of the Indians were mounted; all were bedecked in their brightest colors, their heads crowned with the brilliant war-bonnet, their lances bearing the crimson penant, bows strung, and quivers full of barbed arrows."39 Hancock immediately had his troops deploy into line of battle. Custer's cavalry took the right flank, and he ordered his men to draw their sabers, the bright blades flashing in the sunlight. He was dying to get at the redskins. Everything about the situation invited a cavalry charge, including the level ground and the vast prairie that offered no hiding place.

At this critical moment, when a clash seemed inevitable, agent Wynkoop rode up to Hancock and obtained grudging permission to go forward and talk with the Indians. Wynkoop then rode out alone, a fact Custer failed to mention in his otherwise voluminous account of the campaign. Instead, Custer made it appear that he, Hancock, and a handful of other brave officers rode out to meet the Indians, implying that this was an act of great courage.40 In fact, Wynkoop calmed the Indians somewhat (they knew and trusted him), then signaled for Hancock and his party of officers to come forward. Hancock spoke sharply to Roman Nose, whom he regarded—wrongly —as the head chief, asking if Roman Nose wanted war. The Cheyenne warrior replied sarcastically that if the Indians had wanted war they would not have been likely to come out in the open and face such a force or have come so close to Hancock's artillery pieces. Roman Nose then asked Hancock to make camp where he was, instead of proceeding closer to the village, lest he frighten away the women and children who remembered Sand Creek all too well. Hancock refused the request, the force of Cheyennes turned and rode back toward their village, and the expedition resumed its march.

By late afternoon, Hancock was within sight of the village and he made camp. Roman Nose and some other Cheyennes then rode up to his headquarters to tell him that the women and children had fled—they could not believe the Army's intentions were peaceful in view of all the troops Hancock had with him—and to ask him if the soldiers wouldn't please withdraw. Instead, Hancock ordered the warriors to take some fresh American horses, catch up with the fleeing villagers, and bring the women and children back. Roman Nose said that he would do so.

After darkness fell, Hancock ordered Custer to take the 7th Cavalry and surround the village to make sure that no Indians escaped. Gathering his men together in the dark, Custer ordered them to maintain perfect silence, then proceeded on his hazardous mission. When he had the village surrounded, Custer and three companions crawled toward it. They had no idea what to expect; it was cold (there was a freeze that night), dark, and still. Custer loved the situation; it was almost as exciting as fighting rebels. "While all of us were full of the spirit of adventure," he later wrote, "and were further encouraged with the idea that we were in the discharge of our duty, there was scarcely one of us who would not have felt more comfortable if we could have got back to our horses without loss of pride."[41] Adventure, duty, pride, all wrapped up in one—what more could a man ask?

Inching his way forward on hands and knees, his heart pounding, sweating despite the cold, expecting to meet a savage warrior at any moment, Custer slowly realized the embarrassing truth. The Indians had taken off, leaving all their belongings behind. The village was deserted. When Custer reported the mortifying facts to Hancock, the general solemnly concluded, "This looks like the commencement of war."[42]

Custer did not agree. After some reflection, he decided that "the hasty flight of the Indians and the abandonment of, to them, valuable property, convinces me that they are influenced by fear alone, and it is my opinion that no council can be held with them in the presence of a large military force." He was learning, obviously, and doing so much faster than Hancock. One reason, perhaps, was that he spent all the time he could with Wild Bill Hickok, the famous scout who was working for Hancock. Hickok knew as much about Indians as any white man on the Plains and Custer was wise enough to pump him for all the information he could get. Despite Hickok's presence, however, the Army hardly knew what it was doing. As Custer reported, "Captain Robert M. West, of the Seventh Cavalry, and possessed of great experience with Indians, is firmly of the opinion that they have gone north or south."[43] Wise counsel, indeed.

The following morning Hancock ordered Custer to pursue the fleeing Indians. Delaware scouts found the trail and led the way. The trail led north, but because the Indians had no travois with them (having left everything at Pawnee Fork), it was indistinct. Custer pushed on as hard as he could, heading north in the direction of the Smoky Hill River.

While on this march Custer pulled one of his stunts that left men speechless with rage or admiration, depending on how they felt about him. Custer had a pack of greyhounds along and he was anxious to let them try their speed against an antelope. On the third day, seeing some antelope grazing two miles away and mounted on a fine thoroughbred horse that he had ridden in the Appomattox campaign, Custer gave in to his impulses, left his column, and gave chase. He rode for several miles before giving it up and calling in his dogs, who were unable to gain on the antelope. Looking around, Custer tried to figure out where he was, how far he had ridden, and where his column was, but it was all a mystery. He was lost on the Great Plains—and he had deserted his command in the field.

Custer hoped the dogs could lead him back to the column, but they wandered around aimlessly. Suddenly, about a mile distant, he saw a buffalo bull. It was the first buffalo he had ever seen but he didn't hesitate. With a whoop that would have matched the cry of an Indian about to count coup, he took off after the beast. His magnificent horse soon caught up with the lumbering bull. Together, the buffalo, the thoroughbred, and Custer galloped across the prairie, Custer yelling, shouting, whooping with pure joy. Several times he placed his pistol beside the bull's head, but always withdrew it to allow the chase to continue a little longer. The bull's tongue was halfway to the ground but still the beast pounded on, Custer beside him. Finally Custer's horse began to play out (he estimated they had ridden at top speed for several miles by then) and he decided to finish the business. Placing his revolver alongside the bull's head, he prepared to fire.

At that instant the bull whirled on horse and rider. Custer's horse reared, Custer accidentally pulled the trigger, and he shot his thoroughbred through the head. "Quick as thought," he later wrote, "I disengaged myself from the stirrups and found myself whirling through the air over and beyond the head of my horse." Jumping to his feet, Custer saw the bull trot off, shaking its head at the wonder of it all. "How far I had travelled, or in what direction from the column, I was at a loss to know. In the excitement of the chase I had lost all reckoning. Indians were liable to pounce upon me at any moment. My command would not note my absence probably for hours." It was a desperate situation, but Custer's luck held. Within a couple of hours the column found him, alone (except for a pack of exhausted dogs) and on foot on the prairie, wandering around and wondering which way was north.[44] His men suppressed whatever emotion they felt upon discovering their commander alone on the prairie after having shot his own horse.

The next morning, April 18, Custer resumed his pursuit of the Indians, but the trail soon gave out completely, the Cheyennes having scattered in small groups. Custer pushed on northward, hoping to strike a trail when he hit the Smoky Hill stageline. The only real excitement came the next morning at dawn, when the guards cried out, "Indians!" The men leaped to their horses and Custer rode to the head of a rapidly formed column, while a group of horsemen swept down on the camp. At the last minute, the two sides recognized their mutual mistake—the horsemen were soldiers whom Custer had sent out the previous night to scout for Indian campfires. The detachment had gotten lost, traveled in a semicircle, come upon Custer's camp from the opposite side, in the uncertain light mistaken Custer's tents for tipis, and charged. It was about this time that correspondent Davis noticed that Custer was becoming depressed.[45]

When Custer arrived on the Smoky Hill he discovered that the fleeing Cheyennes had gone on a rampage. Road travel of the whites had come to a halt. The stagecoach stations, located about ten miles apart along the Smoky Hill River route, had been burned. At Lookout Station, fifteen miles west of Fort Hays (the Army's major post in central Kansas), Custer discovered the buildings in ashes and the bodies of three dead station keepers. Hancock had stirred up an Indian war and here was Custer, in the middle of Indian country at the head of a regiment of cavalry, and he had not seen a single Indian since leaving Pawnee Fork. His horses were exhausted, his men were grumbling, Hancock could not believe Custer had not caught at least one Indian, Custer had shot his best horse, his own men had attacked his camp, travel had come to a halt along the Smoky Hill line (and keeping that line open was a major objective of the Hancock campaign), and the Cheyennes were on the loose north of the Smoky Hill, in a mood to kill any whites they encountered.

Matters could not have been much worse, it seemed, but they soon became so. Hancock, furious at the Indians for running away, burned their village at Pawnee Fork. Correspondent Stanley reported that

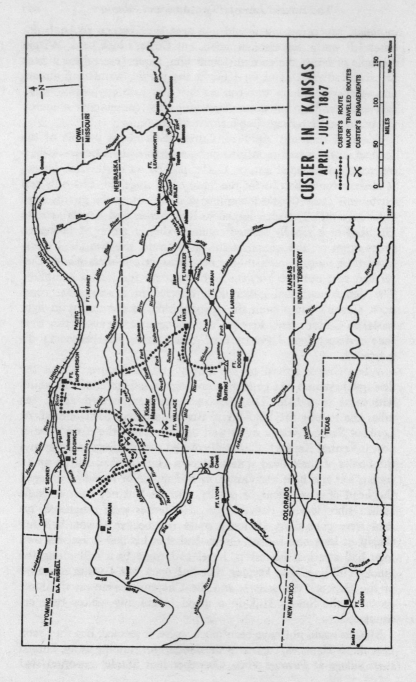

CUSTER IN KANSAS
APRIL - JULY 1867

••••••• CUSTER'S ROUTE
───── MAJOR TRAVELED ROUTES
✕ CUSTER'S ENGAGEMENTS

MILES
0   50   100   150

Walter T. Wilson

1994

251 tipis were burned, along with 942 buffalo robes and all kinds of household equipment. Stanley estimated that it would take three thousand buffalo to replace the skins used in the tipis alone. The cash value of the loss was around $100,000 or close to a million dollars in today's terms.[46] According to George Grinnell, who later interviewed many of the Cheyennes involved, Hancock set the torch to the village *before* the Indians struck the Smoky Hill line, and they went on the warpath in retaliation.[47] Whatever the truth of the matter, the burning of the village hardened the Cheyennes' determination to make war.

Custer, meanwhile, limped into Fort Hays with his troopers on May 2, 1867, hoping to find fresh horses and plentiful supplies. He discovered, instead, a woebegone collection of log shanties and sod huts, with neither horses nor supplies. Custer was immobilized. With no forage available, he would have to stay where he was until the horses fattened up on the spring grass.

Hancock, meanwhile, had marched the infantry back to Fort Larned, where he delivered a war-or-peace ultimatum to Arapaho and Kiowa chiefs from camps south of the Arkansas. The Kiowa war leader Satanta impressed Hancock as being so desirous of peace that the American gave him a major general's dress uniform. Then Hancock left his infantry and traveled north to Fort Hays, where he took one look at the wretched situation, muttered that he would hasten the shipment of supplies when he got back to Fort Leavenworth in eastern Kansas, and shook the dust of the Plains from his heels. And that was the end of the grand Hancock expedition of 1867.

While Custer sat at Fort Hays waiting for the grass to come up, the Indians in Kansas had a fine time. Arapahoes, Kiowas, southern Oglalas, and southern Cheyennes struck repeatedly at mail stations, stagecoaches, wagon trains, and railroad workers on the Platte, the Smoky Hill, and the Arkansas. Railroad construction came to a halt.[48] The Kansas frontier was in a panic. Dozens of whites were killed and women and children captured. Fort Wallace, in westernmost Kansas, was under a state of siege. At Fort Dodge, to the southeast, Satanta put on his major general's dress uniform and then ran off the horse and mule herd. "He had the greatest politeness," Davis reported, "to raise his plumed hat to the garrison of the fort, though he discourteously shook his coattails at them as he rode away with the captured stock."[49]

All the while Custer sat at Fort Hays. His major problem—aside from the embarrassment of knowing that the Indians were running wild while he was immobilized—was the same one Red Cloud and Crazy Horse had faced the preceding winter: Custer's men were deserting in droves. Between October 1, 1866, and October 1, 1867, in fact, the 7th Cavalry lost 512 men by desertion, more than the equivalent of its total field strength.[50] The deserters were replaced, although slowly, but enlistees in 1867 were of a low order and none of the men received any training before being sent to the field. Most could not even sit a horse.

The major reasons for the desertions were beyond Custer's control. Many enlisted men had joined the Army in the east in order to obtain free transportation west. Once in Kansas, the lure of the gold fields in Colorado and Montana was too much for them, and they took off. Secretary of War Stanton once remarked that the best way to populate the West was to keep sending recruits out there. The more general cause of desertion, however, was the Army's wretched treatment of enlisted men, which contrasted so sharply with the relatively decent food and housing available to Custer and the other officers. The men were issued bread that was five years old or older. At Fort Hays and throughout the frontier they slept two to a bunk, on rough wood mounted in two or even three tiers. Kitchen slops were emptied into crude sewers close to the barracks, which soon became clogged with grease, producing foul odors and attracting flies in swarms. Aside from stale bread, the principal staples were beef, salt pork, coffee, and beans, all in insufficient quantity. So inadequate was this diet that many of Custer's men suffered from scurvy.[51] Custer divided his men into teams for competitive events, such as foot and horse races or buffalo hunts, in an effort to maintain some modicum of morale, but it did little good. Each night a few more men left for the gold fields. They took their chances with the Indians, who were practically besieging the fort.

For his own morale, Custer decided to send for Libbie, regardless of the threat of the Indians. The day he arrived at Hays, Custer wrote her, telling her "Come as soon as you can. . . . I did not marry you for you to live in one house, me in another. One bed shall accommodate us both."[52] The next day he told her to bring a good supply of butter for the officers' mess, along with lard, potatoes, and onions. "You will need calico dresses, and a few white ones. Oh, we will be so, so happy." Wagon space was scarce and his men needed every bit of supplies they could get, so Custer told Libbie not to be too outrageous in her requests for space. He advised her to leave her huge clothes-press at Fort Riley. By May 6 his anxiety to be with her was nearly too much for him to bear. "I almost feel tempted to desert and fly to you," he wrote Libbie. "I would come if the [railroad] cars were running this far. We will probably go on another scout shortly, and I do not want to lose a day with you. Bring a set of field-croquet."[53] Libbie came, bringing a young unmarried friend with her, and of course Eliza and the cook stove. Libbie was disappointed with the primitive fort, but she was with Autie and that was enough to make her happiness complete.[54]

With Libbie around, Custer's spirits began to revive. The weather helped, too; there are few places in the world more delightful than Kansas in May. The grass was coming up and his horses were putting on weight; supplies were beginning to arrive from Fort Leavenworth; he had a campaign to look forward to. This time there would be no doubt about the Indians'—or the Army's—intentions. Hancock had started a sure-enough Indian war, and Custer could take the field with the knowledge that any Indian he encountered was fair game. The Army up north might not be able to control the northern Oglalas—Crazy Horse and his associates at this time were again blocking the Bozeman Trail—but down in Kansas, Custer intended to teach the rampaging red men a lesson they would not forget. In the process he hoped to add a little luster to his suddenly tarnished reputation.

CHAPTER FIFTEEN

A Summer on the Plains: 1867

"Whether right or wrong, those railroads will be built, and everybody knows that Congress, after granting the charts and fixing the routes, cannot now back out and surrender the country to a few bands of roving Indians." William T. Sherman to John Sherman, September 28, 1867

Spring came late to the Powder River country in 1867, but when it burst forth it was glorious. By May, when the grass was coming up, Crazy Horse and Little Hawk had rejoined Red Cloud's force near Fort Phil Kearny. The brothers had spent the latter part of the winter harassing the whites farther south on the Bozeman Trail, down by Fort Reno, where they fought a number of sharp little battles, but when the flowers began to bloom, the grass turned green, and the birds returned, Crazy Horse and Little Hawk headed north.[1] They were joined by young warriors from the Laramie Loafers and Spotted Tail's Brulés. There was going to be a big Sun Dance along the Powder, then more fights with the garrison at Fort Phil Kearny. It promised to be a good summer.

When the Sun Dance was over, the headmen of the Oglalas began to discuss their plans. Both the civil and military arms of the Oglala government were represented. Old Man Afraid, the most important of the older chiefs, was there, along with the other Big Bellies. Red Cloud was the highest ranking military officer, backed up by his shirt-wearers, including Crazy Horse. The whites had asked the Oglalas to come down to Fort Laramie to "touch the pen"* to a treaty that would give the Americans the right to use the Bozeman Trail, provide for general peace, and give the Indians lots of beads and other presents. Old Man Afraid and the Big Bellies were willing to go to Fort Laramie to discuss the offer, but Crazy Horse and the shirt-wearers were opposed. Because they represented the fighting

* The phrase indicated that the Indian chief had literally held the pen in his hand; a white man then wrote down the chief's name.

men who were, in addition, the economic providers for the community, their opinion carried great weight. Few of the warriors wanted to give up on a war that had been going so well for them, nor did they feel a need for any white man's presents. The Big Bellies, who had a more realistic view of the power of the whites, wanted peace.

Eventually the Indians reached a workable compromise. Old Man Afraid could go to Fort Laramie to see what the whites had to say, but Red Cloud would accompany him to make sure nothing was done that would displease the warriors. Red Cloud agreed not to speak in the meeting with the whites, but he would be there watching what Old Man Afraid did all the same. The warriors won another concession—Old Man Afraid would sign nothing until the whites had abandoned the Bozeman Trail forts and supplied the red men with some ammunition. The warriors had more guns than they had ever seen before, guns picked up from Fetterman's command, but they had no ammunition nor the materials nor knowledge to make any. Crazy Horse and Red Cloud had insisted on the stringent condition that the whites abandon the forts before any treaty could be signed because they had no faith in the white man's word. Promises would not be enough—the physical fact of abandonment must be accomplished first.

On June 12, 1867, Old Man Afraid met with the white peace commission at Fort Laramie. He said that he represented two hundred lodges of Oglalas, that they all wanted to be friendly, and that he would touch the pen as soon as the whites abandoned the forts and handed over some ammunition. Red Cloud remained in the background, but he watched Old Man Afraid's every move. The whites wanted to know why the Indians needed ammunition. To hunt with, Old Man Afraid replied. But, the whites responded, you have been getting along fine for centuries without guns. Ah ha, Old Man Afraid complained, the game is too wild now because so many whites come and frighten the animals. Ah ha yourself, the white commissioners concluded, you want the ammunition in order to wage a more vigorous war. And with that, Old Man Afraid walked out.[2]

Crazy Horse was not surprised at the failure of the peace negotiations and happily went back to making war on the whites. Along with the warriors, he struck hard throughout eastern Wyoming. Occasionally the main body of warriors would gather near Fort Phil Kearny and either try to wipe out the wood train or to decoy the soldiers out into the open again, but the troops were much more cautious this summer than they had been the preceding winter and nothing was accomplished. Tiring of the war, war chief Pawnee Killer led a band of southern Oglalas down to the Platte River in Nebraska, near Fort McPherson, where he hoped to trade buffalo hides for ammunition. At about the same time that Pawnee Killer left the Powder River camp, Custer set out from Fort Hays, also heading toward Fort McPherson.

Custer started in early June 1867, looking for hostiles. He had three hundred cavalrymen under his command, although on the first day's march Custer was not with the column. Instead, he stayed behind at Fort Hays, where he spent the day with Libbie. At midnight, after one last kiss, Custer embarked on a moonlight ride across the prairie. He galloped for twenty miles, accompanied by a seven-man escort of Delaware scouts, on what he always recalled as a glorious experience. He rode into camp at reveille, just in time to join the column for the next day's march. A night without sleep, followed by a twenty-five-mile march the following day, was small enough price to pay for some extra hours with Libbie.[3]

It was a colorful column. The enlisted men spoke a medley of tongues, representing as they did the vast wave of European immigration to the United States following the Civil War. Immigrants who could not find employment in the cities were a prime target for Army recruiters. So were American criminals, drunks, dead beats, and those who for one reason or another needed to stay a jump ahead of the law. Army recruiters asked no questions and Army examining physicians operated on the principle that if a man could stand up he was fit for active duty.

The officers were all Civil War veterans, primarily men who were afraid to try their luck in civilian life or who had tried and failed. They were divided into pro- and anti-Custer cliques, but that was not so much a reflection on Custer's personality as it was a reflection of the conditions under which they lived. The officers at most frontier posts divided themselves into factions, one side favoring the regimental commander, the other side opposed to him.

Robert Utley has a good description of these men: "As officers aged without advancement, their initiative, energy, and impulse for self-improvement diminished. Their concerns narrowed. They fragmented into hostile factions—staff and line, infantry and cavalry, young and old, West Point and Volunteers, Civil War veteran and peacetime newcomer. They bickered incessantly over petty issues of precedence, real or imagined insults, and old wartime controversies. They preferred charges on the slightest provocation and consequently had to spend a preposterous share of their time on court-martial duty."⁴ Lieutenant Tom Custer headed the pro-Custer clique in the 7th Cavalry, naturally, along with Captain George Yates and the regimental adjutant, Lieutenant William Cooke. Captains Frederick Benteen and Robert West were the leading anti-Custer officers.⁵ But pro- or anti-Custer, they all had one thing in common: to a man they were as ignorant of Indians as Custer himself.

Accompanying the column were numerous scouts, the most colorful being William Comstock, or "Medicine Bill," as the Indians called him. Comstock had lived on the Plains for twenty years. "He is quiet and unassuming in manner," correspondent Davis said of Comstock, "small in size, and compact in proportion. He is one of the best riders on the plains, with which he is probably more familiar than any other white man who roams over them."⁶ Custer cultivated Comstock as he had Hickok. "Comstock messes with me," he wrote Libbie. "I like to have him with me, for many reasons. He is a worthy man, and I am constantly obtaining valuable information from him regarding the Indians, their habits, etc."⁷ Custer had the same problem with Comstock that he had had with Hickok, however; these frontiersmen were terribly quiet and generally contemptuous of regular Army officers. They spoke only when asked a direct question, and Custer hardly knew what the right questions were to ask.

Besides the scouts there were other civilians along, mainly as mule skinners or wagon drivers. The newspaper correspondent Davis was also there. Davis was hoping for a scoop, but after listening to the enlisted men grumble he feared the whole regiment might mutiny or desert.

The commander of the grand expedition was, according to correspondent Stanley, "precisely the man for the job. A certain impetuosity and undoubted courage are his principal characteristics." Custer, Stanley wrote, was "a first-rate cavalry officer, and will no doubt perform any task allotted to him to the entire satisfaction of the western people."⁸ In fact, however, Custer had not yet been in an Indian fight, had seen Indians close up only once, at Pawnee Fork, and later had displayed astonishing misjudgment when he deserted his marching column in enemy territory to go off on a private hunt. Impetuosity and courage had stood him in good stead during the Civil War, but the first was precisely the wrong quality for Indian fighting, while courage was not of much use if he couldn't catch any Indians. To make matters worse, his real job was to assist the Indian agents in maintaining the peace, which required skill and patience, qualities he lacked altogether. As far as the government in Washington was concerned, he was supposed to be acting as a policeman, catching young warriors guilty of outrages but protecting the bulk of the tribe. But his immediate superiors, Sherman and Hancock, wanted him to crush any Indians he met, which is to say that they were egging him on rather than urging caution and common sense.

It was a confusing situation, and as Custer rode north looking for hostiles he had serious doubts as to his proper course of action. Ambivalence had set in. The Indian agents continued to insist that the tribes were peaceful and that the raids on the stagecoach lines were the work of a few young warriors who had been driven to their desperate acts by Hancock's burning of the village at Pawnee Fork. Custer knew that there was some truth in that assessment. He also knew that the cavalry was going to have a hell of a time catching any Indians. If the war continued the 7th Cavalry might spend the entire summer marching aimlessly across the Plains. Such a fruitless effort would do no good for Custer's reputation.

But what really worried him was that he would be without Libbie for months. More in love now than when he had married her, Custer could not abide that thought. He began to work on an idea—if he could induce the tribes to move to the vicinity of the forts, where they could be watched, he could bring about peace on the Plains, then get to see Libbie.

The expedition averaged twenty-five miles a day as it marched north from Fort Hays toward Fort McPherson. Custer frequently left the column to go hunting or to study life on the Plains. He was fascinated by an Oglala funeral scaffold that Comstock showed him, with a warrior's favorite horse lying dead underneath and a lance by the dead man's side.[9] At one campsite the men had no sooner pitched their tents than they discovered they were over an area perforated with rattlesnake holes. The troopers cut off the snakes' heads with their sabers and everyone enjoyed broiled or fried rattlesnake that night. Custer and other hunters killed antelope an occasion, thereby providing fresh meat, and Custer took some young captured antelope and made them into pets.[10]

Custer was hoping to find the Cheyennes who had deserted the village at Pawnee Fork. On June 7 his column crossed the Republican River in southwest Nebraska. When he rode to the top of the bluffs enclosing the valley, Custer saw in front of him one hundred mounted warriors. The Indians immediately turned and fled.

Custer sent a company to chase them; luckily for him, the Cheyennes were not pulling the decoy trick and the company eventually returned safely, although somewhat embarrassed by the fact that it had not gotten close to any red men.[11]

On June 10 Custer looked down on the Platte River Valley. Below him was Fort McPherson. He could see the Union Pacific tracks stretching westward, beside them the telegraph line (which was useless, as the Indians had cut it) and the overland stage road. The road was a shambles and railroad work had come to a halt. Graves were scattered across the countryside. Most were simply mounds, but some were more pretentious; one was marked by a crude board on which had been inscribed UNKNOWN MAN KILLED BY INDIANS.[12]

The commanding officer at Fort McPherson was Colonel Henry Carrington, who had been shifted to the Platte after the Fetterman disaster the previous winter. Carrington had a great deal to tell Custer about Crazy Horse and Oglala fighting tactics, but it is doubtful if Custer let him do so. Custer was contemptuous of the old colonel who had been disgraced by Crazy Horse and Red Cloud, and it seemed obvious that Carrington's military career was over. Custer, despite his bad start as an Indian fighter, was still a rising star. Besides there was the difference in their ages and characters; where Carrington was taciturn, Custer was voluble; where Carrington was cautious, Custer was impetuous.

When the 7th Cavalry appeared at the gates of his fort, Carrington immediately invited Custer to dine with him that evening. Custer declined, muttering that he had to see to his men. It would be difficult to imagine a more cutting insult in the Army than refusing a commanding officer's invitation to dinner. Carrington let it pass, although he did stiffly inform Custer that he had best report officially that his command was present at Fort McPherson, ready for duty. "I peremptorily refused to do it," Custer wrote Libbie that night, on the grounds that his was an independent command responsible only to General Sherman. Again Carrington did nothing —perhaps he figured that the Sioux and Cheyennes would soon teach this insulting young whippersnapper a little humility.[13]

The next day Custer moved his camp ten miles west, officially because there was higher ground and more grass available for his horses at the new site, more likely to get away from Carrington and the possibility of having to take orders from the old colonel. No sooner had camp been made than Pawnee Killer, the southern Oglala who had just left Red Cloud and Crazy Horse, appeared for a talk.

Custer smoked his first peace pipe and did so manfully, even managing to avoid coughing. He gave Pawnee Killer a few trinkets and small amounts of coffee and sugar, then urged him to bring his village to the vicinity of the fort. Custer warned Pawnee Killer that all the territory between the Platte and the Arkansas was, in his view, the battlefield, and if he caught any Indians in the region he would shoot on sight. Pawnee Killer pretended to be impressed, promised to be good, said he would camp by the fort, begged for ammunition—which was refused—and spent most of his time petting Custer's pet antelope. He departed in good humor.[14]

Custer was delighted. Although the Sioux had found him, not vice versa, he was satisfied that Pawnee Killer had no hostile intentions. "I encouraged peace propositions and have sturdy hopes of a successful and satisfactory settlement with the Sioux which will leave us only the Cheyennes to deal with," he wrote Libbie. He hoped the result would be general peace, so "that I will see my little girl much sooner thereby." He expected to meet Sherman, who was visiting the frontier posts to encourage his commanders to kill Indians, the next day.[15]

Sherman arrived at Fort McPherson by railroad on June 16. Custer proudly informed him of his diplomatic victory—Pawnee Killer was coming into the shadow of the fort to camp and Custer had brought it about without bloodshed. Expecting praise for his restraint, Custer was deeply hurt when Sherman exploded. The nervous, excitable, wrinkled, redheaded general was furious with his subordinate. What in hell did Custer mean by meddling in politics? Didn't he know that you can never trust an Indian? How could he have been so stupid? Custer, who had never really had a chance to fight anyway, because Pawnee Killer and a small group had come unexpectedly under a flag of truce, wondered what he could have done. Sherman snapped that he should have held Pawnee Killer and the subchiefs as hostages until the tribe actually made the move to the fort. Sherman wanted Custer to start off immediately and bring back some hostages, but Comstock pointed out that they couldn't possibly catch a few Indians on the open Plains. Sherman then ordered Custer to march to the southwest, toward the headwaters of the Republican River, where he could expect to encounter Pawnee Killer's village and perhaps might run across the Cheyennes. When Custer asked Sherman what the limits of the search should be, Sherman replied that the 7th Cavalry could go to Denver if Custer wished, "or he could go to hell if he wanted to," so long as he was in hot pursuit of Indians. The main point was to find some redskins and shoot them. Sherman explicitly ordered Custer to kill as many Indians as he could, capturing and bringing in the women and children.[16]

Stung by Sherman's rebuke, Custer started out on June 18, pushing his men hard. He rode west, then straight south, toward the Republican River, hoping to find Pawnee Killer or the Cheyennes somewhere in northwestern Kansas or eastern Colorado. Sherman had ordered him to scout the country thoroughly, then move north to Fort Sedgwick, in the northeastern tip of Colorado on the South Platte River, where he could take on supplies and receive further orders. But Custer had already written Libbie, telling her to meet him at Fort Wallace, in western Kansas, 150 miles south of Fort Sedgwick. His desire to be with her had become almost an obsession. By this time he could think of little else, especially since he had just learned that cholera had broken out at Fort Leavenworth and was spreading westward. Libbie might be sick, dying even—he was desperate to know. So when he reached the Republican River he decided to ignore his orders to proceed to Fort Sedgwick. Instead, he would stay where he was, about halfway between Forts Sedgwick and Wallace, and send a wagon train to Fort Wallace to pick up supplies. Libbie would be at Wallace and she could join the wagon train there, then come north with it to meet Custer in camp. Meanwhile, a small column could go to Fort Sedgwick and pick up any orders Sherman might have sent there.[17]

Custer's mistakes were overwhelming, even if understandable. His desire to have Libbie join him had clouded his judgment. He was supposed to be scouting for enemies, not establishing a semipermanent camp on the Republican River while one third of his fighting men escorted his wife safely to his side and another group ran an errand to Fort Sedgwick for him. He was in the middle of the Great Plains, the territory swarming with hostile Indians, and he had divided his relatively small force into three separate parts. He had told Libbie to join him in the field, but he had issued standing orders that if she were about to be captured by red men, any soldier in the vicinity should shoot to kill her.

Although it was a widespread practice in the frontier Army, Custer's orders to shoot Libbie rather than have her captured alive by the savages invites comment. Custer knew that most captives were eventually rescued and that many, especially younger ones, were so happy living with the Indians that they refused to return to civilization even when the opportunity was offered. But it was also true that a woman as young and pretty as Libbie was almost certainly going to be raped if captured, and even though most such victims survived and returned safely to their families, it was a gruesome, horrifying prospect. Still, for Custer to order her killed if capture seemed imminent seems extreme. A psychiatrist might be tempted to speculate that he loved his image of Libbie's purity more than he loved Libbie herself. But if that were true of Custer, it was also true of Libbie, for she knew of the order and approved of it. The Custers believed that capture by the Indians was literally a fate worse than death.

While Custer waited for Libbie on the Republican River, the Indians attacked him. At dawn on June 24 Pawnee Killer led a band of southern Oglalas in an assault on the camp, with the objective of stampeding and stealing some American horses. But Custer had his pickets well placed and the officer of the day, Lieutenant Tom Custer, was properly alert. Within minutes of Pawnee Killer's arrival the entire command was up and fighting—Custer wearing his red flannel night shirt—and they beat off the Indians.

After an hour or so, Pawnee Killer rode up under a flag of truce for a little talk. He wanted to know where Custer was going, and why, and couldn't he please have some sugar and coffee? Custer sharply refused—Pawnee Killer had promised peace, then attacked, and now was begging presents again. Pawnee Killer was much put out. He said he had been ready to come into the shadow of Fort McPherson, but Custer had gone on the warpath before the Indians could do so. After some angry words, he rode off. Custer had his troopers mount up and set off in hot pursuit, but they could not catch the Indians. Pawnee Killer's village, men, women, and children, easily outran the cavalry. Custer, disgusted, returned to camp.[18]

That afternoon a small party of Indians appeared on the horizon. Custer sent Captain Louis Hamilton (a lineal descendant of Alexander Hamilton) with a fifty-man detachment to investigate. The Indians disappeared, only to show themselves again on the next rise. This continued for about five miles, Hamilton riding deeper and deeper into the trap Pawnee Killer was setting. Finally the Indians separated into two parties, each going in different directions. Hamilton divided his troop into two parts of twenty-five men each, retaining command of one and putting the other under Tom Custer. Hamilton then rode forward, directly into an ambush. But Pawnee Killer had only a few rifles among his warriors, so Hamilton was able to fight his way out of the ambush without loss.[19]

For Custer, the important thing about the small skirmish was the lesson it taught. Indians, he reasoned, could not stand up to the fire power of cavalry. The problem of Indian fighting seemed to be as easy as it was frustrating—find the Indians. Once found, the cavalry could overwhelm any number of hostiles armed with bow and arrows. In other words, the trick was to come to grips with the Indians, and if that required following them into an ambush, then that was what must be done. (One hundred years later the United States Army in Vietnam operated on the same principle, i.e., it deliberately walked into Viet Cong ambushes as a way of forcing the enemy to fight, relying upon its superior fire power to win the ensuing battle.)

On June 28 the party that had gone to Fort Sedgwick to pick up Sherman's orders returned to Custer's camp on the Republican River. It had seen no Indians and received no message from Sherman. Everything indicated that Custer's presence on the Republican had forced the Indians to the south, a supposition that was reinforced by word that the Smoky Hill stagecoach line was again a shambles, Fort Wallace under a virtual siege. Custer suddenly realized that Libbie would be coming to him through hostile territory, in company with a loaded wagon train carrying supplies the Indians desperately wanted. Surely they would attack to get at the ammunition, coffee and sugar, and other supplies. Desperate with anxiety, Custer sent out a squadron in the direction of Fort Wallace, with orders to meet the incoming train and help escort it safely to camp.[20]

As Custer's empty wagon train had made its way south to Wallace the previous week, it had passed over an apparently level plateau. The terrain, however, was cut by numerous ravines. Will Comstock, serving as guide, had remarked that the red men would never waste their time attacking an empty wagon train, but rather would wait for it to take on supplies, then hit it on the return trip. "If the injuns strikes us at all," he added, "it will be just about the time we are comin' along back over this very spot. Now mind what I tell ye all."[21]

Sure enough, the Indians struck at the very spot Comstock predicted they would. But the column protecting the northbound wagon train never paused. Infantry moved out on the perimeter, surrounding the wagons and fighting off about five hundred Sioux and Cheyenne warriors, who circled the moving column but dared not come too close because of the superior fire power of the troops. The wagons and infantry slowly worked their way forward, firing as they went, while the Indians dashed around the outside, hoping for an opportunity to sneak in and strike a telling blow. For three hours or more the strange battle went on, the column slowly making its way northward, neither side suffering any serious casualties. Then Custer's relief column appeared and the Indians took off.

As the wagon train came into view of Custer's camp later that day (June 29), Custer sighed with relief. Libbie was safe! He rushed out to meet the escort, only to discover that no one knew anything about Libbie. She was not with the train and had not been at Fort Wallace. Custer figured that she had never received his letter. Knowing that she was safe from Indians, however, did not relieve Custer's worries—he still had the cholera to fret over.[22] Meanwhile, his thought that the troops could shoot their way out of any ambush was reinforced when he heard the details of the wagon-train fight with the Indians.

With his column intact again, Custer set off to scout to the northwest, toward the South Platte River, where he would cross the stage line from Fort Sedgwick to Denver and could obtain supplies from one of the stations. It was dry country, devoid of streams, and the early July sun blazed down on the marching men and horses, who became desperately thirsty. Some of Custer's dogs, plus a few mules, died of thirst that day. Custer pushed the men hard, so hard that they covered sixty-five miles in a day. When the moon came up the column was still marching. From the top of a bluff, Custer could see the South Platte River, seemingly only a couple of miles distant. Taking three men with him, Custer rode ahead of the column, saying he was going to locate a camp along the banks of the river and that the column should follow his trail. He did not explain why he couldn't send the Delaware scouts ahead to do that job, while he stayed with his command. The river turned out to be fifteen miles away, not two or three—Custer thereby learning something about the illusion of distances on the Plains, especially by moonlight—so the Custer party did not reach the South Platte until well past midnight. The men and horses rushed to the water where they quenched their terrible thirst. Using their saddles as pillows, the men almost immediately fell asleep. Meanwhile the column was marching slowly toward them over the prairie, while three miles up stream the Indians were ransacking a stagecoach station, killing three men. Custer slept blissfully. The main body of troops arrived on the South Platte about dawn.[23]

After breakfast Custer rode to Riverside station, where there was an intact telegraph line running to Fort McPherson. Custer sent a telegram to the fort, asking if any orders for him from Sherman had been received. The telegram in reply stated that they had indeed. Sherman had sent an order through channels, which Custer now read for the first time: "I don't understand about General Custer being on the Republican awaiting provisions from Fort Wallace. If this is so, and all the Indians be gone south, convey to him my orders that he proceed with all his command in search of the Indians towards Fort Wallace . . ."[24] Thus did Custer learn that his superior officer was angry with him again, this time for sitting on the Republican River waiting for his wife (a fact Sherman did not know) while the Indians ran wild on the Smoky Hill. Custer also learned that a detachment of ten men, under Lieutenant Lyman Kidder, had set out from Fort Sedgwick to find Custer's column and deliver Sherman's order. Here was fresh cause for anxiety—Kidder was riding toward Fort Wallace with only a few men, right through the heart of hostile territory.

Custer now had three reasons for making a forced march to Fort Wallace: Libbie might have arrived there; Sherman had ordered him there; he needed to find and, it was hoped, rescue the Kidder party, which was headed there. Custer told his men to be prepared to break camp at earliest dawn, July 7, for a march back across the waterless country they had just crossed.

This was too much for the troopers. While in the Indian country they had been afraid to desert, but now they were camped next to the stagecoach line. Not one of them wanted to repeat the terrible march of the previous day, many were tempted by the proximity to the Colorado gold mines, all were disgusted at the rotten rations they had to eat, and only the bravest looked forward to meeting the Indians who had attacked the wagon train from Fort Wallace. That night thirty-five of Custer's three hundred soldiers deserted.[25] Custer was so anxious to find Kidder, and not incidentally to get to Fort Wallace and Libbie, that he decided not to pursue the deserters; instead, at 5 A.M., he started the column southward.

After a fifteen-mile morning march, Custer halted the command and turned the horses out to graze while the men made coffee and had something to eat. When he gave the order to saddle up and prepare to resume the march, thirteen soldiers, seven of them on horseback, began moving north, back along the morning's trail and toward the stagecoach line. They were deserting in broad daylight, right under the nose of Custer and his officers. Custer had the bugler sound "Boots and Saddles," but the deserters continued on their way.

Custer was standing beside a small campfire, surrounded by enlisted men, many of whom intended to desert that night. They were intensely curious to see what their hard-bitten commander would do about this brazen act, while Custer was just as intensely aware that they were watching and that his reputation, the success of the campaign, and possibly even his very life depended on how he met the crisis. If desertions continued at the present rate, he might soon find himself and his officers alone in hostile territory.

The only horses saddled were those of the guard and a few of the officers. Custer called out to Lieutenant Henry Jackson, officer of the day, to take the guard, "follow those men, shoot them, and don't bring one back alive."[26] As Lieutenant Jackson gathered his men, Custer turned to his brother Tom, Lieutenant Cooke, and Major Joel H. Elliott, who were standing nearby and whose horses were saddled, and shouted loud enough for the men to hear, "I want you to get on your horses and go after those deserters and shoot them down."[27] The officers rode off, caught three deserters, shot and wounded them—the others got away—and brought them back to camp. The regimental surgeon started to move toward the wounded deserters to give medical aid, but Custer snapped at him, "Don't go near those men, Doctor. I have no sympathy for them." Custer had the three wounded men loaded into a springless wagon, then resumed his march. Later, out of earshot of the enlisted men, he told the surgeon to attend to the wounded deserters, but because of the absence of fresh water the doctor could not dress the wounds for forty-eight hours. One of the wounded men died, probably as a result of the lack of medical attention.[28] Insofar as he suffered no more desertions for the remainder of the march to Fort Wallace, Custer was satisfied with the results, although the movement away from the stagecoach line and into Indian country was probably more important in bringing about that result than the shooting of the deserters. Still, he had acted decisively at a critical moment and it is difficult to see how he could have done better.

Four days later Custer's column found the remains of Lieutenant Kidder and his men. The tracks told the story. Pawnee Killer and some of his warriors had come up behind Kidder's party. Kidder tried to make a run for it. The Indians caught him, killed everyone (the soldiers managed to bring down two Indians), and mutilated the bodies. It was a sickening sight and a worse smell, as the bodies had been lying in the July sun for days. The lesson seemed to be: if you are caught by Indians, stand and fight, relying on your fire power to keep the enemy out of effective bow and arrow range. Running was almost certain death, for although the American horses were faster than the Indian pintos, they lacked the ponies' endurance. Kidder had galloped for ten miles or more, but eventually his horses gave out and the Indians caught him.[29]

The next day Custer's column reached Fort Wallace. Custer desperately hoped that Libbie was safe inside—signs of Indians were all around, and the fort itself had been attacked twice in the past week—but when he arrived he discovered that she was at Fort Riley, at the other end of Kansas. Libbie, it seemed, had left Fort Hays before Custer's letter telling her to go to Fort Wallace had arrived. That news only added to his worries, however, because the word was that cholera had swept through Fort Riley.

There were no supplies at Fort Wallace, Custer's horses were generally played out and unfit for service, he felt his command was incapable of setting forth on another scouting expedition, and, most of all, he was frantic about Libbie. The Indians had so thoroughly cut the whites' communications that no mail could get through Kansas. Custer decided to call off his campaign, take the hundred best horses and most trustworthy men, and make a forced march to the east, toward Libbie. Since starting out with Hancock in March, Custer had covered nearly one thousand miles. More than 1,400 soldiers had scoured the countryside looking for Indians; the net result of this gigantic effort was two Indians killed, and they had been killed by the Kidder party. Meanwhile the Indians had left two hundred or more dead whites scattered across Kansas. Custer had not gotten off to much of a start as an Indian fighter.

Custer's excuse for calling off the campaign was that his horses were worn out, but that excuse didn't stand up when he immediately marched one hundred of those horses a total of 150 miles in fifty-five hours. His excuse for abandoning his command (not to mention leaving a fort that was under direct attack) was that he needed to get to Fort Harker, in central Kansas, to arrange for the shipment of supplies to Fort Wallace. The Kansas Pacific had reached beyond Fort Harker and there was a telegraph line there. Custer could send for supplies from Fort Leavenworth, which could be shipped to Fort Harker, where wagons could pick up the goods and return to Fort Wallace. The problem with that excuse was that the grazing was good around Fort Wallace; he could have stayed there until the horses recovered their strength. Besides, his enemies were doing just fine living off the countryside—the Indians certainly did not need to send for supplies every couple of weeks—and Custer could have emulated them. His real reason for pushing tired men and worn-out horses on a 150-mile forced march was to get to Libbie.

Custer started out on July 15. Many of his men could not keep up

with the pace and fell behind. Pawnee Killer attacked the stragglers
on the second day and killed two of them. Custer refused to go back
to either recover the bodies or to chase the hostiles, on the grounds
that time was important. Why, he did not say, but the closer he got
to Libbie the more difficult he found it to think of anything but her
health. On the morning of July 18 he reached Fort Hays. There
he left all but two officers and two men, with orders for the other
ninety-four members of the party to rest for a day, then proceed
at a leisurely pace to Fort Harker. Meanwhile he would push on.
By the time the main detachment arrived at Fort Harker, Custer
said, he would have arranged for supplies and wagons for the return
trip to Fort Wallace.

With his brother Tom, another officer, and two troopers, Custer
started off for Fort Harker. He rode sixty miles in less than twelve
hours, without changing horses. At 2 A.M. July 19 he entered Fort
Harker and woke up General A. J. Smith, commander of the military
district. As Smith rubbed the sleep from his eyes, Custer blurted
out some details about the campaign, said that ninety-four members
of the 7th Cavalry would be coming into Harker in two days, asked
to have supplies sent from Fort Leavenworth, and then requested
permission to get on the 3 A.M. train headed for Fort Riley. Smith
muttered his assent and went back to sleep.[30]

So Custer boarded the train for Fort Riley and Libbie. He had
hardly slept for a week, had covered nearly five hundred miles on
horseback during that time, and must have been exhausted. But
a cat nap on the bouncing, jolting train restored his energy and the
prospect of seeing Libbie revived his spirits. At noon the train pulled
into Fort Riley. Libbie was in her quarters, pacing in her room, as
worried about Autie as he was about her. Suddenly she heard the
clank of a saber on her porch rails and the quick, springy steps that
could mean only one thing. The door flew open, "and with a flood
of sunshine that poured in, came a vision far brighter than even the
brilliant Kansas sun. There before me, blithe and buoyant, stood
my husband! In an instant, every moment of the preceding months
was obliterated. What had I to ask more? What did earth hold for
us greater than what we then had? The General, as usual when happy
and excited, talked so rapidly that the words jumbled themselves
into hopeless tangles, but my ears were keen enough to extract from
the medley the fact that I was to return at once with him."[31]

Custer rushed about making preparations. He told Eliza to get
her cook-stove ready—she and it were coming with him and Libbie
to Fort Wallace. He and Libbie spent the remainder of the day

alone. That evening, just as the Custers were preparing to get on the train for the beginning of the trip back to Fort Wallace, he received a telegraph message from General Smith, ordering him to return to Harker and consider himself under arrest. When Smith had awakened later that morning he had realized that he had no authority to give permission to Custer to go to Fort Riley to see his wife, and in any case, what was Custer doing leaving his command in the field? Court-martial charges were being drawn up, accusing him of leaving Fort Wallace without permission. Captain West of the 7th Cavalry was preferring additional charges, accusing Custer of excessive cruelty and illegal conduct when he ordered his officers to shoot the deserters, of abandoning the two soldiers who had been killed on the march from Fort Wallace to Fort Harker, and of pushing the men beyond human endurance.

Custer knew he was in big trouble, but nothing could dampen his spirits now that he had found Libbie safe and healthy and had spent a day with her. Better yet, they were together now. Custer arrived at Fort Harker with Libbie on July 21, 1867. General Smith, who liked the Custers, decided to send them back again to Fort Riley, where the couple would be more comfortable. Custer would wait there, under house arrest, for his court-martial to begin.

Was the visit to Libbie worth the price he was going to have to pay? Libbie gave the answer years later, when she wrote the conclusion to her memoirs of her first year on the Plains: "There was in that summer of 1867 one long, perfect day. It was mine, and—blessed be our memory, which preserves to us the joys as well as the sadness of life!—it is still mine, for time and eternity."[32] If Custer had had an opportunity to do it all over again, he would not have changed a thing.

Back East, meanwhile, the politicians were furious. A senator from Missouri pointed out that "the war is now costing daily at least $150,000 and, if it lasts through the summer, (and at the present rate it will certainly do that) it will cost us $100,000,000 without having accomplished anything."[33] The railroad builders were just as angry. The Cheyennes had derailed a train on the Union Pacific line and thereby obtained vast quantities of supplies. Although this was the first time the hostiles had thought to make a train the target of an attack, the railroad men knew how vulnerable they were to such actions and they told Sherman they would build no farther until he could guarantee peace.

No American believed more thoroughly in the nation's destiny than General Sherman, and none was more committed than he to the idea that the transcontinental railroads were the carriers of that destiny. Despite Hancock's failure, Sherman still thought that forcing the Indians onto reservations was a better policy than bribing them there. On July 16 he wrote his brother Senator John Sherman to explain the problems of fighting Indians: "They operate in small, scattered bands, avoiding the posts and well-guarded trains, and hitting little parties who are off their guard." That was inaccurate— the Indians had attacked Custer's wagon train and hit the post at Fort Wallace. Sherman's explanation of the Army's failure was more to the point. Admitting that he had "a much heavier force on the plains" than any group of Indian warriors, he said the trouble was the vast expanse of the territory.

The truth was that fighting Indians on the Plains was more like naval warfare on the high seas than anything else. In effect, Sherman was lumbering around with battleships and cruisers, chasing pirates in sleek, much faster vessels. Worse, his ships had no staying power; they had to put into port (the forts) every other week or so to replenish their supplies. The pirates could live off the ocean. To continue the image, the wagons were merchant vessels. When they traveled alone, as did the stagecoaches, the pirates gobbled up every one they saw. When the wagons traveled in convoy, protected by fighting men, they got through.

In the Civil War, Sherman's great contribution to the Union victory was to destroy the enemy's resources, but the Indians had no base camps so the Army could not get at their resources. Treaties with the hostiles would do no good, Sherman said, because "they won't last twenty-four hours." Therefore, "we must fight the Indians, and force them to collect in agreed-on limits far away from the continental roads." Finally, to put things in perspective for his brother, who was one of the most influential men in the Senate, Sherman concluded: "I do think this subject as important as Reconstruction."[34]

Congress, however, had no faith left in the Army. Ignoring Sherman's plea for a more active war, it instead (July 20, 1867) provided for a peace commission to meet with the Plains Indians and see what could be done about negotiating an end to the war. In order to take some of the sting out of the Army's objections to this policy, Congress required that four of the seven commissioners be Army officers. Sherman himself was one of them, along with old General Harney, the pre-Civil War Indian fighter.

Sherman agreed to serve because he really had no choice. Further, he was beginning to see a way out of his difficulties, one that would not bring any glory to his beloved Army but which would accomplish the main objective. What Sherman realized was that the coming of the railroad to the Plains would eventually mean an end to the Indian's way of life. The advancing railroad brought settlement with it, and the settlers would crowd the Indians out. More immediately important, the railroad opened the country to the buffalo hunters. Eastern tanners were developing methods of curing buffalo hides and making them into acceptable coats and robes. There was a huge potential market for the hides. As the railroad reached ever deeper into the buffalo country, hunters would reduce the herds, then ship the hides east. By that system, the herds could be eliminated in a decade or less, and without the herds the Indians would have to go to reservations or starve. It would be, in short, a campaign with the enemies' resources, not the enemy himself, as the target.

The white hunters, shooting a thousand and more buffalo a week per gun, were Crazy Horse's and the Plains Indians' real enemies, not the soldiers. The hunters' vulnerability was the railroad line, for without it there could be no great buffalo hunt. Had the Indians concentrated on cutting the railroad line they could have stopped the buffalo hunting and, as a bonus, immobilized much of the Army. But except for the one time the Cheyennes derailed a Union Pacific train, the Indians left the "iron horse" alone, so the hunters were able to get to the range, then ship the hides east. Sherman counted on the completion of the railroads to solve the Indian problem. He did not want to make peace with Red Cloud; rather, he very much wanted to punish the Oglalas and Cheyennes for humiliating the Army. But even more important to him than vengeance was the completion of the railroad, so he agreed to serve on the peace commission. As he told his brother, the commission would have "to concede [to the Indians] a right to hunt buffaloes as long as they last, and this may lead to collisions, but it will not be long before all the buffaloes are extinct . . ."[35]

The program worked. In slightly more than ten years, a continental herd of buffalo numbering fifty million was reduced to a few thousand stragglers. By 1888 there were less than one thousand buffalo in the United States. So many buffalo robes were shipped east that the price quickly fell to $1.00 per hide.[36] The buffalo hunters, not the Army, cleared the Indians off the Plains.

Up on the Powder River in the summer of 1867, Red Cloud's forces had split. Tiring of the endless and fruitless skirmishes with the soldiers in Fort Phil Kearny, the northern Cheyennes had left. They went northwest to try their luck against Fort C. F. Smith. Crazy Horse also got bored with the daily skirmishes and took off a couple of times to steal a few horses from the Crows. Red Cloud may have decided that he had better do something dramatic before his whole force melted away; whatever his reasoning, he decided in late July to make a big effort against the white soldiers. Merely keeping the Bozeman Trail closed was not enough. It was true that the forts protected only their inhabitants, that the road they were supposed to keep open had been deserted by the public, but still the troops were there, in the heart of Oglala territory, and if the white soldiers stayed, more could come the next year. Then the Bozeman Trail would fill up with emigrants, just as the Holy Road had done two decades earlier, and the game would be frightened away. Where could the Oglalas go then?[37]

On the evening of August 1 Crazy Horse, Hump, Red Cloud, the other shirt-wearers, and other war leaders considered their tactical problem. They had so closely blockaded Fort Phil Kearny that the troops had had to fight just to obtain wood and water; eventually Captain J. N. Powell, with a detachment of twenty-six men, had set up a miniature fort on the edge of the Bighorn Mountains, where the pines grew. Powell had taken the boxes off the wagons and placed them in a circle. Inside the enclosure he had some tents for his men and room for the horses and mules at night. Within the corral Powell also had several carefully arranged boxes filled with several thousand rounds of ammunition, and his men were much better armed than Fetterman's had been, as they had the new breech-loading Springfield rifles.[38] The woodcutters had a small camp about a mile away.

The Indians had about one thousand warriors gathered in the area, with perhaps as many as two hundred rifles, but the guns were mostly single-shot muzzle-loaders and the Indians were woefully short of ammunition, with probably less than two bullets per gun. The warriors agreed that a direct attack against Powell's corral was impractical, but perhaps they could lure the soldiers out of the tiny fortress, get them into the open, and then overrun them as they had Fetterman's command. Certainly it was worth a try. Crazy Horse and Hump agreed to lead the decoy party in an attack on the woodcutters; Red Cloud would send the bulk of the warriors into the fight when Powell's men rushed from their corral to protect the woodcutters.

It was a good plan, but its success depended on patience and discipline, qualities the warriors sadly lacked. Crazy Horse and Hump, joined by Little Hawk, Little Big Man, and two others, did their part, setting off shortly after dawn to hit the woodcutters while the thousand warriors waited behind the hills. But when a soldier shot at Crazy Horse, the warriors broke ranks and came streaming out of the hills, whooping and shouting, spoiling everything. Some swept down on the American horse-and-mule herd and drove it off, while others joined the decoy party for an assault on the woodcutters' camp. Crazy Horse attacked with them, killed one white and saw Little Hawk kill another, and then started to chase the fleeing woodcutters into the mountains. But he soon found that he was alone—his comrades had stopped at the camp to scalp, plunder, and then burn the white men's tents. When Crazy Horse rode in from the mountainside he found them squatting in the shade, eating molasses and hard bread. He yelled at them, told them they were fools, slapped one or two, spilled the molasses on the ground, and eventually got them back on their horses. Then he led them over to the corral, where the soldiers and a few woodcutters who had escaped were gathered.[39]

Crazy Horse and Hump now led a grand circling of the corral, the warriors holding onto their ponies with one foot, riding at top speed, firing arrows from under the ponies' necks. The other shirt-wearers made sure no one went too close. Their idea was to get the soldiers to expend their ammunition, then rush the corral as the whites paused to reload. But to Crazy Horse's vast surprise, the firing never slackened. Powell had almost forty men inside the corral and they kept up a continuous fire with their Springfields. After five or six ponies had been shot, Crazy Horse called off the circling and pulled the warriors back into a ravine. He, Hump, and the other shirt-wearers agreed that they were not going to get anywhere with a circling, so they decided to leave the ponies in the ravine and attempt to approach the corral on foot. Red Cloud, watching from a distant bluff, sent a smoke signal warning them to be careful.

At this point in the fight, the Indians suffered from the absence of firm, unified leadership. The ravine narrowed as it approached the corral, so the Indians attacked in a V formation, with Crazy Horse and Hump at the point of the V. The trouble was that the men in front masked the mass of warriors in the rear, making it impossible for them to fire. A second difficulty was that the Oglalas were attacking from one side of the corral only, so Powell was able to shift all his men to that part of the corral. Had Red Cloud signaled for half the warriors to ride around to the other side of the corral and launch a simultaneous attack, Powell's position could have been overrun. As it was, Powell only had to deal with a handful of Indians, Crazy Horse and his fellow shirt-wearers at the apex of the charge.

Despite these handicaps, the Indian charge was a frightening spectacle. They came on painted and dressed for war, their spears and shields held high, chanting war songs, zigzagging, firing arrows ahead, dropping into low places and rising to run closer to fire again. "It chilled my blood," one of Powell's men later recalled. "Hundreds and hundreds of Indians swarming up a ravine about ninety yards to the west of the corral . . . formed in the shape of a letter V. Immediately we opened a terrific fire upon them. Our fire was accurate, coolly delivered and given with most telling effect, but nevertheless it looked for a minute as though our last moment on earth had come."[40]

Crazy Horse was growing desperate. The wagon boxes that formed the corral looked like pincushions, so covered were they with arrows sticking into the wood, but the arrows could not penetrate as a bullet could have done and the fire of the whites still did not slacken. Hunkering down in a low place near the corral, Crazy Horse started motioning the braves back. Just then a tall Oglala named Jipala, stripped to his breechcloth, started walking toward the corral, singing his war song. All the warriors watched this brave deed. When Jipala got close he drew his bow, leaped high in the air, and fired an arrow into the corral. Then he shot another and another, firing faster than even the breech-loading Springfields could. But the soldiers began to concentrate their fire on him and Jipala was cut down. Crazy Horse then led the warriors back down the ravine, away from the murderous fire. He had lost six killed and six wounded, far too many, even though the Indians had killed several woodcutters, one officer, and five enlisted men, and had captured the horses and mules. Powell's fire power was too much for Crazy Horse to overcome, and when he heard from a scout that a hundred-man force was coming from Fort Phil Kearny to relieve Powell, he led the warriors back into the hills. The Wagon Box Fight was over.[41]

That was the last charge Crazy Horse ever led against whites occupying a strong defensive position. He had learned that Indians armed with bows and arrows could not overwhelm whites armed with breech-loaders inside a fortification, no matter how greatly the Indians outnumbered the whites. With arms and ammunition the Indians could do better, he knew, but where were they to obtain them? Besides, if the warriors would not obey orders, it hardly mattered if they had rifles or not. In a running fight over open ground it would be a different story. Though the individual bravery of the Sioux warriors was of little use in attacking a fort defended by breech-loaders, it could be put to good use in combat with troops caught out on the prairie. For the remainder of the summer of 1867 Crazy Horse concentrated on hit-and-run raids against any whites foolish enough to venture out onto the Bozeman Trail, but he left Fort Phil Kearny alone.

This war on the Powder River was just the kind the Sioux liked best. As George Hyde puts it, "The soldiers did not bother them, permitting them to take matters into their own hands and run the war to suit their own convenience. They went to Fort Laramie in the spring to talk, and to attempt to obtain ammunition; then they had their buffalo hunt and Sun Dance; after that they went to Fort Phil Kearny and had a good fight, then to Fort Reno and made some raids, obtaining more horses and plunder. The autumn hunt ended the year's activities, and they then retired to their winter camps, happy and in perfect trust that the white soldiers would not come out and force them to fight at this season, when they wished to be quiet."[42]

In the fall of 1867 Black Buffalo Woman had her third child by No Water. Crazy Horse was often seen hanging around her tipi, exchanging a few words with her, or just watching as she played with her children and did her tasks. Gossips wondered if they would run off together. Eagle Foot's wife had just left him for another man, and Eagle Foot had acted as a Sioux warrior was supposed to act in such circumstances. He had accepted the two ponies that the man who took his wife offered in payment and even had his former wife's mother come to live in his tipi and care for his lodge. But, the gossips said, No Water was a different case. He was a jealous man and if Black Buffalo Woman moved in with Crazy Horse, No Water would be sure to make trouble. As a shirt-wearer, Crazy Horse was under a strong injunction to cause no trouble within the tribe, so he would have to be content with an occasional glimpse of the woman he loved. No Water's brother, Black Twin, had just been made a shirt-wearer too, so Crazy Horse had another reason to keep his distance.[43]

There was already trouble enough in the Oglala camp. The Indians were quarreling. They had been living the wild life for five years and some of them longed for the good things of the white men. These people began to argue that the Oglalas should emulate the Laramie Loafers. Let us go down to Fort Laramie for the coming winter, they said, and enjoy some coffee and sugar, perhaps a little whiskey. Possibly we can get some ammunition. In the spring we can come back up here for a good hunt and a little fighting. Red Cloud, Crazy Horse, and most of the warriors would have none of it. They did not trust the whites and would not move near them under any circumstances. They could no more abide the thought of being penned up on a reservation, even if only temporarily, than Custer could abide the thought of Libbie's being captured alive by savages.

The Oglala women quarreled, too. One afternoon following a successful buffalo hunt, two women were working over the hides. They got into a fight over the question of going down to Fort Laramie and one woman slashed at the other with her skinning knife. When the husband of the woman who did not want to go tried to calm her down, she marched back to their tipi and threw his pipe, his weapons, his medicine bag, his back rest, everything that was his, out of the lodge. "Take your warrior stuff to the white man!" she shouted. "It may be that you are still man enough for a Loafer woman, but not for my lodge!"[44]

But some of the Oglalas were receptive when messengers arrived from General Sherman and the new peace commission, requesting Red Cloud's presence at a big council at Fort Laramie that fall of 1867. Some wanted to go, but most held back. Crazy Horse and the other shirt-wearers were strongly opposed to going to Fort Laramie until the soldiers abandoned the Powder River forts. Sherman was prepared to promise to do just that, as the messengers indicated, but promises were unsatisfactory. The warriors wanted proof.

This was the first time the whites had asked for Red Cloud by name, which caused another problem. Red Cloud was a war leader, not a Big Belly, and besides, no one man could speak for all the Oglalas, not even Old Man Afraid, the acknowledged head of the Big Bellies. So the tribe stayed on the Powder River, sending word that there could be a peace council at Fort Laramie when the forts were abandoned.[45] Old Man Afraid, whom everyone trusted, carried the message.[46]

The whites, meanwhile, were making widely exaggerated claims about the Wagon Box Fight. Powell himself estimated that his men had killed sixty Indians; as was typical of the Army on the frontier, he had inflated the body count by a factor of ten. But that was just the beginning. By the time the story got back to civilization, hundreds of Indians had bitten the dust. Eventually, white writers claimed that Red Cloud lost 1,500 warriors that day.[47]

Sherman knew better. He doubted that the body count could have gone over fifty, and in any case what stood out was the presence of a mass of warriors. Red Cloud had been able to hold his force together and it would have to be whipped in fair fight before it retired from the field. But there was not the slightest chance that Sherman could get the necessary funds from Congress to wage a successful campaign against the Oglalas. Making things worse, the day before the Wagon Box Fight more than five hundred Cheyennes had attacked Fort C. F. Smith. This was a war of an altogether different magnitude than the relatively small affairs on the Republican and Smoky Hill rivers. The hostiles in the Powder River country were simply too strong for the Army.

Besides, Sherman reasoned, it did not matter at the moment, since the Kansas Pacific tracks were far south of Oglala territory. He could leave the Red Cloud forces alone for a while, let them hunt buffalo and fight the Crows for a few more years. Like any good counterinsurgency general, Sherman knew that the only way to win a guerrilla war was to round up the people and put them into concentration camps, where they could be watched and controlled. He would do that to the Indians of the central Plains first, then put the Oglalas on their reservation when the time came. Meanwhile, the Army needed peace in the Powder River country in order to fight in Kansas, the politicians demanded peace, and the Indians seemed ready for peace. Much as he wanted to punish the Oglalas, Sherman himself was willing to accept a truce. He set off from St. Louis in search of one.

Sherman and his fellow commissioners made a whirlwind tour for peace. They went up the Missouri to talk to the wild Sioux of the far-north country, Sitting Bull's people, then down to Fort McPherson, in Nebraska, where in early October 1867 they met with Spotted Tail. The Brulé chief told them to get the white people off the Bozeman Trail and said that although he was one of those who had signed the treaty of 1866, which had provided that he would move onto a reservation and go into farming, he was in no hurry to begin. Spotted Tail indicated that he much preferred hunting to farming and if the commissioners wanted to make him happy, they should give him some guns and ammunition. Sherman said no: Spotted Tail must learn that he could no longer live by the chase. Then Sherman threatened to exterminate the Indians. If the Brulés tried to interfere with the building of the railroads, Sherman said, "the Great Father, who out of kindness for you, has heretofore held back the white soldiers and people, will let them out, and you will be swept out of existence."

Following the lecture to Spotted Tail, Sherman went down to the vicinity of Fort Larned, in Kansas, where in mid-October 1867 the peace commission met with some Apaches, Arapahoes, southern Cheyennes, Comanches, and Kiowas. The Indians took their presents and touched the pen to a treaty that required them to vacate the country between the railroads, moving south of the Arkansas. They also agreed to take up farming as soon as there were insufficient buffalo south of the Arkansas River to justify the chase. When the hunting played out, they would stay within the boundaries of their concentration camps.[48]

With peace seemingly assured along both rail lines, Sherman and the peace commission hurried north to Fort Laramie, where they hoped to persuade Red Cloud to touch the pen. But when the commissioners arrived at Fort Laramie on November 9, they found a few Crows—always friendly to the whites, who after all were enemies of their enemies—but only Old Man Afraid from the Oglalas. Old Man Afraid informed them that the Sioux were making war in order to save the only hunting grounds left to them. He assured the commissioners that when the troops were withdrawn from the Powder River forts the war would cease. Sherman might have been willing to go along, but it was too late in the season to start the infantry at Fort C. F. Smith and Fort Phil Kearny on a 250- or 300-mile march. Besides, Army morale would sink with such an abject surrender. Sherman still hoped the Army could save some face. The council broke up with nothing accomplished.[49]

Crazy Horse spent the winter of 1867–68 on the Powder River, living the free life he loved best. Still unmarried, suffering the pangs of unrequited love, he felt satisfaction and happiness in providing for the helpless ones. Although there was plenty of dry buffalo meat in camp, the old folks and the widows and orphans appreciated it when Crazy Horse would drop by with some elk or other fresh meat. He came to be known as a reliable provider for those in need, a fact that enhanced his reputation. Sitting Bull once explained to a white reporter how reputations were made among the Sioux. The reporter had asked him why the tribe looked up to him. Sitting Bull replied with a question, "Your people look up to men because they are rich; because they have much land, many lodges, many squaws?"

"Yes," the newspaperman replied. "Well," said Sitting Bull, "I suppose my people look up to me because I am poor."[50] Crazy Horse was repaid for his leadership and generosity, in other words, with prestige only, which was just the way he wanted it.

Custer, meanwhile, had gone from Fort Riley to Fort Leavenworth. His court-martial proceedings began in September 1867. At the fort, Lawrence Frost writes, "sides were taken and wagers made. Would they throw the book at Custer? Was he the one selected by the brass to be the goat? . . . Could Custer beat the rap? Was General Grant bucking for President and aiding his political ambitions by placing General Custer on the sacrificial altar so that the blame for the disastrous summer Indian campaign would be taken off the army's ranking general officer?"[51]

Custer was confident, even cocky. Libbie helped him prepare his defense, copying down a fifty-page statement. The main charges were abandoning his command without authority and shooting the deserters without a trial. Captain West, who was responsible for all the charges but one, could not appear because of drunkenness. He had always been in the anti-Custer clique and had smarted under a reprimand given him by Custer on the day they had arrived at Fort Wallace, for "becoming so drunk as to be unfit for the proper performance of his duty." After receiving the reprimand, West preferred charges against Custer, then went back to the bottle, which shortly killed him.

Tom Custer testified for his brother, as did Major Elliott, Lieutenant Cooke, and the regimental surgeon. No other officer of the 7th Cavalry was willing to testify in Custer's behalf, but the 7th was still at Fort Wallace, so the anti-Custerites did not come to Leavenworth to testify against him either, even though most wanted to do so. Despite these advantages, on October 10 the court found Custer guilty on all counts. It suspended him from rank and command for one year, with forfeiture of all pay.[52] Custer hoped to have the decision overturned by a reviewing board, but on November 18 Sherman issued a statement that the "proceedings, findings and sentence in the case of Brevet Major General Custer† are approved by General Grant . . . in which the levity of the sentence, considering the nature of the offenses of Bvt. Major General Custer . . . is to be remarked on." Grant was "convinced that the Court, in awarding so lenient a sentence for the offenses of which the

---

† Post-Civil War soldiers nearly always referred to each other by the highest rank held, no matter what the current rank. "Brevet" means temporary.

accused is found guilty, must have taken into consideration his previous record."[53]

Custer was far from chagrined. As Libbie wrote a friend during the trial, "When he [Custer] ran the risk of a court-martial in leaving Wallace he did it expecting the consequences . . . and we are quite determined not to live apart again, even if he leaves the army . . ." Custer had written her repeatedly during the campaign that he was "tempted to desert" and fly to her before accepting a long separation. Now they were together, happy.[54]

Custer and Libbie spent the winter of 1867–68 at Fort Leavenworth. General Philip Sheridan had taken over Hancock's command of the Department of the Missouri and Sheridan gave the couple his suite of nicely appointed apartments at the fort.[55]

Fort Leavenworth was the largest post on the frontier and the closest to civilization. There were parties, dances, parades, and good hunting available. Sheridan promised to use his connections in Washington to try to get the sentence reduced so that Custer could look forward to another opportunity to prove himself as an Indian fighter. It was a fine winter.

CHAPTER SIXTEEN

The Treaty of 1868 and the Battle of the Washita

"Go ahead in your own way and I will back you with my whole authority. If it results in the utter annihilation of these Indians, it is but the result of what they have been warned of again and again . . . I will say nothing and do nothing to restrain our troops from doing what they deem proper on the spot, and will allow no mere vague general charges of cruelty and inhumanity to tie their hands, but will use all the powers confided to me to the end that these Indians, the enemies of our race and of our civilization, shall not again be able to begin and carry out their barbarous warfare on any kind of pretext they may choose to allege."   Sherman to Sheridan, October 9, 1868

By the spring of 1868 the war on the Powder River had settled into a stalemate. Red Cloud, Crazy Horse, and the Sioux warriors were unwilling to try their luck in any direct assaults on the forts, while the whites were equally unwilling to venture onto the Bozeman Trail. The only fighting Crazy Horse did was during occasional raids against the Crows. The forts belonged to the white soldiers, but the trail and everything else in the Powder River country still belonged to the Sioux. The region contained what may have been, at this time, the largest remaining buffalo herd on the continent, so the Indians lived well while the soldiers ate stale bread and beans.

During the preceding winter the Army had decided it would have to abandon its hard-won positions on the Bozeman Trail. Its reasons were manifold. First, Sherman wanted to launch an extensive search-and-destroy campaign in Kansas in the coming summer and he badly needed the contribution of the regiment of infantry stationed on the Bozeman Trail. The total strength of the United States Army was around 55,000, but more than half these troops were on occupation duty in the former Confederate states, while a significant portion of the rest were on coastal defense duty.[1] The troops at Forts Reno, Phil Kearny, and C. F. Smith represented more than

10 per cent of Sherman's total frontier force—and they were totally wasted, as they could neither guard emigrants nor attack Indians.[2]

Despite these obvious facts, Army officers generally were opposed to abandoning the forts. They had paid a terrible price in blood to establish them and abject surrender hurt their pride. To a man, they expected to have to fight the Sioux again; the idea that the Plains of Wyoming and Montana would be left to the savages for any length of time was inconceivable. Sooner rather than later the Indians would have to be driven onto reservations, and when the time came to settle the score with the Powder River hostiles, the forts would be invaluable as bases of operation. Most of all, the forts represented a threat to the Sioux and there was no point in abandoning them without getting something in return.

Sherman took all these considerations into account as he prepared in the spring of 1868 to resume his peace-making role on the peace commission. He needed troops for Kansas; he had to shut up congressional critics, who were asking embarrassing questions about the cost-effectiveness of the Powder River war; he needed to get the Sioux to agree to something in return for abandoning the forts; he needed to maintain Army morale. He met all these objectives in the peace treaty of 1868.

Sherman was more convinced than ever that eventually the white buffalo hunters would force the Indians to become wards of the government, but the buffalo hunters could not do their work if the railroad did not continue to push west. In the meantime, what he feared most was a resumption of active warfare along the Powder River, which would tie down the Army and make it difficult for it to extract itself. Grant, the General-in-Chief of the Army, had the same fear. On March 2, 1868, after consultation with Sherman, Grant issued an order requiring the abandonment of Forts Smith, Phil Kearny, and Reno as soon as weather permitted. He told Sherman to speed up the movement as much as possible, "because by delay the Indians may commence hostilities and make it impossible for us to give them up."[3]

In drawing up the treaty, Sherman and his fellow peace commissioners seemed to give in to Red Cloud's demands. The Sioux could keep forever all of South Dakota west of the Missouri River, while the territory between the Black Hills and the Bighorn Mountains (the Powder River country) would be "unceded Indian territory." No whites would be allowed to enter it and the Sioux could hunt there as long as there were sufficient buffalo to justify the chase. No changes could be made in the treaty without the consent of three quarters of the adult male Sioux population (how on earth the commissioners thought this clause could ever be fulfilled among wild Indians is a mystery).

The main point was that the Army agreed to abandon the forts. As Doane Robinson puts it, "It is the only instance in the history of the United States where the government has gone to war and afterwards negotiated a peace conceding everything demanded by the enemy and exacting nothing in return."[4] Over the century and more that has elapsed since the signing of the treaty, the Oglalas have argued that this treaty, properly ratified by the Senate and therefore carrying the pledged word (not to mention the good faith and honor) of the United States Government, has been deliberately and illegally ignored by that government, beginning with the theft of the Black Hills in the 1870s. In 1973, Russell Means and other members of the American Indian Movement, at the head of a force of young warriors and in defiance of the tribal elders, took possession of Wounded Knee, South Dakota. Their major demand was restoration of Sioux rights under the treaty of 1868.

But the whites were not the only signatories to the treaty, nor were they the only violators of it. Sherman had put a joker in the deck, a joker that represented the common ground on which both the Indian lovers and the Indian haters on the commission and throughout the nation could stand. The joker was civilization. When the Sioux signed the treaty, they agreed to become civilized (i.e., to take up farming and live in houses). The whites could think of only two solutions to the Indian problem—civilization or extermination. As the Army was not strong enough to exterminate them, Sherman agreed to give civilizing a try.

The civilizing portions of the treaty were like a dream come true to the Indian Bureau and to friends of the Indian everywhere. The Sioux agreed to settle down on farms when the buffalo were gone, and there were complex provisions requiring the government to provide them with wagons, plows, oxen, and other necessary items. Further, the Sioux agreed to compulsory education for their children between six and sixteen years of age. In Sherman's view it didn't hurt to try; in the Indian Bureau's view, cutting the children's hair and teaching them to read the Bible would solve the Indian problem.[5]

But neither side kept its promises. The Indians, however, always claimed that the treaty had not been properly explained to them, and although this point has been disputed,[6] it is difficult to believe that Crazy Horse, Hump, Young Man Afraid, or any of the warriors could have agreed to Red Cloud's touching the pen had they known that they were thereby promising to send their children to the white man's schoolhouse, which had all the appearance of a prison to them.

Sherman had a hard enough time getting Red Cloud to sign as it was. The general and the commission arrived at Fort Laramie in early April 1868, expecting to meet Red Cloud there. But Red Cloud had told the runners from Fort Laramie that he would sign nothing until the forts were actually abandoned. For nearly two months, Sherman sat at the fort and fumed. "The situation was little short of grotesque," James Olson writes. "Here were representatives of the President—the intrepid Indian fighters Sherman, Harney, Terry, and Augur; the distinguished peace advocates Taylor, Henderson, Sanborn, and Tappan. They had come west with wagon-loads of presents and a treaty which conceded everything Red Cloud had demanded, and they could not even get him to come in and talk to them."[7] The commissioners signed up all the friendlies in the area (by this time it was becoming an annual event for these friendlies to sign a treaty of peace between Red Cloud and the Americans and receive handsome gifts in return), but mainly the commissioners sat, impatiently waiting for Red Cloud. The officers at the forts, meanwhile, were dragging their feet on vacating on the excuse that they needed to dispose of valuable property before leaving. In late May, disgusted, Sherman and the commissioners left Fort Laramie, leaving behind a copy of the treaty for Red Cloud to sign when, and if, he ever came in.

On July 29, 1868, the troops at Fort C. F. Smith finally marched away. At dawn the next morning Crazy Horse and his warriors swept down on the post and set it afire. A few days later the soldiers left Forts Reno and Phil Kearny, which the Indians also burned. Red Cloud then started out for Fort Laramie, but stopped to make meat when he ran into a herd of buffalo. He sent word to Fort Laramie that he would come in after his work was done. Not until late October 1868 had he made enough meat for the winter. Then he went down to Fort Laramie to see what the representatives of the Great White Father had to say.

On November 4 Red Cloud and about 125 Indian leaders, representing the Oglalas, Hunkpapas, Sans Arcs, and others (but not Crazy Horse, who stayed in the Powder River country) entered Fort Laramie to begin the conference. After they had settled down, the white representatives entered the lodge. Most of the headmen rose and shook hands cordially, but Red Cloud remained seated and sulkily gave the ends of his fingers to the whites who advanced to shake hands with him. The conference then bogged down in two days of irrelevancies and misunderstandings. Eventually Red Cloud, "with a show of reluctance and tremulousness washed his hands with the dust of the floor" and put his mark on the treaty. Old Man Afraid and the other headmen followed.

Red Cloud then rose to make a speech. He was, he said, ready for peace. It would be difficult for him to control the young warriors, but as for himself he would live up to the treaty as long as the white man did so. He was as good as his word—never again did Red Cloud make war on the whites. He did not, however, fully live up to the treaty. If he ever understood the complex provisions about taking up farming and having the children educated, he had no intention of fulfilling those clauses. Instead, he announced his determination to return at once to the Powder River, where the Sioux would live among the buffalo during the winter of 1868–69 and make war on the Crows the following spring. The Sioux had no desire to abandon the chase at a time when their country abounded in game, they did not know how to farm, and so long as there were buffalo they did not care to learn. With that, Red Cloud marched out of Fort Laramie, the others following.[8] The Powder River war was over.

Crazy Horse had much to celebrate. He had helped conquer from the Crows what was now the Oglala home territory, then played a leading role in turning back the white invaders. He could congratulate himself on a job well done. For the first time in his life he was entirely free of whites, free to live as a hunter and nomad in one of the most spectacular and bountiful wild game areas in the world. His freedom to roam had been somewhat curtailed—Red Cloud agreed in the treaty that the Oglalas would never again go south of the Platte River—but not enough to matter. For the next five years the Powder River Indians did as they pleased. Ho-ka hey! It was a good time to live.

Custer and Libbie, meanwhile, had moved from Fort Leavenworth to Monroe, Michigan, in June 1868, when the 7th Cavalry began its summer campaign in Kansas. In Monroe, Custer wrote his Civil War memoirs and killed time by hunting, fishing, and boating in Lake Erie. He also followed the news from Kansas, which was distressing. Sheridan had sent out search-and-destroy missions but the cavalrymen were still unable to catch any Indians; the hostiles, meanwhile, had killed 124 settlers in Kansas and Colorado. Sherman was nearly beside himself; he raged at the Army's incompetence. "The more we can kill this year," he said pointedly, "the less will have to be killed the next year for the more I see of these Indians the more I am convinced that they will all have to be killed or be maintained as a species of paupers."[9] The Monroe *Commercial* carried stories about outrages in Kansas "too horrible to detail."[10]

The Cheyennes, southern Oglalas, Arapahoes, and other tribes of the central Plains were all on the warpath, a fact that was extremely disconcerting to Sherman and the Army, as these same Indians had signed a peace treaty the previous fall. The Army, indeed the whole frontier, was seized by a mood of self-righteous indignation. The government had lived up to its part of the treaty with the Kansas Indians; then those Indians, without provocation, had gone back to looting, burning, and murdering. Even the Indian agents had to admit that the warriors needed punishing. Frontier posts reverberated with tough talk about what would be done to the Indians, once caught, and it became an article of faith among the Army officers that "you could never trust an Indian." Sheridan's famous remark, "The only good Indian I ever saw was dead," was often and gleefully quoted.

From the Indian point of view, the raids were a necessary part of their defense of their hunting grounds. The railroads were pushing west, bringing fingers of settlement with them, and the buffalo herds were disappearing from Kansas. These Indians of the central Plains were in much worse condition than Crazy Horse's Oglalas because the white buffalo hunters had already reached the Kansas range and were reducing the herds at an alarming rate. Indian communications across the Plains were excellent, and the hostiles south of the Platte River knew about the abandonment of the Powder River forts. Perhaps they figured that if they fought as Red Cloud and Crazy Horse had fought, they too could secure permanent title to their land.[11]

Whatever the cause of the central Plains war, the Army was determined to prosecute it with full vigor. The trouble was the same as the previous summer, however—no one could catch the hostiles. Sheridan had troops roaming throughout Kansas, but the only action came when the Indians discovered and attacked the troops, not vice versa. In September 1868 a party of fifty-two soldiers was almost rubbed out by the Indians near the Republican River in southwestern Nebraska. Totally exasperated, Sheridan consulted with Sherman and the two generals decided to ask Grant to reduce Custer's sentence and allow him to take command of the 7th Cavalry, then at

Fort Dodge. Why they did so is something of a puzzle, since Custer was hardly a proven Indian fighter and indeed had been no more successful at catching hostiles than anyone else. But Sheridan had seen Custer in action in the Civil War and knew that the boy general would fight if he had the opportunity, while Sherman may have reasoned that Custer would be so determined to salvage his reputation that he would either get the job done or die in the attempt. After ten months in disgrace, they could count on Custer's being like a coiled spring, ready to strike.

On September 24, 1868, Custer received a telegram:

> Headquarters Department of the Missouri
> In the Field, Fort Hays, Kansas
> September 24, 1868

> General G. A. Custer, Monroe, Michigan:

> Generals Sherman, Sully, and myself, and nearly all the officers of your regiment have asked for you, and I hope the application will be successful. Can you come at once? . . .

> P. H. Sheridan
> Major General Commanding[12]

Custer was off immediately, on the first train headed west from Monroe. He left Libbie behind, but brought along two Scotch staghounds and a pointer. Early in the morning of September 30 he arrived at Fort Hays, Kansas, where he joined Sheridan for a full day of discussion.

Sheridan had taken command on the Plains after Hancock's disastrous 1867 campaign, just as in the Civil War he had been brought into the Shenandoah Valley to save the situation there for the Union after other generals had failed. Next to Grant and Sherman, he was the most popular general in the country. Thirty-six years old and a bachelor, he liked to think of himself as the hardest-bitten commander in the Army. He cursed as naturally as he breathed; an English nobleman found Sheridan "a delightful man, with the one peculiarity of using the most astounding swear words quite calmly and dispassionately in ordinary conversation."[13] He owed his Civil War reputation, thought a West Point classmate, to his audacity coupled with "a perfect indifference as to how many of his men were killed if he only carried his point."[14] Like Sherman, he believed in the doctrine of total war. His orders from Sherman, quoted at the beginning of this chapter, reflected their mutual belief that all Indians, women and children as well as men, must be made to feel the horrors of war before the warriors would lose their will to fight.

Sheridan now told Custer that he wanted to carry out a winter campaign with the 7th Cavalry in order to hit the Indians literally where they lived. It was intolerable that the hostiles should be free to move near the agencies every winter, draw supplies, rest and refit, and then hit the warpath when their ponies fattened up in the spring. They were much too mobile to catch in the summertime —a fact Custer knew full well—so the thing to do was to locate their winter villages and strike them there, when they were more or less immobile because of the weakness of the ponies. Sheridan confessed that when he talked with the white scouts about the possibilities of a winter campaign, they were all against it on the grounds that if a column of troops were caught by a blizzard on the open prairie, every man in the command would perish. But Sheridan was not ready to give up. What did Custer think?

"How soon do I start?"

No wonder Sheridan and Sherman had pulled strings to get the boy wonder back on active duty! After telling Custer to go at once to Fort Dodge to assume command of the 7th Cavalry, then whip it into shape for a winter campaign, Sheridan concluded, "Custer, I rely on you in everything, and shall send you on this expedition without orders, leaving you to act entirely on your own judgment."[15] Custer dashed off a note to Libbie, telling her to come to Fort Leavenworth at once and promising to go back there and see her at every opportunity. Then he rode off for Fort Dodge.

Custer did a masterful job of getting his men ready. He held target practice twice daily, taught the recruits to ride, saw to it that they were properly equipped, and took them on a two-week shakedown march that put them into fighting trim. He fought a number of skirmishes with marauding Indians who attacked his wagon train or attempted to run off his herd. He regarded the engagements as excellent training for the men. He hired some Osage guides and a number of white scouts, who were paid $75 per month; Custer promised a $100 bonus to the first scout who led the regiment to an Indian village. He maintained formal, but correct, relations with those officers of the 7th Cavalry who hated him and resumed his fun-loving pranks with his friends, most of all with his brother Tom. To get himself into shape, Custer went on long hunts across the prairie, along with some duck hunting on the Arkansas River sloughs. Once he bagged a pelican and sent the specimen to the Audubon Society of Detroit. He obtained special overshoes of buffalo hide with the hair inside and started growing what became an enormous beard. In his fringed leather jacket covered by a buffalo robe and wearing a fur cap, he looked rather like a grizzly bear. By early November he was ready to start. "I do not long for glory or fame," he told Libbie, who knew better. "My reward is centered on ending this trying separation."[16]

On November 12, 1868—a week after Red Cloud signed the Fort Laramie treaty—Sheridan and Custer started off at the head of a mixed force of infantry and cavalry. They marched straight south to the North Canadian River, near the Oklahoma panhandle, where they built Camp Supply, just south of the Kansas boundary. Camp Supply would be the base of operations for a winter campaign against the Indians who had been raiding into Kansas the past summer. Oklahoma was supposed to be safe territory for the hostiles, who had never been attacked there; indeed, the previous summer all the Indians ever heard from the whites was, "Move south of the Arkansas River and we will leave you alone." Complicating matters, the Army had established Fort Cobb on the Washita River, about 150 miles south of Camp Supply. Cobb was more an agency than a fort, its purpose being to provide protection and food for friendly Indians. The tribes camping on the Washita drew their supplies there and felt they were safe. Their hot-blooded young warriors, however, were still making raids north into Kansas and south into Texas and the chiefs could not or would not control them. Sherman had made it clear that in a case of hot pursuit, the troops could attack any villages they encountered near Fort Cobb.[17]

After establishing Camp Supply, Sheridan had to mediate a dispute over rank. The governor of Kansas had raised a force of volunteers for the Indian wars and was bringing it, under his own command, to Camp Supply. Fearful that the governor would claim seniority, Lieutenant Colonel Alfred Sully of the Army's expedition issued an order claiming the command in his capacity as a brevet brigadier general. Lieutenant Colonel Custer promptly countered with an order assuming command in his brevet grade of major general. Sheridan confirmed Custer and sent Sully back to district headquarters at Fort Leavenworth.[18] Custer prepared to march the next day, before the Kansas volunteers arrived.

On the morning of November 23, 1868, Custer woke to find his tent covered with snow. A foot of fresh snow was already on the ground and the wind was howling, bringing more snow with it. Vi-

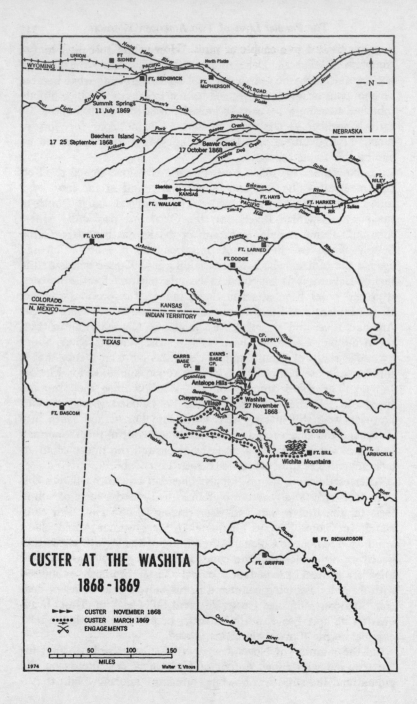

CUSTER AT THE WASHITA
1868 - 1869

▶▶▶▶ CUSTER   NOVEMBER 1868
●●●●●● CUSTER   MARCH 1869
⚔   ENGAGEMENTS

0   50   100   150
MILES

1974   Walter T. Vitous

sion was limited to a couple of yards. "How will this do for a winter campaign?" Adjutant Cooke asked Custer as he delivered the morning report. "Just what we want," was the reply. Custer rode over to Sheridan's tent to say good-bye. Sheridan asked him about the storm. "Just what we want," Custer repeated. "If this stays on the ground a week, I promise to return with the report of a battle with the Indians."[19] The snow was, in truth, a Godsend, for as every hunter knows, tracking game in a fresh snow is child's play—if the hunter is strong enough to keep going—while tracking game for any distance over the bare prairie is almost impossible.

Surrounded by his dogs, Custer had "Boots and Saddles" blown, swung onto his horse, and signaled to the military band that he was bringing along. To the tune of "The Girl I Left Behind Me," the column moved out.[20]

The storm was a challenge to which Custer responded magnificently. Setting his course south by a compass (not even the Osage guides could find their way in the blinding snow) he rode at the head of the column. He kept the men close up, in constant physical touch with each other, so none got lost. Somehow he managed to make fifteen miles that day. He led the men to Wolf Creek, where they dug in the snowdrifts to find fallen trees. When the fires were built and the coffee boiling, the men congratulated each other on how well they had done. Their morale was high. Custer made a bed for himself with a buffalo robe, lay down with a huge dog on each side of him to provide warmth, and slept soundly.[21]

Over the next few days the eight hundred cavalrymen moved steadily south, hoping to strike the fresh trail of an Indian war party returning to its winter camp. Custer caught a buffalo bull floundering in a snow-filled draw and killed it; other soldiers brought down more buffalo and the men enjoyed fresh meat. The nights were bitterly cold, but now that the storm had passed the days were sunny and warmer, so the men's spirits remained high.

On November 26 Custer struck the trail he had been hoping for. Tracks indicated that it was a party of Indians returning from Kansas to their village in Oklahoma. Custer had no idea what the Indians might have been doing in Kansas, what tribe they belonged to, their strength, or their location—indeed, all he knew was that his column was somewhere south of the North Canadian River. But the fresh tracks of the prey are like a magnet to the hunter, and he followed them south through the day and into the night. He cut loose from his wagon train in order to speed up his movement, leaving eighty men to guard it, with instructions to follow his trail.

After darkness fell, Custer joined the Osage guides at the head of the column. The melting snow was freezing again, so the horses made a racket as they broke through the frozen crust. Custer had the men keep a half mile behind the guides in order to minimize the noise. He stopped once to feed the horses some oats and allowed the men to make some coffee to go with their hardtack. It was the only meal the animals or troopers had eaten since 4 A.M., and they would not eat again until noon the next day. That the soldiers could keep going under such conditions was a tribute to Custer's ability as a trainer and leader of men.[22]

When he took up the chase again, Custer passed along orders that no one was to speak above a whisper and that no pipes or cigars could be lit. Silently, except for the crunch of broken snow, his 720 men rode mile after mile. Around midnight, one of the Osage guides smelled smoke. Custer couldn't smell any and wondered if the guide was losing his nerve—Indians did not like to fight at night, he knew, and the Osage guides were fearful of bumping into a big village. Custer sent the other guides forward to investigate while the column followed at a slow walk.

After an hour or so, one of the guides came creeping back to Custer. "What is it?" Custer asked. In his broken English, the Osage replied, "Heaps Injuns down there."

Custer dismounted and crawled forward through the snow to the crest of the hill. Looking down into a valley (he had not known he was near a river) he saw what looked like, in the uncertain light, a large body of animals half a mile away. His first thought was that they were buffalo. Turning to the guide, he asked in a low tone why the Osage thought they were Indian ponies. "Me heard dog bark," was the reply. Still not fully convinced, Custer strained to hear something, anything. He thought he heard a bell, which might mean a pony herd, as the Indians sometimes put a bell on the lead mare. Still uncertain, he hesitated—and then heard the sound that convinced him that he had finally run the prey to earth. A baby cried out in the night.[23]

Quietly returning to his officers, Custer blurted out orders in staccato sentences. He divided his column into four nearly equal detachments. One group would swing around to the far end of the village, while two others would proceed to the sides. Custer would stay with the fourth detachment at his present location. Once they had the village surrounded, they would stay in place until first light, when Custer would give the signal to attack.

Here was audacity indeed. Here was the pay-off for Sherman and

Sheridan in rescuing Custer from disgrace. He was doing exactly what they had hoped he would do. Custer had no idea in the world how many Indians were below him, who they were, or where he was. His men and horses were exhausted. It was freezing cold, but he ordered his men to stand silently, not even allowing them to stamp their feet, for fear the Indians would discover their presence. He was going to attack at dawn from four directions at once. He had made no reconnaissance, held nothing back in reserve, was miles away from his wagon train, and had ordered the most complex maneuver in military affairs, a four-pronged simultaneous attack. It was foolish at best, crazy at worst, but it was also magnificent and it was pure Custer.

This would be Custer's first big fight with Indians and he intended to make the most of it. After catching an hour's cat nap on a buffalo robe on the snow, he walked around among the men, building up their confidence. When the sky began to brighten he had them remove their overcoats and haversacks so they would be able to fight unencumbered.

At the first full light Custer had the band strike up the regiment's favorite tune, "Garry Owen." The music didn't last long, as saliva froze in the instruments, but it hardly mattered, because with a whoop, Custer led his column on a charge down into the village, shooting through the tipis. The other columns were all in place and they attacked, too, firing as fast as they could.

Warriors rushed from their tipis, confused, disorganized, unbelieving. Custer's men shot them down. Some Indians managed to get their weapons and fled to the safety of the Washita River, where they stood in waist-deep, freezing water, behind the protecting bank of the river, and started returning the fire. Others managed to get into some nearby timber and began to fight. But that first assault was overwhelming, and Custer had control of the village. His men were shooting anything that moved. Many of the troopers had been fruitlessly chasing Indians for two years and they poured out their frustrations; everyone was extremely tense after the nightlong approach to the village and the indiscriminate killing relieved the tension. In any event, the soldiers said later, it was hard to tell warriors from squaws, especially because a few of the squaws had taken up weapons and were fighting back. So were Indian boys of ten years of age. The troopers shot them all down. Still, according to George Grinnell, who got his information from the Indians, "practically all the women and children who were killed were shot while hiding in the brush or trying to run away through it."[24]

Within an hour, probably less, resistance was minimal. A few warriors kept up a sporadic firing from the banks of the river, but for all practical purposes the battle was over. Looking around, Custer could see dead Indians everywhere, one hundred or more of them, their blood bright on the snow. He was in possession of fifty-one lodges and a herd of nearly nine hundred ponies.[25]

Custer had won a smashing victory. Best of all, inside the tipis his men found fragments of letters, bits of bedding from Kansas homesteads, daguerreotypes, and other pieces of evidence that these Indians had indeed been guilty of raiding into Kansas. The Indians had held two white captives, too, whom they had killed when the troops overran the village. Now no one could accuse Custer of attacking innocent Indians, of being like Chivington at Sand Creek. And it had all been accomplished with small loss; one officer killed and two officers and eleven enlisted men wounded. Major Elliott and a nineteen-man detachment were missing, but someone had seen Elliott and the men giving chase to a few Indians who were attempting to escape and he was expected back shortly.

While his men reduced the few remaining pockets of resistance, Custer set up a field hospital in the largest tipi and wondered what to do with his victory. He also began to wonder whom he had beaten. Fifty-three women and children had remained hidden inside their lodges when the attack began; they were now all prisoners. Through his interpreter, Custer learned that he had just rubbed out Black Kettle's Cheyennes—the same Cheyennes who had been struck at Sand Creek. Black Kettle himself, always a champion of peace, had been one of the first to die.[26] Custer also learned that he was at the far end of an enormous Indian winter camp; downstream were the villages of the Kiowas, Arapahoes, Apaches, Comanches, and others.[27]

Custer had a long talk with Black Kettle's sister. She said she had told Black Kettle what would happen if he didn't curb the young braves, on whom she blamed everything. She went on and on in that vein, until Custer began to suspect that she was playing for time. Growing impatient, he was about to cut her off when she placed the hand of a beautiful seventeen-year-old Cheyenne girl in his. "What is this woman doing?" Custer asked his interpreter.

"Why, she is marrying you to that young squaw," was the reply. Custer dropped her hand and hurried outside. There he saw an ammunition wagon rattle into the village; the quartermaster of the wagon train had sent it on ahead.[28]

By noon warriors from the downstream villages began to appear on the bluffs surrounding Custer's position. As their numbers increased they began firing into Custer's ranks. He formed a defensive perimeter and decided that the best thing, all in all, was to get the hell out of there and report his victory to Sheridan. "On all sides of us the Indians could now be seen in considerable numbers," he later wrote, "so that from being the surrounding party, as we had been in the morning, we now found ourselves surrounded and occupying the position of defenders of the village." He gave the impression that the Indians were present in overwhelming numbers, but as a close student of the battle, Milo Quaife, convincingly demonstrates, there could not have been more than 1,500 warriors at the outside, and more likely less than one thousand that he had to deal with.[29] This was hardly a force able to stand up to some seven hundred well-mounted and well-armed cavalrymen.

Nevertheless, Custer decided to retreat. First he followed Hancock's example and burned the village, destroying more than one thousand buffalo robes, seven hundred pounds of tobacco, enormous quantities of meat, and other material. Lieutenant E. S. Godfrey later remembered tossing a beautifully beaded buckskin gown decorated with elks' teeth into the flames.[30] While the fires roared, Custer thought about what to do with the captured pony herd. The pintos were afraid of white men and could not be controlled by them; if Custer tried to move out with nine hundred ponies he would never be able to move with any speed, and besides, if he kept the animals, the Indians would attack ceaselessly in an effort to get them back. Dismayed at the alternatives—he loved horses as much as any man—he sadly told the captive women and children to select ponies for themselves, so that they could ride back to Camp Supply with the column. After the captives made their choices, Custer detailed four of his ten companies of cavalry and ordered the men to shoot the ponies. Within minutes more than eight hundred pintos lay on the ground, neighing, kicking, in their death throes, the blood spurting from their wounds, making the snow-covered ground more red than white.[31]

Custer later wrote about the Indians on the bluffs preparing to attack with an "immensely superior force,"[32] but the fact that he could detach 40 per cent of his fighting strength to slaughter the ponies indicates that he was not hard pressed. His next action proved the point. When the butchering was done, he collected his troops—Elliott and his nineteen men were still missing—and began to march downstream along the Washita toward the Kiowa, Apache, and other villages. He hoped the warriors on the bluffs would flee to their camps in order to prepare a defense, thus leaving him alone, and he planned to reverse directions and march back toward his wagon train when darkness fell. He later explained that he was worried about the safety of the wagons, which he had left behind two days before, but that excuse carries no weight, because the wagon train had an eighty-man escort, more than sufficient to take care of itself against almost any force of warriors.

Whatever his real reason for the retreat, Custer's plan worked. As soon as the warriors saw Custer heading downstream they rode as fast as they could back to their camps. When darkness fell, Custer retraced his steps. Elliott still had not been found, but Custer would not waste time looking for him. He marched his men through much of the night and kept them moving until 2 A.M., despite the fact that they had not recovered their overcoats, were drenched with sweat from the morning's fighting, hadn't slept in two nights, and were now freezing. It is a wonder that he kept them going and a tribute to what good shape he had gotten them into before starting the campaign. This night he allowed the troopers to build bonfires to warm themselves, and the next day they met the wagon train. Custer then started for Camp Supply to report his victory to Sheridan.

The battle of the Washita was over. Almost immediately it was surrounded by controversy. Sheridan was delighted, of course, and issued a general field order praising Custer and the 7th Cavalry in the most grandiose terms.[33] Eastern humanitarians, however, compared the Washita to Sand Creek, said that Black Kettle was an innocent victim attacked while living peacefully on his reservation, and denounced Custer as a bloodthirsty monster. Some Army officers had a different complaint; they accused Custer of abandoning Elliott and his nineteen men (who, it turns out, had been surrounded and killed). This charge rankled with the 7th Cavalry from then on, with officers and men taking sides for and against Custer.

The Washita battle raised other questions. Why was there no reconnaissance? Probably because Custer feared that the Cheyennes would escape again, as they had at Pawnee Fork. A reconnaissance would take time, which the Cheyennes might have used to get away. But why attack at all? Custer might have waited until dawn, then ridden into Black Kettle's village under a flag of truce and demanded that Black Kettle turn over the young braves who had been rampaging in Kansas. It probably would not have worked; Black Kettle did not have that kind of authority and the warriors almost certainly would not have surrendered voluntarily. Still, Custer might have tried. That he did not was most likely a reflection of his single-mindedness; having run the prey to ground, his only thought was to finish the hunt. Besides, he needed to prove to Sherman and Sheridan that he could both find and kill Indians.

Given his frame of mind at dawn, why then did Custer decide at noon to retreat? He had plenty of ammunition and was in possession of ample shelter for the winter weather, indeed the finest shelter the Plains afforded—the tipis. His own wagon train was coming up and would be with him shortly, and anyway the tipis were filled with buffalo meat. Custer's force was self-sufficient and nicely stocked for a month's campaign. But for the first time in his career he passed up an offensive opportunity, an opportunity so glittering that had he taken it and succeeded he would have killed more Indians than any other Indian fighter in history. The possibilities, had he continued to move downstream and destroy villages, were staggering, yet he turned around and marched the other way. To add to the mystery, he ignored his obligation, duty even, to search for Elliott and his men.

Why did he abandon the field? Did he think about Libbie, want to get home to her? Was he anxious to get back to Sheridan and claim the victory? Did he feel sorry for the Indians, pity them? Did he shrink from the thought of killing more women and children?

Or, more likely, when the warriors from downstream appeared on the surrounding bluffs, did he think of Fetterman? Most Army officers tended to see one hundred Indians where there were ten; did Custer see ten thousand where there were one thousand? In his own account of his decision to retreat, that was the only excuse he gave that made much sense, but it made sense only in the context of an imaginary, overwhelming force of warriors on the bluffs. Custer retreated, most probably, because he overestimated his enemy, which was the price he paid for attacking without reconnaissance.

It was also the price he paid for ignorance of the enemy. The previous summer he had consistently underestimated the Indians, as he would do again in his next big battle with them, on the banks of the Little Bighorn. He was hardly alone; not a single Army officer on the Plains had anything like an accurate knowledge of the enemy's strength. This really was inexcusable. The Indian agents had a good count of the Plains Indians by this time, and the information was available to the Army. At the Washita, Custer figured he faced at least five thousand and perhaps as many as ten thousand hostiles, but it is extremely doubtful that there were so many warriors on the whole of the southern and central Plains, much less gathered at one spot in the middle of a hard winter. What the Army desperately needed, and never got, was a first-rate intelligence corps. The white scouts, somewhat surprisingly, did not fill the void; they seem to have been as ignorant of Indian numbers as the officers. Custer and the scouts also consistently overestimated the number of guns the Indians had. If Custer had known how many Indians he was likely to encounter in Oklahoma, he would have realized that they had no chance to massacre his column. He could have smashed on into the downstream villages, confident that the warriors would not dare interfere with his bloody work.

Once he had decided to retreat, however, Custer's order to burn the village and shoot the ponies made good sense. It was absolutely within the spirit and letter of Sheridan's orders. It was also within the tradition of the American culture and its consistent policy toward Indians. These Cheyennes were enemies of progress; they stood in the way of the settlement of Kansas and they had to be removed. Custer's destruction of Black Kettle's people and village on the Washita can stand as a symbol of American Indian policy.

From the time of the first landings at Jamestown, the game went something like this: you push them, you shove them, you ruin their hunting grounds, you demand more of their territory, until finally they strike back, often without an immediate provocation so that you can say "they started it." Then you send in the Army to beat a few of them down as an example to the rest. It was regrettable that blood had to be shed, but what could you do with a bunch of savages?

The men of the eighteenth and nineteenth centuries took it for granted that the Indians had to be Christianized and modernized, but how could you do that until you caught them? The problem was more difficult on the Plains than it had been in the eastern woodlands, because with all that space it was hard to catch them. Compounding that problem, each Indian on the Plains required vast amounts of land to feed himself; to accommodate a few thousand Cheyennes on a reservation that would have allowed them to live as they wanted to live, the government would have had to have left them in possession of half of Kansas. In an America on an economic boom unprecedented in history, not to mention an America that was receiving millions of immigrants from Europe, who could abide that thought?

The point is that for all of America's leaders' sincere concern for the fate of the Indians, they had a higher loyalty. The men who made national policy, from the eighteenth century onward, supported by a broad consensus among the white population, have had as their first loyalty the doctrine of material progress. They have believed in that doctrine more than in their Constitution or their treaties or their religion. America's leaders and America's white population have allowed nothing to stand in the path of progress. Not a tree, not a desert, not a river, nothing. Most certainly not Indians, regrettable as it may have been to have to destroy such noble and romantic people.

Well, it was regrettable, but who is to say they were wrong? Who can possibly judge? Who would be willing to tell the European immigrant that he can't go to the Montana mines or to the Kansas prairie because the Indians need the land, so he had best go back to Prague or Dublin? Who wants to tell a hungry world that the United States cannot export wheat because the Cheyennes hold half of Kansas, the Sioux hold the Dakotas, and so on? Despite the hundreds of books by Indian lovers denouncing the government and making whites ashamed of their ancestors, and despite the equally prolific literary effort on the part of the defenders of the Army, here if anywhere is a case where it is impossible to tell right from wrong.

But we can tell truth from falsehood. It is, for example, totally irresponsible to state—as has so often been stated—that the United States pursued a policy of genocide toward the Indians, to cite the Washita as an example, and in the most extreme statements to claim that the Army actually did exterminate the red men. The United States did not follow a policy of genocide; it did try to find a just solution to the Indian problem. The consistent idea was to civilize the Indians, incorporate them into the community, make them part of the melting pot. That it did not work, that it was foolish, conceited, even criminal, may be true, but that doesn't turn a well-meant program into genocide, certainly not genocide as we have known it in the twentieth century. Custer was many things, but he was no Nazi SS guard shooting down innocent people at every opportunity.

To return to the Washita battle, it was typical of the Indian-fighting Army in other ways. Without the Osage guides, Custer would have blundered into the Cheyenne village in the middle of the night, which would have led to an awful confusion and greatly reduced the magnitude of his victory, if he could have won at all. "Divide and conquer" was the watchword, and throughout its Indian-fighting history the United States Army relied on one set of Indians to help it locate and kill another set. The Washita was a surprise assault on a sleeping village, which again was typical; Custer had no idea what the party he had trailed to the Washita had been up to in Kansas—the warriors could have been off on a buffalo hunt, for all he knew, not a raid. Clearly Black Kettle's people as a whole had done the whites in Kansas no harm. Custer's argument was that the village contained men guilty of murder, theft, and other outrages, which justified the attack. But although the city of Denver was also full of men guilty of murder, theft, and other outrages, no one in the Army ever thought to lead a column of cavalry on Denver, shoot it up, and burn it down.

But, of course, the city of Denver represented "progress," not an obstacle to progress. At the Washita, Custer was serving his nation and helping his nation realize its destiny. Every person who has ever taken a train to California, or settled there or in Kansas, or driven an automobile through the area, or eaten the wheat or beef grown on the Plains, has reaped the benefit of the Washita battle. History is not black or white nor is it propaganda. History is ambiguous, if told honestly. It is hard enough to figure out exactly what happened and why; it is impossible to play God and judge the right or wrong of a given action, even the Washita.

Custer spent the remainder of the winter of 1868–69 roaming the Plains, once at the head of a small squadron of cavalry, once with a regiment of infantry added to the 7th Cavalry. He fought no battles, but he did manage to persuade most of the tribes—who had fled their camps on the Washita—to return to the Fort Cobb reservation. On his expeditions, which took him through western Oklahoma and the panhandle of Texas, he brought along three captive Cheyenne women, including the young girl who had almost become his "wife." She seems to have attached herself to him and was a great help as a guide and in persuading the Indians to return to the reservation. Her name was Mo-nah-se-tah. Custer described her as "an exceedingly comely squaw, possessing a bright, cheery face, a countenance beaming with intelligence, and a disposition more inclined to be merry than one usually finds among the Indians. . . . Added to bright, laughing eyes, a set of pearly teeth, and a rich complexion, her well-shaped head was crowned with a luxuriant growth of the most beautiful silken tresses, rivalling in color the blackness of the raven and extending, when allowed to fall loosely over her shoulders, to below her waist."[84] In January 1869 Mo-nah-se-tah had a baby, which she brought with her on Custer's last two expeditions.

The date of Mo-nah-se-tah's delivery is important, because later the Indians claimed that Custer was the father. Custer was a figure larger than life, unbelievable in so many ways, and he attracted myths. In a sense, Custer was part of the Mike Fink-Paul Bunyan tall-tale tradition of America. More nonsense has been said, written, and believed about him than any other Army officer. The Mo-nah-se-tah story is a prime example. The Indians spread the rumor that Custer had fathered her baby; whites picked it up, added embellishments, until it came to be believed that Custer had made her his mistress. Eventually, the story began to appear in serious historical studies and is now firmly established as one of the elements in the Custer myth. All that need be said about it, however, is that Custer first met Mo-nah-se-tah at the Washita on November 27, 1868; her baby was born on January 14, 1869.[35]

Custer's winter campaigning was marked by many difficulties, of which the most significant was keeping the horses and mules going. One major lesson learned was that an extended winter campaign was well-nigh impossible. A short expedition, like Custer's at the Washita, was feasible, but over an extended period of time snow, mud, and cold inhibited movement and caused suffering and exhaustion to the men and even more to the animals. Even after he had reduced his command by weeding out the unfit horses, Custer returned from one expedition with two thirds of his eight hundred men dismounted. On another march Custer had to burn nearly all his wagons because his mules had perished. Frequently his men were reduced to eating mule or horse meat. In March 1869 a New York visitor to one of Custer's camps reported that "the dead carcasses of dozens of horses . . . lay scattered about, tainting the fresh spring air with their disgusting stench."[36] The Army's transportation system, in short, was not much better than that of its enemies; Army horses and mules were no more able to campaign on the frozen prairie than the Indian pintos.

Custer had a personal problem, too. On February 9, 1869, the St. Louis *Democrat* printed an unsigned letter from an officer of the 7th Cavalry criticizing Custer for making no effort to save Elliott and his men. When Custer read the story, he called all his officers to a conference. Tapping his boot top with his whip, he said he intended to horsewhip the author. Captain Frederick Benteen, a leading anti-Custer officer, shifted his revolver to a handy position in his belt and said, "All right, General, start your horsewhipping now. I wrote it." Dumfounded, confused, red-faced, Custer stared at Benteen a moment, then walked out.[37]

The climax to the expeditions came on March 15, 1869, when Custer—with Mo-nah-se-tah's help—found a Cheyenne village, headed by Little Robe and Medicine Arrow, in Texas just west of the Oklahoma boundary, between Sweetwater Creek and the North Fork of the Red River. These Cheyennes had been running all winter.

Custer wanted to force them back to their reservation at Fort Sill, Oklahoma, where they could be watched. He also wanted to rescue two white women held captive by the Cheyennes. Custer, his troopers, and most white Americans had been indignant at the brutal killing of two white captives by Indians in Black Kettle's camp immediately after the 7th Cavalry charged into the village in November 1868. The Cheyennes had had the right idea, however, white indignation notwithstanding, because this time Custer held back from a surprise attack. He wanted to rescue the captives alive, not recover their bodies, and he knew that the first shot fired would be the signal to massacre the white women.

Custer rode toward the village with only his interpreter with him. When in sight of the Indians he rode in a tight circle, the signal that he wanted to parley. The Cheyennes invited him into camp, then sat him down in a circle inside Medicine Arrow's lodge. Medicine Arrow lit a pipe and held it while Custer puffed away on it. As Custer smoked, Medicine Arrow told him in Cheyenne that he was a treacherous man and that if he came there with a bad purpose —to do harm to the people—he would be killed with all his men. Then Medicine Arrow poured the ashes from the pipe on the toes of Custer's boots, to give him bad luck.[88] Custer assured Medicine Arrow of his peaceful intentions and was allowed to leave.

The following day some Cheyennes came to Custer's camp to repay the visit. Custer asked if they were ready to go to the reservation at Fort Sill and if they were willing to trade for the white captives. When the Cheyennes indicated that they were not prepared to do either, Custer seized four men. Holding them as hostages, he said they would be freed when the captives had been released. Custer waited three days; when the Cheyennes made no move to comply with his demands, he told them he would hang the hostages the next morning if the white women were not released. The following day the Cheyennes freed the captives. According to George Bent, the half-Cheyenne who had cast his lot with his mother's people and was living in the Medicine Arrow village, the Cheyennes then paid a friendly visit to Custer's camp. Bent heard Custer give a command. Soldiers started grabbing at the Indians, attempting to take their weapons, while other troopers tried to surround the visitors. All the Indians got away except three men, whom Custer held and sent north to Fort Hays, Kansas, telling the Cheyennes that the hostages would be freed when the village moved onto its reservation. Afterward two of the hostages, eighty-year-old Slim Face and fifty-year-old Curly Hair, were killed by guards at

Fort Hays. The Cheyennes, meanwhile, had gone onto their reservation.[39]

The winter campaign was over. Taken all in all, it had been a success. Operations by the 5th Cavalry in the summer of 1869 completed the job, and Sherman's goal of clearing the territory between the Arkansas and Platte rivers of Indians had been accomplished.

Custer spent the summer of 1869 and the next two years at Fort Hays, with Libbie. A famous Indian fighter now, he was the center of attention. He shot wild turkey, antelope, and elk, became an expert buffalo hunter (hunting buffalo, he declared, was as exciting as hunting Indians), and guided a number of distinguished eastern and European visitors on buffalo hunts. Libbie later wrote a fascinating, detailed description of their years together at Fort Hays, *Following the Guidon*. If she can be believed, they never had a sad day, never got depressed, never missed the comforts of civilization.

The Kansas Pacific Railroad brought congressmen, businessmen, and other members of America's elite to Fort Hays. These men were in a hurry to get to Kansas before the buffalo were gone, fences built, and cattle and wheat had replaced the primeval prairie. The atmosphere was terribly romantic. Custer would turn out a company or two of the 7th Cavalry, along with the band to play "Garry Owen," and lead his guests and troops on a wide-ranging hunt. His stag hounds bounded along beside the column. "One of the guests," Libbie reported, "enthusiastically happy, and fearless in expression of his joy, kept turning to take in the rare sight, declaring that nothing in our prosaic nineteenth century was so like the days of chivalry, when some feudal lord went out to war or to the chase, followed by his retainers."[40] Custer was the knight *sans peur et sans reproche*, while she was his lady fair. Peace brought good times to Custer, just as it did to Crazy Horse, four hundred miles north.

CHAPTER SEVENTEEN

Truce on the High Plains, 1869–73

Hump: "We're up against it now. My horse has a wound in the leg."
Crazy Horse: "I know it. We were up against it from the start."

The Sioux hostiles spent the summer of 1869 on the Powder River. Red Cloud led one big expedition against the Shoshonis, and Crazy Horse led a couple of small parties on raids against the Crows,[1] but for the most part the Indians concentrated on hunting. By fall they had an immense pile of buffalo robes and they set off for the North Platte River, where they expected to trade their robes for guns and ammunition, blankets, coffee, utensils, and a little whiskey. Many of these Indians, including Crazy Horse, had not been near a trading post for five years or more and they badly needed the white man's goods, to which they had become accustomed but which they could not make themselves.[2]

But when the great camp arrived on the North Platte the soldiers there fired at the hostiles, wounding one, and the Indians drew back. Sherman had surrendered the Powder River forts on the understanding that the Oglalas and other hostiles would either move to an agency on the Missouri River or would stay on the Powder River; the whole point to the treaty had been to keep the wild Indians away from the Platte and thus away from the Union Pacific Railroad. The government's orders, therefore, were that there could be no trading along the North Platte. Making matters worse, the traders could not load up their wagons and go to the Powder River to trade. Sherman's attitude was simple; if the Indians wanted white man's goods, let them move to their reservations. If they insisted on living the wild life, let them do so without any help from the whites.[3] The government was especially insistent that none of the Powder River Indians get their hands on firearms, because from Sherman on down the attitude of the Army officers was that the treaty of 1868 was a truce, not a peace treaty. As Sherman put it, "we all know that the time approaches for the battle that is to decide whether they or the United States are sovereign in the land they occupy," and it would be the worst sort of foolishness to give arms to future enemies.[4]

The Indians felt they had been lied to. So did the traders, who had used their influence on Red Cloud to get him to sign the treaty on the understanding that trade would be resumed once peace came. But as far as the government was concerned the scheme worked, because it led to a split in the Oglalas. Red Cloud and half or more of the Powder River hostiles soon moved onto an agency on the White River, south of the Black Hills, called Red Cloud Agency.* Crazy Horse and the other Oglala hostiles stayed in the Powder River country. Within less than a year Red Cloud had so many complaints about his treatment at his agency that the whites took him to Washington to meet the Great White Father, President Grant. They persuaded Red Cloud to come to this 1870 summit meeting by promising him that Grant would listen carefully to his complaints. But their real purpose was to show Red Cloud the enormous power of white society, and they went to great lengths to make sure he saw that power.

"That was an epic journey," George Hyde writes of the trip to Washington by Red Cloud, Spotted Tail, and the other Indians who went along. "By the time they reached the Missouri the Oglalas had grown accustomed to train life; but now they came to Omaha, a hive of white people with hundreds of buildings, some of them very high—four, five stories! The Oglalas liked Omaha; but Chicago stunned them, and as they traveled on their ideas of the world, one by one, toppled and fell in ruins. They reached Washington dazed and rather frightened; that they had any courage left was a splendid compliment to their breed and training."[5]

In Washington, Red Cloud and Spotted Tail made many complaints to the authorities but got little satisfaction. Instead, the government concentrated on showing them such things as the big naval guns, including a fifteen-inch Rodman gun which was fired for them. The great shell went screaming over the Potomac and could be seen skipping over the water miles away. Red Cloud was awe-struck.[6] Later, Red Cloud and the others went to New York, where they were terribly uncomfortable, although Red Cloud managed to make a splendid speech at Cooper Union, much to the delight

---

* The agency was a small group of buildings—warehouse, Army headquarters, agent's house, etc. The area around it, where the Indians set up their tipis—sometimes forty miles or more away from the agency—was the reservation.

of the friends of the Indians.[7] When he got back to the Plains, Red Cloud put away his warrior's clothing and from that time onward played the role of politician, working both for his own advancement and for the good of his people. He looked the other way when his young men sneaked out of the agency in the spring to join Crazy Horse and the hostiles on the Powder River—he knew Indian braves too well to try to stop them—but he himself stayed off the warpath. As far as can be determined, he never again lived in the Powder River country he had fought so hard to defend.

With Red Cloud gone, Crazy Horse's stature among the hostiles rose. As an advocate of war to the bitter end, he was held in high esteem by those warriors who shared his sentiments. His unquestioned bravery and his skill in leading war parties against the Crows or Shoshonis made him a bigger and bigger man. He had not, however, replaced Red Cloud as leader of all the Oglalas on the Powder River—far from it. When the war ended in 1868 with the burning of Fort Phil Kearny, the Oglalas and their allies had no reason to stay together in one big camp and they scattered into small bands, which was much more to their liking, coming together in the spring for a Sun Dance and perhaps again in the fall for a buffalo hunt. Insofar as there was a chief over the Oglalas, it was Old Man Afraid, who had refused to go to Washington with Red Cloud; but even Old Man Afraid was more a respected elder whose sage advice would be fully heard than he was a governmental leader who could give orders. The Oglalas, in short, had no real leader.

Crazy Horse was foremost among the many war leaders, but he was not a chief of a band, much less of the whole tribe. He continued to take his duties as shirt-wearer seriously, so seriously that he still held back from running off with Black Buffalo Woman, even though she wanted to marry him, and he was furious with No Water for not allowing her to have her freedom. But he would not disrupt the tribe.

Despite the United States Government's ban on trade with the hostiles, some traders—mainly half-breeds—did manage to sneak a few wagon loads of goods into the hostile camps, where they exchanged white man's products for beautifully decorated buffalo robes. One of these traders brought in some newspapers and translated them for the Oglalas, reading aloud a report that called the Oglalas "bloodthirsty savages" and "murdering hounds of hell." The word "hell" confused Crazy Horse. What was hell? The trader tried to explain but only confused Crazy Horse more—how could a great power do a bad thing like sending souls to hell? Another newspaper had a picture in it, a pen-and-ink sketch of naked, painted, howling Indians with bloody scalps, dancing around three little white girls tied to the door of a burning house. Crazy Horse was so angry at the misrepresentation that he tore the paper into shreds. Later he learned that the paper had belonged to Billy Garnett, a friendly trader, so Crazy Horse gave Billy a good pinto to make up for destroying his paper.[8]

In 1870 Crazy Horse and Hump led an expedition against the Shoshonis. Years later, He Dog told the story to Eleanor Hinman. It was late autumn, so late that a drizzly rain started turning into snow. Crazy Horse, He Dog recalled, muttered, "I wonder if we can make it back to Cone Creek. I doubt if our horses can stand a fight in this slush. They sink in over their ankles."

He Dog took this word to Hump, who snorted and declared, "This is the second fight he has called off in this same place! This time there is going to be a fight." Hump rode over to Crazy Horse and said, "The last time you called off a fight here, when we got back to camp they laughed at us. You and I have our good names to think about. If you don't care about it, you can go back. But I'm going to stay here and fight."

Crazy Horse's reply, as He Dog remembered it, was, "All right, we fight, if you feel that way about it. But I think we're going to get a good licking. You have a good gun and I have a good gun, but look at our men! None of them have good guns and most of them have only bows and arrows. It's a bad place for a fight and a bad day for it, and the enemy are twelve to our one."

They fought all the same, but the Shoshonis had the best of it. Soon the Oglalas were on the run, with only Hump, Crazy Horse, and Good Weasel acting as a rear guard. He Dog remembered that it was a running fight, "with more running than fighting." In order to check the pursuit and to give the others more time, Crazy Horse charged the Shoshonis from one side, Hump and Good Weasel from the other. When they rejoined, Hump's horse was stumbling.

"We're up against it now," Hump declared. "My horse has a wound in the leg."

"I know it," Crazy Horse replied. "We were up against it from the start."

Despite Hump's crippled horse, the three-man rear guard charged again when the Shoshonis pressed too close. This time Hump's horse went down. The Shoshonis surged over him. That was the last seen of Hump. On the slippery ground, with all those enemies around, Crazy Horse could not even recover the body.[9]

Hump dead! Crazy Horse's oldest friend, with whom he had fought side-by-side in nearly every battle of his life. Hump had been with him at the Platte River Bridge, had rallied the Oglalas against the Crows and Shoshonis on innumerable occasions, had served as a decoy at Fort Phil Kearny. Now he was gone, the boy with whom he had learned to hunt and to make war. Crazy Horse returned to camp with a blackness in his heart.

Red Feather, who was in that fight, told Eleanor Hinman the aftermath: "Four days later Crazy Horse and I went back to find Hump and bury him. We didn't find anything but the skull and a few bones. Hump had been eaten by coyotes already. There weren't any Shoshonis around. When the Shoshonis found out whom they had killed, they beat it."[10]

The next summer, Crazy Horse and He Dog worked up a big war party against the Crows. It was an old-time hunting and war expedition, with some of the women coming along to cook and set up lodges. Crazy Horse and He Dog were the lance bearers of the Crow Owners *akicita* and they carried the two lances of the Oglalas, lances that had been with the people longer than anyone could remember. Worm, Crazy Horse's father, was sure they dated back to the days the Oglalas lived east of the Missouri River. No one could remember, either, how they had acquired their powerful medicine, but it was certain that so long as they were carried by brave warriors and remained in the hands of the Oglalas, there would be fat times for the people. Crazy Horse and He Dog rode at the head of the column, holding the lances high, full of pride in themselves and in the Oglalas.

They found a big Crow camp between the Little Bighorn and the Bighorn rivers. The Oglala women settled themselves on a hillside to watch the fight and to taunt the Crows, making sign-language talk to the enemy, daring them to come on across the valley and take some Oglala women, who were so much better in bed than the Crow women. Crazy Horse and He Dog led an assault, carrying the lances all through the fighting, always making sure that they were first and closest to the enemy, always last to retreat from Crow counterattacks. When they started back home with some captured ponies, the Crows gave chase, getting a few of the ponies back before giving up.

When the Crows broke off the engagement, most of the Oglalas wanted to continue toward home, but Crazy Horse and He Dog decided to follow the Crows awhile. Little Hawk, Crazy Horse's brother, joined the lance bearers, and the other Oglalas then went along—they could not allow the sacred lances to remain unprotected in enemy country. The Oglalas chased the Crows right up to their agency on the Little Bighorn, where the Crows camped under the protection of the soldiers' guns. The Oglalas made camp a little way off and stayed for a week, taunting the Crows, raiding, and hunting. When they finally went back to the Powder River everyone was feeling fine and there was a big victory dance.[11] "When They Chased the Crows Back to Camp," the Oglalas called the fight in their winter-count pictographic history, painted on a buffalo hide.

Custer was becoming bored. He had spent the time from the summer of 1869 to the winter of 1870–71 at Fort Hays, hunting, drilling troops, writing magazine articles and his memoirs, but despite a stream of eastern and European visitors who came for the buffalo hunting there was not enough activity to suit him. Hostilities in Kansas were over, Red Cloud was on a reservation, and the remaining Indians on the Powder River were attacking Crows and Shoshonis, not whites. In late 1869 Custer made a trip to Chicago, where he had an enjoyable visit with General Sheridan, went to the theater, shopped, and lost so badly at cards that he took a vow never to gamble again. Explaining his decision in a letter to Libbie, he wrote with typical exaggeration, "This is a resolution, not the result of impulse, but taken after weeks of deliberation. And in considering, and finally adopting it, I experience a new-found joy. I breathe free'er, and I am not loath to say I respect my manhood more." The vow lasted for nearly a year.[12]

Custer returned to Kansas in high spirits—Sheridan had promised to do all he could to get Custer a promotion—but the dullness of life on a frontier post without Indians to fight soon had him bored again. He considered resigning from the Army but decided to ask for a leave instead; he would go East to see what his prospects in civilian life might be before resigning his commission. He would take along some western mining stock to sell.

After settling Libbie in Monroe, Michigan, Custer went to New York in 1871, where to his delight he found that he had not been forgotten. As far as he could tell, everyone of any importance in the city fawned upon him. August Belmont offered him a position. The Astors thought he was marvelous. He attended dinner parties that began at half past seven and lasted until 2 A.M. and included countless courses of the rarest delicacies. At one banquet he sat between Horace Greeley, editor of the New York *Tribune*, and Bayard Taylor, the writer; Whitelaw Reid, on the staff of the *Trib-*

13. Custer, the Crow scout Bloody Knife (on Custer's right), other Indian scouts, and two of Custer's dogs pose in front of a Northern Pacific Railroad tent during the Yellowstone River expedition of 1873. The dogs loved to chase antelope, and Custer often left the column, even in the middle of hostile territory, to join the hunt.

14. Spotted Tail, the great Brulé leader who had an enormous ego and the talents to back it up. He was Crazy Horse's uncle and reportedly the most fearless of all Sioux warriors. The first to take up arms against the whites (in 1854), he was also the first important Sioux leader to become an advocate of peace (1864). He made frequent trips to Washington to consult with the Great White Father; this photograph was taken in Washington in 1875.

15. Custer's camp at French Creek in the Black Hills, 1874. At this spot, two miles east of present-day Custer, South Dakota, the expedition found gold. In his official report, which he gave to the newspapers, Custer gushed about the Black Hills. Not only was there gold literally at the grass roots, but magnificent scenery, perfect weather, and the best farming and grazing country in the United States—or so he said, thereby helping start the Black Hills gold rush.

16. Custer and Libbie in Custer's study at Fort Abraham Lincoln, North Dakota, 1875. Note the portraits of his two favorite generals—himself and McClellan—on the wall. The two antelopes and the snowy owl are overflows from his trophy room (he did his own taxidermy). Custer always made Libbie sit with him while he wrote his articles.

17. Little Big Man, once the most irreconcilable and hot-blooded of Crazy Horse's Oglala warriors. In 1875 he rode into a council (called by the United States Government to force the Sioux to sell the Black Hills), naked save for a breechcloth and an eagle feather war bonnet, carrying a Winchester repeater in one hand, a fistful of cartridges in the other, and announced with a roar that he would kill any white man who tried to steal Indian land. Two years later he was working for the whites.

18. Elizabeth Bacon Custer in 1874. She spent the summer at Fort Abraham Lincoln while her Autie was opening the Black Hills. Indian scouts, mounted on ponies, carried letters back and forth between Libbie and Autie on a route that they nicknamed the "Black Hills Express."

19. Red Cloud, the Oglala Sioux war leader who took charge of the allied Indian forces during the three-year campaign (1866–68) against the Bozeman Trail and Fort Phil Kearny. After 1868 Red Cloud was a champion of peace, a frequent visitor to Washington for meetings with the Great White Father, and in charge of the largest Sioux reservation, Red Cloud Agency in Nebraska. An able if unscrupulous politician, he managed to stay on top despite the frequent shifts in policy and white agents.

20. Sitting Bull, the Hunkpapa leader, perhaps the most famous of all North American Indians, the man who inspired the Sioux in their defense of the Powder River country. After the battle of Little Bighorn in June 1876 Sitting Bull fled to Canada. When he returned to the United States a few years later he became the chief attraction in Buffalo Bill Cody's Wild West Show (where his photograph was taken). In 1890 he embraced the Ghost Dance and as a result was killed (shot in the back, in fact) by Indian policemen shortly before the massacre at Wounded Knee

21. Libbie Custer at the turn of the century. On social occasions younger women noticed, with jealous eyes, that every male in the room flocked to her side.

22. He Dog in old age, at the time Eleanor Hinman conducted her interviews with him. She said of He Dog at this time: "In spite of his ninety-two years and their infirmities, He Dog is possessed of a remarkable memory. He is the living depository of Oglala tribal history and old-time customs. Anyone digging very deeply into these subjects with the other old-timers is likely to be referred to him: 'He Dog will remember about that.' In interviewing He Dog one can hardly fail to be impressed with his strong historical sense and with the moderation and carefulness of his statements."

une, and Charles A. Dana, owner of the New York *Sun*, were also at the table, along with the Wall Street banker-poet E. C. Stedman, who told Custer he was the beau ideal of the Chevalier Bayard. Custer sold his mining stock for a fat profit and went to Saratoga for the racing season. New York Democrats again held out the promise of a glittering political career. Everyone congratulated him on his great victory on the Washita. Custer, modest as always, said it was nothing.

As usual, Custer wrote page after page to Libbie, describing his triumphs in high society. During the Civil War, when he was in the field and she was in Washington, she had delighted in writing him about her flirtations. Now it was his turn. The women of New York, it seemed, could not leave him alone. He went around the city at night with his actor friend Lawrence Barrett (Custer even considered an acting career for himself but reluctantly decided against it), and between the two of them they knew every woman worth knowing in New York, or so they felt. Custer told Libbie about the hours he spent with the famous singer Clara Louise Kellogg, who gave him the use of her box at the Academy of Music. Custer assured Libbie that "Miss Kellogg is very dainty in regard to gentlemen." "To show you how careful Miss Kellogg is in her conduct with gentlemen," he added, "she told me she has never ridden with a gentleman alone but twice in New York, and on one of these occasions her coachman was along."[13]

How Libbie put up with all this drivel is a wonder, especially since Custer also told her the story of a constant companion who had been, like him, a temporary bachelor. The companion regretted that his wife was coming home in a few days and bemoaned his fate. "Well, boys, school begins on Wednesday," the gentleman sighed (and Custer wrote it all down for Libbie). "No more vacation pour moi. . . . I've had one good winter. I expect I shall never get the old lady to leave me alone for another."[14] A week later, Custer wrote Libbie about his own activities: "There is a beautiful girl, eighteen or nineteen, blonde, who has walked past the hotel several times trying to attract my attention. Twice for sport I followed her. She lives about opposite Mr. Belmont's. She turns and looks me square in the face, to give me a chance to speak to her. I have not done so yet. At her house she enters, then appears at a window, raising this for any attention I may offer."[15]

He went on and on like that. "One of the young ladies has evidently taken a strong fancy to your Bo," Custer informed his wife. "She makes no effort at concealment. She said, 'Oh why are you married?' . . . This fancy of hers was not induced by any advances of mine. She is not fast, is refined and educated. I really think she is a good girl but cannot control herself. She can cause my little one no uneasiness, no regret."[16] Custer assured Libbie that it did not matter that women could not stay away from him: "Girls needn't try to get her dear Bo away from her, because he loves only her, and her always."[17] Libbie seemed to understand her man, even when he wrote her love letters in the third person, filling them with accounts of his flirtations, for she did not complain.

All the glitter and luxury of New York were not enough to turn Custer away from his beloved cavalry. After spending the spring and summer of 1871 in the city he decided to turn down the various offers he had received and remain in the Army. In September 1871 he and the 7th Cavalry were ordered from Fort Hays to the South. The regiment was broken into company and squadron units and assigned to occupation duty in seven southern states. Custer's headquarters were in Elizabethtown, Kentucky, where he killed time by betting his mining stock profits on horse races. The duty was boring, infinitely so, and he longed to return to the Plains, which by now he realized had captured his heart. As much as Crazy Horse, he wanted to be on those vast spaces, where a man could ride all day without seeing a fence or another human being, where the wind blew free, where the air was always crisp and clean, the hunting always good, where a man could test himself against the elements and against the savages. Like Sherman, he knew that sooner or later the United States Government would have to take control of the Oglalas and he wanted to be there when the time came. That was, probably, the major reason he stayed in the Army even though Sheridan was unable to get him a promotion.

Crazy Horse meanwhile was in the biggest trouble of his life. As had been the case with Custer, Crazy Horse's problems came because of his desire to be with the woman he loved; again like Custer, that desire cost him the equivalent of a court-martial and temporary disgrace.

At some point following the death of Hump (it is impossible to establish an exact date), Crazy Horse decided that he had been holding back with regard to Black Buffalo Woman long enough. Perhaps he figured that with the white soldiers gone from the Powder River forts he no longer had to take his vows as a shirt-wearer so seriously. Or perhaps Hump's death caused him to reflect on his philosophy of life and decide that it was too short an existence to pass up the joys of love. Possibly his desire for Black Buffalo Woman grew too strong for him to think about anything else. Whatever his motives and reasoning, Crazy Horse decided to make Black Buffalo Woman his wife.

By this time, Crazy Horse's people had drifted northward and they were now camping near the Yellowstone River in Montana. There they associated with the wild Sioux of the north country, the Miniconjous, Sans Arcs, and Sitting Bull's Hunkpapas. These tribes had not yet been in extensive contact with the whites and they lived in the old ways without the white man's goods. During the winters Crazy Horse's people had only fifty or so lodges, but in the summers they were joined by large groups from Red Cloud Agency, swelling their camp to two hundred lodges or more. These were the Indians who later, in 1872, joined Crazy Horse and He Dog for the fight called "When They Chased the Crows Back to Camp." In the summer of 1871 many Red Cloud Agency Indians had come north once again, No Water and Black Buffalo Woman among them.

Sometime that fall of 1871, after Hump was killed, Crazy Horse worked up a small war party against the Crows. Only a few others were going along, or so Crazy Horse said. It was a feint, however; Crazy Horse did not intend to move against the enemy. Instead, he was running off with Black Buffalo Woman and the war party story was designed to reduce suspicion.

The night before the lovers ran away, Black Buffalo Woman gave her children to trusted relatives to take care of until she returned. But it did not seem likely she would be back soon, because No Water was a jealous man and besides Crazy Horse neglected to pay him for Black Buffalo Woman.

He Dog related that when No Water returned from a hunting trip and found his tipi empty, he went around the village and gathered up his children. "Crazy Horse had been paying open attention to the woman for a long time," He Dog related, "and it didn't take No Water very long to guess where she had gone. He gathered up a fairly strong war party and went after." First, however, No Water went to Bad Heart Bull and borrowed a certain good revolver which Bad Heart Bull owned. No Water said he needed the weapon to go hunting.

Crazy Horse and Black Buffalo Woman were camping on the Powder River. No Water overtook them on the second night. No Water checked each tipi until he finally discovered Crazy Horse and Black Buffalo Woman sitting by the fire in a friend's lodge. Throwing aside the tipi flap, No Water rushed in, waved his pistol, and shouted, "My friend, I have come!"

Crazy Horse leaped up and reached for his knife, but Little Big Man, who was sitting next to him, grabbed his arm and held it, hoping to avoid bloodshed. No Water fired. The bullet hit Crazy Horse just below the left nostril, followed the line of the teeth and fractured his upper jaw. Crazy Horse fell forward into the fire.

Black Buffalo Woman screamed, then crawled out under the back of the tent and fled. She returned to her relatives and begged protection. No Water fled too, running into the night. He jumped on the nearest horse and took off. When he got back to camp he told friends he had killed Crazy Horse. No Water's friends made a sweat lodge for him and purified him of the murder. Then he disappeared. Crazy Horse's friends, meanwhile, not being able to find No Water, killed his favorite mule, slashing it to bits in their anger.

Here was trouble for the Oglalas of the worst possible kind. Crazy Horse was not dead, but he was seriously wounded. No Water was guilty of attempted homicide and of refusing to allow Black Buffalo Woman to live with whomever she pleased, as was the right of a Sioux woman. Crazy Horse had broken the vows he had taken as a shirt-wearer, putting his own interests ahead of the well-being of the tribe. A blood feud might result, or something worse; Crazy Horse was identified with the Hunkpatila band of the Oglalas ("those who camp at the end of the circle"), while No Water was a Bad Face with close connections to Red Cloud. The incident might even set the two bands of the Oglalas at war with each other.

Everything in Sioux culture recoiled at such a prospect. The important, steady men in both bands went to work at once to smooth things over. By the second day after the shooting it was clear that Crazy Horse would recover. He helped keep the peace, too, by signaling in the sign language (he could not speak yet) that there must be no trouble nor should Black Buffalo Woman be punished, for she had done nothing wrong. He fell into a fitful sleep. From time to time, he would stir, then mumble through his broken jaw something that sounded like, "Let go! Let go of my arm!" He was, perhaps, remembering his vision, when his arms had been held by one of his own people.

No Water's friends and relatives in the Bad Face camp wanted to avoid further trouble, too, although they were willing to fight if necessary. Black Twin took his brother No Water into his lodge and said, "Come and stay with me and if they want to fight us, we will fight." But he also encouraged No Water to atone for the injury done, so No Water sent three ponies, including his best bay and his finest roan, to Worm, Crazy Horse's father. By accepting the gifts, Worm signified that he was satisfied and wanted no more shooting.

Crazy Horse's friends, meanwhile, had taken him to the small camp of his uncle Spotted Crow to recover. They were afraid to return him to his own camp and stir up the warriors there; fortunately the hot-tempered Little Hawk was off on an expedition against the Shoshonis. Even so, as He Dog put it, Crazy Horse's friends "were very angry and thought they ought to have No Water turned over to them to be punished, or else wage war on his people. For a while it looked as if a lot of blood would flow."

No Water, meanwhile, told Black Twin that the medicine man Chips was responsible for the whole thing. No Water said Chips had made Crazy Horse a love charm to induce Black Buffalo Woman to run away with him—in No Water's view, nothing else could explain Black Buffalo Woman's leaving him. Black Twin tried to force Chips to admit that he had indeed made such a love charm, but Chips stoutly denied it. Chips said he knew nothing about the matter, although it was true that he had recently made Crazy Horse a protective charm for his war horses and earlier had made him a little medicine bundle to wear around his shoulder. Black Twin was finally convinced and let Chips go; Chips left the Bad Face camp and did not return for a long time.

The peacemakers, meanwhile, were at work. By great good fortune, as He Dog put it, "there were three parties to the quarrel instead of two. Bull Head, Ashes, and Spotted Crow, the uncles of Crazy Horse and the headmen of that band [the band Crazy Horse lived with while he recovered], worked for peace. Also, Bad Heart Bull and I thought we were involved in it, since Bad Heart Bull's revolver had been used for the shooting [and He Dog was No Water's cousin]. We did what we could." There was a grand exchange of horses. Bad Heart Bull had Black Buffalo Woman come live with him in his tent "and left her there on condition that she should not be punished for what she had done. This condition was demanded by Crazy Horse. Then Bad Heart Bull arranged for her to go back to her husband in peace. If it had not been settled this way, there might have been a bad fight."[18]

So the Oglalas managed to get through the crisis without any further spilling of blood or anyone getting killed. But they paid a high price for the incident. As He Dog explained to Eleanor Hinman, "Because of all this, Crazy Horse could not be a shirt-wearer any longer. When we were made shirt-wearers we were bound by very strict rules as to what we should do and what not do, which were very hard for us to follow. I have never spoken to any but a very few persons of what they made us promise then." After a pause, He Dog let a little of his anger show: "I have always kept the oaths I made then, but Crazy Horse did not."[19]

So Crazy Horse lost his position for trying to take another man's wife, but even that was not the end of it. The Big Bellies quarreled over who should replace Crazy Horse, quarreled so badly that the whole organization broke down. Unable to make a selection, the Big Bellies soon split, never to meet again. When Eleanor Hinman asked He Dog who replaced Crazy Horse as shirt-wearer, He Dog replied: "The shirt was never given to anybody else. Everything seemed to stop right there. Everything began to fall to pieces. After that it seemed as if anybody who wanted to could wear the shirt—it meant nothing. But in the days when Crazy Horse and I received our shirts we had to accomplish many things to win them."[20]

The Oglalas had made a promising start in the development of a governmental organization that would have made it possible for them to act together in the face of an outside threat. Now that hope was gone. The Sioux male's concept of property vis-à-vis women had ruined the whole scheme. The loss was not felt immediately, however, because in 1871 the whites were far away from the Powder River and the Crows and Shoshonis had been driven beyond the Bighorn Mountains. But the time would come when the Oglalas would feel keenly their failure to stick together.[21]

When Crazy Horse's wound had healed into a scar, he joined a big camp on a buffalo hunt along the Yellowstone River. He had hardly entered the village when the expedition that had gone out against the Shoshonis returned to camp. The survivors reported that they had had a bad time of it, not from the Shoshonis, but from a band of white miners, well-armed, who had fired at them from behind cover. Little Hawk had been killed.[22]

Crazy Horse was stunned. Little Hawk was dead! The bravest of them all, one who, so it was said, would soon outstrip even Crazy Horse himself, if he managed to live. Little Hawk, to whom Crazy Horse had taught everything he knew and with whom he had shared countless adventures and experiences. Crazy Horse had seen his younger brother take innumerable risks in fights with other Indians and never get hurt; now he was dead, killed by a sneak shot fired by a white man.

The next day Crazy Horse went hunting. It helped ease the pain in his heart a little to drive his arrow through a buffalo and he brought down a fat cow. Late in the afternoon he started back toward camp, walking, with packs of meat loaded on his pony. Closer to camp a man named Moccasin Top who had also been hunting was still dressing his kill. Moccasin Top owned a fast buckskin pony and had it tethered near him while he worked. No Water, who did not know that Crazy Horse was in the vicinity, came along on foot and saw Crazy Horse approaching. No Water untied the buckskin, jumped on, and galloped away.

"Are you still here?" Crazy Horse asked when he reached Moccasin Top. "Then who was the man that just rode off on your buckskin?"

"That was No Water," Moccasin Top answered.

"I wish I had known it!" Crazy Horse exclaimed. "I would certainly have given him a bullet in return for the one he gave me."

Cutting the meat loose from the pack, Crazy Horse leaped on his pony and gave chase. He followed No Water to the banks of the Yellowstone, where No Water forced the buckskin to plunge into the river and swim across. Crazy Horse decided not to follow. No Water rode downstream for some time, then recrossed the Yellowstone and went south, eventually joining Red Cloud at the agency. According to He Dog, "he stayed at the agency all through the war with the white people and had nothing more to do with the hostiles." Black Buffalo Woman returned to No Water. Some months later she gave birth to a light-haired, light-complexioned little girl. Gossips said it was Crazy Horse's daughter."[23]

In January 1872 Custer received a most welcome order from Sheridan. The Grand Duke Alexis of Russia was touring the world, was currently in the United States, and wanted to try his hand at buffalo hunting. The son of Czar Alexander II, only twenty-two years old, was an avid sportsman and the United States Government wanted to show him every courtesy and consideration. Relations between Russia and the United States were excellent, especially because Russia five years before had sold Alaska to the United States at a bargain price, and Alexis had been on a triumphal tour of eastern and midwestern cities. Sheridan was going to make sure the grand duke bagged his buffalo and had arranged for Spotted Tail and some Brulés to join the hunt. He had also signed up the famous scout William F. Cody, later to be famous as a result of Ned Buntline's dime novel *Buffalo Bill*. Sheridan brought Custer along because he had a reputation as an outstanding hunter.[24]

The party, including actor Lawrence Barrett, detrained at North Platte, Nebraska, then rode south fifty miles, accompanied by picked companies of cavalry. There camp was set up on the Red Willow Creek, and what a camp it was! Sheridan had arranged for forty of the Army's best wall tents, plus two gigantic hospital tents for the use of the grand duke and his party. The hospital tents were elegantly carpeted and there was champagne served with the meals.[25] Spotted Tail's camp of six hundred carefully chosen Brulés was just downstream. Sheridan had promised Spotted Tail twenty-five wagon-loads of presents if he would be good, so the Brulés put on quite a show. Both the people and the village were spick and span, with fine tanned-skin clothing and new tipis. Pawnee Killer was along; one wonders if Custer talked with his old nemesis about their skirmishes in Kansas in 1867. The Brulés entertained the imperial party at night with songs and dances. Custer was reported to have flirted shamelessly with Spotted Tail's sixteen-year-old daughter, who was Crazy Horse's first cousin.[26]

On January 13, 1872, the party made its first hunt, Spotted Tail and eight warriors coming along. Sheridan was sick, so Custer, Cody, and the grand duke led the way through snow that in places was eighteen inches deep. A newspaperman reported that Custer wore "his well-known frontier buckskin hunting costume, and if, instead of the comical seal-skin hat he wore, he had feathers fastened in his flowing hair, he would have passed at a distance for a great Indian chief."[27]

Cody located a small herd of buffalo, Custer and the grand duke charged, and Alexis got his buffalo with a revolver shot in the head. Returning to base camp, Alexis sent a runner to North Platte to cable the good news to the Czar.[28]

On the next day's hunt the grand duke killed a few more buffalo, but the herd again was small and it soon scattered and was lost to sight. Both Cody and Custer went scouting but neither could find the buffalo, so Spotted Tail and his eight warriors were given permission to try their luck. They not only found the beasts, but held them together at the entrance of a long and widening canyon. There were broken sides and high hills on either side, forming a magnificent arena. Spotted Tail told the whites to stay on the hills; he and his men would show them an old-time Indian hunt.

With the grand duke, Custer, Barrett, assorted Russian admirals, ambassadors, and generals looking on, the Brulés drove the herd into the canyon. The newspaper reporter described what followed: "Spotted Tail and his chosen Sioux, with a wild whoop, charged into the midst of the fleeing herd, and with unerring aim let fly the feathered arrows from their bows. It was then that the Imperial party were favored with a splendid view of a scene that few white men, who have lived many years upon the plains, have ever witnessed. It was difficult to decide which to admire the more, the skill of the Indian in managing his horse, or the rapidity and accuracy with which he let fly his feathered darts into the side of the doomed buffalo. In some respects the scene resembled a charge of cavalry upon troops already routed and fleeing in disorder; and the Duke was forcibly reminded of the riding of the Cossacks in his native country."[29] Alexis retrieved an arrow that Spotted Tail had shot clear through a buffalo, to take home and show his father.

Luncheon that noon consisted of caviar and other delicacies, along with champagne, brought out to the hunters from base camp. Custer and Alexis had become great friends by this time; the Russian was as much of a practical joker as Custer and the two delighted in pulling childish pranks on the dignified Russian ambassadors and admirals. Custer also regaled Alexis with stories about how it had been in the old days on the Plains, before the coming of the railroad. Alexis was disappointed at not seeing any of the enormous herds he had heard so much about. Custer explained that the grand duke had got there just in time; in another few years there would be no more buffalo left on the central Plains. Hides were being sent east from Fort Riley and other points at the rate of forty thousand per shipment. If the ground had been bare instead of covered with snow, Alexis could have seen for himself—the Plains were covered with buffalo bones (indeed, a minor but flourishing industry was springing up on the Plains; settlers in need of cash would gather wagonloads of bones and take them to the railroad station, where they were shipped on east by the tons to be ground up for fertilizer).[30]

When camp broke up, Cody provided a parting flourish of drama. With the Brulés pretending to chase his wagon, he drove the grand duke at breakneck speed in a four-in-hand over the prairie, Custer along as a passenger, whooping and hollering.[31] Back at North Platte, Alexis asked Sheridan if Custer could stay with the party for the remainder of his tour of the country, and Sheridan readily agreed. So Custer rode the train to Denver (the Union Pacific was across the Plains by this time and a spur ran down to Denver), where he attended a grand ball, then went on another buffalo hunt with Alexis. On January 21, 1872, they took the Kansas Pacific, headed for St. Louis and the East.

Until the previous year the Kansas Pacific and the Union Pacific had advertised that passengers could shoot buffalo as the train sped along, and thousands had been killed and left to the wolves and coyotes by the sportsmen of the day, who realized that it was all coming to a rapid end and that this was their last chance. As the imperial party rattled through Kansas, it saw buffalo along the tracks, nothing like the numbers encountered two years earlier but enough to excite Alexis and Custer. They climbed into the baggage car, each armed with a Spencer rifle, and took pot shots at buffalo as the train sped along at twenty miles per hour. Alexis claimed six kills, while Custer and Sheridan (who soon joined the two hunters) also did their best to eliminate the scattering of buffalo left in Kansas.[32] Barrett wrote that Custer was "enjoying his vacation as keenly as a schoolboy."[33]

Custer's trip with Grand Duke Alexis across the Plains was a dramatic illustration of the conquest of space that the railroad brought about. In the *summer* of 1867 Custer had taken four days to cover the distance from westernmost Kansas to Fort Riley in the eastern part of Kansas, and even then he had ridden the railroad for the last half of the way. In the *winter* of 1872, he covered a much longer distance over much of the same route in less than twenty-four hours, including some stops to pick up the heads of dead buffalo shot by Alexis.[34] Before the coming of the railroad, it took from ten days to two weeks just to cross Kansas.

From ten days at best in the summer to one day in the winter— what an enormous difference! No wonder the men of that era had a sense of bigness about them, an unshatterable confidence in the future, a perfect belief in America and in technology, an absolute faith in their destiny. They had done a remarkable thing in conquering the continent. Custer was proud of his intimate part in the building process, and one supposes that he filled Alexis' ears with old-timer stories about how tough it used to be to get across the Plains, along with only half-joking complaints about how the comforts and conveniences of modern civilization were making men soft. But he surely conveyed something of a feeling of love for those railroad tracks they were bouncing across at twenty miles per hour and all they symbolized; equally probably, Alexis must have been impressed by the railroads across the Plains—Russia had nothing like them.

Libbie joined the party at Louisville, Kentucky, where there was another endless series of grand balls. She danced with His Imperial Highness and was the center of attention throughout the night. A reporter described her, now thirty years old, as "a dark loveliness."[35] Alexis invited both her and Custer to accompany the party on a steamboat trip down the Ohio to the Mississippi, then on south to

New Orleans. The Custers accepted and had a marvelous time, surrounded by all that royalty, being served coffee and rolls in bed in the morning, chatting with the distinguished visitors. "The Admiral is all sunshine and sweet simplicity," Libbie recorded in her diary. "He strives to interest Alexis in the towns we pass, length of rivers, and the like. But in boat or on the train Alexis is not concerned with the outside, only with the pretty girls, with music—he sings magnificently, and has already learned Lydia Thompson's Music Hall ditty—which he renders 'If efer I cease to luf . . .'—in his eternal cigarette, and in joking with his suite and with the General [Custer]."[86]

In New Orleans there were more balls, visits to the restaurants, shopping, and receptions. The imperial party stayed at the St. Charles Hotel and played the horses at the Fair Grounds.[87] The grand duke then took the train to Pensacola, Florida, where a Russian warship picked him up and took him to Havana for more touring.

The Custers went back to Monroe for a short visit and to attend the wedding of Custer's sister Maggie and Lieutenant James Calhoun, whom Custer managed to get appointed to the 7th Cavalry staff. Then they returned to Elizabethtown, Kentucky, where Custer relieved the boredom by wearing a different costume every day. Sometimes he would don a military uniform, then civilian clothes with a dove-gray topper, next fringed buckskins. Barrett came for a visit. Custer lost big money betting on horse races. For the most part, though, he fretted and fumed, wondering when he would get back to the Plains.[88]

In February 1873 he finally got the orders he wanted. He was to gather together the 7th Cavalry and take it to Fort Abraham Lincoln, on the Missouri River just south of the town of Bismarck, North Dakota. The Northern Pacific was moving westward and was about to enter territory the Sioux thought had been promised to them in the treaty of 1868. There was going to be trouble, big trouble, and Sheridan wanted his best man on the scene to protect the advancing railroad. Custer had made it possible to build the Kansas Pacific; now he could do the same for the Northern Pacific.

Custer greeted the assignment with unabashed delight. He strode into Libbie's sewing room in their Elizabethtown quarters, laughing and talking so fast she could not make out a word he was saying, waltzed her around the room, picked her up and put her on top of a table, out of harm's way, and proceeded to throw furniture in every direction, including a chair he tossed into the kitchen. Libbie hopped down from the table, grabbed an atlas, and quietly retired into a safe corner to look up Bismarck. "When my finger traced our route from Kentucky almost up to the border of the British Possessions," she later wrote, "it seemed as if we were going to Lapland."[39]

So, in the spring of 1873, Custer started back toward the land he loved. The Northern Pacific was still short of Bismarck, so it had a long way to go before it reached the Yellowstone River country, home of most of the Sioux hostiles. Custer expected that his services would be needed for a long time to come. His job was to drive the Sioux out of the way. The time had come for Custer to meet Crazy Horse on the field of battle.

Part Four

CHAPTER EIGHTEEN

Crazy Horse and Custer on the Yellowstone, 1873

"My Precious Darling—Well, here we are at last, at the far-famed—and to you far-distant—Yellowstone. How I have longed for you during our march in what seems a new world, a Wonderland."
Custer to Libbie, July 19, 1873

"Sitting Bull had great power over the Sioux. He was a good medicine man. He made good medicine. Many Indians believed him. He knew how to lead them. He told the Sioux many times he was not made to be a reservation Indian. The Great Spirit made him a free Indian to go where he wanted to go, to hunt buffalo and to be a big leader in his tribe."
Lewis Dewitt, a white scout

Sitting Bull is perhaps the most famous of all North American Indians. The whites first knew him as the instigator of resistance to United States Army forays in 1872 into the northern Sioux territory and then as the organizer of the Indian forces that fought Custer at the Little Bighorn in 1876. Later he was a star attraction in Buffalo Bill Cody's Wild West Show. There he made money, most of which, Annie Oakley, another of Buffalo Bill's stars, stated, "went into the pockets of small, ragged boys. Nor could he understand how so much wealth could go brushing by, unmindful of the poor." After looking over much of the eastern United States, Sitting Bull declared that in his opinion "the white man knows how to make everything, but he does not know how to distribute it."[1]

His photograph—the one in which he is wearing a buckskin, fringed shirt, a crucifix around his neck, his braids over his breast, weasel tails hanging from them, his chin jutting at the camera, his broad mouth set, his sharp nose pushing out defiantly, his eyes narrow and hard, watching and wondering, a single feather in his hair —has been distributed worldwide. Books have been written and movies made on his life. He appeals to everyone—to the Indian lover his strength of face and character and the awesomeness of his dignity bear witness to the nobility of Indians, while to the Indian hater his ferocious resistance to the whites entitles him to, if nothing else, deep respect.

Sitting Bull was an extraordinary man for any race at any time, and such a man is of necessity complex. He was all that the whites thought he was, and much more. He was an orator, a philosopher, an adviser, a propagandist for his cause, a lay preacher, a teacher, a husband and father, a healer of the sick, a psychiatrist, a political leader, and a man. He evidently never held any authorized tribal position, either political or military, which may have contributed to rather than detracted from his strength. Something like that had happened with Red Cloud; although Red Cloud was never a chief, the 1865–68 Powder River war was known as Red Cloud's War to the Indians as well as to the whites. It was as if the allied Indian forces at Captain Fetterman's defeat in 1866 outside Fort Phil Kearny had been one big war party, with Red Cloud as its leader.

In somewhat the same way, the struggle that began in 1872 and lasted until 1877 is sometimes called Sitting Bull's War. Sitting Bull was neither the chief nor a war leader in his tribe, the Hunkpapa Sioux, nor did the alliance formed by the Indians grant him any position or power. Nevertheless, he was the Benjamin Franklin of the effort, the adviser to everyone, the man to inspire the resistance, to give it some shape and form, to ask hard questions of the men making the actual decisions, to oversee everything, to be the father of it all. Frank Grouard, the white Army scout and translator who lived with the Oglalas and Hunkpapas for five years, later said that "Sitting Bull's name was a 'tipi word' for all that was generous and great."

But for all his nobility of character and role, Sitting Bull was very human. So, of course, was Crazy Horse, and the two men struck up a fast friendship in the period of 1870–72, when Crazy Horse began to drift northward and come into closer contact with the wilder Sioux tribes, especially the Hunkpapas. Sitting Bull and Crazy Horse drew together, probably, because of their mutual vow to resist any change in their way of life, whatever the cost, for as long as possible. To the Sioux, and increasingly to the whites, Sitting Bull (then in his late thirties) and Crazy Horse (seven or so years younger) symbolized a policy of bitter Indian resistance to white encroachment on Sioux land. Further, each man was ambitious, anxious to occupy first place in the minds of the people. Most of all, Sitting Bull and Crazy Horse were proud to be Sioux and prouder still to be free.[2]

Crazy Horse and Sitting Bull fought together for the first time in the summer of 1872. The Northern Pacific Railroad had pushed as far west as the Missouri River, the town of Bismarck springing up on the east bank at the terminus point of the line. Surveyors pushed farther westward, along the valley of the Yellowstone in eastern Montana. They were protected by a strong military escort, provided by Sherman, who believed that the completion of the Northern Pacific would seal the doom of the hostile Sioux. With the Union Pacific to the south of their territory and the Northern Pacific along the Yellowstone, the Sioux would be trapped between two lines of settlement, their buffalo eliminated, and they would either have to come into the agencies or starve. Sitting Bull and Crazy Horse saw the threat clearly and were determined to resist.[3]

By August 1872 Major E. M. Baker of the 2nd Cavalry, with a mixed force of four hundred infantry and cavalry, had pushed up the Yellowstone from its mouth in western North Dakota. Sitting Bull, Crazy Horse, and most of the Sioux hostiles (Oglalas, Miniconjous, Hunkpapas, Sans Arcs, and Blackfeet) were camped near the mouth of the Powder River in eastern Montana. When Indian hunting parties reported that the soldiers were moving southwest in the Yellowstone Valley, the Indians rode out to meet them. At daybreak, August 14, 1872, they discovered the soldiers' camp at the mouth of Arrow Creek, northeast of the mouth of the Tongue. Crazy Horse had wanted to lay a careful plan for an attack, but the white man's beef and horse herd were too tempting for the young warriors to resist, and a few of them rode down on the camp, whooping and hollering, cutting out cattle and horses. The soldiers started firing. Crazy Horse, angry, advised everyone to pull back—the soldiers had carbines and plenty of ammunition, so nothing could be accomplished now that they knew of the Indians' presence.

But the northern Sioux had only limited experience with white soldiers and they took foolish chances. Plenty Lice charged them on foot and was cut down. Two men who had joined him were wounded. The Indians fell back, but they were not ready to give up. Long Holy, a Miniconjou medicine man with a strong vision, had recently organized an order of seven young men and, following the instructions he had received in his vision, he had made them bulletproof. (In fact, he had wounded several of his young men during a test, but the bullets had not gone through, the reason undoubtedly being that the shells were underloaded. Indians tried to stretch what powder they had and consistently cheated on the powder load. Many a white soldier who was hit by gunfire in a vital spot nevertheless lived through these wars because of that Indian practice.)

Long Holy decided that Arrow Creek was an ideal place to display his power. Stanley Vestal, Sitting Bull's biographer, relates the story. Repeating the bulletproofing ceremony, Long Holy announced that he and his young men were going to circle the soldiers' position four times on their ponies. After that they would charge, the entire hostile force charging with them. So it was done, the bulletproof warriors riding at top speed around the whites, singing the song Long Holy had taught them. But one by one the circling warriors cried out, "I am hit!" or "I am shot!" By the time they finished the second go-round, four of the bulletproof seven were wounded.

As they began their third circle, Sitting Bull galloped out onto the prairie between the lines. He yelled at Long Holy and his young men, "Wait! Stop! Turn back! Too many young men are being wounded! That's enough!" Long Holy protested. No one had yet been killed and only one of the bullets had gone through a warrior (Leading-Him had been shot in the neck, below the chin, and the bullet had passed clear through him). "I brought these men here to *fight*," Long Holy told Sitting Bull. "But of course, if they *want* to quit, they can." Sitting Bull paid no attention to Long Holy; he kept telling the young men to come back, and they did.

For the next couple of hours there was a long-range fight—"Just shooting," as the Indians put it—with no casualties. Then Crazy Horse rode between the lines, slowly, being careful to stay out of effective range of the bullets. He hoped to draw out some white soldiers to fight, but he also wanted to demonstrate his courage to these northern relatives. Long Holy, meanwhile, kept complaining about Sitting Bull's interference. He said that Sitting Bull was getting "mouthy."

By midmorning, Sitting Bull had had enough. He couldn't listen to Long Holy's complaining any more and he was jealous of all the attention Crazy Horse was getting. It was time to show his friends who was the bravest of all. He took his tobacco pouch and long-stemmed pipe and walked coolly out in front of the Indian line, as nonchalant as if he were taking his evening constitutional. He strolled toward the soldiers and sat down on the grass one hundred yards in front of the Indian line, in the middle of the open prairie at the extreme range of the soldiers' bullets. He took out his flint and steel, loaded his pipe, struck fire, lit the pipe, and began to puff away in his usual leisurely fashion. Turning his head toward his astonished companions, he called out, "Any Indians who wish to smoke with me, come on!"

It was a show-off stunt, of the type that led Frank Grouard to say, "No man in the Sioux nation was braver than Sitting Bull." But show-off or not, it was exactly the kind of demonstration that the Indians found most impressive. White Bull, Gets-the-Best-of-Them, and two visiting Cheyennes could not resist the dare. They walked forward and sat down in a row. Sitting Bull was calmly puffing away. He handed the pipe to White Bull, who puffed, then passed it along. White Bull later told Stanley Vestal, "We others wasted no time. Our hearts beat rapidly, and we smoked as fast as we could. All around us the bullets were kicking up the dust, and we could hear the bullets whining overhead. But Sitting Bull was not afraid. He just sat there quietly, looking around as if he were at home in his tent, and smoked peacefully."

It just beat everything. Not one of those Indians had ever seen a braver stunt. After the pipe was finished, Sitting Bull got out his little sharp stick that he used for cleaning, cleared the bowl of ashes, ran the stick through the stem, then carefully put the pipe and stick back into their pouch. Stretching, he rose slowly and sauntered back to the Indian line, White Bull and the other three running ahead of him. Gets-the-Best-of-Them was so excited that he forgot his arrows and White Bull had to run back after them.

It was then about noon and everyone was talking excitedly of Sitting Bull's bravery. Sitting Bull got his horse and mounted up, calling out, "That's enough! We must stop! That's enough!" But Crazy Horse could not ignore the challenge; he too had to demonstrate his courage. So he called out to White Bull, "Let's make one more circle toward the soldier line." White Bull took up the dare and away they charged. All four hundred white soldiers fired at them, filling the air with a constant stream of bullets. Finally one of the bullets hit Crazy Horse's pony and it fell dead on the spot, but by then Crazy Horse was nearly back to the Indian line and he jumped to his feet and ran to safety afoot. White Bull and his horse were untouched. The Indians withdrew.[4]

It had been a show of force, a warning to the whites and not much more. Fortunately for the Indians, the white surveyors had gone about as far west as they wanted to that summer, and shortly after the fight the soldiers turned back, heading east, giving the Indians the impression they had won a significant victory.

It was evidently in that same summer of 1872 that Crazy Horse got married. The evidence indicates that it was a marriage of convenience arranged for him by his friends, especially He Dog. Her name was Black Shawl and she was the sister of Red Feather, a strong warrior and a friend of Crazy Horse. In 1930 Eleanor Hinman asked Red Feather if he could tell her anything about the marriage of Crazy Horse and Black Shawl. "All I can say about that," Red Feather replied, "is that both Crazy Horse and my sister stayed single much longer than is usual among our people."[5] Black Shawl was evidently in her late twenties. What seems to have happened is that He Dog, Red Feather, and others who fought with Crazy Horse decided that he needed a wife. He had recently suffered three grievous blows—the death of Hump, the death of Little Hawk, and the loss of Black Buffalo Woman—and may have been dangerously depressed. Perhaps a wife in his tipi, with the laughter of children soon to come, would cheer him up. So it was arranged.[6]

The marriage was a success. Black Shawl and Crazy Horse stayed together for the rest of their lives. Her mother came to live in the tipi, a common practice among the Sioux, so Crazy Horse was well taken care of, with extra moccasins to take along on war parties; a nicely arranged, comfortable tipi; good, well-prepared food to eat; and a warm atmosphere for his private life. Within a year Black Shawl had a baby, a girl, whom Crazy Horse named They-Are-Afraid-of-Her. The scattered bits of evidence about Crazy Horse as a father are more tantalizing than conclusive, but they indicate that he delighted in the role and played for hours on end with his daughter. He was growing older now, had reached his thirties, the age at which men begin to realize that they are not going to live forever, and he seems to have embraced new responsibilities, especially with regard to the youth of the tribe whose future he was fighting so hard to insure.

Whatever his motivation, Crazy Horse became something like a storyteller, gathering the children around him and filling them up with stories about the Sioux heritage. Black Elk, who would later become famous as a holy man and author (Black Elk Speaks, edited by John Neihardt) was among those who sat at Crazy Horse's feet. Crazy Horse also taught the boys of the village all the lessons they had to master in order to live a free life on the Plains—how to make a bow and arrows, how to track game, how to hunt, how to fight. He was still the best hunter among the Oglalas, and he delighted in leading an occasional war party against the Crows, to keep them pinned back on the Bighorns, or against the white soldiers and surveyors on the Yellowstone. Altogether, despite the loss of his best friend, his brother, and the woman he had loved, the early seventies brought many rewards to Crazy Horse.

In March 1873 Custer gathered the 7th Cavalry at Memphis and began the journey to the far-north country. He had most of the old gang with him, Tom Custer, George Yates, William Cooke, Captain Myles W. Keogh, James Calhoun—and Libbie. His cook, Eliza, had gotten married and left him, so Custer had hired a black couple, Ham and Mary, to accompany him and care for his personal needs. He also brought along cages of mockingbirds and canaries, plus a basketful of puppies.[7]

The 7th Cavalry was headed for Fort Abraham Lincoln, just down the Missouri from Bismarck. Sherman and Sheridan were encircling the northern Sioux with forts, with five on the Missouri River in North Dakota alone, plus others to the west and south of Sioux territory. The preparations were being made, in other words, for the show-down with the hostiles. Custer's initial job was to help protect the Northern Pacific Railroad surveyors as they worked their way westward along the Yellowstone. Whether or not the whites had a legal right to cross these Plains is a moot point, as the treaty of 1868 failed to set a northern boundary for the Sioux. The whites said the Yellowstone was the boundary and they planned to build the railroad along the north bank of the river; the Sioux claimed that the Canadian border was the boundary. Custer had ten troops of cavalry under his command, but that was only part of the total expedition, as Sherman wanted a strong column this summer after the events of August 1872. Colonel (Brevet Major General) David S. Stanley led the full expedition, which included 1,500 soldiers and 400 civilians. Stanley had a train of 275 wagons, supplemented by steamboats plying the Missouri and the Yellowstone.[8]

Stanley was a quiet, competent soldier. He had graduated from West Point in 1852 and had been an Indian fighter on the Plains before the Civil War. He had risen steadily during the war, fighting under Sherman in the Atlanta campaign. Although Sherman blamed some lost opportunities on Stanley's lack of "dash and energy," Sherman must have found him steady, since he made Stanley a corps commander, in which capacity he fought with credit to the end of the war.[9]

Although both Stanley and Custer were successful soldiers, the contrast between them was marked. Stanley was ten years older than Custer, rather quiet and somewhat modest, a man who had a job to do and did it without fuss. He had no stars in his eyes. The contrast between the two men stands out in boldest relief when one compares their reactions to the conditions encountered on the Yellowstone expedition of 1873.

On June 26, from camp on the Heart River, forty-five miles west of the Missouri, Stanley and Custer wrote letters to their wives. (Libbie had gone to Monroe for the summer as there were no suitable quarters for her at Fort Abe Lincoln). Stanley said they were laid over on account of high water on the Heart. Custer said they were laid over to wait for some railroad engineers. Stanley said it had rained four out of the past six days, sometimes in torrents, and that he was miserable. Custer said, "Our march has been perfectly delightful thus far." He had never seen better hunting in his life; the antelope were so plentiful that one bunch actually ran through the wagon train. He was hunting constantly, but assured Libbie that he always stayed within sight of the column. He marveled at the unspoiled prairie. Not many white men had passed over this route, the game was as plentiful as it had once been down on the Platte, Republican, and Arkansas rivers, the grass was waist-high and higher, and Custer was altogether thrilled. He took one look and loved that country for the rest of his life.

To Stanley, meanwhile, it was all just another job on those endless, monotonous Plains. "The winds have been terrible, and the whole prairie has become a swamp," he wrote disgustedly. "I am well," he confessed almost reluctantly, "and wonder that I am as I have been wet nearly every day for nine days." Custer said he had never been in a healthier climate.[10]

When the column reached the Yellowstone in Montana, Custer was overwhelmed. "No artist," he wrote Libbie, "could fairly represent the wonderful country we passed over, while each step of our progress was like each successive shifting of the kaleidoscope, presenting to our wondering gaze views which almost appalled us by their sublimity."[11] Stanley told his wife that while the river itself was beautiful, "the country adjoining is repulsive in its rugged, barren ugliness."

Stanley was no dreamer of dreams. He had penetrated into country seldom seen by white men, a primeval place filled with the marvels of life on this earth, and all he could think to tell his wife was, "These 18 days have been days of as hard work as I ever put in as a soldier."[12]

Custer caught the spirit of the West, the spirit of Cortes, of Lewis and Clark. He gushed about it, simply overflowed. He wrote Libbie one forty-page letter, then followed it with another of eighty pages, mostly devoted to telling her about the country. "What would you think of passing through acres of petrified trees," he asked Libbie, "some with trunks several feet in diameter, and branches perfect?" He described in detail the fossil fish they were finding, the flora and fauna and of course his hunting successes. He wore a brilliant red shirt to let everyone know how good he felt. He became a great booster of the West: "How I have wished that some of our home boys, who possess talent and education, but lack means and opportunity, would cast themselves loose from home and try their fortunes in this great enterprising western country, where the virtues of real manhood come quickly to the surface, and their possessor finds himself transformed from a mere boy to a full-fledged man almost before he realizes his quick advancement."[13]

Most of all, Custer responded to the hunting. The details need not detain us; suffice it to say that he hunted nearly every day and at the end of the expedition reported on the total bag:

"I killed with my rifle and brought into camp forty-one antelope, four buffalo, four elk, seven deer (four of them blacktails), two white wolves, and one red fox.

"Geese, ducks, prairie-chickens, and sage-hens without number completed my summer's record.

"No one assisted me in killing the antelope, deer, or elk, except one of the latter.

"One porcupine and a wildcat I brought in alive. Both of these amiable creatures I intend to send to Central Park."[14]

As the expedition pushed on, Stanley grew more and more irritated at everything, while Custer grew happier and more excited. "I have had no trouble with Custer," Stanley wrote his wife on June 28, "and will try to avoid having any; but I have seen enough of him to convince me that he is a cold-blooded, untruthful and unprincipled man. He is universally despised by all the officers of his regiment excepting his relatives and one or two sycophants. He brought a trader into the field without permission, carries an old negro woman, and cast iron cooking stove, and delays the march often by his extensive packing up in the morning. As I said I will try, but am not sure I can avoid trouble with him."[15] Custer, meanwhile, accused Stanley of near-constant drunkenness.[16]

Trouble was inevitable. Stanley told the story to his wife: "I had a little flurry with Custer as I told you I probably would. We were separated 4 miles, and I intended him to assist in getting the train, his own train, over the Muddy River. Without consulting me he marched off 15 miles, coolly sending me a note to send him forage and rations. I sent after him, ordered him to halt where he was, to unload his wagons, and send for his own rations and forage, and never to presume to make another movement without orders.

"I knew from the start it had to be done, and I am glad to have so good a chance, when there could be no doubt who was right. He was just gradually assuming command, and now he knows he has a commanding officer who will not tolerate his arrogance."[17]

Stanley placed Custer under arrest and ordered the 7th Cavalry to march at the rear of the column, where it could eat the infantry's dust. Custer shrugged, returned to his tent, and took a nap. As he lay dozing, he heard a familiar voice outside say, "Orderly, which is General Custer's tent?" Custer would have known that voice anywhere—it was Tom Rosser! A close friend at West Point, his most resourceful enemy in the Civil War. Rosser was chief engineer on the Northern Pacific survey team now and would be accompanying the column. "We talk over our West Point times and discuss the battles of the war," Custer told Libbie. "I stretch the buffalo-robe under the fly of the tent, and there in the moonlight he and I, lying at full length, listen to each other's accounts of battles in which both had bourne a part. It seemed like the time when we were cadets together, huddled on one blanket and discussing dreams of the future."[18]

When Rosser heard of Custer's difficulties, he went to Stanley and asked to have Custer returned to active duty and his regiment put at the front of the column, where the cavalry belonged in Indian country. Rosser intimated that the Northern Pacific backers would be unhappy otherwise.

Stanley thereupon reinstated Custer, who apparently learned his lesson. He *had* been taking over command of the column, in effect, because the infantry officers were drawn to his mess, which was always so cheerful. There was a permanent poker game going on among the 7th Cavalry officers, which was an additional attraction. Further, the cavalry officers had whiskey aplenty. Colonel Frederick Dent Grant, the President's son, was along as an observer for Sheridan, and rumor had it that he was always drunk. Finally, the infantry officers were drawn to Custer's campfire because his cook made such good meals on her cast-iron cooking stove and there was always fresh meat from the day's hunting. Stanley *did* need to assert himself and re-establish his authority, and he did it effectively. Custer "has behaved very well," Stanley told his wife six weeks later.[19]

Custer's letters to his wife during this expedition provide revealing glimpses of his personality. First, he was more in love than ever. "Good morning, my Sunbeam," he would write when starting a segment of his epic missives (Tom Custer called the 120-page outpouring "Autie's book"), or he would begin, "My Darling Bunkey." He said, over and over, that he could give up anything except her. "Writing to others seems difficult," he continued, "but to you not so. When other themes fail we still have the old story which in ten years has not lost its freshness . . . indeed is newer than when, at the outset we wondered if it would endure in its first intensity."[20]

Next, Custer was generous. "General Stanley," he wrote Libbie, "when not possessed by the fiend of intemperance, is one of the kindest, most agreeable and considerate officers I ever served under." Libbie had heard about her Autie's arrest and was all a-twitter over it, but Custer told her everything was fine. "I suppose you think I am of a very forgiving disposition," he wrote. "Well, perhaps I am. I often think of the beautiful expression uttered by President Lincoln —'With malice toward none; with charity toward all . . .'—and I hope this may ever be mine to say."[21] Perhaps Custer, like General George Patton of World War II fame, needed a strong hand over him to bring out his best.

The letters also reveal that Custer, for all his fame, was still a man on the make. Fred Grant was called home for his grandfather's funeral. Custer, who could not keep himself from fawning on anyone who could help his career and who was always and forever telling Libbie what to do, gave her careful instructions: "If he—Col. Grant— goes to Long Branch from Chicago by way of Monroe to see you, you will, of course, do all in your power to make his stay agreeable. If you know of his arrival in advance you should meet him at the depot with a carriage. Have his father's picture hung in the parlor . . ."[22]

Back in Monroe, Libbie was bored stiff. "I find it hard to rise above depressing surroundings without your help," she wrote Autie. "There are not many joyous people here. The women are so fagged with domestic cares, kitchen drudgery, leading a monotonous life, the men without bright women to cheer them up . . ." She was awfully glad that she had not married a local businessman and spent her life washing, cleaning, and cooking—she much preferred the Army and couldn't wait to get back to the frontier, to excitement and adventure. She said she was trying to "improve to keep up with you, be worthy of you."

Libbie went to visit a childhood friend, Mary Dansard. "Poor Mary," she said, "lingering along with childbirth illness." Mary, with a hint of envy in her voice, remarked, "Just think, Libbie, in ten years I have had seven children—and you not one."[23]

At about the same time, Custer was writing Libbie about his huge dog Tuck, who would go to sleep only on Custer's lap. "She resembles a well-cared for and half-spoiled child," Custer told Libbie after a page of description of Tuck's sleeping habits, "who can never be induced to retire until it has been fondled to sleep in its mother's arms." When he put the sleeping dog down from his lap, Custer added, she was "like a little baby carefully deposited in its crib."[24]

The Custers were childless, a fact they seem never to have discussed in public and never wrote about. Why they had no children is a mystery. To a man of Custer's exuberance and a woman with Libbie's energy, coupled with their mutual love of life and of each other, that fact must have been important, but all one can do is speculate.

On July 31, 1873, the Stanley expedition camped north of the Yellowstone River and the mouth of the Powder River. It was well inside Sioux territory now and Sitting Bull and Crazy Horse were aware of its progress. They, along with other Indian leaders, began to band together and look for a place to set an ambush. Custer proceeded southwestward along the Yellowstone, the surveyors and infantry following. By August 4, Custer was opposite the mouth of the Tongue River (site of present-day Miles City). It was a hot, dusty day, and Custer halted his cavalry to wait for the others to catch up. Pulling off his boots, setting up his saddle for a pillow, his red shirt cushioning the hard leather, Custer took a nap.[25]

He was sleeping, then, when Crazy Horse first saw him. Along with other warriors, Crazy Horse had crawled to the crest of a nearby bluff, from which spot they could look down on Custer's position. The Indians could not have been very hopeful, as there were eighty-five well-armed cavalrymen with Custer and their own force numbered, at most, 350 men, mainly without firearms—bad odds for the red men. Still, there were possibilities. Upstream from the spot where Custer was camping there was a big stand of timber, an ideal place for the bulk of the warriors to hide. Custer's horses had been turned out to graze; perhaps they could be stampeded. Custer would have to follow to get his horses back; perhaps in the process he could be led into the timber, where the soldiers' guns wouldn't count for so much. The Indians decided to give it a try.

Whether or not Crazy Horse was a member of the decoy party is impossible to determine, but it is probable that he was. He had more experience in this sort of thing than anyone else and the details of what he had accomplished against Fetterman in 1866 were known to every Indian in the camp. Further, the actions of the decoy party seem to show the fine hand of Crazy Horse at work.

In any event, after all the preparations were complete, six decoys dashed down into Custer's herd of horses, attempting to stampede it in the direction of the heavy timber and the waiting warriors. But Custer had his guards posted and the men immediately started firing and yelling. Custer jumped to his feet, grabbed his rifle, and ran toward the excitement, wearing only his socks and underwear. The decoys had retreated to a safe distance, from which spot they taunted Custer, shouting insults and occasionally firing at him. The six Indians rode back and forth, making little and big circles, nervous as antelope but showing no disposition to run. Custer ordered his troopers to mount up, pulled on his shirt, pants, and boots, called for a detail of twenty men, put them under the command of his brother Tom, and set off at the head of the small detachment to give chase.[26]

Custer described the ensuing action in his official battle report: "Following the Indians at a brisk gait, my suspicions became excited by the confident bearing exhibited by the six Sioux in our front, whose course seemed to lead us near a heavy growth of timber which stood along the river bank above us. When almost within rifle range of this timber, I directed the squadron to halt, while I with two orderlies, all being well mounted, continued after the Sioux in order to develop their intentions. Proceeding a few hundred yards in advance of the squadron, and keeping a watchful eye on the timber to my left, I halted. The six Indians in my front also halted, as if to tempt further pursuit."[27]

For a brief instant the two parties stared at each other, there beside the Yellowstone. Did Crazy Horse and Custer see each other? There is no direct evidence, but certainly Custer stood out; even without his red shirt he would have caught Crazy Horse's eye, as he was obviously the leader of the whites, a big man among them. Crazy Horse would have been less likely to catch Custer's eye—with his single feather in his hair and his unpainted body, he paled beside his resplendent fellow warriors. Still, Custer had heard of Crazy Horse, knew of his skills as a decoy, and had Fetterman very much on his mind. "Among the Indians who fought us on this occasion were some of the identical warriors who committed the massacre at Fort Phil Kearny," he wrote in his report, "and they no doubt intended a similar programme when they sent the six warriors to dash up and attempt to decoy us."[28]

Whether they saw each other or not, it was a dramatic instant, each side wondering what to do next. Custer was tempted to smash the Indians to bits, to ride into their ambush deliberately and show them what cavalry fire power could do—but he couldn't do it with just two men, nor even with the twenty Tom Custer had in nearby reserve. He would have to wait for the rest of the troopers to catch up; meanwhile he watched, fascinated, as the decoys pulled out their bag of tricks. It was a test of nerves, will, and skill.

But we will never know how it might have come out, for among the warriors in the trees were a few Cheyennes, survivors of Black Kettle's camp on the Washita. They recognized Custer—"Long Hair," as they called him—the hated Custer who had killed their wives and children and brothers, then slaughtered their ponies in November 1868; as soon as they saw him the Cheyennes charged, the other warriors quickly joining them. Whatever chance the ambush had had, it was gone now.

Custer took one look at the oncoming mass of three hundred warriors, all yelling, screaming, firing arrows before them, and he turned and ran. His thoroughbred, called Dandy, outsped the pintos and he reunited with Tom's twenty-man detachment. Leaping to the ground and throwing Dandy's reins to a horse holder, Custer ordered Tom to dismount his troopers and throw them forward into a skirmish line. The grass was tall and they could hide in it.

The Indians came on strong, hoping to get at Custer and his men before they could take up a defensive position. "As the Sioux came dashing forward," Custer wrote in his report, "expecting to ride down the squadron, a line of dismounted cavalrymen rose from the grass and delivered almost in the faces of the warriors a volley of carbine bullets which broke and scattered their ranks in all directions, and sent more than one Sioux reeling from his saddle."[29]

Crazy Horse helped hold the Indians back after that rout and especially after the remainder of Custer's eighty-five men joined him and completed the defensive perimeter, their backs to the Yellowstone. But neither Crazy Horse, Sitting Bull, nor anyone else could do anything to stop the Cheyennes, so hot were they to fight Custer. So while the Sioux circled around cautiously, firing an occasional arrow or bullet at the whites, the Cheyennes rode back and forth between the lines, firing wildly.

Custer called to Bloody Knife, his Rhee scout and increasingly a favorite of his, and together they crawled to a position from which they might get a shot. Lying in the grass, they heard a pony's hoofs galloping toward the soldiers' line. The daring Cheyenne warrior fired, then dashed away.

"If he does that again," Custer said to Bloody Knife, "let's see who's the best shot!"

Again the Cheyenne came on. Both Custer and Bloody Knife rose up and fired simultaneously. The Indian hit the ground with a thud. Each man claimed credit for the lucky shot; Bloody Knife was a saucy fellow with a sharp tongue who delighted in twitting the whites, and he said Custer could not hit a tent from the inside. Custer returned the compliment. Later, in his report, Custer gave the credit to Bloody Knife.[30]

Crazy Horse, Sitting Bull, and the other Sioux leaders knew that they were never going to get anywhere this way, with the warriors dashing out one by one only to get picked off. They decided to set fire to the grass and smoke Custer out, but the wind died, the fire petered out, and nothing came of it. By this time a confident Custer's only worry was that he would run out of ammunition, and in any event he was hardly the soldier to stand and receive an attack when he had an opportunity to take the offensive. So he ordered his men to mount up, then led them on a charge. The Indians, naturally, broke and ran in the face of the awesome fire power of a compact mass of well-armed cavalrymen. Custer called them "cowardly" for doing so, an astonishing judgment but one that was by now firmly established in his mind. He once again concluded that where Indians are concerned, attack, attack, and then attack again—they will always break and run. Custer's losses were three men killed, the Indians' about the same.[31]

Four days later, on August 8, Bloody Knife discovered the trail of a large village. Crazy Horse and the other warriors had gathered together their people and were making their way west, moving upstream along the Yellowstone. They were not running away or retreating, merely following their habitual routine. It is doubtful that they even knew Custer was following; they probably felt that, as had happened the previous summer, the expedition would turn around and go back once it had been challenged.

But Custer did follow their trail, as eagerly as he had followed Black Kettle's warriors back to camp in 1868. With four squadrons of the 7th Cavalry, leaving all tents and wagons behind, he marched through the night of August 8, making thirty miles. He hoped to stumble onto a sleeping village, but had no luck. After a brief halt he took up the pursuit again the following day, reaching the mouth of the Bighorn River as darkness fell. This was about as far west as the Sioux usually went—beyond was Crow territory—and the Indians had crossed to the south bank of the Yellowstone. Custer tried to follow, but the swift current was too much for the white man's horses, and after a full day of effort, with Custer putting his driving energy, his West Point engineering lessons, and the labor of one hundred men into it, they still could not get across. The hostiles, meanwhile, had discovered Custer's presence. They made camp on the south bank, intending to attack the next morning.

At dawn, August 11, the Indians appeared on the bluffs on the south bank and began firing at Custer's camp a few hundred yards across the river. Indian women and children, Black Shawl and They-Are-Afraid-of-Her among them, appeared on the bluffs too. The women wanted to watch Long Hair get rubbed out. Crazy Horse and a couple of hundred warriors, meanwhile, swam the river above and below Custer's position—the feat that had stymied Custer and the cavalry, fording the Yellowstone, was no problem to the Indians—and they began to close in. Sharpshooting across the river continued, with each side taking casualties.

The Indians planned to pin down Custer and overwhelm him with arrow and bullet fire, but most of the warriors who had guns were on the south bank and Custer's men had dug in, so the Indians were being careful. Custer noticed them getting closer to his lines and decided that the time had come for him to charge the enemy on his side of the river. If he could get them on the run, he knew the day would be his, but he had to move fast to disrupt their plans. He rode to the front and started giving orders for the men to mount up and prepare to charge. An Indian bullet picked off his horse (not Dandy), but he calmly took another and remounted.[82]

Tom Rosser was there, and he later told Libbie about it. "The time I would rather have had a picture of George was on the Yellowstone Campaign, when he had a horse shot under him. As the orders were issued and he was making a charge George sat on his horse out in advance, calmly looking the Indians over, full of suppressed excitement, but also with calculating judgment and strength of purpose in his face." In a final tribute to Custer, Rosser, who had fought under Robert E. Lee, declared, "I thought him then one of the finest specimens of a soldier I had ever seen."[83]

Custer ordered the band to strike up "Garry Owen" and away they went. The charge confounded the hostiles, who fled in every direction. Custer chased them for nine miles but came up empty-handed; the warriors recrossed the Yellowstone and that afternoon the big Indian village moved up the Bighorn River, heading south. Custer estimated that he had faced between eight hundred and one thousand warriors, about triple the number that were actually there, and claimed forty killed, which was a grossly inflated figure. His own losses were four killed and four wounded. "The Indians were made up of different bands of Sioux," he reported, "principally Uncpapas [*sic*], the whole under command of 'Sitting Bull,' who participated in the fight, and who for once has been taught a lesson he will not soon forget."[34]

After this skirmish the two sides disengaged. Sitting Bull, Crazy Horse, and their Indians went back to the Powder River country, where they spent a quiet fall and winter. Custer marched overland to the Musselshell River, down that stream to its junction with the Missouri, and then down the Missouri to Fort Abraham Lincoln. There in the fall of 1873 Libbie joined him and they moved into their recently completed home, a handsome frame house built especially for the commanding officer at the fort (Custer), the first home of their own the Custers had occupied.

Both sides were satisfied with the summer's work. The Indians figured they had turned Custer and the advancing whites back, a conclusion reinforced by the fact that for the next two years there were no Army expeditions into the Yellowstone country. (Actually, the reason for the pause in building of the Northern Pacific was the Panic of 1873, which had thrown the stock market into turmoil and led to a bankruptcy of the railroad. Until it was reorganized and refunded, there would be no more railroad building.) Custer figured that he had driven the Indians out of the path of the railroad and taught them a lesson they would not soon forget. Both Custer and Crazy Horse, in short, still had much to learn about each other.

CHAPTER NINETEEN

The Panic of 1873 and the Black Hills Expedition of 1874

"More beautiful wild country could not be imagined."

> William Ludlow, chief engineer of
> the expedition

"An Eden in the clouds—how shall I describe it! As well try to paint the flavor of a peach or the odor of a rose."

> Samuel Barrows, reporter for the
> New York *Tribune*

"It is hardly possible to exaggerate in describing this flowery richness. Some said they would give a hundred dollars just to have their wives see the floral richness for even one Hour."

> Professor A. B. Donaldson, the
> expedition's botanist

"One of the most beautiful spots on God's green earth. No wonder the Indians regard this as the home of the Great Spirit and guard it with jealous care."

> Nathan Knappen, reporter for the
> Bismarck *Tribune*

"In no private or public park have I ever seen such a profuse display of flowers. Every step of our march that day was amid flowers of the most exquisite color and perfume. . . . On some of the water courses almost every panful of earth produced gold. . . . The miners report that they found gold among the grass roots."

> George Armstrong Custer, writing
> from Crazy Horse's birthplace at
> the foot of Bear Butte

America had never seen anything like it. There had been ups and downs in the economy before the Civil War, but the slumps were relatively short and comparatively mild. Besides, prewar America was overwhelmingly rural and thus more or less immune to the crushing effects of an economic depression. By 1873 the country was more urbanized, more industrialized, and therefore more vulnerable. It was also unprepared for any bad economic news.

Since the war the stock market had been on what appeared to be a permanent boom. Railroad stocks led the way; speculation in the stock of the Kansas Pacific, the Union Pacific, the Northern Pacific, and other lines was unprecedented and unrestrained. Infant industries were becoming more mature and there was profitable speculation in their stock, too. Cities were growing, with young men coming in from American farms and from Europe to provide a cheap labor force for the new factories. Growth, prosperity, and progress went hand in hand and most Americans acted as if the boom would last forever.

Then, on September 18, 1873, the banking house of Jay Cooke failed. Other firms quickly followed, including the company of the father of George Bird Grinnell, which had been involved in the manipulation of huge amounts of stock. The crash "came on out of a clear sky," Grinnell later wrote.* "Trusted officers of banks and corporations disappeared with the money of the institutions; the stock market promptly fell to pieces; prices dropped almost to nothing; and the Stock Exchange, to put a period to the ruin that seemed impending, closed its doors."[1] All of this confused and frightened the American people, who hardly understood what was happening to them. Their reaction is best summed up in the name they gave to this depression (which lasted from 1873 to 1877); they called it the "Panic of 1873."

The whole country, not just the stock market, was indeed in a state of panic. Farm prices plummeted. One of the worst grasshopper plagues in history swept the Midwest and the Great Plains; when flying, the insects blackened the sky; when resting or feeding, they were sometimes two or three feet thick on the ground. An epidemic of yellow fever struck the Mississippi Valley. In the cities, meanwhile, there were one million or more unemployed, nearly 20 per cent of the non-farm working force, and in a day when there was no public relief available anywhere. Although farmers could not meet their costs because of falling crop prices, food prices at the city grocery stores dropped only 5 per cent, while factory wages for those lucky enough to hold onto a job were down 25 per cent and more. There were more people in jail than ever before in the nation's history, but

---

* Partly because of the depression, Grinnell went west, to eventually become *the* authority on the Cheyennes.

crime continued nevertheless at unprecedented rates. Tramps were everywhere, wandering the land, wondering what had happened to them and to their nation. Worse, the nation's leaders had no idea what had gone wrong. It was cruel and heartless, this smashing of the American dream, because it was so unexpected and so unexplainable.[2]

Since the political and economic leaders could not explain what had caused the depression, they could hardly come up with any solutions. Normally confident, boastful, swaggering, these men had held to the doctrine of continual progress as to holy writ; now their faith was destroyed and they knew not where to look to find another. They were a curious mixture, these leaders of the Gilded Age; innovative and dynamic in the business world, they had stretched the limits of what was possible in every direction. But for all the changes they had wrought, their political views remained stuck in the eighteenth century. The government's role in the economy, as they saw it, was to pour money into industry (via such means as land grants and direct bonus payments to the railroads) but otherwise to keep hands off. The nation's leaders would not provide unemployment relief or welfare, for they were as hidebound about the functions of government as they were innovative about business.

In trying to understand what had brought on the depression, the leaders tended to put the blame on a lack of circulating money. President Grant had limited the number of greenbacks, which had the effect of putting the country on a gold standard, which was exactly where the most conservative and influential economists of the period wanted it to be. But in an expanding economy the gold supply was insufficient. Farmers' groups and labor unions wanted to expand the amount of paper money in circulation, but such a course seemed blasphemous to the men in power, who were wedded to the gold standard and who thought the issuance of paper money dangerously radical. Still, the powerful wanted more money too, in order to finance the rebuilding of the economy and to get the boom going again. And President Grant and his advisers did want the government to do something about the situation, provide some hope for the tramps, get the country back to normal. The solution to the problem, as the Administration saw it, lay in opening new territories for exploitation. Physical expansion had solved America's problems before and would again. In effect, Grant's relief program was to open new opportunities for the jobless and pump more money into the economy through the development of new gold deposits.

That is where Custer came in. Once again he became the cutting edge of the nation's expansion. By conquering Sioux territory and discovering vast gold deposits, he helped end the depression, and the nation was able to get back to normal without having to examine itself, without having to change the existing cozy relationships between government and business. In the process, Custer added to his own fame.

The Black Hills, *Pa Sapa* to the Indians, had been promised to the Sioux forever in the treaty of 1868. After the Panic of 1873, however, the United States Government began to look on the Hills with greedy eyes. Rumor had it that there were vast mineral deposits in *Pa Sapa*, including gold. A handful of whites had entered the Hills; those who were not killed by Indians returned to civilization with glowing accounts of the riches to be found there. The Indians, knowing that the yellow metal seemed to make whites go crazy, had done their best to keep the whites from knowing of the presence of gold in the Hills. In the 1840s some Sioux brought a few yellow nuggets to Father De Smet, who advised them to bury the gold deep in the earth and forget it. Worm, Crazy Horse's father, had attended a large Indian council where the warriors had agreed that any Indian who revealed the presence of gold in the Hills to the white man, or any white man who discovered it, was to be slain.[8] Nevertheless, the word somehow got out and white Americans began to demand that the government open the Hills for exploitation; these demands grew to a crescendo following the Panic of 1873.

Every level of American society was represented in the demand to open the Black Hills to prospecting. The nation's pride was involved—no patriot could permanently accept the idea of Sioux sovereignty in the vast enclave between the Missouri, the Yellowstone, and the Nebraska boundary. Railroad men generally and the Northern Pacific backers specifically wanted the hostiles subdued. Businessmen, farmers, and laborers wanted to coin the gold found in the Black Hills and put it into circulation. The Army was itching for revenge against the Sioux. Emigrants from the thirty-seven states, and immigrants from Europe, wanted the northern Plains opened to settlement. And President Grant wanted to demonstrate to a suffering, bewildered public that the United States Government could take decisive action to help end the depression.

The United States, like many nations, has started its share of wars on trumped-up charges, but no excuse ever given for the initiation of hostilities—not the Mexican War, not the Gulf of Tonkin—was more absurd than the one given by General Sheridan for the commencement of the Great Sioux War. With the enthusiastic backing of his military and political superiors, Sheridan decided in the spring of 1874 to send a column of troops into the Black Hills in order to establish a fort there, and, although this reason was unacknowledged, to find gold. This was a direct, open, unilateral violation of the treaty of 1868. Sheridan said it had to be done because the Sioux were not living up to their agreements in the treaty. Specifically, he charged that the hostiles were still killing settlers in Nebraska and disrupting the railroads. Although the evidence is fragmentary, it seems clear that Sheridan exaggerated at best, lied at worst. The Indian agents were unanimous in the judgment that the tribes were behaving well, and Sheridan himself had reported officially in 1873 that "The condition of Indian affairs in the Department of Dakota has been remarkably quiet . . ." Bishop William H. Hare protested directly to Grant about the plan to march troops into the Hills; Hare said it would be a "high-handed outrage" and would forever sully the honor of the United States. Democratic newspapers accused Grant of instigating the march as a way of diverting attention from the nation's problems.[4]

Washington ignored the complaints and warnings and went ahead with its plans. As George Hyde wrote, "this proves that very strong influences were back of the project, influences which were willing to risk a Sioux war in carrying out their program. . . . This violation of the treaty was deliberately planned and executed."[5] The proposed expedition received vast publicity—everyone in the West, it seemed, was talking about it. Custer applied for and got command of the entire force; he was immediately besieged with applications from civilian adventurers who wanted to go along.

Fort Abraham Lincoln was base camp for the expedition. There Custer gathered together his column. It was as colorful as its commander. Custer had ten companies of the 7th Cavalry, two infantry companies, a three-inch Rodman gun, and three Gatling guns. His train consisted of one hundred and ten wagons. There were one hundred Indian scouts along, mostly Arikaras (or Rees) and Santee Sioux, and including the Rhee scout Bloody Knife. Two famous white scouts, "Lonesome" Charley Reynolds (so-called "because he preferred to go off and hunt or trap by himself rather than to spend his time in the dreary little frontier towns where cards and whiskey were the sole diversion") and Louis Agard, a guide and interpreter for thirty years in the Sioux country, came along. Captain Luther North and Lieutenant Colonel George "Sandy" Forsyth, both famous Indian fighters, were there, along with Colonel Fred Grant.

Custer hired two miners to accompany the expedition and to look for gold and also brought along a geologist, Newton Winchell, in order to authenticate any gold discoveries. Custer asked Yale University paleontologist O. C. Marsh to make the trip, but Marsh could not go and sent a young osteologist, George Bird Grinnell, instead, thereby starting Grinnell on a career that was of incalculable benefit to every student of Western or Indian history. A stereoscopic photographer joined the party. Finally, to insure publicity, Custer brought along four newspaper reporters. Altogether the column totaled at least one thousand men, with nearly two thousand horses and mules.[6]

On July 2, 1874, the column moved out from Fort Abraham Lincoln to traverse the Plains southward and enter the Black Hills. As usual, the band played "Garry Owen." Custer pushed hard, so hard that the scientists complained that they had no time to make side trips or follow up important discoveries. Custer had written in one of his magazine articles that he was entering "a region of country as yet unseen by human eyes, except those of the Indians." That was typical Custer exaggeration, but it was true that no systematic investigation had ever been made of the country. Winchell and Grinnell found stacks of dinosaur bones and made other fascinating discoveries, but because of the pace Custer maintained they could only barely sample the richness of the region. The troopers were also unhappy; the July sun burned down on the treeless prairie and temperatures consistently rose above one hundred degrees in the shade. Still Custer pushed on; the monotony of the Plains that wearied other men elated him. He had the men up by 3 A.M. and on the march by 4 A.M.; at times they did not make camp until midnight. He often charged ahead on his favorite horse, Dandy, in pursuit of antelope, his hounds bounding along with him. He lied to Libbie about his hunting, telling her that he was obeying her repeated orders to stay within the column at all times.

Returning from his hunting trips, Custer would dash back the length of the column to urge others on, looking magnificent in his buckskin shirt and broad-brimmed hat. He had cut his hair somewhat—it now fell only to the back of his neck, not to his shoulders —and had grown a mustache that covered his mouth and hung down on either side of his chin. His eyes were becoming narrow slits, perhaps as a result of constant squinting into the blazing sun of the Plains. He was trim and fit, as always—no middle-age bulge for the thirty-four-year-old Custer—and even those members of the expedition who disliked Custer marveled at his unbelievable stamina. His enthusiasm for anything new continued, as did his collector's instinct. "I am gradually forming my menagerie," he wrote Libbie at Fort Abraham Lincoln (the phrase indicating that, finally, he was learning to poke a little fun at himself and his unusual habits). He had collected for pets a rattlesnake, two jack rabbits, an eagle, and four owls. His two fine badgers were accidentally smothered. He sent a curlew that he had caught back to Libbie, carried by a courier, with instructions to Libbie to catch grasshoppers for the bird.[7]

Custer had no problem with Indians. Smoke signals surrounded the column, indicating that some of the Sioux in Dakota knew where he was and what he was doing, but there were no attacks. As Sheridan had hoped, the column was too strong for the Indians to risk an assault. Crazy Horse, Sitting Bull, and the hostiles seem to have spent the summer well west of the Black Hills, over toward the Bighorns, and they may not have even been aware of the Custer expedition. Custer's only problems were the heat and dust, which discouraged the men. They relieved the monotony by getting drunk whenever they had a chance. Custer told Libbie that "there has not been a single drunken officer since we left Fort Lincoln," but that was another of his little white lies designed to reassure her. In fact, as one civilian member of the expedition wrote, "the sutler had a wagon with liquor which he sold to the soldiers and everybody who wanted to buy it. Fred Grant . . . was drunk nearly all the time." Indeed, Custer placed Grant under arrest once for drunkenness, an action young Grant greatly resented and which he later reported to his father.[8]

On July 22 Custer, having approached the Hills themselves from the northwest, camped near Inyan Kara, an extinct volcano on the western edge of the mysterious mountains, just inside Wyoming. At this point, his Indian scouts told him to turn back—they insisted that exploration of the Black Hills would be impossible with such a heavy column, and in any event they did not want to invade *Pa Sapa* for fear of Sioux retaliation. When they learned that Custer was going to go ahead anyway, they refused to give him any further information—from that point on, the whites would have to find their own way. Custer argued with them, but to no avail. It seems probable that the Rees and Santees had never been in the Hills anyway, so they could hardly have served as guides. Bloody Knife did remain with Custer, who decided to plunge ahead.

On July 25, 1874, Custer entered the Hills, following a heavily used Indian trail. The trail took him into a valley that moved the aesthetic senses of even the most hardened trooper. Custer named it Floral

Valley, and for once he did not exaggerate. The newspaper reporters were simply dumfounded by the surrounding beauty; so were the others; so are those who go to the Black Hills today. Troopers plucked armfuls of flowers and decorated their horses with garlands.[9] The expedition camped in the valley; within the confines of the campsite alone the expedition's botanist collected fifty-two varieties of wild flowers in bloom. Other flowers had finished blooming, while some were still in bud. Currants, gooseberries, juneberries, huckleberries, strawberries, and raspberries provided sumptuous desserts. The air was clear and cold, clear of flies, gnats, or mosquitoes. Signs of game were plentiful. That night, in this Garden of Eden setting, the band played a concert. A more perfect day could hardly be.[10]

Over the next three weeks Custer explored the Hills, marveling each day at new, breathtaking scenes. He encountered only one small band of Indians, twenty-seven Oglalas from Red Cloud Agency who had come to the Hills for a hunt. A man called Stabber was the chief of the band; his wife was Red Cloud's daughter. Custer tried to bribe them with provisions in order to secure their services as guides, but the Oglalas ran off. Meanwhile, the miners searched for gold, while Custer went exploring and hunting. He climbed the highest point in the Hills (slightly over 7,200 feet, named Harney Peak, in honor of the soldier who had defeated Little Thunder two decades earlier). At the summit, Custer drank a toast to the old Indian fighter. He got lost, killed dozens of deer, and with Bloody Knife's help participated in bringing down a grizzly bear. Although Bloody Knife finished the bear off, Custer posed with his foot on the dead beast. It was the supreme moment of his hunting career. "I have reached the hunter's highest round of fame," he reported proudly to Libbie.[11]

Custer's prowess as a hunter, about which he bragged incessantly, failed to impress George Grinnell, who reported that "Custer did no shooting that was notable. It was observed that, though he enjoyed telling of the remarkable shots that he himself commonly made, he did not seem greatly interested in the shooting done by other people." One day Luther North killed three running deer with three shots. Grinnell took some of the venison over to Custer's tent and reported on the impressive marksmanship. Custer's only response was, "Huh, I found two more horned toads today."

On another occasion, Custer saw some ducks swimming on a pond. Custer got off his horse and announced, "I will knock the heads off a few of them." Captain North also dismounted and sat on the ground beside the general. Custer fired at a bird and missed it; North shot and cut the head off one of the ducks. Custer shot again and missed; North cut the head off another bird. Custer gave North a long, silent look, then shot again. Again he missed; again North cut off a head. Just then an officer came galloping up and complained that Custer's bullets were skipping off the water and singing over the heads of some troopers on the opposite side of the pond. "We had better stop shooting," Custer muttered, and without another word mounted up and rode off.[12]

On July 27 the expedition, then camped in Golden Valley, near present-day Custer, South Dakota, found what it was looking for. The miners reported gold had been discovered on French Creek. Tremendous excitement prevailed. The troopers began to form joint stock companies. Custer wrote that he had before him "40 or 50 small particles of pure gold, in size averaging that of a small pin-head, and most of it obtained today from one panful of earth." After other discoveries were made over the next few days, Custer wrote a preliminary report. So did the newspapermen. Then Custer sent Charley Reynolds on a dangerous ride south to Fort Laramie, Wyoming, in order to telegraph the news to the country. Riding at night, Reynolds made it through the hostile territory to the fort, and by the end of August 1874 the New York *Tribune* and other papers were carrying sensational stories about gold in the Black Hills.[13]

By August 15 Custer had marched out of the Hills and was camping at the foot of Bear Butte, Crazy Horse's birthplace. From that spot he wrote his full report. As Doane Robinson wrote, "It would be difficult to frame language better calculated to inflame the public mind and excite men to enter this country or die in the attempt." Custer said there was gold among the grass roots, gold in paying quantities in every stream. There were other attractions for more permanent settlers. Custer gushed about the Hills: "There are beautiful parks and valleys, through which flow streams of clear, cold water, perfectly free from alkali, while bounding these parks, or valleys, is invariably found unlimited supplies of timber, much of it being capable of being made into good lumber. In no portion of the United States, not excepting the famous bluegrass region of Kentucky, have I ever seen grazing superior to that found growing wild in this hitherto unknown region.† I know of no portion of our country where nature has done so much to prepare homes for husbandmen and left so little for the latter to do as here. The open and timber spaces

† It must have been a rainy summer for the late July grass to have been as luxuriant as Custer said it was. Ordinarily the Hills' grass turns brown in midsummer.

are so divided that a partly prepared farm of almost any dimensions can be found here. . . . Cattle could winter in these valleys without other food or shelter than that to be obtained from running at large."[14]

Custer marched east from Bear Butte, pushing the men hard. After the weeks in the Hills, the Plains seemed even hotter, dustier, and more monotonous than ever. Some Indians tried to burn the prairie grass in order to immobilize Custer, but he managed to find a little grass each night for a campsite. Indian signs were all around. One night, in front of Custer's tent, Luther North remarked that they were lucky the Indians seemed to have cleared out of the way, as there were evidently a great many of them. Custer snorted, then commented, "I could whip all the Indians in the northwest with the Seventh Cavalry."[15]

The expedition arrived at Fort Abraham Lincoln on August 30. The column marched in as it had gone out, with the band playing "Garry Owen." It had covered 1,205 miles in sixty days; as Max Gerber notes, "a truly remarkable achievement from a physical standpoint alone." Custer's preliminary report had already created a sensation; half of Bismarck was planning to go to the Black Hills by the time Custer returned, while the other half was figuring out how to make a fortune by selling wagons, food, and mining equipment to those who planned to take their chances with the Sioux. Yankton, South Dakota, and Sioux City, Iowa, were already advertising that they were the ideal jumping-off place for the new Eldorado.[16] Custer's full report added to the excitement, and all over the country jobless men began the trek toward the Black Hills.

There was one major embarrassment—the treaty of 1868. Friends of the Indians (joined by Fred Grant, still smarting from being placed under arrest by Custer) charged that Custer had exaggerated and insisted that there was no gold in paying quantities in the Hills. The United States Government made pro-forma warnings, telling prospective prospectors that the Black Hills belonged to the Sioux and that no white man could enter. The Army along the Missouri made a half-hearted effort to keep the miners out. Given the condition of the economy, however, nothing was going to stop the gold rush—not the country's honor, nor the pledged word of the government, nor any sense of Sioux rights. The Hills had too much to offer to allow them to remain in the hands of the savages.

Custer provided the classic rationale—the Indians were not using the Hills, so they should give them up to whites who would. "It is a mistaken idea that the Indian occupies any portion of the Black

Hills," he wrote in a message of September 8, 1874, to the War Department (and gave to the newspapers, which gleefully reprinted it). "They neither occupy nor make use of the Black Hills, nor are they willing that others should. . . . If the Black Hills were thrown open to settlement, as they ought to be, or if simply occupied by the military, as they must be at an early date . . . a barrier would be imposed between the hostile camps and the agencies, and the well-disposed Indians of the latter would be separated from the evil influences and war-like tendencies of the hostiles." In other words, it was, as Custer saw it, in the best interests of the Sioux to give up the Black Hills.[17] The Grant Administration could not have agreed more, and it immediately began hatching plots to find a way to relieve the Sioux of their legal title to the Hills.

While on the march back to Fort Abraham Lincoln, Custer had written Libbie to report that, "The Indians have a new name for me, but I will not commit it to paper." The name was "thief," and the route Custer followed the Indians named "The Thieves' Road."[18]

The absence of Sioux opposition to Custer's penetration of the Black Hills is something of a puzzle. In both 1872 and 1873 Sitting Bull, Crazy Horse, and the other leaders had gathered together an impressive force to block the path of the surveyors along the Yellowstone, but in 1874 there was no concerted Indian opposition to Custer's foray. Perhaps the explanation is simple: in 1873 Custer went much farther west than he did in 1874, right into hostile territory on the Yellowstone, and the hostiles did resist. But the wild Sioux hardly used the Black Hills any longer—they lived to the west, along the Powder and Bighorn rivers—and as the presence of Stabber indicated, the Hills were used primarily by the agency Indians. Whatever the reason, Sitting Bull stayed to the north and west of the Hills, and so did Crazy Horse, while Custer stole *Pa Sapa*.

Perhaps, too, Crazy Horse simply did not feel like fighting, for he had suffered another grievous blow. Early that summer he had led a raid to the west against the Crows. When he left, his people were camped near the Little Bighorn River, but when he returned the village had moved. Sticks laid on the ground pointed the way toward the Tongue River and within a couple of days the war party saw smoke rising from the campfires. As Crazy Horse entered the village, Worm grabbed his arm and pulled him away from Black Shawl's tipi. Sadly, Worm informed his son that They-Are-Afraid-of-Her had caught cholera and died.

Frank Grouard was living with Crazy Horse at this time, and he later said that Crazy Horse's grief was pathetic. Late that night, Crazy Horse managed to ask where his daughter's scaffold was located; Worm warned him that it was seventy miles away, deep in Crow country. He urged his son not to go, but Crazy Horse was determined to visit the scaffold of his beloved daughter. Crazy Horse asked Grouard to accompany him. It took them two days to make the journey. When they found the scaffold, Crazy Horse climbed up and lay down beside They-Are-Afraid-of-Her's little body, wrapped tightly in a buffalo robe. Grouard said he stayed there for three days and nights, mourning.[19]

Hump, Little Hawk, Black Buffalo Woman, and now They-Are-Afraid-of-Her—the effect of this succession of tragedies on Crazy Horse seems to have been to intensify his basic personality traits, rather than change them. He became even quieter, evidently almost refusing to speak in public. Certainly he made no attempts to rouse the people with harangues, as Sitting Bull did; instead, when it was necessary, Crazy Horse made plans quietly with his leading warriors. The testimony from his contemporaries is unanimous—he made no attempt to seize power, nor did he seek power in any way. He asked only to be left alone and to be allowed to fight for the people. He became more reckless than ever in combat, so much so that his friends feared he was deliberately seeking death. In battle he jumped off his pony whenever he fired, in order to steady his aim. He took more chances, it was said, than the young and foolish Little Hawk had. But still he was never wounded, as had been promised in his vision. The enemies who knew him best, the Crows, were more afraid of him than ever; one Crow reported that it was well known among them that Crazy Horse had a medicine gun that hit whatever it looked at and that he himself was bulletproof.[20]

Over the next year and a half, until the winter of 1875–76, Crazy Horse often went out from the village alone, disappearing for weeks at a time. No one knew where he went or what he did, but over that time period dozens of white miners who had invaded the Black Hills were found killed, an arrow stuck in the ground beside their bodies, their scalps intact.

The winter of 1874–75 was long and cold on the Plains, with immense snowdrifts and temperatures sometimes below −45 degrees. The Custers, at Fort Abraham Lincoln, with a fireplace in every room and a cavalry private whose sole job was to keep the fires going, had a gay time. Libbie has described it all in "Boots and Saddles," or, My Life in Dakota with General Custer, a classic of western literature. She loved being the Queen Bee at the fort, entertaining, gossiping, riding on sunny days. Custer's niece, Maria Reed, was there—primarily to meet eligible Army officers. They played charades and held amateur theatricals. Custer wrote and wrote and had the intense satisfaction of getting his name on the jacket of a book—*Galaxy* brought out his series of articles on the 1867–68 campaign in book form under the title *My Life on the Plains.* It was a popular success. Encouraged, Custer worked some more on his Civil War memoirs, wrote articles on fighting against the Sioux on the Yellowstone, and generally established himself as something of a literary lion.

He was a complicated man, George Armstrong Custer, as unsure of himself in the study as he was confident on the battlefield. When he wrote, he made Libbie sit across the table from him. He would read aloud to her as he put words down on paper. Overhead he had hung portraits of his two favorite generals, McClellan—and Custer. Antelope heads and horns, guns, stuffed animals (he did his own taxidermy), the head of the grizzly he had helped bag in the Black Hills, and other trophies surrounded him. Everything, in short, reminded him of his accomplishments, but still he could not rest easy. Amazingly, at thirty-five years of age, a veteran soldier, he decided he needed to learn something about the military art, and he began reading Sir William F. P. Napier's six-volume study of Wellington's campaign in Portugal and Spain, *History of the War in the Peninsula.* He found the subject so difficult he had to read the paragraphs over three or four times; if Libbie interrupted him, he had to begin again at the top of the page.[21]

One can fairly assume that Custer found the reading boring. That is hardly surprising—many readers would find such a mass of detailed material boring. The wonder is that Custer kept at it. His persistence provides a fitting symbol for one of the marked contrasts between Custer and Crazy Horse and, beyond them as individuals, for one of the contrasts between their societies. Custer was always trying to improve himself, as were many members of his society, where the traditions of "self-help" and "self-improvement" flourished. So strong were the traditions that even Custer was affected by them, at a time when he was one of the most famous men in the country. That need to improve himself, to do better, to *be* better, permeated Custer's whole life. It is one of the connecting links between the unruly boy, the West Point cadet, the Civil War general, and the world-renowned Indian fighter, just as it was one of the connecting links between Custer and the American tradition.

Crazy Horse felt no such need. It never occurred to him that he needed to, or could, improve himself. Had anyone suggested it to him, he would not have understood. Crazy Horse did not want to be better than he was. He just wanted to *be*.

CHAPTER TWENTY

Politics: Red and White

"If I were an Indian, I would greatly prefer to cast my lot among those of my people who adhered to the free open plains rather than submit to the confined limits of a reservation."

George Armstrong Custer

In 1875 the United States Government began to put pressure on the Sioux to sell the Black Hills. This action caused a political split among the Sioux, who in any event had never been able to present a solid front to the whites. Three major factions among the Sioux emerged over the question of selling *Pa Sapa*. These factions cut across all other divisions; the hostile Brulés, Oglalas, Hunkpapas, Sans Arcs, and other subtribes were divided against themselves, as were the agency Indians. The largest faction consisted primarily of agency Indians who believed that the Hills were lost anyway and that the Sioux ought to get the best price they could for them. Red Cloud and Spotted Tail, by far the most important men among the Sioux, were the leaders of the faction that was willing to sell for a decent price, and they represented a majority of all the Sioux at the agencies. White Swan and Charger told Doane Robinson in 1892, "The Indians at all of the agencies counciled on the matter and we believed that the government would pay us a good big price for the Hills, so we waited."[1]

As the remark indicates, the agency Sioux were beginning to learn how to live in a white man's world. The whites were not going to get *Pa Sapa* for a few beads and a little whiskey, as they had the Holy Road. These agency Indians hardly went hunting anymore—the buffalo had disappeared from the Dakotas and only on the Powder and Yellowstone rivers in Wyoming and Montana were there sufficient buffalo to support a hunting existence. Red Cloud's and Spotted Tail's people lived on the government dole. When they came into the agencies, they gave up their chief asset—their fighting strength—and they had nothing left to surrender in return for the white man's goods. Nothing, that is, except the Hills, which the whites obviously wanted badly and which, Red Cloud and Spotted Tail reasoned, the Sioux could not hold onto anyway.

Not all of the agency Indians agreed. A second faction among the Sioux, led by Young Man Afraid, had abandoned the warpath in order to protect their helpless ones and to save the Sioux nation from total destruction. Young Man Afraid had followed his father to Red Cloud Agency, where he used his impressive skills to work for some kind of accommodation with the whites that would allow the Sioux to live—to live in peace and to live as far as possible in the old ways. In Young Man Afraid's view, selling *Pa Sapa* would be a disaster for the Sioux way of life. Unwilling to fight the whites any longer, he was equally unwilling to sell the Hills.

The third faction, led by Crazy Horse and Sitting Bull, was also unwilling to sell the Hills, but unlike Young Man Afraid, it was determined to fight to keep them. An overwhelming majority of hostiles shared this view, although there were some Sioux on the Powder River who agreed with Red Cloud. Many of the younger warriors in the agencies, however, lent their support to Crazy Horse. These hot-blooded young men scarcely knew there was a political issue involved—they merely wanted a chance to win some honors for themselves. Living on the agencies was dull. The agents would not let the young men go out on war parties against the Crows and there was precious little hunting left in their areas. They were spoiling for a fight, and in the end they provided Crazy Horse with much of his fighting strength. There was a constant flow of Indians between the agencies in Nebraska and South Dakota and the hostile country in Wyoming and Montana, a flow that was highly beneficial to the hostiles, for the agency Indians lived in close contact with the whites and therefore had numerous opportunities to pick up firearms which they could sell to the hostiles. Consequently, the hostiles were better armed than ever before, with possibly as many as one out of four warriors possessing a gun of some type.

Crazy Horse needed the agency warriors for more than just their guns, however; he needed their numerical strength too, because the hostile camps were constantly dwindling. When Red Cloud went onto the agency after the treaty of 1868, he took about five thousand Oglalas with him. By 1874 almost that many more had joined him at his agency on the White River.[2] They were mainly families who found the living too hard or too dangerous in the hostile territory. The whites were always tempting them to come in, as were the agency Indians. Visitors from the agencies would sit around the campfires on the Powder River and tell wonderful stories about life on the agencies. Every five days the Indians came to the agency from their scattered camps, the visitors said, and then the whites would turn the cattle loose. The warriors chased the cattle and killed them like buffalo, the women following with their big knives to butcher the cattle. Then there was feasting. You too can enjoy this good life, the visitors said, and then come out here in the summer for a real buffalo hunt and a little raiding against the Crows. No more hard winters . . . the temptation was difficult to resist.[3] In the winter of 1868–69 there had been fifteen thousand Oglalas living on the Powder River; by the winter of 1874–75 there were only about three thousand left, the others having moved to the reservation.[4] Even Touch-the-Clouds, the leading Miniconjou warrior, had moved down to Red Cloud Agency to try out agency living.[5]

Touch-the-Clouds didn't stay long. Pretending that cattle were buffalo made a mockery of Sioux life, and, besides, the agency Indians were not living fat, no matter what they told the hostiles. The truth was that the agents were corrupt. They accepted diseased cattle, rotten flour, wormy corn, and so on from the white contractors, then took kickbacks when the United States Government paid the bill. There was nothing for the Indians to do at the agencies; the people were undernourished at best, starving at worst. Red Cloud and Spotted Tail argued incessantly with their agents, demanding more and better food, to no avail. Both sides were trying to cheat. The government wanted to make a census, for example, but Red Cloud forbade it. The agents were certain that the Sioux exaggerated their numbers in order to get more rations on issue day, and Red Cloud indeed thought he had fooled the whites. Red Cloud insisted that he had at least six thousand Indians with him, a figure his agent said was much too high. Finally, in 1875, using military force, the whites made a careful census—and it turned out there were 9,339 Sioux at Red Cloud Agency, plus 1,202 Cheyennes and 1,092 Arapahoes.[6] Such foolish bickering, in addition to the conditions on the agencies, soon led Touch-the-Clouds to flee. He moved back to the Powder River country and rejoined the hostiles, camping for a while with Crazy Horse.

Crazy Horse was now the leader of his own band. Whites had started to call him a "chief," but that was not an exact description. He certainly was not a chief in the sense that Bull Bear, Old Smoke, or Old Man Afraid had been, nor was his band a hereditary one. Rather, it was composed of families that shared his sentiments, mostly Oglalas but with other Sioux bands represented. They lived with Crazy Horse because they respected him and wished to follow his leadership. It was a purely voluntary association, as Crazy Horse did nothing to encourage them to follow in his tracks. Nevertheless, by the summer of 1875 the "Crazy Horse people," as they were now called, numbered about one hundred lodges, with between two hundred and three hundred warriors.[7]

The Crazy Horse people, like all the hostiles, embraced an idea. Their loyalty was not to family or band or tribe, but to freedom. Nothing demonstrated this mood better than the association between Crazy Horse and Black Twin, No Water's brother. After the troubles over Black Buffalo Woman, No Water had joined the agency Indians. Black Twin stayed out and became a leading hostile and a close friend of Crazy Horse. They did not allow a blood feud to develop; instead, they worked together for a common good.

In the summer of 1875 the whites invited Red Cloud and Spotted Tail to come once more to Washington for a summit conference with the Great White Father. Red Cloud was anxious to go—he enjoyed such trips and all the attention he received in Washington in 1870—but he was an adept politician who knew that nothing he agreed to would be valid without the consent of the hostiles. So he asked to have Black Twin and Crazy Horse brought along to represent the wild Sioux of the north. Red Cloud wanted these two irreconcilables involved, and he perhaps wanted them to see the power of the whites, as he and Spotted Tail had seen it five years before, so that the hostiles would realize what they were up against. Red Cloud's request to have Black Twin and Crazy Horse brought along also indicates that he regarded them as the most important hostiles, although it is also possible that he realized there was no chance of getting Sitting Bull anywhere near a white man under peaceful conditions. In any event, Red Cloud had misjudged Black Twin and Crazy Horse; they indignantly refused to come to the agency, much less go to Washington. Red Cloud also asked Young Man Afraid to go along, to represent the more militant agency Indians, but he too refused.[8]

The trip to Washington was a fiasco. Red Cloud and Spotted Tail thought they were going to the summit in order to lay before the President their complaints about the dishonest agents, but to their shock the only thing the government wanted to discuss was selling the Black Hills. The Sioux leaders said they had no authority to consider such a proposition and must return home to discuss it with their people.[9]

When the Indian delegation got back to the Plains, Spotted Tail insisted on visiting the Black Hills along with his agent, so that he could make a judgment for himself as to the full value of the Hills. He wanted to see the miners and see how much gold they were getting. The agent himself was anxious for the Sioux to get the best possible price, as that would give him more goods and money to distribute, and thus fatten his profits. Together, after the inspection, Spotted Tail and his agent decided that the Hills were worth $7,000,-000 cash, plus rations and goods for the Sioux for seven full generations.[10]

In September 1875 the whites sent a commission from Washington to Red Cloud Agency to discuss the sale. At all the agencies, and even among the hostiles, there were spirited arguments about what to do. The older Indians wanted peace and security and were willing to give up *Pa Sapa* to get it, but they disagreed among themselves over the price to demand. The younger agency men still would not hear of the sale at all, nor would the hostiles. It was a quarrel that involved every Sioux from the Missouri to the Yellowstone to the White to the Powder.

The council was held about eight miles east of Red Cloud Agency —Red Cloud and Spotted Tail were jealous of each other and engaged in a struggle for leadership, so neither would go to the other's agency. The Brulés, Oglalas, Miniconjous, Hunkpapas, Blackfeet, Two Kettles, Sans Arcs, Yanktons, Santees, northern Cheyennes and Arapahoes were all represented, but not the Crazy Horse people. The agent had sent Young Man Afraid up to Crazy Horse's country to ask him to participate. Young Man Afraid found nearly two thousand lodges in the Powder River country—it was the tag end of summer and there were many agency Indians still there—but no agreement about what to do. Game was scarce, even on the Powder River, and the whites promised a great feast; the temptation to come fill their bellies was alluring. Many hostiles went, but Crazy Horse and Black Twin held back. They said they might come in after a while, which Young Man Afraid knew meant never. Sitting Bull told Young Man Afraid that so long as there was any game left, he would never come in.[11]

Crazy Horse was not a man to hold a grudge, as his close association with Black Twin showed, nor did he allow politics to stand in the way of friendship. Young Man Afraid urged him to come to the council, citing all the reasons why Crazy Horse should be present to represent the hostiles, but Crazy Horse was unmoved. He did not approve of what Young Man Afraid was doing (Young Man Afraid had recently become the head of the Indian police at Red Cloud

Agency) and insisted that any contact with whites spelled disaster for the Sioux. But they parted in friendship, with the crossed handshake of respect. Each man would follow his own trail, respecting the right of the other to do as he saw fit.[12]

The commissioners wanted as many Sioux at the council as possible because of a "three-fourths clause" in the treaty of 1868—no revision could be made in the treaty without the consent of three fourths of all adult Sioux males—but they got more than they bargained for. Perhaps as many as fifteen thousand Indians showed up, mainly Sioux, coming from the Missouri, the Yellowstone, the Powder, and the agencies. They argued constantly among themselves, especially after the commissioners informed them that the government wanted to buy not only the Black Hills, but the unceded Indian territory in Montana and Wyoming as well—the Powder River country. Hardly a single Indian, and none of the leaders, was willing to discuss selling their only remaining hunting grounds, but the request indicated to the more discerning Indians the true implication of white policy. Young Man Afraid and others argued that selling the Hills would not satisfy the whites; nothing short of penning up the Sioux on a narrow reservation, without hunting rights anywhere, would satisfy them. Better to draw a line right here and hold on to the Hills. But Red Cloud and Spotted Tail wanted peace at any price and security for their people—they had seen other tribes, such as the Mandans and Pawnees, refuse to accommodate themselves to the whites and now there were scarcely any Mandans or Pawnees left. They wanted to make the best deal they could in a difficult situation.

A climax of sorts came on September 23, 1875. The commissioners set up their tent fly and sat down under it, their interpreters beside them and 120 cavalrymen, plus Indian soldiers, behind them. Thousands of Indians were riding, walking, or sitting on the nearby hills. At noon a great cloud of dust suddenly billowed up from behind the hills, and a force of two hundred warriors rode into the council area, all mounted on splendid ponies, each man wearing his bonnet and carrying his weapons. "They swept down toward the commission's tent in a column," George Hyde writes, "then whipped their ponies into a run and began circling madly around the seated white men in a whirl of dust, whooping and firing their rifles. Presently they drew off and formed a line facing the commission; then their chief dismounted, walked forward, and sat down facing the white men. A signal was given, and another band of warriors emerged from the hills and repeated the performance of the first band. Band by band the Sioux rode proudly out of the hills, until at length seven thousand warriors were drawn up in a great circle surrounding the commission and its little guard of cavalry and Indian soldiers."[13] There was a great deal of shouting, young warriors shaking their fists or weapons at the whites.

Red Cloud was just getting ready to speak when the thousands of warriors began to seethe with sudden excitement. An opening was made in the circle of warriors and through it shot Little Big Man, a belligerent warrior from Crazy Horse's camp. Whether he was acting on instructions from Crazy Horse or on his own is unknown, but he was an impressive sight. He was riding bareback on a magnificent horse, with a lariat tied to the lower jaw in place of a bridle. Little Big Man was naked, save for a breechcloth and an eagle-feather war bonnet, the long tail sailing out behind him in the wind. He had a Winchester in one hand, a fistful of cartridges in the other. Riding into the open space between the seated chiefs and the commissioners, Little Big Man announced with a roar that he had come to kill the white men who were stealing Indian lands.

Before Little Big Man could do any more than make his threat, Young Man Afraid with a few Indian police rode forward and quickly disarmed him. But the warriors had been roused to a fury by his performance. They began circling the commission and the 120 soldiers, bumping their ponies into the cavalry horses in the hope of starting a fight. They shouted the call for a charge, "Ho-ka hey!" and made little dashes back and forth with their ponies to give them a second wind before the fight started. It was a critical moment, to say the least; Louis Richards, the half-breed interpreter, who knew what the Indians were yelling, was plainly scared. "It looks like hell will break out here in a few minutes," he told the commissioners under the tent fly. "The Indians are all mad, and when they start shooting we'll be the first to catch it."[14] Spotted Tail hurried to the commissioners and urged them to get out of there while they still could.

Just then Young Man Afraid rode into the center of the mass of enraged warriors. The Indians respected him as a great warrior, son of a prominent chief, and a leader of the opposition to selling the Hills. Even though he was a law-and-order Indian now, and a policeman to boot, the hostiles would listen to whatever he had to say. Young Man Afraid knew that if the warriors slaughtered the commissioners and the cavalry, white retribution would be terrible to behold. He ordered the warriors to go home and cool off. After some more milling, arguing, and shoving, they obeyed. The crisis was past.[15]

The question of the Black Hills remained. Following the incident most of the hostiles rode north, thereby ending whatever slim chance the commission had of obtaining the consent of three fourths of the Sioux to the sale of the Hills. But the commissioners could not simply give up—the whites had to have some kind of legal justification for doing what they were going to do anyway. So the commission consulted with the friendly chiefs who were left, principally Red Cloud and Spotted Tail.

The talks took place on September 27, 28, and 29, 1875. The chiefs were becoming skillful politicians. Spotted Tail announced that "as long as we live on this earth we will expect pay. We want to leave the amount with the President at interest forever. I want to live on the interest of my money. The amount must be so large that the interest will support us." Spotted Tail had been among white men long enough by now to know what was what.

So had Red Cloud. He said, "For seven generations to come I want the Great Father to give us Texan steers for our meat. I want the government to issue for me hereafter flour and coffee, and sugar and tea and bacon, the very best kind, and cracked corn and beans and rice and dried apples and saleratus [baking soda] and tobacco, and soap and salt and pepper for the old people. I want a wagon, a light wagon, and a span of horses and six yoke of working cattle for my people. I want a sow and a boar, and a cow and a bull, and a sheep and a ram, and a hen and a cock for each family. I am an Indian, but you try to make a white man out of me. I want some white men's houses at this agency to be built for the Indians.* . . . Maybe you white people think I ask too much from the government, but I think those Hills extend clear to the sky, maybe they go above the sky, and that is the reason I ask for so much. I think the Black Hills are worth more than all the wild beasts and all the tame beasts in the possession of the white people. I know it well, and you can see it plain enough, that God Almighty [Red Cloud had converted to Catholicism] placed those Hills here for my wealth, but now you want to take them from me and make me poor, so I ask so much that I won't be poor."[16]

The other chiefs agreed. Old Spotted Bear said, "Our Great Father has a big safe and so have we. This Hill is our safe. We want $7,000,-

---

* This was done the following year, but the squaws couldn't figure out how to keep a house clean. Brooms, dust rags, and stoves were a mystery to them. They had always cooked over open fires. In a tipi, when dirt accumulated, they just moved the tipi to clean ground and thus in half an hour finished their house cleaning. They could not clean a log house that way, so they moved out, living in the tipis and retaining the log houses to show off to their friends.

ooo for the Black Hills." Somehow the translator turned the sum into $70,000,000, which astonished the commissioners, but it hardly mattered, for, as Billy Garnett said, the Indians "did not know a million from the number of stars in the sky."[17] The whites protested that the Sioux were asking for the impossible, and bickering continued. Finally Spotted Tail, sensibly, asked the whites to state in writing exactly what they were willing to pay for the Hills. The whites responded with an offer of $400,000 annually for mineral rights to the Hills or $6,000,000 for outright purchase but with no annuities or other obligations included. The commissioners also offered $50,000 for purchase of the Powder River country.[18]

The Indians would not accept, wisely enough, as $6,000,000 was far too low a price considering the value of the Hills,† and the commission concluded that "the Indians place upon the Hills a value far beyond any sum that could possibly be considered by the government," so the council broke up with nothing accomplished. The Army then withdrew its nominal opposition to miners going into the Hills, and whites began to fill *Pa Sapa*. By March 1, 1876, there were fully eleven thousand whites in the town of Custer alone, more than fifteen thousand in the Black Hills altogether. In just a year, in short, there were more whites in *Pa Sapa* than there were Oglalas on the Sioux agencies, and thousands more were headed toward the gold diggings.[19]

The United States Government was embarrassed, not at the way its citizens were violating the treaty but by its failure to obtain some legal excuse to take the Hills. It seemed to have little sense of the nation's honor and little morality of its own. On November 3, 1875, President Grant held a high-level Cabinet meeting, with General Sheridan in attendance. It was decided that the hostiles were the ones standing in the way of a Black Hills take-over, so the solution was to drive the hostiles out of the unceded Indian territory in Wyoming and Montana and force them onto the reservations. On December 6 Grant ordered all Indians in the unceded country to move onto the agencies by January 31, 1876. Otherwise, they would be certified as hostile and the Army would come after them. The unceded country would become a free-fire zone. It was a declaration of war, although it should be added that neither Grant nor his advisers thought that the hostiles would put up a fight; in their view,

† Homestake Mining Company, which eventually got a virtual monopoly on the gold fields of the Black Hills, has taken approximately $1.5 *billion* worth of gold out of the Hills. In 1974 alone it extracted $40 million worth of gold. It is the largest operating gold mine in the Western Hemisphere.

the Army would have an easy time of bullying Crazy Horse, Sitting Bull, and the others onto a reservation.[20]

After making the decision to declare war (according to George Manypenny, a former commissioner of Indian affairs) the government then began to look for a *casus belli*. It found its excuse in a report made by Indian Inspector E. C. Watkins, dated November 9, 1875. Watkins accused the wild Sioux of raiding the Crows in Montana! Although such raids had been going on since time out of mind, the government announced with a straight face that it was reluctantly making war on the wild Sioux in order to protect the Crows.[21]

There are two sides to the story, and Robert Utley puts the best possible face on the government's side: "The breakdown of negotiations for the Black Hills capped seven years of mounting frustration with the Sioux hunting bands. They raided all around the periphery of the unceded territory. They terrorized friendly tribes. They contested the advance of the Northern Pacific Railroad. They disrupted the management of the reservation Indians while obtaining recruits, supplies, and munitions at the agencies for these hostile activities. And now they interfered with the sale of the Black Hills. The right to roam outside the boundaries of the Great Sioux Reservation—in the unceded territory—made all this possible." They had to be brought to terms.[22]

The order addressed to the Powder River Indians arrived at Red Cloud Agency just before Christmas. Acting with a heavy heart, the agents—who knew what would happen—sent out runners to tell the hostiles to come in to the agencies before January 31 or face the consequences. "The officials at the Indian Office in Washington must have known that the wild Sioux would take no action on this strange order in time to meet the deadline," George Hyde wrote. "The military officers certainly knew it; and before there had been time to receive any reply from the Indian camps, Major General George Crook went to Fort Fetterman on the North Platte, west of Fort Laramie, and began the work of organizing a column to go and drive the Sioux out of their winter camps on the Powder River."[23] The government was going to make war on the northern Sioux because their relatives at the agencies would not sell the Black Hills to the United States.

The runners found Sitting Bull camped at the mouth of the Powder River. He sent back a friendly message—he couldn't come in just now, but he would consider the order and might come in later on, perhaps next summer, maybe later. The evidence demonstrates that he was just being polite—in fact, he regarded the order as a good joke. So did Crazy Horse and Black Twin. The runner found them camped at the foot of Bear Butte near the Black Hills, less than one hundred miles north of Red Cloud Agency. Crazy Horse let Black Twin do the talking. It was too far, Black Twin said, and besides the village couldn't move in the deep snow and cold. Then, to give the lie to this excuse, Crazy Horse and Black Twin moved in a northerly direction, going almost twice as far as the distance to Red Cloud Agency, and joined forces with Sitting Bull. The Army would have to whip them before they became tame Indians.[24]

January 31, 1876, came and went without a response from the north. On February 1, therefore, Secretary of the Interior Zachariah Chandler, Custer's old friend, notified Secretary of War William Belknap that "Said Indians are hereby turned over to the War Department for such action on the part of the Army as you may deem proper under the circumstances," and, as noted, the Army on the frontier promptly began preparations for a winter campaign.[25]

While the Army of the frontier prepared to march against its enemy, Lieutenant Colonel George Armstrong Custer of the 7th Cavalry was up to his neck in politics in New York and Washington, and thereby hangs a tale.

It began back in the summer of 1875, which Custer had spent quietly at Fort Abraham Lincoln. The Northern Pacific surveyors stayed home during that summer of economic depression, and Sheridan would not allow the 7th Cavalry to interfere with the flow of miners into the Black Hills, so the regiment had nothing to do. Stuck at the garrison, the troopers began to complain, most of all about the high prices charged them by the post trader. The men claimed they could get the same goods for half the price in Bismarck, but Army regulations forbade such purchases; the troopers had to buy from the post trader. Custer knew the complaints were valid because the regulations and prices applied to him as well. It would not be easy to do anything about the situation, however, because behind this swindling of the troopers stood the Secretary of War. It really was a shocking business. The Secretary was solely responsible for the appointment of the post trader, and he sold the appointments for an annual kickback, which forced the traders to jack up their prices. Nor were the traders averse to getting a little extra profit for themselves out of the monopoly. Thus did the government in Washington support a scheme of petty graft at the expense of the troopers who were risking their lives on the frontier.[26]

The Secretary of War was William W. Belknap, a former Civil War general and hack politician with expensive tastes. President Grant continued to trust Belknap for reasons never discovered, but which may have been connected with Belknap's shrewdness in bringing the President's brother Orvil in on the post-trader deals. Orvil Grant was involved in the sale of some traderships at the Missouri River forts and would have had to be included in any exposé. The swindling was common knowledge in the West, but it would have all been hearsay in a court of law. Custer could not prove anything, was not the kind of officer to challenge the Secretary of War directly, and had nothing to gain from taking on the President himself. Custer's stature in the President's eyes was already way down because of the things young Fred Grant had told his father about him, mostly items Fred had made up after Custer had embarrassed him by placing him under arrest for drunkenness.

Evidently, at some time during the summer of 1875, despite the obstacles, Custer decided to do something about the post-trader scandal when and if he could. It should not be thought that he had suddenly taken on a new role, either as champion of the poor or the friend of the enlisted man, for his own fortunes were very much involved in the whole matter. He had no savings, and he and Libbie had to watch every penny. They spent the late fall and winter of 1875–76 in New York, on leave. There they took the horsecars to receptions and dinners, rather than cabs. Custer had only one civilian suit and could afford no more. For entertainment, they went on forty different nights to see their friend Lawrence Barrett in *Julius Caesar*; not that they liked Barrett or the play all that much, but they got in free. They stayed in a boarding house to save money; Libbie told Tom Custer that "We live cheaper than at Fort Lincoln."

When the Custers were preparing to return to Fort Lincoln, Libbie astonished her friends when they asked her why she was leaving so soon and she replied, matter of factly, that they had used up all the money they had saved for the leave of absence.[27] In short, Custer felt the pinch of the traders' inflated prices as much as his men did. He had investigated and discovered that the trader at Fort Abraham Lincoln made a profit of $15,000 per year, of which he kept only $2,000. Custer began calling the traders a bunch of crooks, adding that Secretary Belknap was the chief of the thieves.[28]

In the late summer of 1875 Secretary Belknap had come on an official visit to the fort. The day before his arrival the post trader sent Custer a basket of wine for the distinguished visitor. Custer sent it back, stiffly informing the trader that he himself did not drink and that he did not propose to entertain the Secretary. When Belknap entered the fort, Custer had the appropriate salute fired, but though commanding officer of the post he refused to meet the Secretary at the entrance to the reservation, as was customary. Instead, Custer remained in his office and let Belknap come to him. When the official business was finished, Custer abruptly left Belknap and went to his house, leaving the Secretary to his own devices.[29]

Following this incident, which became a juicy item of gossip at every frontier post, the Custers made their trip to New York. There Custer once again fell in with his old Democratic party friends. These gentlemen were greatly excited by the stories Custer had to tell about Belknap, Orvil Grant, and the traders. It was a presidential election year and the more scandals the Democrats could pin on Grant, the better. This scandal promised to be a hot one, especially with the dashing Custer as the chief witness. On February 10, 1876, James Gordon Bennett, a good friend of Custer's and publisher of the anti-Administration New York *Herald,* demanded a full investigation into suspected corruption in the War Department. Bennett followed it up with a flat declaration that Belknap was selling traderships and that Orvil Grant was implicated. Bennett suggested that Grant ask his brother how much money he, Orvil, had "made in the Sioux country starving the squaws and children."[30]

From this point on, the available information on what happened is sketchy at best. We know what Custer and his Democratic friends did in public, but there is no record of their private discussions. If the unfolding events were part of a conspiracy, it was well hidden and remains obscure. In one way, all the frustrations the historian experiences in trying to get accurate information about what Crazy Horse did, said, or thought pale beside the frustrations of trying to figure out what happened with Custer and the Democrats in 1876. Among the Americans, political plots and schemes were hatched in the dark, and skillful men did their best to keep knowledge of their activities hidden from the public—and from future historians. Even more than when dealing with the Indians, the historian is reduced to speculation in dealing with white politics.

The first question is, did Custer inspire the original Bennett call for an investigation in 1876? The scandal was in the air, was well known in the West, other Army officers were talking about it. But Custer was the one doing the talking in New York, he was close to Bennett, and he did agree privately with Bennett to give the *Herald* his exclusive account of the upcoming Sioux campaign, which Custer expected to command.[31] A further bit of evidence came on March 31, 1876, when the *Herald* published an article entitled "Belknap's

Anaconda," accusing the former Secretary of War of outright corruption and providing details. It was widely assumed that Custer was the author, an assumption reinforced by the later testimony of the post trader, who said he cashed a check from Bennett to Custer shortly thereafter. Custer claimed the check was for another matter altogether, but it looked suspicious.[32] There was other evidence that the *Herald* was getting information obtainable only from someone who knew Fort Abraham Lincoln intimately.[33]

If Custer was responsible for the campaign against Belknap, and beyond Belknap against Grant himself, the next question is why he did so. It is difficult to believe that he would have taken on the Grant Administration simply to save himself a few dollars, and again, it strains the imagination to suppose that he would embark on something this big in order to protect his enlisted men. Perhaps he had the honor of the Army in mind; when asked what effect the alleged corruption had on the Army, Custer said, "I think it one of the highest commendations that could be bestowed on the Service, that it has not been completely demoralized by the unworthiness at the head."[34] These were probably all factors in Custer's decision to act (if he indeed had acted), but perhaps there was something more. Perhaps Bennett and his friends hinted that Custer could earn a reward beyond the satisfaction of exposing the crooks.

Bennett was after big game. He wanted Grant humbled and a Democrat elected to replace him. Custer was a tool Bennett used to get the job done. The question is, how important a tool? The Democrats were in a strong position, for they had taken control of Congress in the elections of 1874, economic conditions were worse than ever as the economic depression ground on, and the public was becoming ashamed of the Grant Administration (there were other scandals the Democrats were exposing). Bennett's problem was that the front-running candidate for the Democratic nomination for President was Samuel J. Tilden, governor of New York and a reformer who had made the destruction of the Tweed Ring running Tammany Hall his chief objective. Tammany controlled the Democratic party in the city, and most city Democrats, including Bennett, were naturally opposed to Tilden's nomination. Bennett needed a candidate who could head off Tilden, which may have been where Custer came into the picture.

Custer was one of the most famous men in the country and extremely popular to boot. While he was in New York, the Redpath Agency offered him a lecturing contract. If he would go on the lecture circuit, the agency would promise him an engagement five nights a week for at least five months, at $200 per performance.[35] That was big money, as much as anyone on the extensive lecture circuit of the day could command on a regular basis, including probably Mark Twain. Further, 1876 was a depression year. In terms of the dollar of the 1930s, Custer was being offered around $1,000 per night; in terms of the mid-1970s, the figure would be $2,000 per night or more. The faith that the Redpath Agency showed in Custer's drawing power indicates that he had that essential qualification of a national politician: instant recognition.

Custer turned down the Redpath offer, as he evidently did any suggestions Bennett may have made to him, and in February he prepared to return to Fort Abraham Lincoln. It is possible that any offers made to him were predicated on a successful campaign against the Sioux, which would add to his laurels. In any event, what he wanted most of all was to be the commander of the expedition. As he wrote Tom Custer in January 1876, "I think the 7th Cavalry may have its greatest campaign ahead," and he would rather have died than missed it.[36]

The Army was planning a three-pronged attack against the hostiles in the unceded Indian territory. One of the columns would start from Fort Abraham Lincoln and eventually follow the Yellowstone River. Another, under General George Crook, would move north from Fort Fetterman toward the Little Bighorn (Crook's proposed winter campaign had not gotten off the ground). The third, under Major General John Gibbon, would follow the Yellowstone down stream from Fort Ellis, Montana. The Sioux, it was hoped, would be caught in this three-way squeeze. Custer was slated to command the column coming from Fort Abraham Lincoln and was anxious to get back to the fort to complete the preparations. Getting to Bismarck from St. Paul, however, proved to be a difficult undertaking. No trains were running, so deep was the snow in Minnesota, but when the Northern Pacific officials learned that Custer needed to get to the fort, they made up a special train for him. These men knew how important Custer was to their plans, so they spared no expense. There were two snowplows and three enormous engines, the usual complement of engineers and firemen, plus forty extra hands to shovel snow. Nevertheless the train got stuck in a gigantic drift and stayed stuck through a severe snowstorm. Libbie described the ensuing discomforts, fears, and dramatic rescue in "*Boots and Saddles.*"[37]

Scarcely had they arrived at Fort Lincoln (late February) when Custer received word that his presence was required in Washington.

As a result of Bennett's call for an investigation, a House committee under the chairmanship of Representative Hiester Clymer, Democrat of Pennsylvania, began digging into the records of the War Department. Clymer wanted Custer to testify. Custer tried to get out of it; he offered to answer questions in writing but begged to be allowed to stay with his command when it took the field. Clymer, however, insisted. Custer was unable to evade the summons.[38]

On his way to Washington, Custer stopped off in New York. There in late March he did some business with his publisher, but he also saw his Democratic friends, including William Endicott, who would later be Grover Cleveland's Secretary of War. What political matters, if any, were discussed we do not know, but Custer did receive an invitation to dinner at the Manhattan Club—"*the* Democratic Club of New York," he wrote Libbie, "with the promise that it would be non-political with no speeches. Congressman Robert Roosevelt signed the invitation."[39]

Custer then went on to Washington to testify, where he also met plenty of prominent Democrats. Senator Thomas F. Bayard of Delaware held a dinner in his honor, with former Confederates now holding political office as the guests. Pro-South Democrat (and former senator from California) William Gwin was there, and Gwin was a political plotter of the first rank. So was Senator John B. Gordon of Georgia, also present. Custer sat to the right of Bayard's daughter at dinner, Representative Clymer to her left. Custer was spending a lot of time with Clymer, walking with him to the Capitol in the mornings, lunching with him, and so on. Custer also returned at least twice to Bayard's home for dinner.[40]

Despite all the attention, Custer was desperate to get out of Washington and back to the 7th Cavalry. His chances looked good, because in early March Belknap had tried to escape the situation by resigning. Grant foolishly accepted the resignation, which added to the foul odor of the whole affair, but Belknap's resignation seemed to preclude an impeachment and trial.[41] Clymer was not going to let Belknap and Grant get off that easily, however, and was pushing ahead with impeachment hearings on Belknap, but Custer hoped that the Senate would decide it had no justification to hear the case in view of Belknap's resignation. In that event, Custer would soon be free to return to the 7th Cavalry.

Custer's testimony before the Clymer committee was a sensation, partly because of what he said, partly because he was the one saying it. He laid out the whole case against Belknap and linked Orvil Grant with the corruption. He got blasted by the Republican press, praised by the Democratic editors, and wrote Libbie: "Do not be anxious. I seek to follow a moderate and prudent course, avoiding prominence. Nevertheless, everything I do, however simple and unimportant, is noticed and commented on. This only makes me more careful."[42]

On April 17 the Belknap impeachment trial began. Custer begged the House managers of the impeachment to release him from Washington, and he got Major General Alfred Terry, commander of the Department of Dakota, to telegraph the managers to ask for Custer's immediate release. As his testimony was all hearsay anyway, the managers let him go, but then President Grant held up his clearance to leave Washington.

Custer was not one of Ulysses Grant's favorite people. Their relations had been strained ever since Custer began writing articles for *Galaxy*, because in the articles Custer was critical of Grant's peace policy toward the Indians. Custer's arrest of Fred Grant had not helped matters, and now Custer was accusing Grant's brother and his former Secretary of War of corruption. While in Washington, Custer had tried on three occasions to have an interview with Grant, but the President begged off each time on the excuse that he had a cold.[43]

The President now refused Custer permission to leave Washington. Custer tried to see him, spent several hours waiting in his anteroom on May 1, but the President still refused. Finally, a desperate Custer sent in a note to the President, saying that he wanted an interview only to correct some unjust impressions that he understood were held by the President regarding him. Still Grant would not see him. Custer then gave up on the President. He decided to rejoin his regiment, whatever the consequences, but he did his best to cover his rear. He wrote Grant another note, protesting the treatment he had received, and reported his proposed departure from Washington to both the Adjutant General and the Inspector General of the Army.

Custer took the train on May 2 to Chicago, his mind filled with thoughts of Libbie, the Sioux, and the 7th Cavalry, which was expected to take the field in a few days. But when he stepped off the train on May 3 a member of Sheridan's staff met him. He was under arrest. The President had given the order. The charge was leaving Washington without permission, and Grant had added specific orders that Custer not be allowed to join the Sioux expedition.[44]

For Custer it was the worst possible development, but for the Democrats it was heaven-sent. Bennett's *Herald* had a field day, denouncing Grant for conduct which appeared "to be the most high-handed abuse of his official power which he has perpetrated yet." On May 6 it declared that Custer was being disgraced "simply because he did not 'crook the pregnant hinges of the knee' to this modern Caesar," and said that Grant's theory of government was that of an "irresponsible despot . . . with an absolute power to decapitate anybody offending his Highness or his favorites."[45] Thanks to Bennett, Clymer, and Grant, Custer was now center stage. The Republicans denounced him, the St. Paul *Pioneer-Press* calling Custer "an extraordinary compound of presumptuous egotism and presumptuous mendacity which makes him the reckless and lawless being he is."[46]

Whatever Custer may have hoped for as a result of a victory over the Sioux, he hardly wanted to be the center of political attention before the military campaign even began. He was free to move about, with the understanding that he should consider himself under arrest, and he took the train to St. Paul. There he met with General Terry, whom Grant had designated commander of the expedition in Custer's place. (There had been a scramble among all the senior officers on the Plains when the news of Custer's arrest broke; Major Marcus A. Reno of the 7th Cavalry, for example, had telegraphed Terry that since it was obvious that Custer would not be available, and since "S. Bull is waiting on the Little Missouri, why not give me a chance as I feel I will do credit to the army.")

Custer regarded his interview with Terry as crucial, for Terry was his last hope. Sherman, now the General in Chief of the Army, had refused to intercede with Grant, and he evidently thought that Custer should have stayed in Washington. Sheridan, always something of a bootlicker, would do nothing to cross the President. Only Terry could help. So Custer went down on his knees, literally, and with tears in his eyes begged Terry to get the orders changed.[47]‡ Terry suggested that Custer write President Grant again; Custer muttered that that wouldn't do any good; Terry insisted that he should give it a try. Custer couldn't think of what to say, so Terry composed a message for him. Custer read it and agreed to send it over his own name. The telegram, addressed to "His Excellency, the President (through

‡ Once again there is a close parallel between George Custer and George Patton. In May 1944 Patton got himself into hot water because of some silly political statements he made about Britain and the United States running the world after World War II. General Eisenhower threatened to relieve him of his command of the Third Army, on the eve of Operation Overlord. Patton got down on his knees, cried, and begged Ike for another chance. Stephen E. Ambrose, *The Supreme Commander: The War Years of Dwight D. Eisenhower* (Garden City, 1970), 344.

Military Channels)," read: "I have seen your order . . . directing that I be not permitted to accompany the expedition to move against the hostile Indians. . . . I respectfully but most earnestly request that while not allowed to go in command of the expedition I may be permitted to serve with my regiment in the field." Then, there was the reminder of the old-school tie and of the honor of the professional soldier: "I appeal to you as a soldier to spare me the humiliation of seeing my regiment march to meet the enemy and I not share its dangers."

Terry, who badly wanted Custer with him on the campaign, endorsed the request. He also promised Grant that he, Terry, would retain command of the expedition even if the President allowed Custer to resume command of the 7th Cavalry, adding that Custer's "services would be very valuable with his regiment." Terry also persuaded Sheridan to ask Grant to change his mind, and Sheridan did ask, although in a way that would not offend Grant. In his appeal, Sheridan recalled 1868, when "I asked executive clemency for Colonel Custer to enable him to accompany his regiment against the Indians, and I sincerely hope if granted this time it may have sufficient effect to prevent him from again attempting to throw discredit on his profession and his brother officers."[48] If these appeals were not enough to move him, the President had an additional motive for backing down—the Democratic press was taking him to pieces for his "abuse of power" and "mistreatment" of Custer. The President relented. Custer could command the 7th Cavalry on the expedition, but Terry would have command of the column.

That fact hardly bothered a jubilant Custer. As he told Colonel William Ludlow, engineer of the expedition, he expected "to cut loose from and make my operations independent of, General Terry during the summer." Custer added that he had "got away from Stanley [in 1873] and would be able to swing clear of Terry" in 1876 without any difficulty.[49] A week later, on May 17, 1876, the 7th Cavalry left Fort Abraham Lincoln with the band playing "The Girl I Left Behind Me."

One evening shortly before the column moved out, Custer had visited the camp of the regiment's Crow and Arikara scouts, and that visit brings us back to speculation about what may have been said to Custer while he was in the East. First, Custer presented his Rhee scout Bloody Knife with several gifts purchased in Washington and told him and the Arikaras of his visit to the capital. Then he said that this would be his last Indian campaign and that if he won a victory—no matter how small—it would make him the Great White

Father in Washington. If the Arikara helped him to a victory, he promised that when he went to the White House he would take his brother Bloody Knife with him. He also told the scouts that he would look after them and see to it that they got houses to live in, and finally promised that as the Great White Father he would always look after the welfare of his children, the Arikaras.[50]

Could the story be true? This biographer must begin by saying that he does not know, that no one will ever know. Only the event itself—a victory over the Indians, followed by a presidential nomination by the Democrats—could have provided proof, and even then we would not know if Custer had planned it that way or if it happened by accident. Still, it is too Custer-like a story to pass by without comment.

Questions arise. Did such a scheme fit in with Custer's character insofar as we understand it? Certainly. Although it is true that he had passed up numerous political opportunities in the past, the presidency was something altogether different. If the Democrats in Washington put that bee in his bonnet while he was testifying against Belknap, it seems probable that the bee would have been just the thing to stir Custer's ambition. President of the United States! The very words have a ring to them that only William T. Sherman has ever been able to resist. Of course Custer would have liked to have been President. Not that he had any program that he was burning to put through for the future benefit of his country— far from it. But the prestige, the glory, the admiration, the sense of being an historic personage—in short, all the things Custer wanted most—would be his forever.

Was it feasible? Could Custer realistically dream of becoming President, or was it all fantasy, whether his or Bennett's or that of the Democrats in Washington? It would seem to have been a realistic enough proposal. After all, Americans since 1789 had been electing one or more war heroes per generation to the presidency—George Washington, Andrew Jackson, William Henry Harrison, Zachary Taylor, and Ulysses S. Grant. The Sioux war had caught the national attention and a victory over them, especially if Custer won it on his own, would cap his military career and make him the most notable Indian fighter of them all. The Democrats, having been licked twice by General Grant, wanted a general of their own to run for the White House, but he had to be a general whose views were acceptable to the South.

What better choice than Custer? He had dozens of highly placed southern friends, was notoriously anti-black, had legitimate Democratic credentials, had stood behind Andy Johnson when the Radical Republicans were hounding him, and besides all that was a Union war hero, the path breaker for the continental railroads, and the man who had opened the Black Hills. New York and New Jersey Democrats knew and liked Custer (McClellan, still Custer's admirer, would become the Democratic governor of New Jersey in 1878). Nationally, he was well known.

In terms of the specifics of 1876, the Democrats could smell blood. They had Grant and the Republicans on the run, and they were going to make an all-out effort to get back into the White House after a sixteen-year absence. Governor Samuel Tilden of New York, a Democrat, had a strong organization and support, but the professionals in the party tended to be against him because of his reform impulses, which they regarded as dangerous. That spring some 120 prominent New York Democrats, following a series of secret meetings, had signed a petition which was printed and widely circulated, stating that they were opposed to Tilden's nomination to the presidency. Some of Custer's supporters were among the signers, including Fernando Wood and August Belmont. The problem these politicians faced was the absence of a viable candidate.

To men desperate for a candidate, Custer must have seemed ideal. The Democrats were scheduled to hold their convention in St. Louis in late June; by then, Custer should have found and whipped the hostiles. News of his victory could have swept the convention like wildfire if handled properly and led to a stampede for Custer. Did Bennett or someone else suggest this possibility to Custer? Despite direct orders to the contrary from Sheridan, Custer was bringing Mark Kellogg, a newspaper reporter, with him on the expedition.[51] Perhaps Custer hoped that Kellogg could get a report of the battle with the Sioux to the Democrats and to the country before June 27, the opening day of the convention.

There was enough reality in the proposition, one could suppose, for Custer to believe his nomination possible. If nominated, could he have won? That is anyone's guess, American politics being as they are, but it may be instructive to recall that the Democrats were able to throw the election of 1876 into the House of Representatives, even when running so faceless a candidate as Tilden and despite widespread Republican fraud at the ballot boxes. And it might also be said that as a President, Custer probably would not have been much worse than the men who did hold the job for the remainder of the nineteenth century. The country would have survived.

But all that is speculation. We don't even know if any important

Democrats whispered about the presidency to him, much less if he took such talk seriously or not. But something prompted him, according to the evidence, to tell Bloody Knife and the Arikara scouts that he was planning to become the Great White Father.

CHAPTER TWENTY-ONE

Crazy Horse Fights on the Rosebud While Custer Closes In

"I now have some Crow scouts with me, as they are familiar with the country. They are magnificent-looking men, so much handsomer and more Indian-like than any we have ever seen, and so jolly and sportive; nothing of the gloomy, silent red-man about them. They have formally given themselves to me, after the usual talk. In their speech they said they had heard that I never abandoned a trail; that when my food gave out I ate mule. That was the kind of a man they wanted to fight under; they were willing to eat mule too."   Custer to Libbie, June 21, 1876

The Sioux hadn't seen anything like it since the Fort Phil Kearny days almost ten years earlier. The flow of movement had been reversed. After the treaty of 1868 the Sioux—individuals, families, and bands—had been slowly, reluctantly, moving south and east into the agencies. So many went that by 1875 the number of hostiles had shrunk from over ten thousand to less than three thousand; meanwhile the population of the agencies doubled and then doubled again, reaching more than ten thousand in 1875. But by February 1876 the tide had turned and by May of that year, its force was almost overwhelming. The agencies lost half or more of their Indian population. Those who stayed behind were old men, women, and children. Spotted Tail and Red Cloud refused to join the hostiles, but Red Cloud's son Jack was one of those who participated in the exodus.

There were almost as many motives for going north as there were Indians making the trek. Some of the agency Sioux made it as a matter of course—they had been wintering on the agencies and spending the summers with the hostiles for years. In 1876, however, many of these Indians left early, moving to the Powder River in February and were joined by others who wanted a chance at some buffalo. This was a direct result of the United States Government

Indian policy, which was almost unbelievably stupid. On the one hand, the government had declared war on the Powder River Indians and was preparing a series of expeditions to march against them. On the other hand, the government was bickering over appropriations to feed the agency Sioux so that no food was arriving at the agencies and the people there were starving. They begged their agents for permission to go hunting up by the Yellowstone and the agents gave it; they had no real choice in the matter—if they had said no, the agency Indians would have starved before their eyes.

But most of the Sioux moving north had more in mind than a good hunt. Some wanted a chance to pick up some coup and horses at the expense of the Crows. Others brought along trading items—white man's goods—to exchange for robes and furs, which commanded relatively high prices at the agencies. Many were just curious, youngsters who wanted to see Sitting Bull, Crazy Horse, and the other famous Sioux for themselves. Some of the young warriors had never been in a fight and wanted to prove themselves—Jack Red Cloud, for example. In his late teens at this time, he had been living on the agency since 1870 and had not been on a war party; there were many other youngsters like him. Older men came along, some with their families, in order to visit relatives they had not seen in years. Some young warriors were mainly concerned with finding a wife among the hostile women, for rumor had it that they were prettier, livelier, and more fun than the agency squaws.

Above and beyond these (and surely other) motives for leaving the agencies, one reason stood out. The Indians were going north to fight the soldiers and to have one last summer of the old wild life. Most of them seem to have held no illusions about the long-term future. The Army certainly made no attempt to hide its preparations for the campaign, which was common gossip among whites at the Red Cloud and Spotted Tail agencies and the agency Indians knew enough about the white man and his power to realize that the end had come: when the Army took possession of the only buffalo range left in the United States, the Sioux would roam no more. It was almost as if the entire Sioux nation (or at least a goodly portion of it) had decided to have one last, great summer before giving in to the whites.

The hostiles played on this sentiment brilliantly. Sitting Bull sent runners to the agencies in February to tell the Indians there to come on north and have a big fight with the whites. There would be a grand Sun Dance, some real old-time buffalo hunts, an enormous get-together (and no race of people enjoyed getting together more than the Sioux), and a good fight against the soldiers, with plenty of coup for everyone. Crazy Horse told the Cheyennes to come join him for a little fighting against the whites.[1]

The appeal was well-nigh irresistible. Crazy Horse's Oglalas and Sitting Bull's Hunkpapas had already joined hands and were camped on the Rosebud Creek, which flowed into the Yellowstone in eastern Montana. Oglalas from Red Cloud's and Brulés from Spotted Tail's agencies swelled their numbers. Then the Cheyennes, who had also been at Red Cloud Agency, came, fifty lodges strong, to camp near Crazy Horse. Some Blackfeet Sioux from western South Dakota rode into camp, enough to have their own circle of lodges. The Sans Arcs were also there with their own circle of lodges. Santees from the Missouri River came, along with some Assiniboines and Arapahoes.

And as the hostile camp increased in size, it became even more of a magnet to other Indians. It was obvious to every Indian in the northwest Plains that the Army was gunning for them, literally, and that any Indian seen anywhere in the unceded Indian territory would be fair game; it didn't take any particular brains to figure out that when you were caught in a situation like that the best place to be was with your comrades. Agency Indians felt the same way. They remembered Sand Creek and the Washita; a number of them indicated to white friends, before leaving the agencies to join the hostiles, that they could not feel safe even on the reservation, not with all those troops about. Their only safety lay in numbers, and by April the camp of Sitting Bull and Crazy Horse was where the numbers were.

Since the opening of the Oregon Trail in the 1840s, this gathering in 1876 was the closest the Sioux ever came to presenting a united front to the whites. But, of course, not all the Sioux agreed with the Sitting Bull-Crazy Horse policy. One defection that particularly grieved Crazy Horse came in early March. He Dog, with ten lodges of Oglala followers, had decided to obey the government and go into Red Cloud Agency. He was joining some forty lodges of Cheyennes, under Old Bear, who were doing the same thing. He Dog explained to Crazy Horse that his women were afraid, that his people had little children who could not run in the snow when the horse soldiers came. He Dog, two years older than Crazy Horse, was in his late thirties. He had no need for any more coup or any excitement of any kind—he had been beside Crazy Horse in almost every battle of Crazy Horse's life. He did not need to prove his courage, but he did need to protect his helpless ones. Crazy Horse made no attempt to stop him, but he watched He Dog go with a heavy heart, certain that He Dog was making a mistake.[2]

Crazy Horse was right; it proved to be a mistake. As the southern prong of the Army's campaign against the Sioux, General Crook was leading a powerful column (eight hundred soldiers) from Fort Fetterman up the Bozeman Trail, in search of Indians. On March 16, 1876, Crook stumbled across the He Dog-Old Bear village. Frank Grouard, once Crazy Horse's white friend, was one of Crook's scouts. Grouard recognized some of He Dog's horses. He assumed that Crazy Horse was, as always, with He Dog, and therefore reported to Crook that they had hit it lucky. Next to Sitting Bull, Crazy Horse was the biggest catch of all, and now Crook had him in his hands, or so Grouard said. Because He Dog and Old Bear were on their way to the agency, they expected no trouble and had neglected to post scouts. Thus Crook was able to achieve complete surprise in a dawn attack reminiscent of the Washita, except that He Dog and most of the people fled to safety. Crook's men got possession of the village and destroyed everything in it, including enormous quantities of fresh and dried buffalo meat. This was remarkably stupid, even for the Army, since Crook was out of supplies. After the battle he had to fall back to Fort Fetterman to replenish his stores.

Crook's success was ephemeral. Unlike Custer at the Washita, he failed to kill many warriors, and after recovering from the initial shock, the Sioux and Cheyennes counterattacked and managed to recover most of their large pony herd. This development, coupled with Crook's retreat after the battle, gave Indian morale a significant boost, for within a week the news of Crook's fiasco was known by every Indian on the northwest Plains. It emboldened the hostiles to the point where they felt they could safely defy the government. The flow of Indians into the Sitting Bull-Crazy Horse camp became a flood. And He Dog, Old Bear, and their followers were a part of it.[3]

How big the great camp became is a matter of speculation that can never be settled. Indian estimates run from nearly one thousand to as many as two thousand lodges and sometimes even higher. The best guess—and it is only a guess—would be that there could not have been less than two thousand warriors or more than four thousand. Whatever their number, there were enough to swell the hearts of the braves, to make them—and their leaders—feel invincible.[4] They were better armed than they ever had been. Agency Indians living cheek by jowl with whites had managed, one way or another, to acquire white man's weapons for themselves. The best estimate is that almost half the warriors had guns. But the Army's claim, after the fact, that the hostiles were better armed than the soldiers was ridiculous. The majority of Indian weapons were old flintlocks, condemned muskets, muzzleloaders, and smoothbores. Sitting Bull's own gun was a forty-year-old Hawken rifle.[5] No matter how deficient the weapon, however, possession of a gun gave the individual warrior confidence.

The Indians knew that the soldiers were coming at them from the south, west, and east, but nevertheless it was a joyous camp, reminding older members of the camps the Sioux used to make at Bear Butte near the Black Hills. Certain that they were strong enough to repel any force of soldiers, no matter how large, the Indians enjoyed themselves. The camp had to move every few days in order to find fresh grass for the gigantic pony herd and to find buffalo, though there was more than enough meat.* Everyone feasted everyone else. Dancing was almost continuous. So was visiting back and forth. Old friends met and embraced, new friends were made. Youngsters raced their ponies from dawn to dusk. Slightly older boys, resplendent in full dress, strutted from circle to circle, showing off. Wherever one looked there were teen-aged boys and girls wrapping themselves inside a blanket, courting. Warriors outdid themselves in bragging about their exploits against the Crows, Pawnees, or Shoshonis and in boasting about what they would do to any white soldiers who might dare to attack the Sioux nation.

The Cheyennes, as honored allies, had first place in the circles of lodges. They led the marches and picked out the camping grounds. So big was the encampment that when it moved in column the

* The presence of buffalo in large numbers in the Powder River country was shown by an experience Crook's column had later that year. By early June Crook was moving north again, looking for the hostiles. When entering the valley of the Rosebud, the troops saw one of the last great North American herds. The following account was written by a newspaperman accompanying the expedition: "All at once we ascended to the crest of a grassy slope, and then a sight burst upon us calculated to thrill the coldest heart in the command. Far as the eye could reach on both sides of our route the somber, superb buffaloes were grazing in thousands! The earth was brown with them. 'Steady men, keep your ranks,' was the command of the officers from front to rear as many of the younger soldiers, rendered frantic by the sight of the noble game, made a movement as if to break from the column in wild pursuit." The Crows and Shoshonis went wild, shooting buffalo throughout the day, bringing them down by the hundreds. "Contrary to their general custom the savages killed the animals in sheer wantonness, and when reproached by the officers said, 'better kill buffalo than have him feed the Sioux!'" The slaughter continued until total darkness. John F. Finerty, *War-Path and Bivouac: The Big Horn and Yellowstone Expedition* (Chicago, 1955), 119–21.

Cheyennes would have their tipis up and their suppers eaten before the Hunkpapas, in the rear, had reached the campground. Yet this huge outfit, with a pony herd of at least ten thousand, could move with remarkable speed. Edgar Stewart, who has done the most intensive research on the subject, writes that the camp was "able to make fifty miles a day despite the presence of women and children and the fact that they were burdened with the lodges and miscellaneous baggage of the camp."[6]

Hanging over the whole camp was the foreboding knowledge that this was the last time it all could be done, the last big encampment of the Sioux. That feeling, however, only fed the joyous mood, as it made individuals more determined to enjoy themselves. Some of the agency Indians hadn't seen a buffalo in years, and the good hunting was pure joy to them. It was one last fling, and the Sioux made the most of it. Every Indian who was there, man, woman, or child, even those who survived well into the twentieth century, always remembered it as the most glorious summer of his or her life.[7]

The irreconcilables among the hostiles did not share the general thought that this was a last fling before moving permanently onto the reservations. Sitting Bull talked about "fighting to the last man," and Crazy Horse agreed. They were determined to stay out forever, if they could, or die trying. They hoped to defeat the whites as badly in 1876 as they had at Fort Phil Kearny in 1866 and thereby, perhaps, win another ten years of freedom for themselves. Having seen only white soldiers, and not many of them at that, they did not believe the agency Indian stories about the power of the whites. Sitting Bull said such stories were part of the white man's medicine, that the agency people had been fooled.[8]

In early June 1876 the camp moved to the Little Bighorn Valley, a favorite resort of the Indians because of its luxuriant grasses and the plentiful buffalo, deer, and elk. But even so favored a place could not support so many people for very long, and after a few days the camp moved back to the Rosebud Valley. There, the Indians held a Sun Dance.

It was a big one, talked about for decades thereafter. All the people, Sioux and Cheyenne, went into one enormous circle. Everything was done in the old way, according to strict and elaborate ritual. Virgins cut the sacred tree; chiefs carried it into the camp circle; braves counted coup upon it. The buffalo skulls were set up, along with the sacred pipes and other paraphernalia. Many men pierced at that dance, undergoing the self-torture so that Wakan Tanka, the All, would smile upon his people. Sitting Bull, his breast already covered with scars from previous Sun Dances, was the sponsor and leader. He sat on the ground with his back to the sacred Sun Dance pole while his adopted brother, Jumping Bull, lifted a small piece of his, Sitting Bull's, skin with an awl and cut it with a sharp knife. Jumping Bull cut fifty pieces of flesh from Sitting Bull's right arm, then fifty more from the left arm.

With blood streaming down both his arms, Sitting Bull then danced around and around the pole, staring constantly at the sun. He danced after the sun had set, through the night and into the next day; for eighteen hours he danced. Then he fainted. When Black Moon revived him by throwing cold water on his face, Sitting Bull's eyes cleared and he spoke to Black Moon in a low voice. His offering had been accepted, his prayers had been heard. He had had a vision.

Black Moon walked into the middle of the circle and called out, "Sitting Bull wishes to announce that he just heard a voice from above saying, 'I give you these because they have no ears.' He looked up and saw soldiers and some Indians on horseback coming down like grasshoppers, with their heads down and their hats falling off. They were falling right into our camp."[9]

Then the people rejoiced. They did not need a holy man to interpret Sitting Bull's vision—clearly it foretold an attack on the camp by the soldiers, who would all be killed by the Indians. Even the most sophisticated agency Indian present at that Sun Dance was impressed by Sitting Bull's performance and made into a believer. Let the soldiers come!

After the dance, the camp moved back to the valley of the Little Bighorn and settled down on Ash Creek. There, on June 16, Cheyenne scouts rode into camp. They reported that General Crook, old "Three Stars," was coming north again, at the head of a one-thousand-man column of white troops, accompanied by 260 Indian allies, mainly Crows and Shoshonis. The hostiles held a council. Some favored moving out of Crook's way; others wanted to start every warrior in the camp moving toward Crook. Crazy Horse rejected both suggestions. He advised leaving half or more of the warriors in camp, to protect the helpless ones and to provide a reserve, while he rode at the head of 1,500 or so warriors to meet and turn back the Crook column. The advice was accepted. Sitting Bull insisted on coming along, although he was still so weak from his Sun Dance ordeal that he could barely sit a horse and needed a man to help him mount and ride. On the afternoon of June 16, the column set off to attack Crook before Crook could attack the camp.[10]

Crook's column was part of a three-pronged offensive that had been under way for a month. From Fort Ellis in Montana Major General John Gibbon was moving east down the Yellowstone River with 450 men, while General Terry was now coming up the Yellowstone from the east with a total force of 2,700 men. Custer rode with Terry, at the head of the twelve troops of the 7th Cavalry. On the march Custer revealed two facets of his many-sided character. In his official capacity he was as tough, as meticulous, and as professional as any general officer could be. He pushed the men hard, but he pushed himself harder. He had the troopers up before dawn and kept them marching until after dark. He held regular inspections, saw to it that his men had the best available equipment and supplies (they were armed with the 1873 model Springfield .45-70s), and generally saw to their welfare while making certain that they were in fighting trim.

But the little boy in General Custer was still very much alive, and he could no more repress his juvenile spirit than he could his ambition. At times it almost seemed that the campaign was a summer camping trip. Custer had his dogs along and he frequently took off on hunting trips. Somewhat like the Sioux on the Little Bighorn, he was enjoying a reunion. Tom Custer was along, of course, along with Calhoun (Custer's brother-in-law), Keogh, Cooke, and other old friends. Boston Custer—"Bos"—the general's younger brother, was there too, serving as forage master. Custer's nephew, Autie Reed, a teen-ager, had joined up and helped drive the beef herd. Mark Kellogg, the correspondent, joined Custer's "family," and together they had a jolly time. They were marching through magnificent terrain—"We are now in a country heretofore unvisited by white men," Custer wrote Libbie with his usual exaggeration—and as always the scenery inspired Custer. The only thing wrong was Libbie's absence, and on May 31 Custer wrote her, "I have about made up my mind that when I go on expeditions like this you are to go too. You could have endured this as well as not."[11]

Custer and Tom delighted in playing practical jokes at the expense of their younger brother. Once the three of them went for a ride away from the column; Bos fell behind. "Let's slip round the hill behind Bos," Custer suggested to Tom, "where he can't find us, and when he starts we'll fire in the air near him." They hid, Bos came over the hill, looked puzzled, and Custer let loose with a bullet that whizzed over his brother's head. Bos turned and fled back toward the column, Custer and Tom shooting over his head as he rode. "Tom and I mounted our horses and soon overhauled him," Custer wrote Libbie. "He will not hear the last of it for some time."[12]

They slept in the open, Tom, Custer, Autie Reed, and Bos, around the campfire. "Tom pelted 'Bos' with sticks and clods of earth after we had retired," Custer wrote Libbie on June 17. "I don't know what we would do without 'Bos' to tease."[13]

Custer maintained his usual literary productivity during the march. He wrote long, descriptive letters to Libbie and articles for *Galaxy*. The steamboat, *Far West*, plying the Yellowstone, picked up the mail and brought letters from Libbie. Custer wrote far into the night and occasionally got up an hour or so before reveille in order to have more time to write. "Bloody Knife looks on in wonder at me because I never get tired," Custer wrote, "and says no other man could ride all night and never sleep."[14] Custer had cut his hair short for the campaign, but he was growing a beard. He wore a red tie, broad-brimmed white hat, and his fringed buckskin shirt.[15]

Throughout the march, Terry leaned on Custer, who was, after all, on his fourth major expedition across the Plains while it was Terry's first. With his wonderful sense of topography—he was almost as good as an Indian—Custer picked out the trail, no easy task as it had to be level enough for the Gatling guns and the wagons. Once, early in the march from Fort Abraham Lincoln, without permission, Custer took four companies on a forty-five-mile scout up the Little Missouri. Terry complained to his diary about Custer's insubordination but did not put him under arrest or, evidently, even give him a verbal reprimand.

By June 10, Terry and Gibbon were in contact at the mouth of the Rosebud. Between them they had covered the upper Yellowstone to the mouth of Rosebud Creek and seen no tracks indicating that the hostiles might have crossed the river, so they were certain that Sitting Bull was somewhere to the south, camping on the Rosebud, the Tongue, the Little Bighorn, the Powder, or the Bighorn. With Crook coming up from the south, they had the Sioux trapped. Now the job was to locate the Indians before they escaped. Terry decided to send Major Reno and half the 7th Cavalry to the south on a scout of the Powder and Tongue valleys. Custer was to move the other half of the regiment back to the mouth of the Tongue, there to await Reno's return.

Custer strongly opposed Reno's making such a scout. He thought it a "wild goose chase," arguing that the hostiles were on the Rosebud or the Little Bighorn. He also thought it dangerous to leave half the regiment behind when a march of a day or two of all twelve troops of the 7th Cavalry would bring them to the Indian camp. Custer feared that the scouting expedition would put the Indians on the alert and make it possible for them to escape. But his real objection was that Reno, not he, would be in command. He evidently had a shouting argument with Terry about it, but Terry would not budge.[16]

While Custer sat at the mouth of the Tongue, he made the last preparations for the battle he soon expected to fight. He was leaving his dogs behind and had officers and men give up their sabers, which were packed in boxes and stored. Custer left the regimental band behind, along with some staff officers and dismounted troopers. On June 16 the shake-down was complete, and Custer waited for Reno to return. That night in camp he finished an article for *Galaxy*. He was about one hundred miles north of Crook, but had no idea where Crook was. Nor did he know that Crazy Horse was marching that night toward Crook.

While Custer, Reno, Gibbon, Terry, and Crook looked for the Sioux, the Sioux found Crook on the Rosebud. On June 16 Crazy Horse led a night march through broken country from the big camp in the valley of the Little Bighorn across the divide to the Rosebud, about thirty miles to the south-southeast. They marched in column formation, with the front, rear, and flanks guarded by Sioux and Cheyenne *akicita*. Crazy Horse was not going to allow any ambitious youngster an opportunity to dash off and put Crook on his guard. At dawn, June 17, the column was close to the Rosebud near the mouth of Trail Creek. Here Crazy Horse stopped to allow the ponies to rest and graze while the men put on their war paint. At about 8:30 A.M. Crazy Horse had his men on the march again.

Crook, meanwhile, had been marching since 4 A.M., June 17. As Crazy Horse was moving forward, Crook was ordering his men to unsaddle their horses and turn them out to graze. He had halted because the Crow and Shoshoni scouts were apprehensive and asked for time to carry out a reconnaissance. Chief Washakie, the great Shoshoni leader whom Crazy Horse had met in battle on a number of occasions, is said to have told Crook at this time that there were too many Sioux ahead for him to fight.[17]

Crazy Horse had his army on the west side of the Rosebud Valley, hidden behind a high hill. Creeping to the top, he could see Crook's 1,200-man force scattered on both sides of the river. The valley was about a mile wide, with the creek running through the middle of it. To the north, the valley narrowed down into a heavily timbered canyon, a perfect place for an ambush if Crook could be lured in that direction. The valley ground below Crazy Horse was very rough and broken, covered with rocks, trees, and bushes.

Crazy Horse had no time to make any plans, for scarcely had he looked down on Crook's scattered troopers than some Crow scouts rode up to his position. The Crows saw Crazy Horse and behind him a mass of Sioux and Cheyenne warriors, and took off as fast as their ponies could run, headed downhill for Crook's camp, yelling "Sioux! Sioux!" at the top of their lungs. Crazy Horse's warriors immediately broke through the ranks of the *akicita* and gave chase. The battle of the Rosebud had begun.

The ensuing action was confused and confusing. There was no over-all leadership on either side; as Robert Utley notes, the broken terrain fragmented the fight and prevented effective central direction.[18] For the most part, it was every man for himself, with the hostiles charging again and again on Crook's divided units. Never had the Sioux or Cheyennes fought so fiercely. Never before had they pressed home even one attack in the way that they did on several occasions that day. Colonel Anson Mills, who was in the battle, said the hostiles were "charging boldly and rapidly through the soldiers, knocking them from their horses with lances and knives, dismounting and killing them, cutting off the arms of some at the elbows in the middle of the fight and carrying them away." The Sioux and Cheyennes had abandoned the old, safe method of hovering, circling at a distance. A new spirit was in them that day, and they came on with their ponies at the dead run, often breaking in among the troops and whipping them in hand-to-hand encounters.[19]

One white soldier later reported that they just kept coming. "They were in front, rear, flanks, and on every hilltop, far and near. I had been in several Indian battles, but never saw so many Indians at one time before, . . . or so brave."[20]

Crook counterattacked when he could, in an effort to drive the Indians from the field, and almost succeeded once. Short Buffalo later said that "Crazy Horse, Bad Heart Bull, Black Twin, Kicking Bear, and Good Weasel rallied the Sioux, turned the charge and got the soldiers on the run. Good Weasel was a kind of lieutenant for Crazy Horse—he was always with him. When these five commenced to rally their men, that was as far as the soldiers got."[21]

The Crows and Shoshonis fought magnificently; indeed, although the Army never admitted it, much less thanked its allies, the Crows and Shoshonis time and again saved Crook from a full-scale disaster. Twice they boldly rode through Sioux lines to save an officer who had been dehorsed and cut off from his men. When young Jack Red Cloud lost his horse and started running on foot, the Crows surrounded him. Recognizing him, they started laughing, whipping him, and jerked off his large war bonnet, telling him he was a boy with no right to wear it. They took his Winchester away, too, an embarrassing loss as it was a special one, engraved and given to Red Cloud by the United States Government. Jack cried out for pity, an unheard of thing among warriors, which only made the Crows laugh harder. Eventually someone—Crazy Horse himself, some say—broke through the Crow ranks. Jack leaped behind his savior on the pony and they rode away safely. Jack then got a horse for himself and fled ignominiously to Red Cloud Agency, where he stayed for the remainder of the summer.[22]

Among the Cheyennes in this battle was Chief Comes-in-Sight, a brave warrior. His sister had followed him out to the battle. He charged the soldiers many times, but finally his horse was killed under him. Comes-in-Sight was near the whites, who began to concentrate their fire on him, while some Crows noticed the dehorsed Cheyenne and began to ride toward him. Suddenly, a rider dashed forward from the Cheyenne lines and swept down on Comes-in-Sight at full speed. The rider reached out a hand on passing, Comes-in-Sight grabbed it, swung himself on up behind the rider, and they made it back to their lines safely. He had been rescued by his sister, Buffalo Calf Road Woman, and ever afterward the Cheyennes called this battle by the name, "Where the Girl Saved Her Brother."[23]

Crook had the idea that Crazy Horse's camp was downstream, and about noon—as the initial fury of the battle eased a bit—he sent Colonel Mills and a detachment of eight troops of cavalry toward the canyon, with orders to locate, capture, and hold the camp until reinforcements could arrive. Mills got started off boldly enough, but his Crow scouts soon refused to go any farther. As the valley became narrower, they became more afraid of an ambush. According to some accounts, Crazy Horse was by then leading them on and had indeed posted warriors on both sides of the canyon for an ambush. Other accounts, however, say that Crazy Horse watched Mills' force march downstream, then gathered together the bulk of the warriors on Crook's flank and rear, with the idea of overwhelming Crook's main body of troops as soon as Mills was beyond supporting distance.[24]

The decoy and ambush tactics sound more like Crazy Horse, but the second account fits in better with what happened next. Perhaps

Crazy Horse was learning. Perhaps he realized that the decoy trick had been done to death, that there was no chance of its working, especially with the Crows and Shoshonis present to give advice to the white soldiers. Crook had done an incredibly stupid thing—with his men hard pressed by a fired-up opponent, he had divided his command and was putting each portion out of supporting distance of the other. Seeing this, Crazy Horse may have decided to apply the basic military principle of concentration of force at the decisive spot. If so, he had learned the fundamental lesson taught by Napoleon— bring all your force to bear against a portion of the enemy, and the day will be yours.

In any event, Crook soon heard from the Crows that the Sioux and Cheyennes were massing on his left flank, and he could see others getting onto his rear. The sight must have appalled him. He abandoned all plans for an offensive movement and sent a staff officer dashing after Mills, to order Mills to come back. Mills swung around to his own left, which after some marching placed him near the flank and rear of the Sioux and Cheyenne lines. When Mills' cavalry appeared behind them, the hostiles were disconcerted. They scattered, and soon thereafter the engagement ended.

Crook claimed a victory, on the grounds that the Indians left the field of battle. The United States Government would soon go broke if the Army won many such victories. First of all, Crook lost twenty-eight men killed and fifty-six wounded (Crazy Horse later acknowledged losing thirty-six men killed and sixty-three wounded, terribly high casualties for Indians).[25] Second, Crook's men had fired away twenty-five thousand rounds of ammunition; counting all the costs of the campaign, the government was paying about $1,000,000 for each Indian killed.[26]

Crook retreated after a day or so, falling back to the south. He was not heard from again until the middle of July. Neither Terry, Gibbon, nor Custer had any idea where he was or what he was doing. Crook was unable to get word through hostile territory to his fellow officers, or so he claimed. Thus they did not know where the hostiles were located or in what numbers. Most important, Crook failed to tell Custer, Terry, and Gibbon that the Indians were displaying new fighting methods, that they were now closing with the Army in combat. After the Rosebud, Crook did nothing; the hostiles had put him out of action.

Crazy Horse and the warriors went back to the big camp near the Little Bighorn, where they mourned the dead, then feasted and danced. They were satisfied with what they had done, especially after scouts reported that Crook had turned around and gone back from where he had come. But the Sioux were under no illusions. From Sitting Bull's vision, and from their own knowledge of all the soldier columns in the northwest Plains, they knew that they would soon be attacked in camp. But they were not afraid—they had shown at the Rosebud what they could do. Their fondest hope was to be left in peace, but if they could not have that, then the soldiers could come—they would stay where they were and fight.

The soldiers were coming. On June 20, Reno returned from his reconnaissance. Though Terry had ordered him only to go up the Powder, then down the Tongue, he had exceeded his orders upon reaching the Tongue, where he found some Indian trails leading to the west, perhaps indicating that the big hostile camp was on the Little Bighorn. Reno followed the trail cross-country to the Rosebud, then left it to march down that creek back to the Yellowstone, then to the Tongue. Terry was furious. So was Custer, but for different reasons. Terry wrote his sisters that Reno "had done this in positive defiance of my orders not to go to the Rosebud, in the belief that there were Indians on that stream and that he could make a success-ful attack on them which would cover up his disobedience. . . ."[27] Custer's complaint was that Reno, having cut loose, then lost heart and returned to the main column. He couldn't imagine how any In-dian fighter could leave a hot trail, and he chewed Reno out in no uncertain terms.[28] He told Libbie he was going to take up the trail where Reno left it, but "I fear that failure to follow up the Indians has imperilled our plans by giving the village an intimation of our presence. Think of the valuable time lost!"[29]

Through his mouthpiece, correspondent Kellogg, Custer managed to get his version of the Reno scouting expedition into the eastern press. Kellogg sent a dispatch to Bennett's New York Herald, which Bennett gleefully printed a few days before the Democratic Conven-tion met in St. Louis. Speaking of Reno, the Herald quoted Custer as saying, "Few officers have ever had so fine an opportunity to make a successful and telling strike, and few have ever so completely failed to improve their opportunity."[30]

The truth was that every senior officer on the three expeditions—Gibbon, Terry and Custer—wanted a crack at the hostiles for himself. Each was convinced that no force of Indians, no matter how large, could stand up to their fire power. They all knew that this would be the last big Indian fight on the Plains and that the victor would become one of the Great Captains: his tactics would be studied in

West Point classrooms and the nation would give him whatever reward he desired. Crook had felt that way. So had Gibbon, who had marched his men well beyond the point of ordinary human endurance in the hope of catching the hostiles and defeating them by himself.[31] In short, the situation was wide open—it was each general for himself and to the victor belonged the spoils.

Terry now moved his command up the Yellowstone and set up base camp at the mouth of the Rosebud, establishing his headquarters on the steamboat *Far West*. There, on June 21, he held a council of war with Gibbon and Custer. The problem they discussed was how to catch the Indians. They estimated the hostile force at between 800 and 1,000 warriors, but Custer thought that figure too low. He felt there would be 1,500 warriors waiting. That was approximately half the actual number in Sitting Bull's camp, but even had Terry, Gibbon and Custer known that there were in fact 3,000 or more warriors waiting for them, they would have changed nothing. Lonesome Charley Reynolds, as well as Bloody Knife and the Indian scouts, thought there were too many Sioux for the Army to handle, but there was not a single officer who had the slightest doubt about what the outcome would be if any sizable force of cavalry or infantry was able to attack the Indians en masse.

Such an attitude was not simply foolish white man's overconfidence. It was based on previous experience, and not only in the United States. Napoleon had concluded as a result of his Egyptian campaign that one European soldier versus one Asiatic or Oriental soldier did not have a chance—the native was far too shrewd and cunning, and regardless of who had the better weapons, the native would best the alien. When a small party of three to five European soldiers met the same number of natives, the Europeans might be able to defend themselves in combat if they were properly dug in on good defensive positions or properly led on an offensive. But twenty or more European soldiers armed with the best weapons could take on fifty or even one hundred natives, because of European discipline, training, and fire control. Custer knew of Napoleon's maxim and thought it exactly right.

So much so, in fact, that when Terry indicated that he wanted Custer to march toward the Indian camp and offered to let Custer take along the Gatling guns as well as four troops of the 2nd Cavalry, Custer refused both. He said he was afraid the Gatling guns would slow his march, and as for the extra cavalrymen, they wouldn't be needed. The 7th Cavalry, 611 men strong, with their powerful American horses, far superior weaponry, and fire control, would be more than sufficient to rub out every warrior in the Sioux nation.[32]

Custer's refusal of the extra cavalry—the four troops would have increased his fighting strength by 30 per cent—was a serious error. They would not have slowed the march and could have added great weight to any attack Custer might make. His decision to go it alone with the 7th Cavalry must be attributed to his ambition, both for himself and for his beloved regiment—he did not want to share the glory with anyone, not even fellow cavalry officers fighting under his own command. But if Custer's motives are difficult to fathom, it is clear enough that this was the biggest mistake he ever made, including leaving Fort Wallace in 1867 to fly to Libbie's side.

The focus of Gibbon, Terry, and Custer during their war council on the *Far West* was not on how to defeat the enemy, but on how to catch him. Its object, recalled Gibbon, was "to prevent the escape of the Indians, which was the idea pervading the minds of all of us." Scouts had reported smoke in the direction of the Little Bighorn; Reno had seen a trail leading in that direction; everything indicated that the Indians could be caught there (it is necessary to recall that none of the generals on the *Far West* knew where Crook was or what he was doing—a classic example of the disadvantage of a divided command). The plan was that Custer would lead the 7th Cavalry up the Rosebud to its head, thus blocking escape to the east, then cross the divide to the valley of the Little Bighorn. Gibbon, meanwhile, would go back up the Yellowstone a way, ascend the Bighorn River, and enter the Little Bighorn Valley from the north. Terry decided to accompany Gibbon, probably because Terry was exhausted from the recent marching and knew that Custer would set a demanding pace. Gibbon's infantry would be easier to keep up with and he could stay on the *Far West* much of the way. He may also have felt that Gibbon had the best chance of finding the hostiles. Mark Kellogg did not. The journalist decided to go with Custer on the grounds that Custer was most likely to find and destroy the enemy (or had publisher Bennett told his reporter to stick with Custer no matter what?).

The following morning, June 22, Terry handed Custer a set of written orders. In some places he was explicit, in others permissive, thereby laying the basis for endless controversy about whether Custer disobeyed orders in the ensuing campaign. Terry ordered Custer to "proceed up the Rosebud in pursuit of the Indians whose trail was discovered by Major Reno a few days ago. It is, of course, impossible to give you any definite instructions in regard to this movement, and were it not impossible to do so, the Department Commander places too much confidence in your zeal, energy and ability to impose upon you precise orders which might hamper your action when nearly in contact with the enemy." That made good military sense—Custer was an experienced commander who had demonstrated his ability to operate successfully when given *carte blanche*. Nor could Terry anticipate what Custer might encounter, and he wisely gave Custer freedom of movement.

If Terry had concluded his orders with that opening paragraph, there would have been no subsequent controversy. But he went on "to indicate to you [Custer] his [Terry's] own views of what your action should be, and he desires that you conform to them unless you see sufficient reason for departing from them." Once again, the phrase "unless you see sufficient reason for departing from them" gave Custer *carte blanche*, but then Terry added "suggestions" that, read in one way, could be construed as binding orders. Terry wanted Custer to proceed past the point where the trail crossed the Rosebud, continue to move south to the headwaters of the Tongue, and only then turn west toward the Little Bighorn, "feeling constantly however to your left so as to preclude the possibility of the escape of the Indians to the south or southeast by passing around your left flank." Terry also outlined Gibbon's route of march, but nowhere in his orders did he mention co-operation between the two columns.[33]

After the meeting, Custer saw to it that the cavalrymen got ready. Then he dashed off a note to Libbie: "My darling—I have but a few moments to write, as we move at twelve, and I have my hands full of preparations for the scout. . . . Do not be anxious about me. You would be surprised to know how closely I obey your instructions about keeping with the column. I hope to have a good report to send you by the next mail. . . . A success will start us all towards Lincoln. . . .

"I send you an extract from Genl. Terry's official order, knowing how keenly you appreciate words of commendation and confidence in your dear Bo. [Here Custer copied the opening lines of Terry's order.] Your devoted boy Autie."[34]

At noon, June 22, the 7th Cavalry paraded past Terry and Gibbon. As Custer marched away, Gibbon called out to him, "Now, Custer, don't be greedy, but wait for us." Waving his hand gaily, Custer called over his shoulder, "No, I will not."[35] As he rode away, an officer claimed he heard Terry say, "Custer is happy now, off with a roving command of fifteen days. I told him if he found the Indians not to do as Reno did, but if he thought he could whip them to do so."[36]

Custer marched twelve miles up the Rosebud, then made camp. That night, June 22, he called his own council of war for the officers of the 7th. After they settled down, Custer made a speech. "We are now starting on a scout which we all hope will be successful," he began. "I intend to do everything I can to make it both successful and pleasant for everybody. I am certain that if any regiment in the Service can do what is required of us, we can." Success would depend on surprise, and Custer ordered the officers to make certain that no man strayed from the column, that there was no shooting at game, no unnecessary noise, and especially no trumpet calls. He asked for their full co-operation and support.

Lieutenant Edward S. Godfrey, who was present at the meeting and who later became *the* authority on the battle of the Little Bighorn, recorded the aftermath. "This 'talk' of his [Custer's] was considered at the time as something extraordinary for General Custer, for it was not his habit to unbosom himself to his officers. In it he showed concessions and a reliance on others; there was an indefinable something that was *not* Custer. His manner and tone, usually brusque and aggressive, or somewhat curt, was on this occasion conciliating and subdued. There was something akin to an appeal, as if depressed, that made a deep impression on all present. . . . Lieutenant Wallace and myself walked to our bivouac, for some distance in silence, when Wallace remarked: 'Godfrey, I believe General Custer is going to be killed.' 'Why?' I replied, 'what makes you think so?' 'Because,' said he, 'I have never heard Custer talk in that way before.' "[37]

On June 23 and 24 the column marched up the Rosebud, making nearly sixty miles on the two days. Indian signs were everywhere— the grass was close-cropped for miles around, indicating a huge pony herd; there were burned-out campfires here and there; trails leading west, toward the Little Bighorn; the frame of the deserted Sun Dance lodge. The Sioux had left drawings in the sand that told the story of Sitting Bull's vision, which greatly excited the Indian scouts, but when they fearfully told Custer what it meant, he shrugged.[38]

Late on June 24 the column reached the point on the Rosebud at which the Indians had crossed the stream a few days earlier, headed toward the Little Bighorn. The trail was a mile wide, the whole valley so scratched up by thousands of travois poles that it gave the appearance of a freshly plowed field. Even the dullest trooper knew now that there were "heaps and heaps of Injins" ahead.

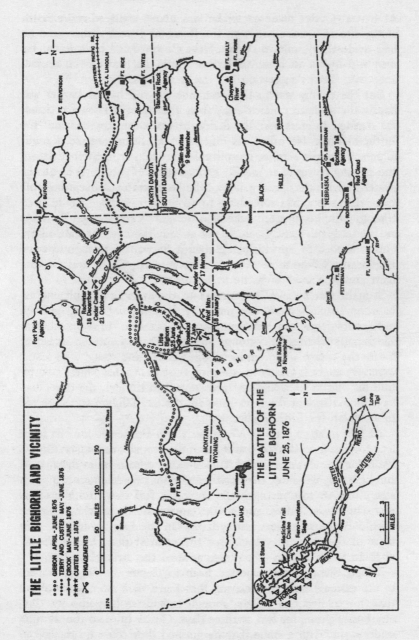

THE LITTLE BIGHORN AND VICINITY

```
0    50   100   150
     MILES
```

ENGAGEMENTS

○○○○ GIBBON APRIL–JUNE 1876
●●●● TERRY AND CUSTER MAY–JUNE 1876
→→→→ CROOK MAY–JUNE 1876
★★★★ CUSTER JUNE 1876
✕ ENGAGEMENTS

1974

Walter T. Vitous

THE BATTLE OF THE
LITTLE BIGHORN
JUNE 25, 1876

```
0   1   2   3
     MILES
```

At 8 P.M. Custer made camp; he was about eighteen miles north of the site of Crook's battle on the Rosebud a week earlier—and he had made thirty miles that day. Here Custer could have rested his men and horses, then moved farther south the next day, in accordance with Terry's suggestion (or was it an order?).

But the enemy was to the west, not the south, and Custer was hardly the soldier to march away from the enemy's known position. He decided to cross over the divide between the Rosebud and the Little Bighorn. He called his officers to him and ordered a night march. This was another inexplicable decision; it further weakened the striking power of an already exhausted 7th Cavalry. Why all the haste? Perhaps the opening date of the Democratic Convention, only three days away, had something to do with it. Kellogg would need time to write his dispatch, take it to the *Far West*, and get the news on the telegraph to St. Louis. It was already the night of June 24–25; Custer needed to fight his battle soon if he wanted to stampede the Democratic Convention. Whatever his reasons, Custer was pushing hard now, the smell of battle in his nostrils.

A night march is, by its very nature, much more difficult and exhausting than the same one made by daylight, but Custer got ten miles out of his men before stopping. At 2 A.M., June 25, he sent Lieutenant Charles A. Varnum and the Crow scouts on ahead to locate the enemy while the men boiled coffee and rested (the scouts were very angry at Custer for allowing the men to make fires). Custer told his officers he would rest the command through the day (June 25), then attack at dawn on June 26, the day Gibbon was expected to arrive on the Little Bighorn.

At first light on June 25 Varnum, Mitch Bouyer (a famous scout lent to Custer by Gibbon), and the Indian scouts were up on Crow's Nest, looking down on the Little Bighorn, fifteen miles distant. As the light strengthened, they saw a sight that made them gasp with astonishment. Intervening bluffs cut off a full view, but the valley was white with lodges, and to the northwest the smoke from the hostile campfires made a murky haze. On the flats beyond the west bank of the river, they could see the greatest pony herd that any of them had ever seen—the pintos covered the earth like a carpet.

When Bloody Knife reported back to Custer, he begged Custer to use extreme caution, declaring that there were more Sioux ahead than the soldiers had bullets, enough Indians to keep the 7th Cavalry busy fighting for two or three days. Custer brushed the warning aside, saying with a smile that he guessed they could do the job in a day. Mitch Bouyer told him that it was the largest encampment ever collected on the northwest Plains and reminded Custer that he, Bouyer, had been in these parts for thirty years. Custer shrugged.

Without finishing his breakfast, Custer, mounted bareback, rode around the camp snapping out orders to his officers. He was wearing a blue-gray flannel shirt, buckskin trousers, long boots, and a regular Army hat over his recently cut hair. He got the column in motion, then rode on ahead to Crow's Nest to see for himself. By the time he arrived, however, a haze had settled over the Little Bighorn and he could see nothing. Custer rode back to the main column. Shortly thereafter, Varnum came in to report that the Indians seemed to be packing up and moving. That was what Custer feared most—that the enemy would get away—and to make matters worse Sioux scouts had been seen riding toward the river. Custer reasoned that they would give the alarm and the Indians would flee. He decided to abandon his plan to rest the men somewhere near the divide, then attack the next morning—instead, he would attack at once.

There was no point to further concealment. He had his bugler sound Officer's Call, the first time a bugle had been blown for two days. Custer informed his officers that "the largest Indian camp on the North American continent is ahead and I am going to attack it." He cautioned them to make certain that each of their men had a full one hundred rounds of ammunition and then he split up the column. Captain Frederick Benteen would take command of three troops, Major Reno another three. One troop would remain with the ammunition train. Custer himself kept five troops.

And away Custer and the 611 men of the 7th Cavalry marched toward the Little Bighorn, where Crazy Horse and 3,000 warriors were waiting. With the difference in weaponry and discipline, the odds were even. This battle would be decided by generalship, not numbers.

CHAPTER TWENTY-TWO

The Battle of the Little Bighorn

"I could whip all the Indians on the Continent with the Seventh Cavalry." George Armstrong Custer, June 25, 1876

"Ho-ka hey! It is a good day to fight! It is a good day to die! Strong hearts, brave hearts, to the front! Weak hearts and cowards to the rear." Crazy Horse, June 25, 1876

The Little Bighorn is a sparklingly delightful stream. Its water is clear, nicely cool in late June, a pleasure to drink. Anywhere from ten to forty yards wide, it has a strong current. Numerous rocks break the flow of the river and cause it to gurgle constantly. The rocks are smooth, the bottom mostly gravel, and the depth seldom over five feet, making it altogether a perfect river for swimming. On the morning of June 25, 1876, hundreds of Sioux and Cheyenne children were bobbing up and down in the Little Bighorn, letting the current carry them along, laughing and splashing, choking when they swallowed too much water. Occasionally a teen-aged girl would cry out to the little ones to be careful, but they paid no attention. Here and there a fisherman tried his luck with a grasshopper for bait. Swallows darted through the surrounding cottonwoods and over the creek— the valley was filled with the birds.

Up on the west bank—and it was a high bank—the children's mothers and fathers went about their business. There was still sufficient grass on the tableland above their camp to feed the ponies for a couple of days, and there was plenty of food in the camp, so the women didn't have any pressing work. Many of them toiled together on hides, chatting about recent events, wondering when the soldiers would come. Some were arguing with their ten-year-olds, telling them they were too young to fight. Most boys of around that age, however, were up on the tableland, keeping watch on the gigantic pony herd. Other women were helping their men prepare for battle. A few just lazed under the abundant cottonwoods, escaping the already hot rays of the morning sun. Black Elk, a brave Sioux warrior, was out with some women gathering wild turnips.

"It seemed that peace and happiness were prevailing all over the world," a Cheyenne warrior later recalled, "and nowhere was any man planning to lift his hand against his fellow man."[1]* Few of the Indians knew much about Custer's approach.

But their leaders knew. The lodges of men like Crazy Horse, Gall and Sitting Bull of the Hunkpapas, Two Moons of the Cheyennes and others became small command posts, with scouts riding in every few minutes to report. The scouts were hanging around Custer's flanks, knew where he was and where he was headed. The only things they didn't know were exactly where, how, and when he would attack the village. But the leaders absolutely expected an attack and even wanted it to come, to fulfill Sitting Bull's vision of soldiers falling into camp. Indeed, on at least two occasions small groups of scouts tried the old decoy trick, hoping to draw Custer into a pell-mell charge into the village. Custer didn't take the bait, although the evidence indicates that the action of the decoys reinforced his *idée fixe* that the Sioux were attempting to escape.

It may be that the single most important fact about the battle of the Little Bighorn was that Custer was doing exactly what the Indians expected and wanted him to do. In any event, as Custer moved to the attack (knowing almost nothing about his enemy's force or position), Crazy Horse stuck to his command post, refusing to commit his men until he knew exactly where, when, and how Custer would make his charge.

Of the four parts of Custer's divided command, Benteen was on the left, Reno in the center, Custer on the right, with the ammunition train following. "You could tell that the plan was to strike the Indian camp at three places," a sergeant in the 7th Cavalry later wrote.[2] About noon, Custer came to the site of a recently abandoned village. One lodge—immortalized today as the Lone Tipi—was still standing, a warrior's body inside—he had just died from wounds re-

---

* In this chapter I shall footnote only quotations. Statements of fact are taken from various sources—the literature on this battle is voluminous—but I have used as a general guide the works of Colonel W. A. Graham, especially *The Custer Myth* (which reprints Godfrey's and Benteen's long accounts, along with those of many other eyewitnesses, red and white), and Edgar I. Stewart's *Custer's Luck*. The serious student who wants to immerse himself in the innumerable controversies about the battle should begin by carefully reading Graham and Stewart about four times through, then go on to the more specialized (and less careful) accounts. One warning—to study this battle is to enter quicksand. Let Graham and Stewart be your guides. Hold to their hands, and abandon them at your peril.

ceived a week earlier on the Rosebud. Custer ordered the tipi burned and evidently decided that the main body of Indians were on the run. The abandoned village had been the site of the full Sitting Bull-Crazy Horse encampment a couple of days earlier, so from the plentiful tracks it was natural for Custer to assume that they had just fled in panic. Bluffs and trees cut off his view of the new campsite.

A scout rode forward to a knoll about fifty yards beyond the tipi, saw great clouds of dust (probably created by the normal activity in the village), and called out, "There go your Indians, running like devils."[3] Custer may have thought, "And there goes the White House with them, if I don't catch them soon." He ordered Benteen to march south, feeling constantly to his left until he reached the Little Bighorn, to make certain that the Indians didn't escape in that direction. He then sent his adjutant, Cooke, to Reno, with verbal orders to "move forward at as rapid a gait as he thought prudent, and charge the village afterward, and the whole outfit would support him."[4]

Custer himself, with his five troops, turned to the north, behind the last line of bluffs (which were thus between him and the camp), with the evident intention of turning the Indians' flank or of preventing their escape down the Little Bighorn. He believed, it appears, that the Indians would fight a rear guard action against Reno while the women and children fled and that Reno's attack would require the warriors' full attention. With the bluff hiding his column from the hostiles, Custer must have thought that his tactics would restore the element of surprise, lost that morning when the Sioux scouts spotted his column, and that he would be able to pitch into the retreating Indians unexpectedly.

Actually, the reverse was true. The hostiles knew all about Custer—but had failed to see Reno break off. Thus Reno's move was the real surprise. Crazy Horse had kept his warriors in hand to meet Custer. Reno crossed the Little Bighorn and came up on the south end of the village. He had open ground in front of him, perfect terrain for a cavalry charge, and his orders were positive and peremptory—charge the enemy. But in sight of the tipis, Reno stopped, dismounted his men, and engaged in some long-range and fruitless firing at the Sioux who were beginning to ride out to meet him.

It was a critical moment. Crazy Horse organized a blocking force —his main concern continued to be Custer's flanking march toward the northern, or lower, end of the village. According to Billy Garnett, who got his information from the Oglalas, "when Reno attacked the village the Indians were almost uncontrollable, so great was their eagerness to press a counterattack, but Crazy Horse rode up and down in front of his men talking calmly to them and telling them to restrain their ardor till the right time."[5] But other Indian accounts suggest that Crazy Horse was still in his lodge when Reno appeared. Short Bull said he and others had Reno's men on the run back across the Little Bighorn when Crazy Horse rode up with his men.

"Too late! You've missed the fight!" Short Bull called out to Crazy Horse.

"Sorry to miss this fight," Crazy Horse laughed. "But there's a good fight coming over the hill. That's where the big fight is going to be. We'll not miss that one." He was not a bit excited, Short Bull said. "He made a joke of it."[6] But Lieutenant William H. Clark, who in 1877 got to know Crazy Horse as well as any white man (see following chapter) and who based his information on interviews with Crazy Horse and other Oglala participants, reported: "Crazy Horse rode with the greatest daring up and down in front of Col. Reno's skirmish line, and as soon as these troops were driven across the river, he went at once to Genl. Custer's front and there became the leading spirit."[7] It is impossible, in short, to make a definitive statement about Crazy Horse's actions versus Reno, in sharp contrast to his abundantly documented activities versus Custer at the other end of the field.

As Reno's men were dismounting, Custer and his staff rode to the top of the bluffs. From that point he could see Reno and a part of the village, although not all of it—the lower, or northern, end being hidden by cottonwood trees. At this moment he must have realized that everything he had done up until now had been based on a faulty assumption. The Indians were not running; indeed, Custer could see normal activity going on in the camp. He had sent Benteen off on a wild goose chase. But he was not discouraged. Reno was— he thought—preparing to charge the upper end of the village. All the warriors would be drawn to Reno's front. Meanwhile, he and his five troops could slip around to the lower end and attack the women and children, causing a general stampede. It would be like the Washita.

"We've caught them napping," Custer called out. Turning in his saddle, he waved his broad-brimmed hat for his men on the east side of the bluff to see, shouting "We've got them!" Riding down to his five companies, he turned to trumpeter John Martini, an Italian immigrant just learning English, and said, "I want you to take a message to Captain Benteen.† Ride as fast as you can, and tell him to hurry.

† Benteen had decided there were no Indians to the south, so on his own he had decided to turn to his right. He joined Reno that afternoon.

Tell him it's a big village, and I want him to be quick, and to bring the ammunition packs." Shifting in his saddle to face his men, Custer called out, "As soon as we get through, we will go back to our station" —that is, Fort Abraham Lincoln.

As Martini prepared to ride off on his mission, Adjutant Cooke stopped the trooper and gave him a written order, scrawled on a notebook pad: "Benteen: Come on. Big village. Be quick. Bring packs. W. W. Cooke. P.S. Bring Packs."[8]

Custer and his five troops rode north, behind the bluffs. On his way to Benteen, Martini passed Boston Custer, who had left the pack train and was going to join his brother. "Where's the general?" Boston snapped. Martini pointed to the north, and Boston put his spurs to his tired horse.

Reno and his men saw Custer wave his hat up on the bluff and thought he was cheering them on. Crazy Horse may have seen Custer too, and it was apparently at this point that he made his own battle plan—i.e., after he knew his enemy's strength, position, and intentions. He would outflank Custer, who was attempting to outflank him. First, however, Reno had to be stopped.

That task proved easy enough. Reno never did attack. The chief reason was that his men were exhausted. It would be impossible to overstate the extent of their weariness, after days of marching with little or no sleep. Sitting Bull expressed it best. "They were brave men," he said, "but they were too tired. When they rode up, their horses were tired and they were tired. When they got off from their horses they could not stand firmly on their feet. They swayed to and fro—so my young men have told me—like the limbs of cypresses in a great wind. Some of them staggered under the weight of their guns."[9]

Reno, having lost one man, ordered a retreat into some cotton-woods along the bank of the Little Bighorn. The Indians did not press him, but they did fire in his direction, and one lucky bullet hit Bloody Knife in the head and splattered his brains all over Reno's face. Reno lost his nerve (remember that he was as exhausted as his men, and a tired commander doesn't think clearly). He ordered a further retreat, back across the Little Bighorn and up into the bluffs, where he could make a defensive stand, and he took off at the head of his men, without making certain that his orders were passed on. It was a rout, not a retreat, and Reno suffered his first serious casualties when his column was getting over the river and up the bluffs. He abandoned sixteen men and one officer in the cottonwoods, but the Indians left them alone and Reno too after he got to the high ground. The Indians had more important business elsewhere; only a few stayed to harass Reno. The whole affair took about thirty minutes.

Custer meanwhile was pushing north, on exhausted horses, hidden by the bluffs. Crazy Horse called to his men, "Ho-ka hey! It is a good day to fight! It is a good day to die! Strong hearts, brave hearts, to the front! Weak hearts and cowards to the rear." He then led them, at a gallop, through the camp, planning to get beyond Custer, ford the Little Bighorn, and hit the 7th Cavalry in the right flank and rear. The Indian force picked up reinforcements as it tore through the camp, until there were as many as one thousand men following Crazy Horse, mainly Oglalas and Cheyennes.

It must have been a sight, that dash through the village on fresh ponies, the animals just as excited as their riders, knocking over tipis, cooking pots, dogs and small children who got in the way, the women screaming out the names of the brave ones. But what was most impressive was that Crazy Horse was getting the warriors to ride *away* from the scene of action, something no one had ever been able to get them to do before.

When Custer reached Medicine Trail Coulee, which cut through the east bank of the river, he must have thought he had reached the lower end of the village. He turned to his left and rode down the coulee, planning to ford the river and attack the hostile rear.‡ But Gall, who had already crossed to the north side of the river, had gathered together some 1,500 Hunkpapas and blocked Custer's path. Custer turned again, to his right, toward the line of bluffs. Gall's warriors pressed him hard, attacking in force.

At this point Custer realized, probably, that he was no longer on the offensive. Suddenly he was in a fight for survival. He had to get to the high ground, dig in, and wait for Benteen (or Gibbon, way to his rear but due the next day) to come to his rescue. The highest ground was in front of him, a hill at the northern end of the bluffs (called Custer Hill today). At the head of his column, he set out for it, Gall and about one thousand warriors pressing him in the rear.

Custer's command got stretched out, Lieutenant Calhoun's company in the rear. Custer was almost on top of the hill. Once there he could set up a defensive perimeter (as Reno had now done four miles to the south) and wait for help. With more than two hundred carbine-carrying troopers, he figured to be able to hold a hilltop in-

‡ All estimates about what Custer did after Martini left him to take orders to Benteen are speculative. There are as many theories as there are accounts of the battle. What follows is my own best guess—but (except for Crazy Horse's actions, which have been authenticated), only a guess.

definitely against almost any force of warriors. He may have realized that although he had lost the victory and thus the presidency, he had not yet lost his command or his life. At that instant, Crazy Horse, who had forded the Little Bighorn beyond Custer's position and come up on the north side of the hill, appeared on its top.

When a group of men on horseback reach the top of a hill after a hard gallop, there is a natural pause; the men want to look around and they pull up, which suits the horses just fine, because they too want to see what's ahead before plunging on. Thus it is likely that when Crazy Horse, his thousand warriors following close behind, reached the top of the hill after a difficult ascent, their horses slightly out of breath and gasping just a little, there was a pause, an instant in which the action was frozen.

What a sight it must have been, especially for George Armstrong Custer, who was—probably—at that instant leading his men toward the spot on which Crazy Horse stood. Behind Crazy Horse, Custer would have seen the thousand warriors, all painted, many with war bonnets, some holding spears high in the air, their glistening points aimed right at Custer. Many braves, as many as one out of five, were brandishing Winchesters or other rifles. Half or more of the Indians held bows and fistfuls of arrows, often with shields in the other hand—they guided their ponies with their knees. The ponies were painted too, with streaks and zigzags and other designs, and with their new coats, sleek sides, and plenty of fat from the spring grass, the animals looked magnificent. They snorted and pranced, caught their second wind, and were ready for battle.

Crazy Horse would have been in front, alone, standing out in that kaleidoscope of shifting color by his apparent plainness. He would have worn only his breechcloth and a single hawk's feather in his hair. Almost surely he had his pebble behind his ear, another under his arm, and had thrown some dust over himself and his pony after painting zigzag marks on his body and some lightning streaks on his pony. He carried his Winchester lightly. His eyes must have sparkled; certainly he must have been proud—of himself, of his warriors, of all the Oglalas, all the Sioux and Cheyennes. Together they had achieved something never before accomplished—an armed mass of Indians, a thousand or more strong, was about to descend from an unexpected direction upon less than 225 regular Army troopers. The warriors had the smell of victory in their nostrils, a smell Custer had known so well, and as Custer also knew, once fighting men begin to smell victory, they are unbeatable.

As at the Yellowstone three years earlier, did Custer and Crazy

Horse see each other? We do not and cannot know. It was certainly possible that they did catch each other's eye, although it is unlikely that they would have recognized one another. Custer might have heard from scouts about the way Crazy Horse dressed for battle, but Crazy Horse could hardly have recognized Custer, whom he knew as "Long Hair," because Custer had cropped his hair for this campaign.

What Crazy Horse saw before him was a long slope with a few more than 200 soldiers on it. With their backs to the top of the hill, they were fighting for their lives, most of them horseless by now, many wounded, hard pressed by Gall's force. The troopers were badly strung out. Hot, tired, dusty, thirsty, afraid, they were slowly working their way up the hill, trying meanwhile to maintain a steady volume of fire in order to hold back Gall's warriors. Just below Crazy Horse§ there was a small knot of men. Tom Custer was there, and Bos, and most of Custer's staff. Custer was at their head, not much more than twenty yards away from Crazy Horse. The officers were making their way to the top, probably looking in that direction, so it is possible that Crazy Horse and Custer looked into each other's eyes.

If so, it was only for an instant. Crazy Horse and his men, making the air fearful with their battle cries, came sweeping down the hill. They crushed everything in their path. They swarmed among Custer's soldiers, killing them with arrows, clubs, lances, and bullets. Gall was simultaneously attacking Calhoun and the troopers on the lower end of the hill. "The country was alive with Indians going in all directions," an Oglala brave later recalled, "like myriads of swallows, yet the great body all the time moving down on Custer." It was almost like hunting buffalo.

Yellow Horse said that "Custer fought and Reno did not; Custer went in to die, and his fighting was superb; I never saw a man fight as Custer did; he was conspicuous in the battle . . . directing his men."[10] An Arapaho brave who was with Crazy Horse said, "Crazy Horse, the Sioux Chief, was the bravest man I ever saw. He rode closest to the soldiers, yelling to his warriors. All the soldiers were shooting at him, but he was never hit."[11]

Two Moons, the Cheyenne leader, recalled that after he topped the hill, following Crazy Horse, "the shooting was quick, quick. Pop—pop—pop very fast. Some of the soldiers were down on their

§ Or so the reported location of the soldiers' bodies on the battlefield two days later led me to believe. This is not conclusive, of course, because the Indians may have moved the bodies after the battle.

knees, some standing. The smoke was like a great cloud, and everywhere the Sioux went the dust rose like smoke. We circled all around them—swirling like water round a stone. We shoot, we ride fast, we shoot again. Soldiers drop, and horses fall on them. Soldiers in line drop, but one man rides up and down the line, all the time shouting. . . . I don't know who he was. He was a brave man."[12]

In twenty minutes, perhaps less, it was over. Custer and his 225 soldiers were dead. Around Custer's body—which lay just short of the crest of the hill he so desperately needed to gain and which Crazy Horse had denied him—lay his closest comrades—Tom and Boston Custer, Autie Reed, Calhoun a little ways off.

There are many versions of Custer's death. The one that sounds most authentic is Sitting Bull's, who freely admitted that he was not there, but who got an immediate after-action report from some young Hunkpapas. Sitting Bull passed the account on to a reporter for the New York *Herald* in 1877.

SITTING BULL: Up there where the last fight took place, where the last stand was made, the Long Hair stood like a sheaf of corn with all the ears fallen around him.
REPORTER: Not wounded?
SITTING BULL: No.
REPORTER: How many stood by him?
SITTING BULL: A few.
REPORTER: When did he fall?
SITTING BULL: He killed a man when he fell. He laughed.
REPORTER: You mean he cried out.
SITTING BULL: No, he laughed. He had fired his last shot.[13]

If his life flashed in front of him, as is sometimes said to happen on the verge of sudden death, no wonder Custer laughed. If he did flash back, he had many achievements to be proud of—his West Point appointment and graduation, his general officer's commission, his string of successful charges in the Civil War, his key role at Appomattox, the Washita, opening the Black Hills—and much to recall of the good life in Washington, New York, on the frontier posts. And of course, most of all, Libbie. He had turned down numerous offers that would have made him a rich man, choosing instead to live the life he loved. He had lived big, thought big, had only big ambitions. He had nothing to regret.

Not even on this last day. The attack had been a gamble, but so had all his attacks. It was a good plan. It could have worked. If only that damn Reno would have charged the camp when he first came upon it! Anyway, one doesn't get to live in the White House without taking some risks. Custer had gambled all his life, and although he usually lost in card games or horse races, he always won on the battlefield. Like all confirmed gamblers, however, he knew that someday he would have to lose. At least, when he lost, all the chips were on the table. It was a winner-take-all game, and Custer would have played it again if given the chance.

He laughed. Then he died.

The world hardly needs another analysis of the battle of the Little Bighorn, but the temptation to comment is too strong to resist. Custer's mistakes, in order of importance, were as follows:

First, he refused to accept Terry's offer of four troops of the 2nd Cavalry. If Reno had had two more troops with him, he might have had sufficient momentum to make a successful charge when he first came upon the Sioux camp. Had Custer had two more troops with him, he might have made it up the hill. But he wanted all the glory for the 7th Cavalry, and it must be said that he managed to make it for generations the most famous outfit in the history of the United States Army.

Second, Custer badly underestimated his enemy, not so much in terms of numbers (where his guess of 1,500 was not a fatal underestimate) as in terms of fighting capability, where he was disastrously wrong. Splitting his force four ways was thus a major error. The point is this: Custer had more than six hundred men. He often boasted that with that force he could whip all the Indians "in the Northwest," and he wasn't far wrong. But he never got a chance to prove it, because of his own overconfidence and inept tactics. Had he kept the regiment together he would have faced three thousand warriors with six hundred-plus well-armed and disciplined troopers, and under those circumstances he should have won. But because he divided his column, and because Crazy Horse and Gall kept their forces close together, Custer faced 2,500 warriors with 225 soldiers. In the first case, the odds would have been five to one against him; in the second case, the odds were ten to one, the crucial difference.

Custer's third mistake was assuming that his men could do what he could do; to put it another way, he attacked too soon. He should have spent June 25 resting, then attacked the next day, when Gibbon could have, on urgent request, reinforced him. All Indian accounts agree that Custer's men and horses, like Reno's, were so exhausted that their legs trembled. It was a hot day, which further cut the troopers' efficiency. A fourth mistake was to commit his command when he did not know his enemies' position, strength, or location. He also lost the element of surprise—his enemies knew more about where he was, in what strength, and with what intentions, than he knew about them. Yet he attacked.

Finally, when Custer lost the initiative, he failed to gain the high ground and dig in, although here one should perhaps blame Custer less and praise Crazy Horse more.

How did Crazy Horse know to swing around the flank? This was not a simple circling maneuver of a small unit caught on the open prairie; it was an intricate series of movements over difficult terrain, planned in advance, requiring exact timing. Crazy Horse had learned the lesson from the Wagon Box Fight of 1867, when he had led an attack up a ravine with all the warriors crowded in on each other, masking their own fire. This time he realized that the way to use his manpower effectively was to spread it out. He had learned, in addition, one of the most basic combat lessons—never attack your enemy directly when you can outflank him. In an Indian-versus-Indian battle, flanking was not necessary, in fact, it did not fit into the scheme of things, as the object in an Indian fight was to win honors, not kill enemies. But if you are involved in an Indian-versus-white soldier fight, Crazy Horse had learned, you damn well better start maneuvering your warriors and striking the flanks. In military affairs it is exceedingly difficult to outflank a flanking force, but when it is achieved it is usually spectacularly successful.

It is even possible to speculate (I would not want to push this too far, but much of the fun of studying this battle is the free rein it gives to the imagination) that if Crazy Horse had not swung around Custer's flank and hit him from an unexpected direction, the 7th Cavalry could have survived the battle of the Little Bighorn. With only enemies in the front to worry about, it would seem that it should have been possible for Custer to make it to the top of the hill, not just near its crest where Crazy Horse caught him. Once on top Custer could have held the high ground, and although the Indians would have attacked in great numbers, Custer should have been able to hold them off. Custer might have been able to rally his troopers and hold Custer Hill long enough to be rescued by Benteen and Reno or by Gibbon. Doubtful, certainly, but it was his best chance, what he almost surely must have had in mind.

Crazy Horse ruined it all. At the supreme moment of his career, Crazy Horse took in the situation with a glance, then acted with great decisiveness. He fought with his usual reckless bravery on Custer Hill, providing as always an example for the other warriors to admire, draw courage from, and emulate, but his real contribution to this greatest of all Indian victories was mental, not physical. For the first time in his life, Crazy Horse's presence was decisive on the battlefield not because of his courage, but because of his brain. But one fed on the other. His outstanding generalship had brought him at the head of a ferocious body of warriors to the critical point at the critical moment. Then with his courage he took advantage of the situation to sweep down on Custer and stamp his name, and that of Custer, indelibly on the pages of the nation's history.

There is some intriguing postfight speculation about this battle. What if Reno had charged, as Custer ordered and expected? He might have put the Indians on the run but that seems unlikely; more probably he would have pinned down Crazy Horse's blocking force and that could have been important. But Crazy Horse had planned for and expected just such a maneuver (the soldiers always tried to hit from at least two directions at once, he had learned through experience). He still, probably, could have outflanked Custer.

What if Custer had followed Reno and supported his attack? Certainly that would have given him a better chance, but his horses and men just didn't have sufficient energy to press home a charge. With a rested command, it might have worked.

What if Benteen had obeyed orders and come quick with the packs?|| That would have helped only if Custer had gained the high ground. As it was, Crazy Horse had rubbed Custer out long before Benteen could have gotten there (if he ever could have made it). As to the charges that Benteen and Reno, who each hated Custer, deliberately abandoned him, such charges are a wholly unjustified slur on them and on the officer corps of the United States Army. These men were professional soldiers who did their best under trying conditions. Of course they made mistakes—who hasn't in a combat situation?—but they were neither cowards nor traitors to their commander. They were hot, sweaty, hungry, thirsty, absolutely spent men, whose mistakes were in large measure a result of the positions Custer had placed them in. They thought (and so did their men) that Custer had abandoned *them*, but they did not abandon him.

|| Benteen did try, after joining Reno, to get through to Custer, but Gall's forces blocked his way and he returned to Reno Hill.

The conclusion is inescapable. At the Little Bighorn, Custer was not only outnumbered; he was also outgeneraled.

All that followed the battle on Custer Hill was anticlimax. The Indians besieged Reno and Benteen, but as always they lacked the killer instinct. Enough had been done. The next day, when Sioux scouts reported to Crazy Horse Gibbon's advance from the north, the great camp—possibly the largest Indian village ever seen in the Great Plains—retired to the south, toward the Bighorn Mountains.

The battle of the Little Bighorn had been a supreme moment in the life of the Sioux nation. Never before had the Sioux people been so united, nor would they be again. Never before had the Sioux warriors been so ably led, nor would they be again.

As the Sioux nation dispersed, Crazy Horse counted up the losses. Forty men dead, or thereabouts. He mourned for them, of course, but not too deeply, because it had been a good day to die.

CHAPTER TWENTY-THREE

The Death of Crazy Horse

"Stab the son-of-a-bitch! Stab the son-of-a-bitch!"
> The Officer of the Day at Camp Robinson,
> Nebraska, September 6, 1877

"Let me go, my friends. You have got me hurt enough."
> Crazy Horse, September 6, 1877

June 25, 1876, had been a good day to die, a better one than Crazy Horse got for himself, and thereby hangs a tale.

Following the battle, the Indians moved south, toward the Bighorn Mountains in Wyoming. After traveling fifteen miles or so, the great camp broke up, Sitting Bull and the Hunkpapas going to the southwest, Crazy Horse with the Oglalas and Cheyennes heading southeast.* The hostiles burned the grass behind them, making cavalry pursuit impossible, and the country was filled with smoke. Soon the Cheyennes left Crazy Horse's camp, and many of the agency Indians did too, as the Sioux continued to scatter. The agency warriors had got what they wanted, a big fight with lots of honors won and plunder captured, and they were ready to go back to the reservation. Many of the Indians were also confident about their future—they figured that such a crushing defeat would teach the Army a lesson it wouldn't soon forget, so that they would be free to hunt the Powder River country once more in their small bands, unmolested. Perhaps there would be a little fighting again next summer, but for now the war was in the bag.

The Army, meanwhile, was refitting before coming after Crazy

* In Chapter 23 I have abandoned the use of specific footnotes altogether. Most of the material in this chapter is drawn from interviews with eyewitness survivors, red and white, primarily in the Eleanor Hinman interviews and the Ricker tablets at the Nebraska State Historical Society, and in various issues of the *Nebraska History Magazine*. To credit each informant properly I would have to have a footnote at the end of almost every sentence. Anyone interested in going deeper into these sources should consult the original interviews, which can be identified from the context.

Horse. Following the Custer disaster, it got everything it wanted. Congress promptly voted funds to build two forts along the Yellowstone, forts that Sheridan had been asking for since 1873. Some 2,500 new recruits were authorized and sent to the Sioux country to reinforce Generals Terry and Crook. Congress took control of the agencies out of the hands of the Indian Bureau and gave it to the Army. Despite all this effort, Crook stayed on the Powder River all through the rest of June and July, while Terry stayed in camp on the Yellowstone. Neither general would move until his command had been doubled in size by reinforcements, saying it would be unsafe to venture into Sioux territory without at least two thousand soldiers.

The hostiles spent the month of July dancing, feasting, going into the Bighorns for lodge poles and deer, coming back to the prairie, and again dancing and feasting. Meanwhile, the same Army officers who for years had been hoping for orders to march against the Sioux and who bragged that they would give the hostiles a five- or even ten-to-one superiority and still whip them, sat where they were. Without overwhelming numerical superiority they dared not enter Sioux territory. The absence of marching troopers in the Powder River country helped convince the warriors that they had won a decisive victory.

But Crazy Horse seems to have realized that he had won a battle, not a campaign. White soldiers were still surrounding the Indians' only remaining hunting grounds, and with so few warriors—Crazy Horse had less than six hundred with him now—he could do nothing about that. Crazy Horse did, however, try to follow up his victory by harassing the white miners in the Black Hills in South Dakota. In early August he moved east from the Bighorns, across the hot, dusty prairie of eastern Wyoming, to attack the intruders in *Pa Sapa*, still legally Sioux territory. Once on the edge of the Hills, camping near Bear Butte, Crazy Horse led small war parties against the miners' camps—small because most of the warriors were tired of fighting. Sometimes Crazy Horse went out on his own. Once he led back into the village some captured mules, loaded with goods; another time he brought home two sacks of raisins, which he had not tasted since he was a child living with Old Smoke along the Holy Road. Crazy Horse called the children of his village to him and held the sack open for them as they grabbed handfuls of raisins.

He Dog strongly opposed Crazy Horse's lone forays. "My friend," he admonished, "you are past the foolish years of the wild young warrior; you belong to the people now and must think of them, not give them such uneasiness." Still Crazy Horse persisted in his raids.

The United States Army, meanwhile, had to do something, and in August it tried. Crook, with two thousand men, double the number he had in his battle with Crazy Horse two months before on the Rosebud, marched overland to the headwaters of that river. Terry, with two thousand reinforcements, moved up the Rosebud. The two forces blundered into each other along the river, then decided that even two thousand men apiece was no guarantee of safety while Sitting Bull and Crazy Horse were loose, and they joined forces. They then made some half-hearted attempts to follow Crazy Horse's trail to Bear Butte near the Black Hills but soon gave it up, Terry returning to the Yellowstone. Crook got lost north of the Hills, his men nearly starved, and he was soon engaged in a struggle against the elements for survival. On September 7 he sent Colonel Anson Mills and 150 men and horses (the other horses had been eaten) on an expedition to the town of Deadwood in the northern Black Hills for supplies. At dawn on September 9, 1876, near Slim Buttes, Mills discovered a Sioux camp of thirty-seven lodges, agency Indians who had left the Crazy Horse people the previous day and were making their way back to the reservation in Nebraska. Mills attacked immediately and drove the occupants of the village to the nearby bluffs. As the starving soldiers gorged themselves on buffalo meat, the Brulés sent runners to fetch Crazy Horse. He got to the scene about noon, with two hundred warriors, and attacked Mills. But the soldiers were well armed and held their ground until late afternoon, when Crook came up with 1,850 more men. Crazy Horse withdrew. The next day he kept up a harassing action against Crook's rear guard, while Crook—after burning the village—made for Deadwood.

The great Army campaign of 1876 was over. Crook and Custer had been defeated, Terry and Gibbon had yet to see an Indian, Crazy Horse and Sitting Bull held the field and thought they had won. But, as Slim Buttes revealed, the future for the Sioux did not look good. The Indian force dwindled steadily while the Army's columns grew in size; at Slim Buttes the soldiers outnumbered the warriors, as would be the case from that time onward.

While Crazy Horse was trying to regain *Pa Sapa*, the United States Government stole the Black Hills. The United States had been unwilling to pay the seller's price for the Hills and unable to defeat the Sioux in war, so it decided to use its ultimate weapon, economic coercion. On August 15, 1876, Congress passed the Sioux appropriation bill. It specified that further provisions would be given the Sioux only if and when the Indians gave up the Black Hills and the Powder River and Bighorn country and removed themselves to an agency on the Missouri River in central Dakota or to Oklahoma. In other words, its Army having lost its biggest battle between Appomattox and San Juan Hill, the government was now demanding unconditional surrender of the Sioux and threatened starvation if the demand was not met!

The inevitable commission sent out to Red Cloud Agency to get the chiefs to sign a treaty managed the impossible—it dragged the honor of the United States even deeper into the mud. Arriving with remarkable haste (appointed by President Grant on August 24, they held their first council at Red Cloud Agency on September 8), the commissioners consistently lied to the chiefs, except about one thing —if Red Cloud, Spotted Tail, and the others did not sign, their people would starve. Young Man Afraid said he was raised in this country and did not want to leave it. He was willing to sell the Hills, if necessary, but only for a big price and only after he had met with the Great White Father. The chiefs then left the council, but they were back on September 19, worn out from arguing among themselves, their people pitiful in their hunger. They all signed the treaty, although only after each one made a speech (Fire Thunder held his blanket to his eyes and made his mark on the treaty blindfolded). Young Man Afraid said, "I give notice it will take me a long time to learn to work, and I expect the President will feed me for a hundred years, and perhaps a great deal longer." After the signing, all the agency Indians were disarmed and dehorsed.

Pa Sapa was gone, even while Crazy Horse continued to fight for it. The Powder River was gone, and the Tongue, and the Rosebud, and the Yellowstone, and the Little Bighorn—all signed over to the whites. Soon even Red Cloud's and Spotted Tail's agencies would be gone, with the Sioux moved back to the Missouri River, which they had crossed four generations earlier. The people and government of the United States had cast their eyes over the Sioux country and found it good. Now it was theirs, won not on the field of battle but in the counting house. Crazy Horse and Sitting Bull had suddenly become aliens, with no right to be where they were.

By late September, Sitting Bull was being chased all over Montana by Colonel (later General) Nelson A. Miles and a force of five hundred infantry and artillery. Miles had built a fort on the Yellowstone at the mouth of the Tongue River, which he used as a supply base. Sitting Bull grew impatient at all the fuss and dictated a letter to a half-breed for Miles. He left it stuck on a stick on the prairie, where Miles found it. The letter read:

> I want to know what you are doing traveling this road. You scare all the buffalo away. I want to hunt in this place. I want you to turn back from here. If you don't I'll fight you again. I want you to leave what you have got here and turn back from here.
>
> I am your friend
Sitting Bull
>
> P.S. I mean all of the rations you have got and all of your powder.

Miles pushed on, fought a couple of skirmishes with Sitting Bull's people, and forced them to scatter.

Crook, meanwhile, was reorganizing to come after Crazy Horse, who had moved to the upper Tongue. "Three Stars," as the hostiles called Crook, was furious. He Dog had gotten away from him in March, Crazy Horse had beaten him in June, he had been sitting on his duff while Custer was wiped out, he had chased Indians all through August without catching any, and when he had finally pinned some down at Slim Buttes, it was only to have them get away. Crook needed to take out his frustrations on someone, and Red Cloud was at hand. Storming into Camp Robinson on the Red Cloud Agency, Crook announced that Red Cloud was deposed from the leadership for refusing to move to the Missouri River; Spotted Tail was now chief of all the agency Sioux.

Crook had yet to capture a single Sioux, but he was a master at ordering prisoners around with a lordly wave of his hand. He told the Red Cloud Indians that all warriors would have to sign on as scouts and help fight Crazy Horse. When Spotted Tail protested, Crook thundered that the government was feeding these lazy bastard braves and they could damn well get off their asses and start working for a living. (Crook's pretense that the warriors lived on the dole was a shocking travesty of the facts. These Sioux had just signed over lands worth their keep for one hundred years or more, and got nothing in return.) Still the chiefs opposed him, but by promising to give each scout a gun and a horse, Crook got sixty Sioux to join up. One at least had a personal motive—No Water, Black Buffalo

Woman's jealous husband, was one of the first to sign on to go looking for Crazy Horse.

No expense was spared in mounting Crook's winter campaign of 1876–77. Each soldier got a buffalo robe, fur mittens and hats, buffalo-hide overshoes, extra pairs of long johns, and so on. Crook had 2,200 soldiers, 60 Sioux scouts, and 350 Shoshonis and Crows. Moving up the old Bozeman Trail from Fort Fetterman, Crook's scouts discovered Dull Knife's and Little Wolf's Cheyenne village at the base of the Bighorn Mountains. The inevitable attack came at dawn on November 25, 1876. The Cheyennes were taken by complete surprise (as Mari Sandoz remarks, if only these Cheyennes could have watched for soldiers the way they could fight them). The Cheyennes fought back—it was rather like the Washita—but Crook was far too strong. Actually, the Indian scouts seem to have done most of Crook's fighting. The Cheyennes lost forty men, women, and children, their ponies, and the village.

Naked on the prairie, the Cheyennes slowly trudged northeast, looking for Crazy Horse, who was back in the Powder River country. The night after the battle the temperature plummeted to −30° F. Eleven babies froze to death in their mothers' arms. For two weeks the Cheyennes plunged through the snow, toward where they hoped Crazy Horse was camped. Occasionally a warrior managed to bring down a buffalo, and the mothers wrapped their babies in green hides to protect them from the cold.

Early in December the Cheyennes found Crazy Horse, and he took them in. The Oglalas shared what little they had; as Billy Garnett put it, "the Indians are a great people in such respects; their natural liberality is almost unbounded." Or, as Short Bull said more modestly, "We helped the Cheyennes the best we could. We hadn't much ourselves." At least the starving, freezing Cheyennes could sit by a fire, under shelter, and chew on some dried buffalo meat.

In mid-December, shortly after the Cheyennes found him, Crazy Horse decided to give up. The buffalo were too scarce to replenish the losses the Cheyennes had suffered. The children were coughing, the women's ribs showing, the old men downcast. His young men were short on guns and shorter on ammunition. He had only five hundred or so warriors left. His own wife, Black Shawl, had tuberculosis. His responsibility was to his people, not to his own reputation. It was time to surrender.

Colonel Miles, from his fort on the Tongue River, had sent out several runners to ask Crazy Horse to come in, promising him fair treatment. Around Christmas, Crazy Horse led his people down the

Tongue. When almost within sight of the fort, he stopped the moving column and made camp. Then he sent eight men on ponies ahead, with a white flag and a string of American horses stolen from the fort the preceding month. Miles' Crow scouts saw the peace delegation first. Whooping and hollering, the Crows sprang to their ponies and rode down on the Oglalas before Miles could stop them. They killed five Sioux. Miles, furious, took away the Crows' horses and sent them, along with some tobacco and an apology for the mistake, to Crazy Horse as a gift. But he refused it. With the other warriors, he turned away from the fort.

"So the men rode back to their people," Mari Sandoz writes, "waiting not far away for the good news of peace. And when Black Shawl saw the face of her man she went silently to strike her lodge for more wandering through the snow, chopping cottonwood for the horses, the men hunting buffalo for the kettle, everybody ready night or day to run from the horse soldiers brought against them by their own people."

It was a terribly cold winter, the wind howling through Montana, piling up immense drifts. The hunting was poor, the people hungry. A small group of families tried to break away, to go into Red Cloud Agency and surrender. Crazy Horse would not allow it. He called for the *akicita* and had the warriors break up the lodge poles of the runaways and shoot their ponies. The next night, two or three days before New Year's Eve, more messengers arrived, some from Miles, others from Crook at Red Cloud Agency. They said to come on in and be fed and get warm. Many wanted to go, but Crazy Horse declared that all deserters would be followed and punished. Nevertheless, the next morning some thirteen families started out for the agency. "We got quite a ways," one of them later recalled, "supposing we had got quite away when all at once Crazy Horse appeared with a good many warriors who shot our horses, took our guns and knives and all our powder, and then told us if we want to go to the whites to go on." They all turned back.

The whole sad business must have caused Crazy Horse great pain. It was a very un-Indianlike thing for him to do, forcing people to stay with him in a situation of extreme danger (Miles had been seen marching from his fort on the Tongue toward the village). No Sioux had ever done anything remotely like it before, and Crazy Horse wasn't even a real chief, not like Bull Bear or Old Smoke or Old Man Afraid. His motivation may have been simple—he evidently believed that anyone from his band who went to an agency would be shot, as his peace envoys to Miles had been shot. Further, he couldn't afford any deserters, not with Miles coming. The women and children could hardly make it into the agency alone, so they would have to stay where they were, all of them, together. But if the motivation is simple, Crazy Horse's feelings must have been complex, as, like Custer in Kansas, he forced deserters back onto the firing line.

On New Year's Day 1877 Miles found Crazy Horse on the Powder River. He attacked at dawn, with infantry and artillery. Crazy Horse fought a rear-guard action while the women packed what they could and fled. Miles followed with bulldog tenacity, attacking again and again through the entire week. Casualties were light, but losses in food and equipment devastating. Crazy Horse's people were eating their horses now, and some of the children had frozen limbs.

Although Crazy Horse and his two thousand or so Indians, mainly women and children, were capable of staying out on the Powder River through the winter, Miles and his soldiers could not cope with the weather, and after a fight on January 8 Miles called off the campaign. He was convinced that Crazy Horse was finished, that he would surrender in a couple of days or starve. Miles himself had to limp back to the warmth and security of his fort. Crazy Horse found a small buffalo herd and kept going, but he was a defeated man now, and he knew it. He no longer had the heart or the energy to stop deserters—he was tired of killing and running—and one by one little groups broke away and made their way to the agency.

The commanders of the various Army forts, meanwhile, kept sending runners to get Crazy Horse to come in. From the flood of telegrams exchanged between the forts, one might have supposed it was 1865 and that the officers were negotiating over Lee's surrender of the Army of Northern Virginia. Crazy Horse will come in, one would say. Then, Crazy Horse isn't coming in. He is. He isn't. On and on it went, generating excitement and tension. A typical Crook-to-Sheridan telegram read: "There is some little difference of opinion here as to whether Crazy Horse will come in or not. I have sent runners to learn positively and to report back here with the least possible delay." Miles was also sending out runners, asking Crazy Horse to surrender to him on the Yellowstone—there was a tug of war between the two officers for the honor of capturing Crazy Horse.

Sitting Bull, meanwhile, paid a visit to Crazy Horse to urge him to join the Hunkpapas in a flight to Grandmother's Land—Canada— where the red coats would treat them with kindness and respect and allow them to live the free, wild life. Crazy Horse must have been tempted, but in the end he said no. His people were coughing already and it was too cold in Canada. He told Sitting Bull that he was staying where he was, in a sheltered valley where there was a little hunting, until spring, when he intended to surrender. Crazy Horse was sure he was safe for the remainder of the winter, because Miles wouldn't dare venture out in such weather. Sitting Bull said Crazy Horse was a fool and left.

During this winter, Crazy Horse often went out alone, to hunt or to think. The others worried about him. The elder Black Elk, father of the holy man-author, found Crazy Horse one day, alone on a little hill. When Crazy Horse saw the concern in Black Elk's face, he said: "Uncle, you notice the way I act, but do not worry. There are caves and holes for me to live in, and perhaps out here the powers will help me. The time is short, and I must plan for the good of my people."

In midwinter, Crook persuaded Spotted Tail to go to Crazy Horse to see what he could do. Crazy Horse, Crook hoped, would listen to Spotted Tail. Crook was so anxious to steal Crazy Horse from Miles that he authorized Spotted Tail to make a series of promises, none of which Crook was in a position to fulfill. Crook said that if Crazy Horse would surrender to him at Camp Robinson on the Red Cloud Agency, Crazy Horse could have his own agency in the Powder River country. Further, Crook would see to it that the Red Cloud and Spotted Tail Indians would not be forced to make the hated and dreaded move to the Missouri. This last point put great pressure on Crazy Horse to surrender and come in, because it linked the fate of the Red Cloud Oglalas and the Spotted Tail Brulés with Crazy Horse's actions.

Spotted Tail, accompanied by two hundred fifty Brulé warriors, started out for the Powder on February 15, 1877. It was a long and hazardous journey—it is instructive to recall that no Army column, no matter how well equipped, and even if commanded by Custer himself, could possibly have made the trip. Spotted Tail found Touch-the-Clouds and his Miniconjous on the Little Missouri, north of the Black Hills, and they agreed to come in as soon as the weather permitted. Spotted Tail then moved west. He found the Crazy Horse camp on the Powder, but Crazy Horse was out alone on a hunt, whether because he wanted to avoid Spotted Tail or by accident is not clear (Spotted Tail thought he had been deliberately insulted by his nephew). Spotted Tail sent some scouts out to find Crazy Horse, but they could not locate him. Worm, Crazy Horse's father, meanwhile told Spotted Tail that his son had left a message saying that he shook hands with his uncle through his father and that he would bring his camp of Cheyennes and Oglalas, about four hundred lodges now, into Red Cloud Agency as soon as weather permitted. In early April, Spotted Tail returned to General Crook with this good news.

By this time the agencies seethed with political plots and intrigues. So it has always been with a conquered people—some do their best for all the people in a bad situation, while others try to advance themselves. The conquered split into factions and contend among themselves for the petty favors of their oppressors. But except for the headman of the oppressors, no one has any real power.

Red Cloud was jealous of Spotted Tail, and Lieutenant William H. Clark, the military head of Red Cloud Agency (which was administered separately from Camp Robinson), was jealous of Crook. In addition, Clark wanted Red Cloud reinstated as head of the Oglalas, so that his agency would be as important as Spotted Tail's. So, when Spotted Tail came back to Crook with the great news that he had convinced Crazy Horse to surrender, Clark and Red Cloud were furious. They thought the honor of bringing in Crazy Horse should have been theirs. Clark called Red Cloud to his office, where he reviewed events since Crook had stripped Red Cloud of his chieftainship. Clark then said, "Now, I want you to go out and bring Crazy Horse in . . . I don't want Spotted Tail to get ahead of you." Clark added that after Crazy Horse came in, both chiefs would make the trip to Washington to consult with the Great White Father about their new agency. The Army wanted Crazy Horse in the delegation, to prove to the Great White Father and to the American public that it really had won the Sioux war. If Red Cloud would bring in Crazy Horse for him, Clark said, "I will recognize you as the highest officer among the chiefs; so that you can have control of your people. I will assist you with all the rations you think you will need." This last was the key—the whites distributed rations via the chiefs, and the chief who controlled the rations was, without question, the big chief. Spotted Tail had stolen Crazy Horse from Miles for Crook; now Red Cloud was to steal Crazy Horse from Spotted Tail for Clark.

Red Cloud was well pleased. Clark let him take one hundred men and lots of food and other presents, and he set off to escort Crazy Horse in. By April 27 Red Cloud had found Crazy Horse and his people already on their way to his agency. They were moving slowly because of the condition of their ponies, Red Cloud reported to Clark by runner, but they would be in within ten days. The Cheyennes under Two Moons, Ice, and Little Wolf were also coming in by a different route. They surrendered, too, in late April—109 families of Cheyennes, a total of 524 people (about 150 warriors) and 600 ponies. That made a total of 752 Cheyennes who had come in since March 1, plus 243 Sioux from scattered bands, all formerly members of the Crazy Horse camp.

Red Cloud fed the Crazy Horse people with the agency rations he had brought with him and then told them, "All is well, have no fear, come on in." Crazy Horse spread his blanket for Red Cloud to sit on and gave him his shirt, as a signal that he was surrendering to Red Cloud. It must have been a poignant moment. Together Red Cloud and Crazy Horse had planned the defeat of Fetterman eleven years before; together for three years they had kept up the pressure on Fort Phil Kearny, eventually winning what seemed to them to be a decisive campaign. But then the paths of these comrades-in-arms had split, and now the once mighty Red Cloud was a lackey for the whites, eager to do their bidding, and Crazy Horse was his prisoner. One wonders if Red Cloud, who had not seen Crazy Horse since the Fort Phil Kearny days a decade earlier, asked Crazy Horse why he stayed out so long and brought so much trouble down on the Oglalas. If he did, Crazy Horse may have responded with a question of his own: Why did Red Cloud give up so easily?

When Clark heard from Red Cloud that Crazy Horse was coming in, he dispatched Lieutenant William Rosecrans of the 4th Cavalry, with Billy Garnett as interpreter, fifty Indian scouts, and ten wagonloads of rations plus one hundred cattle. Rosecrans met the Red Cloud-Crazy Horse group on the Laramie-Black Hills stage line. American Horse, an Oglala elder, led the scouts and, as Garnett later put it, "true to his instincts as ever to help himself, Chief American Horse posed his scouts in line in front of all the others and had them sitting down facing the Indians coming in from the north." Rosecrans did not understand, but the Sioux custom compelled the Crazy Horse people to give a pony to each of the scouts. (The irony was that though Crazy Horse was surrendering for the good of his people, they were better off, at least in ponies, than the agency Indians, whose ponies Crook had taken. Although they had from time to time eaten horseflesh to survive that winter, the Crazy Horse people still had 2,500 ponies.) Then Rosecrans shook hands with Crazy Horse, the first white man to do so. The Crazy Horse people made camp and rested and feasted for three days before taking up their final march.

On May 6, 1877, on a flat two miles north of Camp Robinson, Lieutenant Clark and an escort met the column. Crazy Horse and his headmen sat in a row and motioned for Clark to come forward and shake hands. Crazy Horse used his left hand, telling Clark, "Friend, I shake with this hand because my heart is on this side; the right hand does all manner of wickedness; I want this peace to last forever." Crazy Horse had never had a war bonnet, so he could not present one to Clark as a token of surrender; He Dog stepped forward and put his bonnet on Clark's head and his shirt on Clark's back, and he gave the lieutenant his pipe.

Then began the march to the fort itself. Crazy Horse and the chiefs led the way, most wearing their war bonnets, all carrying their arms. Their ponies and their bodies were painted for war. Crazy Horse had the single hawk's feather in his hair, his brown, fur-wrapped braids falling across his plain buckskin shirt. His Winchester rested easily across his lap. He Dog was on one side of Crazy Horse, Little Big Man on the other. Behind them came the warriors in a tight military formation. Then came the women and children. Altogether the column stretched out for two miles.

When they came within sight of Camp Robinson, the chiefs began to sing, the warriors and then the women and children taking it up, filling the White River Valley with their song. Thousands of agency Indians lined their route, and they too began to sing and to cheer for Crazy Horse. One of the watching Army officers put down his binoculars and complained to those around him, "By God, this is a triumphal march, not a surrender."

It must have been at this moment that the officers, and Red Cloud, knew that although Crazy Horse was captured, their troubles were far from over. Suddenly they realized that Crazy Horse was a hero, the greatest hero of them all, idolized by nearly every Indian on the agency. He might very well upset the cozy relationships that existed between Red Cloud and the military; he certainly would be a rival for leadership.

Clark had Crazy Horse move to an area about a mile south of Camp Robinson, then disarmed and dehorsed his people. Crazy Horse surrendered about three hundred families, totaling 889 Oglalas (250 warriors). Between them, the warriors had forty-six breech-loaders (an eloquent commentary on the Army's claim that at the Little Bighorn the Indians were better armed than Custer's men), thirty-five muzzle-loaders and thirty-three revolvers.

After all the ponies were taken, the arms collected, and the people counted, Clark sat down with Billy Garnett and Crazy Horse for a talk. Crazy Horse said he wanted his promised Powder River Agency set up right away. "There is a creek over there they call

Beaver Creek," he said, referring to a site near present-day Gillette, Wyoming. "There is a big flat west of the headwaters of Beaver Creek. I want my agency put right in the middle of that flat." The grass was good there, and some buffalo were still in the area. Clark said all that could be decided later—right now he wanted Crazy Horse to go to Washington to meet the Great White Father. Crazy Horse responded that if he couldn't have Beaver Creek, there was another site near the Bighorns (present-day Sheridan, Wyoming) that would do. Clark replied that there would be no agency for Crazy Horse before he went to Washington—until then he would stay where he was and take orders from Red Cloud. Crazy Horse said he would go to Washington *after* he had his own agency in his own country, as Crook had said he could if he would surrender. Clark wouldn't give in—go to Washington, he said with some heat, and then get your agency. This was the first in a series of broken promises. For Crazy Horse was now a prisoner, and prisoners have no rights.

The day before Crazy Horse surrendered, Sitting Bull made it to Canada. At dawn the day after Crazy Horse's surrender, Miles attacked the only hostiles still out, a small camp of Miniconjous, under Lame Deer, near the Tongue River. Miles inflicted a crushing defeat. There were no more Sioux in the Powder River country. The Great Sioux War was over.

And now Crazy Horse was an agency Indian. Deprived of his horse and gun, he no longer was his own man. His wanderings across the Plains, which had taken him five hundred miles and more in every direction from his birthplace at Bear Butte, were over. He was dependent on others for his food, his clothing, his shelter.

All in all, he handled the situation well, his natural dignity forcing his jailers to respect and even stand in awe of him. He and his people ate beef now,* and beans and flour, instead of buffalo; they lived under canvas instead of skins; the women wore cloth dresses instead of buckskin; but throughout his four months at the agency Crazy Horse remained what he had always been, a man who asked no favors of anyone and who answered to no one but himself.

The Army officers were, naturally, fascinated by the warrior who had defeated Fetterman, Crook, and Custer, and they flocked to his lodge, with Billy Garnett along to interpret. Crazy Horse didn't say much, but he impressed most of the officers deeply. He fit their image of what an Indian should be like, especially when contrasted with

* Clark reported on August 1, 1877, that "the Indians, especially the northern fellows, seem to be ravenous for meat, really suffering from the want of it."

Red Cloud, Spotted Tail, and their partisans, who were always engaged in little plots and intrigues for preference and advancement.

One officer reported on a visit he made to Crazy Horse's lodge, with Frank Grouard along to interpret. "Crazy Horse remained seated on the ground, but when Frank called his name in Dakota, he looked up, arose, and gave me a hearty grasp of his hand. I saw before me a man who looked quite young, not over thirty years old [Crazy Horse was between thirty-five and thirty-seven years old], five feet eight inches high, lithe and sinewy, with a scar in the face. The expression of his countenance was one of quiet dignity, but morose, dogged, tenacious, and melancholy. He behaved with stolidity, like a man who realized he had to give in to Fate, but would do so as sullenly as possible. While talking to Frank, his countenance lit up with genuine pleasure, but to all others he was, at least in the first days of his coming upon the reservation, gloomy and reserved. All Indians gave him a high reputation for courage and generosity. In advancing upon an enemy, none of his warriors were allowed to pass him. He had made hundreds of friends by his charity towards the poor, as it was a point of honor with him never to keep anything for himself, excepting weapons of war. I never heard an Indian mention his name save in terms of respect."

Lieutenant Clark described Crazy Horse as "remarkably brave, generous and reticent, a pillar of strength for good or evil." Another officer was sure Crazy Horse would become as great a leader of his people in peace as he had been in war.

Crazy Horse seems to have enjoyed talking about hunting and old battles with the officers. Clark reported to Crook that "Crazy Horse and his people are getting quite sociable, and I reckon I shall have to be considered one of their tribe soon, as I have been invited down to three feasts."

Red Cloud was terribly jealous of Crazy Horse because of the attention the officers showered upon him and because of the respect which the warriors held for him, and he set about to cut the upstart down to size. Almost as soon as Crazy Horse came in, Red Cloud and his sycophants began to spread rumors that he was planning to break out and go back to the warpath. The officers dismissed such stories out of hand—without horses and guns, what could Crazy Horse do? —but the white agent who controlled the Oglalas via Red Cloud swallowed the rumors whole. This agent, James Irwin, told the Commissioner of Indian Affairs and any officer who would listen that "Crazy Horse manifests a sullen, morose disposition; evidently a man of small capacity, brought into notoriety by his stubborn will and brute courage. His dictatorial manners, and disregard for the comfort of his people, have caused dissatisfaction among them and his want of truthfulness with the military department has rendered him unpopular with the leading men of his band, who have drawn off from him, and say that they are determined to carry out their promise to General Crook, and their original intention to obey orders and keep the peace." Throughout this report, one can see the fine hand of that master politician Red Cloud at work—he might almost have dictated it.

During this period Irwin worked on Crazy Horse to persuade him to go to Washington to see the Great White Father. The officers, too, urged him to make the trip. No, said Crazy Horse, not until he had his own agency west of the Black Hills, in the center of Sioux territory. Always the response was the same—first the trip, then the agency. In late May, Crook came to Red Cloud Agency to meet with the chiefs about the trip. To his great irritation, Crazy Horse refused to attend the council. What good was a Sioux delegation to Washington if Crazy Horse wasn't along? Crook left, disgusted, after giving orders that everyone at the agency should keep working on Crazy Horse.

Crazy Horse's closest white friend was Major V. T. McGillicuddy, the post surgeon, who had successfully treated Black Shawl for tuberculosis. (The Red Cloud people even made a fuss about this, saying Crazy Horse should have stuck to Indian medicine men; Crazy Horse replied that they had done his wife no good and he would try anything.) McGillicuddy had two or three long talks with Crazy Horse and he gave a verbatim report on what must have been the longest speech Crazy Horse ever made. It is suspect as a genuine document for precisely that reason. With that caveat, however, the following is McGillicuddy's report on what Crazy Horse said to him:

"His complaint regarding the coming of the white man was, 'We did not ask you white men to come here. The Great Spirit gave us this country as a home. You had yours. We did not interfere with you. The Great Spirit gave us plenty of land to live on and buffalo, deer, antelope and other game; but you have come here; you are taking my land from me; you are killing off our game, so it is hard for us to live. Now you tell us to work for a living, but the Great Spirit did not make us to work, but to live by hunting. You white men can work if you want to. We do not interfere with you, and again you say, why do you not become civilized? We do not want your civilization! We would live as our fathers did, and their fathers before them.'"

Like the other whites, McGillicuddy urged Crazy Horse to go to Washington. Crazy Horse replied that he "was not hunting for any Great Father; his father was with him, and there was no Great Father between him and the Great Spirit."

By early July 1877, however, Crazy Horse was beginning to weaken. For the first time in his life, he was bored. There was nothing to do at Red Cloud Agency, and he wanted an agency of his own in good hunting territory—the little stringy beef he got at Camp Robinson was a poor substitute for juicy buffalo ribs roasted over an open fire. The white soldiers, whom he trusted, kept telling him that he could move to Wyoming as soon as he returned from Washington. Crazy Horse decided he would have to go. He began dropping by Billy Garnett's place to ask questions about the trip. What was it like, riding on a train? How long did it take to get to the Great Father? How did you eat? Relieve yourself? What did you do when you got there? Crazy Horse had Billy teach him how to use a fork, so that he would not embarrass the Oglalas when he sat at a table for a feast with the Great White Father.

Now that Crazy Horse showed a willingness to co-operate, the agents couldn't do enough for him. They promised to allow Crazy Horse and his people to go on a big buffalo hunt on the Powder River.† When? Soon, soon. On July 27, 1877, Indian Inspector Benjamin Shapp held a council to make plans for the Washington trip. At the conclusion, he announced that he would provide enough cattle for a great feast. Young Man Afraid, working as always to hold the Oglalas together, suggested that it be held at Crazy Horse's lodge, thus making Crazy Horse the giver of the feast. It would help integrate him into agency life. No one objected, but Red Cloud and two or three others abruptly left the council. That night two Indians called on agent Irwin. They said that Red Cloud was greatly dissatisfied at this development; Crazy Horse had only recently come in and there was no reason at all why he should be allowed to give a feast. Red Cloud wanted Irwin to know that Crazy Horse was unreconstructed and would cause trouble at the first opportunity. Red Cloud also warned that if Crazy Horse were given horses and guns and allowed to take his warriors off on a hunt, he would never return.

Spotted Tail, back on his own agency, took up the refrain. Like

† How odd it is to think of Crazy Horse being "allowed" to go hunting.

Red Cloud, he regarded Crazy Horse as a troublemaker who had brought much grief and misery down on the Sioux because of his intransigence. He too made solemn warnings—if his nephew were allowed to go to the Powder River, he would never return to the agency. And so the white authorities called off the feast, and the buffalo hunt too.

Still Red Cloud was not done with Crazy Horse. He did not want Crazy Horse to go to Washington, to be feasted and petted by the United States Government, made into a big man, perhaps elevated to the chieftainship of all the Sioux (rumor had it that the government intended just that; like all concentration camps, the Red Cloud Agency was a breeding ground for wild rumors). So Red Cloud's lieutenants began to whisper to Crazy Horse that if he went to Washington, the government would put him into chains and ship him off to an island prison off the Florida coast. (They were quite right about this point—Crook planned to send Crazy Horse to a prison cell on the Dry Tortugas, a thought too painful for the mind to hold.) Red Cloud also arranged to send a young woman to live in Crazy Horse's lodge. Garnett described her as "a half-blood, not of the best frontier variety, an invidious and evil woman." But she was young and pretty, and Crazy Horse took her in. She too filled his mind with poison, convincing him that the Washington journey was a trap. But the real trap was the one Red Cloud had been setting to keep him out of Washington, and Crazy Horse fell into it. He told the officers he had changed his mind—he would not go to Washington.

The Nez Percés, meanwhile, had broken out of their reservation and headed toward eastern Montana. They were defeating everything the Army sent against them. Crook was ordered to round them up, and he came to Red Cloud Agency to enlist Oglalas to help him. Lieutenant Clark tried to get Crazy Horse to join up as an Indian scout, but Crazy Horse refused. Clark kept pestering him, promising a horse, a uniform, and a new repeating rifle—strong inducements, indeed. Still Crazy Horse replied, "I came here for peace. No matter if my own relatives pointed a gun at my head and ordered me to change that word I would not change it."

Crazy Horse's warriors, however, were signing on as scouts, proudly riding through the agency with their new horses and guns. And Clark kept putting the pressure on Crazy Horse. "I have only my tent and my will," Crazy Horse told Clark. "You got me to come here and you can keep me here by force if you choose, but you cannot make me go anywhere that I refuse to go." Clark persisted, until

Crazy Horse, exasperated, snapped that he would go to the Powder River with Crook and fight until there wasn't a Nez Percé left.‡

He never meant it. Crazy Horse was convinced that Crook was lying again, that Crook's real intention was to campaign against Sitting Bull. On August 31, the day after Crazy Horse said he would become a scout, Clark prepared to march off with the Oglalas to join Crook to fight the Nez Percés. Crazy Horse told his warriors to stay home—it was unthinkable that they should fight Sitting Bull —and threatened to take his people and head north if Clark persisted.

It was an idle threat, but so frightening was Crazy Horse's reputation that it terrified the whites. Lieutenant Colonel L. P. Bradley, commanding at Camp Robinson, telegraphed Sheridan, "There is a good chance of trouble here and there is plenty of bad blood. I think the departure of the scouts will bring on a collision here." Sheridan then telegraphed Crook, ordering him to interrupt his preparations for the Nez Percé campaign and hurry to Camp Robinson to straighten things out. Sheridan also ordered Bradley to hold the scouts at Camp Robinson until Crook arrived.

Crook got to the camp on the morning of September 2, 1877. He ordered all the Indians to move their camps to the base of the white butte (site of present-day Crawford, Nebraska), where he intended to hold a big council. Crazy Horse refused to go. He told his people he wanted nothing to do with Crook. He Dog disagreed. He told the village, "All who love their wife and children, let them come across the creek with me [to Crook's council]. All who want their wife and children to be killed by the soldiers, let them stay where they are." Most began packing up. Crazy Horse asked He Dog to come to his tipi; there Crazy Horse admitted that he was expecting trouble but he wouldn't go looking for it. He would stay where he was and hope to be left alone. He Dog asked, "Does this mean that you will be my enemy if I move across the creek?"

Crazy Horse laughed in his face, and said, "I am no white man! They are the only people that make rules for other people, that say, 'If you stay on one side of this line it is peace, but if you go on the other side I will kill you all.' I don't hold with deadlines. There is plenty of room; camp where you please."

He Dog moved to the white butte. Clark gave him some presents

‡ Grouard, for reasons of his own, willfully mistranslated this statement, to make it appear that Crazy Horse said he would fight until there wasn't a white man left. The error was straightened out, but it hardly helped the atmosphere around the agency.

to send to Crazy Horse. He Dog sent the goods by messenger, with a request that Crazy Horse change his mind. Again, Crazy Horse laughed in the messenger's face.

By the time of Crook's council with the Sioux, September 2, the Nez Percés had emerged from the newly designated Yellowstone Park area and come to the Bighorn River. Crook was anxious to get at them, so he was in an impatient mood as he drove in an ambulance from the agency to the council site. On his way, he was accosted by Woman's Dress, the *winkte*, who whispered in his ear that Crazy Horse planned to kill him at the council (Woman's Dress was a uniformed scout at this time). Crook was filled with anxiety. Crazy Horse had made a fool of him on the Rosebud and indeed throughout the previous summer and fall.

Crook turned back from his proposed council after listening to Woman's Dress, returned to Camp Robinson, and ordered the chiefs to come meet him in the post stockade. The agency chiefs all came, and Crook told them that if they did not assist the Army, Crazy Horse would cause big trouble for the Sioux. He wanted Crazy Horse arrested. Red Cloud, Spotted Tail, and the others conferred among themselves, then told Crook that Crazy Horse was a desperate man who would start a civil war among the Sioux if anyone attempted to arrest him. Better to kill him outright, at once.

Crook was tempted—one quick shot in the back and the Crazy Horse troubles would be over—but whatever else he was, Crook was not a man to condone outright murder, especially in this situation, when he would have a hard enough time explaining on what grounds he was ordering Crazy Horse's arrest. Just go ahead and arrest Crazy Horse, Crook said to the chiefs—he'd give them a strong force of cavalry to assist the warriors in the job. Crook told Bradley to ship Crazy Horse to Omaha, via the Union Pacific Railroad, as soon as he was arrested. Then Crook went off to fight the Nez Percés. (And to be away from the scene when the dirty work was done?)

On the morning of September 4, the chiefs set out from Camp Robinson to arrest Crazy Horse with four hundred agency warriors. With them were eight full companies of the 3rd Cavalry. Truly Crazy Horse inspired fear; the force sent out to arrest him was more than twice as large as the one Custer had with him on the Little Bighorn, and this time Crazy Horse had neither arms nor warriors. Fortunately, Young Man Afraid was along, to make sure Crazy Horse wasn't shot while "attempting to escape."

The mixed force of Indians and soldiers rode up to Crazy Horse's village, about six miles from Camp Robinson, only to find that Crazy Horse had fled. Red Feather, Black Shawl's younger brother, had warned him of what was coming. Crazy Horse had somehow obtained two ponies, and he and Black Shawl set out to the northeast for Spotted Tail Agency, with the hope that he could live in peace there. They were just disappearing beyond the buttes as the soldiers and scouts rode up.

Clark immediately offered a $200 reward to the Indian who captured Crazy Horse and brought him back. They all set off with a whoop, No Water leading the way. No Water had an extra pony with him. He rode so hard that his first mount dropped dead of exhaustion. He pushed his spare pony just as hard, and soon it too collapsed and died.

Billy Garnett explained Crazy Horse's method of retreat, which he said was much talked about by the Sioux. "Crazy Horse always ran down hill and across the level country but slowed down to a walk at the foot of a hill, and when he got to the top his horses were fresh, and in this way he conserved the strength of his animals. While the scouts kept about so near to him for a long time, they noticed toward the end he was lengthening the distance between them, because of his way of using his steeds saved them, while his pursuers raced up hill and down wearing theirs out, when at length ten miles from Spotted Tail Agency they were played out."

Crazy Horse's arrival at Spotted Tail Agency generated the wildest excitement. Touch-the-Clouds and his Miniconjous were there, and these former hostiles lined up on one side, Spotted Tail's Brulés, agency Indians, on the other. The two groups of Indians shouted threats at each other. Spotted Tail got some of his men to surround Crazy Horse and lead him into the agency stockade. When the scouts who were chasing Crazy Horse finally rode up, a Touch-the-Clouds warrior who had a lance made blood-curdling sweeps and passes at them with it. Spotted Tail then brought Crazy Horse out to the parade ground to show that no harm had come to him. When the Indians quieted down, Spotted Tail made a speech: "We never have trouble here!" he said, looking directly at Crazy Horse. "The sky is clear; the air is still and free from dust. You have come here, and you must listen to me and my people! I am chief here! We keep the peace! We, the Brulés, do this! They obey ME! Every Indian who comes here, must obey me! You say you want to come to this agency to live peaceably. If you stay here, you must listen to me! That is all!"

That evening Crazy Horse explained to Spotted Tail, the agent (Lieutenant Jesse Lee), and Touch-the-Clouds that he had never threatened to go back on the warpath or to murder Crook. He only wanted to get away from Red Cloud Agency, where so many bad things were said about him. He had done nothing, absolutely nothing, but a thousand and more armed men had come to arrest him. He asked Lee to explain all this to the authorities at Red Cloud Agency. Lee said Crazy Horse should do so himself and promised that if he gave himself up voluntarily, he, Lee, would see to it Crazy Horse had an opportunity to explain. Touch-the-Clouds and Spotted Tail offered to go with him, back to Camp Robinson, to insure that no harm was done. Crazy Horse asked his uncle Spotted Tail if he could live at Spotted Tail Agency afterward, and Spotted Tail said he could if he would obey orders. So it was arranged that Crazy Horse, Lee, Spotted Tail, and Touch-the-Clouds would go together to Camp Robinson the next day, September 6, 1877.

In the morning, however, Crazy Horse had changed his mind. Lee later recalled that Crazy Horse was like a "frightened, trembling wild animal brought to bay, hoping for confidence one moment and fearing treachery the next. He had been under a severe strain, and it plainly showed." Crazy Horse said he feared trouble if he went back —couldn't Lee go and explain for him? Lee insisted that he must go himself, and after some discussion Crazy Horse reluctantly mounted up and set out, Touch-the-Clouds and Spotted Tail beside him, surrounded by Spotted Tail's warriors.

It was a long ride, forty-five miles, and dusk was coming on when Crazy Horse topped the last butte and looked down on the White River Valley. It was a breathtaking sight. Camp Robinson was located in a gigantic natural amphitheater, surrounded by majestic bluffs which were capped by Ponderosa pines. Once the home of uncountable buffalo, it was a fitting stage for a tragedy to be played out for the gods. This day it was filled with Indians—all the Oglalas, former hostile and friendly, had heard the news and were down there on the flat where the frontier post was, between Soldier's Creek and the White River. Next to Soldier's Creek there were a few log Army buildings and a couple of newly built officers' quarters, a warehouse, sutler's store, and infantry barracks, all enclosing a large, flat parade ground.

As Crazy Horse's party made its way toward the adjutant's office, the assembled warriors parted to make room. There were thousands of them. Everyone was extremely tense. He Dog rode up to Crazy

Horse's left side, shook hands, saw that he did not look well, and said, "Look out—watch your step—you are going into a dangerous place." Little Big Man, once the most irreconcilable of Crazy Horse's warriors but now a man determined to co-operate with his captors and thus rise to leadership on the agency, slipped up on Crazy Horse's right hand.

As Crazy Horse dismounted and walked across the parade ground, it was suddenly deathly quiet. A Red Cloud warrior broke the silence. He called out that Crazy Horse was supposed to be a brave man, but now everyone could see that he was a coward. Crazy Horse lunged for him, but Little Big Man grabbed Crazy Horse's arm and pulled him back.

Lee had Crazy Horse go into the adjutant's office, explaining that he would arrange for an interview with Colonel Bradley. But when Lee got to Bradley's office, the commanding officer told him to have Crazy Horse locked up in the guardhouse. It was too late for explanations, Bradley said—first thing in the morning, September 7, Bradley was going to ship Crazy Horse off to Omaha, on his way to the Dry Tortugas. Lee went back to the adjutant's office and evidently told Crazy Horse that he was being taken to talk to Bradley. The guardhouse was right next to the adjutant's office. When they came out, Little Big Man stepped up to Crazy Horse's side and took his arm, guiding him into the guardhouse.

Crazy Horse's sense of smell told him first that he was in a bad place. They had entered the guardhouse, and as he turned, or was turned, to his right, the odor overwhelmed him. Prisoners were *never* allowed out of their cells; the place stank. His nostrils flaring, Crazy Horse's eyes caught the dreadful sight of a ball and chain. He saw in a glance that they were putting him into a three-foot-by-six-foot cell, with no windows, only a little air hole too high up to afford a view of anything but sky. Crazy Horse knew then that he was being penned up in solitary confinement.

Caged! The very thought of it made the heart sick, the stomach turn, and led to instantaneous action. Crazy Horse smelled, looked, realized what was happening, and struck out against his captors, all in an instant. He jerked his arm loose from Little Big Man, pulled a concealed knife, and began a rush toward the door, slashing at anyone in his way. He cut Little Big Man's wrist, but Little Big Man got behind him and grabbed both his arms and pinioned them.

Crazy Horse's momentum had carried them outside, where the officer of the day started shouting, "Stab the son-of-a-bitch! Stab the son-of-a-bitch!" Other officers were yelling, "Kill him! Kill him!" Soldiers standing guard began thrusting toward Crazy Horse with their bayonets. Crazy Horse could not fight back because, just as it had been foretold in his vision twenty-three years before, his arms were held by one of his own people. He gave a desperate lunge and broke free. At that instant, a bayonet cut through his side and into his guts. Another thrust entered his back and went through his kidney.

Crazy Horse fell to the ground. Little Big Man and some soldiers reached for him, grabbed his arms again, but he said, "Let me go, my friends. You have got me hurt enough." And suddenly it was deathly silent again, down there on the parade ground, beside the White River, as the sun set over the surrounding buttes. A passing hawk, on his way to his roost, screamed.

The soldiers wanted to carry Crazy Horse's bleeding body into the guardhouse, but Touch-the-Clouds would not allow it. "He was a great chief," Touch-the-Clouds said, "and he can not be put into a prison." Bending his seven-foot body, Touch-the-Clouds gently picked up Crazy Horse and carried him to a bed in the adjutant's office. Dr. McGillicuddy gave Crazy Horse some morphine while Touch-the-Clouds shooed everyone but Worm out of the building.

Crazy Horse spoke once. Worm had leaned over him and said, "Son, I am here." Crazy Horse replied, "Father, it is no use to depend on me. I am going to die." An hour or so later, with only Worm and Touch-the-Clouds present, Crazy Horse died.

Touch-the-Clouds, his great back bent, went outside to tell the mighty host of Sioux warriors. Most of those assembled there were men who had followed Crazy Horse to Custer's rear at the Little Bighorn or had been with him at the Platte Bridge, Fort Phil Kearny, on the Yellowstone, or on innumerable war parties against the Crows and Shoshonis, men of brave hearts and strong bodies, warriors any commander would be proud to lead, the mightiest armed force, man for man, if equally armed, this continent has ever seen. It was also the least disciplined. These were the braves who had freely chosen to fight beside Crazy Horse, who had entrusted him with their lives and reputations.

Behind the warriors, out there on the moonlit parade ground, stood the women. These were the women who had made it possible for the men to fight, the ones who saw to it that the society remained intact, that the children were cared for, the old ones too. They had endured much misery, these Oglala women; they had lost their possessions time and again, had seen six months' hard work burned up by the soldiers in a minute, had hugged their babies to their breasts as they trudged through the snow, following Crazy Horse. They had also followed of their own free will, for they too thought that freedom was more important than anything else. Black Shawl was there, way at the back, and Black Buffalo Woman too, her hand holding tightly to that of her little light-haired daughter.

This night the red men and women were confused. They knew if they broke for freedom, they would be caught and killed, that if they made a move against the soldiers at Camp Robinson, even if they won, other soldiers would come and kill them all. Besides, they didn't know what to believe, so thick were the rumors. Some said Crazy Horse really did conspire to go on the warpath—or murder Crook. No one knew, either, what had happened—it had all taken place so quickly. One rumor had it that Little Big Man did the killing. Another said that Crazy Horse had fallen on his own knife. All the Indians facing Touch-the-Clouds feared another Indian war, yet almost all of them found living on the agency intolerable and, if Crazy Horse was now out of the way, the United States Government would be sure to move them to the hated Missouri.

One thing the Oglalas did know: Crazy Horse's way, Sitting Bull's way, could no longer be tolerated. The Indians had to make adjustments, learn to walk the white man's road. The "savage" in them had to be molded, tempered, abandoned. They knew they were no longer free, which is to say that they had taken the first step toward civilization. There was no room on this new road for Crazy Horse, the greatest warrior of them all.

Perhaps Touch-the-Clouds had this in mind as he looked down on those courageous, confused people. "It is well," he said quietly, reassuringly. "He has looked for death and it has come." The Oglalas filed away, silently, into the night.

CHAPTER TWENTY-FOUR

What Happened to the Others

"There never was a good war, nor a bad peace."
                                                Benjamin Franklin, 1773

Custer's body was found at the Little Bighorn by Gibbon's men on June 27, 1876. It had been stripped naked. He had a bullet hole through his left breast and another in his left temple—either wound would have been fatal. His body was just short of the highest point of the hill. He had not been scalped nor mutilated. He was buried there on the field; a year later his body was disinterred and brought to West Point, where he was reburied with full military honors.

Crazy Horse's body was taken away from Camp Robinson on September 7, 1877, by his parents in a wooden coffin to Spotted Tail Agency. A few days later, when the Spotted Tail and Red Cloud Indians were forcibly moved to the Missouri, Worm put the body on a travois. Then Worm and Crazy Horse's mother broke away from the others and took their son out onto the prairie to the north, beyond Pine Ridge, South Dakota, along the valley of Wounded Knee Creek. Somewhere out there, no one knows where, Crazy Horse's parents wrapped his body in a buffalo robe and placed it on a scaffold.

Libbie Bacon Custer learned on July 5, 1876, of her husband's fate. Margaret Custer Calhoun was with her—Maggie had lost a husband, three brothers, and a nephew at the Little Bighorn. Together the two women helped carry the terrible news to the other thirty-seven widows at Fort Abraham Lincoln who had lost husbands at the Little Bighorn. That fall Libbie moved back to Monroe; later she lived in New York City, where she earned her living by serving as a secretary to the Society of Decorative Arts, an organization that sold artistic works of other widows who, like Libbie, were "ladies" and thus prevented by custom from taking a job. Her widow's pension from the

United States Government was only $30 per month; later General
Sheridan got it raised to $50 per month. For years Libbie skimped
in order to have enough money to purchase a bust of Custer that
artist Vinnie Ream was creating. Libbie once told Vinnie, when
Vinnie had asked her to come to Washington to supervise the finishing touches, that she lacked the courage to show herself in public.
"A wounded thing must hide, and I cannot go to Washington and
stay among the general's friends."

Eventually Libbie got the bust, which she kept on her desk the
rest of her life, and she began a writing career, one that was so successful that it brought her a handsome living, so that she could afford
trips to Europe and a series of homes, and hobnobbed at summer
writing conferences with such writers as Mark Twain, John Bur-
roughs, and Frank Stockton.

Throughout her fifty-seven years of widowhood, Libbie defended
her husband's reputation, concentrating especially on the events of
June 25, 1876. Her version, which became the most widely accepted
one because of her extraordinary efforts and determination, put the
blame squarely on Major Reno and Captain Benteen. If Reno had
continued his charge or if Benteen had obeyed orders and come on
with the ammunition train, Custer would have won the battle. In
short, Custer was betrayed. Many participants in the tragedy—especially Reno and Benteen—withheld their own comments about the
various controversies, saying that they would wait to tell their version
until Mrs. Custer died. But she outlived them all.

In 1908, at the age of sixty-seven, Libbie went for a motor-car tour
of Europe. Young women still noticed, with jealous eyes, that wherever she went in a drawing room, the gentlemen followed, eager to
engage her in conversation. She deeply disapproved of Margaret Calhoun's remarriage, and when Maggie died shortly thereafter, Libbie
insisted that the inscription on her grave should read MARGARET, SIS-
TER OF GEN. GEO. A. CUSTER.

Libbie's loyalty to her Autie never flagged. To the end, she labori-
ously answered by hand any letter from a veteran who had ever spent
a day in the 7th Cavalry. She started a movement to preserve as
monuments the frontier forts. Death came on April 6, 1933, at the
height of Franklin Roosevelt's Hundred Days of the New Deal—
surely a world away from that hot dusty day on the Little Bighorn,
fifty-seven years earlier. She was buried at her husband's side at West
Point, with a small marker which rests in the shade of Custer's gigantic memorial.

Black Shawl remained a widow. Dr. McGillicuddy had done his work well; she lived at Pine Ridge until 1930, when she was in her mid-eighties.

Major Reno, like Libbie, spent the remainder of his life haunted by the events of June 25, 1876. A lengthy Army Court of Inquiry was insisted upon by Libbie, and by Reno himself after Custer's first biographer, Frederick Whittaker, blamed him for Custer's death. The court held Reno blameless for the disaster, but few others were convinced. In 1880 he was dismissed from the Army for drunkenness and conduct unbecoming an officer and a gentleman. It was said that he had ordered a subordinate away on special duty and in his absence made advances toward the subordinate's wife. He died, a bitter man, in 1889.

Young-Man-Afraid-of-His-Horses became what was known as a "progressive chief." In 1889–90 he opposed the Ghost Dance and tried to dissuade the adherents; he brought some bands back to the Pine Ridge Agency after they had gone to the Bad Lands to practice their religion. But he was never a bootlicker. When the Army demanded that he turn in some of his warriors for murdering two white men, he replied: "No, I will not surrender them, but if you will bring the white men who killed Few Tails I will bring the Indians who killed the white soldier and the herder; and right out here I will have my young men shoot the Indians and you have your soldiers shoot the white men, and then we will be done with the whole business." In 1883 the Oglalas had elected Young Man Afraid to be president of the Indian Council; he beat Red Cloud in the election by a three to one margin. The whites later reinstated Red Cloud.

Captain Benteen took the lead in criticism of Custer's tactics, writing many articles and letters to various newspaper editors. In 1877 he fought the Nez Percés well enough to win a promotion to brevet brigadier general. He retired from the Army in July 1888 to live in Atlanta, Georgia, where he died in 1898.

He Dog lived to be a very old man, highly respected by both red and white. He became the judge of the Court of Indian Offenses at Pine Ridge Reservation in South Dakota. In the early 1930s he was Eleanor Hinman's chief informant. She said of He Dog, "In spite of his ninety-two years and their infirmities, He Dog is possessed of a remarkable memory. He is the living depository of Oglala tribal history and old-time customs. Anyone digging very deeply into these subjects with the other old-timers is likely to be referred to him: 'He Dog will remember about that.' In interviewing He Dog one can hardly fail to be impressed with his strong historical sense and with the moderation and carefulness of his statements."

General Sherman remained General-in-Chief of the Army until 1883. In 1884 the Republicans tried to nominate him for the presidency, but he absolutely refused ("If nominated I will not run; if elected I will not serve"). He died in New York City in 1891. Sherman was converted to Roman Catholicism on his deathbed, so he and his old adversary Red Cloud were members of the same faith at the end.

Sitting Bull went to Canada to stay; he much preferred Grandmother Victoria to the Great White Father. But it was cold in Canada and the buffalo were scarce, so in 1881 he surrendered. He was held prisoner at Fort Randall, South Dakota, for two years; in 1883 he was allowed to join the Hunkpapas at Standing Rock Agency in North Dakota. There he and his people began to starve because of government neglect. Sitting Bull rose to address one set of visiting stuffed-shirt commissioners from Washington and said, "It is your own doing that I am here; you sent me here and advised me to live as you do, and it is not right for me to live in poverty." Senator John A. Logan of Illinois told him to sit down, that he had no right to speak because he had "no following, no power, no control, and no right to control."

SITTING BULL: I wish to say a word.
LOGAN: We do not care to talk anymore with you.
SITTING BULL: I would like to speak. I have grown to be a very independent man, and consider myself a very great man.
LOGAN: You have made your speech. And we do not care to have you continue further.
SITTING BULL: I have just one more word to say. Of course, if a man is a chief, and has authority, he should be proud, and consider himself a great man.

Buffalo Bill Cody knew that Sitting Bull was a great man and made him the star attraction in his Wild West Show. Cody treated Sitting Bull with respect and earned his friendship. But Sitting Bull quarreled incessantly with the agent at Standing Rock and from the Indian Bureau's point of view he was a disruptive force. He became something of a leader in the Ghost Dance, which terrified the whites, and in December 1890 the Army ordered him arrested. Indian police tried to do the dirty work at dawn on December 15. Sitting Bull resisted, was shot in the back by an Indian policeman, and died immediately.

President Grant tried for the presidency again in 1880, but the Republicans rejected him for the nomination, choosing James A. Garfield instead. Grant's last years were overshadowed by misfortune, poverty, calumny, and illness. His income failed. He was exploited in business and humiliated by bankruptcy. In the last year of his life, however, Grant triumphed; with the enthusiastic support of Mark Twain, he undertook to write his Civil War memoirs. Stricken with cancer, he wrote from his sickbed in his home in New York State and died on July 23, 1885, shortly after completing the best set of memoirs ever written by a professional American soldier.

Red Cloud, always the consummate politician, remained as head of the Oglalas after they moved to Pine Ridge Reservation. He was criticized by the Indians for giving in too easily to the whites, and by the whites for being an obstinate enemy of progress. He did his best. He died peacefully, on December 10, 1909.

General Crook went to Arizona to fight Chief Geronimo and his Apaches. He chased Geronimo all over the southwest, but in 1886 Geronimo surrendered to General Miles, thus giving Miles some revenge for Crook's "stealing" of Crazy Horse from him in 1877. After 1888 Crook served as commander of the Division of the Missouri. He died in Chicago in 1890.

Spotted Tail remained the head of the Brulés. He sent his children to Carlisle Barracks, Pennsylvania, to be educated, but after visiting them there and learning how much they hated it, he pulled them out, to the great consternation of the white friends of the Indian. Spotted Tail was also involved in constant political machinations at Rosebud Reservation in South Dakota, usually emerging triumphant, at least until August 15, 1881, when one of his rivals, Crow Dog, shot him to death from ambush.

General Miles captured Chief Joseph and the Nez Percés shortly after Crazy Horse's death. In 1886 he fought the Apaches under Geronimo, chasing them into Mexico. After holding various Army posts, he commanded the forces that put down the Sioux after the

Ghost Dance outbreak in 1890, culminating in the massacre at Wounded Knee Creek. Later, in 1894, from his Chicago headquarters, Miles was called upon to quell the Pullman strikers and subsequent rioting. In 1895 he became General-in-Chief of the Army and in 1898 took over Puerto Rico from Spain for the United States during the Spanish-American War. He retired from the Army in 1903 and died in Washington, D.C., in 1925.

Black Buffalo Woman's fate is unknown, but her pale-skinned daughter, born less than a year after she ran off with Crazy Horse and having his light hair and complexion, lived at Pine Ridge Reservation until World War II.

General Sheridan succeeded Sherman as General-in-Chief of the Army in 1884 and was promoted in 1888 to four-star rank. He completed his memoirs a few days before his death in 1888.

No Water, Black Buffalo Woman's husband, became leader of a small band and was a participant and something of a leader in the Ghost Dance of 1890. He put in a claim to the United States Government for the two horses he had killed attempting to capture Crazy Horse on September 5, 1877, but it apparently was not paid.

Woman's Dress, the *winkte*, remained an enlisted scout for the Army. In 1879 he was wounded at Camp Robinson by the Dull Knife Cheyennes, who were attempting to break out of the reservation. He was a great favorite with the Army officers and lived in glory until his death in 1920.

The Oglalas ended up on Pine Ridge Reservation, South Dakota, where there are today 11,500 of them. The Brulés are just to the east, on Rosebud Reservation; their population is 7,400. The Hunkpapas are on Standing Rock Reservation, North Dakota (4,890). Shoshonis and Arapahoes (4,280) share Wind River Reservation in Wyoming. The Crows (4,100) remain at Crow Agency, Montana, in the Crow Reservation, near the site of the Little Bighorn battle. The once mighty Pawnees are reduced to 3,390 and have no reservation of their own. The northern Cheyennes, after their forcible removal to Oklahoma, fled in October 1878 and fought their way back to Montana (Dull Knife and Little Wolf were the leaders). Eventually the United States Government allowed them to have their own reservation, of which Lame Deer is the center, where today there are 2,490 of them.

All these Indians live under conditions of dire rural poverty. It makes no difference what their ancestors did or what their attitude toward the whites was—the United States Government treats them all alike. Thus Spotted Tail's Brulés, who quit fighting in 1860, are no better off than Red Cloud's Oglalas, who fought until 1868, or Crazy Horse's people, who continued the struggle until 1877. Nor are the Crows, who were allied with the government throughout the Indian wars, much better off than the northern Cheyennes, who fought the government until 1878.

ACKNOWLEDGMENTS

Although it is not customary to thank authors who are dead or whom one has never met or corresponded with, in this instance I must at least attempt to indicate my debt to those whose labors made my work possible. And while I am grateful to all those listed in the bibliography, I must single out three women and three men, who between them were the *sine qua non* of this study. They are Eleanor Hinman, Mari Sandoz, Elizabeth Bacon Custer, Jay Monaghan, George E. Hyde, and George Bird Grinnell.

I want also to thank Dan Davis, Noni Carey, Henry Blake, and Arti Blake, for introducing me to the Great Plains; Ron and Louise Kroese for leading me to the Black Hills; and Dr. Clyde Ferguson for teaching me about life on the Plains. My typist, good friend, and former student, Josephine Sibille Kuntz, was absolutely indispensable.

My students at the University of New Orleans have been extraordinarily helpful, in ways too numerous to elucidate. Dr. Joseph Logsdon provided many insights on Civil War and Reconstruction politics; Dr. Jeffery Kimball helped me put the Indians in perspective. Dr. John Fluitt was a careful critic. Colonel Roger Willock, USMC, provided me with expert guidance on the frontier Army and gave me many tips on Custer's tactics and leadership. Dr. William A. Williams, who has forced all American historians to rethink their assumptions and attitudes, and whose example has encouraged us to take risks in our attempt to understand American history, read large parts of the manuscript. As always, his insights were sharp, his questions penetrating. John Homer Hoffman shared with me his knowledge of the Sioux and his own great good humor. My colleagues at the University of New Orleans read the early chapters and, in a department seminar, made numerous helpful suggestions.

The librarians at the University of New Orleans, Tulane University, and Kansas State University, along with that marvelous institution the interlibrary loan system, were exceedingly kind. So were the staffs of the Nebraska State Historical Society, the Custer Battlefield National Monument, and the Denver Public Library.

John Ware and Sam Vaughan of Doubleday & Company made me believe that the idea of a dual biography was feasible at a time when I had serious doubts and, indeed, thought the whole project pure madness. Throughout the writing, they provided me crucial support and important ideas.

My children, Stephenie, Barry, Andrew, Grace, and Hugh, were cheerful participants in the search for Crazy Horse and Custer. Moira was indispensable. Custer used to make Libbie sit with him while he wrote. I'm not quite that bad, but I did make Moira stop what she was doing at 6 P.M. and sit back and listen while I read aloud to her the day's outpouring. I can't think of a change she suggested that I did not make. If there appears to be rather a lot about women in this book on two men of violence, it is because of what Moira has taught me.

Most of all, Moira and the kids put up with me—and with Crazy Horse and Custer—and beyond that made it all seem worth while.

NOTES

1. Walter P. Webb, *The Great Plains* (Boston, 1931), 10–47. Readers who know this classic will realize how dependent I am on Webb's great work.
2. Ibid., 22.
3. Ibid.
4. Ibid., 39.
5. Wayne Gard, *The Great Buffalo Hunt* (Lincoln, Neb., 1959), 4–7.
6. Clark Wissler, *Indians of the United States* (rev. ed., New York, 1966), 8. Folsom points were chipped dart points, named after the New Mexico town where they were first found in 1926.
7. Robert H. Lowie, *Indians of the Plains* (reissue, Garden City, N.Y., 1963), 15–16; Ruth M. Underhill, *Red Man's America* (rev. ed., Chicago, 1971), 144–48.
8. Frank Gilbert Roe, *The Indian and the Horse* (Norman, Okla., 1955), 78.
9. Ibid., 135–55, for an excellent summary.
10. Ibid., 135–55; Thomas E. Mails, *The Mystic Warriors of the Plains* (Garden City, N.Y., 1972), 218.
11. Walker D. Wyman, *The Wild Horse of the West* (Lincoln, Neb., 1945), 90.
12. Doane Robinson, *A History of the Dakota or Sioux Indians* (Minneapolis, 1904), chaps. 2 and 3; Underhill, *Red Man's America*, 144–53.
13. Webb, *The Great Plains*, 48.
14. George E. Hyde, *Spotted Tail's Folk: A History of the Brulé Sioux* (Norman, Okla., 1961), 3.
15. Lewis O. Saum, *The Fur Trader and the Indian* (Seattle, 1965), 38.
16. Ibid., 164.
17. Ibid., 165.
18. Ibid., 95.
19. Francis Parkman, *The Oregon Trail* (Washington Square Press, 1967), 215.
20. Saum, *Fur Trader*, xi; italics in original.
21. Robinson, *History of the Dakota or Sioux Indians*, 112–14.
22. Wissler, *Indians of the United States*, 182.
23. Saum, *Fur Trader*, 197.
24. See the James D. Hart introduction to Parkman, *The Oregon Trail*.
25. Parkman, *The Oregon Trail*, 222.
26. George E. Hyde, *Red Cloud's Folk: A History of the Oglala Sioux Indians* (Norman, Okla., 1937), 60.
27. Parkman, *The Oregon Trail*, 74.
28. Ibid., 89.
29. Ibid., 190.
30. Ibid., 166.

31. Ibid., 86–87.
32. Ibid., 200.
33. Roe, *Indian and the Horse*, 376–77.
34. Saum, *Fur Trader*, 245.

CHAPTER 2

1. J. D. B. DeBow, ed., *Statistical View of the United States . . . Being a Compendium of the Seventh Census to Which Are Added the Results of Every Previous Census, Beginning With 1790 . . .*, in the *Demographic Monographs* series (New York, 1970), 61, 117.
2. Ibid., 63, 74.
3. Ibid., 125, 128.
4. Ibid., 163.
5. Ibid., 51.
6. Ibid., 133.
7. R. Carlyle Buley, *The Old Northwest: Pioneer Period, 1815–1840*, I (Bloomington, Ind., 1950), 385.
8. Henry Steele Commager, *The American Mind: An Interpretation of American Thought and Character Since the 1880's* (New Haven, 1950), 5.
9. Ibid., 4–5.
10. R. E. Banta, *The Ohio*, in *Rivers of America* (New York, 1949), 10.
11. DeBow, *Statistical View*, 155–56.
12. Max Lerner, *America as a Civilization* (New York, 1957), 48.
13. D. S. Stanley, *Personal Memoirs* (Cambridge, Mass., 1917), 1–2.
14. Ibid., 2–3.
15. DeBow, *Statistical View*, 292.
16. Arthur K. Moore, *The Frontier Mind: A Cultural Analysis of the Kentucky Frontiersman* (Lexington, Ky., 1950), 56.
17. Ibid., 95.
18. See Henry Nash Smith, *Virgin Land: The American West as Symbol and Myth* (Cambridge, Mass., 1950), 61–63 for a discussion.
19. The text for such beliefs was Vattel's classic *Law of Nations*, the standard authority for Americans on international law. E. de Vattel, *Le Droit des Gens*, trans. Charles G. Fenwick (Washington, 1916), III, 37–38, as quoted in Roy Harvey Pearce, *The Savages of America: A Study of the Indian and the Idea of Civilization* (rev. ed., Baltimore, 1965), 70.
20. Moore, *The Frontier Mind*, 187.
21. Merle Curti, *The Growth of American Thought* (2d ed., New York, 1951), 403–7, has a good discussion on this point.
22. Reuben Gold Thwaites, ed., *Original Journals of the Lewis and Clark Expedition*, VI (New York, 1959), 98.
23. Pearce, *The Savages of America*, 68.

24. Alexis de Tocqueville, *Democracy in America* (Mentor Books ed., New York, 1956), 26.
25. Ibid., 52.
26. Ibid., 194.
27. Ibid., 256.
28. Quoted in D. A. Kinsley, *Favor the Bold: Custer: The Indian Fighter* (New York, 1968), 34.

CHAPTER 3

1. John Stands-in-Timber and Margot Liberty, *Cheyenne Memories* (New Haven, 1967), 27–41.
2. The date of Crazy Horse's birth is disputed. Mari Sandoz puts it circa 1842–45; see her *Crazy Horse: The Strange Man of the Oglalas* (Lincoln, Neb., 1942), xiii. Chips, however, an Oglala who grew up with Crazy Horse, said in an interview in 1930 that Crazy Horse was born "in the year in which the band to which he belonged, the Oglalas, stole one hundred horses, and in the fall of the year"; see Chips interview, in the Eleanor Hinman interviews, Nebraska State Historical Society. A Sioux winter-count—a pictographic history—kept by Iron Shell puts 1841 as the year of the Big Horse Steal, when the Sioux captured many horses from the Shoshonis; see Royal B. Hassrick, *The Sioux: Life and Customs of a Warrior Society* (Norman, Okla., 1964), 348. This is not, of course, conclusive, for He Dog told Hinman that both he and Crazy Horse were born in 1838.
3. Hassrick, *The Sioux*, 310; Erik H. Erikson, "Observations on Sioux Education," *The Journal of Psychology*, Vol. VII (1937), 134–36.
4. Hinman interview with He Dog; Ricker interview with Chips, in Ricker tablets, Nebraska State Historical Society.
5. Hyde, *Spotted Tail's Folk*, 11–13; Sandoz, *Crazy Horse*, 18.
6. Erikson, "Observations on Sioux Education," 136–37; Hassrick, *The Sioux*, 313–14.
7. Erikson points out that under the Sioux system "the tension from the ambivalent fixations on the parents most probably cannot accumulate to the dangerous point which is often reached in our narcissistic use of the one-family system as a system of self-chosen prisons." See Erikson, "Observations on Sioux Education," 146.
8. "In their bewilderment," Erikson writes, the Sioux "could only explain such behavior [the physical chastisement of white children] as part of an over-all missionary scheme—an explanation also supported by the white people's method of letting their babies cry themselves blue in the face. It all must mean, so they thought, a well-calculated wish to impress white children with the idea that this world is not a good place to linger in and they had better look to the other world where perfect happiness is to be had as the price of having sacrificed this world." Erik Erikson, *Young Man Luther* (New York, 1958), 69.

9. Erikson, "Observations on Sioux Education," 141.

10. Ibid., 134. It is Erikson's opinion that "the Sioux system of child training tended toward that pole of education where the child in most respects . . . is allowed to be an *individualist* while quite young . . ."

11. Ibid., 146.

12. Hassrick, *The Sioux*, 317–19; Luther Standing Bear, *My People the Sioux* (Boston and New York, 1911), 28–48; Mails, *The Mystic Warriors of the Plains*, 516; Robert H. Lowie, *Indians of the Plains* (Garden City, N.Y., 1954), 131–36.

13. Hassrick, *The Sioux*, 216.

14. Ibid., 191.

15. Mails, *The Mystic Warriors*, 519, 544; Hassrick, *The Sioux*, 319.

16. There is a good discussion of Sioux myths in Stephen Return Riggs, *Dakota Grammar, Texts, and Ethnography* (Washington, D.C., 1893), Vol. IX of *Contributions to North American Ethnology*.

17. Sandoz, *Crazy Horse*, 19, makes Hump considerably older than Crazy Horse, but both He Dog and Red Feather told Hinman that these intimate friends were close in age; see Hinman interviews, Nebraska State Historical Society.

18. Hassrick, *The Sioux*, 319.

19. Mails, *The Mystic Warriors*, 531; Claude Lévi-Strauss, *The Savage Mind* (Chicago, 1966), 37.

20. Ibid., 510–37.

21. Parkman, *The Oregon Trail*, 170–71.

22. Sandoz, *Crazy Horse*, 17.

23. Parkman, *The Oregon Trail*, 133.

24. Hassrick, *The Sioux*, 320.

25. Ibid., 134–35.

26. Erikson, "Observations on Sioux Education," 150–51; Hassrick, *The Sioux*, 134; Sandoz, *Crazy Horse*, 16–17.

27. Hassrick, *The Sioux*, 321.

28. Ibid., 73.

29. Ibid., 17.

30. Lowie, *Indians of the Plains*, 112.

31. Parkman, *The Oregon Trail*, 204.

32. Robert H. Lowie, *The Origin of the State* (New York, 1927), 76–107.

33. Lowie, *Indians of the Plains*, 125.

34. There is a vast literature on Plains Indians' government; incredibly small details are known, recorded, analyzed. I have not gone into the subject in any depth because, first, the experts disagree with each other over the names of offices, functions, authority, and everything else. Second, I am in full agreement with Lowie, who takes a common-sense view: "So far as essentials go, it is therefore of no significance whether there was one chief, or a pair of chiefs, or, as among the Cheyenne, a council of forty-four in a population of about 4,000, nor whether a man by virtue of his lineage could or could not ever qualify for the title of chief"; Lowie, *Indians of the Plains*, 125. The standard authority on Sioux government

is Clark Wissler, "Societies and Ceremonial Associations in the Oglala Division of the Teton-Dakota," American Museum of Natural History *Anthropological Papers*, XI (1912). See also James O. Dorsey, "The Social Organization of the Siouan Tribes," *Journal of American Folk-Lore*, IV (1891); Hassrick, *The Sioux*, Chap. 1; and the various works by George Hyde. Central to study of Plains Indians' government is the classic work by K. N. Llewellyn and E. Adamson Hoebel, *The Cheyenne Way: Conflict and Case Law in Primitive Jurisprudence* (Norman, Okla., 1941); the title is formidable, but the text is absolutely fascinating and, as a bonus, beautifully written.

35. This sketch of Crazy Horse's character is based on Eleanor Hinman's interviews with his contemporaries, now in the Nebraska State Historical Society, especially the ones with He Dog, Short Bull, Red Feather, and Little Killer. All these men lived with Crazy Horse and two were closely related. All agree that he was unusually reserved, quiet, not boastful—in short, not a hail-fellow-well-met back-slapping type—and that he was that way as a youth. And, obviously, my view of Crazy Horse is much influenced by Mari Sandoz' great work.

36. Hyde, *Red Cloud's Folk*, 54–55; see also James C. Olson, *Red Cloud and the Sioux Problem* (Lincoln, Neb., 1965), 20–21.

37. Parkman, *The Oregon Trail*, 165.

38. Hyde, *Red Cloud's Folk*, 56.

39. Ibid., 58.

40. Hyde, *Spotted Tail's Folk*, 44.

41. Robinson, *A History of the Dakota*, 221. Sandoz, *Crazy Horse*, Chap. 1, emphasized the extreme hunger the Indians underwent before the wagons arrived with the goods; so does Hyde, *Spotted Tail's Folk*, 44–45. But De Smet was there, and he wrote: "Notwithstanding the scarcity of provisions felt in the camp before the wagons came, the feasts were numerous and well attended."

42. Robinson, *A History of the Dakota*, 222.

43. Ibid., 223.

44. Hyde, *Spotted Tail's Folk*, 47.

45. Ibid., 47–48.

46. Hinman interview with Short Bull, Nebraska State Historical Society.

47. Hinman interview with He Dog.

48. Chips interview, Ricker tablets, Nebraska State Historical Society.

CHAPTER 4

1. Hyde, *Red Cloud's Folk*, 86.

2. Hyde, *Spotted Tail's Folk*, 50.

3. Precisely what happened with the Mormon and his cow (or ox in some accounts) is impossible to state accurately. I base this account on an interview with Frank Salaway (Ricker tablets, Ne-

braska State Historical Society), because Salaway was there. For the different versions, see Sandoz, *Crazy Horse*, 3–12; Hyde, *Spotted Tail's Folk*, 47–54; Hyde, *Red Cloud's Folk*, 72–79; and Olson, *Red Cloud*, 8.

4. Salaway interview, Ricker tablets.
5. Hyde, *Red Cloud's Folk*, 73.
6. Salaway interview, Ricker tablets.
7. Ibid.; Hyde, *Red Cloud's Folk*, 74–75.
8. Sandoz, *Crazy Horse*, 29.
9. Hyde, *Red Cloud's Folk*, 75–77; Sandoz, *Crazy Horse*, 30–39; Salaway interview, Ricker tablets.
10. Sandoz, *Crazy Horse*, 39–41.
11. The dreams "represent the culture's demand that the individual shall conform to its ways along certain limited lines which it lays down by its specific tradition defined in its myths"; Jackson S. Lincoln, *The Dream in Primitive Cultures* (New York and London, 1970), 193. See also Hassrick, *The Sioux*, 266–95.
12. The following account of Curly's dream is taken from a Ricker interview with William Garnett, a fur trader who often translated for the Army. Garnett heard it from Crazy Horse (Curly) in 1868 when he was visiting Crazy Horse's village. John Stands-in-Timber, a Cheyenne, saw and was told about the sand rock drawing; see his *Cheyenne Memories*, 105.
13. Aside from the Garnett interview, see also Sandoz, *Crazy Horse*, 104–5. Sandoz knew many of Crazy Horse's contemporaries and heard the dream second-hand from them.
14. Sandoz, *Crazy Horse*, 45–62.
15. Hyde, *Spotted Tail's Folk*, 56.
16. Hyde, *Red Cloud's Folk*, 77; Robinson, *A History of the Dakota*, 223–24.
17. He Dog interview with Hinman, Nebraska State Historical Society; see also Sandoz, *Crazy Horse*, 69–70, and Hyde, *Spotted Tail's Folk*, 56–57.
18. Robinson, *A History of the Dakota*, 224; Hyde, *Spotted Tail's Folk*, 60–61.
19. Hyde, *Spotted Tail's Folk*, 59.
20. Robinson, *A History of the Dakota*, 224.
21. Ibid., 224–25; Hyde, *Spotted Tail's Folk*, 61.
22. Sandoz, *Crazy Horse*, 76–78, 92.
23. Hyde, *Spotted Tail's Folk*, 62–63; Robinson, *A History of the Dakota*, 225–26.
24. It took great courage for Spotted Tail and the others to give themselves up; they expected to be killed. The prisoners spent the next year at Fort Leavenworth in Kansas, where Spotted Tail learned many of the white man's ways and became deeply impressed with the power of the United States—from that time on he was an advocate of peace.
25. Robinson, *A History of the Dakota*, 225–26; Hyde, *Spotted Tail's Folk*, 63–65.
26. Robinson, *A History of the Dakota*, 227.

27. George Bird Grinnell, *The Fighting Cheyennes* (Norman, Okla., 1955), 119–20.
28. Grinnell, *The Fighting Cheyennes,* 120; Sandoz, *Crazy Horse,* 95–98.
29. Hyde, *Spotted Tail's Folk,* 78.
30. Sandoz, *Crazy Horse,* 99.
31. Ibid., 105. On the number of firearms held by the Sioux at this time, see Hyde, *Red Cloud's Folk,* 132.
32. Robinson, *A History of the Dakota,* 227–30, reprints Warren's report.
33. Details on Curly's preparation for battle come from a Ricker interview with Chips, Ricker tablets.
34. Hinman interview with He Dog, Nebraska State Historical Society; Sandoz, *Crazy Horse,* 115–18.

CHAPTER 5

1. George A. Custer, *My Life on the Plains,* ed. by Milo Milton Quaife (Lincoln, Neb., 1952), x–xiii.
2. Jay Monaghan, *Custer: The Life of General George Armstrong Custer* (Lincoln, Neb., 1959), 4–5.
3. Robert Sunley, "Early Nineteenth-Century American Literature on Child Rearing," in Margaret Mead and Martha Wolfenstein (eds.), *Childhood in Contemporary Cultures* (Chicago, 1955), 152–57. "Since moral virtues were associated with cleanliness, order, and regularity of all habits," Bernard Wishy writes, "it is not surprising that doctors . . . stressed the earliest possible rigorous toilet training; control by the age of one month was the goal! Even bladder and bowel control represented moral victories, and regular or controlled 'habits' as making life easier for mother and child were usually viewed as subsidiary ideals at best. What we call infantile masturbation was classified in a familiar way; it was the first sign of moral and physical degeneration"; Wishy, *The Child and the Republic: The Dawn of Modern American Child Nurture* (Philadelphia, 1968), 40. See also Ronald G. Walters, ed., *Primer for Prudery: Sexual Advice to Victorian America* (Baltimore, 1973).
4. Marguerite Merington, ed., *The Custer Story: The Life and Intimate Letters of General George A. Custer and His Wife Elizabeth* (New York, 1950), 6.
5. Ibid., 4.
6. Ibid., 5; Kinsley, *Favor the Bold,* 2.
7. Kinsley, *Favor the Bold,* 2–3.
8. DeBow, *Statistical Review,* 291.
9. Erich Fromm, "Individual and Social Origins of Neurosis," in Clyde Kluckhohn and Henry A. Murray (eds.), *Personality in Nature, Society, and Culture* (New York, 1949), 409, as cited in David

M. Potter, *People of Plenty: Economic Abundance and the American Character* (Chicago, 1954), 11.

10. Merle Curti, *The Social Ideas of American Educators* (Paterson, N.J., 1959), 60.

11. Ibid., 62.

12. Ibid., 63. After an intensive study of nineteenth-century American educators, Curti concluded that "on the whole there prevailed an attitude of reverence and respect for what had been achieved . . ." See also Wishy, *The Child and the Republic*, 75.

13. Curti, *The Social Ideas*, 80.

14. Ibid., 85–86.

15. Kinsley, *Favor the Bold*, 3.

16. Merington, *The Custer Story*, 5–6; Kinsley, *Favor the Bold*, 3; Monaghan, *Custer*, 8.

17. Custer, *My Life on the Plains*, xvi–xvii.

18. Kinsley, *Favor the Bold*, 3.

19. Custer, *My Life on the Plains*, xvi–xvii.

20. Merington, *The Custer Story*, 25; Talcott E. Wing (ed.), *History of Monroe County, Michigan* (New York, 1890).

21. Kinsley, *Favor the Bold*, 3.

22. Merington, *The Custer Story*, 7.

23. Memo at Custer Battlefield National Monument, cited in Monaghan, *Custer*, 9.

24. Kinsley, *Favor the Bold*, 4; Monaghan, *Custer*, 10–11.

25. Monaghan, *Custer*, 11–13; Kinsley, *Favor the Bold*, 5–7. Custer's correspondence with Bingham is in the Elizabeth Custer Collection, Custer Battlefield National Monument, Crow Agency, Montana; this source is hereinafter cited as Custer Mss.

26. Merington, *The Custer Story*, 6. Wishy, in *The Child and the Republic*, 78, has a good description of the pre-Civil War American males: "Their characters were like rocks. They had the ability to resist temptation, the easy way, the lures of the world. They did not go 'round about but straight through. Pre-eminently, they were people with at least a genuine aspiration to principle. Many had moral dignity and some were even capable of tragedy. But inseparable from these qualities that may now seem, nostalgically, so admirable, there was, we must not forget, a persistent moral fanaticism, a crippling hunger for absolutism, for the hundred per cent return on a hundred per cent investment in life."

CHAPTER 6

1. George A. Custer, "War Memoirs," reprinted in Frederick Whittaker (ed.), *A Complete Life of General George A. Custer* (New York, 1876), 42; hereinafter cited as Custer, "War Memoirs." Whittaker was a close friend of Custer's and worked with Elizabeth Custer on the preparation of his book. Custer's "War Memoirs" was also

printed in *Galaxy*, XXII, September 1876. The original is in the Elizabeth Custer Collection.

2. Frederic F. Van de Water, *Glory-Hunter: A Life of General Custer* (Indianapolis, 1934), Chap. 2.
3. See the Quaife introduction to Custer, *My Life on the Plains*, xvii.
4. Monaghan, *Custer*, 36.
5. Ibid., 42.
6. Stephen E. Ambrose, *Duty, Honor, Country: A History of West Point* (Baltimore, 1966), 148.
7. Cadet James W. Schureman to sister, October 14, 1840, James Wall Schureman Papers, Library of Congress, and Cadet Cullen Bryant to father, June 17, 1860, Bryant Family Papers, New York Public Library; both quoted in Ambrose, *Duty, Honor, Country*, 148–49.
8. Ambrose, *Duty, Honor, Country*, 150–51.
9. Kinsley, *Favor the Bold*, 9.
10. Custer, "War Memoirs."
11. Monaghan, *Custer*, 35.
12. Cadet Thomas Hartz to sister, December 11, 1852, Hartz Papers, Library of Congress, quoted in Ambrose, *Duty, Honor, Country*, 151.
13. Ambrose, *Duty, Honor, Country*, 153.
14. Ibid., 154.
15. Morris Schaff, *The Spirit of Old West Point* (Boston, 1907), 194.
16. K. Bruce Galloway and Robert B. Johnson, Jr., *West Point* (New York, 1973), 64.
17. Oliver O. Howard, *Autobiography* (New York, 1908), I, 50–51.
18. Schaff, *Old West Point*, 80–81.
19. Cadet Henry A. Du Pont to mother, October 16, 1856, Du Pont Papers, Wilmington, Delaware, quoted in Ambrose, *Duty, Honor, Country*, 149.
20. Ambrose, *Duty, Honor, Country*, 131–32.
21. Cadet George W. Cushing to father, November 28, 1854, George W. Cushing Papers, USMA Library, quoted in Ambrose, *Duty, Honor, Country*, 133.
22. Ambrose, *Duty, Honor, Country*, 133.
23. Cadet Thomas Hartz to sister, July 30, 1852, Hartz Papers, Library of Congress, quoted in Ambrose, *Duty, Honor, Country*, 131.
24. Monaghan, *Custer*, 19.
25. Merington, *The Custer Story*, 8.
26. Monaghan, *Custer*, 20, 33; Kinsley, *Favor the Bold*, 9.
27. Monaghan, *Custer*, 33.
28. Schaff, *Old West Point*, 194.
29. Ibid., 86.
30. Ibid., 67.
31. Monaghan, *Custer*, 35.
32. Ibid., 29, 32.
33. Custer Mss.
34. Ibid.
35. Monaghan, *Custer*, 36.

36. Merington, *The Custer Story*, 9; Custer Mss.
37. Ambrose, *Duty, Honor, Country*, 167–69.
38. Lynwood M. Holland, *Pierce M. B. Young* (Athens, Ga., 1964), 43.
39. Custer, "War Memoirs."
40. Monaghan, *Custer*, 37.
41. Schaff, *Old West Point*, 175; Custer, "War Memoirs"; Ambrose, *Duty, Honor, Country*, 169–70; Monaghan, *Custer*, 37.
42. Schaff, *Old West Point*, 207–8.
43. Ibid., 84.
44. Monaghan, *Custer*, 39.
45. Kinsley, *Favor the Bold*, 13; Monaghan, *Custer*, 39; Custer Mss.
46. Ambrose, *Duty, Honor, Country*, 175–76.
47. Kinsley, *Favor the Bold*, 13; Merington, *The Custer Story*, 10; Custer Mss.
48. Merington, *The Custer Story*, 10; Custer Mss.
49. Custer, "War Memoirs"; Monaghan, *Custer*, 43; Kinsley, *Favor the Bold*, 15–16.
50. Custer, "War Memoirs."
51. Schaff, *Old West Point*, 260; Kinsley, *Favor the Bold*, 17–18; Monaghan, *Custer*, 43.

CHAPTER 8

1. For general accounts of the Oglalas during this period, see Hyde, *Red Cloud's Folk*, 101–87; Sandoz, *Crazy Horse*, 121–52; and Olson, *Red Cloud*, 27–214. On Crazy Horse, see Sandoz' biography; and the Hinman interviews and Ricker tablets, Nebraska State Historical Society. Helen H. Blish, *A Pictographic History of the Oglala Sioux*, with drawings by Amos Bad Heart Bull (Lincoln, Neb., 1967), contains the Sioux "history" of the period. Bad Heart Bull, who was much younger than the participants in these events, drew or sketched scenes from various battles on the basis of information given him by the older men. Delightfully precise in detail, they are frustratingly vague about what happened when. On Plains Indian warfare, consult W. W. Newcomb, "A Re-examination of the Causes of Plains Warfare," *American Anthropologist*, 1950, 317–29, and Peter Farb, *Man's Rise to Civilization as Shown by the Indians of North America from Primeval Times to the Coming of the Industrial State* (New York, 1968), 112–32.
2. Hinman interview with Short Bull, Nebraska State Historical Society.
3. Ibid.; see also Sandoz, *Crazy Horse*, 125–26.
4. Hinman interview with Red Feather, Nebraska State Historical Society.
5. Hinman interview with He Dog, Nebraska State Historical Society.
6. Hinman interviews, Nebraska State Historical Society; see also Blish, *A Pictographic History*, 389.

7. Ricker tablets, Nebraska State Historical Society. This information comes from Ricker's own work on Crazy Horse, prepared from various Indian and trader sources.

8. Hinman interview with Red Feather, Nebraska State Historical Society.

9. Billy Garnett interview, Ricker tablets, and Hinman interview with He Dog, Nebraska State Historical Society; see also Sandoz, *Crazy Horse*, 174–78.

10. Hinman interview with He Dog, Nebraska State Historical Society. On the Crow Owners Society, see Wissler, "Societies and Ceremonial Associations of the Teton-Dakota," 23–25.

11. Sandoz, *Crazy Horse*, 131–34.

12. Hassrick, *The Sioux*, 121–24; Llewellyn and Hoebel, *The Cheyenne Way*, 169–71.

13. Hassrick, *The Sioux*, 125.

14. Llewellyn and Hoebel, *The Cheyenne Way*, 172–74; Hassrick, *The Sioux*, 129–34.

15. Llewellyn and Hoebel, *The Cheyenne Way*, 187; Hassrick, *The Sioux*, 136.

16. Llewellyn and Hoebel, *The Cheyenne Way*, 192.

17. Hassrick, *The Sioux*, 136.

18. Ibid., 136–37.

19. Erikson, "Observations on Sioux Education," 130.

20. Sandoz, *Crazy Horse*, 173.

21. Ibid., 133–35; Hinman interviews with He Dog and Short Bull, Nebraska State Historical Society.

22. Hinman interviews with He Dog and Little Shield, Nebraska State Historical Society.

CHAPTER 9

1. On Lieutenant Collins, see Agnes Wright Spring, *Caspar Collins: The Life and Exploits of an Indian Fighter of the Sixties* (New York, 1927), and Sandoz, *Crazy Horse*, 136–37.

2. Spring, *Caspar Collins*, 171.

3. Ibid., 172–73.

4. Ibid., 165–67.

5. Ibid., 165.

6. Hyde, *Red Cloud's Folk*, 103.

7. Ibid., 104.

8. Garnett interview, Ricker tablets, Nebraska State Historical Society.

9. Robinson, *A History of the Dakota*, 351.

10. Grinnell, *The Fighting Cheyennes*, 154.

11. Ibid., 143.

12. The best account of the Sand Creek massacre is Grinnell, *The Fighting Cheyennes*, 149–80; see also Hyde, *Red Cloud's Folk*, 108–11.

13. Hyde, *Red Cloud's Folk*, 110; Grinnell, *The Fighting Cheyennes*, 181–203.

14. Grinnell, *The Fighting Cheyennes*, 191; Hyde, *Spotted Tail's Folk*, 96.
15. Eugene F. Ware, *The Indian War of 1864* (Lincoln, Neb., 1960, reprint), 372.
16. Grinnell, *The Fighting Cheyennes*, 193; Hyde, *Red Cloud's Folk*, 111.
17. Hyde, *Red Cloud's Folk*, 112.
18. Ibid., 112; Grinnell, *The Fighting Cheyennes*, 194–203.
19. Hyde, *Red Cloud's Folk*, 113.
20. Ibid., 116.
21. Ibid., 118.
22. Hyde, *Spotted Tail's Folk*, 100.
23. Interview with Frank Salaway, Ricker tablets, Nebraska State Historical Society; Sandoz, *Crazy Horse*, 158–59.
24. Sandoz, *Crazy Horse*, 161; Hyde, *Red Cloud's Folk*, 121; Hyde, *Spotted Tail's Folk*, 103.
25. Hyde, *Spotted Tail's Folk*, 106.
26. Ibid., 106; Sandoz, *Crazy Horse*, 162–63.
27. Ricker tablets, Nebraska State Historical Society; this information comes from Ricker's own short biography of Crazy Horse, prepared from various Indian and white sources.
28. Hyde, *Red Cloud's Folk*, 123–24.
29. Sandoz, *Crazy Horse*, 164–65; Hyde, *Red Cloud's Folk*, 124–25.
30. Most of these details come from Grinnell, *The Fighting Cheyennes*, 221–23; Grinnell got most of his information directly from the Cheyennes, shortly after the turn of the century. See also Sandoz, *Crazy Horse*, 164–65.
31. Sandoz, *Crazy Horse*, 166–67; Hyde, *Spotted Tail's Folk*, 125.
32. Grinnell, *The Fighting Cheyennes*, 125–26.
33. Hyde, *Red Cloud's Folk*, 125; Sandoz, *Crazy Horse*, 173–74.

CHAPTER 10

1. Custer to parents, March 17, 1862, Custer Mss.; Merington, *The Custer Story*, 27–28.
2. Bruce Catton, *Mr. Lincoln's Army* (Garden City, N.Y., 1955), 155–59, is the best discussion.
3. James Harrison Wilson, *Under the Old Flag* (New York, 1912), I, 126; Whittaker, *Custer*, 133; Catton, *Mr. Lincoln's Army*, 336–37.
4. George B. McClellan, *Report on the Organization and Campaigns of the Army of the Potomac* . . . (New York, 1864), 238–39; for a good discussion, see Warren W. Hassler, Jr., *General George B. McClellan* (Baton Rouge, 1957), 320–25.
5. Monaghan, *Custer*, 113–14.
6. Custer to Lydia Reed, May 5, 1862, Custer Mss.; Merington, *The Custer Story*, 29–30.

7. Monaghan, *Custer*, 245.

8. Custer to Lydia Reed, September 21, 1862, Custer Mss.; Whittaker, *Custer*, 125–29; Monaghan, *Custer*, 90–92.

9. Whittaker, *Custer*, 51–52; Custer, "War Memoirs"; Monaghan, *Custer*, 45–46.

10. Wilson, *Under the Old Flag*, I, 101–2; see also Monaghan, *Custer*, 77–80, for two somewhat different versions of the incident.

11. Monaghan, *Custer*, 81–83; George B. McClellan, *McClellan's Own Story* (New York, 1887), 364–65.

12. Quoted in Catton, *Mr. Lincoln's Army*, 117.

13. Bell I. Wiley, *The Life of Billy Yank* (New York, 1951), 124.

14. Ibid., 92.

15. Custer, "War Memoirs"; Whittaker, *Custer*, 65–69.

16. Wiley, *Billy Yank*, 72.

17. Bell I. Wiley, *The Life of Johnny Reb* (New York, 1943), 72.

18. Custer to Lydia Reed, August 8, 1862, Custer Mss.; Whittaker, *Custer*, 122–24.

19. Custer to Lydia Reed, April 20, 1862, Custer Mss.; Merington, *The Custer Story*, 29.

20. Custer to Lydia Reed, May 2, 1863, Custer Mss.; Merington, *The Custer Story*, 53; Monaghan, *Custer*, 116.

21. Wiley, *Billy Yank*, 199.

22. Ibid., 115.

23. Ibid., 247–48.

24. Custer to Isaac Christiancy, May 31, 1863, and to Lydia Reed, same date, both in Custer Mss.; see also Monaghan, *Custer*, 123.

25. Monaghan, *Custer*, 108.

26. Merington, *The Custer Story*, 46–47.

27. Ibid., 47.

28. Even when she was sixty years old, Libbie's eyes belied the sweet gentle lady she always tried to be. In a photograph taken about 1900, when she had put on some weight, was dressed in black, and wore one of those horrendous turn-of-the-century hats, her eyes still sparkle, still tell the observer that here is an extraordinary woman. As indeed she was. The best series of Libbie Bacon photographs is in Lawrence A. Frost, *The Custer Album* (Seattle, 1964).

29. Merington, *The Custer Story*, 38–40.

30. Ibid., 44.

31. Whittaker, *Custer*, 91.

32. Monaghan, *Custer*, 158.

33. Merington, *The Custer Story*, 50–51.

34. Ibid., 58.

35. Custer to Lydia Reed, June 8, 1863, Custer Mss.; Monaghan, *Custer*, 124–25.

36. Custer to Lydia Reed, June 19, 1863, Custer Mss.; Whittaker, *Custer*, 159.

37. Whittaker, *Custer*, 161–62; Monaghan, *Custer*, 132–33.

38. Merington, *The Custer Story*, 69.

39. Wiley, *Billy Yank*, 303.

40. Monaghan, *Custer*, 134–35.
41. Ibid., 162.
42. Merington, *The Custer Story*, 67; the originals of all these letters are in the Custer Mss.
43. Ibid., 65.
44. Ibid., 71.
45. Ibid., 74.
46. Ibid., 75.
47. Ibid., 79.
48. Ibid., 75.
49. Ibid., 77.
50. Ibid., 80.
51. Ibid., 81.
52. Monaghan, *Custer*, 179.
53. Merington, *The Custer Story*, 81.
54. Ibid., 84–85.

CHAPTER 11

1. *War of the Rebellion, Official Records of the Union and Confederate Armies* (Washington, D.C., 1880–1901), XXVII, Pt. 1, 991–98, 919. Hereinafter cited as O.R.
2. O.R., XXXVI, Pt. 1, 110, 128, 163, 177.
3. For an excellent discussion, see Russell F. Weigley, *The American Way of War: A History of United States Military Strategy and Policy* (New York, 1973), especially Chap. 7, "A Strategy of Annihilation: U. S. Grant and the Union."
4. O.R., XLVI, Pt. 1, 475, 1111. The details of Custer's campaigns are admirably recounted in Monaghan's *Custer*.
5. Custer to Libbie, June 21, 1864, Custer Mss.; Merington, *The Custer Story*, 104.
6. Custer to Nettie Humphrey, October 12, 1863, Custer Mss.; Merington, *The Custer Story*, 65–66.
7. Custer to Nettie Humphrey, October 9, 1863, Custer Mss.; Merington, *The Custer Story*, 65.
8. See Custer to Daniel Bacon, November 12, 1864, Custer Mss., for a full description of his staff; see also Merington, *The Custer Story*, 133, and Monaghan, *Custer*, 159.
9. Monaghan, *Custer*, 220.
10. Merington, *The Custer Story*, 151; Monaghan, *Custer*, 238.
11. Libbie Custer to Richmond, November 15, 1864, Custer Mss.; Merington, *The Custer Story*, 133.
12. Elizabeth Custer, *"Boots and Saddles": or, Life in Dakota with General Custer* (New York, 1904), 223.
13. Merington, *The Custer Story*, 60.
14. Monaghan, *Custer*, 136.
15. Ibid., 236.

16. Merington, *The Custer Story*, 153.
17. Custer to Libbie, March 30, 1865, Custer Mss.; Merington, *The Custer Story*, 146.
18. Merington, *The Custer Story*, 160.
19. Monaghan, *Custer*, 141.
20. O.R., XXVII, Pt. 1, 998; Monaghan, *Custer*, 148–49.
21. Merington, *The Custer Story*, 66.
22. Monaghan, *Custer*, 166–67.
23. Ibid., 194–95; O.R., XXXVI, Pt. 1, 813–17.
24. Monaghan, *Custer*, 211–12; Custer to Libbie, October 10, 1864, Custer Mss.
25. Merington, *The Custer Story*, 125, 137; Monaghan, *Custer*, 217.
26. New York *Times*, March 20, 1865.
27. Libbie Custer to parents, October 25, 1864, Custer Mss.; Merington, *The Custer Story*, 125–26.
28. Merington, *The Custer Story*, 127; Monaghan, *Custer*, 219.
29. Custer to Libbie, October 5, 1864, Custer Mss.; Merington, *The Custer Story*, 119.
30. Custer to Libbie, August 21, 1864, Custer Mss.; Merington, *The Custer Story*, 115.
31. Monaghan, *Custer*, 223.
32. O.R., XXXIII, 161.
33. S. L. A. Marshall, *Men Against Fire* (New York, 1947), 57, and Chap. 5 generally.
34. Wiley, *Billy Yank*, 205.
35. Ibid., 209.
36. Ibid., 205–6.
37. Libbie Custer to parents, December 4, 1864, Custer Mss.; Merington, *The Custer Story*, 134.
38. Wiley, *Billy Yank*, 201–2.
39. Libbie Custer to parents, March 28, 1864, Custer Mss.; Merington, *The Custer Story*, 87.
40. Merington, *The Custer Story*, 91.
41. Ibid., 145.
42. Ibid., 91, 101, 112.
43. Ibid., 103.
44. Ibid., 121.
45. Ibid., 99–100.
46. Ibid., 120.
47. See Monaghan, *Custer*, 158–59, for details.
48. Merington, *The Custer Story*, 68–69.
49. Ibid., 69.
50. Custer to Nettie Humphrey, November 1, 1863, Custer Mss.; Merington, *The Custer Story*, 71.
51. Monaghan, *Custer*, 188.
52. Custer to Libbie, May 16, 1864, Custer Mss.; Merington, *The Custer Story*, 97.
53. Custer to Libbie, July 1, 1864, Custer Mss.; Merington, *The Custer Story*, 110–11.

54. Monaghan, *Custer*, 196.
55. Wilson, *Under the Old Flag*, I, 424.
56. O.R., XLIII, Pt. 1, 33, 453, 526.
57. Libbie Custer to parents, March 28, 1864, Custer Mss.; Merington, *The Custer Story*, 87.
58. Monaghan, *Custer*, 189.
59. Libbie Custer to Noble, August 18, 1864, Custer Mss.; Merington, *The Custer Story*, 113–14.
60. Libbie Custer to Custer, March 8, 1865, Custer Mss.; Merington, *The Custer Story*, 136.
61. Quoted in Monaghan, *Custer*, 246.
62. Ibid., 247.
63. Quoted, ibid., 250–51.

CHAPTER 13

1. Robert M. Utley, *Frontier Regulars: The United States Army and the Indian* (New York, 1973), 2–3. This outstanding work became the standard source on the frontier Army immediately upon its publication.
2. Quoted, ibid., 94.
3. Robinson, *A History of the Dakota*, 362–63.
4. Hyde, *Spotted Tail's Folk*, 113; Olson, *Red Cloud*, 10.
5. Quoted in Utley, *Frontier Regulars*, 93.
6. Olson, *Red Cloud*, 33.
7. Frances C. Carrington, *Army Life on the Plains* (Philadelphia, 1910), 46–47; Hyde, *Red Cloud's Folk*, 138–39.
8. James D. Richardson, comp., *Messages and Papers of the Presidents, 1789–1897* (Washington, D.C., 1897), VI, 454.
9. Cyrus T. Brady, *Indian Fights and Fighters* (Lincoln, Neb., 1971), 10.
10. Ibid., 23.
11. Olson, *Red Cloud*, 43; Hyde, *Red Cloud's Folk*, 145; Grinnell, *The Fighting Cheyennes*, 236; Dee Brown, *Fort Phil Kearny: An American Saga* (New York, 1962), 149.
12. Brady, *Indian Fights*, 19; Robinson, *A History of the Dakota*, 355.
13. Carrington, *Army Life on the Plains*, 121.
14. Robinson, *A History of the Dakota*, 358–59. The information on Crazy Horse's role at the siege of Fort Phil Kearny is based on the statements of White Bear, an associate of Red Cloud, to Doane Robinson, secretary of the South Dakota Department of History, in 1904. See Robinson, *A History of the Dakota*, 361.
15. Ibid., 361.
16. Brown, *Fort Phil Kearny*, 149; Hyde, *Red Cloud's Folk*, 145.
17. Brady, *Indian Fights*, 19–23; Brown, *Fort Phil Kearny*, 162–67; Sandoz, *Crazy Horse*, 195–96.
18. Sandoz, *Crazy Horse*, 195–96.

19. Brown, *Fort Phil Kearny*, 166.
20. Ibid., 170–71.
21. Grinnell, *The Fighting Cheyennes*, 237–38.
22. Brown, *Fort Phil Kearny*, 174–75.
23. Ibid., 159–203, is the most complete account from the white man's point of view, while Hyde, *Red Cloud's Folk*, 146–49, Sandoz, *Crazy Horse*, 198–203, Grinnell, *The Fighting Cheyennes*, 238–43, give the Indian side. See also Brady, *Indian Fights*, 24–32, and J. Cecil Alter, *James Bridger* (Columbus, Ohio, 1951), 458–59.
24. Grinnell, *The Fighting Cheyennes*, 233–34, and Sandoz, *Crazy Horse*, 202–3.
25. Quoted in Brown, *Fort Phil Kearny*, 188.
26. Frank Grouard, "An Indian Scout's Recollections of Crazy Horse," *Nebraska History Magazine*, XII (January–March, 1929), 72.
27. Quoted in Brown, *Fort Phil Kearny*, 191–92.

CHAPTER 14

1. Quoted in Utley, *Frontier Regulars*, 111.
2. See Elizabeth Custer, *Tenting on the Plains* (Norman, Okla., 1971), 27–92.
3. Merington, *The Custer Story*, 168.
4. Libbie Custer to parents, July 20, 1865, Custer Mss.; Merington, *The Custer Story*, 169.
5. Custer, *Tenting on the Plains*, 139–40.
6. Ibid., 204.
7. Custer to Bacons, October 5, 1865, Custer Mss.; Merington, *The Custer Story*, 174–75.
8. Quoted in Monaghan, *Custer*, 260.
9. Custer, *Tenting on the Plains*, 110; Monaghan, *Custer*, 257–59.
10. Merington, *The Custer Story*, 172–73.
11. Custer to Bacons, October 5, 1865, Custer Mss.; Merington, *The Custer Story*, 174–75.
12. Monaghan, *Custer*, 266.
13. Custer to Libbie, March 12, 1866, Custer Mss.; Merington, *The Custer Story*, 177–78.
14. Custer to Libbie, March 16, 1866, Custer Mss.; Merington, *The Custer Story*, 179.
15. Custer to Libbie, March 18, 1866, Custer Mss.; Merington, *The Custer Story*, 179.
16. Custer to Libbie, April 1, 1866, Custer Mss.; Merington, *The Custer Story*, 180.
17. Monaghan, *Custer*, 270.
18. Ibid., 271.
19. Custer to President Andrew Johnson, August 13, 1866, Custer Mss.

20. See Howard K. Beale, *The Critical Year: A Study of Andrew Johnson and Reconstruction* (New York, 1930), 299. Beale felt that Johnson's failure to make economics, instead of race and the status of former Confederates, the issue of the campaign was "a fatal error in political judgment."

21. For an excellent discussion, see LaWanda Cox and John Cox, *Politics, Principle, and Prejudice, 1865–66* (New York, 1963), preface.

22. Quoted, ibid., 195–96; see also Eric L. McKitrick, *Andrew Johnson and Reconstruction* (Chicago, 1960), Chap. 10.

23. Monaghan, *Custer*, 272–77.

24. Ibid., 277–78.

25. Whittaker, *Complete Life of Custer*, 631–33; Monaghan, *Custer*, 279–80.

26. Charles Godfrey Leland, *Memoirs* (New York, 1893), 333; quoted in Monaghan, *Custer*, 283.

27. Sandoz, *Crazy Horse*, 207.

28. Grinnell, *The Fighting Cheyennes*, 245–46.

29. Rachel Sherman Thorndike, ed., *The Sherman Letters* (New York, 1894), 287.

30. Ibid., 289.

31. Utley, *Frontier Regulars*, 111–14.

32. Ibid., 114.

33. Quoted in Lawrence A. Frost, *The Court-Martial of General George A. Custer* (Norman, Okla., 1968), 8. This work is much the best source on Custer's campaign in Kansas.

34. Utley, *Frontier Regulars*, 120.

35. Custer, *My Life on the Plains*, 34.

36. Frost, *Court-Martial*, 35.

37. Ibid., 13–16; Utley, *Frontier Regulars*, 115–16.

38. Grinnell, *The Fighting Cheyennes*, 248–49.

39. Custer, *My Life on the Plains*, 37, 44.

40. Ibid., 48–49; Grinnell, *The Fighting Cheyennes*, 250–51.

41. Custer, *My Life on the Plains*, 58.

42. Utley, *Frontier Regulars*, 116.

43. Frost, *Court-Martial*, 21.

44. Custer, *My Life on the Plains*, 79–82.

45. Ibid., 88–93; Monaghan, *Custer*, 289.

46. Henry M. Stanley, *My Early Travels and Adventures* (London, 1895), I, 46.

47. Grinnell, *The Fighting Cheyennes*, 253.

48. Utley, *Frontier Regulars*, 117–19.

49. Theodore Davis, "A Summer on the Plains," *Harper's Weekly*, XXXVI, February 1868, 298.

50. Frost, *Court-Martial*, 35.

51. Jack D. Foner, *The United States Soldier Between Two Wars: Army Life and Reforms, 1865–1898* (New York, 1970), 18–20.

52. Merington, *The Custer Story*, 199.

53. Ibid., 201–4.

54. Monaghan, *Custer*, 290.

CHAPTER 15

1. Robinson, *A History of the Dakota*, 371.
2. Hyde, *Red Cloud's Folk*, 151–54; Robinson, *A History of the Dakota*, 371–73.
3. Custer, *My Life on the Plains*, 115; Monaghan, *Custer*, 291.
4. Utley, *Frontier Regulars*, 21.
5. Monaghan, *Custer*, 282.
6. Davis, "A Summer on the Plains," 303.
7. Custer, *Tenting on the Plains*, 579.
8. Stanley, *Early Travels*, I, 87.
9. Custer, *My Life on the Plains*, 119–20.
10. Davis, "A Summer on the Plains," 299–301.
11. Frost, *Court-Martial*, 41; Custer, *My Life on the Plains*, 121.
12. Davis, "A Summer on the Plains," 301.
13. Merington, *The Custer Story*, 206.
14. Frost, *Court-Martial*, 45–46; Custer, *My Life on the Plains*, 124–25.
15. Frost, *Court-Martial*, 46–47.
16. Ibid., 191; Custer, *My Life on the Plains*, 125–27.
17. Frost, *Court-Martial*, 49–51; Custer, *My Life on the Plains*, 133–34; Monaghan, *Custer*, 293–94.
18. Frost, *Court-Martial*, 53–56; Custer, *My Life on the Plains*, 135–44.
19. Custer, *My Life on the Plains*, 145–47.
20. Ibid., 151–55; Frost, *Court-Martial*, 59–60.
21. Custer, *My Life on the Plains*, 156; Frost, *Court-Martial*, 60.
22. Frost, *Court-Martial*, 61–64; Custer, *My Life on the Plains*, 160–65.
23. Custer, *My Life on the Plains*, 172–77; Frost, *Court-Martial*, 66–67.
24. Quoted in Frost, *Court-Martial*, 53.
25. Davis, "A Summer on the Plains," 306.
26. Frost, *Court-Martial*, 185.
27. Ibid., 151.
28. Ibid., 165–68.
29. Custer, *My Life on the Plains*, 190–201.
30. Ibid., 203–13; Frost, *Court-Martial*, 78–85.
31. Custer, *Tenting on the Plains*, 699–702.
32. Ibid., 702.
33. Frost, *Court-Martial*, 87.
34. Thorndike, ed., *The Sherman Letters*, 291.
35. Ibid., 320.
36. Gard, *The Great Buffalo Hunt*, is an excellent account of the slaughter of the buffalo.
37. Hyde, *Red Cloud's Folk*, 158.
38. Brown, *Fort Phil Kearny*, 223.
39. Sandoz, *Crazy Horse*, 212; Hyde, *Red Cloud's Folk*, 159.
40. Quoted in Brown, *Fort Phil Kearny*, 223.
41. Sandoz, *Crazy Horse*, 212–13; Hyde, *Red Cloud's Folk*, 159; Brown, *Fort Phil Kearny*, 223.

42. Hyde, *Red Cloud's Folk*, 160.
43. Sandoz, *Crazy Horse*, 216.
44. Ibid., 223.
45. Olson, *Red Cloud*, 67–69; Sandoz, *Crazy Horse*, 224; Hyde, *Red Cloud's Folk*, 161.
46. Robinson, *A History of the Dakota*, 383.
47. Hyde, *Red Cloud's Folk*, 159–60.
48. Utley, *Frontier Regulars*, 132–35; Olson, *Red Cloud*, 66–68.
49. Olson, *Red Cloud*, 69; Utley, *Frontier Regulars*, 134.
50. From an interview with Sitting Bull, New York *Herald*, November 16, 1877.
51. Frost, *Court-Martial*, 164.
52. Ibid., 245–46.
53. Ibid., 247.
54. Merington, *The Custer Story*, 212.
55. Frost, *Court-Martial*, 256.

CHAPTER 16

1. Utley, *Frontier Regulars*, 12.
2. Ibid., 135; Olson, *Red Cloud*, 71.
3. Quoted in Olson, *Red Cloud*, 72.
4. Robinson, *A History of the Dakota*, 387.
5. Ibid., 382–87, for a full account of the treaty; see also Olson, *Red Cloud*, 72–76, Utley, *Frontier Regulars*, 134–35, and Hyde, *Red Cloud's Folk*, 162–65.
6. See Olson, *Red Cloud*, 80.
7. Ibid., 74.
8. Ibid., 80–82.
9. Monaghan, *Custer*, 304; Robert G. Athearn, *William T. Sherman and the Settlement of the West* (Norman, Okla., 1956), 213–23.
10. Frost, *Court-Martial*, 266.
11. For an excellent discussion of the origins and causes of this war, see Utley, *Frontier Regulars*, 138–43.
12. Custer, *My Life on the Plains*, 216.
13. Quoted in Utley, *Frontier Regulars*, 142.
14. Stanley, *Personal Memoirs*, 23.
15. Merington, *The Custer Story*, 217; Monaghan, *Custer*, 306–7.
16. Custer, *My Life on the Plains*, 218–60; Monaghan, *Custer*, 308–9.
17. Utley, *Frontier Regulars*, 149; see also General W. B. Hazen, "Some Corrections of 'Life on the Plains,'" *Chronicles of Oklahoma*, III (1925), 295–318.
18. Utley, *Frontier Regulars*, 150.
19. Custer, *My Life on the Plains*, 281–84; Monaghan, *Custer*, 310.
20. Custer, *My Life on the Plains*, 284.
21. Ibid., 286–88.
22. Ibid., 310–15.

23. Ibid., 316–20.
24. Grinnell, *The Fighting Cheyennes*, 302.
25. Custer, *My Life on the Plains*, 334–45; Utley, *Frontier Regulars*, 150–51; Monaghan, *Custer*, 316–18; Merington, *The Custer Story*, 222–23.
26. As George Grinnell writes, "Black Kettle was a striking example of a consistently friendly Indian, who, because he was friendly and so because his whereabouts was usually known, was punished for the acts of people whom it was supposed he could control" (*The Fighting Cheyennes*, 309).
27. Ibid., 304–5; Monaghan, *Custer*, 319; Custer, *My Life on the Plains*, 347.
28. Custer, *My Life on the Plains*, 358–64.
29. Ibid., 347; Quaife's long note on the subject is on pp. 353–55.
30. Monaghan, *Custer*, 319–20.
31. Custer, *My Life on the Plains*, 356–58.
32. Ibid., 346.
33. Custer reprinted the order in *My Life on the Plains*, 388–89.
34. Ibid., 415.
35. See Monaghan, *Custer*, 327–28, for a full discussion of the myth.
36. Utley, *Frontier Regulars*, 158–59.
37. Monaghan, *Custer*, 322.
38. Grinnell, *The Fighting Cheyennes*, 307.
39. Ibid., 308.
40. Elizabeth Custer, *Following the Guidon* (Norman, Okla., 1967), 263 64.

CHAPTER 17

1. Hyde, *Red Cloud's Folk*, 171.
2. Sandoz, *Crazy Horse*, 225–26.
3. Hyde, *Red Cloud's Folk*, 167.
4. Olson, *Red Cloud*, 174.
5. Hyde, *Red Cloud's Folk*, 175.
6. Ibid., 176.
7. Olson, *Red Cloud*, 96, 112; Hyde, *Red Cloud's Folk*, 176–78; Robinson, *A History of the Dakota*, 396–99.
8. Sandoz, *Crazy Horse*, 227.
9. Hinman interview with He Dog, Nebraska State Historical Society.
10. Hinman interview with Red Feather, Nebraska State Historical Society.
11. Hinman interview with He Dog, Nebraska State Historical Society; Sandoz, *Crazy Horse*, 237–38.
12. Merington, *The Custer Story*, 231; Monaghan, *Custer*, 332.
13. Merington, *The Custer Story*, 234–35.
14. Ibid., 237.
15. Ibid., 235.

16. Merington, *The Custer Story*, 237.
17. Ibid., 237–38.
18. Hinman interview with He Dog, Nebraska State Historical Society.
19. Ibid.
20. Ibid.
21. It must be added, however, that Crazy Horse was hardly the only one responsible for the dividing of the Oglalas. That division had been building for a long time, essentially from the beginnings of the Holy Road, and its basic cause was less internal than external. The whites tempted the Oglalas to come down to the reservation or drove them there; when Red Cloud moved to his Nebraska agency he helped complete the split.
22. Sandoz, *Crazy Horse*, 246–47.
23. Hinman interview with He Dog, Nebraska State Historical Society. He Dog said that "many people believe this child was Crazy Horse's daughter, but it was never known for certain."
24. Monaghan, *Custer*, 336; Merington, *The Custer Story*, 246; William Tucker and Jeff C. Dykes, *The Grand Duke Alexis in the United States of America During the Winter of 1871–1872* (New York, 1973). This rare book was originally published in 1872; it is a compilation of newspaper accounts of the grand duke's tour.
25. Tucker and Dykes, *The Grand Duke*, 157.
26. Ibid., 158; Hyde, *Spotted Tail's Folk*, 180.
27. Tucker and Dykes, *The Grand Duke*, 161.
28. Merington, *The Custer Story*, 246; Tucker and Dykes, *The Grand Duke*, 162.
29. Tucker and Dykes, *The Grand Duke*, 167.
30. Ibid., 170; Hyde, *Spotted Tail's Folk*, 180–81.
31. Merington, *The Custer Story*, 246.
32. Tucker and Dykes, *The Grand Duke*, 189–90.
33. Quoted in Dykes's introduction, ibid.
34. Ibid., 189.
35. Monaghan, *Custer*, 337.
36. Merington, *The Custer Story*, 247.
37. Tucker and Dykes, *The Grand Duke*, 219.
38. Monaghan, *Custer*, 338.
39. Elizabeth Custer, "*Boots and Saddles*," 5.

CHAPTER 18

1. Stanley Vestal, *Sitting Bull: Champion of the Sioux* (Norman, Okla., 1957), 250–51, a fine biography.
2. Ibid.; Utley, *Frontier Regulars*, 236.
3. Utley, *Frontier Regulars*, 242.
4. Vestal, *Sitting Bull*, 125–30; Sandoz, *Crazy Horse*, 273–74; Utley, *Frontier Regulars*, 236, 242; Robinson, *A History of the Dakota*, 401.

5. Hinman interview with Red Feather, Nebraska State Historical Society.
6. Ibid.; Hinman interview with He Dog, Nebraska State Historical Society; Sandoz, *Crazy Horse*, 253–55.
7. Monaghan, *Custer*, 339.
8. Utley, *Frontier Regulars*, 242.
9. Lloyd Lewis, *Sherman, Fighting Prophet* (New York, 1932), 407.
10. Stanley's letters are in Stanley, *Personal Memoirs*, 238–39; Custer's are in Custer Mss., Custer Battlefield National Monument, Crow Agency, Montana, and are reprinted in Merington, *The Custer Story*, 248–50, and Elizabeth Custer, *"Boots and Saddles,"* 225–30.
11. Elizabeth Custer, *"Boots and Saddles,"* 232.
12. Stanley, *Personal Memoirs*, 241.
13. Elizabeth Custer, *"Boots and Saddles,"* 233.
14. Ibid., 257–58.
15. Stanley, *Personal Memoirs*, 239.
16. Merington, *The Custer Story*, 252.
17. Stanley, *Personal Memoirs*, 240.
18. Elizabeth Custer, *"Boots and Saddles,"* 230; Monaghan, *Custer*, 343.
19. Stanley, *Personal Memoirs*, 241.
20. Merington, *The Custer Story*, 259.
21. Ibid., 265, 267.
22. Ibid., 258.
23. Ibid., 251.
24. Elizabeth Custer, *"Boots and Saddles,"* 234.
25. Monaghan, *Custer*, 345.
26. Ibid., 345–46; Custer's battle report, reprinted in Elizabeth Custer, *"Boots and Saddles,"* 237; Sandoz, *Crazy Horse*, 275.
27. Custer's battle report, in Elizabeth Custer, *"Boots and Saddles,"* 237–38.
28. Ibid., 240.
29. Ibid., 238.
30. Ibid., 239.
31. Ibid., 239–40; Monaghan, *Custer*, 347; Utley, *Frontier Regulars*, 242–43.
32. Custer's battle report, in Elizabeth Custer, *"Boots and Saddles,"* 241–47.
33. Merington, *The Custer Story*, 261.
34. Custer's battle report, in Elizabeth Custer, *"Boots and Saddles,"* 247–48.

CHAPTER 19

1. John F. Reiger, ed., *The Passing of the Great West: Selected Papers of George Bird Grinnell* (New York, 1972), 79.
2. Robert V. Bruce, *1877: Year of Violence* (Indianapolis, 1959), Chap. 1.

3. Edgar I. Stewart, *Custer's Luck* (Norman, Okla., 1955), 61; Sandoz, *Crazy Horse,* 287.
4. Max E. Gerber, "The Black Hills Expedition of 1874: A New Look," *South Dakota History,* June–July, 1970, 8.
5. Hyde, *Red Cloud's Folk,* 217.
6. Gerber, "The Black Hills Expedition," 10; Monaghan, *Custer,* 353; Reiger, ed., *The Passing of the Great West,* 81; Stewart, *Custer's Luck,* 62–63.
7. Merington, *The Custer Story,* 272–73; Monaghan, *Custer,* 354–55; Gerber, "The Black Hills Expedition," 11; Elizabeth Custer, "Boots and Saddles," 261.
8. Merington, *The Custer Story,* 273; Gerber, "The Black Hills Expedition," 10.
9. Gerber, "The Black Hills Expedition," 12.
10. Monaghan, *Custer,* 355; Gerber, "The Black Hills Expedition," 12.
11. Merington, *The Custer Story,* 275.
12. Reiger, ed., *The Passing of the Great West,* 105–6.
13. New York *Tribune,* August 28, 1874; Gerber, "The Black Hills Expedition," 14; Monaghan, *Custer,* 355.
14. Custer's report was printed as Executive Document No. 32, 43d Congress, Second Session, Washington, D.C., 1874. Reprinted in Robinson, *A History of the Dakota,* 289.
15. Reiger, ed., *The Passing of the Great West,* 106.
16. Gerber, "The Black Hills Expedition," 19.
17. Bismarck *Tribune,* September 8, 1874.
18. Merington, *The Custer Story,* 274.
19. Grouard, "An Indian Scout's Recollections," 70–72; Sandoz, *Crazy Horse,* 284–86. All sources agree that Crazy Horse mourned his daughter deeply; but Grouard is the sole source for the claim that he went with Crazy Horse, and Grouard is not the most reliable witness.
20. Hinman interviews with He Dog, Red Feather, and others, Nebraska State Historical Society; Sandoz, *Crazy Horse,* 290.
21. Whittaker, *Custer,* 636; Monaghan, *Custer,* 358–59; Frost, *Custer Album,* 135–47, has some striking photographs taken that winter.

CHAPTER 20

1. Robinson, *A History of the Dakota,* 416.
2. Hyde, *Red Cloud's Folk,* 253.
3. Sandoz, *Crazy Horse,* 280.
4. Hyde, *Red Cloud's Folk,* 253.
5. Sandoz, *Crazy Horse,* 281.
6. Hyde, *Red Cloud's Folk,* 223.
7. Hinman interview with He Dog, Nebraska State Historical Society; Sandoz, *Crazy Horse,* 222.
8. Olson, *Red Cloud,* 177; Robinson, *A History of the Dakota,* 414–15; Hyde, *Red Cloud's Folk,* 230–31.

9. Olson, *Red Cloud,* 177–98.
10. Hyde, *Spotted Tail's Folk,* 210–11.
11. Olson, *Red Cloud,* 203–4.
12. Sandoz, *Crazy Horse,* 293.
13. Hyde, *Spotted Tail's Folk,* 213.
14. Hyde, *Red Cloud's Folk,* 243–44; Hyde, *Spotted Tail's Folk,* 213–14; Olson, *Red Cloud,* 204–5.
15. Robinson, *A History of the Dakota,* 418; Hyde, *Spotted Tail's Folk,* 214.
16. The fullest account is Robinson, *A History of the Dakota,* 418–20; see also Hyde's books and Olson, *Red Cloud,* 204–12, which is the best analysis of the council.
17. Garnett interview, Ricker tablets, Nebraska State Historical Society.
18. Robinson, *A History of the Dakota,* 420.
19. Ibid., 421; Utley, *Frontier Regulars,* 246; Hyde, *Red Cloud's Folk,* 250.
20. Robinson, *A History of the Dakota,* 422–23; Utley, *Frontier Regulars,* 246–47; Hyde, *Red Cloud's Folk,* 250.
21. Hyde, *Spotted Tail's Folk,* 219; Olson, *Red Cloud,* 214–20.
22. Utley, *Frontier Regulars,* 246.
23. Hyde, *Spotted Tail's Folk,* 220.
24. Ibid., 221; Utley, *Frontier Regulars,* 248; Sandoz, *Crazy Horse,* 300–1.
25. Utley, *Frontier Regulars,* 248.
26. Stewart, *Custer's Luck,* 120–21.
27. Elizabeth Custer, "*Boots and Saddles,*" 207–9; Merington, *The Custer Story,* 277.
28. Stewart, *Custer's Luck,* 123–28.
29. Ibid., 127; Monaghan, *Custer,* 361.
30. Stewart, *Custer's Luck,* 121.
31. Monaghan, *Custer,* 368.
32. Stewart, *Custer's Luck,* 121; Merington, *The Custer Story,* 289.
33. Stewart, *Custer's Luck,* 121.
34. Merington, *The Custer Story,* 294.
35. Ibid., 277.
36. Ibid.
37. Elizabeth Custer, "*Boots and Saddles,*" 211–13.
38. Stewart, *Custer's Luck,* 124.
39. Merington, *The Custer Story,* 284.
40. Ibid., 283–85, 291.
41. William B. Hesseltine, *Ulysses S. Grant: Politician* (New York, 1936), 395–96.
42. Merington, *The Custer Story,* 293; for Custer's testimony, see Stewart, *Custer's Luck,* 124–31.
43. Merington, *The Custer Story,* 281.
44. Stewart, *Custer's Luck,* 132–33; Monaghan, *Custer,* 367.
45. *New York Herald,* May 6, 1876, quoted in Stewart, *Custer's Luck,* 134.
46. St. Paul *Pioneer-Press,* May 11, 1876, quoted in Stewart, *Custer's Luck,* 135.

47. Stewart, *Custer's Luck*, 136.
48. Ibid., 135-37.
49. Quoted, ibid., 138.
50. This story appears in Orin G. Libby, ed., *The Arikara Narrative of the Campaign Against the Hostile Dakotas, June, 1876* (North Dakota Historical *Collections*, VI, Bismarck, 1920), 58-63, and is based on Arikara sources. It is summarized in Stewart, *Custer's Luck*, 181.
51. Stewart, *Custer's Luck*, 138.

CHAPTER 21

1. Stewart, *Custer's Luck*, 188; Olson, *Red Cloud*, 219-22; Hyde, *Red Cloud's Folk*, 258-61.
2. Hinman interview with Short Buffalo, Nebraska State Historical Society; Sandoz, *Crazy Horse*, 303-4; Stewart, *Custer's Luck*, 90.
3. Telegram, Lieutenant Ruhlen to Adjutant General, April 19, 1876, War Department Records, AGO, Division of the Missouri; Stewart, *Custer's Luck*, 90-91, 309; Olson, *Red Cloud*, 217; Robinson, *A History of the Dakota*, 423-24.
4. The best discussion is Stewart, *Custer's Luck*, 309-12; see also Hyde, *Red Cloud's Folk*, 261, and Utley, *Frontier Regulars*, 255.
5. Vestal, *Sitting Bull*, 146; Utley, *Frontier Regulars*, 71.
6. Stewart, *Custer's Luck*, 192.
7. For a good discussion, see Vestal, *Sitting Bull*, 142-43.
8. Stewart, *Custer's Luck*, 187.
9. Ibid., 192-95; Vestal, *Sitting Bull*, 149-51.
10. Sandoz, *Crazy Horse*, 314-15; Vestal, *Sitting Bull*, 152-53; Hyde, *Red Cloud's Folk*, 263.
11. Elizabeth Custer, *"Boots and Saddles,"* 270.
12. Ibid., 270.
13. Ibid., 274.
14. Ibid., 268.
15. Ibid., 270-71; Monaghan, *Custer*, 370.
16. Stewart, *Custer's Luck*, 226.
17. Ibid., 201-2; Utley, *Frontier Regulars*, 255; for an eyewitness account by a newspaperman of the ensuing battle, see John F. Finerty, *War-Path and Bivouac: The Big Horn and Yellowstone Expedition*, ed. by Milo M. Quaife (Chicago, 1955), 124-52.
18. Utley, *Frontier Regulars*, 255.
19. Hyde, *Red Cloud's Folk*, 264.
20. David Mears, "Campaigning Against Crazy Horse," Nebraska State Historical Society *Publications*, XV (1907), 68-77.
21. Hinman interview with Short Buffalo, Nebraska State Historical Society.
22. Sandoz, *Crazy Horse*, 318-19.
23. Grinnell, *The Fighting Cheyennes*, 336.

24. See Stewart, *Custer's Luck*, 204–6; Stands-in-Timber, *Cheyenne Memories*, 186–87; Hyde, *Red Cloud's Folk*, 264; Sandoz, *Crazy Horse*, 318–21; various Hinman interviews, Nebraska State Historical Society; Grinnell, *The Fighting Cheyennes*, 334–45.
25. Utley, *Frontier Regulars*, 256.
26. Stewart, *Custer's Luck*, 206.
27. Quoted, ibid., 234.
28. Ibid., 237.
29. Elizabeth Custer, *"Boots and Saddles,"* 275.
30. Quoted in Stewart, *Custer's Luck*, 238.
31. Ibid., 285.
32. Ibid., 255.
33. Ibid., 249–50.
34. Elizabeth Custer, *"Boots and Saddles,"* 275–76; Monaghan, *Custer*, 376.
35. Brady, *Indian Fights and Fighters*, 223.
36. Quoted in Stewart, *Custer's Luck*, 253.
37. W. A. Graham, *The Custer Myth: A Source Book of Custeriana* (Harrisburg, Pa., 1953), 135.
38. The following account of Custer's march to the Little Bighorn is based on many sources, but primarily Stewart's careful and exciting account in *Custer's Luck*, 263–82; see also Utley, *Frontier Regulars*, 258–59, Monaghan, *Custer*, 382–84, and especially Graham, *The Custer Myth*, 135–38, which reprints Godfrey's narrative.

CHAPTER 22

1. Stewart, *Custer's Luck*, 315.
2. Quoted in Graham, *The Custer Myth*, 248.
3. Quoted, ibid.
4. Quoted from Lieutenant E. S. Godfrey's account, ibid., 138–39.
5. Garnett interview, Ricker tablets, Nebraska State Historical Society.
6. Hinman interview with Short Bull, Nebraska State Historical Society.
7. Clark to the Assistant Adjutant General, September 14, 1877, War Department Records, AGO, Division of the Missouri.
8. Monaghan, *Custer*, 384–86; Graham, *The Custer Myth*, 287–95; Stewart, *Custer's Luck*, 341.
9. Graham, *The Custer Myth*, 71.
10. Yellow Horse interview, Ricker tablets, Nebraska State Historical Society.
11. Graham, *The Custer Myth*, 110.
12. Ibid., 103.
13. Ibid., 73.

BIBLIOGRAPHY

Manuscripts

Elizabeth Custer Collection, Custer Battlefield National Monument, Crow Agency, Montana. Cited as Custer Mss.

Eleanor Hinman interviews, Nebraska State Historical Society, Lincoln.

Ricker tablets, Nebraska State Historical Society. These consist of transcripts of interviews with nineteenth-century red and white residents of the Plains (mainly Nebraska and South Dakota), newspaper clippings, letters from various sources, and some writing by Judge Daniel Ricker himself, who collected all the material.

Printed Sources

Alter, J. Cecil. *James Bridger*. Columbus, Ohio, 1951.

Ambrose, Stephen E. *Duty, Honor, Country: A History of West Point*. Baltimore, 1966.

Athearn, Robert G. *William T. Sherman and the Settlement of the West*. Norman, Okla., 1956.

Banta, R. E. *The Ohio*, in *Rivers of America*. New York, 1949.

Beale, Howard K. *The Critical Years: A Study of Andrew Johnson and Reconstruction*. New York, 1930.

Blish, Helen H. *A Pictographic History of the Oglala Sioux*. Lincoln, Neb., 1967.

Brady, Cyrus T. *Indian Fights and Fighters*. Lincoln, Neb., 1971.

Brown, Dee. *Fort Phil Kearny: An American Saga*. New York, 1962.

Bruce, Robert V. *1877: Year of Violence*. Indianapolis, 1959.

Buley, R. Carlyle. *The Old Northwest: Pioneer Period, 1815–1840*. Bloomington, Ind., 1950.

Carrington, Francis C. *Army Life on the Plains*. Philadelphia, 1910.

Catton, Bruce. *Mr. Lincoln's Army*. Garden City, N.Y., 1955.

Commager, Henry Steele. *The American Mind: An Interpretation of American Thought and Character Since the 1880's*. New Haven, 1950.

Cox, LaWanda and John. *Politics, Principle, and Prejudice, 1865–66*. New York, 1963.

Curti, Merle. *The Growth of American Thought*. Second edition. New York, 1951.

——. *The Social Ideas of American Educators*. Paterson, N.J., 1959.

Custer, Elizabeth (Bacon). *"Boots and Saddles": or, Life in Dakota with General Custer*. New York, 1961.

——. *Following the Guidon*. Norman, Okla., 1967.

——. *Tenting on the Plains*. Norman, Okla., 1971.

Custer, George A. *My Life on the Plains*, ed. by Milo Milton Quaife. Lincoln, Neb., 1952.

——. "War Memoirs," *Galaxy*, XXII, September 1876; reprinted in Frederick Whittaker, ed., *A Complete Life of General George A. Custer* (New York, 1876).

Davis, Theodore. "A Summer on the Plains," *Harper's Weekly*, XXXVI, February 1868.

DeBow, J. D. B., ed. *Statistical View of the United States . . . Being a Compendium of the Seventh Census to Which Are Added the Results of Every Previous Census, Beginning with 1790 . . .* , in the *Demographic Monographs* series. New York, 1970.

De Tocqueville, Alexis. *Democracy in America.* Mentor Books, New York, 1956.

Dobie, J. Frank. "Indian Horses and Horsemanship," *Southwest Review*, XXXV, Autumn, 1950.

Dorsey, James O. "The Social Organization of the Siouan Tribes," *Journal of American Folk-Lore*, IV (1891).

Erikson, Erik H. "Observations on Sioux Education," *The Journal of Psychology*, VII (1937).

———. *Young Man Luther.* New York, 1958.

Farb, Peter. *Man's Rise to Civilization as Shown by the Indians of North America from Primeval Times to the Coming of the Industrial State.* New York, 1968.

Finerty, John F. *War-Path and Bivouac: The Big Horn and Yellowstone Expedition*, ed. by Milo M. Quaife. Chicago, 1955.

Foner, Jack D. *The United States Soldier Between Two Wars: Army Life and Reforms, 1865–1898.* New York, 1970.

Frost, Lawrence A. *The Court-Martial of General George A. Custer.* Norman, Okla., 1968.

———. *The Custer Album.* Seattle, 1964.

Galloway, K. Bruce, and Robert B. Johnson, Jr. *West Point.* New York, 1973.

Gard, Wayne. *The Great Buffalo Hunt.* Lincoln, Neb., 1959.

Gerber, Max E. "The Black Hills Expedition of 1874: A New Look," *South Dakota History*, June–July 1970, 6–20.

Graham, W. A. *The Custer Myth: A Source Book of Custeriana.* Harrisburg, Pa., 1953.

Grinnell, George Bird. *The Fighting Cheyennes.* Norman, Okla., 1955.

Grouard, Frank. "An Indian Scout's Recollections of Crazy Horse," *Nebraska History Magazine*, XII, January–March 1929.

Hassler, Warren W., Jr. *General George B. McClellan.* Baton Rouge, 1957.

Hassrick, Royal B. *The Sioux: Life and Customs of a Warrior Society.* Norman, Okla., 1964.

Hazen, General W. B. "Some Corrections of 'Life on the Plains,'" *Chronicles of Oklahoma*, III (1925).

Hesseltine, William B. *Ulysses S. Grant: Politician.* New York, 1936.

Holland, Lynwood M. *Pierce M. B. Young.* Athens, Ga., 1964.

Howard, Oliver O. *Autobiography.* New York, 1908.

Hyde, George E. *Red Cloud's Folk: A History of the Oglala Sioux Indians.* Norman, Okla., 1937.

———. *Spotted Tail's Folk: A History of the Brulé Sioux.* Norman, Okla., 1961.

Kinsley, D. A. *Favor the Bold*, Vol. 2, *Custer: The Indian Fighter.* New York, 1968.

Leland, Charles Godfrey. *Memoirs*. New York, 1893.

Lerner, Max. *America as a Civilization*. New York, 1957.

Lévi-Strauss, Claude. *The Savage Mind*. Chicago, 1966.

Lewis, Lloyd. *Sherman, Fighting Prophet*. New York, 1932.

Libby, Orin G., ed. *The Arikara Narrative of the Campaign Against the Hostile Dakotas, June 1876*, in North Dakota Historical Collections, VI, Bismarck, 1920.

Lincoln, Jackson S. *The Dream in Primitive Cultures*. New York and London, 1970.

Llewellyn, K. N., and E. Adamson Hoebel. *The Cheyenne Way: Conflict and Case Law in Primitive Jurisprudence*. Norman, Okla., 1941.

Lowie, Robert H. *Indians of the Plains*. Garden City, N.Y., 1954 and 1963.

———. *The Origin of the State*. New York, 1927.

Mails, Thomas E. *The Mystic Warriors of the Plains*. Garden City, N.Y., 1972.

Marshall, S. L. A. *Men Against Fire*. New York, 1947.

McClellan, George B. *McClellan's Own Story*. New York, 1887.

———. *Report on the Organization and Campaigns of the Army of the Potomac*. . . . New York, 1864.

McKitrick, Eric L. *Andrew Johnson and Reconstruction*. Chicago, 1960.

Mead, Margaret, and Martha Wolfenstein, eds. *Childhood in Contemporary Cultures*. Chicago, 1955.

Mears, David. "Campaigning Against Crazy Horse," Nebraska State Historical Society *Publications*, XV (1907).

Merington, Marguerite, ed. *The Custer Story: The Life and Intimate Letters of General George A. Custer and His Wife Elizabeth*. New York, 1950.

Monaghan, Jay. *Custer: The Life of General George Armstrong Custer*. Lincoln, Neb., 1959.

Moore, Arthur K. *The Frontier Mind: A Cultural Analysis of the Kentucky Frontiersman*. Lexington, Ky., 1950.

Newcomb, W. W. "A Re-examination of the Causes of Plains Warfare," *American Anthropologist*, Vol. 52, July–September 1950.

Olson, James C. *Red Cloud and the Sioux Problem*. Lincoln, Neb., 1965.

Parkman, Francis. *The Oregon Trail*. New York, 1967.

Pearce, Roy Harvey. *The Savages of America: A Study of the Indian and the Idea of Civilization*. Revised edition. Baltimore, 1965.

Potter, David M. *People of Plenty: Economic Abundance and the American Character*. Chicago, 1954.

Reiger, John F., ed. *The Passing of the Great West: Selected Papers of George Bird Grinnell*. New York, 1972.

Richardson, James D., comp. *Messages and Papers of the Presidents, 1789–1897*, Vol. VI. Washington, D.C., 1897.

Riggs, Stephen Return. *Dakota Grammar, Texts, and Ethnography*, Vol. IX of *Contributions to North American Ethnology*. Washington, D.C., 1893.

Robinson, Doane. *A History of the Dakota or Sioux Indians*. Minneapolis, 1904.

Roe, Frank Gilbert. *The Indian and the Horse*. Norman, Okla., 1955.

Sandburg, Carl. *The People, Yes*. New York, 1936.

Sandoz, Mari. *Crazy Horse: The Strange Man of the Oglalas*. Lincoln, Neb., 1942.

Saum, Lewis O. *The Fur Trader and the Indians*. Seattle, 1965.

Schaff, Morris. *The Spirit of Old West Point*. Boston, 1907.

Smith, Henry Nash. *Virgin Land: The American West as Symbol and Myth*. Cambridge, Mass., 1950.

Spring, Agnes Wright. *Caspar Collins: The Life and Exploits of an Indian Fighter of the Sixties*. New York, 1927.

Standing Bear, Luther. *My People the Sioux*. Boston and New York, 1911.

Stands-in-Timber, John, and Margot Liberty. *Cheyenne Memories*. New Haven, 1967.

Stanley, D. S. *Personal Memoirs*. Cambridge, Mass., 1917.

Stanley, Henry M. *My Early Travels and Adventures*. London, 1895.

Stewart, Edgar I. *Custer's Luck*. Norman, Okla., 1955.

Sunley, Robert. "Early Nineteenth-Century American Literature on Child Rearing," in Margaret Mead and Martha Wolfenstein, eds. *Childhood in Contemporary Cultures*. Chicago, 1955.

Thorndike, Rachel Sherman, ed. *The Sherman Letters*. New York, 1894.

Thwaites, Reuben Gold, ed. *Original Journals of the Lewis and Clark Expedition*. New York, 1959.

Tucker, William, and Jeff C. Dykes (comps.). *The Grand Duke Alexis in the United States of America During the Winter of 1871–1872*. New York, 1973.

Underhill, Ruth M. *Red Man's America*. Revised edition. Chicago, 1971.

Utley, Robert M. *Frontier Regulars: The United States Army and the Indian*. New York, 1973.

Van de Water, Frederic F. *Glory-Hunter: A Life of General Custer*. Indianapolis, 1934.

Vestal, Stanley. *Sitting Bull: Champion of the Sioux*. Norman, Okla., 1957.

Walters, Ronald G., ed. *Primer for Prudery: Sexual Advice to Victorian America*. Baltimore, 1973.

Ware, Eugene F. *The Indian War of 1864*. Lincoln, Neb., 1960.

War of the Rebellion, Official Records of the Union and Confederate Armies. 128 vols. Washington, D.C., 1880–1901. Cited as O.R.

Webb, Walter P. *The Great Plains*. Boston, 1931.

Weigley, Russell F. *The American Way of War: A History of United States Military Strategy and Policy*. New York, 1973.

Whittaker, Frederick, ed. *A Complete Life of General George A. Custer*. New York, 1876.

Wiley, Bell I. *The Life of Billy Yank*. New York, 1951.

———. *The Life of Johnny Reb*. New York, 1943.

Wilson, James Harrison. *Under the Old Flag*. New York, 1912.

Wishy, Bernard. *The Child and the Republic: The Dawn of Modern American Child Nurture*. Philadelphia, 1968.

Wissler, Clark. *Indians of the United States*. Revised edition. New York, 1966.

Wissler, Clark. "Societies and Ceremonial Associations in the Oglala Division of the Teton-Dakota," *American Museum of Natural History Anthropological Papers*, XI (1912).

Wyman, Walker D. *The Wild Horse of the West*. Lincoln, Neb., 1945.

INDEX

ABOUT THE AUTHOR

Stephen E. Ambrose is the author of twenty-four books on political and military history, including the number-one *New York Times* bestseller *D-Day, June 6, 1944,* the award-winning biography *Eisenhower,* and a three-volume life of Richard Nixon. In preparation for *Crazy Horse and Custer,* the author, accompanied by his wife, five children, and two dogs, spent four years and traveled over fifteen thousand miles across America by pickup truck, canoe, horse, and backpack. His most recent book is *Undaunted Courage: Meriwether Lewis, Thomas Jefferson, and the Opening of the American West.*